THE MODERN LANGUAGE ASSOCIATION OF AMERICA

MONOGRAPH SERIES

X

MILTON IN CHANCERY

Approved for publication in the Monograph Series of the Modern Language Association of America.

CHRISTIAN GAUSS
JAMES H. HANFORD
FRANCIS P. MAGOUN, JR.
G. T. NORTHUP
LAWRENCE M. PRICE
Committee of Award

Sir Anthony Cope, co-defendant with his mother Lady Elizabeth Cope against Milton's bill in 1654, and his brother John Cope. From the portrait at Canon-ffrome Court, Ledbury, Hereford-shire. Used by the kind permission of Mrs. Sybil Hopton.

MILTON IN CHANCERY

NEW CHAPTERS IN THE LIVES OF THE POET AND HIS FATHER

BY

J. MILTON FRENCH

Assistant Professor of English
Queens College

NEW YORK
THE MODERN LANGUAGE ASSOCIATION
OF AMERICA
MCMXXXIX

COMPOSED, PRINTED AND BOUND BY

The Collegiate Press

GEORGE BANTA PUBLISHING COMPANY

MENASHA, WISCONSIN

To the
sole partner and sole part
of all these joys

Sancho. But if this is hell, why do we see no lawyers?
Clarindo. They won't receive them, lest they bring lawsuits here.
Sancho. If there are no lawsuits here, hell's not so bad.

—Lope de Vega, *The Star of Seville*, III, ii.

Lussurioso. Tell me, what has made thee so melancholy?
Vindice. Why, going to law.
Luss. Why, will that make a man melancholy?
Vind. Yes, to look long upon ink and black buckram. I went me to
law in *Anno quadragesimo secundo*, and I waded out of it in *Anno sex-
tagesimo tertio*.
Luss. What, three and twenty years in law?
Vind. I have known those that have been five and fifty, and all about
pullen [poultry] and pigs.
Luss. May it be possible such men should breathe,
     To vex the terms so much?
Vind. 'Tis food to some, my Lord. There are old men at the present,
that are so poisoned with the affectation of law-words (having had many
suits canvassed), that their common talk is nothing but Barbary Latin.
They cannot so much as pray but in law, that their sins may be removed
with a writ of error, and their souls fetched up to Heaven with a sasarara
[certiorari].

—Tourneur, *The Revenger's Tragedy*, IV, ii.

Surely, my Lords, this lawyer here hath swallowed
Some 'pothecary's bills, or proclamations.
And now the hard and undigestible words
Come up like stones we use give hawks for physic.
Why, this is Welsh to Latin!

—Webster, *The White Devil*, III, i.

. . . some allured to the trade of law, grounding their purposes not on
the prudent and heavenly contemplation of justice and equity, which
was never taught them, but on the promising and pleasing thoughts of
litigious terms, fat contentions, and flowing fees . . .

—Milton, *Of Education.*

     wherefore should not strength and might
There fail where virtue fails, or weakest prove
Where boldest? . . . nor is it aught but just
That he who in debate of truth hath won,
Should win in arms, in both disputes alike
Victor; though brutish that contest and foul,
When Reason hath to deal with force, yet so
Most reason is that Reason overcome.

—Milton, *Paradise Lost*, VI, 116–126.

PREFACE

A PROFOUND though incidental satisfaction arising from this book is the excuse it offers me of publicly thanking numerous friends. However dubious they may have felt of my wisdom or skill in this second disinterment of Milton's bones, they have been long-suffering in help and encouragement. A grateful mind, as Milton prophetically explained, by owing owes not, but still pays. It is therefore with great pleasure that I venture here to express a lifelong debt to Professor Hyder Rollins of Harvard University, who first set my feet on the scholar's path which they very stumblingly tread. I am also grateful to Professor Leslie Hotson of Haverford College, who generously gave me many references which I might otherwise have missed; to Mrs. Sybil Hopton of Canon-ffrome Court, Ledbury, Herefordshire, who has taken a cordial interest in this investigation and who graciously sent me photographs of several Cope portraits in her possession, here used as illustrations; to Mrs. E. E. Cope of Finchampstead Place, Berkshire, who provided many genealogical notes about her family; to Professor Thomas O. Mabbott of Hunter College for support and inspiration in this and other Miltonic enterprises; to Mr. Edmund Burroughs of Akron, Ohio, for helpful information about the laws and courts; and to my mother, whose unwavering confidence in me has always remained serenely oblivious to the meagerness of my actual achievements. Such glimmerings of readability as the book may possess are owing in no small measure to generous criticism of the manuscript by Professor James Holly Hanford of Western Reserve University, Professor Hyder Rollins, Professor Douglas Bush, and Professor James Buell Munn of Harvard University, Professor Frank Allen Patterson of Columbia University, and the members of the Monograph Series Committee of Award—though all of them are innocent of any of its shortcomings. My investigations of parish records in the Milton-Powell country was made easier and more pleasant by the hospitable co-operation of the Reverend Hubert W. Ottoway, vicar of Forest Hill; the Reverend Eric Graham, vicar of Cuddesdon; the Reverend Julius B. White, rector of Holton; the Reverend John A. Davies, rector of Stanton St. John; the Reverend Richard D. Budworth, vicar of Horsepath; and the Reverend Owen S. E. Clarendon, vicar of Iffley. Miss Nellie O'Farrell of London has been a constant guide to me in these wandering mazes lost. The directors and staffs of the Public Record Office, the British Museum, the Bodleian Library, and the Harvard College Library have been uniformly helpful. Professor Harlan W. Hamilton of the University of

Akron has voluntarily struggled through the Serbonian bog of proof with
me and has in this way helped materially to reduce the number of glaring
errors. The Columbia University Press and the Harvard University Press
kindly allowed me to make use of portions of this book previously published by them, and the Macmillan Company courteously permitted the
reproduction of the illustration used as a frontispiece. In view of the
large element of pure luck which attends all researches into ancient
records, I must in all fairness also lay a wreath of gratitude on the altar
of that power which erring men call Chance. Finally, my wife has not
only shared the combined drudgery and excitement of this work from
beginning to end, but what in me was dark has illumined, what was low
has raised and supported.

J. M. F.

Queens College
September 1, 1939

TABLE OF CONTENTS

PART IV

APPENDIX: TRANSCRIPTS OF ORIGINAL DOCUMENTS

LIST OF ILLUSTRATIONS

INTRODUCTION

INTRODUCTION

IT might seem unlikely, now that John Milton has been dead nearly three centuries, that buried details of his life could be recovered. Yet the blending of sheer optimism with good fortune in a series of excursions into English archives has made it possible to offer in the present book chapters in the lives of Milton and his father only a few bits of which have ever seen publication. Brief accounts of two of the five suits concerning the elder Milton have previously appeared; and I have recently printed a few samples of other representative documents. Ninety per cent of the total, however, is now offered for the first time to readers interested in Milton.

I

Some explanation of the documents comprising the book seems necessary. Most of them consist of law suits arising from financial transactions. The common situation underlying them was somewhat as follows. A lent B a sum of money, say fifty pounds, which B undertook to repay with interest in six months. As security for repayment A took from B a bond or recognizance, made out in a sum approximately double the amount of the loan, but defeasanced for, or conditioned on, the payment of the original fifty pounds with interest. If B repaid the fifty-three pounds agreed on at the given day, A handed back the bond, and the transaction was complete. If he did not, one of two results followed. Either he retained the principal and paid regular "forbearance," or interest, usually to the complete satisfaction of both sides, who regarded it as a profitable or necessary investment; or else he threw up his hands and paid nothing at all. Neither of the first two cases would lead to difficulties, and neither is therefore of much use or interest to the biographer. But the third usually led to litigation, and in litigation untold possibilities of interesting information opened up.

It should be noticed that bonds or recognizances always carried a penalty, by which, on the debtor's failure to conform to the terms of the bond, the creditor had a right to take the possessions and usually the body of the debtor and hold them till the debt was satisfied. The process of doing so was somewhat complicated. One method is illustrated in the normal procedure for suing a recognizance at common law, as explained in Thomas Powell's *The Attourney's Academy* (1630 edition). The creditor, in case such a bond is forfeited, should take a copy to the clerk of the petty bag, who will make out writs of *scire facias* on it. These the creditor delivers to the sheriff of Middlesex, who will return them.

When they are returned, they are carried back to the clerk of the petty bag. Next the creditor retains a clerk as attorney and gives the defendant a day to appear. If he fails, the creditor receives a judgment against him. If he does appear, the creditor declares against him, and he must answer as in other courts of common law. If the creditor goes to trial, he must have the whole proceedings written into parchment and sent by an officer of the petty bag sealed up to be tried in the court of Common Pleas or of King's Bench, or unsealed to the lord keeper or the lord chancellor. The proceedings in the suit between Milton's father and Rose Downer given below illustrate some steps in this procedure.

On the other hand, most of the proceedings which are presented here do not take place in the court of common law, but in one of the courts of equity or chancery. The distinction lies in the remedies which the court may grant, and also in the nature of the evidence which may be taken. As to the remedies, equity through desire to soften the severity of the principles of the common law gave to the chancellor in his discretion the right to make certain exceptions in the interests of justice and of fairness to the parties. As to the evidence, it was possible in equity to examine the defendants and other persons in accounting matters through interrogatories, in a manner which was not generally followed in the law courts. The legal experiences of the Miltons as here presented were thus confined chiefly to equity.

II

Milton was himself at least a dilettante in legal matters. His father, it will be remembered, pursued the vocation of scrivener, which involved him in extensive money-lending, so that a reasonable knowledge of the law was indispensable to him. Though the poet declined to become a lawyer, he could not have been his father's son without picking up a certain acquaintance with the subject. The inheritance and investment of considerable amounts of money would necessitate such familiarity. In a recent edition of his *Epitaphium Damonis*,[1] to be sure, it has been pointed out that he disliked the law. He scorned the "fee'd gamester" (*An Apology*) and "litigious terms, fat contentions, and flowing fees" (*Of Education*); and in thanking his father (*Ad Patrem*) for not dragging him to a legal career and to the badly guarded laws of the nation, and for not condemning his ears to insipid pleadings, he almost put his father in his place for even dreaming of his becoming a lawyer. On the other hand, he probably possessed a copy of Fitzherbert's *Natura Brevium*,[2] and his widow's inventory mentions his eleven law-books.[3]

A more interesting link with the law, formerly unknown, may now be added. There has recently come to light one of his commonplace books, in which he kept (or had kept) copies of most of his letters of state; this collection has been drawn on in the recent edition of those letters in the Columbia *Milton*.[4] In another volume of the same series[5] several other essays from the same collection have been published. The following notes on procedure in the court of Chancery were not included in that series because they were felt to be not Milton's work, but merely gathered by him for his information or interest. But their close connection with the present subject makes them of unusual value here, so that the inclusion of substantial selections will probably be welcomed.[6] Thus Milton says:

In the time of Henry IV the court of Chancery was then fled unto, as to the only altar of help and refuge . . . in sum the written law is like to a stiff rule of steel or iron which will not be applied to the fashion of the stone or timber whereunto it is laid. And equity (as Aristotle saith well) is like to the lead rule of Lesbian artificers, which they might at pleasure bend or bow to every stone of whatsoever fashion, and thereby it may also appear what use there ought to be of positive or written law, as also of equity itself. For seeing that the positive and common is made meet for the most part, and that equity is added in some few and singular cases, it followeth by reason that commonly and regularly the positive law should be put in use, and that equity should be appealed unto but only in rare and extraordinary matters, lest on the one side if the judge in equity should take jurisdiction over all, it should come to pass (as Aristotle saith) that a beast should bear the rule, for so he calleth man whose judgment, if it be not restrained by the chain of law, is commonly carried away with unruly affections. And on the other side if only strait law be administered, the help of God, which speaketh in the oracle of equity, should be denied unto men that need, and therefore even as two herbs being in extremity of heat or cold be by themselves so many persons, and yet if they be skilfully tempered will make a wholesome medicine, so also would it come to pass if either the arithmetical government (as they call it) by rigor of law only, or this geometrical judgment at the pleasure of the Chancellor (or Prætor) only should be admitted, and yet if they be well compounded together, a most sweet and most harmonical justice will follow of them.

Milton goes on to quote rules for the procedure in Chancery.

There is no formality or precise order of proceeding required in Chancery as at the common law . . . nevertheless the bill in Chancery must contain sufficiency of matter both to entitle the court and charge the defendant or otherwise it shall abate. . . . It must also yield good certainty of all such things as by the knowledge of the complainant . . . except it be in some special case where he shall not be forced to charge himself as in crime and such others. By late order taken in Easter term, 38 *Elizabethæ*, no bill ought to be of needless length upon pain to have a fine set on the counsellor, with some penalty also on the plainant, and the like order also standeth for answers, replications, rejoinders, etc. The original process here is the *subpœna certæ summæ*, which albeit the party shall never pay . . . yet upon affidavit made before a Master of Chancery of the serving thereof, and upon the default of the defendant, an attachment shall be awarded against him, and then if he cannot excuse the contempt, he shall be remitted to the Fleet. In this taking of the affidavit, the Master is forbidden to swear him that maketh it upon any point tending to the proof or disproof of the matter or title in question, but only concerning the default or contempt. . . .

If the defendant come not in after attachment, then proclamation *sub pœna ligeantiæ* to the sheriff and county of rebellion, to other persons whom the plaintiff may name shall be awarded; and those may break the house where he is and take him out as in case outlawed, *quia similis contumacia, et contemptus idem est, quod* Master Lambert.

Being come in upon the commission, it is the manner to examine upon interrogatories (query, whether he shall not be committed upon the commission and examined upon the attachment) drawn concerning the special manner of the contempt informed against him. Albeit the contempt was expounded by Parliament, yet the Lord Keeper awarded costs against the contemner, *Pasc. 40 Elizabethæ Reginæ.*

Where it is informed after diverse proclamations that the defendant hath not certain dwelling, but runneth to and fro and covereth himself, it hath been seen that the land in question hath been sequestered or otherwise the possession thereof awarded to the complainant *quousque.* The like process of attachment, proclamation, etc., is awarded upon the breach of any decree, for execution of certificate into this court by commission upon the statute 39 *Elizabethæ* for gifts to charitable uses. There was a special writ to the parties devised Trinitate 41 *Elizabethæ Reginae* by commandment of the Lord Keeper, the form whereof passed my pen, etc. And the same was for a school at Waybridge in Suffolk sealed and set forth. The newly devised *subpœna de executione ordinis* may be reckoned among judicial process because an order is an interlocutory decree.

If upon a demurrer the bill be adjudged insufficient, the defendant shall not have any costs . . . for the statute . . . giveth damage only where the suggestion is found false, which is not done here, for it cometh not to trial. Howbeit, the manner is now by good direction to award costs in such cases lest place be given to vexation.

A demurrer upon a bill is properly where the bill is, and yet is no cause of suit true, in which case the defendant shall not need to answer upon the oath, for it is a plea *plede per le mannre nulla*, etc. But if the defendant do in words demur, and yet do speak over or do object matter not contained in the bill, and yet will demur, these be not properly demurrers, and therefore he ought to answer these upon oath, though many do call them demurrers, which be either pleas to the jurisdiction or some other peremptory matter of bar or answer.

The answer likewise must be good to common intent, which is afforded the pleas in bar at the common law, and needeth not to be enlarged in Chancery. Such things also as be directly in the knowledge of the defendant by his own acts he ought to disclose there, avoiding all cautelous evasions and proffering the simple truth, except in cases where he is not to charge or betray himself, and if he do trifle or use, he is upon report thereof fined the first time 20s., and double the second, etc. For making answer he hath convenient time after his appearance, or may do it by commission upon affidavit of impotency to travel.

The replication is by late order to be put into the court within [blank], etc.

A woman was admitted to sue *in forma pauperis* and at the hearing of the cause it fell out that after many clamors she had no good cause of suit, but did it partly for vexation, and partly for countenance to live thereby. And therefore Sir Thomas Egerton, Lord Keeper, ordered that she should be whipped, *Trinitate*

38 Elizabethæ, William Lambert *tunc assidente*, for he said so was the opinion of all the justices by the equity of the statute . . . both for the Chancery and Star Chamber. Yet the statute mentioneth only actions at the common law.

If a witness depose a manifest contrariety or falsity in any material part, he shall be wholly rejected, and the party must produce others.

III

To pass on now from Milton's notes to a more systematic description of legal procedure, we may notice that the typical Chancery action involved several steps.[7] First came the bill by the plaintiff. It usually appeared as a large parchment sheet, written closely on one side only, addressed at the top to the lord keeper of the great seal or some corresponding official, stating the plaintiff's grievances in detail, and asking the issuance of a writ of subpœna against the defendant or defendants, to compel them to set forth certain specified facts in answer to the plaintiff's questions. This bill was usually (but not always) signed, not by the plaintiff but by his counsel, and was then sworn to before one of the masters in the Court of Chancery. It was then filed with one of the so-called six clerks in Chancery, whose business it was to act as attorneys for the parties to the suit and to receive, file, and keep track of the proceedings. The clerk affixed his name, and theoretically the subsequent documents in the case were filed with him, or with the defendant's six clerk. The cost of the bill was not inconsiderable, since the counsel's fee to begin with was at least ten shillings, and there were various lesser expenses, such as the oath, the engrossing of the bill, and the attorney's fee.

The next step was the issuance of the writ of subpœna or privy seal, which was automatic on the filing of the petition or bill. This was a summons of full authority, issuing from the very seat of government as vested in the sovereign. It was addressed to the commissioners or justices or other responsible officials of the county concerned, and commanded the defendant or defendants to appear at a certain time, at a certain place, and under a certain penalty, to answer the charges of the plaintiff. It was written on a comparatively small sheet of parchment, with a label or detachable strip at the bottom for each defendant named in the suit. The officer who served the subpœna detached one of these labels for each defendant served except the last, and delivered it to him or to some recognized representative, or left it at his dwelling. To the last defendant he delivered the body of the writ itself, having first showed it to each of the others. He then returned to the court and made oath that he had so delivered the writ.

Usually the defendant or defendants appeared in the fashion specified, bringing a written answer. The answer resembled the bill in many ways. It too was written on a large sheet of parchment, signed and sworn like the bill. It bore a heading showing that it was the answer of B to A, and as with the bill the date of swearing to the answer was usually entered. The answer might reply carefully to all the questions raised in the bill, in which case the way was then open for a quick decision and disposal of the case. An answer cost ten shillings in counsel's fees, plus various minor costs.

But often the answer did not appear as directed. There might be various legitimate reasons for this failure. The defendant might not be able to answer properly within the short time allotted because he might need to consult various records or documents not quickly available. Or he might need to have conference with some person at a considerable distance. Or he might not be physically able to travel to the place designated for an answer. In case of simple neglect to answer, the plaintiff could procure an attachment against the defendant to compel his appearance. Otherwise, if the failure was due to distance, sickness, or the like, the defendant's attorney could procure a writ of *dedimus potestatem* by which his patron could deliver his answer in the country wherever he might happen to live. The fee for this writ was two shillings sixpence.

When the answer had come in, the plaintiff had a certain length of time (till the beginning of the third law-term thereafter) to put in a replication, or rebuttal. Some replications were elaborate affairs, pointing out defects in the answers, and indicating the need of more satisfactory answers. Others were weak attempts to uphold the original bill by mere asseveration, unconvincing reiterations that the bill was true and the answer false. In form the replication resembled the answer, though usually shorter. The fee was as for the original bill.

Following the replication might come the defendant's rejoinder, which bears the same relation to the answer which the replication does to the bill. The form and fees were similar. Most suits did not run to these last two parts, ending rather with the simple bill and answer, but a considerable number did so continue.

Other possible pleadings to a bill included a demurrer, which was an objection to the bill on the ground that it was defective for failure to state a cause of action. Another was a plea, based on the assertion that the bill contained foreign matter, that the cause had formerly been dismissed, that the plaintiff had been outlawed or excommunicated, or that another bill was depending for the same cause. Various other ramifications include injunctions, petitions, and so forth, which do not concern the reader of this book.

If either side so desired, provision might be made for the examination of witnesses on one or both sides. These depositions might be taken either

Court of Chancery.

The Court of Chancery in the time of Henry VI. From a manuscript in the Inner Temple, London, reproduced in F. A. Inderwick, *The King's Peace* (1895), facing p. 122. Used by permission of the Macmillan Company, New York.

in London or elsewhere; in one case they were called "town depositions," in the other "country depositions." If witnesses were called, the party calling them provided interrogatories, or questions for them to answer on oath. The answers might be helpful or worthless, depending on the character of the questions or on the knowledge and intelligence of the witnesses. Frequently much interesting information about the parties to the suit comes out in these depositions. When completed, they were handed in sealed to the judge.

At various times during the progress of the suit, the parties through their counsels might appeal to the court on a variety of points, and secure a decision or decree on them, often successively postponing final hearings over a considerable time. Thus a decree might appear in a case without in any way being a final judgment or even particularly important. A decree might pronounce on the permissibility of a writ of *dedimus potestatem*, on a delay in submitting an answer or other action, on submission of some moot point to a master in Chancery for resolution, or on numerous other details. Thus it frequently happened that a suit of some difficulty might acquire in its progress a large number of decrees. All these were duly entered in a large decree book, and indexed. If a matter was referred to a master for consideration, his report or certificate was submitted within a short time, and entered in a special book kept for the purpose.

IV

Most of the suits described in this book are based on the lending of money at interest; in other words, on usury. Now usury was a subject of perennial satire and vicious attack among Elizabethan and later writers, and calls up in our own minds unconsciously visions of Shylock and his pound of flesh or of Barabbas and his monstrous crimes. According to the zealous Phillip Stubbes, usurers are "merciless tigers," who delight in allowing their poor debtors to rot in prison, and who before they will release one, will "make dice of his bones." A usurer, says Stubbes, is "worse than a thief . . . worse than a Jew . . . worse than Judas, worse than hell itself."[8] Dekker agrees with him in his tirade: usurers lure young novices into a fool's paradise till they have signed away their lands by mortgage, "and then like pedlers go they (or some familiar spirit for them, raised by the usurer) up and down to cry commodities, which scarcely yield the third part of the sum for which they take them up."[9]

Milton himself, in his *Commonplace Book*, interestingly enough straddles the fence by quoting opinions both in favor of and adverse to usurers.[10] First he records Dante's opinion that usury is a sin both against nature and against art: against nature because it makes money beget money, which is an unnatural birth, and against art because it does no work. Almost immediately, however, he presents the judgment of Rivetus, who upholds usury. Thus he remains neutral as to one phase of his father's occupation.

According to the prevailing notion, the creditor is always cruel like the usurer, whereas the debtor is invariably an innocent lamb at the mercy of these roaring tigers. Dekker levels the finger of accusation at creditors:

You have another cruelty in keeping men in prison so long, till sickness and death deal mildly with them . . . when you see a poor wretch that to keep life in a loathed body hath not a house left to cover his head from the tempests, nor a bed (but the common bed which our mother the earth allows him) for his cares to sleep upon, when you have (by keeping or locking him up) robbed him of all means to get, what seek you to have him lose but his life? The miserable prisoner is ready to famish, yet that can not move you; the more miserable wife is ready to run mad with despair, yet that cannot melt you; the most of all miserable, his children, lie crying at your doors, yet nothing can awaken you to compassion. . . . I would . . . that every miserable debtor that so dies, might be buried at his creditor's door, that when he strides over him he might think he still rises up (like the ghost in *Jeronimo*) crying "Revenge!"[11]

By the same criterion, lawyers are the scum of the earth, and the law a net of unadulterated villainy. According to Harrison's *Description of England*,

now all the wealth of the land doth flow unto our common lawyers, of whom, some one having practised little above thirteen or fourteen years is able to buy a purchase of so many thousand pounds.[12]

It is the old and yet still familiar story of graft and extortion. Stubbes, as might be expected, rubs it in even more vehemently:

. . . the lawyers, they go ruffling in their silks, velvets, and chains of gold; they build gorgeous houses, sumptuous edifices, and stately turrets; they keep a port like mighty potentates; they have bands and retinues of men attendant upon them daily; they purchase castles and towers, lands and lordships, and what not. And all upon the polling and pilling of the poor commons. . . . If you have *argent* . . . then your suit shall want no furtherance; but if this be wanting, then farewell client; he may go shoe the goose for any good success he is like to have of his matter; without this, sheriffs and officers will return writs with a *tarde venit* or with a *non est inventus*, smally to the poor man's profit.[13]

William Parkes draws a similarly hostile picture:[14]

> There's lawyers, that by virtue of the tongue,
> Draw to themselves great wealth, yet right not wrong.
> And therefore rather than by law contend,
> Give half thy right to make quiet end.
> Who tired and wasted thought this counsel bad
> In the beginning, wished in the end he had.

He reinforces the doggerel caution with plain prose:[15] ". . . by thy

tedious deferments much paper hast thou blotted with expenseful needless lines, to no other use but only to fill black boxes, and buckram bags,
and to be paid by the sheet."

Of still more interest in connection with the elder Milton is the
commonly received opinion of a scrivener. Dekker dismisses the class
nonchalantly: "Upon Usury hast thou [*i.e.*, London] begotten Extortion . . . then hath she sons in law, and they are all scriveners."[16]
Stubbes describes their supposed enormities with relish:

And if it be true that I hear say, there be no men so great doers in this noble
faculty and famous science [*i.e.*, usury] as the scriveners be. For it is said (and I
fear me too true) that there are some to whom is committed a hundred or two
of pounds, of some more, of some less, they putting in good sureties to the owners
for repayment of the same again, with certain allowance for the loan thereof;
then come there poor men to them, desiring them to lend them such a sum of
money, and they will recompense them at their own desires, who making refusal
at the first, as though they had it not (to actuate the minds of the poor peti-
tioners withal), at last they lend them how much they desire, receiving of the
poor men what interest and assurance they lust themselves, and binding them,
their lands, goods, and all, with forfeiture if they fail of payment; where note,
by the way, the scrivener is the instrument whereby the Devil worketh the frame
of this wicked work of usury, he being rewarded with a good fleece for his labor.
For first, he hath a certain allowance of the archdevil who owns the money, for
helping him to such vent for his coin. Secondly, he hath a great deal more usury
to himself, of him who borroweth the money, than he alloweth the owner of the
money. And, thirdly, he hath not the least part for making the writings between
them.[17]

Wye Salstonstall's character of a scrivener is so exuberantly vituperative
than I cannot resist quoting a few sentences. A scrivener, he assures his
readers, is

a Christian cannibal that devours men alive. He sits behind a desk like a spider
in a cobweb to watch what flies will fall into his net. . . . To conclude, his life
is so black that no ink can paint it forth, he is one of the Devil's engines to ruin
others, he is a paper-worm, or a rack for honest men, and his *ultimum vale* is a
deceitful breaking.[18]

William Parkes makes usurers and scriveners the procurers to his villainous lawyers:[19]

> There's usurers and scriveners, and they draw
> Men into bonds, and compass of the law.
>   And therefore warily eschew their gin,
>   For pain brings forth what pleasure ushered in.
>   The bird with ease into the net doth glide,
>   But out she cannot get, for there she's tied.

Middleton's picture of the scrivener Bursebell is amusing:[20]

Whereupon entered master Bursebell, the royal scrivener, with deeds and writings hanged, drawn, and quartered for the purpose: he was a valiant scribe, I

remember; his pen lay mounted between his ear like a Tower-gun, but not charged yet till our young master's patrimony shot off, which was some third part of an hour after.

Various other pictures of this black and villainous world of law and lawyers could be extracted from the writings of the time. Almost every writer with any imagination added his little drop of gall to the general sea of bitterness. But the present book is unusually illuminating in that it furnishes a totally different view of the whole situation. It is not so much that the quotations given are entirely wrong, but that they rest upon the exceptional instance. Some lawyers did then, as they will always, batten on the miseries of others; some scriveners were then, as brokers may occasionally be now, unscrupulous and vicious. But the majority of men in these occupations, like those in all other legitimate walks of life, were reasonably honest and faithful. Creditors are human beings like debtors, and often fully as deserving of sympathy. Indeed, in the instances which follow, the creditor is sometimes less luxurious in his mode of life than the debtor. It is as often as not the debtor who alienates our sympathy, and the creditor whom we pity. And the lawyer and the judge usually appear hard-working, colorless persons. The whole story which will follow, then, is a useful corrective to that romantic sentimentalizing which grows up all too easily, and which still holds its ground just as does our instinctive repugnance to various other occupations and situations which spell discomfort to us. Nine tenths of mankind instinctively distrust doctors, dentists, undertakers, and lawyers, not because they are actually worse than teachers, insurance men, and grocers, but because they are less customary parts of our lives and are seldom called to our aid except in difficult and vexatious situations, in which we tend naturally to identify the trouble we suffer with the people whom we then call on for aid.

V

The events to be described below need to be put into their proper place in relation to the lives of the Miltons. Though they cover fairly thoroughly the period from about 1600 to the Restoration, the active periods are somewhat more concentrated. The proceedings which affect the elder Milton fall chiefly within the years 1624, 1626, 1631–32, and 1636–38. Though one suit stretches on to 1640 before it reaches a conclusion, practically speaking the activity closes in 1638. Those touching the younger Milton fall for the most part within the years 1646–47 and 1653–59. But the total period is long, covering the mature lives of both men—a full two generations.

Against what background shall we think of these events? Milton's father, as we know, became free of the Scriveners' Company in 1599, thus entering into his position as a mature man and master of his own life. We know something about his interests and his tastes, both from biographical sources and from his son's description of him. He enjoyed reading, he was a skilled musician and composer, he gave his son unusual leeway in education and in the choice of a profession, and he won the affection and admiration of that son. He trained several apprentice scriveners, retired to Horton some time in the 1630's, and died in 1647, about ten years later than his wife, Milton's mother.[21]

A good deal more is known about his professional activities than appears in Masson's biography. I shall venture to summarize very briefly the still scanty records of his work. The known is still scarcely more than one per cent of the unknown, for only occasionally do the documents which reveal his activities come to light; and there are doubtless still in existence in private collections ten times as many as can be listed, since many of them have never been mentioned in print. But the gathering of the following items may possibly induce some of these private collectors to examine their holdings more carefully, and, in case they find interesting papers, to make them public. The following transactions, then, to which Scrivener Milton was a witness or which were drawn up at his shop in Bread Street, London, are known:

1602/3 March 4 Heigham-Sanderson bond, witnessed by Milton, and payable at his shop.[22]

1606/7 January 21 Scudamore-Calton bond, witnessed by Milton, and payable at his shop.[23]

1607 May 12 Williams-Shelley bond, witnessed by Milton.[24]

1607 July 20 Throckmorton-Huntley bond, witnessed by Milton's servant.[25]

1615 December 2 Shelley-Stone bond, witnessed by Milton's servant, and payable at his shop.[26]

1622/3 March 2 Webber-Cowper bond, witnessed by Milton.[27]

1623 May 26 Coppinger-Randolph deed, witnessed by Milton's servants.[28]

1628 October 22 Oakley-Macie deed, witnessed by Milton.[29]

Something is also known of the elder Milton's dealings in real estate. A summary of these runs as follows:

1621 May 25 Buys land of Leonard Poe in Gray's Inn Lane.[30]

1622 April 3 Sells the above property to James Kent.[31]

1627 May 25 Buys land in St. Martin's-in-the-Fields (in the tenure of Sir Matthew Lyster) from Anthony Rudd.[32]

1627 June 23 Buys land in St. Martin's-in-the-Fields from Ann Westrawe.[33]

1628 June 14–30 Concord of fine with Rudd.[34]

1629 April 1 License to sell land in St. Botolph's, Aldersgate, to Alexander Dorington.[35]

1629—Leases land in St. Botolph's to Caleb Rawlins.[36]

1629 June 19 Sells the St. Botolph's property to Alexander Dorington.[37]

1629 July 18 Buys land in Ludgate from Sir John Suckling.[38]

1638 May 7 Sells land in St. Martin's-in-the-Fields to Lyster.[39]

It may be noticed that the peak of activity in Milton's professional work comes near to coinciding with the chief dates concerned in the Chancery proceedings to be related.

The younger Milton entered the world after a certain amount of his father's work had been done. Born in 1608, he was admitted to Christ's College, Cambridge, in February, 1624/5, and received the B.A. in 1628/9. In 1632 he received his M.A. and probably removed to Horton. During the thirties he wrote his famous Latin poem "Ad Patrem," which may perhaps be read as a pledge of loyal affection to a parent suffering from a multitude of vexatious legal actions. In 1635 he seems to have received an M.A. from Oxford. This honor occurred just half way between two interesting events in the life of his father, who was chosen a master of the Scriveners' Company in the spring of 1634,[40] and resigned from his office in the spring of 1636 on account of his "removal to inhabit in the country."[41] In 1638, at about the termination of the active part of his father's suits, Milton went abroad. In the same year (probably), his brother Christopher, who had entered the Inner Temple in 1631,[42] and who was to be of great assistance to him later in legal work, married.[43] Shortly after John returned from abroad, Christopher was called to the bar.[44] Two years later, in 1642, Milton himself married. In 1644 he began attempts to foreclose on his father-in-law's debt of 1627;[45] the business was not completed until 1647,[46] when he secured an extent on Powell's Wheatley property and took it over to his own use. In 1649, as the climax to nearly ten years of political pamphleteering, he was appointed Latin Secretary, an office which he was to retain till the Restoration. In 1650 he arranged to compound for the land he held from Powell, and in 1651 paid the requisite fines on it. Throughout the 1650's he was engaged in constant business as secretary, consulting officials of the state and visiting diplomats (as the German Mylius), writing books (as his various *Defences*), and prosecuting the business of the suits already mentioned. If any statement ever made about Milton was more untrue and misleading than Wordsworth's famous dictum, that Milton was "like a star and dwelt apart,"[47] it must be difficult to discover. However useful such a characterization of his personality as a poet may be, it is utterly untrustworthy as applied to his ordinary life. Constantly in touch with people of all classes and stations and nationalities, suing and being sued, he was very decidedly a man of the world during the years from 1640 to 1660. His subsequent career was indeed different, and to that period the characterization may possibly be applied. But during the Commonwealth his life was active and demanding.

VI

From a consideration of the ensuing documents the question naturally arises, what effect had these experiences on Milton's character, personality, and writings? One might expect that such constant battles with lawyers and adversaries might have left a very definite impression on them, coloring his views of life and affecting the subject matter and style of his writing. And to some extent they did. They certainly emphasized the controversial bent which had already been encouraged by his earlier ventures into scholastic and political tiltyards. While one would hesitate to argue that the stream of Milton's poetry lost itself in a desert of legal quibbles and that lawsuits diverted him into twenty years of pamphleteering, one may safely say that from this forced attention to legal matters, and from the incidental study of the law which it entailed, he must have acquired some interest in and knowledge of law which gave him a richer and more vital background for his later writings.[48]

For his prose works are liberally documented with legal learning. References to the laws of England, to Fleta, to Bracton, to Fortescue, to Coke, and to similar source books recur frequently. His *Commonplace Book* and the Columbia MS devote several sections to quotations concerning laws, usury, and the like. The documentation of the divorce books is exhaustive. Most of his prose, in short, is presented with a meticulous care in preparation and a methodical step-by-step refutation of adverse views which is distinctly legal in approach. And it may be mentioned in passing that his picture of the great lawyer Bradshaw in his *Defensio Secunda* is one of his most glowing eulogies.

Aside from these more or less general effects, his writings are curiously devoid of references to judicial proceedings. In this one respect, at least, he was reticent, and failed to make that blend of public and private interests which often pervades his writing. Seldom does he mention lawyers, and if casually they slip in, it is without either noticeable scorn or praise. His enemies, too, though they grasped at any chance to twit him with possible insults, never mentioned his or his father's affairs in court.

The one noticeable exception to this statement is *Colasterion*, in which he gives his nameless opponent so devastating a tongue-lashing. The attack in this pamphlet is directed against his enemy, not principally as a lawyer, but merely as an impudent buffoon who has dared to attack him, Milton. One would give something to know the name of the poor fellow, but it appears to be hopelessly lost. The chief handle for attack is his position as a serving-man, but incidentally Milton makes merry with him as "the lowest person of an interlude . . . turned solicitor."

With his "huckster at law," "opiniastrous sub-advocate," "paltry solicitor," "serving-man both by nature and by function, an idiot by breed-
ing, and a solicitor by presumption," "lunacy of law, and [one who]
speaks revelations out of the attorney's academy," "John-a-Noaks and
John-a-Stiles," "[man] nothing refined since his law-puddering," "mere
and arrant pettifogger," "right handicraftsman . . . of petty cases,"
"hackney of the law," "folkmooter," "barbarian, the shame of all honest
attorneys," "cockbrained solicitor," "tradesman of the law," and a
torrent of equally overwhelming epithets, Milton simply swamps him in
a flood of abusive laughter, from which, so far as we know, he never
emerged to utter another word of criticism. It is one of the most hilarious
examples of Milton's satire on record, one of the most abusive and ques-
tionable as to taste, perhaps, but certainly also one of the most exuberant
and smashing. Milton was elsewhere frequently a giant with a flail, a
veritable Talus of invective, but never elsewhere does he crush his enemy
with such a cloudburst of combined vituperation and animal spirits.[49]
It is an interesting coincidence, if nothing more, that Milton's most
ridiculous antagonist should have been a petty lawyer. It may have
been with a touch of wistfulness that Milton said in his *History of Mos-
covia* that there were no lawyers in Russia!

In general, the effect on Milton's writings of his and his father's legal
experiences is not so much specific as general. His own most strenuous
affairs in this field came too late to affect a good deal of his writing. The
Cope and Ashworth cases date from about 1654 onwards, when he was
in the thick of the international controversy with More, the successor of
Salmasius. Some echoes of Chancery procedure may be traced in the second and third *Defences*, but the attempt to make positive connections is
precarious. A more alert sense of the weaknesses in the opponent's armor,
a restricted courtesy, a heightened unscrupulousness in aiming at victory
at any cost, a fertility in mustering arguments, an easier acquaintance
with ways and methods of presenting telling arguments, a sense of a
judge or judges always in the background (in this case readers) to be
influenced—these are some of the more indefinite and yet probably more
certain effects of the experiences of these years.

VII

It may not be amiss to speak very briefly of the English system of
land tenures and property in Milton's time. Under English law all landed
property was understood to be held feudally of the crown. These holdings are divided by Littleton into estates held by common law and estates
held by custom.[50] Common law estates are again subdivided into freehold
and less than freehold. The highest form of tenure is fee simple, under

which the estate belongs to the owner and to his heirs forever, without limitation to any particular class of heirs. This condition is virtually the equivalent of the absolute possession of land which obtains in both theory and practice in the United States. Under this status if an owner of land dies, the land descends to his children according to the law of primogeniture; if he dies without issue, however, the land goes to his next cousin collateral, so that his uncle would inherit before his father, on the principle that inheritance may not ascend. His father's family inherits before his mother's, etc. The many intricacies in this law need not delay us here.

Purchase or transfer of land under this condition was accomplished frequently by means of a fine, which was the compromise of a fictitious or collusive suit for the possession of lands. A fine barred further dispute as to previous rights to alienate possession. Such fines, being a branch of procedure at Common Pleas, are filed and indexed in that department in the Public Record Office. The various parts or steps in the levying of a fine were the following:[51] (1) the writ of covenant (C.P. 50), (2) the concord (C.P. 24), (3) the note of the fine (C.P. 26), and (4) the foot and indentures of fine (C.P. 25). There are careful indexes to records of fines, arranged by counties and then chronologically by terms. Thus it is not difficult to follow the successive ownerships of a given piece of land; but to trace the land holdings of an individual, who might hold estates in various counties, would be extremely laborious.

Transfer of property also frequently involved the obtaining of a license from the Crown for alienation of land, which meant entries in the Patent Rolls (C. 66). These rolls are long sheets of parchment, considered "open" as opposed to the "closed" or private nature of the Close Rolls. They contain much public, governmental matter in addition to these licenses to alienate. Of the full manuscript indexes to the Patent Rolls in the Public Record Office, only the earlier reigns have been printed, the present set ending with that of Henry VII. The Close Rolls (C. 54), which are very similar in appearance, contain among other matters many enrolments of private deeds. Thus they offer another repository in which to search for information about land transfer. Like the Patent Rolls, they are fully indexed in manuscript and partly in print.

Fee tail, the next most absolute form of land holding, may be either general, where lands are given to a man and to the heirs of his body begotten, by whatever wife; or special, where the lands are given to a man and his wife and to their heirs of their two bodies begotten. If a tenant in general tail dies without heirs, the donor or his heirs enter into the property as in reversion. Other special arrangements may be made whereby the inheritance may be limited to heirs male, heirs female, etc.

The next class is tenure for life, under which a man holds lands during the term of his life, with possession after his death passing back to some former holder. Under this classification come also tenants in tail after the possibility of issue is extinct, tenants "by the courtesy" (*i.e.*, by inheritance from a wife after her death), or tenants in dower. Under the last-named a wife inherits all or part of an estate from her husband under various conditions; such an arrangement is impossible if his holdings are below the grade of fee simple or fee tail general.

Next down the scale comes tenure for a term of years, which is simply a lease for a specified time. It may be noted in this connection that owners of property under a higher grade frequently transferred them to others under a lower grade, and often for a date of future entry. Thus A might hold an estate for life, might lease it for twenty years to B, and then shortly afterwards and before the expiration of this lease, also lease it to C for a term of ten years to commence at the expiration of the first lease. Milton's and Powell's holdings in and around Forest Hill were complicated by such dealings.

Littleton gives various minor forms of tenure which have little relation to the following book. The explanation just given, however, will help to steer the reader through such mazes of ownership and transfer as he may meet in the following chapters. For more detailed information he will need to consult Blackstone's *Commentaries*.

VIII

The following chapters, one to a suit, are arranged chronologically according to the date of the first bringing of the action. In any arrangement there must of necessity be some overlapping, for one suit does not always conclude before another begins. But it seems wisest to adopt this order, and very little confusion will be experienced in following the thread of action. The first five chapters concern the elder Milton. Then two chapters deal with financial transactions of a slightly different sort, and with a hasty survey of lands which were for a time in Milton's possession. The later chapters follow the younger Milton through his actions. In the appendix the records from which the story is taken are printed in virtually their entirety, and in as nearly as possible their original form.

PART I

JOHN MILTON, SCRIVENER

CHAPTER I

THIS WICKED WORK OF USURY
Ayloffe *vs.* Milton, 1624

"The Scrivener is the instrument whereby the Devil worketh the frame of this wicked work of usury."—Stubbes, *Anatomy of Abuses.*

ON May Day of the last year of the reign of King James I, John Milton the elder, scrivener, gentleman, and citizen of London, was for the first time, so far as we know, the object of a legal action. On this most inappropriate day one James Ayloffe of Cambridge brought into the court of Chancery a bill against Milton alleging a serious misapplication of funds by the scrivener.[1] It was the first in a long series of actions either brought against or initiated by the Milton family.

The trouble began with a simple loan of fifty pounds. In February, 1621/2, or thereabouts, Milton, in his capacity as broker or money-lender, lent fifty pounds to one Edward Raymond.[2] Ayloffe was sufficiently confident of Raymond's integrity and financial standing to be willing to act as his surety to repay the loan.

In the regular form Raymond and Ayloffe bound themselves to repay the said fifty pounds to Milton on the eleventh day of the ensuing August, with interest at the rate of five per cent. In other words, they bound themselves in a bond of £100 to pay £52–10–0 at the end of that time. The recognizance or bond, however, instead of being made out to Milton, was, by a device common at the time, made to his friend John Lane.[3] Whether this system proceeded from a disinclination to have one's name appear too often on legal documents, or whether Lane was the one who furnished the money is not clear; but many such documents follow this method. The bond was, as usual, made out in a sum almost double the debt, to provide a sufficient margin for expenses if legal action should become necessary.

The bond with which we are now concerned has not itself come to light. It does not seem to be among the oceans of recognizances in the Public Record Office nor among those catalogued in the British Museum. But it may very likely be surviving in some out-of-the-way hiding place, and may yet appear. There is no doubt of its reality and of its provisions, on which both parties to the suit agree.

When August came, instead of paying the debt, Raymond did what was the customary thing to do—renewed it for another six months.

Ayloffe says, and Milton does not deny, that the interest on the loan for the first six months was paid. The continuation was a perfectly natural step, and there was no objection to it. Presumably all the parties were satisfied.

But Raymond soon became negligent in his payments. Milton and Lane became growingly suspicious, and watched him with increasing sharpness. By the spring of 1624 it had become evident that the investment was not a good one to continue. Milton thereupon had an interview with Raymond, and informed him that the money must be paid back in full at the next interest day. After hedging for a time, Raymond finally confessed that he neither had the money nor could get it by the date indicated. He pleaded for further time. Milton resisted his plea, and threatened to go to law for recovery of the debt. Raymond still begged further respite, and offered to get some of the money for early repayment, and the rest as soon as possible. The final arrangement was that Milton should take out a technical judgment before the lord mayor and aldermen of London, ordering seizure of the goods of Raymond, but that action should be stayed if Raymond paid ten pounds in August and the remaining forty pounds at the rate of ten pounds each quarter.

This original judgment has not been found, but the summaries of it by both parties in their proceedings agree on its details. Ayloffe says that Raymond, having before the 26th of March, 1623/4, "paida great part of the said debt to the said Milton" (a misleading statement by the way),

did acknowledge a judgment before the Lord Mayor and aldermen of the City of London in the chamber of Gin Hall, London, to the said John Lane for one hundred pounds debt and one penny costs, which the said John Lane remitted to forty pounds. . . . And the said John Milton according to the said former agreement did agree under his hand by way of defeasancing the said judgment to stay execution for the residue of the said debt . . . to be paid at four several days then to come . . . after the acknowledging of which judgment the said Raymond satisfied and paid to the said Milton all or within a small deal of the residue.

Milton's story agrees except omitting the item of having paid "a great part of the said debt," which is nonsense, and specifying that the forty pounds was to come by quarters.

Within a short time of this arrangement Raymond died. The next step was to try to collect the debt from his estate. Milton accordingly promptly sued out a *scire facias* on Raymond's administratrix on the basis of the aforesaid judgment, but was met by the confession from her that she had paid Raymond's debts as far as the money had gone, but that there were no funds remaining to pay further claims. Milton was thus balked in his attempt to recover.

The Lord Mayor's court, Milton had said, had been selected as a personal favor to Raymond because it was less onerous on the defendant. But there was no further reason to be lenient. So Milton and Lane went next to the Court of Common Pleas, and brought an action in that court against Ayloffe as Raymond's security. Since Raymond had defaulted in payment, his guarantor would now have to step in and make good the failure. Presumably the demand was for the forty pounds already named, and the date must have been in April, 1624. But this action was hastily interrupted. Between March 26 and May 1, Milton had procured the action against Raymond, Raymond had died, Milton had sued his administratrix, she had refused payment, and he and Lane had gone to common law. Now the case took a new turn. Ayloffe, who was a co-signer of the bond with Raymond, and who was of course involved in Milton's action, countered by bringing a bill against Milton in the court of Chancery.[4]

Ayloffe's bill is dated May 1, 1624. It is addressed to John, Lord Bishop of Lincoln, lord keeper of the great seal.[5] Ayloffe's story, part of which has already been drawn on for the preceding narrative, is as follows.

After rehearsing the original borrowing, Ayloffe takes the precaution of stating that he made it plain to Milton at the time that as security to Raymond's signature he was unwilling to allow the loan to be renewed beyond the original six months. But, he charges, Milton "for some reward given to him by the said Raymond and by some agreements between them did at the end of those six months notwithstanding your orator's said declaration receive the interest then due for the said money and continued the said money at interest for six months longer." Ayloffe pretends a good deal of virtuous indignation over this flouting of his express direction, and explains how it happened that he never objected before, despite the lapse of nearly two years of time. If Ayloffe may be believed, Raymond told him that he had discharged the debt at the end of the period, and that the slate was now clear.

The reader need not feel too much alarm over this apparently underhanded behavior of the scrivener. Chancery bills, as one quickly finds after a little study of them, are much like political speeches. The best defense is thought to be an aggressive offensive. In these proceedings the parties may be truthful, but even if they are the best people in the world, either their lawyers or the atmosphere of the courts will inevitably bring out in their papers the tendency to shoot at the most vulnerable parts of their opponents' armor. Certain devices become almost entirely commonplaces. Wherever possible one always as a matter of course charges the other side with conspiracy to defraud or with slander. If the charges are not founded on truth, as they usually are not, no great harm is done; if they happen to contain a germ of fact, one may succeed in collecting damages, which will be so much clear gain. It is always good tactics to let a few darts fly blind in the hope that they may find a target. So Milton's alleged collusion may never have existed at all, or may have been nothing more than persuasive pleading on Raymond's part. Ayloffe's warning as to the six-months limitation, on the other hand, may have been a mere oral suggestion, little more than a suggestion, perhaps, which might easily have been forgotten or disregarded. But a disgruntled plaintiff in Ayloffe's position might well have grown to believe Milton guilty of underhanded action and naturally charged him with it.

Ayloffe's further accusation that the agreement between Milton and Raymond over the suit in the Lord Mayor's court was arrived at without consulting him may be true. Next, Ayloffe charges, Milton surrendered the original obligation (now replaced by the new judgment) to Raymond, who with great cunning but for no discoverable reason showed it to Ayloffe as proof that the debt of fifty pounds had been entirely paid. Thereafter Raymond paid Milton "all or within a small deal of the residue of the said debt . . . on or very near to the days agreed upon" —which makes Raymond's actions more than ever puzzling. For that matter, asserts Ayloffe, Milton could have collected the whole amount from Raymond during the latter's lifetime if he had been sufficiently awake and had "prosecuted execution against him upon the said judgment."

But Milton and Lane pretend that "all or the greatest part of the said debt for which your Orator stood bound as surety for the said Raymond as is aforesaid is yet unsatisfied." They are well aware that "the said Raymond is lately dead, so as your Orator cannot make proof of the said agreement or payments," and by some hook or crook have "gotten into their or one of their hands the said obligation which was formerly delivered up" to Raymond.

And now they are suing Ayloffe at common law and seek to recover the whole amount of the bond from him. (Again this original action has not been found; the information is from Ayloffe's bill.) Since Ayloffe cannot plead anything in bar to the suit in that court and cannot be relieved anywhere except in a court of equity, he is obliged to have recourse to Chancery. He therefore begs for a writ of subpœna against Milton and Lane, requiring them to appear in that court and answer the accusations herein brought against them. The bill is signed by Ayloffe's lawyer William Gilbert,[6] and marked at the head with the name of George Evelyn.[7]

The writ was issued accordingly within a few days, and was duly served on Milton. He answered promptly, his answer being sworn on May 10, 1624.[8] Like Ayloffe, he rehearses the circumstances of the loan and its subsequent developments; and in general outline his story agrees with Ayloffe's. He admits that Ayloffe was only a surety for Raymond, and that he used Lane's name only in trust for himself. But he vigorously denies that Ayloffe ever told him that he would not consent to let the debt run longer than six months. He recounts repeated attempts to persuade Raymond to pay the debt, and tells of finally turning it over to an attorney to collect by suit. Raymond, it now appears, was also an attorney in the Court of Common Pleas. He enlarges also on the selection of the Lord Mayor's Court for his action. He asserts that Raymond begged him either to wait for his money or at least to bring action in a court in the city of London (the technical seat of the Court of Chancery being at that time in Westminster, not in London, though cases were often heard in the Temple or in Lincoln's Inn) to spare him unnecessary expense. Milton, willing to oblige him, did so. Apparently Raymond put it very strongly, not to say melodramatically, to Milton, painting a lurid picture of himself lying in prison, utterly undone, if sued at common law. Milton then admits that Raymond promptly paid ten pounds of his debt, and almost immediately afterward died. Since then no payment has been made. Milton also categorically denies that he ever gave up or surrendered the original obligation to Raymond, though he admits that his attorney had it for some time.

Milton really thinks that Ayloffe knew he was still bound for the debt, because after Raymond's death he came to Milton's house to learn whether the debt was still owing, and was told by a servant during Milton's absence that it was. So Milton thinks that "his conscience . . . accused him, or at least persuaded him that he was not discharged." Milton protests that Ayloffe does him a great wrong to put him to all this unnecessary vexation and expense (another stock charge!), since Milton never asked anything but his just debt and reasonable interest. He is still willing to discharge Ayloffe from the bond and the suit if he merely repays the debt, which now amounts to thirty pounds plus interest. (Evidently Raymond or his executrix had succeeded in producing ten pounds more in addition to that previously mentioned.) So with the usual peroration confessing, avoiding, traversing, denying, averring, and the like, and humbly praying "to be hence dismissed with his reasonable costs and charges in this behalf most wrongfully sustained," he closes his defence. The document was signed by his counsel Edmund Breres,[9] sworn to before James Hussey,[10] and filed with Valentine Sanders.[11]

Here, unfortunately, the case abruptly breaks off. If it were a normal, full record, there would be reports and certificates from masters in Chancery, depositions of witnesses, and decrees and orders. We should learn whether Ayloffe was forced to pay the sum demanded, whether Milton was denied his plea, or whether some other disposition of the case was made. But no judgments or depositions have been found. Possibly the case was settled out of court. A careful search of the decrees and depositions yields no references to Milton's name. One would surmise that Milton's defence would be upheld, but one can never be sure. Until some further evidence is discovered, the case is adjourned.

CHAPTER II

FOR FASHION'S SAKE
Burton *vs.* Milton, 1626[1]

Easy. Why, sir, you know Master Blastfield is the man.
Quomodo. Why, sir, I know Master Blastfield is the man; but is he any
more than one man? Two entered into bond to me, or I'm foully
cozened.
Easy. You know my entrance was but for fashion's sake.
Quomodo. Why, I'll agree to you: you'll grant 'tis the fashion likewise,
when the bond's due, to have the money paid again.—Middleton,
Michaelmas Term, III, iv.

THIS second chapter appears somewhat like an imitation of the
first. Loans, judgments, suits, countersuits, and writs are the
burden of its drama. As in the previous instance, not all the materials
have come to light, but we can learn enough from the documents which
we have to form a moderately accurate picture.

The first move was made before the end of the Ayloffe affair. In or
about May, 1623, when Milton was peacefully collecting the interest
on Edward Raymond's bond, he managed another similar loan for the
Willoughby family for a hundred pounds. Much of our knowledge of this
transaction comes from a bill which Samuel Burton brought against
Milton in the Court of Requests on May 10, 1626.[2] Burton tells how
about three years earlier Robert Willoughby, late citizen and grocer of
London, Thomas Willoughby the elder of Sutton Coldfield, Warwickshire, gentleman, and Edward Willoughby the younger, citizen and linen
draper of London,[3] borrowed a hundred pounds of William Smith, citizen
and mercer of London,[4] and in security became bound to him in the
amount of two hundred pounds for the payment of one hundred at a
day agreed upon but not known to Burton.

Apparently the Willoughbys treated their loan exactly as Raymond
had his. When the day came for payment of interest (and principal if
they so chose), they defaulted. Probably there were the usual reminders
from Milton or his servants, the same refusal on the part of the borrowers, perhaps the same pleas for time. In the meantime trouble blew
in on the Willoughbys from another quarter. On the Plea Rolls for 21–22
James I appears the following entry, originally in Latin but here
translated:[5]

London, ss. Edward Willoughby, late of London, esquire, otherwise known

27

as Edward Willoughby of Sutton Coldfield in the county of Warwick, esquire, was summoned to reply to Thomas Paradine[6] about a plea which he brings against him for £300 which he owes him and unjustly detains, etc. And whereupon the said Thomas, by his attorney Henry Hodgkinson,[7] says that whereas the aforesaid Edward on the sixth day of November in the twentieth year of the reign of our lord the now king of England [i.e., 1622], in London in the parish of St. Mary of the Arches in the ward of Cheapside, conceded that he was bound by a certain writing obligatory to the said Thomas in the aforesaid £300, to be paid to the said Thomas when it should be required, but the said Edward though often required, has not yet repaid the said £300 to the said Thomas but has hitherto refused to yield it to him and still refuses. Further he says that he is injured and he has damages to the value of £40. And so the said party brings this suit, etc., and presents here in court the aforesaid writing, which aforesaid debt is witnessed in form aforesaid, which is given on the day and year aforesaid, etc.

And the said Edward through Thomas Shakespeare[8] his attorney came and denied force and injury, etc. And the said attorney says that he is not instructed by the same Edward his master as to any response for the same Edward to be given to the aforesaid Thomas in the aforesaid plea. And he says nothing else, by which the said Thomas remains undefended against the said Edward. Therefore it is awarded that the said Thomas may recover against the said Edward his debt aforesaid, and his damages by reason of the detention of that debt, to 100s. . . . And the said Edward in mercy, etc.

This form is then repeated word for word for Thomas Willoughby. Then comes the epilogue:

And because the said Thomas Paradine in the court of the lord King here recovered his debt and damages aforesaid against a certain Edward Willoughby of Sutton Coldfield in county Warwick, esquire, who together with the aforesaid Thomas Willoughby is held and bound by the said writing to the said Thomas Paradine in the aforesaid debt, as appears on this same roll . . . therefore the aforesaid Thomas Paradine shall have one such execution against the said Edward and Thomas Willoughby or either of them on the aforesaid debt and damages.

Following this affair as recorded on the Plea Rolls, and entered on the same membrane, comes the entry which concerns our present story more closely. In brief form it reads as follows:

Edward Willoughby was summoned to reply to William Smith about a plea which he has brought against him about two hundred pounds which he owes him and unjustly detains. And whereupon the said William by Henry Hodgkinson his attorney says that whereas the said Edward on the sixteenth day of October in the twentieth year of the reign of the now lord King of England [1622], etc. . . . And the said Edward by Thomas Shakespeare his attorney came, and denied. . . . Therefore it is awarded that the said William shall recover his debt . . . and damages . . . to 80s. . . . [Similar records follow, substituting the names of Thomas and Robert Willoughby for Edward].

And because the said William in the court of the lord King here has recovered his debt and damages aforesaid against one Edward Willoughby of Sutton Coldfield in county Warwick, esquire, and Thomas Willoughby, citizen of London, who together with the aforesaid Robert Willoughby are bound and obliged through the aforesaid writing to the said William in the aforesaid debt, as appears on this same roll, therefore the said William may have one such execution against the said Edward, Thomas, and Robert or any of them for the debt and damages aforesaid, etc.

The language of these proceedings is complex, difficult, and dull. Its purport, briefly, is as follows. Paradine (in the second instance, Smith) brought suit at common pleas through his attorney Henry Hodgkinson for recovery of the face amount of the bond plus damages. The court admitted the validity of the debt, authorized its recovery, and awarded Paradine 100s. damages and Smith 80s. The judgment was granted against all three Willoughbys (in the first instance, only two), so that if one slipped through the creditor's fingers, he could still get his money from the others. The Willoughbys, represented by their attorney, Thomas Shakespeare, offered no defence or rebuttal other than the perfunctory denial of force and injury. The court, to make its judgment effective, then granted an execution or attachment, by which the plaintiff could seize the lands of the defendant and hold them until recovery of the principal, interest, and expenses. For all practical purposes, the incident was closed.

But though the affair just described may have seemed to be closed, actually it was not. It was rather just beginning. Possibly Smith was unusually good-natured; possibly the Willoughbys were tricky persons who found means to slip out of the judgment; perhaps they had no real estate, so that the court attachment was so much worthless paper. At any rate, according to Burton's story later, Smith's next move was to approach the Willoughbys confidentially and attempt an improvement of the situation. Smith, he alleges, after causing their arrest, told them that if they could procure other security they should be not only set free but also released from their debt. Unexpected good fortune, this, for the Willoughbys.

They thereupon looked about for friends with money to loan, and picked on Samuel Burton[9] and Sir George Peckham.[10] Their sales talk must have been convincing, for the new friends responded. In May, 1624, Burton signed a bond to Smith for two hundred pounds, conditioned for the payment of one hundred and ten pounds at Milton's house in Bread Street on April 20, 1625. The Willoughbys presumably heaved a sigh of relief, went home, and forgot their troubles.

Next, Smith turned his fire on Burton. There seems to be something tricky and collusive about the proceedings; certainly, as Burton tells it, it is one mass of injustice crying to Heaven for correction. From the archdeacon's point of view, Smith and Peckham almost at once began to plot against his peace of mind, gathered in Milton as fellow conspirator, and "combined and confederated" to make Burton pay the whole debt of £110. Burton was pained at this rascally proceeding, partly because Smith, says Burton, never furnished a penny of the sum so lent to him by Burton, and partly because Smith bears no expense in the suit which the confederates have contrived against him at common law. On the contrary, it is Milton and Peckham who are the chief actors, Smith being only an intermediary, a figurehead. Milton, however, violently denies that he is prosecuting any suit at all against Smith, or has any hand in the prosecuting of any. However, Milton admits that he has heard that Thomas Paradine, citizen and haberdasher of London, used the name of Smith in trust in such a bond, and he offers his opinion that Burton is wilfully trying to perplex and hinder a lawful suit which Paradine in the name of Smith has taken against Burton and Peckham.

Here is a perplexing mix-up. Smith sues Burton on his bond; Burton denies the propriety of the suit; Milton suggests the suit is not by Smith but by Paradine in the name of Smith. There is evidently some connection with the other suit just summarized. In one of them Paradine sues the Willoughbys for £300; in the other, Smith sues them for £200; in both cases judgment is granted. The two follow each other on the rolls; the defendants are the same; the language and the judgments are similar. These facts argue close connection between Smith and Paradine, and support Milton's suggestion. Perhaps the two suits by Smith and Paradine were actually different statements of the same action: two suits under different names for recovery of the same money. Still, as the amount named in the two is not the same, one cannot be sure. What is certain is that Burton was dragged into the business, was vexed by legal actions, and decided to defend himself by attacking in another quarter.

On May 10, 1626, then, he brought action in the Court of Requests against all three of his supposed persecutors.[11] Like the Court of Chancery, this was a court of equity; and though originally devised for the suits of paupers and poor men, it had long before this time been thrown open to equity proceedings of nearly all kinds. Burton, then, could legitimately bring his bill into this court.

In his bill he rehearses the circumstances of the original loan from the three Willoughbys to Smith, describing their arrest by Smith "about two years since," and their arrangement with him to procure a new security. Robert Willoughby thereupon, he says, addressed himself to Burton, begging him to join with Sir George Peckham to guarantee the one hundred pounds to Smith—assuring Burton that he (Willoughby) and Peckham would really attend entirely to the matter, leaving Burton's name only "to satisfy the curiosity of the said Smith." This happened in

May, 1624, as already described. In the bond, he says, Willoughby was the first signer, Peckham the second, and Burton himself the last. The bond, he states rather inconsistently, was dated April 18.

Now Smith and Peckham, he complains, having persuaded Burton thus to enter bond, combine with Milton, "a scrivener in London and a broker for the letting out of the moneys of the said Smith" (whom he has just called a "common usurer" himself), to "lay the whole penalty of the said bond of two hundred pounds upon your said subject." What is worse, Burton thinks that Smith is now dead, and that Milton knows it. Not only conspiracy but fraud! Burton quickly qualifies this accusation with an alternative; namely, that Smith is in hiding, and by Milton's advice conceals his place of lodging so that Burton cannot possibly find him to serve him with due process of court. Milton, however, he protests, visits him almost every day ("if he be living"!), knows where he lodges, but, though entreated by messengers from Burton to reveal the address, utterly refuses, merely out of spite and to prevent Burton from having any means of relief from his persecutions. In fact, Milton seeks only one thing: to secure as quickly as possible a judgment at common law against Burton.

Still worse frauds than these, however, are being perpetrated. Milton and Peckham also combine together to relieve Peckham of all responsibility in the bond so as to throw all the responsibility on Burton. Burton also goes further in his charges, though evidently thinking better of it after having written them. He accuses Smith of receiving a bribe from Peckham to avoid taking lawful action against him, and asserts that though in order to avoid conspicuous favoritism he has sued Peckham to an outlawry, it is in such mild fashion as "he intendeth shall not be prejudicial to him, nor any way compel him to make payment of the said debt." After writing this last part, Burton evidently feared that it might be libelous and revert on his own head; so he crossed it through. It might well have cost him heavily to make such wild statements.

Therefore, since Burton was drawn into the tangled business through the fair promises of Willoughby and Peckham, since it was Peckham's security and not Burton's which was the principal affair, since the first bond is not delivered up by Smith as it should have been when replaced by the second, since Peckham is a rich man, having lands worth at least a thousand pounds a year and no children to cause him expense, and since Peckham is Willoughby's own brother-in-law, it is only right that Smith should proceed against Peckham rather than against Burton.

Accordingly, in order to force Peckham and Milton and Smith to appear and tell all they know about the whole matter, and to answer such questions as Burton wants to ask them, he begs the King to issue

a writ of privy seal addressed to them, commanding them to appear in
the Court of Requests at Whitehall, there to abide such further order
and direction as the court shall direct. He also begs an injunction to
stay Smith's proceedings against himself at common law. The questions
he wants answered are as follows. From Peckham he wants to know
whether he or Willoughby has received any money from Smith, whether
the first bond of Willoughby's was given up at the time of the exchange,
and why Peckham should not discharge the present debt. He wants
Milton to tell whether Smith paid any money to Willoughby on the bond,
whether Smith is alive or dead, where he resides if alive. The bill is
signed by his counsel, Richard Townesend.[12] It is endorsed, in addition
to the simple statement of the names of plaintiff and defendants, "the
defendant notified by messenger."

The court duly summoned the defendants to appear and answer these
charges. Nothing happened. Smith could not be found; Milton did not
appear; Peckham faded from the memory of the court. Consequently
the court issued further orders. On June 27, 1626, after reviewing briefly
the state of the case, the court ordered the defendants Smith, Peckham,
and Milton to desist from prosecuting their suit at common law until
after answering the present bill, and also issued an injunction (addressed
to Smith and Milton only) to enforce compliance with this order.[13]

The effect was instantaneous. The very next day Milton appeared
personally in court. In the records of the Appearance Book of the Court,
under this date, is the laconic statement, "John Milton personally
appears before the king's commissioners by command of the messenger
of the chamber at the suit of Samuel Burton, Doctor of Theology."[14]

But what happened next we cannot say. Milton certainly appeared;
but for all the records show, he disappeared without leaving a trace.
No account of what he did or said or of what was said or done to him
is available. The records of this court's business are unfortunately frag-
mentary and none too orderly. For the next five months we are utterly
in the dark.

On November 15, as if time had simply slipped by without leaving a
trace, Milton again appeared personally in court as before, but with this
difference, that this time the mysterious William Smith, formerly supposed dead or in hiding, was with him. The Appearance Book again
tells the story:[15]

William Smith and John Milton personally appear before the commissioner of
the king by command of the messenger of the chamber at the suit of Samuel
Burton, clerk. And on their response they are admitted to be represented by
Peter Langley, gentleman, their attorney,[16] together with Master Hakewill.[17]

Their joint answer, dated the same day, is preserved with Burton's bill.[18] They begin in the usual fashion by complaining that the bill has been brought against them for no good reason, but only to cause them bother and expense. Smith protests that he knows neither Robert nor Thomas Willoughby, has never heard of any bond of theirs to himself, has no knowledge of their having been arrested, never told them that he would free them if they could find other security, and never had any conference with them or Peckham. (He does not, however, deny doing business with Edward Willoughby, but ignores him.) He indignantly denies that he is a common usurer, though unfortunately without stating clearly just what is his actual business. Both he and Milton deny that they or Peckham (to their knowledge) persuaded Burton to stand surety on the bond, or that they conspired to lay the whole penalty of the bill on Burton. Still, they know no good reason why, if he signed the bond, he should not stand to it.

Speaking for himself personally, Milton explains that he never knew Smith till recently, when he met him for the first time in putting in this answer. He says that he never put out any money for Smith. As to the bond in question, he has heard that Thomas Paradine, citizen and haberdasher of London, used Smith's name in trust for such a bond, and thinks that Burton has been told of this fact long ago and knows it to be true. It is Milton's guess that Burton is wantonly bothering all the defendants merely to hinder Paradine's lawful legal action against himself and Peckham for recovery of his just debt. As for the matter of collusion or confederacy, Milton and Smith are so very far from anything of the sort that they believe that Paradine is suing Peckham as well as Burton, and that Peckham has been so stirred up over this action that he has already actually paid fifty pounds of the one hundred. Milton even denies absolutely that he is prosecuting any suit at all against Burton. He further charges that Burton has, as he believes, often been told where Paradine lives, and that the bond concerns him. Furthermore he thinks that Burton has sent a messenger to confer with Paradine.

Reverting to their joint answer once more, Milton and Smith together deny all combination, confederation, or conspiracy with Sir George Peckham. Whereupon they pray to be "dismissed with their reasonable costs and charges in this behalf wrongfully and without cause sustained." The answer is signed by William Hakewill, headed with the name of Peter Langley as counsel for the plaintiff, and sworn to before Sydney Mountague.[19]

To sum up this rather tangled story, here is the situation. Burton complains that he has been inveigled dishonestly into signing the Willoughby-Smith bond. He claims that the Willoughbys have slipped out, that the other guarantor, Sir George Peckham, has bribed the prosecutor to keep himself out of trouble, so that the penalty falls unjustly on Burton. He complains that the whole thing is a conspiracy among the trio of defendants, and demands relief. In replying, Milton and Smith deny combination and suggest that Burton, who is simply trying to crawl out of a perfectly just and well understood obligation, may very justly be held to his signature.

What are we to conclude from these records? That Milton was underhanded, winking on collusion with a dishonest usurer to defraud an innocent clergyman of a hundred pounds? That he was the dupe of unscrupulous and shady brokers? That being in the money-lending business he must inevitably run into occasional perplexing and difficult situations? That he was the innocent bystander injured in a brawl? That Burton was too easy-going in signing obligations and too reluctant in honoring his signature? That he was making up most of his story out of whole cloth? From the facts thus far given almost any of these interpretations might be justified. The only way to be sure of the interpretation is to have the final decision of the court.

But this decision is lacking. The books of decrees and orders are very incomplete, running sometimes for a long time in perfect sequence, and then dropping out a whole block of entries. In the present case no final decision can be found. With our tentative summary, and with no chance of working out the probable decision, we must leave Milton just as he speaks his final word. We can hardly believe that he was guilty of particularly sharp practice, and his answer sounds quite frank and genuine, whereas Burton's bill is open to many defects and doubts. It does not seem convincing that all the chicanery which he alleges should have taken place. He sounds pained and hurt rather than confident. One would like to know what became of Sir George Peckham, who seems to have been a rather elusive character, and how the Willoughbys managed to elude the difficulty which overtook men apparently less personally concerned in the financial deal at stake. But the gaps in the legal records leave all these questions without an answer. Until further information is discovered, the curtain rings down on this particular suit.

CHAPTER III

DEVOURING WIDOWS' HOUSES
Downer *vs*. Milton, 1631

[The scrivener] is a Scribe by profession, for he devours widows' houses, and a Pharisee in his religion.—Wye Salstonstall, "A Scrivener."

At about the time when Milton was busily engaged in dealing with the Willoughbys, he was entering on still another transaction which was likewise to become a thorn in his flesh. In November, 1624, a certain Rose Downer came to him with fifty pounds to invest, an amount which seems to have represented the better part of her estate. Milton found a borrower named Leigh,[1] and took a bond of him dated in the same month.

Rose Downer was the widow of John Downer, tallow-chandler of London, who had died in the same year, and whose will (56 Byrde) is filed in the Prerogative Court of Canterbury. She lived in the parish of St. Andrew's by the Wardrobe, London, on Audlin Hill, with a trusted servant, on the small estate which she had inherited from her husband. She had at least one daughter Rebecca, perhaps already married to the Mr. Wainwright whose name she bore in 1632, when she proved her mother's will (90 Audley). Her house was but a few blocks southwest of St. Paul's Cathedral, and not much farther from Milton's house in Bread Street.

This investment is related on the authority of Milton's partner Thomas Bower,[2] later to be quoted more fully. The original record of the loan from Rose Downer to Leigh, like so many others, has disappeared. Rose Downer's own account does not tally exactly with Bower's, since she seems to place it in 1626 rather than 1624; but Bower is perhaps the more likely to be accurate since he probably had the documentary evidence at hand when he wrote. At any rate, the money was lent and everyone seemed satisfied.

Nothing more was heard of it for several years. Then in August, 1626 (assuming Bower's chronology now to be correct), it was paid, principal and interest, so that the widow had the money to reinvest. Again she went to Milton, who this time found her a customer in the person of the famous Sir Fulke Greville, Lord Brooke, the friend of Bacon, of Elizabeth and James I, a poet and the biographer of his cousin Sidney, and a relative of the Willoughbys of the preceding chapter. Greville kept

the loan, paying interest, till about June, 1628, when according to
Bower it was voluntarily paid in with all interest and principal—probably after Greville had been stabbed to death by a disgruntled servant.[2a]
Rose Downer, on the other hand, spoke of it as having been called in
by Milton. Whichever alternative was true, the money came intact.

Milton thereupon proceeded to reinvest it. The third borrowers were
Matthew Ewens[3] and William Keymer.[4] The fifty pounds were lent to
them on a bond dated June 10, 1628, in which they were bound in the
sum of one hundred pounds to repay the fifty with interest on the following December 12.

The bond from Ewens and Keymer to Rose Downer, which called for
repayment of the sum of £52 the following December at John Milton's
house in Bread Street, was signed (as Rose Downer says) in the presence
of Milton and his servants or partners, Thomas Bower and James
Fisher.[5] According to Bower's information, Rose Downer's money was
sufficient to furnish but half of what Keymer and Ewens needed, the
rest coming from one Bulteel,[6] "who liked them well." But the widow
felt somewhat skeptical, and charged later that Milton kept a good deal
of the money to pay debts already owing to him from his clients.

The business was highly unsatisfactory, and proved increasingly so.
The interest failed to come in as it should have come; the widow called
for her money back; she got fair promises instead; she called more in-
sistently. Still nothing happened. Six months passed, and then a year;
another year followed. What was she to do? She was poor; she needed
the money; but it did not come. Finally she took the desperate course
that so many others had taken and were to take: she brought legal action.

On April 26, 1631, she presented her bill against Milton and Bower
in the Court of Chancery.[7] It is addressed to Thomas Lord Coventry,
lord keeper of the great seal, and bears at the head the name of Robert
Henley.[8] She tells her story in some detail. About five years ago (Bower
and she do not agree in this detail) she had on hand, of her own money,
"the greatest part of her estate," the sum of £50. The first step in investing this sum, we learn, came from Milton:

the same being come to the knowledge of John Milton of London, scrivener, he
repaired to your said oratrix about the said time and advised her to put out the
said fifty pounds at interest rather than to employ it any other ways, and used
divers persuasions unto your said oratrix that he might have the putting of it
forth, telling her that she should have good security for the payment of the same
to her again, by means whereof your oratrix was drawn to consent.

By her story, Milton was not a man who sat calmly in his office and
waited for business to come to him, but went out and sought it. He
wanted, as she says, to "have the benefit of the brokage thereof, and of

the making of the bonds for the same," in which his profits and income consisted. She had insisted on knowing who the prospective borrowers were and on having time to think it over. He agreed, and shortly afterwards sent her the names of the borrower and his two sureties—which are not given in her bill. This reference may be to either Leigh or Lord Brooke. All went well at first. When the money fell due, in June, 1628 (she seems to have forgotten the several years between), she went to Milton's office and asked him to call in the money, because she had "urgent occasion to use the same." Whether she merely distrusted the borrowers, having possibly heard some tales about them, or whether she genuinely needed the principal for household or other expenses is not quite clear. Milton agreed to call it in, merely asking her to leave the bond with him.

What happened next is hard to be sure of. She says that he called in the money and turned it over to his "then servant" Thomas Bower, to pay to her. But since Thomas Bower was not actually his "then servant" but rather a partner, the widow may have been wrong about other matters than his status. He had by that time been "free" for some four years since his apprenticeship with Milton had terminated. So also she may have erred slightly when she said that the next day after the money was thus paid in, she went to Milton's house and demanded the money. But go she undoubtedly did, only to find Bower there instead of Milton. One gains the impression from these documents that Bower was a somewhat unreliable person, perhaps over-suave, perhaps not absolutely the soul of rectitude. Milton appears upright, if perhaps slightly careless of the way in which his associates managed clients' money-affairs. Bower, says Rose Downer, had the money then in his desk, and admitted having it; but nonchalantly refused to give it to her, saying that he would invest it for her again. She begged, he denied; she reminded him of her great need for it, he pooh-poohed her. She then grew angry and began to abuse him.

Just then, to her immense relief, Milton came in. She at once appealed to him, confident that he would set all right, and he did not fail her— at least not much. He ordered Bower to pay her the money, and seemed much offended that he detained it from her. At the same time she felt that this brusqueness was assumed rather than real; he acted "with such gesture and subtle carriage as your said oratrix did plainly perceive that it was a mere confederacy and a combination between them to detain her money from her." Much disgruntled, she was obliged to return home without her money.

The next morning came another unpleasant surprise. A messenger arrived from Milton's office bringing a new bond for her signature. Here was no money for her, but in its place a new investment. This was the Ewens-Keymer obligation, made for £100 for repayment of £52 on December 12 following. James Fisher, the messenger who brought it, gave her the package. She inquired what it was. A bond for her money, he answered. But, she protested, she needed the money and had no wish to reinvest it. Well, replied he, it was good security and she would have to be satisfied with it. Saying which, he "cast the bond to your said oratrix and departed."

She refused to take it, and went and told Milton as much. He evidently hushed her up, assured her the borrowers were reliable men, and further—so she says—declared that he would guarantee the money himself. There being no better alternative, she went home and was forced to borrow money from her friends till it should come back. Apparently she was pretty badly in need of cash. She seems to have distrusted the new borrowers chiefly on instinct, partly because they were "utterly disliked by your said oratrix," and partly because they were men not known to her, and perhaps most of all because they "dwelt far remote in Somersetshire." One wonders whether the story of being in dire need and reduced to borrowing may not be slightly exaggerated for effect on the court.

This encounter took place in June, 1628. Enduring the delay as patiently as she could, Rose Downer came eventually to the end of the six months—December, 1628. She then appealed to Milton again for her money. Again Bower the villain confronts her. No, unfortunately her money is not ready, nor the interest; but if she will only wait till next June, it will all come in serenely. Again the discontented return home with empty pockets.

Six months pass. In June, 1629, she again makes the semiannual pilgrimage to Bread Street. Again she demands her money. Again Bower meets her with a shrug of the shoulders, and the regret that the money has not come in. But this time there is one change. Milton now frankly confesses that the money has not been paid, and advises her to resort to law to collect her money. The good debt has become a bad debt. To be sure, he still offers to pay her if she cannot collect otherwise (at least, this is her version); but his advice is to sue out the bond at common law. Her comment on this final indignity is almost lyrical. She is sure that they both realized that she was an "ignorant poor old woman," and took advantage of the fact, hoping for her death and combining to defraud her. Their injustice and inhumanity are too much for her.

Apparently from that time she even ceased hoping to collect her money. She trudged faithfully over to Bread Street occasionally, but met with no success. She called for her money periodically between 1629 and the time of submitting this bill two years later, but received in return only "fair words and promises." The scriveners, on their part, grew more and more curt, if not disgusted. They told her she must stick to her bond and get payments as best she could, despite the fact, which she emphasizes, that she never consented to the bond.

She goes on to assure the court that Keymer and Ewens were of very dubious financial standing. They were, for instance, in debt to Milton at the very instant they signed the new obligation, or if not to Milton, at least to some of his clients. Ewens' lands were fallen to decay and insufficient to cover his indebtedness, and he was in the very process of trying to sell them. Moreover, Ewens "did obscure himself," a doubtful phrase, meaning perhaps that the widow Downer could not find him to talk to, and perhaps that he had moved away. This state of affairs has become intolerable to her. She is forced to act.

So she brings this bill into the Court of Chancery. She is concerned primarily to recover her money, but she has some questions for the defendants to answer. She wishes them to tell whether she did not call in her money from the former securities, whether they did not receive it and put it out again, whether she assented to the transfer, what promises they made to her, how they disposed of the £50, and what money Ewens owed them at the time. For that purpose she asks for a writ of subpoena on Milton and Bower, summoning them at a specified time to appear and give their answers. Her bill is signed "Goldsmythe."[9]

In just a week Milton submitted his answer.[10] It was sworn to on May 3, 1631, before Thomas Eden,[11] and filed with Lawrence Maydwell.[12] This time he makes an individual answer, and not a joint one with the co-defendant. First he admits the loan to Keymer and Ewens, but he disclaims any knowledge that Rose Downer did not lend the money willingly. In fact, as she received both the bond and later the interest on several occasions, she gave him no intimation that she was at all dissatisfied till very lately.

We learn a new angle to the situation now for the first time. Milton mentions that for a long time previous to this affair John Downer, husband of the plaintiff, who had for a long time been acquainted with Milton, had come to Milton for investments. He had apparently for years been bringing in money for Milton to place, and had always been satisfied with Milton's management of his funds. After he died, "long since" [actually 1624], Mrs. Downer continued her money along at interest as before, and was perfectly satisfied to do so. But of late, when the widow became restive under this arrangement, he finally "persuaded" her to take in her moneys, "that this defendant might be alto-

gether quit of her and her moneys." Evidently he had not found her a
saint to deal with, nor her funds an unmixed delight.

He categorically denies that he ever solicited her to invest her money
with him, or persuaded her as she had asserted. On the contrary, the
money was lent out to men whom she approved of, and was paid in
satisfactorily in June, 1628, to Thomas Bower for her use. He believes
that she afterwards asked Bower for the money, but what answer he gave
her or why he did not pay it to her at once, Milton cannot say but leaves
such questions for Bower to answer. Milton here digresses long enough
to inform the court that Bower was not then his servant, but a partner,
as he still is. Indeed, Bower is well enough off to answer to her for any
wrong he may have done her, though Milton thinks there is no such
damage. He denies, of course, all confederacy and combination, and
ridicules the idea of his having used any "subtle gesture or carriage"
toward Bower to lead him to retain her money.

Furthermore, Milton believes the money was lent to Ewens and
Keymer with her full approval. He knows that the bond was later sent
to her, but does not know that she refused to accept it, or that James
Fisher virtually threw it in her face. If he had known of such behavior,
he would have reproved Fisher, and given him "due correction." Indeed,
if he had known that she disliked the negotiation, and if she had brought
back the bond at once to him (as she, however, intimates she did do),
he would have seen that she was paid back her money. But he thinks
that all was done fairly between her and Bower; he believes that she
consented to the loan; and he knows that for a long time she showed no
dislike. He denies that he ever promised to pay her himself, that Ewens
was at the time (at least to Milton's knowledge) in decayed circumstances, or that Ewens "did obscure himself." He admits that Ewens
owed money at his shop, and that some of the new loan was used to
repay older debts. But he maintains (as would a modern economist in
most such cases) that Ewens was not thereby barred from being a good
risk.

As a possible explanation of her bill, Milton next suggests that perhaps
Rose Downer is merely the creature of some designing person. It is unlikely that she should do such a thing of her own initiative, for she
often, in his hearing, has cleared him of any fault. She must be a stalking-
horse for some enemy with a grudge.

With these exceptions he has nothing further to say to the bill, other
than that he humbly prays that his reasonable costs and charges, wrongfully sustained in this suit, may be reimbursed to him. His answer is
signed by W. Greene.[13]

On the same day with Milton's answer Thomas Bower submitted his, swearing to it before John Michell.[14] Like Milton's answer it was filed with Lawrence Maydwell. Bower begins by accusing the widow Downer of filing this bill out of pure spite, on purpose to "vex, molest, and trouble this defendant, and to put him to unnecessary charge." In general, the tone is much more querulous and touchy and less reassuring than Milton's. He goes on to say that he was for about eight years servant to Milton, and has for about six years been his partner, investing money concurrently with him. He agrees with Milton that John Downer in his lifetime invested money through Milton, and that this £50 was by common consent lent to Master Leigh. Who this Leigh was, however, Bower does not help us to discover. After this loan, which lasted till 1626, the loan to Sir Fulke Greville was managed, and was repaid in 1628. Thereupon, while the money remained in Milton's shop, in came Ewens and Keymer looking for money. The money, which had been paid in "voluntarily" by Greville, Bower thought he was within his rights in lending out again, especially since Ewens and Keymer were both "then reputed gentlemen of good worth and sufficiency, and the meaner of them to have about five hundred pounds per annum, and both of them formerly having taken up moneys at interest, and dealt fairly and squarely therein from time to time." He advised the widow to let them have her fifty pounds (along with another fifty which they secured from Bulteel), and she consented. Not only consented, indeed, but approved of the extension of the loan "for two or three six months [i.e., two or three periods of six months each], and the interest duly paid her for the same time, and by her accepted of, without any dislike at all." Part of the money Bower paid by Ewens' direction to his creditors, part of it he gave to Ewens himself. So far, in fact, was the widow from distrusting this negotiation, that she readily consented during this time to lend £30 more to a Master Waring, and continued it to him until about June, 1630.

But Ewens and Keymer eventually failed to pay their interest. The plaintiff then called for her money. Since that time Bower has frequently called on Ewens and Keymer for repayment, and they have frequently given fair promises. He feels confident that within a reasonable time the money may be secured, and he will do his best to procure it. He utterly denies having detained the money from the widow, or having delivered the bond to her in the brusque manner she describes. As for guaranteeing the money, he denies that also, and explains that neither he nor Milton "use for to do to any, having little reason for it (in these evil times)." However, they do their best; they "take good security for moneys lent, and afterwards with much travail, pains and care, do seek to get such moneys in again to give the lenders what content they may."

He denies all combination and confederacy with Milton, "as is most scandalously set down" in the bill, hopes for his "reasonable costs and damages in that behalf wrongfully sustained," and ends his answer. His counsel is Stephen Atterbury.[15]

Here is a most tangled and conflicting tissue of statements, though all were made under oath and under the penalties for perjury, to say nothing of the moral compulsion to strict truth. In few details is there perfect agreement among the various parties. Rose Downer says that Milton solicited her to lend the money; he says that she solicited him, and that her deceased husband had for years invested through him and that this loan was merely a continuation of the former. She maintains that she often demanded her money; he and Bower protest that she approved their investments till very recently. She avers that Ewens and Keymer had the reputation of being bad borrowers; the scriveners assert they were of good credit. She says she protested from the start against lending the money to Ewens and Keymer; Milton and Bower claim she approved of it for the first year or more. She feels that he and Bower were taking advantage of her inexperience; they deny any such duplicity. She resents the slamming of the new and unapproved bond in her door; they deny such action. She complains of being in dire need of money; Bower says she even brought him £30 more to invest and left it with him for a year or more. She is angry with Ewens and Keymer for "obscuring themselves"; Milton and Bower contradict the charge. With so many points at variance, and such diametrically opposite statements on so many topics, the stage is set for a long battle.

The reasonable step to take next was to secure corroboration of the various stories. Additional information was desirable—the opinions and knowledge of other people than Milton and Bower and the widow Downer. Witnesses were therefore sent for and summoned to testify. On the following September four people appeared and told what they knew of the facts in the case. To those depositions we now turn.[16]

The interrogatories to be submitted to the witnesses are not to be found with the depositions where they should be, but they can be fairly safely reconstructed from the answers. They seem to have run somewhat as follows:

1. Do you know the plaintiff and the defendant? How long have you known them? Tell what you know about them.
2. Was Milton trusted by Rose Downer with investing her £50?
3. Did she in June, 1628, call in her money?
4. Did Milton promise her the money?
5. Did Milton tell her her money was in good hands? Did she admit that she had no objection to the borrowers, but insist that she needed the money for urgent present use?

6. Was the £50 paid in at the time due? Did Milton call it in?

7. Did Rose Downer go to Milton's office and demand her money? Did he seem annoyed at her insistence and order Bower to pay her? Did Bower say he had promised it to a friend, and did she go away much discontented?

8. Did Milton send a servant to her with the bond to Ewens and Keymer? Was she angry, and did she refuse to accept it? Did he say she could have no money, only the bond, and leave it with her? Was the plaintiff then sick in bed?

9. Did Ewens and Keymer enter into the bond without the consent of the widow Downer? Was it entered into to offset a debt of theirs to Milton or others? Were they insolvent and of no credit? Was it the intention of the defendants to cheat the plaintiff of her money?

10. Did she tell Bower shortly before this time that he had dealt badly with her, that she was old and ignorant, that Milton had blamed him for the trouble? Was Bower then angry with Milton, and did he threaten to tell something to Milton's discredit? Did he or Milton advise her to sue Ewens and Keymer?

11. Did Ewens ever admit that the loan was to be used chiefly in paying back other debts, and that little of the money came to him? Did he confess that without this loan he would not have been able to pay the other debt? Did he admit paying no interest? Did he say that Milton must have paid the interest out of his own pocket if any were paid?

12. Did Milton tell her that since she had accepted interest on the loan he was absolved of his promise to see her paid the money, and that she would have to collect her money as best she could?

Such was the tenor of the questions. The first deponent to appear in reply was Olive Street, an embroiderer, aged twenty-six, living in Rose Downer's parish of St. Andrew's. He stated that he knew all the parties concerned: he had been acquainted with the widow for some twenty years, with Milton and Bower for about six. He testified that the widow lived on her small means with one maid servant, that Bower, formerly Milton's servant or apprentice, was now "writing under him in his shop," or at least was doing so three months ago; that the widow lived on Audlin Hill, in St. Andrew's parish, Milton in Bread Street, and Bower (six months ago, the present residence being uncertain) in Long Lane, Smithfield. He testified that Milton (who had the reputation of an honest man in his profession) was entrusted with the investing of the widow Downer's £50, which was her chief capital. This practice must have covered an extended period, for Street mentions that the plaintiff was made acquainted, from time to time, with the various borrowers, whom she regularly approved before the actual lending. In June, 1628, she came to the Bread Street shop and earnestly entreated Milton to call in her money because of her pressing personal needs. Street testified that he was present at the time, and therefore knew it at first hand. Probably he went with her as friend and helper. Moreover, he says, he frequently went from her to Milton as messenger, to urge him to call in the money. When he so went, Milton promised to oblige her, saying that she should have it when it was due. She told Street several times, however, that it was not the borrowers to whom she objected, but merely to the unwarranted detention of her money, which she needed; otherwise she would heartily have approved of them.

Milton told Street that the money had been paid in to his shop. Street was not present when Mrs. Downer went just afterwards to see about it, but he heard about the interview on credible authority. She hurried over to Bread Street immediately after the money had been paid, and asked for it. Milton replied, angrily:

"What a stir is here about your money! [To Bower] Pay her her money. I will be rid of her, and her money too."

Bower replied, "I have promised to furnish a friend of mine with this amount of money, and I must have this money of hers. I knew that when she got it, she would put it forth again. She might as well let my friend have it as another man."

So he refused to let her have it. Not long afterwards, as Mrs. Downer's servant Frances Stacy told Street, Milton or Bower sent a messenger (probably Fisher) to the widow with a bond made out to Ewens and Keymer. She, as Frances told him, was very angry, protesting,

"I will not accept of the bond! I must have in my money to serve my occasions, as I have oftentimes told them before."

"The security is good," retorted Fisher. "My master will make it good, as reason is he should."

Thereupon Fisher, against her will, left the bond with her, repeating what he had said before:

"You can have but good security for your money, and here it is."

But the widow was at the time sick in her bed, as the servant confided to Street, and not fit to take the obligation back again.

Here Street's deposition broke off, though he had answered only the first eight of the questions. It had been directed that he should be examined only on the first eight. Whether he was not expected to know about the last four, or whether it was feared that what he answered to them might be derogatory to the cause of one of the parties is not clear. At any rate, his information stopped at this juncture, and he was thereafter dismissed, having signed his name to each sheet of answers. They were sworn to before Martin Basil.[16a]

The second witness was George Broome of the parish of Blackfriars, a scrivener of the age of fifty-one, who was examined on the same day as Street, and probably in the same place.[17] Broome was an old friend of Milton's, having known him twenty-seven or twenty-eight years, whereas he had known Rose Downer only six or seven. Bower he knew not at all, but he thought it was true that he had formerly been Milton's apprentice and now "wrote under him" in his shop. Milton, he asserted, had the reputation of an honest man in his profession of scrivener. As Milton had told him, the widow had entrusted her money to him to invest, and Milton had disposed of it to her satisfaction. He had never known whether Milton had informed her of the manner of its investment.

He had heard from Milton that the fifty pounds had been paid in, as formerly described, to Bower, with the interest, and that she had come for it not long afterwards. Milton told him that he had instructed Bower to pay her, and had been angry with her and wanted to get rid of her. He had heard the widow say that Bower refused, and that she was forced to return home discontented without the money.

Unlike Street, Broome had talked with Ewens since the beginning of this suit; that is, since last April. Possibly Ewens had carried on his financial dealings with Broome as well as with Milton. At the time of their discussion Ewens, he said, seemed very sorry that the fifty pounds was a widow's, though he really cared little where he got the money, since it was to be used to pay debts owed by him at Milton's shop, and that very little if any of the fifty pounds came into his hands. Ewens had never seen the widow. If it had not been for this loan, Ewens had confessed, he would not have been able to pay his creditors. Ewens told him, moreover, that Milton or Bower had urged him to enter into the bond, hoping that they should not be losers through him. Ewens further confessed to him that he had never paid any interest on the money, but that if any had been paid to the widow Downer, Milton or Bower must have paid out of their own pockets. He hinted that they would not have dared not to pay it, since that was the only way they could persuade her to accept the bond. Since this conference, Broome said that as an emissary of the widow and on her behalf he had demanded the money of Milton and reminded Milton of his promise to see her paid. But Milton had replied,

"Whatsoever promise I made her at the first, yet in regard she has accepted of interest for the said money, I hold myself to be discharged. She may get her money where she can."

Further than this Broome was not examined. He had replied only to questions 1, 2, 6, 7, 11, and 12. He of course signed his name to his answers.

Four days later Frances Stacy, the girl who has already been mentioned as Rose Downer's servant, came up for examination. She was twenty-two years old, a spinster, living with the widow in St. Andrew's parish, and was directed to answer only interrogatories 1, 2, 5, 6, and 8.

She had known Rose Downer, she said, ever since she could remember, the widow being her aunt and having educated and bred her since childhood. Milton and Bower she had known for some four years, presumably through carrying messages back and forth from her aunt relative to investments. The widow, she testified, lived on her small income on Audlin Hill, whereas the two scriveners both lived, she thought, in Bread Street. Bower was servant, she believed, to Milton; of his having gained his freedom some seven years earlier she seemed not to be aware.

From living with her aunt Downer, Frances Stacy knew that the widow had gone to Milton originally because of his reputation for honesty, and had turned over the £50—"a great part of her estate"—to him. From time to time Milton had made her acquainted with her securities, which she was accustomed to approve before he invested the money. She had known it to happen that Milton would send to the widow to know whether she would accept such or such borrowers; and she would either consent or refuse, as she pleased.

The rest of her deposition adds little to the previous versions. She does, however, make the visit of Milton's servant to the widow's house slightly more vivid. After the discussion between the widow and the messenger and her angry rejection of the new bond, he told her the security was good, and that his master would make good any failure to pay. Thereupon he left the bond "on a table in the room."

As might be expected, Frances made her mark rather than signing, being doubtless unable to read or write.

Three days later Richard Sheratt furnished the fourth and last of the depositions. He was a haberdasher aged about sixty-seven, living in the unsavory precinct of Bridewell, only a few steps from Broome's precinct of Blackfriars. He had been acquainted with all the parties for a long time: Rose Downer for twenty years, Milton twelve, and Bower ten. Milton he called a "notary" rather than a scrivener, though the terms are practically synonymous. He knew far more than any of the others about Bower, who, he said, had been a servant two years ago (though the figure is wrong) to Milton and had "written under him in his shop," but of late had become an attorney, practising in the court of Common Pleas—information which we shall see later was correct. His residence, at least during the preceding Hilary term, was at an upholsterer's house in the Strand.

The story that Sheratt tells agrees in most respects with those already described. We need notice here only the additions or variations; otherwise, though somewhat more detailed and circumstantial, it repeats. He said that he, like Broome and Frances Stacy and Olive Street, had been sent to Milton to ask for the widow's money, and had accordingly performed this errand "sundry and often times," both with the widow and alone. Milton had finally become angry, exclaiming,

"You do not need to fear your money, for the security is good enough!"

He was certain that the money came in by Milton's calling for it and not by any other means. He repeated the story of the refusal by the scriveners to give her her money, echoing the "What a stir is here!" conversation, but adding the opinion that they could just as well have paid her if they had wanted to, since they had the money in their hands at the moment. He was sure that the loan to Ewens and Keymer had not been approved by the widow. Of the £50 lent, he had heard that not more than £14 actually came to the hands of Ewens and Keymer, since they were "men insolvent and careless in what and to whom they became bound, and indebted, being both of them far more indebted than their estates did amount unto, and were unworthy of credit for any such sum of money; but what their estates were at the time when the said money was lent unto them as aforesaid this deponent doth not know."

He added that he had, since the beginning of this suit, conferred with Bower and accused him of bad and harsh dealing, since the widow was but an ignorant and simple woman. Sheratt thought that Bower was hard in lending the money against her will and to men unknown to her, and told Bower that Milton also thought so and laid the fault entirely on Bower. Bower thereupon seemed to grow very angry with Milton, saying,

"If he [meaning Milton] tells, I will tell something also!"

Sheratt also charged Bower with duplicity:

"All but a small part of this money is to stop and pay debts due to you and Milton by Ewens! But a small part of the money came to the hands of Ewens!"

Bower made little answer, but admitted,

"Indeed, I think Ewens had but little part thereof."

After this conference, Milton and Bower advised Rose Downer to put the bonds in suit against Ewens and Keymer. Whether this advice was a trick between the scriveners to pay themselves or others some weak debt due from Ewens and Keymer, Sheratt was not able to say, but he insisted it was very hard dealing. So ended his deposition.

What had been gained by these examinations? On certain points the deponents were fairly well agreed, so far as they answered the questions. They had no differences of opinion about Rose Downer's having entrusted £50 to Milton to invest. It was clear that he had invested money for her over a considerable length of time to her entire satisfaction, that he had the reputation of an honest broker, and that she finally asked for her money not because she distrusted his investments, but because she needed it for use. The money was undoubtedly paid in to his office, and laid aside for her. The next day she came and asked for it, but was told that it had been reinvested. He had appeared angry with her for her insistence, her often nagging him for it, and had told Bower to pay her. Bower in turn had told her that the money had already been reinvested and could not then be given to her. She had gone home discontented, only to be followed shortly by a messenger from the scrivener bringing the new Ewens-Keymer bond.

But much of the disagreement and uncertainty persists. Only two witnesses say anything about Rose Downer's calling in her money; the other two know nothing, or at least testify nothing on this point. For all they say, the money may have come in in the ordinary course of investments. If so, it was perhaps routine business for Milton to reinvest it at once. Only one witness has anything to say about Ewens' solvency; the others make no mention of the matter, either knowing nothing about it, or disagreeing with the plaintiff. Only one witness has any information about the amount of money that came to Ewens and Keymer. Only one mentions Milton's promise to stand behind the bond, and he says that Milton considered himself absolved by the payment of the interest.

Certain other points which we should like to know about are not touched at all. No one mentions the reputation—if any—of Bower as to his honesty and good judgment. Milton's integrity is agreed to by all, but Bower is ignored. No one describes Rose Downer, to discuss whether she is patient or irritatingly nagging. One gathers the impression from the documents that she was a nervous, fluttery old woman, constantly running in to Milton's shop to bother him with trivial apprehensions and questions about her money, till he was heartily sick of her and her fifty pounds. No one tells how much interest was paid to her, or what she wanted to do with the money when she got it. A discussion of these problems would assist us greatly.

Meanwhile, Milton and Bower were anxious to have the testimony of James Fisher, who, it will be remembered, was one of the witnesses of the bond and Milton's messenger to the widow. He had been Milton's servant, and had undoubtedly been well informed about the progress of the dealings. An attempt was therefore made to have him examined, but the move was unsuccessful. The failure was unfortunate, because it must be understood that the previous depositions were all "ex parte," that is, selected in the hope that they would confirm the contentions of the plaintiff. Henry Fisher, however, father of James, was found, and his testimony is recorded among the affidavits of the Court of Chancery under the date of November 21, 1631.[18] In answer to the insistence by Milton and Bower that James Fisher was "a very material witness to be examined in this cause on the said defendants' behalfs," he could

only say that his son "is at this time residing in the kingdom of Ireland."
So there was no hope of bringing him into court. This affidavit of Fisher's
was sworn to before Robert Rich.[19]

Though one could not be brought into court, however, his testimony
could; and the court proceeded to arrange for his examination *in ab-
sentia*. On November 28, one Maundrell,[20] lawyer for Milton and Bower,
moved in court that a commission be awarded into Ireland to examine
James Fisher, returnable the last day of the next (Hilary) term.[21] The
motion was acted on favorably by Rich, and the questions were presumably sent over for Fisher to answer.

From this point forward the records become sketchy. Whether the
examination provided for was made, and if so what the result of it was,
we have no way of knowing. There is no evidence that James Fisher was
reached by the examining officer. No report seems to have been turned in
as ordered on the last day of Hilary term. The nearest approach we have
to it is the merely mechanical copying of the depositions for the use of
Rose Downer. On the cover of the bundle of depositions which we have
been using is the notation, "Copied the 14 April, 1632, for Down' by
Waad'."[22] Below this is the endorsement corresponding to the date when
the depositions were taken: "Michaelmas, Anno septimo Caroli Regis."

The case came up for decision on June 2, 1632, over a year after the
bill had been filed, and about nine months after the depositions. It is
just possible that some decrees and orders, not listed in the indexes,
might be found by a patient search through the Decree and Order Books
themselves, for even this final decision has appeared only through a
summary of it later. The books are not accurately or completely indexed,
and many orders are entirely omitted from the indexes. But the books
are too large to be searched through save in exceptional instances. In a
decree of June 20, 1632, however, the court alludes to its own decision
of June 2 in order to establish the basis for a further decree.[23] It is there
stated that it was ordered and decreed on June 2 that "the defendants
should before the end of this term pay unto the plainant 50 pounds, and
thereupon the plainant should assign over unto the defendants the bond
in question to help themselves against the obligers." Rose Downer had
been successful in her suit, and Milton and Bower had been held to
blame in handling her money. They were therefore ordered to "be her
paymasters," as it was claimed in the proceedings that Milton had
offered to do.

On June 20 comes the final chapter. Through the representation of a
new counsel, Thomas Estcot (or Estcourt),[24] Milton protested that
whereas the court had ordered the defendants to pay the £50, now
Bower, even though it had been shown that he lent the £50 without

Milton's consent and that Milton had ordered him to pay it back to the widow, refused to pay his just share of the money. This action, Milton's counsel pointed out, was patently contrary to the intent of the court, which contemplated that they should pay equally, £25 apiece. But Bower, noticing that the order did not indicate what proportion each should pay, and being evidently a cunning person, had refused to pay his half. Yet the court was not to be deflected from its decision that between them they must make good the £50. The final arrangement was that Milton should assume the whole debt, so that the widow Downer should at least not have to suffer further for her misfortune. Then to reimburse Milton a subpœna was ordered against Bower, to see whether he could show good cause why he should not pay his half. If he could not do so, then he should pay Milton his £25. This final decision is signed "R," presumably once more for Robert Rich.[25] So ended the Downer-Milton suit.

In judging Milton we naturally shrink from finding him guilty of robbing a destitute widow; yet the court unmistakably found the part-ners at fault. Between them, Milton and Bower detained Mrs. Downer's money against her will and put it into the hands of borrowers who never repaid it. Whether they miscalculated the reliability of Ewens and Keymer is a legitimate question. In view of the respectable social position of the Ewens family such an error would not be unnatural. It also seems possible that Rose Downer may have been fussy, busybodyish, irritating. Yet despite all the charity which we can muster, we can at best only regret that Milton should have allowed himself to become involved in so unsavory a transaction.

The proper division of guilt between Milton and Bower remains still more uncertain. Though the court treated them as equally involved, the records picture Bower as the active partner and Milton as a shadowy figure in the background. At this time Milton was nearing seventy and laying his plans to retire soon to Horton. More and more he must have relinquished the active guidance of the business to his younger partner. We may be permitted some suspicion of the honesty of Bower, who in this instance seems to have been the moving spirit. We may be pardoned a distinct irritation with the records for not informing us whether Milton ever recovered his £25 from Bower. But so long as Milton re-mained in partnership with him, he must share the blame for the bad faith of the firm.

CHAPTER IV

BONDS LIKE FLIES IN WINTER
Cotton vs. Milton, 1636

[A scrivener] works upon the occasions of other men, and his bonds are
like flies in winter, which lie dead for a time, but afterwards recover life,
and contrary to other things, they have most force when they are ready
to expire.—Wye Salstonstall, "A Scrivener."

WHEN John Cotton[1] turned in most of his bonds and other investments at Milton's shop in Bread Street on November 25, 1630,
the scrivener must have thought of this act as marking the end of a
pleasant and profitable relationship. But he was destined to find such an
opinion very wrong. It was to prove in the sequel neither pleasant nor
the end. Not for seven or eight years was the matter to conclude, and
then only after tumultuous struggles.

The relationship had begun some thirty years before, when Milton
was newly setting up for himself in his profession as notary and broker.
It must have been about 1600 that Milton and Cotton first met in a
business way, for in his answer to Cotton in 1637 Milton said that
Cotton had invested money at his shop "for the space of near forty
years," and his associate Thomas Bower bore similar testimony by saying that "the said John Cotton for thirty years or thereabouts [ending
about 1630] did employ the said John Milton to let out at interest
divers great sums of money."[2] The amounts invested over this period
were considerable, for when the bonds were finally turned in, their
value at the most conservative estimate was some £2,000.

What investments Milton made for Cotton in the first two decades of
the century we cannot at present tell. But in Sir Thomas Cotton's bill
against Milton in 1636, a long list of bonds covering the years from
1620 is given. Though some of the names are illegible, they can be supplied from other sources; others, having no surnames or being those of
obscure people, are not now easily identifiable. Some are those of well-
known people. For example, Milton managed a loan of two hundred
pounds to the fantastic Sir Kenelm Digby in 1626; one of £100 (about
1626) to Sir Robert Heath, chief justice of common pleas and King's
Bench and a puritan sympathizer; and one in 1623 to Sir Richard
Molineux, receiver-general of the Duchy of Lancaster. Evidently Cotton
was a highly valuable customer, and Milton a trusted adviser who was
thought to be not only an honest but a keen business man.

51

Unfortunately a depression began to creep on. What with taxes and growing political and economic bitterness and division, some of the borrowers became poor risks. In Bower's words, many of those who borrowed money of John Cotton "did much decline in their estates . . . and did neglect to pay the principal or interest for two or three years together." It became necessary for Milton to break this ominous news to Cotton, whereupon "the said Mr. Milton did in Easter term one thousand six hundred and thirty acquaint John Cotton therewith."

He must have deplored this unfortunate outcome of the congenial relationship. An onerous duty in any case, it would have been doubly so now, for he was thinking of retiring from business soon. It was to be only a short time now before he was to leave London for Horton, to live a retired life, and he may well have been looking forward to it. It was highly distasteful to him to bring his career to a close with a melancholy attempt to salvage the ruins of a broken fortune.

But since it had to be done, Milton did it. Whether because of ill health or not, he followed a procedure similar to that which had been fraught with trouble in his relations with Rose Downer: he let Bower do it. Bower, who is to appear more and more the smartish young upstart, apparently saw a chance to make a little money on the side. He wrote to Cotton in the fall of 1630 and offered to take all the bonds off his hands for £2,000. Their face value being £3,600, this figure meant a severe loss and consequent disappointment for Cotton. But he was growing old, being already eighty-three, and perhaps felt his inability to cope with changing conditions. Here was an opportunity to rescue over half the face value of his investments; it might be wise to grasp at it, and resolutely forget the loss. Accordingly, he accepted Bower's offer, and closed the deal. The bonds were duly turned in at the Bread Street shop, and a receipt signed by Thomas Bower was given for them. This receipt, which is dated November 25, 1630, lists the individual bonds which were delivered at the shop on that day, and which total well over £3,000 face value. It is now among the Cottonian charters in the British Museum, together with several other documents in the case.[3]

As long as John Cotton lived, the negotiation gave no dissatisfaction, at least none which can now be discovered. But he died in 1635, and his will (2 Pile) was proved on January 29, 1635/6, by his grandnephew and executor, Sir Thomas Cotton. Sir Thomas immediately saw that the investments had diminished in value, and suspected the investors of fraud. So he took counsel with his lawyer, prepared a petition for submission in the Court of Requests, and submitted it on May 28, 1636.

A good deal of the documentary material in this case has been known for some time. It was first brought to light in 1860,[4] enlarged in 1874,[5] and incorporated in Masson's revised first volume in 1881.[6] One set of documents, incomplete but fairly extensive, is among the Cotton papers in the British Museum, another in the Public Record Office.[7] The former, which is from the papers of the Cotton family, consists of the original drafts made by the plaintiff, whereas the latter is the official set filed in the archives.

Sir Thomas Cotton's bill, addressed as usual to the king, begins by explaining that he is the executor of the will of John Cotton, his uncle— "being an old decrepit weak man of the age of fourscore years and up- wards." He lists the bonds which Milton had arranged for Cotton, naming some thirty, most of them for £100 apiece, but an occasional one for somewhat more or less.[10] On these investments, he continues, Milton and Bower regularly brought to Cotton yearly interest at the rate of eight per cent "for some years." Moreover, they exercised constant oversight over the principal, changing it whenever desirable— "and did often renew, call in, and put out the said sums as they thought best themselves, ever pretending to the said John Cotton that the said parties to whom the money was put out were very sufficient and able men." On the heels of this remark, which sounds rather dubious, Cotton is forced to add practically a vindication in blank—"as in truth most of them were (as your subject hath since learned)." The real quarrel which we can see looming ahead here is over the fact that Milton and his partner managed the reinvestment of money which had been called in without asking Cotton's advice, simply selecting what they themselves thought was good security and letting it go at that. John Cotton appears to have been satisfied enough with that procedure; when anything went wrong afterwards, it was a very agreeable handle with which to bludgeon the broker.

Now appears the customary accusation of collusion and conspiracy to defraud. Milton and Bower, it is alleged, finding that Cotton was becoming old and decrepit and "constrained altogether to keep his chamber," did cunningly, with the "practice and direction of one Thomas Holchar [or Houlker],[11] an attorney who was used by the said John Cotton in suing bonds, forbear to bring him in either the principal or most part of the interest of the said sums, pretending that the parties to whom the said sums were let out were not sufficient" (*i.e.*, insolvent). The way was being paved for cheating Cotton out of a good deal of his estate.

Houlker had presumably been Cotton's intermediary in the routine procedure of conveying messages back and forth between him and his brokers; so, when the eye of suspicion was opened, he was a natural victim. Houlker now began to make to Cotton the suggestions which

brokers always have to offer during a depression: sell, even at a loss, but avoid leaving money in collapsing securities till everything is swallowed up. "Thomas Holchar used persuasions to the said John Cotton that it would be more for his profit and ease if he took some competent sum of money and delivered up to them or one of them his said bonds, whereupon they would endeavor to get the principal money." There *may* have been malice in the suggestion, but it may equally well have been sound business judgment.

At this point another conspirator enters: "one Thomas Colwell Esq.,[12] in whose house the said John Cotton then lay." By a bribe of £200, alleges the plaintiff, the Milton-Bower-Houlker ring lured Colwell into their nefarious scheme, to act the part of inside tipster. He often warned Cotton that the borrowers were "desperate, and the parties to be dead, non-solvent, or beyond the seas, and resident in the County Palatine of Chester and Lancaster, where writs could not easily be served." Here was enough of a warning to frighten off any lender. The plaintiff does not say whether there was any truth in the information; one or more of the allegations might easily have been true. Indeed, though the names of most of the borrowers are too vague for identification,[13] Sir Richard Molineux was receiver-general of the Duchy of Lancaster,[14] and his family was connected with the counties of both Lancashire and Chester.[15] The name of Sir William Norris is found associated with his on a fine in Lancashire.[16] William Welby was also of Lancashire.[17] Very likely several others of Cotton's debtors lived in one of these two counties.

In any case, Cotton was persuaded to make a settlement for £2,000 cash. For this amount he agreed to surrender all his bonds, of the face value of £3,600, to Thomas Bower (it is significant that Bower is so frequently the one named rather than Milton; it is never Milton alone, but often Bower alone), with the proviso, necessary of course, that Bower was free to renew any or all of the said bonds, and to collect the principals in the name of either himself or any other he pleased. This transaction evidently was completed in the fall of 1630, for the receipt signed by Bower, listing the individual bonds, and dated November 30, 1630, is preserved in the Cotton papers.[18]

Since that time, to the indignation of Cotton, Bower and Houlker (here again Milton's name is not mentioned) have been able to collect at least £500 of back interest (due before the time of the transfer), which Sir Thomas feels has been taken almost out of the mouth of his weak, decrepit old uncle. Old John Cotton, however, has in the meantime died, leaving Sir Thomas named in his will as executor. Sir Thomas thinks that, now that the old man has passed out of the way, he himself ought to be able to accomplish something. First, therefore, he has gone through the formalities of urging Milton and Bower to sell the securities

back to him for the price they paid him, namely £2,000, and to turn
over to him the interest which they have received during the interim.
He has requested Houlker to tell him what moneys have been received,
and what changes in investments have been made since the transaction;
"it being no reason that the said Holchar, Milton, and Bower should by
such practices and undue carriage make so great profit to themselves."
But they quite naturally failed to see the point, and "refused to enter
into the said account."

Baffled by these repulses, Sir Thomas complains that he has no recourse other than a court of equity. He accordingly prays for a writ of
Privy Seal to compel Milton, Bower, Houlker, "or such others as your
said subject shall hereafter learn to be interested in the said money" to
appear before the Court of Requests to answer the charges. The signature
of the lawyer is not legible, but presumably it was the Henry Perry to be
mentioned in further documents in the case.[19] The bill bears the date
May 28, 12 Charles I [1636].

Of this bill two versions are extant. One, done in a large easy spacious
hand on sheets of paper, is in the Cotton papers;[20] another on parchment
in the usual legal hand and form is among the Requests Proceedings.[21]
The Requests copy is badly torn and worn, so that much of it is entirely
illegible; but it is considerably fuller than the Cotton copy, adding not
only the full list of bonds (of which only the first few are given in the
other) but also all the references to Houlker, which are written in above
the lines as if afterthoughts.

There must have been something wrong with Cotton's bill. For eight
months scarcely any attention was paid to it. Two minor exceptions have
been discovered, but one of them is merely a later allusion to a document
not now known, and the other is, like Melchizedek, without parents or
progeny. The first is an allusion in a later letter from Henry Perry to his
employer, which records that "in Easter term we served Bower by the
messenger, and filed our bill the same term."[22] The other is a decree of
the court, dated five days before the date of the bill, and penalizing
Milton for contempt of a writ of summons which has not been found.
Not only that, but the decree itself has now disappeared, and is known
only through being quoted in a later order.[23] In a decree of March 22,
1636/7, the court recalled that

it was ordered upon the 23rd of May last upon pretence that the defendant
stood in contempt and living within 17 miles of London, that an attachment
should be awarded against him . . . and that the defendant for his delays should
pay the plainant 20 shillings costs.

But no amount of searching has brought to light this original order, nor
has any writ of a date near this time been found.

On the following January, however, a writ was served. But the dates

remain confused. The writ itself is dated in March, but there are several references to serving it dated in January. Either the clerk who kept the records bungled his dates, or else there were several writs, not all of which have survived. The first item in point of time is a record under date of January 23, 1636/7, of the serving of a summons on Milton.[24] "23tio die Januarii . . . A P[rivy]. S[eal]. rendered to John Milton at the suit of Sir Thomas Cotton Baronet." This was apparently the day of *issue;* according to the affidavit of the messenger it was actually served four days later, on the 27th. On February 13 William Witherington[25] made affidavit that "on the 27th of January last he served John Milton the elder with his Majesty's process of Privy Seal."[26] It is interesting to notice the qualifying epithet "the elder"; the younger Milton was already beginning to be heard of.

Masson seems either to have made a mistake or to have known of a document in this action which I have not been able to find. He quotes an order of the court dated February 18, 1636/7, which mentions the serving of the writ on Milton three weeks earlier, and on a motion of one Bernard, counsel for the plaintiff, fines him twenty shillings and orders his goods seized as surety.[27] This lawyer was probably Robert Bernard, of the Abingdon family, who occasionally incurred Cromwell's ire for his disaffection to the Parliament.[28]

Meanwhile Milton had appointed one George Miller[28a] to represent him as attorney on account of the distance from the city and of his growing feebleness. In a court order of March 22 it is stated that he had appointed Miller at the beginning of the last law-term, which would mean about the last week in January.[29]

On March 10, 1636/7, the writ for Milton's examination was issued.[30] It authorized the commissioners for Buckinghamshire to call Milton before them, to receive his answers on oath, to certify them, and to transmit them so certified to the court within three weeks of Easter. It was signed by William Parker and Thomas Parker,[31] and addressed to John and Thomas Agar.[32]

In the matter of the writ, as more than once previously, the dates seem confused. There can be no doubt about the date on the writ; yet in the Court of Requests Order Book there is recorded a decree under the date of March 22, 1636/7, authorizing the taking of Milton's answer. Whether the previous writ had for some reason failed to be delivered or failed to produce effect we cannot be sure; more likely it had been made out but not served. The order of March 22 first sums up the history of the case. It recalls the decree of May 23 last that whereas the defendant seemed to be in contempt of court and living within seventeen miles of London, an attachment should be awarded against him and that as a penalty for his delay he should pay the plaintiff 20s. costs. But new developments have arisen since that time. It has been alleged by the plaintiff [probably an error for "defendant"] in a petition to Sir Edward Powell,[33] one of His Majesty's counsel for the court, that Milton is an old man about fourscore years old, infirm, and unfit for travel; that he had sent up to his attorneys to appear in due time for him; and that about the beginning of the last term Milton had retained George Miller to appear for him. Also that Miller soon made a copy of Cotton's bill upon affidavit that the defendant was aged and unable to travel, and had a writ of *dedimus potestatem* made out for taking his answer in the country. This writ is probably that of March 10, which has just been described; in substance such a writ was an order empowering specified commissioners in the country to take the answer of a defendant to a bill and transmit it in parchment to the court.

In view of these mitigating circumstances, the court ordered that the costs of 20s. previously levied against Milton should be suspended, and that the writ so prepared should issue forth. One wonders whether there could be any possible connection between Milton and Sir Edward Powell in this affair, which may have worked to the advantage of the scrivener. There had been dealings between the two families years before, and within a few years young Milton was to marry Mary Powell. Such a connection is therefore entirely possible.

On April 1, 1637, for the first time, if our dates are correct, Milton's son Christopher, brother of the poet, enters on the stage. The Court of Requests Affidavit Book records under date of April 1 an affidavit the substance of which is as follows.[34] Whereas Milton has been served with a writ of privy seal to answer Cotton's bill, Christopher Milton his son makes oath that "his said father, being aged about 74 years [not 80], is not by reason of his said age and infirmity able to travel to the City of Westminster to make his perfect answer to the said bill without much prejudice to his health, he living at Horton in the County of Buckingham, about 17 miles distant from the City of Westminster." From what we have already seen, this affidavit must actually have come earlier than the date it bears, for the wording of it is so exactly like that of the undiscovered "petition" of the "plainant" alluded to in the court's order of March 22. But in any case it is only a matter of a few days' variation one way or the other. If, as seems likely, there is some error in dating several of these items, it is fairly clear that by April 1, 1637, there had been a good deal of jockeying for position on both sides, writs and counterwrits, affidavits and petitions, until the case had become ready for Milton to submit his answer to Cotton's bill from Horton, nearly a year after the filing of the suit.

The progress of the case to date is summarized in a letter from Cotton's attorney, Henry Perry, to Sir Thomas on April 3, 1637.[35] He mentions the filing of the bill (Easter term), the serving of Bower with a writ (Easter term), the serving of Milton—three writs being issued, of which only the last was served—, an attachment against Bower for want of an answer (the last term), an order for his commitment and an increase of charges for his delays and contempt, a similar order for Milton, Milton's obtaining of an order for suspension of costs against himself ("since the term"), and the *dedimus potestatem*. Perry also hastens to show his alacrity and faithful solicitude for his employer in that he "sent the name of a gent that lives thereabouts who [is] to be put into the dedimus for you, who I hope will be present when the answer is taken." He assures Sir Thomas that by the beginning of the next term both answers will have been secured, and the case will then "stand in a right and ready way for further proceedings as shall then be advised." He is sending Sir Thomas copies of all the orders, and makes a further rather cryptic statement: "when your other bill comes, I shall be as careful in that as [I] may be." This may refer to the amended form of the bill as described above, in which the name of Houlker has been added above the line in a number of places.

On April 8 Thomas Bower gave in his answer.[36] Here, as we might expect, we begin to see the case from a different angle. Bower concedes the truth of many of the plaintiff's statements: Cotton invested money with Milton for thirty years or so, Bower was Milton's "servant" till some seven years ago, and he helped to invest Cotton's money (but only with Cotton's consent). When the depression came, it was Milton and not Cotton who took the initiative, and in Bower's version the situation seems entirely changed. As some of the borrowers "did much decline in their estates," Milton reported this circumstance to Cotton, who, apparently in a panic, tried to unload his holdings on Milton at half price— £3,600 worth for £1,500. But Milton was too distrustful, and "would by no means condescend to compound" on these terms. Cotton's next step was to send for the younger man, Bower, and try to make a deal with him. In this he was successful. Indeed, he got Bower to pay him £2,000, or £500 more than the amount which Milton had been unwilling to consider. Thereupon Cotton sent the £3,600 worth of bonds to Bower, who borrowed most of the money for his venture at 8% interest. Milton, he is careful to explain, was not present when this agreement was made, and one wonders whether Bower was not committing something very near a breach of trust. But it was profitable business. He set to work so energetically that within a short time he had collected all but a few hundred pounds of the £3,600. Apparently a little hard work over these

few months netted him between £500 and £1,000, a profit which,
if actually realized, would be entirely unreasonable. And this account
is based on his own testimony.

However, it is important to note that he goes on to testify that
neither he nor Milton ever invested any of the money without Cotton's
consent. Moreover, he says that neither he nor Milton worked on
Cotton to persuade him that the debts were "desperate," or insolvent.
He denies any collusion with Colwell, but entirely omits the name of
Houlker, a fact which may possibly indicate that he was answering the
earlier version of the bill, to which Houlker's name had not been added.
He concludes by protesting that he has undergone enough expense and
trouble to be allowed to keep the money which he has received on the
principal debt, and hopes that he may be dismissed with costs.

His answer is signed with the names of two lawyers: Francis Walsted[37]
and Pedaell Harlowe.[38] An abstract of Bower's answer, considerably
condensed and perhaps made for Cotton by his lawyer, is among the
Cotton papers.[39]

Bower submitted with his answer on the same day an impressive as-
sortment of excuses and defences, which were entered in the Affidavit
Book.[40] He swore that he had procured a copy of Cotton's bill about the
end of Easter term last, that he had taken it to his counsel to draw up an
answer, that the counsel shortly afterwards had left town, that by
reason of the sickness and the consequent adjournment of both Mid-
summer and Michaelmas terms he had not come back to town again
until the beginning of Hilary term, that when he had finally come he had
lost the copy of the bill, that therefore Bower had been forced to procure
a new copy "about Candlemas [February 2] last," and that what with
all these lets and hindrances, sickness, and "his extraordinary occasions
in his other business," he had been unable to present his answer till the
present time. All these explanations are plausible enough, but such an
aggregation of good reasons is almost too much. However, we are grateful to him for the reminder of the "sickness," which helps to explain
much of the delay and confusion of the steps in the suit. In 1636, as on
certain occasions previously, the most memorable of which were 1377,
1603, and 1625, London had been swept by the bubonic plague, which
killed thousands of its inhabitants and created a reign of desolation and
horror comparable to that resulting from an efficient, modern war.
The plague undoubtedly explains why the case dragged out so long
before the answers were turned in.

Finally on April 13, 1637, Milton himself turned in his answer.[41] He
furnishes no great amount of new information, agreeing for the most part
with Bower as to the facts of the case. Cotton, he says, often walked to

his shop in London; and though Milton denies that Cotton gave him great sums to be lent out at 8% interest, yet for "near forty years" he did bring in money to lend at Bread Street, to a total of about £3,000. Cotton was always satisfied with these investments, and no losses occurred. Milton does not remember the names of the various borrowers, "his employment being great that way, and long since he gave over his trade." All these investments were made earlier than five years ago (*i.e.*, before 1632, the probable date of his removal to Horton). He takes sharp issue with Bower on one point, which is that he never told Cotton his investments were bad. Cotton, he agrees, was a timorous soul, and once attempted to persuade him to buy the lot for £2,000 [not £1,500, as Bower puts it], but Milton never *offered* him that amount for them, and refused to accept Cotton's proposal. After Cotton left him, he does not know what his client did. He has heard, of course, that Cotton dealt privately with Bower, and that Bower joined with Houlker to invest the money, but he does not actually *know* anything about it. Though Bower and he were "co-partners in the trade of a scrivener, yet they were never partners in or concerning the said bargain or agreement." So he begs to be dismissed "with his reasonable costs and charges in this behalf wrongfully sustained." The answer is signed by "Whitfield."[42]

The answer was sworn to on April 13 before John and Thomas Agar, though the Requests copy is endorsed with a later date: "Responsio Miltoni ad sectam Cottoni vi Maii 1637 per Johannem Agar generosum armigerum Commissionarium."[43] There is a further note to the same effect opposite the heading on the Requests copy. There is no accounting for the discrepancy in dates except by the general confusion throughout the case. After studying the other papers, one would not be at all surprised to have the answer received on April 13 by the commissioners, and held until May 6 before being sent in to London.

Then for seven months the suit drops out of sight. On November 30, 1637, according to the records in the Appearance Book of the Court of Requests, Bower appeared in court and got permission to be represented the following December 5 by his counsel Noel Boteler or Butler,[44] together with Francis Walsted. Evidently his previous answer had been excepted to by the Cottons, who had convinced the court that he had evaded some issues.

Bower's further answer, signed however only by Francis Walsted and not by Noel Butler, was presented on December 5 as contemplated by the previous entry. It is rather short, and is concerned chiefly with explaining that Bower has since the beginning of the negotiations received about £160 interest, which he considers rightfully his, as also any interest which was due before the transaction and is not yet paid.

This answer was evidently intended to meet two interrogatories or exceptions which Cotton had presented. Among the Cotton papers these questions, together with abstracts of Bower's answer, are still preserved.[45] Cotton has two questions to ask about Bower's answer. The first is what principal and interest Bower has received. The answer as noted on the sheet of interrogatories is illegible, but Bower asserts that Milton offered £1,500 for the bonds. The second asks what interest Bower got before receiving the principal of the bonds; the answer is none. The document bears no date, but from its close resemblance to the foregoing must be assigned to some date before the "further answer."

On the first day of the following February the case came to an end, this time with a complete vindication of Milton. The decree of that date has not been found in the order books of the court, but a copy among the Cotton papers may be accepted as reliable.[46] Dated February 1, 1637/8, it rehearses how Cotton had put in his bill "long since" and how Milton had answered during the "same term." This last item gives us pause. According to the dates given on our documents the bill had been submitted in May, 1636, the answer in April, 1637. Either the dates again are badly mistaken, or else the plague of 1636, which caused the suspension of several law-terms, had jammed business into a confusion from which it never recovered. The case, however, was now ready for settlement. The court noted that the plaintiff had not replied or in any other way proceeded after the defendant's answer for over two full terms, which was the limit of time allowed. According to Thomas Powell, when the defendant had put in his answer, the plaintiff then had till the beginning of the third term thereafter to put in his "replication." After that time, and after the defendant's attorney had given the plaintiff's attorney seven days' notice, the defendant should have costs. If, on the other hand, the plaintiff should reply, the defendant could then put in his rejoinder, and so force the plaintiff to go to a commission.[47] In this instance, however, the court deemed that the plaintiff "resteth satisfied, for that he hath by the space of two whole terms last past and upwards failed to reply or otherwise to proceed in the said cause, whereby to bring the same to hearing as by the ordinary course of this court he ought to have done." The court therefore decided that the case should be

from henceforth out of this court clearly and absolutely dismissed for ever for want of prosecution, and the said defendant as concerning the same is discharged of any further attendance in this behalf and licensed to depart at his liberty (sine die) and that the said complainant Sir Thomas Cotton shall presently upon sight or knowledge hereof content and pay unto the said defendant Milton or to his assigns demanding the same the full sum of twenty shillings of current English money for his costs herein wrongfully sustained.

CHAPTER V

CRYING "REVENGE!"

MILTON *vs.* DUCK, 1637

I would . . . that every miserable debtor that so dies might be buried at his creditor's door, that when he strides over him he might think he still rises up (like the ghost in *Jeronimo*), crying, "Revenge!"—Dekker, *The Seven Deadly Sins.*

MONTHS before the Cotton action had been disposed of, Milton and Bower had set about recovering from the effects of the adverse decision in the Downer case.[1] What arrangement the partners had arrived at between themselves we can only guess at; whatever it was, it satisfied neither of them. They had felt, rightly or wrongly, that they had been dealt with unjustly, and they had been turning over in their minds plans for recouping their losses. After all, if we count the pound in 1632 as worth between six and ten today, £50 in 1632 would be worth $1,500 to $2,500 today, an amount not to be dismissed lightly. With the original bonds now at their disposal, they now set out to remedy their losses.

The logical person to attack was the borrower, Matthew Ewens, or his associate William Keymer. But unfortunately, Ewens had died, and Keymer was not to be found. Ewens, however, had at least died testate, and his estate was being administered by his son Matthew, who seemed to be willing to pay his father's debts. To do so, he had sold considerable holdings in land and estates, some of them having been purchased by Arthur Duck[2] and William Child[3] of London.

Though Duck and Child were formidable antagonists, Milton (and Bower) resolutely attacked them. Milton filed his bill in Chancery on February 16, 1637.[4] The first section of it relates the history of the Downer-Ewens transaction. Without adding anything new to what we now know, it relates how Rose Downer lent £50 to Ewens and Keymer in 1628, how they furnished as security for the money their bond for £100, how Ewens shortly thereafter died without paying either principal or interest, having first made his will and appointed his son and heir Matthew his executor, how Matthew the son failed to repay the debt, how Rose Downer brought action against Milton and Bower, how Ewens and Keymer had paid interest for two periods of six months to Milton and Bower (this glaring inconsistency stands thus in Milton's bill),

62

how Ewens and Keymer became insolvent, how Milton and Bower answered Rose Downer's bill, how the court decided against the defendants in June, 1632, how Milton and Bower paid Rose Downer her fifty pounds on June 20, 1632, and have a receipt to prove it, and how in return, and in accordance with the decree, she assigned the bond over to them for their collection.

Now emerges the story as carried on from this point, where it stopped before. Milton and Bower, as the bill sets forth, learned shortly afterwards that young Ewens had sold some of his lands to Duck and Child, thereby raising a great sum of money, sufficient to pay all his father's debts "with a great surplusage." He in turn shortly afterwards made his will (8 Russell, proved February 14, 1632/3, by his brother Alexander), appointing his brother Alexander and his sisters Barbara and Catherine executors, and then died. His money, they aver, he left in the hands of Duck and Child. Alexander Ewens thereupon proved the will and possessed himself of the lands and moneys of his brother, including that held by Duck and Child.

In the autumn of 1633 Milton and Bower brought a bill in Chancery against Duck, Child, Alexander Ewens, and the latter's two sisters Barbara and Catherine. What has become of this bill I cannot tell. I have looked through the indexes of all actions of this period, but nothing of the sort has come to light. The only discoverable bill of Milton against Duck and these others is the present one. Duck and Child replied, however, confessing that they had money to the sum of £2,000 as charged. But the case never came to a hearing, and herein probably lies the reason for its nonappearance among the records. Before it came to trial, Rose Downer died "far remote from the city of London," so that Milton and Bower could not learn how she disposed her estate or who took administration of it. Actually her will (90 Audley) was proved on August 7, 1632, by her daughter Rebecca Wainwright, but they seem not to have known this fact.

Certain other closely related documents may however be mentioned at this point. On May 8, 1635, despite her having died three years earlier, Rose Downer was named as plaintiff in a bill against Duck and Ewens.[5] She (or another writing in her name) recounts how she lent £50 to Ewens and Keymer in 1628, and how they failed to repay the debt. After Ewens's death his son sold his property to Arthur Duck and William Child, and then soon died. He left a considerable sum of money with them to cover his debts, but they failed to satisfy them. She therefore begs a writ against them. The bill is signed by R. Estcott.[6] Duck and Child answered on June 13, acknowledging such matters as the death and settlement, but pointing out that they had no official knowledge of Rose Downer's claim, and denying that they were liable for the debt. Their answer is signed by Thomas Gardiner.[7]

The situation is strange. The evidence already presented seems to prove irrefutably that Milton settled the debt to Mrs. Downer years earlier. Furthermore, she was indisputably dead by 1632 (when her will was proved), three years before presenting this bill. Oddly enough, too, Milton's name is nowhere mentioned in the bill. One is forced to the conclusion that since the original obligation was made out in Rose Downer's name, Milton prepared a bill, using her name as plaintiff. If one accepts this guess, the lost bill, though misdated, is accounted for. But it seems like an unusual procedure, and I am not confident that this explanation is correct.

There is undoubtedly some connection here with a suit brought by Arthur Duck and William Child against the Ewenses, with actions brought by the Ewenses against Duck and Child, and with various others which I have not examined. As one item in this history, Duck was ordered on November 31, 1636, to pay Ewens £50,[8] and later on June 9, 1637, Child was ordered to pay him £20.[9] No decree in the Downer-Duck suit has appeared.

To resume the summary of Milton's bill, he continues that since the administrators of Rose Downer's estate are unknown, he and Bower are unable to prosecute suit on the bond at Common Law or to procure any assignment of the bond by which they could bring such a suit. Consequently they feel it necessary to appeal to the Court of Chancery, which decides such matters on equity rather than on strict literal interpretation of the law. The questions which they wish answered, the consideration of which is essential to recovery of their money, are the following. How much personal estate did Ewens the father leave behind him, what lands did he possess, and what estate came to his son Matthew? How much money remains in the hands of Duck and Child for payment of the debt to Rose Downer? To obtain the answers to these and other questions, the plaintiffs beg the usual writ of subpœna addressed to Duck, Child, the Ewenses, and the executors or administrators of Rose Downer when that person or persons shall be discovered. The bill was filed with Lawrence Maydwell, and was signed by an attorney whose name is now illegible beyond the initial letter R. It may possibly stand for R[oberts], or the R[ichard Estcott] who drew up the Downer-Duck bill just mentioned.

Duck and Child answered (part of their answer, however, being a demurrer) on March 16.[10] They begin, as a conventional precaution, by disclaiming any actual knowledge that Rose Downer lent £50 to Matthew Ewens—using the word "knowledge," of course, in the customary legal sense of first-hand information. Neither do they know—still speaking in a legal sense—about her assignment of the debt to Milton and Bower. They agree with the plaintiffs that Ewens the elder left his son Matthew as his executor, and that the latter in turn made his brother Alexander his executor; but what estates either of them bequeathed, the defendants know not. Duck further admits that in December, 1629, he bought of Matthew Ewens the son the manors of North Cadbury and South Cadbury in Somersetshire and paid all but about £2,000 of the agreed price, that sum being delivered to Child to be held for seven years for the purpose of meeting any incumbrances which might be discovered during that period. The purchase price, to judge from this fact, must have been high. The inference from the statement is that £2,000 was a comparatively small portion of the entire price, which must therefore have amounted to at least £10,000, the equivalent today of nearly $300,000 to $500,000. This is a very tidy sum, and one, as we shall see, which is not far from the correct figure.

The seven years here mentioned terminated in December, 1636, just a few months before the present suit was brought. During that period, and out of the £2,000, Child explains that Matthew Ewens received at one time or another, "for the supply of his occasions," about £500. No other draft against it is mentioned. But the defendants hasten to make it clear that they never understood that any of the sum was to be used to pay the debt (the unknown debt!) to Rose Downer or to the plaintiffs, and that Matthew Ewens never instructed them to pay any such debt. They do confess, however, that several persons, "pretending themselves to be creditors to the said Matthew the father and Matthew the son for divers sums of money far surmounting in all the aforesaid sum of two thousand pounds," have either entered suits in Chancery against the defendants or have obtained judgments at common law against them or the executors of the estate. (Some of these are doubtless included in the list given above.) They confess also that Rose Downer put in a bill against them as the present bill charges, and that they answered it; but they also emphasize the fact that this suit, "as these defendants are informed by their counsel, is abated by the death of the said Rose Downer."

The plaintiffs' assertion that Duck and Child ought to settle the debt for £50 and accumulated interest, they contend, is absurd. Duck and Child do not even know that such a debt exists, or if it does that Milton and Bower are rightfully possessed of the title to it. Besides, it is for young Ewens rather than for them to worry over such matters. He is the executor of the estate, and by the showing of the plaintiffs themselves he has received most of the money from Duck and Child. So they are or should be free from such claim. In short, with a high tone of injured innocence, they demur to the manifest imperfections of the bill, and trust that a fair-minded court will see their point of view and dismiss them with "their reasonable costs and charges in this behalf wrongfully and without just cause sustained." Swearing to their answer before John Page,[11] and leaving it to be filed with Edward Robinson,[12] they marched off to more important matters.

For several months nothing happened, and when we next hear of them, it is in connection with another suit. Mention has already been made of suits of Duck against Ewens, and of Ewens against Duck, both of 1637. A decree in the former case, dated June 9, 1637, rehearses the arrangement by which Duck bought North and South Cadbury, and mentions incidentally that the price was £11,300—the equivalent of $350,000 to $550,000 today. It alludes also to a current action, already noted above among others, by which Thomas Farewell is suing Duck for debts of Ewens to him and others. On consideration of these circumstances, the court orders Duck and Child, out of their nest egg of £2,000, to pay Alexander Ewens the whole sum due him, the exact amount of which is to be reckoned up by Mr. Page, the Master in Chancery already mentioned. Since, according to Mr. Fountain,[13] Ewens's lawyer, the creditors of the estate were pressing for payment, and since there was some danger that the remainder of the said £2,000 might not last to go around, Mr. Page is ordered to expedite his certificate and report, and in the meantime Child is ordered to advance £20 for "present necessities."[14] Page proceeded as he was instruced, and during Trinity term turned in his report, which is still among the records. It takes him three folio pages simply to list the suits which are pending against Duck and the creditors of Ewens, by which it becomes clear that Child has far too little money to meet all the claims on the estate. Of interest is the entry part way through the list, in which Rose Downer's bill against Ewens, and Milton's and Bower's bill against Duck and Child are mentioned.[15]

To match this account, one is interested to turn back the pages for a few months and find that on November 31, 1636, Duck had been fined the large sum of £50 costs for want of a bill against Ewens.[16] Either he had escaped this penalty by filing an amended bill, or had continued with his action despite the setback.

The end of the action was not to come for years. Presumably the situation became so tangled that all manner of inquiries became necessary— depositions, reports, and the like. I have not investigated all these, but either they or some other unusual circumstance staved off a final verdict in the case till the summer of 1640. Then finally, on June 12, 1640, over three years after the action had opened, the decree was handed down.[17]

The defendants were again represented by Mr. Fountain. The decree is brief and to the point. After summarizing the bill and answer and noting that the remnant of the £2,000 in Child's hands has now been turned over to Ewens, from whom the plaintiffs may seek satisfaction, the court orders that

unless the said plainant shall by the end of this term show good cause to the contrary, then the said bill shall stand clearly defaulted out of this court, and the plainant paying the defendant the ordinary costs.

No more being heard of the action, we may assume that Milton gave it up as a bad job, paid the twenty shillings costs, and retired wearily to Horton. After nearly twenty years of law-suits, Milton the scrivener was at last out of Chancery.

PART II

ABOUT FOREST HILL

CHAPTER VI

GOOD DEEDS IN PARCHMENT
Milton, Powell, and Forest Hill

Though he [a scrivener] do no good, yet he loves good deeds in parchment.—Wye Salstonstall, "A Scrivener."

IN the next chapters, the theater of action moves from London to
the neighborhood of the Powell[1] estates at Forest Hill, Oxfordshire.
At Stanton St. John, a few miles away, Milton's family had been settled
for several generations. Since the younger Milton, on whom our attention
is hereafter to be concentrated, was to be closely concerned with the
property for many years, a sketch of its history will not be amiss. The
tale of its ownership or possession is very tangled and complicated, but
I will try to make it as clear as possible.

In 1545 the manor and rectory of Forest Hill were granted to Robert
Brome, a goldsmith of London, whose family had been settled in the
nearby Holton since the middle of the fifteenth century.[2] In 1547 he
disposed of these and other neighboring properties to Sir John Brome.[3]
In 1567, however, large grants in Forest Hill, Shotover, Wheatley,
Horsepath, Stanton St. John, and elsewhere were made to Sir Edward
Powell of Sandford, who had previously received a grant in Cuddesdon
in 1542.[4] In 1589 Sir Christopher Brome, a relative of Robert, died,
leaving extensive possessions in Holton, Headington, Marston, and other
places in Oxfordshire to his son Edmund,[5] the date of whose birth I have
not found, but who had several children. In 1591 Edmund Brome appears as owner of the manor and the manor farm of Forest Hill,[6] in
which he was assessed for £12 in 1599.[7] About 1603 George Brome (son
of the above-named Sir Christopher) claimed to be seized in his demesne
as of fee of the manors and lordships of Holton, Headington, and
Marston, of various messuages in Holton, Forest Hill, and Wheatley,
and certain other properties;[8] and already in 1592 he had sold land in
Oxford as George Brome of Holton.[9] In 1604 Edmund Brome initiated
a long series of suits about Forest Hill. He brought in three separate
bills: (1) against William Whetcombe,[10] (2) against Alice Chamberleyn,[11]
and (3) against Thomas Ayloffe.[12] The last may be taken as typical.[13]

Edmund Brome of Forest Hill, Esquire, brings suit in Chancery on
June 26, 1604. He is lawfully seized in all the manor of Forest Hill and
the messuages thereto belonging. He formerly had all the charters and

71

muniments and other documents pertaining to this property, but he
has by mischance lost them. Thomas Ayloffe of Lincoln's Inn, counselor-
at-law, he asserts, has by indirect practice got them into his possession,
and secretly contrives to defraud Brome of his inheritance. In order to
prosecute his suit against Whetcombe, Brome must have these papers,
which Ayloffe refuses to give him. So he asks a writ against Ayloffe.
Ayloffe answers on June 29, confessing that he has a box, contents
unknown, which he would be glad to hand over to Brome, but the latter
has never come for it. He did send a servant, but not with authorization,
and Ayloffe refused to deliver the papers to him. Presumably the matter
was easily settled.

Except for a suit by Edmund Brome against John Graves in 1605[14]
nothing of further interest arises till 1610. On June 25 of that year
George Brome brought suit against Sir William Whorwood.[15] As the
Bromes were the reigning family of Holton, so the Whorwoods were of
Sandwell, Staffordshire, and of Headington, Oxfordshire.[16] The suit concerned an alliance between the two families. George Brome's daughter
Ursula had been contracted to marry Thomas, son of Sir William Whorwood of Sandwell, and various settlements had been made on her and
on him to that end. But Brome now claims that Thomas, though understood to have been of age, was not actually twenty-one, and that his
father schemed thus to recover the property settled on the son by fraudulent means. What came of the suit I cannot say, though both parties
died within the next five years.

Henry Brome of London and his sisters Jane and Margaret brought
suit on November 29, 1615, against Thomas Whorwood about this
settlement.[17] Their story is that George, who was of "near kindred" to
them, had agreed as long ago as the first year of James I's reign (1602–3)
to the proposed marriage, and had settled on the couple the manors of
Headington and Marston. He had also granted to the plaintiffs an annuity of £10 a year for life out of these estates. They bring suit to enforce
this bequest.

A year later, on April 25, 1616, Edmund Brome "of Forest Hill,
Esquire," sued Roger Shirte for putting a bond in suit unjustly, as he
claimed, at common law against him and others. Shirte in his answer
denied any illegality in the matter.[18] The inquisition post mortem of Sir
Thomas Whorwood (not the husband of Ursula Brome) is dated in this
same year, 1616;[19] that of Sir William Whorwood in 1618;[20] and that of
George Brome in 1619.[21]

In 1620 Richard Powell, Milton's future father-in-law, first comes into
view, though hazily. In Hilary term of 1619/20 he acquired from Sir
George Symeon by fine for £120 two messuages in Wheatley and Cud-

Oxfordshire in the time of Milton. (Forest Hill, not shown here, is near Wheatley and Stanton St. John.) From William Camden, *Britannia* (1607), pp. 262–263.

desdon.[22] In Easter term, 1620, he obtained another messuage in Wheatley from John Robinson.[23] In the same year Edmund Brome sued George Lusher in regard to Forest Hill.[24] Hunter remarks that Powell's name occurs on a tax list of the hundred of Bullingdon in 1620, but I have not found the original.[25] By a bond of September 1, 1621, he also became bound to Abraham Archdale of Wheatley for £2,000, conditioned on Powell's settling on his wife Anne Moulton before Michaelmas, 1622, a freehold estate worth £100 a year.[26] The marriage "succeeded," but Powell never settled the estate on his wife; with the result that over thirty-five years later, long after Powell's death, the widow was still struggling for it. The treaty for the marriage is said to have taken place in 1621, but since Richard Powell, Jr. was born on June 10, 1621, the ceremony presumably was solemnized as early as 1620.[27]

On October 2, 1621, Edmund Brome is said to have demised Forest Hill to Powell for twenty years.[28] The original records of this transfer have not appeared, but it is frequently referred to at second hand. Presumably this arrangement was made in recognition of Powell's marriage to Anne Moulton. There were at least two such real-estate transactions between Brome and Powell, the second coming in 1623. Further confirmation of that of 1621 appears in Hunter's manuscript note to the effect that in a schedule of Easter term, 1636, Edmund Brome was set down as being in possession of Forest Hill on January 21, 1621/2,[29] and in a similar statement in the inquisition post mortem of Edmund Brome in 1631.[30] The value in both instances is given as £5 a year. In Hilary term, 1621/2, Powell was assessed as "of Forest Hill, gentleman."[31]

On March 23, 1622/3, something went wrong. According to the last-named inquisition, Powell and Brome became indebted on February 21 to the commissioners for causes ecclesiastic for forty marks (i.e., £26-13-4) and £50, for which on March 23 the manor of Forest Hill was seized into the hands of the king. Powell appeared in the court of the king's exchequer thereupon, and pleaded that he was grievously bothered, that Brome had demised him the manor for the term of twenty years, and that on the strength thereof he had entered. His pleading was so effective that he was restored to it.

On July 21, 1623, the already complex situation became further entangled, when Brome granted Powell a second lease of Forest Hill for a term of thirty-one years to begin at the expiration of the first lease (which was to expire on November 1, 1641), at the annual rent of £5.[32] Two days later John Brome turned around and conveyed the same property to Thomas Whorwood.[33] Thus the Bromes had disposed of the same premises to two different customers within two days. There is always the possibility that the terms covered by the two leases were entirely distinct, in which case the transaction would be completely legitimate; but in view of the succeeding squabbles one is inclined to suspect some sort of duplicity. In rehearsing some of these circumstances a recent commentator has accused Powell of shifty conduct;[34] but it seems only fair to Powell to recognize that the overlapping in leases had begun before he got possession of the property.

What makes the matter still more puzzling is that the license to alienate the property was procured, not before the conveyance, but afterwards. On September 1, 1623, Edmund Brome received the royal patent to demise his holdings,[35] and even here the negotiations were conducted through intermediaries. The substance of the patent as found on the Patent Rolls is as follows. In return for eighty shillings the king grants a license to Edmund Brome, Esquire, and Elizabeth his wife to concede and alienate or acknowledge by fine or recovery the manor of Forest Hill with its appurtenances, and ten messuages, ten cottages, and 260 acres of meadow and pasture with their appurtenances in Forest Hill and Cuddesdon, which they hold in chief from the crown, to James Chesterman[36] and William Hearne;[37] to have and to hold to them and their heirs and assigns forever. The corresponding concord of fine, dated Michaelmas, 1623, follows the lines of the patent.[38] In the inquisition post mortem of Edmund Brome, on the other hand, there is mentioned an indenture of September 9, 1625, by which Brome granted to William Hearne (with no mention of James Chesterman) the manor of Forest Hill for 48 years at an annual rent of one peppercorn, and Hearne entered and became possessed of it. Chesterman and Hearne presumably acted as trustees for Powell, since when Powell transacted a later piece of business with Milton he acted through Hearne; and Chesterman was sufficiently close to Brome to draw up his inquisition post mortem in 1631.

Whatever degree of culpability, if any, was involved in the Brome-Powell lease, things moved smoothly enough for some time. Powell was taxed in Forest Hill in 1624,[39] lent money to John Gadbury in 1624,[40] and on November 8, 1625, was named in Edmund Brome's will as executor, an office which he fulfilled by proving the will some three years later (78 Barrington). In the latter document, by the way, Brome is described as "of Forest Hill but now inhabiting in Westwellowe," Wiltshire. The only disturbing event had been the curious flurry of April 25, 1625, when Brome had filed against Roger Shirte almost the identical bill in Chancery which he had submitted nine years before—and on the same day of the same month.[41] The duplication may be a clerical error.

In 1626 John Robinson again made over to Powell property in Wheatley,[42] and in 1627 Buton Croke granted property in Headington to Sir Thomas Whorwood.[43] In 1626 Powell secured from All Souls' College, Oxford, another lease of property in Forest Hill or the vicinity, which was later to lead to further litigation.[44]

Milton enters the story in 1627. On June 11 of that year, preliminary arrangements presumably having been previously attended to, Milton's father lent Powell £300, in return for which Powell gave the younger Milton a recognizance in the form of a statute staple for £500.[45] Since this action, with its subsequent developments, will be treated more at length in the following chapter, it need only be added now that William Hearne here reappears as co-debtor with Powell. On the same date he in turn acknowledged a recognizance in the form of a statute staple to Powell for £600.[46] There must be some connection between the two transactions. Presumably Powell was buying Hearne's share in the Forest Hill property which Hearne had acquired in 1625, and was borrowing the money for the purpose from Milton's father, who was professionally a money-lender and an old neighbor of the family to boot.

In passing it may be mentioned that in 1628, for neither the first nor the last time, a survey of Shotover Forest near Forest Hill was being made under the direction of the crown to estimate the condition of the underwoods and copses, to reckon the damage to them, and to decide on a future policy.[47] This fact is mentioned here because some few years later Powell was to take out a lease of this property and to keep it for many years. Similar surveys had been conducted under Elizabeth, and were to be continued in 1629, 1635, and later years.[48]

In 1628 Powell made a loan (amount unknown) to John Brome,[49] and another to Oliver Gadbury,[50] probably a relative of the John Gadbury previously mentioned. Elmer Gadbury, in turn, probably another member of the same family, conveyed property in Wheatley to Powell in the same year.[51] It was in August of this year, it will be remembered, that Powell proved Edmund Brome's will.

On July 15, 1629, according to a later suit, John Brome, son of Edmund, borrowed £500 of Powell and gave him in return an indenture of lease of Forest Hill for ninety-nine years, presumably to begin at the expiration of Powell's present lease.[52] There is probably a confusion between this loan and that of 1628, caused by some inaccuracy in Powell's version or elsewhere, but the fact of the new lease is important. This business was carried on indirectly, again through William Hearne in trust for Powell, the latter being "not willing to impeach his former leases." Powell agreed that if the money was paid within two years, he would return Brome the lease, which therefore in effect was a mortgage. Brome assured Powell that the title to the premises was clear. Apparently, however, it become clear that the lease was imperfect because of a previous conveyance from Brome to the Whorwoods during the former's minority. Trouble in plenty was to come of this duplicity, if such it was. The wind had been sown; the whirlwind was yet to be reaped. I have not been able to find the original indenture from Brome to Powell nor any record of it in the Close Rolls or in the Patent Rolls. Yet there is no doubt that such an action was taken. The close relation between the Brome and Powell families still held, however, as is proved by Powell's acting as one of the two executors to the will of Edmund Brome's widow Elizabeth made in September 8 of this year. With Sir Edward Master, son-in-law of Brome Whorwood, he proved it on February 6, 1634/5 (18 Sadler). She left him, as her "loving friend," three silver bowls marked E.P. [Edmund Powell?] and a dozen of her best silver spoons. She also gave to Richard Powell, Jr. the beds and all the furniture in her own bedroom.

About this time (the papers not being precisely dated) the attorney-general, Sir Robert Heath, brought action against Sir Thomas Whorwood for unlawfully intruding on the royal forest of Shotover, digging quarries in it, seizing woods, and making a profit by carrying away timber and erecting cottages, doing damage altogether to the extent of £1,000.[53] In Michaelmas of 1629 he brought further suit against Whorwood for similar damages, as well as for having threatened and arrested His Majesty's servant Edward Stonte.[54] Whorwood replied on the following January 26, acknowledging that he had built cottages, but claiming the right to do so under royal grant in Shotover. He denied the other charges except for admitting that he had sued Stonte at law.[55] The attorney-general replied, finding fault with the answer as untrue and insufficient.[56]

In 1630 new complications began to develop in the Forest Hill property. On December 10 John Brome sold his holdings in Forest Hill to his brother Christopher, who was apparently a somewhat more shrewd business man than himself. By indenture of that date in the Close Rolls John Brome, Esquire, of Sarum, Wiltshire, son and heir apparent of Edmund Brome, late of Forest Hill deceased, made an agreement with Christopher Brome, citizen and salter of London, and in return for £750 paid him by Christopher acquitted to him forever the manor and lordship of Forest Hill and all messuages thereto pertaining, as also the manor of Mynch Court in the parish of Stanton St. John and the Vent in Cuddesdon. The indenture was enrolled the following May 26.[57] But Christopher evidently acted merely as a friend or intermediary. Three months later, on March 5, 1630/1, he resold the same properties for the same amount to his cousin Thomas Whorwood the younger, son of Sir Thomas of Headington.[58]

On May 23, 1631, an inquisition post mortem was taken on the estate of Edmund Brome, deceased, and signed by James Chesterman.[59] It rehearses that Brome was seized in fee of the manor and appurtenances of Forest Hill, that he conveyed it to Powell in 19 James I (1621) for twenty years, that he and Powell became indebted in 1621/2 to the commissioners for causes ecclesiastic in forty marks and fifty pounds, for which in 20 James I (1622/3) the manor was seized by the king, and redeemed by Powell only after severe effort, that Brome conveyed it again to Powell in 1623 for thirty-one years to follow the previous twenty years, that in 1 Charles I (1624–5) he granted it to William Hearne for forty-eight years. If the latter grant, as previously, was in trust for Powell, this makes a total length of ninety-nine years in the three leases, which agrees well with information from other sources.

In 1631 also Powell acquired property from George Horseman (or Furseman).[60] On October 3, 1631, Abraham Archdale died.[61] On January 10, 1631/2, Powell borrowed £400 from Edward Ashworth, giving him as security a ninety-nine year mortgage on his Wheatley property.[62] On February 27, 1632, Richard Powell served as one of the official witnesses in an impressive ceremony. In the chancel of Cuddesdon church he attended the confirmation of John Bancroft, bishop of Oxford, as to the holding of Cuddesdon *in commendam*, vacant by the death of Edmund Underhill. The fact that the other witness was Thomas Iles, professor in divinity, prebendary of Christ Church, and principal of Hart Hall, shows that Powell was by now a man of some social standing.[63] In Michaelmas, 1632, Powell conveyed to Richard Archdale property in Wheatley which earlier in the same term he had apparently acquired from Thomas Carpenter.[64]

Meanwhile in Easter term, 1632, Christopher Brome, not finding his business venture with Sir Thomas Whorwood to his liking, had sued him in Chancery for corrupt practices.[65] The suit, however, was of no avail because of Whorwood's privileged status as an officer of the king, and before long Christopher found himself in prison, where he was to stay over three years. Shortly afterwards John Brome, agitated at finding his holdings in Forest Hill slipping into the Whorwood family, sued both Thomas Whorwood and his own brother Christopher, only to find that the premises had been estated on Whorwood's infant son and were therefore unrecoverable.[66] On November 30, 1632, and July 6, 1633, Edmund Brome was granted a license of entry on lands in Oxfordshire.[67]

On July 10, 1633, Richard Powell brought suit against John Brome.[68] His bill set forth that Edmund Brome, late of Forest Hill deceased, had leased Forest Hill to him by several leases for fifty-one years and had died some seven years ago. After his death John Brome had offered Powell the reversion of the lease for ninety-nine years, and in 1629 had conveyed it to William Hearne, goldsmith, in trust for Powell. Powell had agreed that if within five years Brome repaid to him the £500 spent on this transaction, he would reassign the lease to him; but Brome not doing so, the conveyance had become absolute. In fact, Powell had let him have an extra £140, in return for which Brome released to Hearne and Powell the aforesaid agreement. Powell subsequently had spent some £500 in improvements, building, etc. But now Brome was combining with Sir Thomas Whorwood to present fraudulent conveyances pretended to be previous to Powell's, and intending to get the property away from him. Powell protests that if any such exist, they were got from Brome during his minority and without substantial consideration. So he begs a writ of privy seal against John and Christopher Brome.

John Brome replied in a moderate and conciliatory tone, proving that he had not attempted any fraud, but placing his brother Christopher in a rather bad light.[69] He admits the lease to Powell—fortunately for us. He asserts that his father died four years ago. (Incidentally, it seems curious that neither Edmund Brome's son nor his executor knew definitely when he died!) He admits that by the indenture of 1629 he got £500 of Powell and conveyed the premises to Hearne in trust for ninety-nine years. Of the £500 he gave £100 to his brother Christopher and more to his other brothers, none of which has been repaid to him. He says also that by a writing of the same day Powell bound himself in £1,000 to reassign the property to Brome when the £500 should be repaid. But not only was it not repaid; Powell also gave him (as he asserts) £140 additional, for which Brome conveyed him the deed and confirmed the premises to Hearne and Powell. But in 1623 Whorwood had secured from John Brome, during the latter's minority, a conveyance of the premises, in return for which John Brome got no benefit whatsoever. In 1630 his brother Christopher Brome, employed therein by Whorwood, got from him another such conveyance, mentioning £750 as the price, but of this amount John Brome never got more than £35. Christopher Brome conveyed it in a few months to Whorwood for a trifling consideration. So John Brome has sued both his brother Christopher and Whorwood, only to find that the estate has been settled on an infant son, and that John Brome can recover nothing. Thus the web grows more and more tangled.

Meanwhile, probably as a result of this suit, Christopher Brome was on his way to prison, to remain there for some three and a half years.[70] His brother John at least, one feels, would have felt that justice had been triumphant.

In Trinity term of 1633 Richard Powell acquired property in Wheatley from W. Wase.[71] On April 25, 1633, his infant son was baptized as Archdale Powell, as a compliment to his wife's family.[72]

In Easter term, 1634, Powell acquired other property in Forest Hill from Richard Huggins.[73] On October 2, 1634, on the death of Sir Thomas Whorwood, the Whorwood share in the manor of Forest Hill descended to his son Brome Whorwood, named of course for the related Brome family.[74] There is a monument to Sir Thomas dated 1634 in the church at Holton.[75] Brome Whorwood's son Brome was baptized at Forest Hill in 1635.[76] In 1634 Richard Powell procured a new lease from All Souls' College, without (it was alleged) surrendering that of 1626.[77]

On February 6, 1634/5, Richard Powell proved the will of Elizabeth Brome, relict of Edmund and brother of John and Christopher Brome (18 Sadler). The will was contested by Ursula Whorwood, daughter of George and Elizabeth Brome, but upheld. Meanwhile Richard Archdale, son and heir of Abraham Archdale, who had died in 1631, had obtained letters of administration for his father's estate, and had put in suit against Anne Powell as executrix and Richard Powell as heir thereof the bond for £2,000 which Powell had given to Anne on their marriage.[78] This process was brought in the Court of Common Pleas, and in 1635 Archdale had obtained several judgments against the estate in trust for Anne. But Richard Archdale had died before any money had been paid thereon, so that the question of Anne's settlement remained open as before.

In 1636 Richard Powell embarked on an ambitious venture to recoup the family fortunes. He turned to land as his salvation and acquired a large area of woodland with the idea of developing it. By an indenture of July 8 between the king on the one part and John Bancroft, D.D., bishop of Oxford, Bryan Duppa, D.D., dean of Christ Church Cathedral, Oxford, Gilbert Sheldon, D.D., of Oxford University, Henry King, John King, and Richard Powell of Forest Hill, Esquire, on the other part, it is rehearsed that the King's forest of Shotover is much spoiled and decayed in the underwoods, many stems and stowells (*i.e.*, stools or stoles: saplings or young shoots) are dead and worn out, and the whole place much trespassed on.[79] Now whereas the bishop has built himself a fair house of stone for his see at Cuddesdon, five miles from Oxford and half a mile from Shotover, and has spent £2,400 on it, and whereas the king gave him fifty tons of timber out of the forest for it and remitted the first fruits to him, and since the expense of repairing the forest will exceed the income for the next ten years, they humbly beg the grant of it for the use of the see for the next sixty years, paying the king no rent for the first ten years, and £100 a year thereafter. Powell is to take a lease from the bishop for fifty-nine years, and to pay in addition another

£100 a year to the king. Powell will also quickset the mounds, having stakeboot, gateboot, and stileboot allowed, and being assured that the keepers will not meddle with the underwoods. Consequently the king grants to them the woods called Rowe Coppice, Horsepath Coppice, Elderston Coppice, Wheatley Coppice, Redding *alias* Rydinge Coppice, Thornehill Coppice, Borowe Hill Coppice, Quarry Coppice, Lodge Coppice, all in Shotover and Stow Wood, Oxford. The total is 832 acres. In addition are included Wike Coppice, Lodge Coppice, Beckley Coppice, Steeplehill Coppice, Lynchhill Coppice, Groundsill Coppice, Principal Coppice, and Wadley Coppice, all lying in Stow Wood, and totaling 642 acres. These are for the grantees to have and to hold from the feast of the Blessed Virgin last past (May 25, 1636) for sixty years, and they are to grant the same to Richard Powell for fifty-nine years on condition that he pay to His Majesty's receiver-general in Oxford £100 a year on the feasts of St. Michael (September 29) and of the Annunication of the Virgin (May 25), beginning at Michaelmas, 1646. Powell agrees so to plant and pay or to forfeit the said forest lands. A further but unimportant indenture concerned with the same properties was made on March 30, 1637, and dealt with the right to enclose certain areas and plant them with hops, as also to kill conies in these areas.[80] This undertaking was to be a losing venture for Powell, primarily because of the war; but at the time it must have seemed hopeful. The lease was enrolled on June 10, 1637.[81]

The Calendars of State Papers for years before 1636 show a dreary record for the Shotover woods. For many years they had been a steady irritation to the crown, for though they were a principal source of timber for building ships, they had been badly wasted by careless or criminal handling. The principal oversight of the tract had for some time been, as it was long to remain, in the hands of Sir Timothy Tyrrell and Montague Bertie, Earl of Lindsey. Powell's position, under them, was that of "verderer."[82]

In 1638 Powell assigned his lease of property in Wheatley (obtained from All Souls' College in 1634) to Richard Bateman for £200.[83] In Hilary term, 1638/9, he was sued by Sir Thomas Edolph of St. Radegund, Kent.[84] The complaint was that while certain lands had been wrongfully seized by the royal prosecutor on account of failure to pay regular rents, though without seriously falling behind or intending not eventually to pay, Powell had stepped in and snapped up these inconsidered trifles and made off with them wrongfully. This had occurred on the preceding July 20, and had included lands and messuages in Stanton St. John and Woodperry, which Powell had secured by royal lease. Evidently Powell had further plans for rehabilitation. In his answer he denied any wrong dealing, and said that as the lands were up for sale he had bought them.

For further investments he had rented from the Dean and Chapter of Westminster Abbey two messuages and tenements in Paul's Alley, parish of St. Michael's, Wood Street, London. One was a three-room messuage with a garret, the other six rooms and garret. The indenture, extending over forty years from the feast of St. John the Baptist last preceding (June 24, 1638 or 1639) at an annual rent of 30s. and two capons (or 5s.), is now among the Abbey muniments.[85] Part of the cost of this lease was recovered by Powell from George Hearne, I think, since on September 30, 1639, Powell surrendered to him the (worthless?) 1626 lease of Wheatley in consideration of £340.[86] Hearne immediately redemised it to Powell for £40 a year. It soon appeared that the title was not clear, that Richard Bateman of London, merchant, had a better title, and that Sir Edward Powell at least thought that his own title was better still.[87] But Richard Powell got his money; and once again the Powells and the Hearnes had touched.

He was now becoming hard pressed for funds. Perhaps, though it is not likely, he was trying to get money ahead for a dowry for his daughter Mary, soon to marry John Milton; or perhaps he needed it for more immediate and pressing purposes. At any rate, he went to Sir Robert Pye of Farringdon Magna, Berkshire, who had already advanced him £1,000, and got from him £300 more, in return for which plus a "consideration" (i.e., interest) of £100 he indented to Pye, on June 30, 1640, the manor of Forest Hill for the remaining thirty-one years of its then lease, on condition that if he paid Pye £1,510 on July 1, 1641, the indenture was to be void. But the money was not to be paid, and Pye was to possess himself of the estate.[88] This transaction was to lead to suits with Milton later. The £1,000 just mentioned had been used by Pye to buy in a debt, or lease, to George Furseman (or Horseman).[89]

At various times through 1641, if we may trust Hunter's manuscript notes,[90] Powell was assessed as of Forest Hill, Stanton St. John, and Wheatley, chiefly for subsidies. Entries occur under dates of March 20, April 21, May 20, August 17, and November. On June 28, 1641, poor Christopher Brome, after several years in jail, entered suit in Chancery against Thomas Whorwood the younger, his wife Ursula, and another person to straighten out the ownership tangle over the Forest Hill property.[91] Christopher recounts how his brother John had, in consideration of £600 which Richard Powell of Forest Hill advanced to him, leased the manors, rectory, and premises of Forest Hill to William Hearne of London, since deceased, for ninety-nine years for the use of Richard Powell, on the condition that if the £600 were repaid on or before a certain day agreed on, the lease should be reassigned to Brome. This document may offer a partial solution of the difficulties which have hitherto perplexed us over the ownership. Immediately afterwards, continues Christopher, brother John had qualms over thus alienating the family possessions and asked counsel of brother Christopher. Christopher, feeling similar repugnance and considering his own credit good, promised to get the money for John. John, with some queer streak of reasoning, then (December 10, 1630) immediately conveyed the same property to Christopher—forever! He must have felt that as long as he had the money to pay off Powell, he was sure of recovering the lease and could safely turn it over to another person. His action was silly, but not so unfathomable as it has previously appeared. Yet as one might have foreseen, it is far easier to promise money than to get it, and Christopher had his difficulties. His credit was not so good as he had counted on. Finally he went to Sir Thomas Whorwood, whose wife was his relative, and who had often made great protestations of love and helpfulness to Brome. When Whorwood immediately offered more of the same fair promises, easily undertaking to pay off the £600 when it became due, Christopher like a simpleton conveyed his aforesaid lease of the property to Whorwood. From that day forward, he laments, Whorwood never lifted a finger to pay off the debt, but allowed the property to go to Powell without a murmur. Christopher of course sued Whorwood for recovery, but attachments and writs simply slid off Whorwood's back because he was the "king's servant in ordinary"; and Christopher, unable to pay his debts, went to prison. Since then Sir Thomas has died, and his son has come of age, but despite promises no aid appears. So he begs a writ against young Thomas and his mother and the Charles Guest[91a] who conspired along with them. We have not the outcome of the business, but we know that whatever came of it, Powell retained the property as of course he had the legal right to do.

Within a few months Powell was scheming to make more money in real estate. On October 29, 1641, turning over his hard-worked lease of 1626, he procured a new lease of a tenement and forty acres in Wheatley from Gilbert Selden, D.D., warden of All Souls' College.[92] The lease was for twenty years, in consideration of 40s. and "one quarter and four bushels of good clean sweet and dry wheat and two quarters of good clean sweet and dry malt" on the feast of the Purification of Our Lady and on Michaelmas, or a money commutation therefor, which was settled at £26-13-4.[93] In consideration of £100 (Stevens says £300) Powell made over this lease on December 18, 1641, to Sir Edward Powell, a relative and perhaps Richard's brother,[94] on the condition that if Richard Powell should pay him £312 on the following June 22, the transfer should be void. But Powell was not to pay it, and the possession was to be complete. Perhaps the money was needed towards work on the royal coppices which Powell had recently taken over, and on which his widow later estimated that he had spent £1,500 in the first ten years.[95]

On November 3, 1641, Thomas Whorwood answered Christopher Brome's bill. He says that he came of age only very recently, that he was young at the time of the treaties between his father and the plaintiff, and that he knows nothing about them. He personally does not have possession of the indenture in question; his mother or Guest does. He has promised since coming of age to reassure the premises to Brome and to assist him in regaining it from Powell. He is still willing to do all in his power.[96]

During the next few years, for obvious reasons, the Powell financial activities were restricted. We know that on January 8, 1641/2, Powell borrowed about £200 of one Acton Drake,[97] and entered into bond to him for £440 conditioned on the repayment of £228 on the following January 9.[98] This bond, like so many of Powell's other transactions, was later to give rise to a law-suit. In May, 1642, Powell paid Sir Robert Pye £110 on account.[99] In Michaelmas, 1644 (his daughter in the meantime having married John Milton and soon afterwards having returned home to live), he was found to be in arrears to the crown in the trivial amount of four shillings fourpence. The details do not appear, nor is the source of the information clear, but the note occurs among Hunter's exasperatingly illegible and undocumented jottings.[100]

In June, 1646, Sir Robert Pye, to whom the Forest Hill premises had become forfeited, sent his servant Lawrence Farre to enter them, and thus became "quietly possessed thereof."[101] In her bill of 1657 Anne Powell states that he has "since enjoyed it."[102] Powell's household goods were confiscated and sold in June, 1646.[103] Troubles were closing in from all sides. During the king's stay in Oxford, if we may trust Anne Powell, his followers raided Powell's forests in Shotover to the extent of £800 damage.[104] Several hundred pounds' worth of his timber was granted to the town of Banbury on July 15. In Michaelmas, 1646, the royal surveyor-general, Joseph Barber,[105] seized the coppices into the king's hands and took the rents from them thereafter. The lands in Wheatley which Powell had leased from All Souls' College were sequestered and then taken over by George Hearne,[106] who later relinquished possession to Richard Bateman or others. And on December 8, 1646, in common with royalists everywhere, Powell found his lands sequestered and a heavy fine before him. The fine was fixed at £180, or two years' value.[107] According to the account which accompanies this statement, he lost by reason of the war a total of £3,000. As early as June 10 a careful inventory of his goods had been taken by Henry Maundrell, John Webb, Richard Vivers, John King, and Thomas Cox. Every pot and pan, each book and shovel and dustcloth in the house was listed in this financial X-ray.[108] The next winter Richard Powell, worn out with the struggle, died, and his son Richard Powell, who had fought on the king's side during the war, went abroad to stay until 1649 or 1650.[109] Thus poor Anne Powell was left to fight her battles alone: debts piled up in all directions, most of her property confiscated or alienated, her income decreased, and both her men beyond her reach for help.

On January 14, 1646/7, Sir Edward Powell appointed his nephew William Powell *alias* Hinson his attorney to enter the Wheatley premises on his behalf, but because of the pretended title of Richard Bateman and George Hearne he was unable to get in.[110]

About this time Milton took a hand in the proceedings. Richard Powell, it will be remembered, had borrowed three hundred pounds from Milton's father, and in return had given young Milton a statute staple or bond for £500 on June 11, 1627.[111] From 1627 to 1644 Powell had paid regular interest on this debt.[112] Upon cessation of these payments Milton had immediately attempted to take out an extent on the property of Powell in order to levy his debts on the real estate, but had not succeeded in accomplishing his purpose till after Powell's death. If it seems that he acted very hastily and harshly, we must remember that it was war-time, that feelings ran high, and that Milton felt especially bitter towards the Powells because his wife had deserted him. But on August 5, 1647, the machinery functioned, and the extent and inquisition were effected. Powell's holdings in Wheatley were appraised and seized, and on November 20, 1647, delivered over to Milton to hold in satisfaction of his debt.[113]

Early in 1647 another creditor was also pressing the Powell estate for satisfaction. In answering Sir Edward Powell's bill on February 15, 1648/9, Anne Powell stated that the old bond from her husband to Abraham Archdale dating from 1621 had been put into the Court of Common Pleas in March, 1646/7, by his son Richard Archdale.[114]

In a tax-list of October 18–21, 1647, of property in Bullingdon, Thame, and Dorchester hundreds, Sir Robert Pye was assessed in Forest Hill for £4-7-0 and William Powell for 1s., with no other Powell or Milton mention mentioned.[115] At the same time Anne Powell was assessed 6/9 in Wheatley, Thomas Powell 1s., and no other Powell or Milton mentioned.[116] On December 3, 1647, Sir Robert Pye indented Forest Hill to his son John Pye.[117]

In Michaelmas, 1648, in the annual report of the surveyor-general, the estate of Richard Powell was found delinquent again, this time in £250,

covering a period of two and a half years.[118] This delinquency has reference to the grant of Shotover and the other coppices to Powell in 1637, on
which rents of £100 a year, beginning in 1646, were supposed to have
been paid by him, but had never been. Not long afterwards Sir Edward
Powell brought in a bill in Chancery which has already been referred
to from time to time.[119] On October 23, 1648, he rehearsed that Richard
Powell by indenture of 1641 had been granted by the warden of All
Souls' College, Oxford, a tenement and land in Wheatley for twenty
years at an annual rent of 40s. and a specified amount in kind. In the
same year, in consideration of £100, Richard Powell had transferred
this to the plaintiff, on condition that if on the following June Richard
paid him £312, the transfer should be void. Richard failed to pay, and
hence the estate became forfeited to Sir Edward, who in 1646/7 attempted to enter, only to be balked by Richard Bateman and George
Hearne, who pretended a better title. He begs a writ against them all.

George Hearne (spelled Heron) maintained in answer, on November
24, 1648, that he knew nothing of Sir Edward Powell's title, but that he
himself, in return for £340 paid to Richard Powell in 1639, had received
an indenture of Wheatley to himself. But finding that Bateman had a
better title than he, he relinquished it to him.[120] Bateman's answer is
unfortunately missing. But Anne Powell answered on February 14,
1648/9, at great length.[121] She explained that in December, 1646, after
Richard Powell's death, Bateman and Hearne took possession, but by
what title she knew not. In 1621, she explains, there was a treaty of marriage on foot between Richard Powell and her friends and herself, and
that in consideration of her dowry of £2,000 brought him, Powell became bound to Abraham Archdale of Wheatley, since deceased, for
[blank] thousand pounds on the condition that if before Michaelmas,
1622, Powell should assure her of an absolute freehold estate of £100 a
year for life, this bond should become void. She brought him the money,
but he never fulfilled his part, and died without having done so. So in
proving his will she confessed a judgment on the said bond to Richard
Archdale, who put it in Common Pleas about March, 1646/7. Then the
sequestrators seized Powell's goods and chattels at Forest Hill, and sold
a considerable amount of property, from which she received only slightly
over £200. She recounts that Forest Hill was mortgaged to Sir Robert
Pye the elder for £1,400 several years ago, and that he still enjoys possession of it; that by indenture of 1629 John Brome demised the manor
of Forest Hill to William Hearne in trust for Powell for ninety-nine years,
but that to satisfy Pye's debt the sheriff of Oxford had seized it by a *scire
facias;* and that on his death Powell had been indebted to several persons, among them John Milton for £300. She pleads that in view of her

family of nine children and no jointure she should not be liable to pay her late husband's debts without enjoying his estate. Attached is the inventory of his goods taken June 10, 1646.

On September 29, 1649, Powell was again listed as in arrears for the Shotover property. The entry on the Pipe Roll for Michaelmas, 1649, lists all the various coppices before mentioned, and concludes that Powell is at present indebted to the king in the total sum of £400.[122] On the same roll is another entry concerning other property of Powell's in Iffley, Stanton St. John, and elsewhere, including one messuage occupied by Philip Pitts, gentleman, all of which has been seized into the king's hand—the total due on these pieces being £345. On October 1 his fine was reported as being £180.[123] The latter, of course, is a Parliamentary fine, levied against him as a royalist. On December 24, 1649, incidentally, the fine of Christopher Milton, brother of John the poet, was reported due; the amount, £200.[124]

On June 1, 1650, the commissioners for Oxford reported to the commissioners for compounding with delinquents that the greatest part of Powell's personal estate had been given to the church and town of Banbury some years ago, that Sir Robert Pye was in possession of the real estate, and that the rest was in question before the commissioners for articles of war.[125] Eleven days later a substantial order for her relief appeared.[126] Some time in the same year Richard Powell Jr. returned from abroad to take up his position as head of the house.[127]

In August, 1650, Milton formally petitioned to compound for his Wheatley holdings, and his petition was duly filed and approved.[128] On August 23 John Pye also put in his petition to compound;[129] on August 28 Elizabeth Ashworth presented hers;[130] and on August 28 Sir Edward Powell gave in his.[131] Pye's concerned Forest Hill, the other two Wheatley. Sir Edward's was on the grant to Richard Powell from All Souls' College, Elizabeth Ashworth's on the tithes of Wheatley.

On January 1, 1650/1, John Reading found that John Pye held lands, formerly Powell's, to the value of £272-15-8 yearly, and that Powell's debt to him at that time amounted to £1,238.[132] On January 24, as one set of records indicates, Sir Robert Pye paid his fine of £658-15-3.[133] But this seems to be a mistake, since on March 25 the commissioners were calmly ordering him to pay it as if nothing had happened.[134] One or the other entry must be wrong. On March 29 John Pye paid £329-7-6, the first moiety of his fine.[135] On April 8 his fine was reduced from £658-15-3 to £554-18-0.[136] On September 5 it was altered to £576-12-3.[137] On October 11 he paid the second moiety of £247-4-9, thus clearing the manor of Forest Hill.[138] Much later this fine was reduced again to £384-8-2, the overplus already paid in to be refunded to him or to Anne Powell.[139]

We have followed the fortunes of Pye somewhat beyond our chronological scheme. To return again, we note that on February 25, 1650/1, Milton, whose first petition had not been followed through because of his "having had important business ever since, by order of the Council of State," put in a second petition to compound.[140] He showed then that he had received toward his debt and expenses the sum of £180.[141] On March 11 he paid in £65, the first half of his fine, whereupon his sequestration was suspended the next day.[142] This was of course the fine levied on Wheatley property as belonging to the delinquent royalist Powell. On March 24 he paid in the second half, £65 more, and on March 27 the property was declared cleared.[143]

On April 19, 1651, John Pye, son of Sir Robert, brought suit against Anne Powell.[144] He summarizes how Edmund Brome indented Forest Hill to Richard Powell in 1621 for twenty years, how he extended this lease in 1623 for thirty-one years more, and how in 1629 the son John Brome confirmed it to him; how on June 30, 1640, for £1,400, Powell assigned it to the plaintiff's father Sir Robert Pye of Farringdon Magna, Berkshire, for the thirty-one-year period by mortgage; and how Pye conveyed it on December 3, 1644, to the plaintiff, and entered it and took possession in June, 1646. John has paid the fine set on the property (£658-15-3, since amended), but now Anne Powell seeks to prevent his enjoying it. He begs a writ against her.

She answered on May 31, 1651.[145] She does not know that her husband ever so mortgaged the property to Pye, or that Pye actually paid any such fine as he says. She therefore demurs to that part of his bill. The court considered her answer, and decided on October 14, 1651, that he should amend his bill and she her answer.[146] She accordingly presented her further answer on November 19, 1651, avowing her willingness to pay any fine which was justly her own, but protesting against paying Pye's for him.[147]

From now on Anne Powell was very busy seeking relief from sequestrations.[148] According to her later account (1662) she spent some £53 in vexatious suits and in attendance on the committee for the relief of persons on articles of war in 1649–1650. For messengers, lawyers, and the like she paid £57. In soliciting a review of these proceedings she lived near Westminster from November, 1651, to September, 1652, and spent in food and lodgings at least £39. In the next two and a half years thereafter she spent (with her son Richard) for orders, reports, and other necessities at least £30, plus £93 more for living expenses. Accordingly her time was occupied off and on in this business nearly six years, and she spent on it nearly £300. Her various petitions and the actions taken on them are printed by Hamilton and by Masson.[149] By about 1654 she had finally succeeded in freeing the estate from sequestration.[150]

In 1656 Sir Edward Powell (through his nephew and executor William Powell *alias* Hinson) brought suit in the Chancellor's Court of the University of Oxford against All Souls' College and others for fraudulent dealings with the leases which the elder Richard Powell had obtained as early as 1626. The court decision was adverse to the plaintiffs.[151]

In the meanwhile, the charges against Powell for the Shotover and other woodlands had been steadily mounting, as we can see from Anne Powell's statement in a bill of 1657, where she says that in the Great Roll of the Pipe for Michaelmas, 1657, Richard Powell was charged with £1,150 rent for eleven and a half years.[152] It should be mentioned also that although about 1654 Powell's estate at Forest Hill had finally been discharged from sequestration, the Pyes were still in possession, so that the Powells were not free to enjoy it.[153] And now the Shotover grant was causing Anne Powell active trouble. By a patent from the king Sir Timothy Tyrrell[154] had for some time enjoyed the herbage and the pannage (*i.e.*, pasturage for swine) and a good deal of firewood; and since Michaelmas, 1646, the government surveyor, Joseph Barber,[155] had received all the rents. So Anne made up a full account of her grievances, got her son-in-law's brother Christopher Milton to prepare it in the form of a bill, and submitted it in the court of the Exchequer in Michaelmas, 1657.[156] She mentions the indenture of 1637 by which Powell acquired Shotover, his expenses in upkeep for the first ten years (over £1,500), the inroads made by the king during his siege at Oxford (amounting to £800), and the sequestration of Forest Hill, which however she says that Pye entered in 1646 and still enjoys. She mentions the recent bothers described above, and protests against such injustices. The attorney-general, Edmund Prideaux,[157] answered, disclaiming knowledge of any reasons for non-payment, but insisting that she stands charged with £1,050 in the Pipe Rolls.[158] He knows nothing about Barber's seizure, and denies any letters patent to Tyrrell. He concedes, however, that if Anne has paid anything at all, he will gladly have that amount deducted from the debt recorded in the Roll. Anne replied in the following Hilary term, insisting that her bill was true, his answers untrue, and so forth.[159]

Shortly after the last action, the attorney-general countered against Anne Powell by bringing a bill against her.[160] He rehearses the story of the leases, and asserts that during the ten rent-free years Powell must have received many thousands of pounds of revenue, also that any woods seized by the king during his occupation of Oxford were paid for. He charges that she has confederated with other persons to defraud the government, and begs a writ of privy seal to compel her to submit all her accounts of receipts during the period in question. She submitted her answer on February 2, 1658/9, protesting that she had no records or accounts as described in his bill; that if there had been any such, they had been seized with other Powell properties during the sequestrations.[161]

Meanwhile, now that Milton had received from rents in Wheatley the full value of his loan to Powell, there was no reason why the bond should not be cleared. Accordingly, on November 29, 1659, Richard Powell, Jr. and Milton went together to the lord chamberlain's office and formally concluded Milton's earliest business transaction.[162] Wheatley thereby returned to the Powells.

But their distresses, like Milton's, by no means ended with the Restoration. About 1661 they conveyed the property in Wheatley and Forest Hill to one Gilbert Jackson[163] for £1,700. It was agreed that of this amount £700 should go to Matthew Archdale, executor of Abraham Archdale, to satisfy a debt to him; that £470 should be paid to Elizabeth Ashworth,[164] executrix of Edward Ashworth, for a mortgage on Wheatley property; and that the balance should remain for five years with Jackson till the time for all claims should have passed.[165]

Not long after the time of the conveyance to Jackson, possession of the Shotover forests passed away from the Powells. According to their answer to Thomas Whorwood's bill in 1662 they had been "much disturbed" in their possession by Montague, Earl of Lindsey,[166] who "pretends" a title thereto.[167] In a later answer to George Lowe's suit, however, they admit that they finally had to surrender it to the king, who later granted it to the Earl, since deceased.[168]

The State Papers enable us to discover more details of this change. On July 24, 1660, Anne and Richard Powell's petition (in which they are mentioned as "late of Forest Hill") for discharge of the late Richard Powell's arrears of rent as tenant of the forests of Shotover and Stowood was referred to the surveyor-general of crown lands to certify a valuation.[169] On September 22, 1660, the treasurer, the Earl of Southampton, issued a warrant to Sir Thomas Fanshawe, the king's remembrancer, to stay all process arising in the Court of Exchequer from this debt.[170] On March 27, 1661, Southampton authorized the surveyor-general to take a "particular" of the king's holdings in Shotover and Stowood, and to determine the rent to be paid the crown by Sir Timothy Tyrrell for his share.[171] An attached report makes it clear that both timber and deer, formerly abundant, were destroyed by the war. Meanwhile, despite the presentation of a bond by the younger Richard Powell and his son John that they would abide by the judgment of the said Court, government officials had seized the manor of Forest Hill.[172] Southampton thereupon issued on June 17, 1661, another warrant, to supersede all process on the debt.[173] It was pointed out at the same time by the surveyor-general that the elder Powell had made no profit on his lease since 1642, and but little previously.

Though the decree of the court has not been found, some satisfactory settlement must have been reached, for it was not long before the Powells were making fresh negotiations. On November 16, 1661, the bishop of London received a petition from "Mr. Powell of Forest Hill" (i.e., Richard the younger) requesting the discharge and remission of arrears of rents due to the king on the Shotover lands.[174] The lord chancellor expressed his favorable opinion. On January 17, 1661/2, the lord treasurer received from the bishop of Oxford, Anne Powell, and Sir Timothy Tyrrell a joint petition for the continuing to the bishop of the augmentation of £100 a year out of the herbage and pannage and the like of Shotover and Stowood, as long as Sir Timothy and Mrs. Powell should renew their patents for them.[175] By February 4, 1661/2, Sir Timothy and Mrs. Powell had applied for a new lease of thirty-one years of the herbage and pannage of Shotover and Stowood, on the usual payment of £100 a year to the king and £100 to the bishop.[176] A week later, in a memorandum to the king, the lord treasurer Southampton lamented that Shotover and Stowood were so reduced in wood, explained that he had reserved a portion of them for the king, and announced the lease of the rest to Sir Timothy Tyrrell. Anne Powell is mentioned, but not as of equal standing with Sir Timothy; rather she seems to be a relic of a previous arrangement, since the lord treasurer speaks only of a part being "reserved on a lease of the wood to Anne Powell."[177] On March 10, 1661/2, however, the king, writing to the lord chancellor, and mentioning a report by the attorney-general on the petition of Tyrrell and Mrs. Powell, ordered leases to both of them at rentals of approximately the previous amounts.[178] The leases, however, must have struck a snag in Parliament; and probably this point marks the end of the Powells' possession of the forests. For on October 3, 1662, the king, after deploring the waste in the lands, which was so great that they were no longer fit for parks and must be enclosed, described the opposition of the House of Commons to the leases.[179]

We do not again hear of the Powells in connection with Shotover. We can follow the leases of Shotover for some time through the State Papers, but the names are not theirs. Thus on March 31, 1663, Sir Timothy Tyrrell received his grant of the coppices and the like in Shotover and Stowood at a rent of £50 a year to the king and £50 to the bishop of Oxford.[180] At the same time the corresponding lease, such as had previously gone to the Powells, was this time given to the Earl of Lindsey.[181] A year later, on February 2, 1663/4, the two men received additional privileges in these grounds, including waifs, the goods of strays and felons, and other casualties of the crown.[182] On December 23, 1665, Sir Timothy Tyrrell applied for an extended lease of thirty-one years at the same rental, and received it on January 13, 1665/6.[183] A similar extension was granted to the Earl of Lindsey on May 23, 1666.[184] Both claimed huge expenses in improving and renovating the grounds.

In 1662 there appeared another of the perennial suits. On December 1 Thomas Whorwood and four others filed a Chancery bill against the Powells.[185] The others were James Parcall[186] of Westminster, gentleman, Anne Jackson of Stanton St. John, administratrix of Richard Eldridge[187] of Brightwell, Berkshire, Thomas Tipping[188] of Wornall, Bucks, yeoman, and John Frinnor[189] of Abingdon, Berkshire, executor of George Ball, who was executor of Thomas Ball.[190] Several old obligations of Richard Powell the elder are mentioned: to Thomas Whorwood for £40 on May 21, 16—[illegible]; to Richard Eldridge for £200 in 1644; to Edward Tipping for £200 in April, 1628; and to Thomas Ball and John Edwards[191] for £600 in March, 1633/4. Powell failed to pay them, and the plaintiffs have become legally possessed of them. The history of Powell's death, his will, and its probate are rehearsed, as well as the recent conveyances to Gilbert Jackson, and the circumstances of Powell's marriage. The plaintiffs complain that Jackson, though he has £530 for just such purposes, refuses to pay them a penny. They beg a writ of privy seal.

In their joint answer to Whorwood's bill the two Powells rehearse Richard Powell's holdings, their troubles during the rebellion and since, and the matter of the marriage.[192] They emphasize how much money they have spent in vexatious suits and attendance on the various parliamentary committees—in all some £200 or £300. They maintain that all discoverable bills of Powell's have been paid. They enclose an inventory of Powell's goods which came to Anne since the list of 1646, this one being dated 1656/7. They also admit that Sir Robert Pye has paid them certain moneys, chiefly in return for loans to him from Powell and partly for assistance in getting in his harvests for him. Matthew Archdale's answer, dated June 20, 1663, adds nothing new except a few details of the Powell marriage, with which he was chiefly concerned.[193] His answer was signed by Christopher Milton, who was therefore still in close relationship with the Powell circle. Gilbert Jackson also answered on May 30, 1663.[194] He matter-of-factly recounts the details of the Powell-Jackson transaction of 1661, says that he has paid the two amounts to Archdale and Ashworth, and that if no further debts arise he is ready to surrender the remaining £530 to the Powells.

On September 29, 1666, Richard Powell was assessed on seven hearths in Forest Hill.[195]

Soon another suit arose, though a simpler one than usual. John

Spicer[196] sued the Powells on November 8, 1667,[197] for failure to repay a debt incurred by the elder Powell to Mary Morrison.[198] The Powells answered on January 17, 1667/8, admitting the debt, but denying that Powell had mortgaged any lands for it.[199]

We now skip half a dozen years, with no entry other than that in 1672 Pye's lease of Forest Hill expired, and he relinquished possession of it.[200]

In 1673 an amusing series of transactions occurred. On April 30 Mary Roberts[201] of Isleworth, Middlesex, and William Chilcott,[202] with the consent of the Powells, made over their rights in the manor and lands of Forest Hill to Elizabeth Newman[203] of St. Giles-in-the-Fields. What they had was the remainder of a lease for ninety-nine years. Elizabeth Newman then reconveyed the same to the Powells for nine hundred and ninety-nine years at a rent of £130 a year for the first twenty-two years and a peppercorn each year thereafter. On June 17, 1673, Elizabeth Powell, administratrix of the will of William Hearne, goldsmith, late of London, assigned to Elizabeth Newman her share in the first of these leases of Forest Hill, which Elizabeth Newman then immediately assigned over to Powell as above.[204]

Since the later events in this story are not too well dated, we may anticipate a trifle here and follow the thread somewhat further. Subsequently Osbaston Newman, son of Elizabeth, who was entitled as above to £130 a year annuity, agreed with Powell to commute this annuity into a cash payment. Powell was to pay her a lump sum of £910 plus £170 arrears. But inasmuch as some of the legatees concerned in the distribution of this money were minors, Powell was obliged to bring suit against them in order to force the legal appointment of trustees for them. This action he brought in 1683, the court appointed trustees for them in May of that year, they answered the bill, and Powell's act was ratified by the court. Powell paid the £910 and extras, Newman acknowledged it and distributed it as agreed on, and conveyed Forest Hill back to Powell. So far as that affair was concerned, the Powells were settled again as normal.[205]

To return again to the thread of our chronology, we find at once another suit. On June 19, 1673, George Lowe[206] of Oxford brought in a bill as executor of the will of Jane Drake his deceased wife, who in turn was the executrix of the will of her former husband Acton Drake,[207] deceased.[208] Here a long and wearisome law-suit hangs on a slight original transaction. On January 18, 1641/2, Richard Powell was bound to Acton Drake in £440 to pay him £228 the next July 19. He paid interest for 6 years, and then stopped on account of the seizure of his estate by the usurpers. Then he died, his son Richard went abroad, and Anne refused to pay the debt and has since continued so to refuse, pretending various excuses. So he begs a writ on them.

They answered by a demurrer on October 31.[209] They protest that they do not think that Powell ever entered *singly* into such a bond, and that hence other parties ought to be dealt with first. If he signed such a bill at all, it was merely as surety. For that matter, the bond is too old to be brought up now.

The court argued the point on December 15.[210] The lord keeper decreed that the demurrer should be overruled but without costs, and that the defendants should answer the bill. He also ordered that if the plaintiff should amend his bill, he should pay the defendants costs; and if he did not amend it, and if subsequently other persons bound in the bond should be found, he should have no relief in this court.

The Powells, perhaps over-confident through inclusion among the notable gentry in Blome's *Britannia* (1673),[211] took their time about answering. In fact, they took too much, for on February 12, 1673/4, the court took cognizance of their failure to answer and issued an attachment against them to compel an answer by Easter term.[212]

Spurred on by this prodding, the two Powells, Anne and Richard, answered on February 26, 1673/4.[213] They reiterate their belief that the debt was no true obligation of the elder Powell's, and recount the story of his sequestration, which was removed only in 1654. They tell also of their great expense in and final surrender of Shotover Forest. The Forest Hill lands are still encumbered with debts. The answer is signed by Hope Shuter.[214]

George Lowe evidently considered this second answer still imperfect, for he put in a replication.[215] On April 1, 1674, the court took this document under advisement, and referred the matter to a master in Chancery, Sir Miles Cooke.[216] He found the answer insufficient and ordered a fuller one.[217]

On May 21 the lawyers for both parties appeared in court, and Shuter and Keck[218] for the defendants begged that since the plaintiff had offered to produce the bond in question, proceedings be stayed till it appeared. The court concurred and ordered the plaintiff to produce it.[219]

On June 25 the lawyers appeared again, and Keck and Shuter, showing the bond triumphantly with its list of other signatures, demanded that in accordance with the previous decree the bill should now be dismissed. Thereupon the plaintiff's lawyer, Phillipps,[220] smoothly proposed that the plaintiff should, with the court's permission, now include these other names in the bill. And the court calmly allowed the request, merely charging the plaintiff five marks for so doing.[221]

Some time later Sir Timothy Baldwin[222] brought in a report on the case which I have not found, and the defendants entered exceptions to it. Their lawyer Hewler[223] requested in an appearance in court on January 18, 1674/5, that proceedings be stayed till the result of these exceptions should be determined. The court so ordered.[224]

A week later, on January 25, 1674/5, Lowe put in his amended bill.[225] This time he adds two names to Powell's as signatories: William Freeman[226] and Ralph Manwaring.[227] But he claims that they are both dead, leaving no real estate, and that their personal estates are being administered by John Clement.[228] Moreover, Clement, together with the Powells, Ann Roberts,[229] William Chilcott, George Clarkeson,[230] Matthew Archdale, and Gilbert Jackson (the parties in previous suits), combine to defraud Lowe. His wife's former husband Acton Drake died in 1651, and she married Lowe in 1652, but died some years since, leaving him as her executor. The conspirators, he complains, deny that Powell was ever bound and try to foist upon Lowe a judgment of £200 [i.e., £2,000] said to have been obtained years ago by Archdale against them; and they have caused Powell's estates to be extended and have voluntarily confessed other judgments and "ancient mortgages" and alleged debts for great sums of money, and pretend that the estate is not sufficient to pay these debts. Lowe claims that as for the Archdale bond, Anne has got more than her £100 a year already out of the estate, and also that the Powells have made many private and fraudulent conveyances (meaning perhaps the Newman affair). So he begs a writ of privy seal.

The Powells answered this latest bill on April 31, 1675.[231] They deny any knowledge of the original debt, but insist that if there were any such it was not Powell's debt and that it is too old to be credited. They have heard that it was paid long ago out of Freeman's estate. They doubt whether the other signatories died intestate, and charge that the pretended executor Clement is merely a puppet of the plaintiff's.

After all this voluble protesting, the plaintiff's lawyer Phillips appeared in court and innocently complained that the defendants had furnished no amended answer![232] It begins to seem like a contest between deaf-mutes. By June 29, however, the defendants had submitted exceptions to Sir Timothy Baldwin's reports, for on that day they were ordered considered.[233]

On December 18, 1675, the defendants put in still another answer, this time of monstrous size.[234] They rehearse everything included in the previous answers touching Powell's sequestrations in Forest Hill, Wheatley, and Shotover, his will and probate, Pye's seizure of Forest Hill (he is since deceased), the expiration of John Pye's possession in 1672, the

leases in Wheatley taken by George Hearne, and Richard Powell's war
service and years abroad. In addition Anne Powell sets forth that since
her husband never made settlement on her as provided in his marriage
bond, she took £700 out of the proceeds of the conveyance of Wheatley
to the Jacksons, though there was actually owing to her £2,800. She lists
debts owing by Powell at the time of his death, in addition to those already recounted in other actions: £120 to Henry Ashworth,[235] £200 to
Simon Cleaver,[236] £400 to Thomas Bennett,[237] £400 to Margery Lupworth (or Lapworth),[238] £200 to Jane Cholder,[239] £600 to Thomas Overman,[240] £300 to Robert Style[241] and James Heath,[242] and many more. The
total comes to some £2,600 and interest. All these they have discharged
before April, 1670, and they have all the cancelled bonds except two or
three which were mislaid. Richard Powell the younger tried once to sell
Forest Hill for £3,600, but not finding any purchasers who would offer
more than £3,300, he held it. They hope to enjoy it in peace till the expiration of the lease. The answer is signed by Hope Shuter. Attached is
a copy of the will of Richard Powell the elder.

On February 11, 1675/6, with confusing incoherence, the plaintiff's
lawyer again complained that no amended answer had appeared.[243] The
matter was again referred to a master. On May 25 the lord chancellor
ordered, on a petition of the plaintiff, that a day should be set for arguing
the matter.[244] On June 6 the lord chancellor found the answer sufficient
and ordered 40s. paid the defendants.[245] So ended a long and tiresome
suit.

But the Powell distresses were by no means ended. In 1683 the Newman affair burst forth again, with Powell acting this time as plaintiff. On
May 31, 1683, he submitted a bill.[246] He rehearses how he himself, Mary
Roberts, William Chilton (i.e., Chilcott?), and George Clarkeson, acting
as trustees for him, and Elizabeth Newman (since deceased) signed an
indenture on April 30, 1673, whereby Powell and his trustees conveyed
to Elizabeth Newman the manor house and all buildings and appurtenances of Forest Hill for a thousand years at the rent of £130 a year for
the first twenty-two years and a peppercorn annually thereafter; how
on June 7 Elizabeth Powell, administratrix of William Hearne, conveyed
to Elizabeth Newman her share in the same property; how on June 9
Elizabeth Newman leased it to Powell for nine hundred and ninety-nine
years at the aforesaid rent; and how Elizabeth Newman made her will
on January 3, 1681/2, bequeathing to her son-in-law Thomas Powell,
his wife Mary Powell, and their daughter Elizabeth an annuity of £30
a year out of the aforesaid £130 annual income from Forest Hill, intending this to be effective only so long as the said income continued. But
now, although it has ceased, they still demand their annuity. He begs a
writ of privy seal on them.

On June 16, 1683, Osbaston Newman, executor of Elizabeth Newman his mother, Thomas Powell, Mary Powell, and a host of others combined in an answer to this bill.[247] They again rehearse the circumstances of the indenture, without giving Richard Powell—or us—any particular satisfaction.

For four years the action then lay dormant. Then on October 26, 1687, Theophilus Eyton of Gray's Inn and his wife Elizabeth sued Richard Powell.[248] Eyton explains that his wife is the daughter of Elizabeth Guise (née Newman), who was the daughter of Elizabeth Newman, and one of the legatees named in her will of 33 Charles II (1681–82) of the much-discussed annuity of £30; that his wife is similarly another legatee; and that his wife and Osbaston Newman were executors of her will and Richard Powell overseer. On her marriage to him, Eyton applied to Powell for arrears of £100, but Powell refused to give it to him, alleging either that the estate was not equal to such payment, that there was no such annuity, that it was voided by court decree, or that it had expired. So he begs a writ of privy seal on Powell.

On November 9, 1687, Powell and Osbaston Newman answered.[249] In one of the increasingly mammoth answers which this business engendered, they rehearse again the whole story of the indenture: how Powell and Mary Roberts and William Chilcott and George Clarkeson indented their share in Forest Hill to Elizabeth Newman on April 30, 25 Charles II (1673), how Elizabeth Powell similarly made over William Hearne's share on June 17, and how in the same month Elizabeth Newman made over all these shares to Richard Powell for £130 a year for twenty-two years and a peppercorn for the remainder of the long term; how Elizabeth Newman bequeathed £30 a year to Elizabeth Guise and to the plaintiff Elizabeth; how Powell bought up the leases for £910 plus £170 arrears, of which £210 was for Edward Guise, his wife, and their daughter Elizabeth in full discharge of their legacy, plus £45 arrears; how Powell sued some minors in Chancery to force the appointment of guardians for them; and how after he had paid the £910 the court had ratified the arrangement, and the property had been confirmed clearly back to Powell.

Then the two defendants began to fight among themselves. On May 28, 1688, Osbaston Newman brought in a bill against Richard Powell, complaining that Powell had not used him fairly.[250] Powell duly replied in an answer as astronomically huge as the bill.[251]

On November 3, 1691, Gilbert Jackson was brought back into the picture when Richard Powell filed another bill against him.[252] Powell rehearses how he had conveyed the Forest Hill property to Jackson in consideration of nearly £2,000, out of which Jackson was to pay debts to various people, and to keep some £500 for such debts as might appear.

Jackson satisfied all the debts. Then he married Elizabeth Towersey, whose father, Richard Towersey of Holton, he now pretends held a bond of Powell's for £40 dated November 19, 1659, and has recently sued Powell at Common Pleas on it. Powell protests that this was thirty years ago, that he signed only in escrow (*i.e.*, conditionally) and never got any of the money, that they could have satisfied it out of the said £500 if they had desired to, that though they live only some two miles from Forest Hill and could easily have come over and asked for it, as they often came for other purposes, they have never done so; and that they also frequently came to London where Powell is a bencher of the Inner Temple and similarly never demanded it there.

He then comes to another grievance. Jackson has recently brought action against various tenants at Forest Hill for breaking his mounds by walking with Powell and the Forest Hill minister along "their usual perambulation[253] or procession" where the inhabitants usually go for this purpose. Now Jackson has recently altered the time-honored perambulation in Cuddesdon parish and "changed the place of the minister's reading or saying one of the said perambulation gospels which anciently . . . was accustomed to be read and said" in Jackson's (formerly John Ellston's[254]) house, "in a room heretofore called the old little parlor." The location of the "way" is specified in detail. So he begs a writ of privy seal on Jackson and the minister Symons.[255] The bill is signed by Edward Hillyard.[256]

Samuel Symonds, clerk, answered on November 20, 1691.[257] He knows nothing of the matter except that he has heard Jackson claim the ground in question. He says that Powell was often told the land was in Cuddesdon, but insisted that the ministers and parishioners of Forest Hill take it in their perambulation. He protests that Powell has no right to vex him with such tremendously long bills as he has lately brought (he mentions two), one of which consisted of 146 sheets of paper!

Similarly Jackson replied on February 3, 1691/2, with his wife Elizabeth.[258] Jackson admits buying the premises as rehearsed, but adds that he discovered only later that Anne Powell (now deceased) was entitled to part of the premises as her dowry and refused to convey it to him. So he says it was agreed that he should be paid his expenses and the deed be void. But later, on her agreement to pay her part of the purchase money, he had it conveyed to her and agreed to accept £20 for his expenses and trouble. Then he paid all the purchase money and accepted a bond from Powell to Richard Towersey[259] for the £20. He maintains he has often demanded the amount from Powell, both in his chamber in the Temple and in his house in Red Lion Court near Fleet Street. Powell promises but pays nothing. The "way" mentioned in the bill is in Cuddesdon, and was railed in by John Elstone, gentleman, over forty years since. The house and green are named "Vent House" and "Vent Green." Powell has confessed to Elizabeth Jackson that he can claim no title to it or to any lands in Cuddesdon. They never in thirty years have heard of any perambulation of parishioners into any room or parlor in their now dwelling house. He confesses he has now an action of trespass pending against various inhabitants of Forest Hill for breaking a hedge belonging to Vent Farm and attempting to take Vent Green into the perambulation of Forest Hill, and he hopes his action is lawful.

The answers did not satisfy Powell, and the Jacksons were compelled to make a further one, which was presented on June 4, 1692.[260] Jackson here gives further details about the purchase of the manor. Out of the £1,700 purchase money, he paid Anne Powell £700, Elizabeth Ashworth £470, John Finnor of Abingdon £200, James Parcall of Westminster £104-7-0, Richard Eldridge and Anne Jackson of Shotover £105, Thomas Whorwood of Headington £25, Thomas Tippinge of Worndall, Bucks., £32, his counsel in Chancery and other assistants £35, and Powell himself £29-4-0—all with Powell's consent. Thus all the purchase money was "swallowed up." He says that Powell sealed and delivered the bond to Towersey as his personal act and deed and not as escrow, and so Jackson is entitled to both principal and interest.

Meanwhile the Court had been considering the closely related Powell-Newman suit. On January 25, 1691/2, the defendants had been granted a month's respite to answer, since they needed time to consult deeds and documents in the plaintiff's possession.[261] Then on March 7, 1692/3, the plaintiffs having failed to respond to the defendants' answer, which had been submitted on April 12, the court dismissed the case with costs of seven nobles (equivalent to £2-6-8) to the Newmans.[262]

Richard Powell made his will on December 29, 1693, leaving the bulk of his estate, aside from a few trifling legacies, to his wife, who by an interesting coincidence was also named Ann. He died some two years later, and on February 3, 1695/6, she proved his will (18 Bond). She in turn must have died before 1705, for in the margin of the entry of his probate in the will books is the note that administration of her goods was granted on January 27, 1704[/5], to Jane Brokesley (or Brokesby)[263] and on January 24, 1705[/6], to Samuel Grascom[264] and Richard Holt.[265] So comes to an end the story of the struggles and suits of the Powell family.

It remains only to be said that in 1700 one Francis Heywood was owner or tenant of the manor and manor farm of Forest Hill.[266] Since that date the Powells and the Miltons have had little if any connection with the village. The manor house was bought in 1808 by Lincoln College, Oxford, and pulled down in 1854.[267] The only relics of Milton which still remain are the so-called Milton gateway in the vicarage garden, and the Milton stone, on which, as it lay outside the door of the manor house, Milton used to sit and smoke.[268] The authenticity of both stories is of course highly dubious.

So we leave this sketch of a country manor in the seventeenth century. Its history is astonishingly tangled and litigious, and to no inconsiderable extent confused. The documents here summarized are obviously far from representing all that could be found by painstaking search, but they reveal a constancy and prickly cantankerousness very different from the peaceful pastoral life which the casual visitor to even the modern village of Forest Hill would expect to find. They serve to confirm the point, which is the central fact of all this book, that life in the time of Milton, and his life like that of others, required a good deal of attention to financial matters, to law and courts, and to investments. Even a poet could not live a life apart, but must be swept into the rushing current of life, either to fight for his rights or to sink.

CHAPTER VII

NOVERINT UNIVERSI
Milton and Powell

He [a scrivener] is so impudent in his art of undoing others, that he begins with Noverint universi, let all men know it.—Wye Salstonstall, "A Scrivener."

> Well, push him out of doors,
> And let my officers of such a nature
> Make an extent upon his house and lands:
> Do this expediently and turn him going.
> —Shakespeare, *As You Like It*, III, i.

IT has long been known that on June 11, 1627, Richard Powell the elder borrowed £300 from John Milton Jr., and gave him as security for principal and interest a bond of £500. Speculation about the possible relation between the loan and another Milton-Powell incident of a different character which culminated some fifteen years later has baffled biographers, who have sometimes facetiously suggested that Milton married Mary Powell in order to collect the debt from her father. Be that as it may, the original documents in the transaction have never hitherto come to light.[1]

The bond was described as a "statute staple," which is one of various kinds of obligation current in Milton's time. It was therefore a bond of record, acknowledged before the mayor of a "staple" town or a chief justice of England or a recorder of London; on default of payment the creditor might have execution, or disposal, of the body, lands, and goods of the debtor.[2] In the Public Record Office there are several groups of documents under the classification of statutes staple, and a little search among those known as "Certificates and Recognizances" revealed the original obligation from Powell to Milton.[3]

It is a parchment bond, roughly the size of a sheet of type-writing paper, disfigured by slashes, and so blackened by time as to be in part illegible. The few words or letters which are not readable, however, may easily be filled in by comparison with other examples from the same bundle, so that we may be certain enough of the wording. It is written in Latin, beginning with the familiar "Noverint universi"; and a transcript of the original will be found in the appendix. For present purposes an English translation will be more useful.[4]

Remains of Milton's House at Forest Hill, near Oxford;
the scenery around which is described in L'Allegro.

The manor of Forest Hill as it appeared in the nineteenth
century. From Robert Chambers, *Cyclopædia of English
Literature* (edition of 1851), I, 335.

Forest Hill Church, showing the so-called Milton gateway. From
Skelton's Engraved Illustrations of the Principal Antiquities of Oxfordshire
(1823 ff.), "Bullington Hundred," p. 5.

Know all men by these presents that we, Richard Powell of Forest Hill in the county of Oxford, gentleman, and William Hearne,[5] goldsmith, of London, hold ourselves firmly bound to John Milton of the University of Cambridge, gentleman, in five hundred pounds of lawful English money to be paid to the said John (or to his specified attorney on presentation of this writing), his heirs or executors, on the feast of the Nativity of St. John the Baptist next ensuing after the date of these presents [i.e., June 24], and if we shall fail to pay the aforesaid debt, we are willing and consent that there shall fall on us and both our heirs and executors the penalty in statute staple ordained and provided, in case of disputed debts, for the recovery of the said sum. Given this eleventh day of June, in the third year of the reign of our Lord Charles [i.e., 1627], by the grace of God King of England, Scotland, France, and Ireland, Defender of the Faith, etc.

Richard Powell [seal]
William Hearne [seal]
[blank] [seal]
Nicholas Hyde[6] [seal]

On the back are several endorsements which furnish information about the subsequent history of the debt. The first may be translated as follows:

Certified in the Chancery of our Lord the King by me Thomas Hampson,[7] Baronet, Clerk, etc., the sixteenth day of December in the twenty-second year of the reign of Charles [i.e., 1646].

Next comes a later endorsement, written by a different clerk, since the handwriting is dissimilar, and this time in English:

Memorandum that upon the nine and twentieth day of November in the year of our Lord one thousand six hundred fifty and nine, before the keepers of the liberty of England by authority of Parliament, did come the within-named John Milton and did acknowledge himself to be fully satisfied the within-mentioned five hundred pounds and all the damages, costs, and expenses any ways sustained in and about the recovery thereof. And thereupon he the said John Milton instantly requireth that this writing obligatory may be cancelled and made void. At whose instance this said writing obligatory is altogether cancelled, vacated, and made void.

Just below follows an affidavit by some nonentity of the time:

I know the above-named John Milton.
Thomas Gemm.[8]

Hearne's name is included for safety's sake. In Thomas Middleton's *Michaelmas Term*, when the young gull Easy is about to sign a bond, he is told he must have a citizen sign with him. He asks why, and the sharper Shortyard answers that it is "a custom they're bound to o' late by the default of evil debtors; no citizen must lend money without two be bound in the bond; the second man enters but for custom's sake."[9] As many guileless souls discovered to their sorrow, however, one who nonchalantly signed a bond merely as a good fellow often found himself haled to court and forced to pay the debt himself. Such an affliction is exactly what we have discovered happening to Samuel Burton.[10] Middleton's Easy learns the same lesson. Arrested for the unpaid bond of the pretended Blastfield, he protests, "You know my entrance was but for fashion's sake." Quomodo, the Shylock of the play, gleefully exults over this naiveté: "Why, I'll agree to you: you'll grant 'tis the fashion likewise, when the bond's due, to have the money paid again."[11]

Two other short endorsements on the back of the bond must be mentioned, one of them a real find. The first must be transcribed largely by guess work (the bracketed readings being illegible), but it is patently an abbreviated version of the preceding note.

Discharged the [29th day of November] 1659: because I saw [the said recognizance] in the hands of Richard Powell [esquire].

Not for some time after I first saw the document did the significance of certain faint lines appearing just below the foregoing endorsement become apparent, but I then realized that they represented Milton's own signature. Written in a sprawling hand and with an extremely fine pen, it is nevertheless legible up to the last two letters: "J o h n M i l t [o n]." The J is not wholly formed (or at least visible), but the long down-stroke is clear and black, and the first up-stroke faintly discernible. The right-hand side of the o is missing, but the h and the n are quite clear except for having been written over the endorsement. The first four letters of M i l t o n are perfectly clear, and one can imagine traces of the o in the midst of the endorsement. Written parallel to the certificate of 1646, it nevertheless must of course be Milton's signature to the cancellation, and as such represents one of a very few signatures extant from the period of his blindness.[12]

The transaction covered a period of more than thirty years. During the interval much had occurred to alienate the two parties: civil war, an unsuccessful marriage, parliamentary seizure of royal estates, including Powell's, the rise and death of Cromwell, and the looming across the Channel of the shadow of the Stuart Restoration. Milton had changed from an undergraduate of nineteen, writing academic exercises and pleasant little verses, to a veteran of fifty-one, blind, busy, and the most famous controversialist in England. His father, who had helped to arrange the loan in the beginning, and his father-in-law Powell, as well as William Hearne, had long been dead. The matter had virtually passed from the hands of one generation into those of the next. For it need hardly be pointed out that the Richard Powell mentioned in the endorsements is the *son* of Milton's father-in-law, not the elder Powell.

Turning now to the records of the Lord Chamberlain's office, where such obligations were often recorded, we find this one listed in the index to the Recognizance Books as "R. Powell–J. Milton—265." On page 265 of the corresponding book the entry of the bond is recorded, together with copies of the further endorsements which have already been given.[13] The wording is so similar to those already given that it need not be repeated here.

Further light on the proceedings of 1646 is desirable, and fortunately also available. In answer to a Chancery bill brought against him by Elizabeth Ashworth in 1654[14] Milton stated that after the signing of the original statute Powell had paid interest regularly on it for some seventeen years, and had then failed to continue payments:

... the said twelve pounds interest was paid upon the said twelfth day of December or soon after. And ... the growing interest for the forbearance of the said principal debt was for some years then following likewise paid, and so continued to be paid until June in the year of our Lord one thousand six hundred forty and four. At what time the said Richard Powell failed ... in the payment of the interest then due and payable and from thence growing due and payable ...

Powell's income was undoubtedly feeling the pinch of the war, and he may have had a suspicion that a favorable outcome to that struggle might automatically ease off any little unpleasantnesses like debts to defeated parliamentarians. But Milton was not of the breed to take such setbacks with simple resignation. The future antagonist of Salmasius and More, and the son of a seasoned veteran of the courts like the scrivener Milton, was not likely to let a Cavalier sap his income with impunity. Milton went to law.

The regular procedure in such cases is outlined in *The Attourney's Academy* by Thomas Powell.[15] First the creditor goes to the clerk of the staple, shows him the date of the statute, and has him make a certificate. Next, he takes this certificate to the clerk of the crown and has an "exigent" made on it. This exigent is defined by Cowel as a "writ that lieth where the defendant in an action personal cannot be found, nor any thing within the country, whereby to be attached or distrained, and is directed to the sheriff, to proclaim and call five county days one after another, charging him to appear under the pain of outlawry."[16] The creditor next has an obligation made, and his exigent endorsed. This latter he then delivers to the sheriff, who impanels a jury to "enquire, extend, and apprehend as well the body as the lands, goods, and chattels of the party so bounden." These effects the sheriff holds in his possession till the creditor brings a "deliberate" (or "liberate") from the clerk of the petty bag, which is to be procured on surrender of the statute. Milton undoubtedly followed these steps religiously. He had already, as we have seen, taken his bond to the clerk of the staple, Sir Thomas Hampson, and got the certificate; from the clerk of the crown (who might be his brother-in-law Edward Phillips or his successor Thomas Agar, also Milton's brother-in-law) in return for this certificate he would next obtain an extent, which he would then deliver to the sheriff.

Fortunately for the completeness of this story, these papers too prove to be extant. There are two of them. The first is a writ of July 16, 1647, authorizing the sheriff of Oxford county to take an extent or inventory of Powell's real estate in Wheatley. The following is an English translation from the original Latin.[17]

Charles by the grace of God King of England, Scotland, France, and Ireland, Defender of the Faith, etc. To the Sheriff of Oxford, greeting. Whereas Richard Powell of Forest Hill in your county, gentleman, and William Hearne, citizen and goldsmith of London, on the 11th day of June in the third year of our reign [i.e., 1627], before Nicholas Hyde, knight, then our Chief Justice, at a session appointed to be held before us, acknowledged that they owed John Milton of the University of Cambridge, gentleman, five hundred pounds which they were bound to pay to the said John at the feast of the Nativity of St. John the Baptist then next ensuing [i.e., June 24]; and whereas they did not pay it to him, as is said: by our writ we have commanded you that the bodies of the aforesaid Richard Powell and William Hearne (if they were laymen) should be taken and held safely in our prison till they should have satisfied the aforesaid debt to the said John, and that all the lands and chattels of the said Richard and William in your county should be diligently extended and appraised by the oath of honest and lawful men of your said county by whom the truth of the matter might be the better known, according to the true value of the same, and that they should be seized into our hand in order that the same might be delivered over to the said John until full satisfaction should be made for the aforesaid debt according to the form of the statute published and provided at Westminster for the recovery of men's debts. And that you should make known to us in our Chancery on a certain day now past, wherever it should then be, by your sealed letters, how you executed our said order, and that you should have there our said writ. On which day as specified in our said writ you returned to us in our Chancery that the aforesaid Richard Powell was dead. We ordered you therefore that the body of the aforesaid William Hearne (if he were a layman) should be taken and safely held in our prison till he should have fully satified the said John of the aforesaid debt, and that all the lands and chattels of the said William in your county, and also all the lands and tenements which belonged to the aforesaid Richard Powell at the said time of the recognizance of the said debt or the inquisition afterwards, unless they had descended by any law of inheritance to any heir under age then living—that all these goods and chattels which were possessed by the aforesaid Richard at the time of his death in your said county should be diligently extended and appraised, by the oath of honest and lawful men of your said county by whom the truth of the matter might be the better known according to the true value of the same, and seized into our hand, that they might be delivered to the said John Milton till full satisfaction should be made to him for the said debt according to the form of the statute aforesaid. And you are to make known to us in our Chancery aforesaid within three weeks of the day of St. Michael next to come [i.e., September 29], wherever it shall then be, by your sealed letters, how you have executed this order of ours. And you shall have there this writ. Witness myself at Westminster, the sixteenth day of July in the twenty-third year of our reign [1647].

Lenthall, Speaker.[18]

The execution of the same writ appears in a certain inquisition annexed to this writ.

William Cope,[19] Esq., Sheriff.

The second paper, dated August 5, 1647, is the inquisition or inventory itself taken by a jury of twelve good men and true. In English translation it follows.

Oxford, ss. An inquisition drawn up and taken at the city of Oxford in the aforesaid county on the fifth day of August in the twenty-third year of the reign of our Lord Charles by the grace of God King of England, Scotland, France, and Ireland, Defender of the Faith, etc. [i.e., 1647], before me, William Cope, Esq., Sheriff of the said county, by virtue of a writ of our said Lord the King directed to me and annexed to this inquisition, and the oaths of John Hunt,[20] Richard Phillips, [21] William Sadler,[22] Triumph de St. Paul,[23] John Slatford,[24] William Cooper,[25] William Yanning,[26] John Wild,[27] James Colkyer,[28] William Michell,[29] Thomas Hore,[30] and Anthony Slatter,[31] honest and lawful men of my county. Who say on their oath that Richard Powell, gentleman, named in the aforesaid writ, on the day of the recognizance of debt mentioned in the aforesaid writ, that is on the eleventh day of June in the third year of the reign of our said Lord the now King of England, etc. [1627], mentioned in the aforesaid writ, was seized in his demesne as of fee of and in all that portion of the tithes of corn with the appurtenances in Wheatley in the parish of Cuddesdon in the said county, of the clear annual value in all issues over and above reprises of £26-3-4; and of and in one messuage, two barns, one cottage, and one yard and a half of land, containing thirty-seven acres and one rod of land, three acres of meadow and eight acres and a half of pasture with the appurtenances lying and being in the town and fields of Wheatley aforesaid in the parish of Cuddesdon aforesaid, of the clear annual value in all issues over and above reprises of £15; and further the jurors aforesaid on their oath aforesaid say that the aforesaid Richard Powell after the said day of recognizance of debt aforesaid mentioned in the same writ, that is on the said eleventh day of June in the third year aforesaid, and before the day of the taking of this inquisition, was seized in his demesne as of fee of and in two yards of land with appurtenances lying and being in the said Wheatley, containing forty-eight acres and one rod of arable land and four acres of meadow with appurtenances, of the clear annual value in all issues over and above reprises of £13-6-8; and of and in one cottage with appurtenances in Wheatley aforesaid now in the tenure or occupation of one Walter Symons,[32] of the clear annual value in all issues over and above reprises, of 20s.; and of and in one other cottage with appurtenances in Wheatley aforesaid, now in the tenure or occupation of one Richard Clarke,[33] of the clear annual value in all issues over and above reprises, of 20s.; and of and in one messuage with appurtenances in Wheatley aforesaid in the tenure or occupation of one Thomas Church,[34] of the clear annual value in all issues over and above reprises, of 20s.; and also of and in one other cottage with appurtenances in Wheatley aforesaid in the tenure or occupation of one William Platt,[35] of the clear annual value in all issues over and above reprises of 13s. 4d.; and further the jurors aforesaid on their oath

aforesaid say that Anne Powell, widow, who was the wife of the aforesaid Richard, stands possessed of and in a third part of all and singular the premises
aforesaid with the appurtenances as of freehold for the term of her life as her
portion from the endowment of the aforesaid Richard her former husband, and
that the said Anne now survives and exists in full life at Wheatley aforesaid.
All which premises aforesaid with their appurtenances I, the aforesaid sheriff, on
the said day of the taking of this inquisition, have taken and caused to be seized
into the hands of our Lord the King. Finally, the aforesaid jurors on their aforesaid oath say that the aforesaid Richard Powell at the time of his death had no
goods or chattels and had no other or further lands in my said county to the
knowledge of the said jurors which could be extended or seized. In testimony of
which matter both I, the aforesaid sheriff, and the aforesaid jurors have affixed
our seals to this inquisition on the day and year first above written.

William Cope, Esq., Sheriff.

From other sources we learn that these legal measures taken by Milton
became really and finally effective on November 20, 1647, when he
stepped into full possession of the attached property. Our authority is
the same Chancery proceeding quoted before:[36]

By vertue of which extent, inquisition, and a liberate thereupon . . . the said
portion of tithes with the appurtenances, and also all and singular the lands,
tenements, cottages, and premises with their appurtenances, upon the twentieth
day of November in the twenty-third year aforesaid, were delivered to this defendant by the said sheriff, to hold to him and his assigns as his freehold until he
should be fully satisfied of his said debt.

The returns from this newly acquired property were at first somewhat
slow. In the winter following the seizure he received only two pounds
thirteen shillings, not being able to rent most of the premises until the
following spring. Thereafter, to summarize from the same document,
his receipts were as follows:

1648, Michaelmas	£31-13- 8	1651, Michaelmas	45-18-11
1649, March 25	31-14- 9	1652, March 25	47- 2- 7
1649, Michaelmas	31- 3-10	1652, Michaelmas	48- 6- 0
1650, March 25	31-10- 0	1653, March 25	47-15- 4
1650, Michaelmas	32- 2- 0	1653, Michaelmas	47-14- 6
1651, March 25	47-12- 4		
		Total	£445- 6-11

The sudden increase of 50% in 1651 was caused by the fact that in that
year Anne Powell, widow of Richard Powell, stopped receiving her legal
third of the income of the estate. Previously, as the inquisition shows,
she had been allowed one third in satisfaction of her unpaid dowry, but
the parliamentary committee had recently refused to continue her
allowance.[37]

Milton estimated that there was yet owing to him £114-6-1. If the
rents continued to be paid to him about as shown in the schedule above,

his debts would be satisfied in something over two years. This was exactly what happened. We have no record of payments in such detail after Michaelmas, 1653, for the answer from which we have been quoting was submitted in February, 1654. But by a decree of the Court of Chancery, dated in 1657, it was decided that by Michaelmas, 1656, Milton had received enough to satisfy his debt, with a surplus of £4-17-4, which he agreed to turn back to Richard Powell, Jr.[38] The transaction was now complete except for the formalities of cancellation. Why it required two years more to arrange those details I cannot say; but, as we have seen, in November, 1659, the bond was formally cancelled, and the score was settled.

PART III

JOHN MILTON, POET

Specimen bill in Chancery (Pye *vs*. Milton). From the original in the Public Record Office, London.

CHAPTER VIII

A GREAT BUYER OF LAND
Pye *vs.* Milton, 1647

This fellow might be in's time a great buyer of land, with his statutes, his recognizances, his fines, his double vouchers, his recoveries. . . .—
Shakespeare, *Hamlet*, V, i.

FOR some years the law courts left the Miltons in peace. Not long before Scrivener Milton had been finally released from trials and answers, Poet Milton had returned from his grand tour and set up a school in London for training young Miltons. In a few months, however, he had been sucked into the devouring maw of war-work, and had poured out his energies, not in sword-blows, but in pen-drops. Pamphlet after pamphlet, many of them long and erudite, and all of them fiercely sweeping opposition before them, rushed from his studies in Aldersgate and the Barbican. There seemed to be no time for legal actions. But time had to be found, for shortly after the fall of Oxford, young Milton received his first writ from the Lord Chancellor's office. For the first time he was to discover how it felt to be a defendant.

The suit was brought against him by Sir Robert Pye, an influential member of Parliament.[1] Pye was the son of a Sir Roger (or William) Pye of the Mynde in Herefordshire, the father of Sir Robert the parliamentarian, and an ancestor of Henry James Pye the poet-laureate. Our Sir Robert, who was to remain a staunch royalist during the commonwealth, began his career through the favor of Buckingham as remembrancer of the exchequer. He was knighted in 1621 and bought the manor of Farringdon, Berkshire, which he fortified and later defended spectacularly during the war from an attack on it led by his republican son of the same name. In early life he "loved the Muses," as Ben Jonson averred in his whimsical verse petition.[2] He had a reputation for snobbishness, and John Aubrey, who disliked him, dismissed him as "haughty." John Hoskyns, sergeant-at-law, hearing of his death on Christmas day, exclaimed satirically, "The Devil has a Christmas Pye."[3] Wood tells how his son and Lord Say quietly and perhaps a trifle ignominiously slipped out of Oxford on hearing of Prince Rupert's approach.[4]

Aubrey tells an amusing story of Sir Robert, the parliamentarian, and Captain Carlo Fantom, a Croatian officer under his command and a "hardman" (*i.e.*, hard to kill, impervious to bullets). Fantom, a great swaggerer, dueller, thief, and ravisher of women, stole a horse. Pye shot his pistol at him, and the bullets went through Fantom's coat, setting it on fire; but he calmly took them back to Pye, saying, "Here, take your bullets again." Fantom was eventually hanged for rape, having boasted, "I care not for your cause, I come to fight for your half crown and your handsome women."[5]

Milton became involved in this action through his loan to Richard Powell, which had resulted, as we have seen, in his taking over Powell's property in Wheatley in 1647. The negotiations had been in process for some time preceding this action. Pye in his turn had apparently first become financially connected with Powell in 1640. In June of that year he had taken over Powell's debt to one George Furseman for £1,000, and had also assumed several hundred pounds' worth of other obligations. Powell in return had given him a mortgage bond for £1,510, the terms of which were that if Powell failed to repay his debts to Pye by July, 1641, the estate of Forest Hill should become forfeited to Pye.[6] But being hard pinched by the war, Powell had been forced to let this debt slide as he had the bond to Milton, until in 1646 Pye determined to foreclose. He took the necessary steps preparatory to entering the property. But when he entered, he came into conflict with Milton, who was just in the act of taking over the Wheatley property. The result may best be told by a summary of Pye's bill, which was filed on February 11, 1646/7—a little over a month after Powell's death.[7]

Pye's bill is addressed to the commissioners of the great seal of England, who now had charge of Chancery proceedings, the lord keeper being of course no longer recognized. He recites the course of his business relations with Powell. By a deed dated June 13, 1640, in consideration of £1,400 paid by Pye, Powell granted him the manor or lordship of Forest Hill with various other lands and premises for the term of thirty-one years, with the proviso that if Powell should pay Pye £1,510 on July 1, 1641, the transfer should become void. The money, however, was not paid, and so the lease became absolute.

But on taking possession, Pye protests, he has been "hindered and interrupted in the peaceable enjoyment" of his estate by "one John Melton of London, gentleman, who pretends that he hath some former interest and estate" in the premises. Pye has often in a friendly manner (a mere legal fiction which frequently appears in such suits) desired him to explain what title he has in the premises, but Milton doggedly refuses to make known his claim. Completely balked in his peaceful enjoyment of the forfeited estate, Pye begs a writ of privy seal to compel Milton to recite his claims and defend his action. The bill was drawn up by Bulstrode Whitelocke,[8] sworn to before "Kel. sen.,"[9] and filed with Lawrence Maydwell.[10]

Milton's answer appeared promptly,[11] being sworn on February 22 before Robert Aylett.[12] Incidentally, he met Pye's challenge of a big name for counsel with another equally important. His counsel was John Bradshaw.[13] In his answer Milton formally denied knowledge that Powell had ever conveyed to Pye the manor of Forest Hill or any lands within the neighborhood. He pointed out, however, that Powell had become bound to Milton in 1627 in an obligation of £500, which had never been paid. Consequently, Milton had put the bond in execution, as he conceived it was right for him to do, and had thereby gained a title to the premises superior to Pye's because prior in time. So he hoped that he should be maintained in his action and awarded reasonable costs "in this behalf most wrongfully sustained."

The curious fact about this proceeding is that so far as we can ascertain, the two antagonists were talking at cross-purposes. They appear not to have realized the discrepancy even themselves, but actually they were concerned with two wholly distinct properties. Pye had a title to the manor of Forest Hill, Milton to a messuage in Wheatley; there should have been no overlapping and no conflict. It seems incredible that the trouble could have arisen in the first place, and still more so that the action could have proceeded so far as it did without discovery of the mistake. Yet nowhere in the records is there any recognition of this comedy of errors. Whether Milton actually gained some sort of foothold in Forest Hill itself which is not mentioned in the documents is a possible question that comes into our minds. It is conceivable that some *sub rosa* understanding about this estate (which was not mentioned by the inquisitors, it will be remembered) might have been arrived at between Milton and the Powells. Only by some such hypothesis does this proceeding make sense at all.

Pye took his time to meditate over Milton's answer. It was nearly a year before he finally put in his "replication," which even then was totally worthless.[14] Even the date of it is somewhat uncertain. In a later decree of the court it is given as November 27, 1647,[15] but the document itself is dated more vaguely as Hilary, 22 Charles I [1646–47], which must be a clerical error for 23 Charles I [1647–48]. Hilary term extended from January 24 to February 12,[16] which would of course rule out any possibility of a replication in 1646/7, since Milton's answer is dated February 22, 1646/7. The dating in Hilary term would, however, carry on the reply several months later than the dating in November. Since both the decree and the reply contain mistakes, one is uncertain which to place the greater credence in; but I incline to the replication. If my interpretation is correct, Pye waited nearly a year before answering Milton's reply.

When he did finally respond, he had nothing worth saying. He made just two points: Milton is a liar, and Pye is right. Nothing else. More explicitly, he maintained that his bill of complaint was "just, true, certain, and sufficient in the law to be answered unto," and that Milton's answer was "very untrue, uncertain, and insufficient in the law to be replied unto for the manifest faults and imperfections therein contained." It sounds very offhand and careless.

One suspects that Pye had lost confidence in his cause, and that his uncertainty caused the weakness of his replication. Probably he had begun to discover the fundamental mistake on which his bill had rested. It is still more clear that what little confidence remained soon waned. Whether he discovered that he had made a fool of himself, or whether his royalism rendered him too unpopular to continue, he quietly dropped the case. The replication was feeble and vague, taking the defensive rather than the offensive; it was virtually an admission of defeat. Thereafter Pye made no moves whatsoever.

Yet it was nearly two years before the case ended. It was not till June 16, 1649, that the lawyers for the two sides appeared in court to receive the decree.[17] These were not the distinguished counsel who had helped to draw up the proceedings; the services of those luminaries had ended when the bill and answer were ready. On this occasion, Pye was represented by one Wilcox;[18] Milton's lawyer is unnamed. The presiding officer (who would be either Bulstrode Whitelocke, John Lisle, or Richard Keble) summed up the previous steps in the case to date, making at least one and probably two mistakes in the process. According to his summary, the bill had been put in during Hilary term, 1646/7, the answer in March following [an error for February], and the replication on November 27, 1647 [an error for January–February, 1647/8?]. Milton's attorney also supplied a certificate that the plaintiff had not proceeded in the cause since that time.

The decision was brief, simple, and logical. The case was ordered dropped, with costs to the defendant. "It was therefore prayed [by counsel for the defence] that the said bill might be dismissed with ordinary costs, which is ordered accordingly." Milton's first adventure in Chancery had ended easily and almost farcically.

CHAPTER IX

MERCILESS TIGER

Ashworth *vs.* Milton, 1654

... some merciless tigers are grown to such barbarous cruelty that they blush not to say [of debtors], "Tush! he shall either pay me the whole, or else lie there till his heels rot from his buttocks."—Stubbes, *Anatomy of Abuses*.

FOR the present chapter we need to retrace our steps some years and recall one or two events in the career of Richard Powell, the inveterate borrower. In January, 1631/2, Powell had borrowed £400 of Henry Ashworth,[1] and had given him the usual bond for it, securing it by a messuage, a cottage, the moiety of three yards of land, and all the tithes of corn and other things in Wheatley and Groveleyes situated in Wheatley and Cuddesdon, worth £100 a year. As usual, he failed to repay the money. The lender, feeling a natural desire to recover his money, took legal action. The property in question had been obtained by Powell by fine from Sir George Symeon[2] in Hilary term, 1619/20.

To bind the bargain with Ashworth, Powell had given him a lease of this property for ninety-nine years, to commence from January 13, 1632/3,[3] the indenture being dated January 10, 1631/2.[4] The understanding, according to the usual arrangement, was that if Powell paid back the loan, as he hoped to do, before January 13, 1632/3, the demise should be void. As a second alternative, it was of course understood (though it is never explicitly stated in the documents) that so long as he should continue to pay interest on the loan, his property should remain in his own possession. But as so often in similar cases, Powell's expectations surpassed his powers of fulfilment, and when the time for repayment came, the purse was empty and the creditor had to go without. Ashworth, however, with unusual lenience (though we cannot be sure that the interest was not paid regularly), allowed Powell to retain his estate, and, dying, made Edward Ashworth his son his executor. Years later—in fact, about 1648—Edward Ashworth received £100 on account towards the accumulated interest and principal, which by that time should have amounted to some £528. Who paid this we cannot be sure, but it could not have been Richard Powell, who had died one or two years earlier. Perhaps the money was paid by Richard Powell, Jr., to whom his father's estate had descended. In 1648, however, Edward

Ashworth himself died, leaving his interest in the transaction to his wife and executrix Elizabeth.

In the midst of this game of hide-and-seek a new figure stepped into the arena—the poet Milton. It has been shown elsewhere how he lent Powell £300 in 1627, how he took out an extent on Powell's estates in Wheatley for failure to repay the loan, and how it was finally settled in 1659. In November, 1647, after some months of formalities, he calmly stepped in and helped himself to the Wheatley holdings. To the Ashworths the prospect of easy settlement of their affair, or even of any settlement at all, suddenly appeared precarious. So they took the natural step by bringing suit against Milton to compel him to show what his claims against the estate were, to what extent they had already been satisfied, and why he should not move out and let them walk in.

The bill in which Elizabeth Ashworth stated her grievances has unfortunately been lost or mislaid, so that it is not now available. There is so good a summary of it in a later Chancery decree in the case, however, that we can get along quite comfortably without the original. In fact, the story of the affair which has just been given is taken in considerable measure from sources which are two removes from the facts: it comes from the court's summary of Elizabeth Ashworth's summary of the actual events. Since it has been possible, however, in many details to check this information from other sources, and since there seem to be no very wrong statements, I believe we can trust it. We do not know the exact date of her bill, nor the name of her counsel, but the date must have been about February 11, 1653/4.

From the decree and from Milton's answer, we can infer the principal claims that must have been contained in the bill:

1. That Richard Powell gave a recognizance to Sir John [*rectius* Edward] Powell which should take priority over Milton's.
2. That Milton has given out in speeches that he obtained his recognizance in some way different from the above.
3. That Milton's recognizance has been fraudulently antedated.
4. That he has already received more than his due debt.
5. That he wrongfully caused the lands to be charged with the dower-thirds of Elizabeth [*rectius* Anne] Powell, widow.
6. That Anne has already received a jointure from her husband Richard Powell.
7. That Powell had other lands besides these subject to action but overlooked.
8. That Milton has failed to collect his debt as speedily as he could or should have.
9. That he has been guilty of combination (or collusion) to defraud.

In framing his answer to this bill Milton found himself in one respect in good fortune: he could now go to his brother Christopher for assistance. Christopher Milton, it may be remembered, was some years younger than John, but he was by now a man of thirty-eight, who had been admitted to the bar at the Inner Temple some fourteen years before, and had in the meantime married Thomasine Webber and had three children.[5] Politically, he had been on the opposite side from Milton during the war, but the brotherly friendship had apparently not been impaired.[6] When Milton needed a lawyer to draw up his answer, he called on Christopher.

The answer was sworn on February 22, 1653/4, before Thomas Estcourt.[7] The answer is of considerable length, and gives us a good deal of interesting information about Milton's affairs.[8]

With the usual caution Milton begins by disclaiming any knowledge of Powell's lease to Ashworth or of any borrowing by Powell from Ashworth. He denies having possessed himself of or meddled with any of Powell's cattle, household stuff, money, plate, or jewels, as the plaintiff has intimated in her bill. He then recounts how Powell and Hearne had acknowledged a recognizance of statute staple to him in 1627 for a debt of £300 principal and £12 interest, which had been loaned, he said, by his father. The principal (as might have been expected) had never been paid, but the interest, at the same rate of 8%, had been regularly paid until June, 1644. There is no indication in the document of any reason why Powell should have failed in payment after that time, but explanations are not far to seek.[9]

Milton, however, was far from accepting defeat or loss of income. Rather he went directly to law to force an action on the defaulted recognizance. In his own words, he "did take out several extents upon the said statute before he could get any of the lands and tenements of the said Richard Powell duly extended." After Powell's death (December, 1646) he achieved his end, and obtained an inquisition on Powell's estates. This was taken in August, 1647. The inquisition made no mention of Powell's estate in Forest Hill, but confined itself to the Wheatley property.

We need not follow the account of this procedure in detail, since it has been summarized in a previous chapter.[10] It will suffice to say that the inquisitors appraised the property, the sheriff seized it, and it was delivered to Milton in November, 1647. The account of Milton's receipts from the property up to the time of submitting his answer, which follows this story of the inquisition, has also been summarized above. The net result of his accounting is to find £114-6-1 still due to him at the time of writing the answer.

Milton then goes on to deny that he knew of any statute or other debt acknowledged from Richard Powell to Sir John [or Edward] Powell or to any one else named in the bill. He hotly denies another insinuation in the bill to the effect that he had antedated his recognizance to make it appear anterior to its real date, and he hopes that the court will allow him liberal financial consolation for such scandalous aspersions.

The rest of the answer is rather verbose and taken up with cautions and hedgings. Milton wants it understood that he has not in any way failed in acting honestly and justly, and many sentences are consumed in the effort. He denies that he has caused the lands to be charged with Anne Powell's dower, explaining at length that this act was ordered by the jury. He denies knowing of any jointure which Richard Powell has allowed her, though he has heard of some such bond entered into by him to that effect (a veiled reference to the Archdale business).[11] He denies knowing what benefit if any she has reaped from this bond. He states that he knows of no property of Powell's other than those listed which is liable to such debts. And he denies forbearing collection on his debt in any way, asserting on the contrary that he has used all possible means to speed the process (as it truly seems he had). Finally he denies conventionally the conventional charge of collusion.

Now both the bill and the answer were in the hands of the court, and it should have been only a matter of a term or at the most two terms before some decision was handed down. Actually, however, nothing happened for nearly two years. The records of that period have been carefully searched without results. For the rest of 1654 and most of 1655 the action seems to have drifted along without any kind of notice: no decrees, no reports or certificates, nothing whatever. Finally, when one might have supposed the whole affair had been totally forgotten, activity began and for some time was brisk.

On December 3, 1655, a year and nine months after the filing of Milton's answer, a writ was sworn out to examine witnesses on the part of both plaintiff and defendant.[12] It issued from the crown, and was signed by Henry Marten, the violent and dissipated member of the council of state who was on the threshold of being expelled from political life. Addressed to Richard Crooke,[13] George Bainger,[14] Charles Holloway the younger[15] and Edward Astyn,[16] it gave them or any three or two of them power and authority to examine witnesses called on behalf of either plaintiff or defendant on certain interrogatories to be exhibited to them. They were accordingly ordered to summon these witnesses, administer the questions to them, take their answers, "reduce them to writing in parchment," and after sealing them with their official seals, send them together with the interrogatories in to the Court of Chancery within eight days of the following St. Hilary's Day (January 14).

The interrogatories (which are on the plaintiff's part only) accompany the writ.[17] There are nine in all, many of them long and breathless in style. They may be summarized as follows:

1. Do you, or did you, know Milton, Powell, or the Ashworths? If so, how long? When did the Ashworths die?

2. Do you know the messuage in Wheatley which Powell procured from Sir George Symeon? What is its value?

3. How much rent would you pay for it?

4. Are you now tenant to Milton? What rent do you pay? How much have you paid in all to him? How much will be due on Lady Day next (May 25)?

5. What portion of the taxes do you pay?

6. Do you know the witnesses to the Powell lease of January 10, 1631/2, now showed to you, or any person present at its sealing? Are any of them living? Are they people of good credit?

7. Did Edward Ashworth outlive his father Henry? How did he dispose of his interest in this messuage?

8. How much, if any, did Milton pay on his composition for these premises as being the property of Powell, a royalist?

9. If you have any other pertinent information, tell it.

These questions are signed by two of the men to whom the writ had been directed—Charles Holloway, Jr. and George Bainger. The interrogatories are endorsed on the back several times, showing the names of the parties, the year, and the filing memoranda.

The commissioners at once proceeded to examine the witnesses selected at Oxford. The first to come was John Robinson of Wheatley,[18] who appeared to give his depositions on January 11, 1655/6.[19] He gave no answers on most of the questions, replying only to numbers 4, 5, and 8. His answers were purely statistical and financial, not personal. He deposed that he was a tenant as stated, that he had rented the messuage and lands for about a year and the tithes for seven years. He said he was paying Milton £70 a year for messuage, lands, and tithes (contributions and taxes being deducted), that he had paid Milton in all for the tithes from the beginning about £280, and that on the following Lady Day (May 25) he was to pay about £65. He knew nothing at first hand about Milton's fine for sequestration, but he had heard that it amounted to £133 (actually £130). Further he could not depose.

The next witness was George Ball of Forest Hill, aged fifty-four, whose examination was taken on the same day, January 11. Like Robinson he is described as a gentleman. He has already come once under our consideration, and at that time all the important facts discoverable about him were recounted.[20] He answered questions 1, 2, and 6 only, and his remarks even on those are not very helpful to us. He stated that he knew all the parties, but told nothing about them. He knew that Richard Powell had acquired the messuage from Symeon, and had heard Powell say that the tithes were worth £50 a year, and had heard that Milton had been offered £34 a year for them. He knew the names of the witnesses to the indenture, and thought that though they were all dead, they had been men of good credit in their lifetimes.

Next appeared John Gadbury of Wheatley,[21] gentleman, aged forty-

five, to answer questions 2 and 3. Gadbury's testimony, taken on the
same day as the others, was of little service to any one. He knew that
Powell owned the messuage in question, and that it had been let for the
last six years for £80 a year. But from whom Powell acquired it he was
ignorant. Personally he would be willing to pay £90 a year for the property. Further he could not depose.

The final deposition was furnished by John Trevis of Wheatley,[22]
gentleman, aged somewhat over fifty. His deposition is worth exactly
nothing. It is, indeed, almost a gem of futility. He says that he does *not*
know that Powell purchased this messuage from Symeon, he does *not*
know its value, and he does *not* know what yearly rent has been paid for
it. Having offered these helpful remarks, he made his mark and went
home.

The depositions seem to have taken eleven days to reach the court
at Westminster, for they are endorsed on the back, "Ashworth against
Milton . . . 22th of January, 1655[/6], by the oath of Abraham Dickinson, gentleman.[23] Nathaniel Hobart."[24]

The parties to the suit must have been as disappointed as we over the
net result of the depositions. They contributed little definite factual information in the first place, and in the second place, what they do offer
is strikingly inconsistent. When Ball estimates the value of the Wheatley
messuage as £50, Robinson as £70, and Gadbury as £80, no one is likely
to be much wiser as to its true value. Mrs. Ashworth had very little com-
fort from her witnesses.

At this point occurs another of the lacunæ which have already become
familiar from previous records. Though these depositions were submitted in January, nothing happened till May 10. On that day the court
passed a decree to the effect that if Milton did not show cause within a
week, publication should be granted.[25] In other words, if he did not request further time to examine witnesses, the hearings should be closed,
and both parties should be at liberty to take out the depositions of the
witnesses to prepare for a hearing.[26] Milton thereupon immediately be-
stirred himself by bringing up what was little more than a technicality;
namely, that there were other defendants to this suit who had never
answered the bill as they should have.[27] Through his brother, who was
acting as his counsel, he protested on May 13 that the plaintiff had
named Anne Powell and her son Richard as co-defendants merely to
prevent Milton's having their testimony as deponents; but that, since
they had been named, it was wrong not to have served them, like himself, with writs to answer the bill. So he requested that they might be
examined "de bene esse" (*i.e.*, subject to possible future disqualifica-
tion[28]) on his behalf, and that he might have till the first day of the

next term (which would be June 13) to examine them. The court agreed
to this proposal and ordered publication to be stayed accordingly.

What happened next we cannot be sure. Apparently Milton did not
take the Powells' depositions, for when June 13 came around, nothing
occurred. The summer and the fall passed: nothing. Not till December 2
did another step materialize, and then it was at a complete tangent
from the previous line of activity. On that day Christopher Milton again
appeared in court with a complaint that the bill against Milton contained
much matter which was either irrelevant or definitely scandalous against
Milton. Though the ground of the objection is not stated, it is a reasonable guess that Milton was offended by the charge of antedating his
papers. The complaint was referred in routine manner to a master in
Chancery to investigate and report on.[29]

Here occurs another lacuna. No report from a master has been found,
and no decree such as usually accompanies such a report. The "Reports
and Certificates" (C 38) and the "Decrees and Orders" (C 33) have been
searched in vain. No action is discoverable for months.

On May 4, 1657, the court again took cognizance of the case. This
time it was to revert to a point made long before, but to ignore the
recent events.[30] Counsel for both sides being in attendance, the court
applied itself to the matter as if it were almost a fresh case:

This cause standing in the paper to be heard this day, and counsel on both sides
attending for that purpose, upon entering into the hearing thereof, forasmuch as
it appeared that the scope of the plainant's bill is to redeem a mortgage, and
that the heir of the mortgagee and his mother, who are parties to this suit, and
whom the matter properly concerns, have not as yet answered,—it is ordered
that the said defendants Richard and Anne Powell shall in a fortnight next answer the said bill and examine their witnesses so as publication may pass the first
day of the next term [June 13], and the cause be heard the last week of the same
term [June 25–July 2].

Thus a year since Milton had pointed out the reasonableness of summoning the Powells to answer the bill, the court acted on his suggestion.

The Powells' answer was duly filed—not within a fortnight, as
ordered by the court, but within about three weeks. On May 26, to be
exact, mother and son appeared before William Harrington[31] and swore
to their answer, which like Milton's had been drawn up by Christopher
Milton.[32] Their answer does not add a great deal of new material to our
knowledge of the history of the transaction, but it is so long that it
deserves a considerable summary.

In their joint answer, the Powells admit that the elder Powell was in
his lifetime seized in his demesne as of fee by purchase from Sir George
Symeon of the messuages or tenements named in the bill, situated in

Wheatley, Groveleyes, and Cuddesdon, and that in return for £400 borrowed from Henry or Edward Ashworth, Powell demised these estates to them for ninety-nine years subsequent to January 13, 1632[/3]. The condition of the loan was that if he should repay the said £400 before that day, the demise should be void. They deny, however, that Powell agreed to pay 8% interest or any other specified rate. They believe that Powell failed to repay the loan, though they think that he paid back about £100 of it. They formally deny any collusion with either Milton or the Sir John Powell mentioned in the bill, "if any such person there be." Like Milton, they deny the charge of antedating any or all of the mortgages, statutes, recognizances, or other deeds or evidences whatsoever, and hope that the court will allow them substantial "costs" as balm for their wounded feelings. They believe that Powell and William Hearne became bound to Milton for £500 by a statute staple dated June 11, 1627, defeasanced for the repayment of £300 principal which was lent to Powell by "John Milton, deceased, father of the other defendant John Milton," and £12 as interest. This statement is highly important as settling a detail of this important episode in Milton's career. It definitely establishes the fact that it was Milton's father who started him on his financial career, and not the poet himself.

The defendants continue that by virtue of Powell's failure to settle his debt to Milton, the latter extended his lands for the values set out by Milton in his answer. They say that Anne Powell received her thirds of the income for about two years. Then on December 13, 1646, Powell made his will and bequeathed the lands to his son and made him executor, with the proviso that in case he refused the executorship it should pass to her. Accordingly, she proved the will and thus inherited both his lands and his debts. They now hold themselves ready to pay to the plaintiff any money which is justly due her as the court shall award. If, moreover, Milton has received enough to cover his debt, as should appear by the account he should render, then the said lands ought to return to the Powells; and if Milton has made any lease for a term yet to come, it ought to be cancelled and made void, always provided that his tenants should be allowed a reasonable time to vacate the premises. In addition to Christopher Milton's signature, this answer was signed by Edward Peck.[33]

The court had suggested that the Powells examine what witnesses were necessary to their presentation of the case, but apparently they felt confident they needed none. No records of any depositions are to be found, and the final decree of the court appeared in so short a time later that there must have been none.[34] The answer was submitted on May 26, 1657; the decree was dated June 5, only about ten days later.

It is rather long, containing an extended summary of the proceedings to date. But since these have been dealt with in their proper places, they need not detain us again here.

The decree mentions the hearing of May 4, at which the Powells had been ordered to reply, and gives a digest of the plaintiff's bill (which has already been drawn on above) and of the answers of Milton and of the Powells. Then the court considers the pros and cons. It orders: (1) that the Powells shall pay to Elizabeth Ashworth £560, being principal, interest, and damages due to her; (2) that since Milton has received all the money due to him plus £4-17-4 in addition, he shall deliver up the premises to the Powells and pay them this overplus; (3) that the Powells shall have and receive all the income of the estates due at Lady Day (May 25) past; and (4) that Milton shall be discharged from making any further accounting to Elizabeth Ashworth or any one else, and from all suits and troubles over the premises. The decree is signed, quite unlike the usual fashion, by the three defendants to the suit, probably as a guarantee of their acceptance of the conditions involved in the decree, and by Antony Collins, counsel for Mrs. Ashworth.[35]

So ended an action of some length and complexity, apparently to the satisfaction of all concerned. No one lost or gained any money to speak of, and no one suffered in reputation or person, at least to any severity. Some expense and a fair amount of time had been consumed, but these were inevitable. Milton's connection with the Powell premises, which had begun as early as 1627, was not even yet fully ended, as has been shown in a previous chapter. But this particular action had closed calmly and with no severe penalties to any party.

CHAPTER X

DICE OF THEIR BONES
Milton *vs*. Cope

Before I will release him [says the grinding creditor of the poor debtor],
I will make dice of his bones!—Stubbes, *Anatomy of Abuses*.

IN the last action which we shall meet, the incongruity between the
small amount of money involved and the bulk of the proceedings is
more than ever apparent. The affair sprang from a simple loan of £150
from Milton to Sir John Cope in 1638; but in complexity and size this
is the most important action to be considered in this book. It is also the
latest, extending as it does nearly to the Restoration.

When, in 1654, Milton brought suit against Lady Elizabeth Cope and
her minor son Sir Anthony, he was pitting himself against one of the
most litigious families in England. I have noted well over a hundred
separate (often related) actions in which they were involved, and a more
intensive search might easily double that number. Their family being
prominent in English society and their possessions being extensive, the
question of titles to estates became growingly intricate, until it seems at
times that half of England was disputing with them some point of
ownership. Readers who are curious for detailed information may be
referred to the notes below;[1] it may suffice here to mention those members of the family who are of most importance in our story.

The Copes were an old established family, which can be traced back
at least to John Cope, who died in 1415. One of his descendants, Sir John
Cope of Hanwell, Oxfordshire, is the central figure in the Milton connection. By borrowing money from Milton and failing to repay it, he
set off a train of legal fireworks which continued to explode till long
after his death. His wife Elizabeth, daughter of Francis Fane, first Earl
of Westmoreland, and their son Sir Anthony carried on the contest with
Milton till the eve of the Restoration.

It was in 1638, during the most active period of the Cope litigations,
that Milton's connection with them began. At that time he lent £150
to Sir John Cope, who gave him as security a bond for £300 dated
February 1, 1637/8, signed by himself, by Robert Lee of Billesley,
Warwick,[2] and by Thomas Offley of Great Dalby, Leicestershire.[3] The
condition of the obligation was that if Cope paid Milton £153 on May 3,
1638, it should become void. The original bond has not been found

despite considerable search, but the details are taken from Milton's bill of June 16, 1654, and are not contradicted by Cope's answer.

As usual, the money in this loan was not repaid on the date specified, but was allowed to run as long as the interest continued to be paid. But since Sir John Cope died in 1638, and since his will mentions various people who will be heard of later, it may be well to summarize it briefly at this time.

The will (179 Lee) was dated October 11, 1638, and was proved on October 25, 1638, by his relict Lady Elizabeth Cope. After expressing a wish to be buried (as he was) in Hanwell church, Sir John provides that all the lands entailed on him may go to his eldest son (Sir Anthony, then about six years old), whose guardian during his minority is to be the testator's wife (Lady Elizabeth). His lands that are not entailed are to be disposed of for the payments of his debts, for the raising of portions for his younger children (*i.e.*, Anne and Elizabeth), and for payments to his sisters Mary and Ursula Cope of £700 and £500, respectively. As trustees for this purpose he appoints his wife, his friend the Countess Dowager of Westmoreland (his wife's mother),[4] Lord Say and Sele,[5] his cousin Richard Knightley,[6] and Giles Harris,[7] gentleman, to whom he has conveyed the lands by deed. An undated codicil provides that if any accident befalls the £2,000 assigned to his daughter Anne out of the income of the Custom House in London, the amount shall be made up to her by the executors. After various small legacies he appoints his wife his executrix, and the will is witnessed by Robert Harris,[8] Edward Raleigh,[9] John Draper,[10] Thomas Chaundler,[11] Richard Deane,[12] and Elias Jackman.[13]

The interest due on Sir John Cope's debt to Milton continued to be paid by the executors, apparently, till the fall of 1641. In his bill Milton states that "neither the said principal debt of £150 nor any part thereof nor any interest due for the forbearance of the same since November, 1641, hath been paid or satisfied unto your orator."[14] He therefore proceeded shortly to take legal action towards recovery of the debt, by putting the bond into action at common law. I have not found the records of this action, but it is referred to in both Milton's bill and Lady Cope's answer. Milton alludes to it (in 1654) as "an action of debt long since brought by your orator upon the said bond or writing obligatory," and by Sir Anthony Cope as "the action brought at law by the said complainant against this defendant as heir to his father Sir John Cope." Whatever the course of the action was, it seems to have extended over many years, for Milton speaks of it in 1654 as a matter of recent concern: "And the said Sir Anthony Cope also . . . hath lately pleaded to your orator in bar of an action of debt long since brought . . . that no lands, tenements, or other hereditaments are descended upon him in fee simple as heir unto the said Sir John Cope." And this plea was probably true, since the lands which he received were for the most part, as Sir John Cope's will indicates, entailed and not fee simple possessions.

Milton was therefore obliged to give up the idea of collecting his debt by this means, and to resort to Chancery. His next step was the submission of a bill in that court. Prepared and signed by his brother Christopher and by a certain Staunton,[15] it was dated June 16, 1654, and filed with Philip Smythe.[16]

The bill[17] opens by recounting the circumstances of the loan to Sir John Cope, Cope's death about a year later, and the provisions of his will, which have already been summarized. Next follows an accusation that Lady Elizabeth Cope (after being remarried to another Cope, whose name is left blank in the bill [actually William Cope of Icombe]) has secretly conveyed and disposed of her husband's fee-simple estates to unknown persons in order to defraud Milton of his just debt. She has thereupon, he charges, given out in speeches that she has administered all her husband's assets and has none left to cover any further debts, though many creditors have commenced actions at law against her. Actually, says Milton, she has far more assets in her hands than are necessary to settle all his debts.

Milton further charges that the other trustees, Lord Say and Sele, the Countess Dowager of Westmoreland, Knightley, and Harris, together with Sir Anthony Cope, are guilty of similar collusion and fraud, in keeping back part of the income of the estate for their own use despite the provision of Sir John's will. In particular he maintains that they have kept out rents to the value of £500 issuing out of the Custom House messuage in London and the wharf or quay there, and out of various pieces of property adjacent to it, of which Sir John Cope was seized in his demesne as of fee during his lifetime. Indeed, Lady Cope is accused of having "embezzled" these moneys. Yet she and all the other trustees unanimously refuse to pay Milton a penny of his debt, though they well know that nothing has been paid to him since 1641. Both Lady Cope and Sir Anthony go about protesting that they have no funds with which to pay him, and so they prevent his bringing action against them in court.

This procedure, protests Milton, though gaining some color of truth by the literal application of the common law, is a patent attempt to defraud him of his just dues, and to avoid the clear implication and wishes of the testator Sir John Cope. As a matter of fact, Sir Anthony reaps the benefit of many sources of income from which he ought in equity to make good the debt to Milton. As for her having satisfied other debtors to the full assets of the estate, Lady Cope is mistaken. She may have selected a few private friends and paid their debts, but that is all.

Since as the result of these underhanded and fraudulent practices Milton is unable to charge Lady Elizabeth or Sir Anthony Cope directly with sufficient assets to make them liable to action at common law, he must perforce have recourse to the Court of Chancery. In order, therefore, that they may be obliged to reveal what personal estate of any sort has come to their hands from Sir John Cope, what its value is, how they have disposed of it, what debts of his they have settled, whether there are any assets left in their hands, what messuages have descended to Sir Anthony Cope, whether he has conveyed any such to another person and if so to whom, whether he still receives the income of them and if so of what value, whether Sir John Cope at the time of his death owned in fee simple properties in or near the Custom House and if so of what value, whether these did not descend to Sir Anthony, if not who does own them and receive their incomes, whether the Copes have at any time received such incomes, what estates they received by deed from Sir John Cope and what their worth is and who receives the income from them, whether they have disposed of any of these properties and if so to whom, what money they have realized by such disposal if any, what debts they have satisfied, what money remains in their hands, and why they should not satisfy Milton his debt—to accomplish these purposes, Milton begs a writ of subpœna to be issued against Lady Elizabeth Cope, her husband [William] Cope, her son Sir Anthony Cope, Lord Say and Sele, the Countess Dowager of Westmoreland, Richard Knightley, and such other "confederates" as may later be discovered.

The desired writ was promptly issued.[17a] Dated June 22, 1654, it was addressed to John Draper, John Warren,[18] William Webb,[19] John Jordan,[20] and William Hastings,[21] who were thereby commanded to take the answers of the Lady Elizabeth Cope and Sir Anthony Cope to the questions raised in the bill. It was signed "Len Len," which probably stands for William Lenthall, speaker of the House of Commons and parliamentary keeper of the privy seal. The examiners were directed to take the answers of the defendants, "reduce them into writing in parchment, and send them to the Court of Chancery within three weeks of the ensuing feast of St. Michael" (*i.e.*, before October 20). The ends of the writ are still attached, and on the back is the usual endorsement to the effect that the execution of the commission appears in the answer annexed to it. This note is signed by John Draper and William Webb, the commissioners who conducted the examination.

Faced with this summons, Lady Elizabeth Cope prepared to submit a full and convincing answer. She had nearly four months in which to do it, and she used her time fruitfully. First, she prepared two very

elaborate inventories of Sir John Cope's estate as it was at the time of
his death: the first a list of his goods and chattels, and the second a
schedule of his debts. These were submitted later with her answer on
October 21, 1654, and they are still filed with it.[22] The sum total of
estimated value of Cope's real and personal estates was £2,932-14-5;
of his debts, £16,220-15-0. Both inventories were signed by Lady Cope
herself.

These inventories are both very detailed and highly interesting. Such
inventories were of course not uncommon; and indeed Milton's widow
made an inventory of his possessions which is of great interest to students of his life. But the Cope inventory is far more extensive than
Milton's, because the estate described was far more ample. By reading
it intelligently we may form a vivid idea of the scale on which a country
gentleman of the time lived. It is a social document of real importance.

Since the complete inventories are printed in the appendix, we may
pass them over with a brief comment. The mere list of rooms at Bruern
and at Hanwell is impressive, the former amounting to between fifty
and sixty and the latter to more than thirty. One proud memento in the
Hanwell house was "the Queen's chamber," undoubtedly the room
assigned to Queen Elizabeth on one of her visits. Sir John Cope left £100
in wearing apparel, £337 in ready money, £800 in rents due, £500 in
silver plate, and £24 in pewter. The furnishings of the rooms as in-
ventoried are lavish. Most interesting are perhaps the items of about
£275 in horses and cattle at Bruern, the hundreds of sheets and other
bed-linens, and £100 worth of arms and armor.

The list of debts adds up to the considerable total of some £20,000.[23]
Though one bond alone accounts for nearly a third of this amount, the
most common figure is £200. In settling or reducing these debts, Lady
Elizabeth Cope's method was by no means uniform. If any rule guided
her, it was apparently that she should pay about half of the debt. But
in some instances she paid in full and in one or two even more than the
total amount due. Her husband's legacies received similarly erratic
treatment. Some bequests were paid, others omitted; and one or two
payments not mentioned in the will were inserted as if entirely natural.

Lady Elizabeth's arithmetic betrays the same erratic process as her
treatment of debts and legacies. Her totals are never very far from the
correct figures; on the other hand they are never accurate. Perhaps we
are unduly uncharitable or cynical; but her constant unreliability in
figures renders us suspicious of her utterances in the law-suit.

Together with these two inventories, then, Lady Elizabeth Cope and
her son Sir Anthony submitted their joint answer to Milton's bill on
October 21, 1654.[24] It is a very long document, and very wordy. With

all the repetitions weeded out, it is easily reduced to a comparatively tidy compass. They begin, conventionally, by casting doubts on the existence of any bond from Cope to Milton; or if there was any, they suggest that Cope was rather a mere surety than a real debtor. They say that Sir John was seized in fee simple only of the estates mentioned below, and deny that he died possessed of a great personal estate, referring themselves for proof to the accompanying inventory, which they say is correct except for one item. That exception is a messuage in Covent Garden which Sir John disposed of during his lifetime to the Countess of Westmoreland. The Countess made this over to Sir Francis Fane and the Lady Elizabeth, who sold it for £820, which, with some £600 more, she made over to Sir Francis to cover a debt. They say that Sir John's legacies amounted to £3,145. They deny that his estate was undervalued; indeed, the appraisers confess that it was overvalued to increase Sir John's reputation. Then they quote part of Sir John's will, especially the portion bearing on his legacies to his daughters and sisters, and his appointment of trustees. Lady Elizabeth then recounts how she took over the execution of his will. She denies that she has defrauded any creditors or "embezzled" any of the estate. On the contrary, she maintains that she has paid her husband's debts by the amount of many thousand pounds more than his assets amounted to, contributing for the purpose much of her own fortune. She firmly states that she has administered all his assets. The only estate of which he was seized in fee simple at the time of his death was Tangley in Oxfordshire, which he had mortgaged during his lifetime, in 1637, to John Moore[25] for ninety years as security for a loan of £500. On the forfeiture of the mortgage Moore took the property, which, however, Lady Elizabeth bought back with her own money for £598, and then she borrowed £1,500 on the lands from one Loggin[26] to obtain money to settle Sir John's debts.

Sir Anthony on his part explains that he was an infant during all these affairs, having come of age only a year or so ago; and he had nothing to do with all these transactions except that he has hired the house at Tangley to live in with his family, and pays £30 a year rent for it. As for the Custom House, Lady Elizabeth says that long before Sir John's death his father Sir William mortgaged it and the adjacent wharves and quays to one Timberlake[27] for a debt of some £4,000. After Sir John's death Lady Elizabeth herself bought in this piece also and paid £4,200 for it. Further, in 1631 when she married Sir John, bringing him a portion of £5,500, Sir William entailed these properties on their son. The adjoining property of Hartshorn Key was only a short-time lease, but that also she has bought in from the school of Sevenoaks in Kent. Hence Sir Anthony enjoys the income of the property by right. Aside from these

items, Sir John had no fee-simple estates except some lands at Marshland in Norfolk. Furthermore, in 1628 Sir William assured all his manors,
messuages, lands, and hereditaments to Sir Cope Doyley.[28] Hence they
repudiate any debt to Milton or any necessity of paying it.

The answer of Lady Elizabeth and Sir Anthony Cope is signed, contrary to the usual custom, by the two defendants themselves. One
wonders at first whether Sir Anthony himself had been trained as a
lawyer and may have prepared the answer as counsel for himself and
his mother. But although Sir William Cope (probably grandfather of
Sir Anthony) had entered Lincoln's Inn in 1614,[29] a Sir Anthony of
Hanwell had been admitted to Gray's Inn in 1606 (perhaps a belated
entrance by Sir Anthony's great-grandfather),[30] John son of Sir Anthony
had been enrolled on the books of Gray's Inn in 1613,[31] by his uncle
Walter Cope, "that carried little law from this house!"[32] and Richard
son of Richard of Hanwell had followed in 1629, I have found no record
that the present Sir Anthony ever attended any of the Inns of Court.
It seems more likely, then, that he and his mother had the services of a
lawyer in the conventional way. This conclusion is made more probable
by two facts: first, that she frequently refers in her answer to her
"counsel," and second, that she was represented at a hearing in the
following year by a Mr. Sanford.[33] It is a fair guess, then, that Sanford
drew up her bill in this instance, but for some inexplicable reason did not
sign it in the customary fashion.

The answer was sworn to before John Draper and William Webb, two
of the commissioners addressed in the writ (two being sufficient for a
quorum), on October 21, 1654, and signed with their signatures. Presumably it was then sent to London and filed in the office of the six
clerk who had already had the custody of the previous papers.

Milton dealt promptly with the answer by filing exceptions to it. The
records of this move have not come to light, but we learn of them through
later papers. The Copes, however, failed to amend their answer to suit
his desire. Consequently, his brother Christopher appeared in court on
February 6, 1654/5, to protest further and to speed up matters.[34] He
reminded the court that the exceptions had been submitted, and that
the defendants had not revised their answer within the time limited by
the court's order (which, like the exceptions, has not been found). The
court thereupon decreed that one of its masters, Thomas Estcourt,
should examine the bill, the answer, and the exceptions to decide whether
the answer was sufficient in the points excepted to. If not, a subpoena
was to be issued to compel the defendants to amend their answer.

In the course of his consideration of the case, Estcourt heard counsel
on both sides. After carefully considering all the documents also, he

reported on February 28 that the answer was *not* sufficient, since Lady Cope had not made clear to whom the deed of settlement mentioned in the bill for payment of debts was made out, nor what lands were thereby conveyed nor to what value, nor the particular properties in the neighborhood of the Custom House which were mortgaged by Sir William Cope.[35] Presumably these were among the points mentioned in Milton's exceptions, which thus proved to be well founded in law.

The next step was the issuance of a writ of subpœna as threatened. It appeared on May 28, 1655, and except for the date and two changes in the names of the commissioners was practically identical with the writ of June 22, 1654.[36] For the name of William Hastings that of Thomas Blagrave[37] has been substituted; and that of Elias Jakeman (or Jackman, formerly noticed as a witness to Sir John Cope's will) was added.

Lady Elizabeth Cope's further answer was submitted on June 18, 1655.[38] In it she comes directly to the points. (1) The deed of settlement from Sir John Cope, she explains, was a deed poll (*i.e.*, a deed made and executed by one party only) dated October 10, 1638. It recites that in return for a consideration of five shillings (a legal formality) he sells to Mary Countess Dowager of Westmoreland, William Lord Say and Sele, Richard Knightley, and Giles Harris the manor or farm of Tangley, Oxfordshire; the rectory of North and South Marnham, Nottinghamshire; a parcel of land in the Norfolk Marshland called Cross Keys; a messuage in Hounslow, Middlesex; the rectory of Merthyr Cynog, Brecknock; the rectory of Winteringham with certain tithes in Winteringham, Lincolnshire; Newton Lincoln; Knapton, Yorkshire; the tithes of corn in Knottingley, Yorkshire; the "tithes of the sea" (*i.e.*, of fish) in Withernsea, Yorkshire; the rectory of Middle Rasen, Lincolnshire; the rectory of Kidwelly, Caermarthenshire, with the tithes thereto belonging; the rectory of Mylor and Mabe, Cornwall; and the parsonage of Mount and Lledred, Cardiganshire, with their appurtenances.[39] (2) The manor or farm of Tangley is worth £100 a year, Marshland 40s., Hounslow £4, Marnham £30, Mylor and Mabe £20, Merthyr Cynog unknown, being sold by Sir William Cope before Sir John Cope's death, the sea tithes of Withernsea unknown, Winteringham £6, Kidwelly £35-16-5, Mount and Lledred £5, Middle Rasen £14, Knottingley £9, the rest unknown. (3) The properties near the Custom House she is rather hazy about, but she mentions by name the New Wool Key and the Old Wool Key. Out of the Hartshorn Key there is payable yearly to the school of Sevenoaks in Kent £120, and a fee farm rent from the two Wool Keys of £53-13-4 a year. The entire lot have been demised recently for a yearly rent of £400 over and above these amounts.

This second answer is again signed, not by counsel, but by the defendant herself, "Eliza: Cope." It was sworn to at Bruern before two of the commissioners, William Webb and Thomas Blagrave, on June 18, 1655. It is endorsed (the date of its reaching the office of the clerk in London) under the hand of William Webb on June 20.

The next incident came about a month later. On Saturday, July 14, William Lenthall, master of the rolls, unexpectedly turned the tables on Milton by deciding that his exceptions to the defendants' answer should be overruled, and ordered Milton to pay the defendants 46/8 costs.[40] No reasons for his decision are offered.

Meanwhile there were other defendants named in Milton's bill who had been lying quiet before answering. One of these, Viscount Say and Sele, was now summoned to answer. Why he had not been so ordered previously does not appear, unless perhaps because the real quarrel was with the Copes and not with their friends and helpers. But on November 27, 1655, probably as the result of a renewed effort by Milton, a writ of subpœna was issued for Lord Say and Sele's answer.[41] It was addressed to James Fiennes,[42] Richard Fiennes,[43] William Dalby,[44] and Barnabas Horseman,[45] and ordered them to examine the defendant and send in his answer within eight days after the ensuing Hilary (January 23). The endorsement shows that it was James and Richard Fiennes who took the commission and carried it out.

Lord Say and Sele's answer was submitted on January 16, 1655/6, and reached London by the hands of Barnabas Horseman on February 6.[46] Lord Say and Sele disclaims knowledge of the Milton bond entirely. He admits being selected by Sir John Cope as one of the trustees under his will, and he explains that the indenture confirming the transfer of Cope's property to the trustees named was dated October 10, 1638. Richard Knightley, incidentally, he refers to as "since deceased." By this indenture, says this defendant, Cope demised Tangley, Marnham, Cross Keys, Hounslow, Merthyr Cynog, Winteringham, Middle Rasen, Kidwelly, Mylor and Mabe, and Mount and Lledrod. This deed, however, was made without the knowledge of Lord Say and Sele, and he neither then nor at any time since agreed to or accepted the trust therein arranged. On the contrary, he refused it, and released and by a formal disclaimer surrendered by quitclaim to Giles Harris all his estate therein. The reason for his refusal was that Sir William, father of Sir John Cope, made an indenture with Lord Say and Sele, Sir Cope Doyley, and Richard Knightley, granting to them several estates in Oxford, Nottingham, Essex, and other counties with the provision that from the sale of such lands they pay all the debts of Sir William Cope. By his will dated May 3, 1637, Sir William Cope gave to his son Jonathan Cope his estates in Great and Little Wakering, Essex, and various others in other counties, including such messuages and properties in the Custom House and the Wool Keys as were not settled on Sir John. Lord Say and Sele denies all combination or confederacy with the co-defendants and any dishonest use of any of the estates of Sir John Cope. He has sold, it is true, several pieces of property for the benefit of persons mentioned by Sir William Cope, but under authority of Sir William's deed and not under Sir John's. And he has not satisfied any of Sir John's debts, having refused to meddle in the latter's affairs at all. This answer is subscribed as having been delivered "upon his honor" (it being unnecessary for a nobleman of his rank to be sworn) before James and Richard Fiennes.

From this point there stretches another long hiatus, covering two full years. One would give something to be able to find "Milton's affidavit" of Michaelmas, 1657, which is calendared among the indexes to Reports and Certificates;[47] but no amount of search, either on my part or on that of the authorities of the Public Record Office, could bring the document itself to light. The next record of proceedings is merely a brief note of an order in the case made on January 12, 1657/8. John Williams[48] appeared in court and made oath that John Draper had not attended to be examined as a witness on the plaintiff's behalf. An attachment was accordingly authorized, directed to the sheriff of Oxford, returnable by February 5.[48a]

Much had evidently been going on during the two years that have dropped out of our records. Milton had apparently made arrangements for examining witnesses, had prepared interrogatories for them, had summoned John Draper among others, and had possibly received and turned over to the court several such depositions. None of them has come to light, however, and we should not know about these were it not that Draper neglected to appear for his quizzing.

The attachment, furthermore, proved ineffectual. It seems that the sheriff of Oxford was as remiss in his duties as Draper. The secret of this negligence may lie in the fact that at this time the sheriff of Oxfordshire was William Draper, no doubt a relative of John, who may possibly have tried to shield him from bothersome questioning, or who may have been amenable to John's quiet efforts on the part of his patrons to discourage too much inquisitiveness.[49] At any rate, the court, which had been very lenient in allowing the matter to ride till May 17, some three months beyond the date set for the return, abruptly set a sharp limit of five days within which he must produce his return; otherwise he was to be fined £5.[50]

One feels puzzled in encountering the next record. As if nothing had previously been done about depositions, but as if this were a new idea, Lenthall on September 21, 1658, issued a writ ordering the examination

of witnesses for both the plaintiff Milton and the defendant Lady Elizabeth Cope.[51] One would not of course in such a stereotyped document
expect any reference to previous endeavors to obtain witnesses, but one
might wonder that this particular writ was not dated earlier. It is just
possible, of course, that the date 1658 is an error for 1657, and that in
this way we might account for the hiatus already noticed. But there is
no doubt of the actual reading of the writ, which is 1658. The writ is
issued by authority of Richard the Protector, and directed to William
Dobinson,[52] George Roberts,[53] Thomas Chamberlaine,[54] and Richard
Coxeter,[55] ordering them to examine witnesses on both sides (or on
either side), to take their answers, and to send in the written records of
the same by the following October 20. It is signed by Lenthall as keeper
of the seal, and endorsed as having been executed by Dobinson, Roberts,
and Coxeter.

The interrogatories administered by both parties are extant and may
be summarized here.[56] Lady Cope's questions are extremely detailed.
There are altogether nineteen groups of interrogatories, each one consisting of from one to six parts. They have been a great deal marked
over, and the erased portions are almost totally illegible, so thoroughly
has the deletion been made. Altogether the questions cover the financial
affairs of the Copes with considerable thoroughness.

After the usual query whether the witness knows the parties to the
suit, Lady Cope begins by asking about the Wool Keys or the Custom
House in London, and specifically whether they were not settled by a
Chancery decree on Timberlake for a debt of £3,000 owing to him
from Sir William Cope; whether the debt was paid, or how much of it;
whether the decree has since been bought in by one of the Copes; what
interest Sir John Cope had in it and in the part called the Hartshorn
Key; how much the lease of it is worth, and who now owns it; what part
of the Custom House Sir Anthony Cope has bought; who were witnesses
to the bond now showed to the deponents, signed and sealed at the time
of Sir John Cope's marriage to Lady Elizabeth; whether Sir John mortgaged Tangley to John Moore, and whether the document now exhibited
is the mortgage deed in question; whether Moore took it for non-payment
of interest, and whether Lady Elizabeth Cope bought back the mortgage
and for how much; whether Lady Cope really borrowed the £1,500 for
this purpose from Thomas Loggin; what Sir Anthony Cope has paid
his mother for the reversion of the inheritance of Tangley; whether Sir
John Cope mortgaged his house in Covent Garden, and to whom, and
how the debt was secured, and whether the lease was sold for its full
value and for how much; what rectories or parsonages of Sir William
Cope's in England or Wales have been sold by Lord Say and Sele or

others and under what authority; who owned the houses in Hounslow at Sir John Cope's death and how much rent he received for them; when Sir John died; what arrangement there was between Lady Elizabeth Cope and Robert Lee to pay Sir John's debts, and how each disengaged the other from such responsibilities; whether Lady Cope's account annexed to her answer is a true and just one; whether she has not paid a great deal more for his debts than his estate amounted to, and how much more, and out of what estate; and whether the witness has ever seen any documents relating to the estates of either the Lady Elizabeth or Sir Anthony Cope. The interrogatories are signed by William Dobinson, Richard Coxeter, and George Roberts.

Milton's interrogatories are even more elaborate. After the formal query whether the deponents know the parties, Milton presents the original obligation from Sir John Cope for identification. Do you recognize this document, he asks, and did you sign it as a witness? What messuages or estates did Sir John Cope hold in lease at the time of his death, and what were their yearly values? Is the inventory of Sir John's debts and estates accurate, or is any part omitted? Are any particulars undervalued? Did the Lady Cope actually and *bona fide* pay the amounts there said to have been paid for debts? What provision for payment of his debts did Sir John make, and where is the deed or will making such provision? Who made or had engrossed Sir John's deed? What lands did he own in fee simple? What is the true yearly value of Tangley, and who enjoys the income from it? What is the value of the rectories of North and South Marnhead [Marnham], and who has received the income from them since Sir John's death, and what profit has been made on them by fines or leases? Similar information is asked about the properties at Cross Keys, Hounslow, Merthyr Cynog, Winteringham, Newton Lincoln, Knapton, Knottingley, Withernsea, Middle Rasen, Kidwelly, Mylor and Mabe, and Mount and Lledrod (though with almost unrecognizable spellings of some of the names). Did Sir John at his death possess the Custom House in London, and what was its value? Who now enjoys the income from it? Who enjoys similarly the Old and New Wool Keys, and Hartshorn Key? What leases or fines in any of these properties have taken place since eight years before Sir John's death? Did Sir John at his death possess any house in Covent Garden, what is its value, and who now enjoys it? What debts to the Countess of Westmoreland did Sir John owe, on what consideration and what security, and how have they been settled? What did Sir John owe John Moore and why and how has it been paid? Did Sir John have any estate liable to pay his debts but not already revealed? What is the yearly value of Tangley, was it rented under its true value, and if so why? What money did Sir John Cope borrow from Dr. Clapton and Mr. Greenwood for the use of William Joyner, and what part of it has been repaid?

It will be seen from this summary that Milton approached his task with fully as practical and vigorous a determination as did the Copes. He made as detailed and careful preparation for the fray as he had in his contest with Salmasius and More. Whether any witness could be found who could answer all his questions was another matter, but he at least provided an opportunity for his witnesses to disclose all information that they could furnish which was at all relevant to the suit. It is a thoroughly workmanlike set of interrogatories.

It may be pointed out that though Lady Cope and Milton in general ask questions about the same properties and situations, their approach is, naturally enough, quite different. Roughly speaking, Lady Cope is more concerned with the past history of the various estates, Milton with the present ownership, value, and profit. Thus where in questioning the deponents about the scattered rectories and tithes she emphasizes Sir William's transfer of them to Lord Say and Sele and the latter's disposal of them, Milton inquires systematically into the value, present possession, and profit of each. Whereas she tries to elicit information about the mortgaging and redemption of Tangley, he aims at the facts of its ownership and value. Similarly with the Covent Garden messuage it is the mortgage which interests her, and the value and present enjoyment which appeals to him. The Wool Keys and the Custom House lead her into several questions about the history of previous possession, but he is content with the insinuating query what leases or fines of it have been arranged since 1630. About the Hounslow property Milton does not even ask any questions at all.

In other respects the questions are at much greater divergence. Lady Cope asks about the marriage bond of herself and Sir John, which Milton ignores. He, on the other hand, questions about the bond from Cope to himself, which she ignores. In working for information about Sir John Cope's death, will, possessions at the time of his death, and debts, their implications are radically in conflict. Her questions attempt to demonstrate that his debts were far greater than his assets, and that she contributed large amounts from her own pocketbook to make good the deficiency. His queries insinuate that she has omitted some parts of his assets from her inventory, that she has undervalued others, and that not all her payments have been *bona fide*. There is even a hint, though probably merely precautionary, that the will may not have been properly made or witnessed.

It is interesting to discover that there exists also a revised set of interrogatories designed to be administered by Lady Cope to her witnesses.[57] Substantially the questions are the same as in the previous set (which had already undergone extensive modifications and erasures and substitutions in its present form), but some minor variations have been introduced. The numbering of the questions has been slightly altered, for no discoverable reason, and occasionally a phrase has been added, such as "and conceal nothing," or "of your knowledge herein at large." Occasionally the purpose of the revision is greater clarity. In several places the word "inventory" has been added to go along with the "accompt" in describing the papers annexed by Lady Cope to her answer. In question 17 a clause is added to ask whether the paper book now showed to the deponent is a true copy of her inventory and account. In question 18 the whole latter part, which inquires about Lady Cope's payment of her late husband's debts out of her own pocket, is omitted; and in its place has been added a query about the mortgaging of Tangley.

Finally, it may be seen from the transcripts given in the appendix below that the examiners have used various blank spaces near the head of these new sheets just described on which to enter brief records of the time and appearance and identity of the deponents. This fact proves conclusively that this copy is not a first draft or closet copy, but the actual one used in conducting the investigation. It also serves to date the use of this particular version of the interrogatories, and to prove that it was considerably later than the other. In fact, both the stylistic changes and these notes support this opinion. The notes are as follows:

(1) At the head, before question 1: "John Draper, sworn 10th February, 1658 [/9], Wm. Harington."[58]
(2) After the first interrogatory: "Thomas Chaundler,[59] sworn 24th February, 1658[/9], Edm. Gyles."[60]
(3) After the second interrogatory: "Hugh Candish,[61] sworn 10th June, 1659, Wm. Harington."
(4) On the back: "The paper book or inventory mentioned was received back by me this 11th of February, 1658[/9]. John Draper. Received C [?J] Draper."
(5) On the back: "Cope *adversus* Milton. Received 10th February, 1658[/9]. Show Staunton,[62] Mr. Warren,[63] Johnson.[64] No fees, Mr. Warren. No fee, Chandler. No fee, Candish." Elsewhere nearby: "All the several deeds and writings in this cause mentioned I received back again this 21th of June, 1659. John Draper."

These interrogatories have carried us somewhat beyond the steady pace of strict chronology. The first witness to be examined on Lady Cope's part was one Thomas Richards of Lynt, Wiltshire, gentleman, aged about sixty.[65] He testified on one point only, the mortgage by Sir John Cope to Moore of the farm or grange of Tangley for ninety-nine years.[66] Asserting that he knows Sir Anthony Cope and did know Sir John, he deposes that he knows the property was so mortgaged, because as witness he signed the deed to that effect now shown to him. His deposition, undated but undoubtedly taken in September or October, 1658, was signed by Dobinson, Coxeter and Roberts.

Milton, shrewdly enough, had chosen for questioning a very important acquaintance of the Copes,—one who, as we shall soon discover, knew more about their affairs than perhaps even they themselves. Among the notes of the interviews later with Lady Cope's witnesses comes the statement: "John Draper of Brewengrange in the county of Oxford, gentleman, aged 58 years or thereabouts, being formerly sworn and examined on the part and behalf of the now complainant. . . . " It will be recalled that for several months John Draper had been anxiously and vainly sought. On January 12, 1657/8, Draper had been ordered attached for not appearing as a witness for Milton, and on May 17, 1658, his relative (?) William Draper the sheriff had been ordered penalized for not serving the attachment. It looks like protection or collusion of some kind. Eventually, however, Draper had evidently appeared and taken the interrogatories. But whether his answers were not satisfactory and hence had been discarded, whether they have been lost, or whether they have strayed from their proper place and will some time come to light elsewhere, they have not been found. We have simply this note, and nothing further. We regret extremely the loss of what may have been Milton's most valuable deposition.

On October 12, 1658, however, two other witnesses were examined on his behalf at the house of one Richard Vesey, keeper of the George Inn at Burford.[67] The three commissioners whose names have been signed so often to the interrogatories—William Dobinson, George Roberts, and Richard Coxeter—were present to examine them. Neither deponent contributed enough information to be of much assistance.

The first deponent interviewed at the George Inn was Edward Lyde *alias* Joyner of Horsepath,[68] a little village near Wheatley and less than five miles from Forest Hill. He described himself as a gentleman, aged thirty-nine. Edward Lyde deposed that he knew personally none of the parties in the suit, though he said that he had often heard of them. Consequently, he knew little of the matters under debate, his knowledge being limited chiefly to one minor point, that of one item in Lady Cope's inventory of Sir John Cope's debts. Lyde testified under oath that whereas Lady Cope had mentioned the sum of £402 which she had paid to George Greenwood and Dr. Clapton on their bond, the sum paid was actually far less, probably not more than half. The source of his knowledge was the fact that Greenwood and Clapton (among others) had been executors of the will of his mother Anne Lyde, and that he himself had perused several accounts of theirs, among which was one item to the effect that they had lent to Sir John Cope in 1638 the sum of £200. These records showed that Lady Cope had paid £16 interest on this loan in 1639 (at the rate of 8%), £16 more in 1640, and a further £8 in 1641. Further, Greenwood told Lyde in 1643 that he had received from Lady Cope £200, which he had paid to Lyde's brother William on account of his legacy from his mother, and that he had received no more than this sum from her. The inference seems to be either (1) that Lady Cope was padding her schedule in order to conceal assets, or (2) that Greenwood was falsifying his accounts to feather his own nest. But since this is only one item out of a long list of interrogatories, and since Lyde could offer no information on any other detail, his testimony must have carried comparatively little weight. It must have been just barely enough to excite a faint flicker of suspicion—all the fainter for the reason that he was an obscure person whereas the Copes were an important family with large financial dealings and influential friends and large holdings of real estate.

The other witness was John Robinson, also of Horsepath, gentleman, aged fifty-five.[69] Robinson had, he said, been acquainted with Milton for about ten years [*i.e.*, since the time of the publication of Milton's *Tenure of Kings and Magistrates* or thereabouts], but not with the Copes. His only information was second-hand, and worth little in a court of law. Answering the ninth question, as to the value of Tangley, he deposed that though he did not know at first hand, he had "diligently inquired" among the neighbors, who were agreed that its value was about £160 a year. Lady Cope, it will be remembered, estimated it at about £100 a year.[70] This deposition would show her to be rather far wrong in her valuation—if we could accept it as authoritative.

Altogether, the net result of Milton's depositions (omitting that of John Draper, which is missing) was to show Lady Cope seriously astray in her valuations of real estate and in her account of moneys paid. If the deponents could be accepted as trustworthy by the examiners, grave suspicion had been thrown on the veracity and accuracy of the defendant's whole account, and certainly enough discrepancies had been offered to cover more than the amount of Milton's debt.

Whether the next move of the defendants resulted from strategy or from carelessness is not clear. What happened is that the Copes lost the sheet of interrogatories and were unable to proceed with their examinations. They had already examined various witnesses, but they could not go on further with the others whom they wished to interview, they said, unless they had a fresh copy of the questions. They therefore appeared in court on November 11, 1658, and begged that the court would order the clerk for the plaintiff to produce the original interrogatories before some master in Chancery so that their own clerk might take a copy of them. The master of the rolls, Lenthall, ordered Master Eltonhead to attend to the matter and supply the desired papers.[71]

The Copes, however, once they obtained them, were in no hurry to use them. It was three months before they examined witnesses. Altogether three deponents then gave in their answers, which were far more detailed and valuable and illuminating than any that had previously been offered.[72] Incidentally, whereas Milton's had been "country depositions," taken by commission, these were "town depositions," taken in London. They were conducted by Robert Shiers (or Shire), examiner in Chancery, and are labeled "showed by Mr. Johnson," though in the first set of answers this label has been crossed through.

The first and best witness was John Draper of Brewengrange, aged fifty-eight, who was examined on February 10, 1658/9, and who answered all the questions with impressive fullness, showing a thorough knowledge of all the complicated details of the Cope affairs. First he testified that he knew all the parties, including Sir John Cope and Sir William Cope, deceased, but that his acquaintance with Milton was only slight. He then proceeded to confirm Lady Elizabeth Cope's statements in almost every particular. He knew that the Custom House had been settled by a decree in Chancery on Timberlake for a debt of £3,000 from Sir William Cope; that the debt was unpaid at the time of Sir William's death; that Timberlake's executors after his death had assigned the debt to Lady Elizabeth Cope for about £4,000, the difference being accumulated interest at 9%; that Sir John Cope had no interest in Hartshorn Key at the time of his death, the lease of it to Sir William or to Sir Walter Cope from the free school at Sevenoaks, Kent, having expired about the time of Sir William's death (a year previous to Sir John's); that shortly afterwards Lady Elizabeth procured a new lease for forty years at £120 a year; that Sir Anthony bought of his uncle Sir Jonathan the latter's interest in the Custom House; that the deed now showed to him, dated January 20, 1631/2, was the same which was made between Sir John Cope and the Lady Elizabeth on their marriage; that he knew all the signatories thereto, namely Sir William Cope, the late Lady Westmoreland, the late Sir Cope Doyley, the late Richard Knightley, William Viscount Say and Sele, Mildmay Earl of Westmoreland, and Lady Elizabeth Cope; that he was familiar with the handwritings of Sir William Cope, Lady Cope, and Viscount Say and Sele; that in addition to the last three named, he believed that Giles Harris, William Banister,[73] William Lynn,[74] and William Sprigg[75] signed as witnesses, and that he recognized their signatures on the deed as genuine; that Sir John Cope mortgaged the farm of Tangley to John Moore for ninety-nine years, and that it became forfeited to Moore for non-payment of interest during Sir John's lifetime, and that Lady Elizabeth Cope purchased the mortgage after his death for £580; that Sir Anthony Cope paid Thomas Loggins (who had in the interval purchased this mortgage) £1,500 for the mortgage, and that the premises had been let for £120 a year; that Sir Anthony agreed with Lady Elizabeth to buy from her the reversion of the inheritance of Tangley, after the expiration of this lease, for £1,550, being the amount owed by Sir John Cope to various people by bond, and that since that time he had paid about £1,400 of that sum and given bond for the remaining £150; that Sir John Cope mortgaged the leases of his houses in Covent Garden to Mary Countess Dowager of Westmoreland for £1,450 by a bond to be paid at the rate of £200 a year, and that after his death Lady Cope sold the leases for £820, which was as much as they would bring; that Sir John Cope conveyed by deed of trust in October, 1638, all the rectories or parsonages in England or Wales which were formerly Sir William Cope's, and that William Viscount Say and Sele had since disposed of all of them; that at the time of Sir John Cope's death the right and interest in the house in Hounslow was in Robert Lee and his wife Frances, sister to Sir John, and that Sir John received no income therefrom; that Sir John Cope died in October, 1638; that he and Robert Lee were mutually engaged as securities for each other in several obligations, and that after Sir John Cope's death Lee and Lady Cope secured the discharge of these obligations, she having made the rounds of all the scriveners' shops in London where they used to take up money together in order to make sure of missing no outstanding obligations; that he had carefully perused her inventory and account and believed it correct, all the more so because he had kept his own careful record of all her financial transactions, and because careful comparison of her account with his showed the two to be in perfect accord.

The transcripts of the interrogatories described above furnish several pertinent notations on this examination. They show that Draper was sworn for his examination on February 10 by William Harington, and that on the following day, February 11, he received back again "the paper book or inventory mentioned" in the questions. The latter was probably the original of the account and inventory of Lady Cope, particularly the inventory of debts, annexed to her answer; and it would have been given back to Draper as her steward, while the copy which we now have available remained in the files of Chancery.

Two weeks after John Draper had given his deposition, Thomas Chandler appeared for examination. He described himself as a gentleman of St. Andrews Holborn, London, aged about seventy. He had for a

number of years been a servant to Sir John Cope during the latter's
lifetime, and was therefore fairly well acquainted with many of Sir
John's affairs.

After stating that he knows all the parties to the suit, Chandler
testifies that he knows the Custom House in London, and that he believes the premises were assigned by decree of Chancery from Sir William
Cope to Timberlake for a debt of £3,000; that on being shown the
marriage settlement of Sir John Cope and Lady Elizabeth Cope, to
which he was *not* a witness, he is certain that he wrote one of the endorsements on the back concerning the ancient ownership of Tangley;
that he can identify as genuine the signature of Sir John Cope on the
mortgage deed of Tangley to John Moore now shown him, as also the
signatures of Thomas Moore and Giles Harris, witnesses; that in order
to pay Moore for the mortgage of Tangley Lady Elizabeth Cope borrowed £1,500 of Loggin, giving him as security a deed to the property
at Tangley; that he has read over the copy of Sir John Cope's deed of
settlement of October 10, 1638, now shown him; that this is a true copy
of the original, and that livery and seisin (*i.e.*, the act of delivering
actual possession) were executed thereon the following day; that Sir
John Cope died in 1638; and that he cannot depose as to the annexed
inventory since it is not produced for him to see. A note on the interrogatories informs us that Chandler was sworn on February 24 before Edmund Gyles. His depositions are considerably less important than
Draper's.

The last witness was Hugh Candish, gentleman, of Shipton under
Wychwood, aged forty. He appeared much later than the others, not
coming to London for his examination till June 10, 1659. According to
the revised interrogatories he was sworn before William Harington.
Aside from the facts given in his deposition we know nothing whatever
of Candish. Milton must by this time have become somewhat discour-
aged about his suit, having watched five years roll by since he first
entered his bill, and the end being hardly nearer in sight than then.
Candish, however, had a good deal to say—less than Draper but more
than any other deponent.

First he testified that he knew the Cope family well, but Milton not
at all. Incidentally, it seems odd that a resident in the Oxford district
so near the ancient homes of both the Miltons and the Powells should
not know the great Latin Secretary of England and the author of many
famous books; but the statement undoubtedly means simply that though
Candish had heard of him, he had never met him personally. His next
answer gives us valuable information about one or two persons previously mentioned. Giles Harris, he says, was formerly a steward to the

Copes, and then lived on his means in the country as a gentleman till his death. William Sprigg he identifies as an attorney. William Lynn, he says, is now steward to the Countess of Bath and Middlesex. These persons were all witnesses to the marriage settlement of Sir John and Lady Elizabeth Cope, and their signatures he identifies as their own handwriting. He answers further that Sir John Cope mortgaged Tangley to Moore; that Lady Elizabeth Cope borrowed £1,500 of Loggin to redeem Tangley from Moore, and that she secured the money to Loggin by a mortgage or other conveyance of the property, and that she paid Moore the £1,500; that when Loggin assigned the lease of ninety-nine years (from Sir John Cope to Moore, the property being worth £140 a year) to Sir Anthony Cope, Draper as steward for Lady Cope paid him £1,500; that Sir Anthony has paid his mother £1,500 for the reversion of the inheritance of Tangley; that he has heard that Lord Say and Sele, as feoffee in trust for Sir William and Sir John Cope, has sold several rectories, including Midwim [Kidwelly?], Llanghangell (Carmarthen) [Lledrod?], Llangahangell (Brecknock), Merthood [Merthyr?], and others in Yorkshire and near Bristol; that it is twenty years since Sir John Cope died; and that he has recently seen the deeds and other documents concerning the possessions of the Lady Elizabeth Cope and Sir Anthony Cope, but he cannot remember where and when.

One or two points in this deposition raise difficulties. Making due allowance for discrepancies in spelling, we can identify some of the properties mentioned towards the end as identical with some in Lady Cope's list in her second answer. Midwim may be a garbled form of Kidwelly (the reading is almost illegible anyhow), since both are assigned to the county of Carmarthen; Merthood in Brecknock is probably Merthyr Cynog; but the two mouth-filling Llangahangells, one in Brecknock and the other in Carmarthen, have little correspondence to any names there, with the possible exception of Llethered (or Lledrod), which, however, is in Cardiganshire. Either Candish got badly tangled in his geography or else Lady Cope omitted several locations from her list. One may at least allow himself to become slightly more alert in watching her statements.

It is difficult to assess the net result of all these depositions. For the most part Lady Cope's witnesses had been able, whenever they testified at all, to corroborate her statements. They had not been able to prove what she was intent on demonstrating, that the assets of the Cope estate were unequal to its liabilities, so that the debt to Milton, if it were indeed an actual debt at all, could not be paid; in other words that the estate had become insolvent before Milton's turn had come, and that there was unfortunately no recourse for him except to pocket his indigna-

tion and make the best of a bad debt. On the other hand, in one or two
particulars, not of much importance but at least cautionary, her witnesses had disagreed with her figures to the extent of perhaps a hundred
pounds out of a total of several thousand. Milton's witnesses, on his
side, had been of next to no use to him. One had testified that Lady
Cope had actually paid £200 less than she claimed to have paid; but
Draper, her steward, had counterbalanced this assertion by his sworn
statement that she had truly paid all amounts which she had itemized.
Another of Milton's witnesses had offered hearsay evidence that the real
value of Tangley was far higher than Sir Anthony Cope was paying for
it, but hearsay evidence is notoriously unacceptable at law. What Draper
testified for Milton we have no way of knowing. Milton had therefore
not been able, to our knowledge, to prove either that his debt was a true
and unpaid one, or that Lady Cope was financially able to pay it—the
two cardinal points in his argument. Neither party seemed much better
off after the six months or more devoted to these elaborate testimonies
than before. What we need to fall back on is the opinion of the court as
to the merits of the case. Courts are not infallible, but they are more
likely to be right than wrong.

But here again, as once or twice before, we are unfortunately without
the ultimate decision in the case. Only two further items in the record
of this story are discoverable, and neither is final. On June 11, 1659, the
day following the Candish deposition, the court contemplated consulting
the accumulated depositions. It ordered that if the defendant showed no
cause for stay of publication of the depositions within a week, publication
should then be granted.[76] In other words, unless there was reasonable
cause for further delay, the depositions should be opened to both parties
preparatory to a more or less final hearing.

This is the last official record. I have searched the indexes for further
entries, and another competent searcher has followed me, but both of us
have worked without result. One further record appears, but it is so
minor and trivial as hardly to deserve mention, and it is not strictly
official like the others. It is merely a receipt, dated June 21, 1659, and
signed by John Draper (on the back of the revised sheet of interrogatories) to show that he had received back from the examiners "all the
several deeds and writings in this case mentioned."[77] Obviously the
examinations were concluded, and there was no further need of the various deeds of mortgage and of settlement which had been shown to the
deponents. John Draper had packed up his records and retired to the
country.

Did the parties settle the case out of court? Did the impending
Restoration hasten their agreement? Did Lady Cope in hopefulness and

Milton in resignation wait for the results of that far-reaching overturn in government? Did the Restoration when it came quash Milton's chances of collecting his debt? The silence of the records is most exasperating. We may feel entitled to our opinion that his case was just and that he presented it with sufficient energy to persuade the court of his rights. We may permit ourselves to feel that Lady Cope, who dealt so airily in sums mounting into the thousands of pounds, could without much suffering have found £150 to set herself right with this important statesman and author. But we do not know; and we may never learn the outcome.

CONCLUSION

BY way of conclusion we may permit ourselves a brief glance back over our findings. Scrivener Milton, except for a stray deposition in someone else's suit, first entered the courts as a defendant to Ayloffe's bill in 1624, as the result of business which had begun some two years earlier. His legal activity continued more or less regularly until the final decree in his suit against Duck in 1640. Thus he was in and out of court with some regularity for a quarter of a century. A skeleton of the proceedings, omitting all but the most important items, runs as follows:

(1600 Milton begins to invest money for John Cotton)
1622 Raymond borrows money through Milton
1623 Deposition in Walthew *vs*. Shares action
1624 Ayloffe sues Milton
"   Milton answers Ayloffe
"   Milton invests money for Rose Downer (continuing his practice of investing formerly for her husband)
1626 Burton sues Milton
"   Milton answers Burton
1630 Deposition in Peck-Randolph action
1631 Rose Downer sues Milton
"   Milton answers Rose Downer
1632 Decree in Downer-Milton case
1635 Decree in Downer-Duck case
1636 Cotton sues Milton
1637 Milton answers Cotton
"   Milton sues Duck
"   Duck answers Milton
1638 Decree in Cotton-Milton suit
1640 Decree in Milton-Duck suit

Poet-Secretary Milton, having had his financial career begun for him by his father's loan to Powell in 1627, first entered the courts about 1646, and did not emerge till about 1660. The chief milestones in his litigious career are:

(1627 Loan to Powell)
(1638 Loan to Cope)
(1646 Attempts to extend Powell's estate)
1647 Proceedings on and possession of Powell's Wheatley
"   Pye sues Milton
"   Milton answers Pye
1649 Decree in Pye-Milton suit
1654? Elizabeth Ashworth sues Milton
1654 Milton answers Elizabeth Ashworth
"   Milton sues the Copes

146

"   The Copes answer Milton
1657 Decree in Ashworth-Milton case
1659 Cancellation of Powell-Milton bond
"   Last discoverable record in Milton-Cope case

The substance of all these suits is financial. It need hardly be pointed out that none of them is criminal. However thrilled one might be to find Milton or his father involved in a shooting affray or an embezzlement, there is no suggestion of any such situation here. All these legal tilts were purely civil. They almost always revolved around a loan of money which was not duly repaid. But the loan was like shrapnel: when it burst, small as it originally was, it spread over considerable territory. So loans usually dragged lands in their wake, until at times it seems as if every pound of debt had the power of exploding about a square mile of disputable land. Just as our federal investigators, on pretext of examining the income-tax returns of notorious malefactors, succeed in reaching into their most private affairs, so failure to repay a borrowed £50 might eventually lay open most of the unfortunate defendant's personal possessions—furniture, curtains, dishes, clothes, pictures, and even debts. Chancery suits remind one of the earthquake in Browning's "House":

> The whole of the frontage shaven sheer,
>   The inside gaped; exposed to day,
> Right and wrong and common and queer,
>   Bare, as the palm of your hand, it lay.

Milton senior becomes revealed as a broker of far-flung interests, trusted by men of wealth, and handling for them many thousands of pounds in investments. His personal traits come less under our observation than his professional; but at least it is self-evident that he was busy and successful. However opinions may vary as to his conscientiousness, and however negligent he may perhaps be considered at some times in looking after the interests of his clients, it seems to me that he was usually doing his best for them. He clearly had a reputation for honesty. I think he chose unwisely in his assistant and partner, Bower, and that it was this choice more than any other factor which dragged him into court. But there is no doubt that his shortcomings, if any worthy of the name have been exposed in this chronicle, are in judgment rather than in ethics.

Technically, out of his five cases in court, the scrivener was proved to be right once, and wrong twice, with verdicts missing in the other two cases. He won his defence against Cotton's bill, thus apparently proving to the satisfaction of the court that he had acted in good faith towards his wealthy client during the generation in which he served him. He was considered wrong in his behavior towards Rose Downer and ordered to make good her loss of £50, and when he attempted to recoup from Duck, he was again defeated. The latter being probably a forlorn hope anyhow, we find practically just one count against him. The Burton and Ayloffe cases are a draw, since we do not have the decrees.

Milton junior emerges as a complete man of business. The qualities of his character most conspicuous are neither imagination nor religion, but tenaciousness. Having loaned £300 to his father-in-law Powell, he hung on for thirty years till he recovered it. For the sake of making good his loan of £150 to Cope, he fought steadily through five years of bills, answers, decrees, reports, depositions, inventories, and innuendoes. When other claimants on the Powell property tried to shoulder him out of the way, he turned on them and forced them to respect his claims. His score is rather better than his father's: twice right, once settled to mutual satisfaction, and once postponed. If no new instance of saintliness or affection or idealism comes into view from these pages, no one should be surprised, since the law court is hardly the nurse of such virtues. Hardheadedness and dogged British mastiff-perseverance are the predominant traits developed in its halls.

This is not the place in which to offer an interpretation of Milton's poetry in the light of these new biographical episodes. This book confines itself to the presentation of the facts, from which the reader is free to draw his own conclusions. Personally, I feel confident that the years spent in bills and answers, in decrees and depositions, no less than the energy poured out in Salmasian controversy and Smectymnuan dialectics, stamped ineffaceable traces on his poems. The conflict in Heaven must be, in part at least, a reverberation of its author's struggles in the law courts. But the purpose of this book is biographical, not critical. Our interest in the facts of Milton's life is legitimate, regardless of any demonstrable effect on his writings. One unassailable inference, however, may be drawn from these experiences. Milton was certainly not a star who dwelt apart from the workaday life of the world. He lived in no remote ivory tower. On the contrary, he was continually plunged into the most trying conflicts. His character was built to no small degree on the years in Chancery.

NOTES

NOTES

INTRODUCTION

[1] Translated by Walter Skeat and edited by E. H. Visiak (1935), pp. 69–70.

[2] Masson, I, 327; Columbia *Works*, XVIII, 576.

[3] These books are not mentioned in printed transcripts of the inventory, but are included in the "true copies" in the New York Public Library (among the Dati MSS) and in B.M. Add. MS. 24,501, ff. 51–54.

[4] *The Works of John Milton*, edited by Frank A. Patterson and others (Columbia University Press: New York), Vol. XIII.

[5] *Ibid.*, Vol. XVIII.

[6] The so-called Columbia Manuscript, formerly in the library of Sir Thomas Phillipps, the English collector, now in the library of Columbia University. It is a vellum-covered notebook of 156 pages, of which about 105 are written on. In addition to 156 letters of state, of some of which no other records are known, the book contains short discussions of statues and antiquities, of Genoa, of differences in rank in England, of the functions of a secretary of state, a constable, a marshall, and a chancellor, of the privy council, of procedure in Chancery, and of a Spanish ambassador. Some of these are acknowledged to be taken from writings of Thomas Sheres, the Earl of Salisbury, the Duke of Bedford, and Sir Robert Cotton. There are also early drafts of Milton's *Letter to General Monk* and of his *Letter to a Friend*. At the other end of the book, among accounts kept by Bernard Gardiner, warden of All Souls' College, Oxford, from 1703, is a brief collection of Latin quotations about the law (the "Index Legalis"). None of the writing can be ascribed to Milton's own hand. The letters, as was explained in the Columbia *Milton*, must have been copied after 1659, but some of the other writing may be earlier.

[7] Thomas Powell, *The Attourney's Academy;* M.S. Giuseppi, *A Guide to the . . . Public Record Office*, I (1923), 1–70; Margaret Dowling, "Public Record Office Research: The Equity Side of Chancery, 1558–1714," *R.E.S.*, VIII (1932), 1–16. An interesting account of some of the steps in a Chancery action of the mid-seventeenth century may be found in *The Letters of Dorothy Osborne*, ed. C. G. Moore-Smith (Oxford, 1928), pp. 185 ff.

[8] Phillip Stubbes, *Anatomy of the Abuses in England*, ed. F. J. Furnivall, part I, New Shakspere Society Transactions (1877–79), p. 127. I have modernized this and the following quotations.

[9] Thomas Dekker, *The Seven Deadly Sins*, in *The Non-Dramatic Works of Thomas Dekker*, ed. A. B. Grosart, II (1885), 64–65.

[10] *Commonplace Book*, fol. 160.

[11] Dekker, p. 72.

[12] Harrison's *Description of England*, ed. F. J. Furnivall, New Shakspere Society Transactions, part I, book II (1877), p. 204.

[13] Stubbes, p. 117.

[14] William Parkes, *The Curtaine-Drawer of the World*, 1612, ed. A. B. Grosart (1876), "To the Reader."

[15] *Ibid.*, p. 34.

[16] Dekker, p. 37.

[17] Stubbes, pp. 128–129.

[18] Quoted in Gwendolen Murphy, *A Cabinet of Characters* (1925), pp. 220–222.

[19] Parkes, "To the Reader."

²⁰ Thomas Middleton, "Father Hubburds Tales," *The Works of Thomas Middleton*, ed. A. H. Bullen (1886), VIII, 72.

²¹ For the familiar facts of the elder Milton's life, the reader is referred to Masson's *Life of John Milton, passim*. References will here be given only for the less common or more recently discovered facts.

²² B. M. Lansdowne MS. 241, fol. 58; Masson, I, 1.

²³ Dulwich College Muniment 503; *Athenæum* (1880), I, 376.

²⁴ In the possession of Mr. Perceval Lucas in 1910: *N & Q*, XI, ii (1910), 427.

²⁵ B. M. Add. Ch. 23,574; *Athenæum* (1880), I, 376.

²⁶ B. M. Cart. Harl. 112. D. 19; *Athenæum* (1880), I, 376.

²⁷ Records of the Corporation of London in the Guildhall; *Athenæum* (1884), I, 20.

²⁸ S.P. 14/145/36; Hamilton, p. 44.

²⁹ Westminster Abbey Muniment 28,515; *Athenæum* (1902), II, 722.

³⁰ C 54/2477/34; Stevens, *Milton Papers*, p. 1.

³¹ C 54/2525/32.

³² C 54/2715/20; Stevens, pp. 39–40.

³³ C 54/2715/19; Stevens, pp. 40–41.

³⁴ C.P. 24. (3). 4; C.P. 25. (2). 457.

³⁵ C 66/2527/70.

³⁶ C 54/2803/18; Stevens, pp. 41–44.

³⁷ *Ibid.*

³⁸ C 54/2800/7; Stevens, pp. 44–46.

³⁹ C.P. 25. (2). 458, Easter, 14 Charles I.

⁴⁰ Bodleian MS. Rawl. Misc. 51, pp. 29–30; *Athenæum* (1880), I, 565–566.

⁴¹ *Athenæum* (1880), I, 760–761.

⁴² *Students Admitted to the Inner Temple, 1547–1660*, p. 270.

⁴³ *N & Q*, XI, vii (1913), 21.

⁴⁴ *A Calendar of the Inner Temple Records*, ed. F. A. Inderwick, II (1898), 254.

⁴⁵ Milton's answer to Elizabeth Ashworth's bill (C 10/44/2); see p. 117.

⁴⁶ *Ibid.;* Milton's extent (C 228/6); see p. 104.

⁴⁷ "London, 1802."

⁴⁸ In this connection see J. Milton French, "Milton as a Historian," *PMLA*, L (1935), 469–479.

⁴⁹ On Milton's satire, see J. Milton French, "Milton as Satirist," *PMLA*, LI (1936), 414–429.

⁵⁰ *Littleton, His Treatise of Tenures*, ed. Sir Thomas E. Tomlins (London, 1841). See also the *New English Dictionary* under "fee," "fee-simple," "fee-tail," "foot," "fine," "tenure," "concord," etc.

⁵¹ Giuseppi, I, 248 ff.

CHAPTER I. THIS WICKED WORK OF USURY

¹ In the county of Cambridge Ayloffe was a man of some importance, whose pedigree is given in considerable detail in the Visitations of 1575 and 1619. He came of an old Essex family, being the son of Sir William Ayloffe of Bretaynes, Essex, and Catherine, daughter and heir of Thomas Sterne of Meldreth, Cambridge, whose estate became that of her son James. James was twice married, like his father; his first wife was Jane, daughter of Sir William Harris of Sherley, Essex, and his second was Elizabeth, daughter of Thomas Penyston. By his first wife he had one son, and by his second, four children. A Thomas Ayloffe, perhaps a relative, was sued in 1604 by Edmund Brome in connection with Forest Hill, the estate near Milton's ancestral home at Stanton St. John. Brome accused Ayloffe, a counselor-at-law, of Lincoln's Inn, of defrauding him of his inheritance and his title deeds. Perhaps the Forest Hill connection may have served to introduce the Milton and

Ayloffe families. See B. M. Harl. MS. 1534, printed in the Publications of the Harleian Society, XLI (1897), 129; C2 James I/B11/20. The following pedigree is taken from the Harleian Society Publication just mentioned.

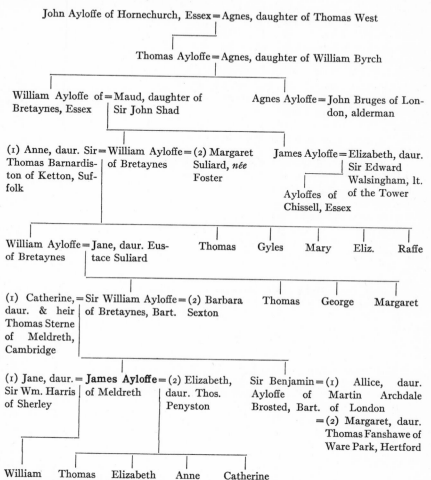

² Who this Raymond was is not certain. A John Raymond, citizen and poulterer, died in 1624; his will was registered in the Prerogative Court of Canterbury as 110 Byrde. One Edward Raymond had surrendered, before January 30, 1600, the office of bowstring-maker in the Tower, with a fee of sixpence a day, which was on that day granted to Robert Offley. Either he or another Raymond figures several times in letters of his cousin Edward Reynolds. Reynolds wrote him a long letter in 1597 (?), warning him to be careful in dealing with one Dimmery about selling a house. Reynolds wrote again in 1612 to advise him how to proceed against Dimmery, who had evidently cheated him despite the warnings, and again about a similar difficulty in 1615. Reynolds wrote to another cousin, John Castle, in 1614, deploring Raymond's carelessness in getting into debt. This Raymond may be our man; he at least shares some of his qualities. See wills proved in the Prerogative Court of

Canterbury (for which no references will be given in these notes, since they are adequately indexed in the lists of Matthews and of the British Record Society); *Calendars of State Papers, Domestic Series, 1598–1601*, p. 388; *ibid.*, 1595–1597, pp. 560–561; *ibid.*, 1611–1618, pp. 125, 257, 309.

³ On John Lane, the friend of the elder Milton, see Masson, I, *passim; Athenæum* (1880), I, 760; B. M. Harl. MS. 5243; MS. Reg. 17 B, p. xv; Bodl. MS. Rawl. Miscell. 51, ff. 29–29v.

⁴ C2 James I/A6/35.

⁵ John Williams, appointed lord keeper and bishop of Lincoln in 1621, later to be tried in Star Chamber, fined, suspended, imprisoned, but subsequently appointed archbishop of York.

⁶ William Gilbert was a member of Lincoln's Inn, who was called to the Utter Bar in 1623, and elected pensioner in 1641. See *The Black Books of Lincoln's Inn*, II, 238, 356.

⁷ George Evelyn was six clerk from 1606 to 1636.

⁸ C2 James I/A6/35.

⁹ Edmund Breres was called to the "grand company" of Gray's Inn in 1622. In 1628 Sir Richard Fleetwood was engaged in the sum of two thousand pounds as his security, and was to prosecute a suit in Chancery for his relief. See *The Pension Book of Gray's Inn*, p. 246; *CSP Dom 1628–1629*, p. 380.

¹⁰ James Hussey, Doctor of the Civil Law, died in 1626; his will is 20 Hele. His son James was admitted to the Middle Temple in 1640. See *Middle Temple Records*, II, 903.

¹¹ Valentine Sanders was six clerk, 1607–1629.

CHAPTER II. FOR FASHION'S SAKE

¹ A brief description of the proceedings to be given in greater detail in this chapter was offered by Mr. Ernest G. Atkinson in the *Athenæum* (1897), II, 160–161.

² Req 2/387.

³ The difficulty in tracing the Willoughbys is that the pedigrees, though numerous, stop too soon or omit our brothers. There seems to be little doubt, however, that they were more closely related to the Willoughbys of Wollaton, Nottinghamshire, of Middleton, Warwickshire, and of Boreplace, Kent (descended from Richard Bugge of Willoughby, Lincolnshire, who adopted the name of the town as his surname), than to the branches of Eresby or Parham. Sir Percival Willoughby of Lincolnshire and Kent, who married Bridget, daughter of Francis Willoughby, builder of the manor of Wollaton, and who was the great-grandson of Sir Thomas Willoughy, chief justice of the king's bench, had three brothers Edward, Thomas, and Robert, who may be our men. He also had a son Edward (of Cossall, born about 1592), a son Robert, and various other children, including Sir Francis of Middleton (1591–1665), father of Francis the naturalist (1635–1672). Fulke Greville, the friend and biographer of Sidney, was a distant relative. Our most likely candidates seem to be the sons of Sir Percival and Bridget, who would have been about thirty years old at the time of this action. In default of certain evidence, however, it seems worth while to offer such scraps of additional information about men of their name as has come to hand.

Robert Willoughby, here designated as "late citizen and grocer of London," may have been dead in 1626 or simply removed from London, perhaps to Sutton Coldfield, Warwickshire. He may have been the Robert Willoughby who wrote to Secretary Conway on November 30, 1625, craving his aid in recovering the manor of Castle Cary, sold by his elder brother to the late Earl of Hertford, though it was entailed on the writer's great-uncle Robert Willoughby, Lord Brooke, whose heir the writer was. It may have been the same man who was taxed £30 in Buckinghamshire in 1604. A Robert Willoughby is mentioned in the will of his brother George, merchant (91 Lee), in 1638, and a Robert Willoughby died in Gloucestershire in 1641 or 1642 (his will is 10 Cambell). Since Robert, son of

Thomas Willoughby of Boreplace, who was admitted to Magdalen College, Oxford, in 1587 at the age of eighteen, and who became bachelor of medicine in 1603, had a brother George who was admitted at the same time, he was probably identical with the brother of the merchant George mentioned above.

Thomas Willoughby the elder of Sutton Coldfield was almost surely the grandfather of Richard and Thomas Willoughby, who entered Pembroke College, Cambridge, in 1653 and 1655 respectively, both at the age of seventeen. In the registers they are called the sons of Thomas Willoughby of Sutton Coldfield, but though the dates make it impossible for him to be "the elder" in 1626, it seems strongly probable that his father was the man we seek. Either (or another) may have been the high sheriff of Warwickshire in 1656. However, a Thomas Willoughby was living in London, in Red Lion Alley, in 1638, and was rated in his property at £12; it was very likely his son Hugh who matriculated at Lincoln College, Oxford, in 1665/6 at the age of eighteen. A Thomas Willoughby who was the son of Sir Francis (but obviously not the Sir Francis of Middleton mentioned above) took part in the expedition to Rhé and Rochelle.

In addition to the Edward Willoughbys already listed, one was a member of the warden and society of Sutton Coldfield in 1619; another proved the will (125 Evelyn) of his brother Henry of London in 1641; and a third, called a girdler, took out a license in 1613 to marry Margaret Hickman, spinster. In 1638 an Edward Willoughby, whose occupation is not given, was living in St. Dunstan's in the East, London; curiously enough, he was a next-door neighbor to a John Milton, who, however, cannot be either our scrivener or his son.

A brief pedigree may serve to clarify some of these relationships:

Sir Francis Willoughby (built Wollaton) ═ Elizabeth dau. Sir John Littleton

Thomas Willoughby   Robert Willoughby   Edward Willoughby

Sir Percival Willoughby ═ Bridget   Winifred ═ Edward Willoughby
of Lincolnshire and Kent

Sir Francis Willoughby ═ . . .   Edward Willoughby ═ Elizabeth dau. John
.of Middleton and   of Cossall   Atkinson of Nottingham
Wollaton, 1591–1665   b. 1592

Percival Willoughby   Robert Willoughby   Henry Willoughby
b. 1599

Francis Willoughby,   Thomas   Sir Francis   Francis   George
naturalist, 1635–1672 b. 1665? b. 1668   b. 1633   b. 1627

Thomas Willoughby ═ . . .   Thomas Willoughby ═   Thomas Willoughby ═
of Sutton Coldfield   of London   of Kent

Richard   Thomas   Hugh   Robert   George
b. 1636   b. 1638   b. 1648   b. 1569   b. 1571
at Sutton   in Stafford-   B. Med. 1603
Coldfield   shire

Authorities for the above facts are: *D.N.B.*, *s.v.* "Willoughby, Francis," and "Willughby, Francis"; Joseph Edmondson, *An Historical and Genealogical Account of the Noble Family of Greville* (1766); Thomas Bailey, *Annals of Nottinghamshire* (1852 ff.), II, 437, 443, 481–484; *ibid.*, III, 944; Robert Thoroton, *The Antiquities of Nottinghamshire* (1677), pp. 220 ff.; the visitations of Nottinghamshire in 1569 and 1614, Publications of the Harleian Society, IV (1871), 145–149, 184–185; *Alumni Oxonienses*, IV, 1651; Venn and Venn, *Alumni Cantabrigienses*, IV, 423; *The Verney Papers*, Publications of the Camden Society, LVI (1853), 278, 280; The Visitation of Warwick, Publications of the Harleian Society,

XII (1877), 186; *Black Book of Warwick*, ed. Thomas Kemp (1898), p. 413; T. C. Dale, *The Inhabitants of London in 1638*, pp. 50, 217; *Allegations for Marriage Licenses issued by the Bishop of London, 1611–1628*, Vol. II, ed. J. L. Chester and G. J. Armitage, Publications of the Harleian Society, XXVI (1887), 23; *CSP Dom 1625–1626*, p. 164; *CSP Dom 1628–1629*, p. 465.

⁴ Though Burton calls William Smith a "common usurer," I can trace few records of him. Curiously enough, a William Smith, mercer, figures in another case in the same Court of Requests a hundred years earlier; and a William Smith who is probably the Willoughbys' creditor appeared there in the spring of 1627 at the suit of William Hughes. The will of a William Smith was proved in 1632 (104 Audley), of another in 1637 (104 Goare), of another in the same year (137 Goare), and of another in 1635 (28 Sadler). Myriads of William Smiths can of course be found; the difficulty is to link the name with certainty with our mercer-usurer. See *Select Cases in the Court of Requests*, pp. 11–14; Court of Requests Appearance Book, Req 1/111, part 2, folios 16, 19v.

⁵ C. P. 40/2137/m. 3030.

⁶ Thomas Paradine, who appears in these records, was a citizen of London and a haberdasher, who died in 1628 leaving a widow Mary. His will (42 Barrington) and hers (80 Essex, proved 1648; a codicil to it, 188 Pembroke, proved 1650) are in the Prerogative Court of Canterbury. He is very likely the Thomas Paradine who lent £100 on bond in 1604 to William Steward, who paid neither principal nor interest. In 1636 Paradine's son-in-law Robert Wright petitioned dolefully from King's Bench, where he was prisoner, for an order of the House of Lords directing its repayment. The Robert Paradine mentioned in the parliamentary composition papers may be his son or some other relative. The Earl of Cumberland and his son the Earl of Cork gave him a bond of statute staple for £3,000, which in 1649 was unpaid after the death of both Robert and his wife. See *CSP Dom 1636–1637*, pp. 310–311; *Calendar of the Committee for Advance of Money*, pp. 1084–86.

⁷ Henry Hodgkinson has not been identified. The name occurs frequently among the lists of jurors in Lancashire inquisitions post mortem of the Stuart period, and a James Hodgkinson was at one time an apprentice to Milton in his scrivener's business. But Henry's name does not occur among the lists of admissions to the various Inns of Court. See Publications of the Record Society of Lancashire and Cheshire, Vols. III (1879), XVI (1887), XVII (1888), *passim; Athenæum* (1880), I, 565.

⁸ Thomas Shakespeare, attorney for the Willoughbys, was probably a remote relative of the dramatist, from Lutterworth, Leicestershire, who was admitted to Staple Inn on February 15, 1607. He was involved in court proceedings in the year 1604. He or another of the same name gave bond to James Whitlocke for 28s. 6d. in 1606, and a John, son of Thomas, was baptized in St. Gregory by St. Paul's in 1619. See *Admission Books of Staple Inn*, quoted by C. C. Stopes, *Shakespeare's Family* (1901), pp. 133–134.

⁹ Samuel Burton was a man of some dignity. A graduate of Christ Church and a kinsman of Bishop Joseph Hall, he had received the M.A. at Oxford in 1591, and had become rector of Dry Marston (or Marston Sicca), Gloucestershire, in 1598. He later became archdeacon of Gloucester, paying the first fruits for it on May 9, 1607, and justice of the peace for Gloucester. He died possessed of the archdeaconship on June 14, 1634, and was buried in Marston Sicca. His will (113 Seager) was proved on December 5, 1634, by Michael Rutter (with Thomas Bushell renouncing). Before his death he served as surety for another bond, for which he was sued by his brother John Burton of Essex in 1629. Richard Corbet's "Iter Boreale" gives a satirical picture of him. Visiting Fulke Greville at Warwick Castle, Corbet found with him *"Arch-deacon Burton,"*

> Arch-deacon to the Byshopp, by his face
> A greater man; for that, did counterfeit

Lord Abbot of some Covent standing yet,
A corpulent Relique; maery and tis sinne
Some Puritan gets not his face *call'd in;*
Amongst Leane Brethren it may Scandall bring,
Who seeke for parity in every thing.

See Clement Barksdale, *Memorials* (1675), p. 79, in which Joseph Hall in his autobiography expresses his deep gratitude to Burton for procuring for him the living of Wolverhampton; Wood, *Fasti Oxonienses*, I, ed. Bliss (1815), col. 255; John LeNeve, *Fasti Ecclesiae Anglicanæ*, ed. Sir T. D. Hardy (1854), I, 446; C8/85/210; Corbet, *Poetica Stromata* (1648), p. 62.

[10] Sir George Peckham, though a brother-in-law of the Willoughbys, was a frail reed to lean on and a most unpromising prospect from whom to solicit money. As George Peckham of Stanley Grange, Derbyshire, he married Dorothy, daughter of Walter Powtrell of West Hallam, who was born in 1574; and he entered his pedigree in the Visitation of Derbyshire in 1611, which has been published only in part. By 1597 he was deeply in trouble, for on January 16, 1596/7, he wrote a woful complaint to Sir Robert Cecil, lamenting that his lands had been extended for the past twelve years for a bond of £6,500 to the queen, which was part of £26,000 owed her by Thomas Gardiner, sometime a teller of exchequer. He had consequently been obliged to sell the clothes off his and his wife's backs, and even the bed he lay on, and had kept the last Christmas more like Lent. Even so he was in extremities, having been forced to live on his friends for two years. Worse still was in store, however: sickness and prison. On July 24, 1602, he wrote again to Cecil, telling how he had been sick and in prison for two years, and needed to return to the country and to his wife, who was visiting the Lady Mary Arundell in Wiltshire. The latter's husband, however, refused to have Peckham around on account of his dangerous religious views. From his lodging in Fleet Street, Peckham begged Cecil to use his good services to effect a reconciliation. Years later he was still in hot water. In 1621 Sir John Michell (a master in Chancery) petitioned to the Council for a writ of *ne exeat regnum* against him, calling him a recusant because he refused to fulfil the award made by arbitrators appointed by the Court of Chancery as to payment for the manor of Shipley and the sale of Bilborough and Strelley. The Strelley connection came through Peckham's having married as a second wife a Willoughby girl, whose first husband, Francis Strelley, brother-in-law of Sir John Michell, lived in Wollaton, Nottinghamshire. An indenture between Peckham and George Strelley and others, dated January 22, 1608/9, which may have related to this marriage, is recorded. See the *Journal of the Derbyshire Archæological and Natural History Society*, XIV (1892), 96; *ibid.*, XXIII (1901), 68; *ibid.*, XLIII (1921), 40; *Historical Manuscripts Commission. Calendar of the Manuscripts of the . . . Marquis of Salisbury . . . at Hatfield House*, VII (1899), 23; *ibid.*, XII (1910), 243–244; L. T. Golding, *An Elizabethan Puritan* (1937), pp. 88–89; *CSP Dom 1619–1623*, p. 329; J. Hunter, *Familiæ Minorum Gentium*, I, Publications of the Harleian Society, XXXVII (1894), 303.

[11] Req 2/387.

[12] Richard Townesend was admitted to the Middle Temple in 1605, called to the Utter Bar in 1613, chosen reader in 1631, and made treasurer in 1639. See *Middle Temple Records*, II, 454, 563, 781, 883.

[13] Req 1/32, p. 966.

[14] Req 1/111, pt. 2, fol. 6.

[15] *Ibid.*, fol. 10v.

[16] Peter Langley was a member of the Middle Temple, who on his death in 1651 was buried in St. Clement's. See *Inner Temple Records*, II, 363.

[17] William Hakewill of Devon was admitted to Lincoln's Inn in 1598. William Hakewill of Buckinghamshire was a bencher in 1634, when his son, also named William, was ad-

mitted on May 10. The present attorney was probably the bencher, who was master in Chancery 1646–1652. See *Lincoln's Inn Admission Registers*, I, 127, 224.

[18] Req 2/387.

[19] Sydney Mountague, the sixth son of Sir Edward Mountague of Bowghton, Northamptonshire, was admitted to the Middle Temple in 1593 and called to the bar in 1601. In 1616 he was chosen a master of the Court of Requests extraordinary and later was knighted. In 1619 he was deferentially elected a reader of the Middle Temple, "if he will read." See *Middle Temple Records*, I, 333, 413; II, 602, 641, 832.

CHAPTER III. DEVOURING WIDOWS' HOUSES

[1] It is useless to attempt to identify Leigh without knowing his Christian name: the name is far too common.

[2] Thomas Bower was probably a relative, perhaps a son, of the scrivener Geoffrey Bower, who was chosen by the Scriveners' Company with Milton in 1622 as an "assistant." Geoffrey later moved to the Rye, Stanstead Abbey, Hertfordshire, and died there in 1629; his will (61 Ridley) was proved in that year. William Bower, who was admitted as an apprentice of the company in 1621 under Milton, may also have been a relative. Thomas Bower himself, who had been Milton's apprentice, took his freedom as a scrivener in 1624 and became Milton's partner. He may have been the Thomas Bower whose will (528 Wootton) was proved in 1658. See Bodl. MS. Rawl. Miscell. 51; *Athenæum* (1880), I, 565–566.

[2a] *The Obituary of Richard Smyth*, Publications of the Camden Society, XLIV (1849), 3; *D.N.B.*

[3] Matthew Ewens belonged to a Somersetshire family of some importance. A Matthew Ewens who had been a baron of the exchequer had died and been buried in North Cadbury (not far from Bristol) in 1598, but he had had no issue. His brother Alexander, however, who had married a member of the family of Brooke of Wiltshire, had a son Matthew. Probably the Brooke-Ewens marriage influenced the change of bond, since it was very likely that when Lord Brooke or his administrator paid back the money it might become known that another member of the family was looking for a loan. Alexander's son Matthew, who died at North Cadbury and was buried there in 1628 or 1629 (his will is 65 Barrington), had a large family. In addition to our Matthew, who was baptized at North Cadbury on March 15, 1602/3, it comprised Jane, Hastings, Gertrude, Anne, Alexander, Barbara, and Katherine. It may be mentioned that a brother of Matthew's grandfather Alexander, John Ewens of Wincanton, married Elizabeth, daughter of Henry Keymer of Pendomer, and thus paved the way for the association of the two families which appears in the present bond. The Baron Ewens already mentioned had purchased the manors of North and South Cadbury, Somerset, from Sir Francis Hastings, and bequeathed them in his will to his brother Alexander, grandfather of Matthew Ewens, father of our present Matthew. Alexander, a justice of the peace, was constantly occupied with his judicial duties, as is evidenced in the quarter sessions records for the county of Somerset. His name having dropped out about 1616, we may presume that he died about this time. Shortly afterwards Matthew Ewens his son became a member of the commission of the peace, a position which he retained till 1627. Thus the Ewens family was one of some social solidity, and, as one would suppose, a fairly good risk in money-lending. The only evidence which I can find to the contrary is that of a recognizance for £600 entered into by Matthew Ewens in 1628, which was protested in 1629 and listed in the records as "not paid." But this came just at the time of or after the death of Matthew the elder, and may have been settled later. See Publications of the Somersetshire Record Society, Vol. XXIII (1907), *passim*, covering the reign of James I; *ibid.*, Vol. XXIV; L.C. 4/200/390; pedigree by A. J. Jewers, Proceedings of the Somersetshire Archæological and Natural History Society, XXXVI (1891), part II, 153–155, from which I take the following chart.

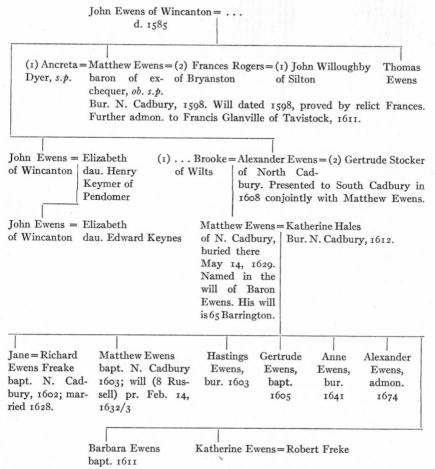

John Ewens of Wincanton = . . .
d. 1585

(1) Ancreta = Matthew Ewens = (2) Frances Rogers = (1) John Willoughby   Thomas
Dyer, *s.p.*   baron of ex-   of Bryanston   of Silton   Ewens
chequer, *ob. s.p.*
Bur. N. Cadbury, 1598. Will dated 1598, proved by relict Frances.
Further admon. to Francis Glanville of Tavistock, 1611.

John Ewens = Elizabeth   (1) . . . Brooke = Alexander Ewens = (2) Gertrude Stocker
of Wincanton   dau. Henry   of Wilts   of North Cad-
Keymer of   bury. Presented to South Cadbury in
Pendomer   1608 conjointly with Matthew Ewens.

John Ewens = Elizabeth   Matthew Ewens = Katherine Hales
of Wincanton   dau. Edward Keynes   of N. Cadbury,   Bur. N. Cadbury, 1612.
buried there
May 14, 1629.
Named in the
will of Baron
Ewens. His will
is 65 Barrington.

Jane = Richard   Matthew Ewens   Hastings   Gertrude   Anne   Alexander
Ewens Freake   bapt. N. Cadbury   Ewens,   Ewens,   Ewens,   Ewens,
bapt. N. Cad-   1603; will (8 Rus-   bur. 1603   bapt.   bur.   admon.
bury, 1602; mar-   sell) pr. Feb. 14,   1605   1641   1674
ried 1628.   1632/3

Barbara Ewens   Katherine Ewens = Robert Freke
bapt. 1611

[4] There is less information about the Keymers. William seems to have been one of the sons of Clement Keymer of the parish of Blandford Forum, Dorset, who died about 1601. He made no will, but administration of his estate was granted to Christopher Gawler, vicar of Sturminster Newton Castle, on July 7, 1601, during the minority of his sons Christopher and William. William must therefore have been born later than 1580, which would make him somewhere between twenty-seven and forty-seven at the time of the loan —let us say for a guess about thirty-five. In 1631 it was noted that "William Keymer hath sold his lands and is gone out of the county." He too took out a recognizance in 1628, but unlike his friend Ewens, paid it. See *Notes and Queries for Somerset and Dorset*, II (1891), 271; *ibid.*, IV (1895), 116; L.C. 4/200/256.

[5] I have found no trace of James Fisher, though a John Fisher, who may have been a relative, witnessed the 1667 contract between John Milton the poet and Matthew Simmons for the publication of *Paradise Lost*.

[6] A Peter Bulteel, one of the merchant strangers, was appealed to under writ of privy seal in 1626 by Sir Robert Pye in regard to loans owed by them; he sent in his letter of excuse on August 5. See *CSP Dom 1625–1626*, p. 422.

[7] C2 Charles I/D39/47.

[8] Robert Henley was six clerk, 1618–1632.

[9] Several Goldsmiths were lawyers. This may have been the Goldsmith of Gray's Inn who in 1621 was charged with a plot to ruin Sir Edward Coke, and was found guilty by the House. Or he may be Clement Goldsmith, who was admitted to the Utter Bar in Gray's Inn in 1583, elected "in magnam Societatem" in 1589, chosen pensioner (or treasurer) in 1598, and elected reader in the same year. Or possibly he might be Henry Goldsmith, chosen utter barrister of Gray's Inn in 1595, fined twenty shillings in 1602 for excusing a suspected recusant, and appointed reader of Barnard's Inn in 1604 and of Gray's Inn in 1615. See *CSP Dom 1619–1623*, pp. 316, 318, 320; *Pension Book of Gray's Inn*, pp. 57, 83, 112, 138, 139, 158, 159, 168, 218.

[10] C2 Charles I/D39/47.

[11] Thomas Eden was master in chancery 1625–1640.

[12] Lawrence Maydwell was six clerk 1629–1662.

[13] Greene's identity is not certain. One William Greene was admitted to Gray's Inn in 1621, the son of Humphrey Greene of Stanningston, Northumberland, clerk. Another, son of Thomas Greene, reader in the Middle Temple, was called to the Utter Bar in that house in 1629. See *Gray's Inn Admission Register*, p. 163; *Middle Temple Records*, II, 665, 752.

[14] C2 Charles I/D39/47. John Michell was master in Chancery 1619–1644.

[15] Stephen Atterbury was admitted to the Middle Temple in 1610. The son of Lewis Atterbury of Houghton Magna, Northants, he was called to the Utter Bar in 1618. He later fell into arrears and forfeited his rooms in the Temple. See *Middle Temple Records*, II, 529, 629, 784, 791.

[16] C 24/574/40.

[16a] Martin Basil was examiner in chancery 1619–1635.

[17] George Broome may have been related to the Bromes of Oxfordshire, who will come into our story later on in connection with Milton's land-holdings in Forest Hill and Wheatley, and of whom several went to the Middle Temple. This George is pretty certainly the attorney whose death in 1652 is noticed by "Obituary" Smith in his funereal diary. See *Middle Temple Records*, I, 253, 319; *The Obituary of Richard Smyth*, p. 32.

[18] C 41/7, Michaelmas, 1631, #469.

[19] Robert Rich was master in chancery 1618–1646.

[20] Maundrell was probably either Henry Maundrell of Wiltshire, who was admitted to Lincoln's Inn in 1607, or Thomas Maundrell, who was admitted in 1598. See *Lincoln's Inn Admission Registers*, I, 126, 144.

[21] C 33/161, f. 171.

[22] Waad was probably Armagil, son of Sir William Waad (1546–1623), lawyer, clerk of the council, diplomat, and lieutenant of the Tower; and grandson of Armagil Waad (died 1568), "the English Columbus." The younger Armagil entered Gray's Inn in 1608 and would thus be about forty-five at this time. He might alternatively be James Waad, son of Sir William of Battleswade, Essex, who entered Gray's Inn in 1621; but the former identification is more likely. See *D.N.B.*, s.v. "Waad, Sir William"; *Gray's Inn Admission Register*, pp. 117, 162.

[23] C 33/161, f. 704.

[24] Thomas Estcourt was master in chancery 1652–1683; examiner in chancery 1674–1682.

[25] C 33/161, f. 704.

CHAPTER IV. BONDS LIKE FLIES IN WINTER

[1] Cotton came of an old and important family, who traced their pedigree back to Robert Bruce and earlier. The best-known member of it is the famous antiquary Sir Robert Bruce

Cotton, whose great library of manuscripts and books, still one of the most important constituent elements of the British Museum, contained the priceless and unique manuscript of *Beowulf,* and who was one of the first Englishmen to use a third name. Our John was his uncle. The following pedigree, based in part on a genealogy prepared by Sir Thomas Cotton (1594–1662), is taken from an extensive one printed in *Miscellanea Genealogica et Heraldica,* New Series, I (1874), 337–340. See also *ibid.,* V (1894), 202; *D.N.B., s.v.* "Cotton, Sir Robert Bruce"; H. R. Moulton, *Palaeography, Genealogy, and Topography* (1936), pp. 107, 128–129, 260–261.

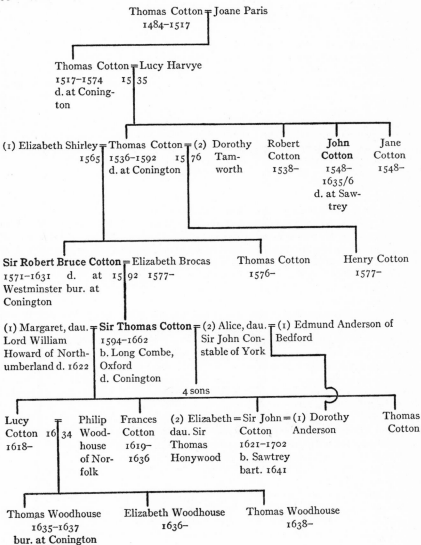

Thomas Cotton ⊤ Joane Paris
1484–1517

Thomas Cotton ⊤ Lucy Harvye
1517–1574   15|35
d. at Coning-
ton

(1) Elizabeth Shirley ⊤ Thomas Cotton ⊤ (2) Dorothy   Robert   **John**   Jane
1565   1536–1592   15|76   Tam-   Cotton   **Cotton**   Cotton
d. at Conington   worth   1538–   1548–   1548–
1635/6
d. at Saw-
trey

Sir Robert Bruce Cotton ⊤ Elizabeth Brocas   Thomas Cotton   Henry Cotton
1571–1631   d.   at   15|92   1577–   1576–   1577–
Westminster bur. at
Conington

(1) Margaret, dau. ⊤ **Sir Thomas Cotton** ⊤ (2) Alice, dau. ⊤ (1) Edmund Anderson of
Lord William   1594–1662   Sir John Con-   Bedford
Howard of North-   b. Long Combe,   stable of York
umberland d. 1622   Oxford
d. Conington

4 sons

Lucy   ⊤   Philip   Frances   (2) Elizabeth ═ Sir John ═ (1) Dorothy   Thomas
Cotton   16|34   Wood-   Cotton   dau. Sir   Cotton   Anderson   Cotton
1618–   house   1619–   Thomas   1621–1702
of Nor-   1636   Honywood   b. Sawtrey
folk   bart. 1641

Thomas Woodhouse   Elizabeth Woodhouse   Thomas Woodhouse
1635–1637   1636–   1638–
bur. at Conington

[2] See pp. 58, 60.

[3] B. M. Cott. Ch. 1/5/4. In a nearby bundle (Cott. Ch. 1/3/1) is an amusing bill brought by Sir Robert Cotton against John Stevenson and John Wilcock and others, which however bears neither endorsement nor date. The plaintiff complains that the defendants have attempted to blackmail him for £40, threatening to publish abroad that he and Amphyllis Fermor were incontinent together in her upper chamber. I have found no other documents in this particular action.

[4] N & Q, II, x (1860), 341.

[5] Academy, VI (1874), 560–561.

[6] Pp. 627 ff.

[7] B. M. Cott. Ch. 1/5/1–5; P.R.O. Req 2/630. The existence of the latter documents has been known for many years, but since the press-mark has not been mentioned, it seemed almost hopeless to attempt to find them. Since the proceedings of the Court of Requests comprise over 800 parcels, each containing several hundred bills and answers, since only a small portion are calendared and those chiefly from the reign of Elizabeth or earlier, and since there is virtually no system of arrangement for most of them, the prospects for putting one's hand on a desired case among the possible 200,000 offerings is negligible. Only weeks of industry or else a stroke of sheer luck as unpredictable as lightning would survive such odds. In my case it was the latter alternative; for when I called for a bundle chosen almost blindly, these proceedings were the first to catch my eye at the very top of the pile.

[8] Omitted.

[9] Omitted.

[10] This list is found in the Requests copy of the bill, but not in the B.M. copy.

[11] Thomas Holchar (or Houlker) was a member of the Middle Temple, into which he had been admitted as "of London, gentleman," on April 16, 1630. Though the date of his admission to the bar does not appear, he was listed in June, 1635, as among those who were practising as common attorneys. In 1639 he was one of many members of the Middle Temple who, after many unsuccessful attempts on the part of the treasurer to collect their arrears, were "put out of commons" until they should have paid them. Houlker's bill was £5-3-9. He was dead by June 16, 1648, when Francis Rowland was admitted to the chamber which had been his. He may have been the Thomas Houlker, brother-in-law of "Obituary" Smith, who died in 1643 as of Kings Langley. See Middle Temple Records, II, 763, 837, 882, 968; The Obituary of Richard Smyth, p. 21.

[12] A Thomas Colwell, late of Barnard's Inn, was admitted to Gray's Inn on May 29, 1584. He may have been the same Thomas Colwell, described as of Feversham, Kent, whose grandson Norton Bold, sometime fellow of Corpus Christi College, Oxford, impressed Anthony Wood as "good for nothing." See Gray's Inn Admission Register, p. 65; Wood, Life and Times, II, 347.

[13] See the list in the appendix, p. 257.

[14] D.N.B.

[15] Lancashire and Cheshire Inquisitions, Publications of the Record Society of Lancashire and Chester, III (1879), passim, and XVII (1888), 383–391.

[16] Ibid., XVII, 188.

[17] Ibid., III, 4, 49; XVI (1887), 148; XVII, 297.

[18] B.M. Cott. Ch. 1/5/4.

[19] Henry Perry was admitted to the Middle Temple in 1580, after being enrolled for a time in New Inn, and was admitted to the Utter Bar in 1590. He was the son of Nicholas Perry (or Purye) of Potterne, Wiltshire. A Henry Perry who may be Cotton's attorney was in 1633 a resident of St. Ives, Huntingdonshire, and on April 22, with Oliver Cromwell

and others, signed a document nominating several surveyors of streets in that town. See W. C. Abbott and C. D. Crane, *The Writings and Speeches of Oliver Cromwell*, I (Cambridge, Mass., 1937), 77–78; *Middle Temple Records*, I, 235, 311. A Henry Perryn was called to the bar in Lincoln's Inn in 1625; see *Black Books*, II, 258.

[20] B.M. Cott. Ch. 1/5/5.

[21] Req 2/630.

[22] B.M. Cott. Ch. 1/5/5.

[23] Req 1/71, p. 227.

[24] Req 1/186, f. 1 *verso*.

[25] William Witherington was probably William Widdrington (1610–1651), sheriff of Northumberland in 1637, member of Parliament in 1640, knighted in 1642, created baron in 1643, and a victim of wounds at the battle of Wigan in 1651. He was reader of Gray's Inn in 1641. His son William, who was admitted in 1641, succeeded him as second baron. It is interesting to find the names of William Witherington and Sir Thomas Cotton of Connington associated in an indenture of 1658. See *D.N.B.; Gray's Inn Admission Register*, p. 229; Moulton, p. 128.

[26] Req 1/141, f. 198v.

[27] Masson, I (1881), 630.

[28] Mrs. Napier Higgins, *The Bernards of Abingdon*, I (1903), 77; W. C. Abbott and C. D. Crane, *The Writings and Speeches of Oliver Cromwell*, I (Cambridge, Mass., 1937), 67–69, 209–210, 225–226.

[28a] Nothing has been discovered about George Miller.

[29] Req 1/71, p. 227.

[30] Req 2/630.

[31] Thomas Parker was called to the bar in the Inner Temple in 1616 and chosen steward in 1634. Thomas, son of Thomas Parker, was a clerk of the privy seal in 1629, and is occasionally mentioned in connection with the Court of Requests later. The Parkers may have come from Lancashire, since many of their name are mentioned in Lancashire inquisitions. A Thomas Parker was also Bailiff of Derby in 1637, and another Thomas, son of Thomas Parker of Anglesey, Cambridge, deceased, entered Gray's Inn in 1649. William Parker and Thomas Parker were parties in various indentures of 1658. See *Inner Temple Records*, II, 95, 96, 213; *CSP Dom* 1628–1629, p. 583; *ibid.*, 1635, p. 445; *ibid.*, 1636–1637, p. 399; Publications of the Record Society of Lancashire and Cheshire, III, *passim*, and XVII, 307, 391, 461; *Gray's Inn Admission Registers*, p. 252; Moulton, pp. 99–100.

[32] The Agars are of particular interest as being connected with the Milton family. Thomas Agar, it will be remembered, succeeded Edward Phillips the elder, both as clerk in the Crown Office and as husband of Ann Milton, daughter of the scrivener. Other details about the two Agars are also available, though it is not wholly certain that all of them belong rightfully to the two men of that name concerned here. A Thomas Agar was a member of the Inner Temple, but deceased before 1636. His son John was admitted on May 27, 1636, but there is no record of his having been admitted to the bar. He probably, however, became the attorney at common pleas noticed by the indefatigable Richard Smith as having died in Barnes, Surrey, in 1671. His name occurs frequently among the records of the Inner Temple, because he often petitioned about his chambers. He entered John Norden's rooms in 1652 or 1653 and refused to give them up, accepted others in Pump Court in their place in 1654, built new rooms in Essex Court in 1655, and surrendered claim to the former chambers in 1658. He was almost certainly the John Agar whose son Thomas entered Gray's Inn on February 26, 1657/8, but transferred almost immediately to the Middle Temple, which he entered on June 30, 1658. He was admitted to the brick building in Essex Court in 1661, was called to the bar in 1663, and was stew-

ard in 1675. Several law-suits later arose over these chambers, the discussion of which would lead us too far afield at present. More to our purpose is the fact that Thomas and John Agar are mentioned in 1630 as having drawn up the will of one Thomas Harding, in connection with which they were sued by Awdrey Harding. See Helen Darbishire, *Early Lives of Milton*, p. 53; *Middle Temple Records*, II, 850; *ibid.*, III, 1038, 1039, 1055, 1059, 1081, 1111, 1125, 1163, 1164, 1176, 1177, 1191, 1251, 1253, 1291; *The Obituary of Richard Smyth*, p. 91; *Gray's Inn Admission Register*, p. 285; C 8/70/154.

[33] Sir Edward Powell was a man of some importance and even notoriety. Admitted to the Middle Temple in 1601 and called to the bar in 1613, he was "discharged of his vacations" (*i.e.*, exempted from staying in London) on account of his "great occasions of business in the country" in 1614. Incidentally, for ten years between 1613 and 1623 he shared a chamber with Richard Townesend, whom we have met before as the lawyer representing Samuel Burton. On June 22, 1625, he was made master of the Court of Requests with an annuity of £100 a year for life. He was involved in a most complicated and scandalous quarrel with Sir Peter Vanlore, his father-in-law, and the accounts of their bickerings recur frequently in the Calendars of State Papers and Chancery proceedings. He may have been Richard Powell's brother. See *Middle Temple Records*, I, 412; *ibid.*, II, 563, 566, 570, 576–577, 580, 680; *CSP Dom 1625–1626*, p. 541; Moulton, p. 258; above, Chap. VI, *passim;* below, p. 167.

[34] Req 1/141, f. 216.

[35] B.M. Cott. Ch. 1/5/5.

[36] B.M. Cott. Ch. 1/5/2.

[37] Francis Walsted, son of Thomas Walsted of Walsted Delves, Staffordshire, gentleman, went to New Inn, was admitted to the Middle Temple in 1613, was called to the bar in 1621, and was classed as an "ancient" in 1654. See *Middle Temple Records*, II, 570, 669; *ibid.*, III, 1064.

[38] Pedaell Harlowe, son of Robert Harlowe of London, was admitted to Gray's Inn in 1609. See *Gray's Inn Admission Register*, p. 127.

[39] B.M. Cott. Ch. 1/5/5.

[40] Req 1/141, f. 220.

[41] Req 2/630.

[42] Whitfield may be any one of several lawyers of that name. Several Whitfields from Tenterden, Kent, were admitted to Gray's Inn: Ralph in 1608, Herbert in 1612, Robert in 1622, another Herbert and another Robert in 1625, Henry and still another Herbert in 1632, and Roger and another Ralph in 1633. A John Whitfield was called to the bar in Lincoln's Inn in 1615. Another Ralph Whitfield was admitted to Gray's Inn in 1607, called to be of the "grand company" in 1627, elected reader of Staple Inn in 1628 and of Gray's Inn in 1633, and appointed to various committees until at least 1636. It was perhaps this Ralph, later knighted and made sergeant-at-law, who was buried in the Temple in 1645. Again a John Whitfield of Beaconsfield was admitted to the Middle Temple in 1639 and called to the bar in 1646. It is impossible to say with any certainty which was the lawyer in question here. See *Gray's Inn Admission Register*, pp. 119, 130, 168, 176, 195, 197, 200, 202; *Black Books of Lincoln's Inn*, II, 173; *Inner Temple Records*, II, 361; *Pension Book of Gray's Inn*, pp. 276, 283, 315, 317, 326; *Middle Temple Records*, II, 883, 940.

[43] Req 2/117, p. 124.

[44] Noel Butler was a member of the Middle Temple, who gave up his chambers there in 1652. See *Middle Temple Records*, III, 1041.

[45] B.M. Cott. Ch. 1/5/5.

[46] B.M. Cott. Ch. 1/5/5.

[47] *The Attourney's Academy* (1630 edition), p. 14.

CHAPTER V. CRYING "REVENGE!"

[1] See above, Chapter III.

[2] Arthur (later Sir Arthur) Duck was born in 1580, proceeded B.A. at Exeter College, Oxford, in 1599 and M.A. at Hart Hall in 1602, was appointed fellow of All Souls' in 1604, and was granted an LL.D. in 1612. He became an advocate in Doctors' Commons in 1614, a member of Parliament for Minehead in 1624 and later, chancellor of the diocese of London about 1628, chancellor of Bath and Wells in 1635, and a master in chancery in 1645. He died in 1648. A member of a Devon family, the son of Richard Duck and the grandson of Philip Duck of Heavitree, he had several influential relatives in law and commerce. His brother Nicholas (1570–1628), recorder of Exeter in 1617 and a bencher of Lincoln's Inn in 1620, had married Grace, daughter of Thomas Walker, alderman of Exeter; a sister Katherine had married Geoffrey Waltham, also alderman of Exeter; and his wife Margaret was the daughter of Henry Southworth, a merchant of London and Wells. Sir Arthur himself later accumulated large holdings of land and a sizable income, for he was able during the interregnum to compound for £2,000 and to lend Charles I the large sum of £6,000— the equivalent of $200,000 to $300,000 today. He wrote several books, the most important ones being a life of Archbishop Chichele and a treatise on Roman civil law. Charles I thought highly enough of his ability to summon his assistance in drafting the treaty of peace in the Isle of Wight. He held other offices also, among them being that of master of the Court of Requests; and Fuller asserts that he just missed being made master of the rolls. Fuller's characterization of him is vivid enough to deserve quoting:

One of most smooth language, but rough speech; so that what a comedian saith of a fair maid in mean apparel was true of him:

> " . . . nisi vis boni . . .
> In ipsâ inesset formâ, vestes formam extinguerent."

Had there not been a masculine strength in his matter, it had been marred with the disadvantage of his utterance.

He inherited from his parents, and passed on to his children, a great estate.

But he was involved in constant legal squabbles. Not only are the Calendars of State Papers rich in references to cases which he handled, as master of the Court of Requests or otherwise, but the files of Chancery similarly abound in cases in which he appeared as either plaintiff or defendant. He was sued by the rector of North Cadbury in 1647 in regard to debts involving Matthew Ewens; he borrowed £5,000 of John Cary in 1638 and was brought to heel for failure to repay in 1650, though he did make the debt good in 1654; he was sued by Peter Dubois between 1626 and 1639 in connection with his holdings in Cadbury; he was sued, together with William Child, in 1637 by two sons of the Ewens family, John and Andrew; judgment against him as plaintiff against Alexander, John, and Andrew Ewens to the sum of £50 was granted on November 31, 1636; he brought action against one Farewell over the Ewens affair in 1637, and was sued by James Farewell presumably on the same grounds at some date unknown; and, to continue the list no further, he was involved in a very complicated triangular skirmish with Sir Edward Powell and Sir Peter Vanlore in 1640, the records of which cover too many actions to be listed here. Though several of these had not yet begun at the time of our present suit, it is fairly obvious that in bringing this bill Milton had again not hesitated to attack a formidable antagonist. See Anthony Wood, *Fasti Oxonienses*, part I, ed. Bliss (1815), col. 296; Thomas Fuller, *History of the Worthies of England*, I, ed. P. A. Nuttall (1840), 420–421; *D.N.B.; Miscellanea Genealogica et Heraldica*, New Series, I (1874), 317; C2 Charles I/C 108/39; L.C. 4/202/67; C 3/400/152; C2 Charles I/E 28/40; C2 Charles I/C 38/26; C 33/171, f. 4v; C2 Charles I/D 59/26; C2 Charles I/F 44/1; C2 Charles I/P 32/51; C2 Charles I/D 36/14; C2 Charles I/D 59/26; C2 Charles I/D 42/22; C2 Charles I/D 53/29; C2 Charles I/D 57/25.

[3] William Child, Duck's associate, is not to be confused with Sir Francis Child, banker and lord mayor of London, nor with William Child the Shropshire Doctor of Laws who was to become master of chancery in 1639 and was to be knighted later, though the latter may have been a relative, even a son. But "Obituary" Smith records that on February 27, 1638, "Mr. Child, scrivenor," who must have been our defendant, "died sodenly." Whether the shock of Milton's suit killed him or not, he apparently died just in time to escape more serious difficulties. For on January 11, 1640/1, a group of his creditors petitioned to the House of Commons against "one William Childe, a scrivener, and his son, who had cousened divers persons of near upon £40,000." Sir Thomas Browne still remembered him in 1679 as a large-scale swindler. Sir Simonds D'Ewes spoke against the petition on the ground that it was not Parliament's business to bother with it since there had been no evidence of any denial of justice in the courts. If the charge was true, Milton was pitted against a formidable adversary, one who had made away with well over a million dollars. It is not certain whether Duck's associate was the William Child who in 1627 obtained lands in Buckinghamshire from the Dean and Chapter of St. George's, Windsor, and whose son in 1645 acquired other property nearby. See *D.N.B.*, *s.v.* "Child, Sir Francis"; *Lincoln's Inn Admission Register*, I, 263, 289; *The Obituary of Richard Smyth*, p. 14; *Journals of the House of Commons*, II, 66; *The Journal of Sir Simonds D'Ewes*, ed. Wallace Notestein (1923), p. 238; Moulton, p. 340; Sir Thomas Browne, *Works*, ed. Keynes, VI (1931), 152.

[4] C2 Charles I/M 78/26.

[5] C 8/39/39.

[6] Estcott is probably Richard Escott of Cornwall, who entered Lincoln's Inn in 1613, was called to the bar in 1620, and became reader in Furnivall's Inn in 1630, or else Richard Escott who was called to the bar in Lincoln's Inn in 1633 and to the bench in 1648. See *Lincoln's Inn Admission Register*, I, 164; *Black Books of Lincoln's Inn*, II, 219, 293, 309, 379.

[7] A Thomas Gardiner entered the Inner Temple about 1610, later became bencher and treasurer, and was in 1636 Recorder of London. At least two other men of the same name entered Gray's Inn in time to be eligible as counsel for Duck and Child. A Sir Thomas Gardiner of Cuddesdon who died about 1656 offered depositions in 1651 concerning Milton's extent on Powell's property. See *Inner Temple Records*, II, 107, 145, 164, 224, 241, 252; *Middle Temple Records*, II, 999; *Gray's Inn Admission Register*, pp. 182, 186; Hamilton, *Milton Papers*, pp. 48–49.

[8] C 33/171, f. 4v.

[9] C 33/171, ff. 414–414v.

[10] C2 Charles I/M 78/26.

[11] John Page was master in chancery 1627–1655.

[12] Edward Robinson was six clerk 1628–1639.

[13] There were several lawyers named Fountain at this time. Brigg Fountayne was called to the bar in 1620 in the Inner Temple, and was chosen steward for the Reader's dinner in 1640. Hugh Fountain was called to the bar of Lincoln's Inn in 1591, but may have been dead by 1640. John Fountain was called to the bar in Lincoln's Inn in 1629, was restored after being ousted for his political affiliations in 1653, was called to the bench in the same year, and was sergeant-elect in 1656. Wood mentions him as a sergeant-at-law. Since the Christian name of Duck's lawyer is nowhere mentioned, he may be any of these, or even some other. Sergeant John would seem the likeliest guess. See *Inner Temple Records*, II, 120, 256; *Black Books of Lincoln's Inn*, II, 20, 286, 398, 414; Wood, *Parochial Collections*, pp. 205–206.

[14] C 33/171, ff. 414–414v.

[15] C 38/86.

[16] C 33/171, f. 4v.

[17] C 33/173, f. 349.

CHAPTER VI. GOOD DEEDS IN PARCHMENT

[1] Since all the remaining chapters involve the Powell family, it seems advisable to furnish here a fairly complete genealogy. There were several families of Powells, the chief for our purposes being those of Sandford, Forest Hill, and Fulham (Middlesex). The precise connection between them is not clear, though it seems possible that Milton's father-in-law Richard Powell of Forest Hill may have been brother to Sir Edward Powell of the Fulham branch. In addition to these three, there was at least one other family of Powells at Forest Hill, and various stray names come to light here and there. The chief sources of the following consolidated pedigree are: Masson, *passim; D.N.B.; Calendars of State Papers, passim;* probates of wills; Chancery suits summarized in chapter VI; parish registers of Forest Hill; Wood, *Life and Times, passim;* Wood, *Parochial Collections,* p. 250; Bodl. MS. Rawl. B. 400. b, folios 213 ff.; *The Visitation of Middlesex in 1663,* ed. W. Ryley (1820), pp. 31, 42; *Gentleman's Magazine,* LXXXV (1815), pt. I, pp. 22–25; *Calendar of the Committee for Compounding,* p. 1970. (See facing insert for Powell pedigree.)

[2] Wood, *Parochial Collections,* pp. 177–179; *Forest Hill and Shotover/1933/The Village Book,* ed. Ella Miller, p. 25. The latter book, which will be quoted frequently hereafter, will be mentioned as *Forest Hill Book.* It is compiled from many records. See also G. A. Coppock and B. M. Hill, *Headington Quarry and Shotover* (Oxford, 1933), p. 12. The following pedigree of the Brome family is taken from Wood, *Parochial Collections,* pp. 177–179; wills; registers of Forest Hill; *The Visitation of Oxfordshire in 1634,* Publications of the Harleian Society, V (1871), 229–231, 263–264.

Christopher Brome = . . . Hampden

Robert, goldsmith of London, of Forest Hill in 1545

John d. 1558 buried at Holton = Margaret Rous of Warwick

William of the Vent in Forest Hill = . . . Hampden

(1) Elizabeth, dau. Sir Thomas Weynman = Sir Christopher d. 1589, buried at Holton = (2) Eleanor, dau. William, Lord Windsor of Bradenham

Nicholas = Audrey, dau. of the Vent Robert Man of Lincolnshire

George of Headington and Holton, of the Middle Temple, 1591, dead in 1615 = Elizabeth

Thomas

Henry of London

Edmond in Forest Hill in 1591 and 1621, of the Middle Temple, 1582 d. 1628 = Elizabeth d. 1634/5

eight daughters

Ursula = **Sir Thomas Whorwood** d. 1653 d. 1634

William d. 1599

| Jane b. 1595 | Frigwith b. 1597 | George 1600–01 | Elizabeth b.d. 1600 | **John** b. 1602 | Mary b. 1605 | **Christopher** b. 1608 |

³ *Calendar of Patent Rolls, 1547–1548*, p. 99. Robert's name here appears as "Browne."
⁴ B.M. Add. MS. 24,501, f. 21.
⁵ C 142/221/106; Bodl. MS. B. Rawl. 400. b, folios 217ff.
⁶ *Forest Hill Book*, p. 16.
⁷ E 179/163/395.
⁸ C2 James I/B 33/20 (bill of 1610).
⁹ Salter, *Oxford*, p. 254.
¹⁰ C2 James I/B 39/42.
¹¹ C2 James I/B 39/39.
¹² C2 James I/B 11/20.
¹³ Incidentally, Thomas Ayloffe had a dubious reputation. Though the son of a Justice of the Queen's Bench, he had been first fined and later expelled from Lincoln's Inn for beating a butler. He had later been reinstated and admitted to the bar. The will of Thomas Ayloffe of Essex, probably the same man, was proved in 1657. He may have been the son of the James Ayloffe who brought action against the elder Milton. See above, Chapter I, note 1; *Black Books of Lincoln's Inn*, II, 7, 9, 11, 31, 34.
¹⁴ C2 James I/B 39/8.
¹⁵ C2 James I/B 33/20.
¹⁶ The Whorwoods are an interesting family, whose later history may here be cursorily sketched. Thomas, later Sir Thomas, succeeded in marrying Ursula Brome, by whom he had three sons: Brome, Thomas, and William. Brome married Jane Ryder or Ryther of Kingston-upon-Thames, who was a perfect story-book heroine. Anthony Wood tells how, red-headed and appropriately fiery in her loyalty to Charles I, she visited the astrologer William Lilly in 1647 to discover by magic divination the spot of greatest safety for Charles to hide in. Before she could arrange to have him conveyed there, he had unfortunately surrendered. Nothing daunted, she smuggled saws and acid to him in Carisbrooke Castle, by means of which he cut through the bars of his window and almost escaped. Unfortunately this attempt, like the former, was abortive, but the king gave her his casket of jewels to keep for him. Gossip had it she was the mistress of Sir Thomas Bendish the diplomat. Her son Brome became a member of Parliament but was involved in seditious disturbances in 1680 and later. Wood, who disliked him intensely as a "clownish and ill natured person," "of no religion," tells how he came to Oxford in 1681 in the train of Lord Lovelace, with crowds lining the streets and shouting, "A Whorwood! A Whorwood!" He achieved his election in this year, though he had failed in 1680. When he died in 1684, his death was certified in court by an attorney. The appended pedigree is taken from the following sources: *Miscellanea Genealogica et Heraldica*, New Series, IV (1884), 38; *Alumni Oxonienses*, IV (1625); Wood, *Parochial Collections*, pp. 177–179; *Life and Times*, I, 184, 204, 226, 256, 399; *ibid.*, II, 331, 485; *ibid.*, III, 403; and wills. See also Mary Sturge Gretton, *Oxfordshire Justices of the Peace in the Seventeenth Century*, Publications of the Oxfordshire Record Society, Vol. XVI (hereafter referred to as *Oxford Justices*), pp. xlvii–iii; Wood, *Life and Times*, II, 439, 476–477, 516, 522–523; *ibid.*, III, 93–94; *The Nicholas Papers*, Publications of the Camden Society, New Series, Vol. XL (1886), pp. 78, 80. (The pedigree is printed on p. 169.)
¹⁷ C2 James I/B 2/47.
¹⁸ C2 James I/B 4/49.
¹⁹ C 142/354/104.
²⁰ C 142/367/101.
²¹ C 142/379/87.
²² C.P. 25 (2), Oxon., Hilary, 17 James I.
²³ C.P. 25 (2), Oxon., Easter, 18 James I.

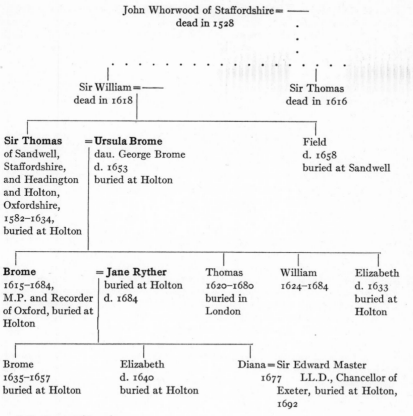

John Whorwood of Staffordshire = ——
dead in 1528

Sir William = ——
dead in 1618

Sir Thomas
dead in 1616

Sir Thomas = **Ursula Brome**
of Sandwell,   dau. George Brome
Staffordshire,   d. 1653
and Headington   buried at Holton
and Holton,
Oxfordshire,
1582–1634,
buried at Holton

Field
d. 1658
buried at Sandwell

Brome   = **Jane Ryther**   Thomas   William   Elizabeth
1615–1684,   buried at Holton   1620–1680   1624–1684   d. 1633
M.P. and Recorder d. 1684   buried in   buried at
of Oxford, buried at   London   Holton
Holton

Brome   Elizabeth   Diana = Sir Edward Master
1635–1657   d. 1640   1677   LL.D., Chancellor of
buried at Holton   buried at Holton   Exeter, buried at Holton,
                                                 1692

[24] C2 James I/B 17/9.

[25] Hunter, *Milton: A Sheaf of Gleanings*, p. 29.

[26] C 5/2/65 (Anne Powell's answer of 1648/9); C 5/44/90 (Thomas Whorwood's bill of 1662); C 7/476/93 (Matthew Archdale's answer of 1663).

[27] Forest Hill registers.

[28] S.P. 23/109, p. 52 (John Pye's petition of August 23, 1650); C 5/13/94 (John Pye's bill, 1651).

[29] B.M. Add. MS. 24,501, f. 35.

[30] C 142/472/92.

[31] E 179/289/31.

[32] C 142/472/92; Hamilton, pp. 55, 85.

[33] C2 Charles I/P 49/2 (Brome's answer to Powell, 1633).

[34] Stevens, *Milton Papers*, pp. 9–11.

[35] C 66/2318/40.

[36] James Chesterman was an attorney of St. Martin's parish in Oxford, the son of John Chesterman of Cleve, Wiltshire, sometime fellow of New College. James's brother John's daughter Grace married another attorney of St. Martin's parish, Edward Asteyn. James himself married a wife named Grace, who survived him by many years. He died in January,

1645/6, and was buried in St. Martin's church. His will, 14 Fines, was proved by his wife in March, 1645/6, and later in February, 1646/7; she died in 1659/60. I have noticed several records of land-transfers in which he participated in and about Oxford during the reign of Charles I. One with Richard Edwards concerns property in Oxford itself; another with Thomas Gilder concerns Newnham Courtney; and another with John Pollard concerns Marchbaldington. He had leased a brewhouse in Oxford in 1616. A somewhat earlier transaction with John Whilton concerned Headington. Apparently Chesterman was a man of some standing locally. He was at least sufficiently well-to-do, and of sufficiently pronounced royalist leanings, to subscribe £108 for the king's service in (?)1648; an action which of course stood him in no good stead with the Parliament later. See Wood, *Life and Times*, II, 269; Wood, *A Survey of the Antiquities of the City of Oxford*, III (1899), 234; Salter, *Oxford*, p. 196; *Calendar of the Committee for the Advance of Money*, pp. 998, 1004; C.P. 25 (2) Oxon., Mich., 7 Charles I; *ibid.*, Easter, 11 Charles I; *ibid.*, Easter, 12 Charles I; *ibid.*, Trinity, 18 James I.

    37 William Hearne is a more shadowy person. Many Hearnes (often spelled Heron or Herne) may be found in the indexes to wills, in Wood's *Life and Times*, and in similar lists. The family was well represented in Oxfordshire, as records of fines show. Thus, to name only a few examples, Anthony Hearne appears on a fine of Drayton in 1633; John Hearne in a fine of Tainton in 1637 and in a Chancery action of a later period concerning affairs in Oxfordshire; another John Hearne's inquisition post mortem (Oxfordshire) is dated 1631; a Richard Hearne appears on a fine of Stokenchurch in 1638; and Thomas Hearne on a fine of Shutford in 1634. But these are not William, who was a goldsmith of London. He may possibly be the William Hearne who proved the will of his father William of Basingstoke (45 Seager) in 1634. He may have been the William Hearne who in 1610 witnessed an indenture between Sir Edward Heron and John Smyth of Dartford, Kent. One of the very few facts that we positively know about him is that he was dead by 1641, when Christopher Brome alluded to him as "since deceased." There is a strong likelihood that he was connected by marriage with the Powell family, since his will was administered by Elizabeth Powell, spinster. See C.P. 25 (2) Oxon., Mich., 9 Charles I; *ibid.*, Mich., 13 Charles I; *ibid.*, Mich., 14 Charles I; *ibid.*, Mich., 10 Charles I; C 3/447/44; C 142/638/80; Moulton, p. 255; C 7/572/42 (Powell's answer to Eyton, 1687); C 7/55/146 (Christopher Brome's bill of 1641).

    38 C.P. 25 (2) 340, Michaelmas, 21 James I.
    39 B.M. Add. MS. 24,501, f. 31.
    40 Ind 8961/7; the book to which this is an index is lost.
    41 C2 Charles I/B 145/35.
    42 C.P. 25 (2) Oxon., Trinity, 2 Charles I.
    43 C.P. 25 (2) Oxon., Hilary, 3 Charles I.
    44 Bodl. MS. Wood 515, p. 3; Stevens, pp. 9–11.
    45 L.C. 4/200, f. 265; C 152/61.
    46 L.C. 4/200, f. 265v.
    47 S.P. Dom., Charles I, Vol. CXXIII, #38.
    48 S.P. Dom., Charles I, Vol. CL, #35; E 178/5584; E 178/1839.
    49 Ind 8961/7.
    50 *Ibid.*
    51 C.P. 25 (2) Oxon., Mich., 4 Charles I.
    52 C2 Charles I/P 49/2 (Powell's bill, 1633); C 5/2/65.
    53 E 112/232/46.
    54 E 112/232/34.
    55 E 112/232/34.

[56] E 112/232/34.

[57] C 54/2900/6.

[58] C 54/2901/27.

[59] C 142/472/92.

[60] C 54/2902/24.

[61] Forest Hill registers.

[62] Hamilton, pp. 76, 87–88, 97.

[63] From a document in the diocesan registry at Oxford which I have not seen; quoted by Masson, II, 498n.

[64] C.P. 25 (2) Oxon., Mich., 8 Charles I.

[65] C 7/55/146 (Brome's bill of 1641).

[66] C2 Charles I/P 49/2 (Brome's answer to Powell, 1633).

[67] Bill in the Court of Wards, as calendared in the *48th Report of the Deputy Keeper of the Public Records*, appendix, p. 467.

[68] C2 Charles I/P 49/2.

[69] *Ibid.*

[70] C 7/55/146 (Brome's bill of 1641).

[71] C.P. 25 (2) Oxon., Trinity, 9 Charles I.

[72] Forest Hill registers.

[73] C.P. 25 (2) Oxon., Easter, 10 Charles I.

[74] *Forest Hill Book*, p. 25.

[75] Bodl. MS. Rawl. B. 400. b, folios 217 ff.

[76] *Ibid.*

[77] Stevens, p. 10; Bodl. MS. Wood 515, pp. 2–3.

[78] C 7/476/93 (Archdale's answer to Whorwood, 1663).

[79] C 66/2736/7; Masson, II, 497–499.

[80] C 66/2763/19.

[81] Hunter, pp. 29–31.

[82] *CSP Dom, passim;* especially 1628–1629, p. 344; 1637–1638, pp. 563–564; *38th* and *43rd Reports of the Deputy Keeper of the Public Records, passim.* Tyrrell had been granted custody of the Shotover and Stowood forests in 1628 (*43rd Report*, appendix, p. 117), and Lindsey had received a lease of part of them in 1629 (*ibid.*, p. 144).

[83] Stevens, p. 10.

[84] E 112/232/96. See the *39th Report of the Deputy Keeper of the Public Records*, appendix, p. 498, for a reference to depositions in this action.

[85] Westminster Abbey Muniment 18181 (a survey of 1654).

[86] Stevens, p. 10; Bodl. MS. Wood 515, p. 3.

[87] Stevens, p. 10; C 5/2/65 (Hearne's answer to Powell, 1648).

[88] C 5/13/94 (Pye's bill of 1651); Hamilton, pp. 55–56.

[89] Hamilton, pp. 55–56.

[90] B.M. Add. MS. 24,501, ff. 30, 34.

[91] C 7/55/146.

[91a] Nothing has been found out about Charles Guest.

[92] C 5/2/65 (Powell's bill, 1648); Bodl. MS. Wood 515, p. 3; Stevens, p. 10.

[93] *Ibid.*

[94] See above, note 1.

[95] E 112/328/55 (Anne Powell's bill, 1657).

[96] C2 Charles I/B 7/67.

[97] Acton Drake, of Charlbury, Oxfordshire, was gentleman of the bedchamber to Henry Danvers, Earl of Danby, ranger of the forest of Wychwood, and later one of Danby's

executors. In the latter capacity he was heavily assessed by the parliamentary commissioners, and was more than once called in for questioning. Aubrey states that he died in 1642, but Lowe gives the date as 1651. See *Calendar of the Committee for Advance of Money*, pp. 697, 1388; *Calendar of the Committee for Compounding*, pp. 2525, 1638; John Aubrey, *Wiltshire. The Topographical Collections*, ed. J. E. Jackson (Devizes, 1862), p. 228; C 7/598/77 (Lowe's bill, 1674/5).

98 C 7/598/77 (Lowe's Bill, 1674/5).

99 Hamilton, p. 106.

100 B.M. Add. MS. 24,501, f. 36.

101 C 5/13/94 (John Pye's bill, 1651); Hamilton, p. 56.

102 E 112/328/55.

103 Hamilton, pp. 92–94.

104 E 112/328/55 (Anne Powell's bill, 1657).

105 Little is known of Joseph Barber. There was a man of that name in Essex (1622–1679), but his occupation is unknown. In 1634 there were Barbers in Adderbury, Oxfordshire, but no Josephs. The surveyor-general in 1640, however, was Sir Charles Harbord; in 1650, Colonel William Webb. See *Miscellanea Genealogica et Heraldica*, I, 58; Visitation of Oxfordshire, Publications of the Harleian Society, V (1871), pp. 324–325; *CSP Dom 1650*, p. 713; *ibid.*, 1640, p. 18.

106 C 8/203/48 (Anne Powell's answer to Lowe, 1675).

107 S.P. 23/54, p. 973.

108 C 5/2/65 (accompanying Anne Powell's answer to Powell, 1648); Hamilton, pp. 92–94.

109 C 8/203/48 (Anne Powell's answer to Lowe, 1675).

110 C 5/2/65 (Powell's bill, 1648).

111 C 152/61; L.C. 4/200, f. 265.

112 C 10/44/2 (Milton's answer to Elizabeth Ashworth, 1654).

113 See below, Chapter VII.

114 C 5/2/65.

115 Oxfordshire Assessment Rolls.

116 *Ibid.*

117 Hamilton, p. 56.

118 B.M. Add. MS. 24,501, f. 22.

119 C 5/2/65.

120 *Ibid.*

121 *Ibid.*

122 E 372/493.

123 S.P. 23/39.

124 *Ibid.*

125 S.P. 23/251/100.

126 Hamilton, pp. 82–83.

127 C 8/203/48 (Anne Powell's answer to Lowe, 1675).

128 Hamilton, pp. 51, 92.

129 Hamilton, pp. 85–86.

130 Hamilton, pp. 87–88.

131 Hamilton, pp. 86–87.

132 Hamilton, pp. 55–57.

133 Hamilton, p. 90.

134 Hamilton, pp. 100, 108.

135 Hamilton, p. 102.

136 Hamilton, pp. 90, 107.

137 Hamilton, p. 108.

138 Hamilton, p. 108; S.P. 23/43, p. 73.

139 Hamilton, pp. 121–124, 127.

140 Hamilton, pp. 51–52.

141 Hamilton, p. 95.

142 Hamilton, pp. 98–99; S.P. 23/43, p. 73.

143 Hamilton, p. 100.

144 C 5/13/94.

145 *Ibid.*

146 C 33/196, f. 1104.

147 C 5/13/94.

148 C 5/44/90 (Anne Powell's answer, 1662).

149 Hamilton and Masson, *passim.*

150 See p. 93.

151 Bodl. MS. Wood 515, a printed pamphlet of eight pages; Stevens, p. 11.

152 E 112/328/55.

153 C 5/519/35 (Anne Powell's answer to Lowe, 1673/4).

154 Sir Timothy Tyrrell came of an interesting family. One ancestor, Sir John Tyrrell, was sheriff, member of Parliament, speaker, and treasurer in the time of Henry VI; another, Sir James, was the supposed murderer of the princes in the Tower of London, for which act he was beheaded in 1502; another, Anthony, was a renegade priest and spy in the reign of Elizabeth; James, the historian, was the grandson of Milton's antagonist Archbishop Ussher; and a contemporary, Sir Thomas, was a judge and a justice and held various legal offices. Sir Timothy himself obtained the rangership of Shotover Forest by a curious accident. When as master of the buckhounds to Prince Henry, son of James I, he held the head of a buck for the prince to cut it off, the prince cut awkwardly and took off Tyrrell's hand by mistake. In reparation Tyrrell received by letters patent in 1613 the rangership and bailiwick of the forest, a rank which his family retained till 1742. He married the daughter of James Ussher, archbishop of Armagh and primate of Ireland. At his house in Shotover the ambassador from Morocco was entertained at a banquet en route from Windsor to Oxford in 1682. See *D.N.B.;* G. A. Coppock and B. M. Hill, *Headington Quarry and Shotover* (Oxford, 1933), pp. 12–13; Wood, *Life and Times,* III, 17; *43rd Report of the Deputy Keeper of the Public Records,* appendix, p. 16; *Forest Hill Book,* p. 21.

155 See above, note 105.

156 E 112/328/55.

157 Sir Edmund Prideaux was a lawyer and politician, who became successively a barrister of the Inner Temple (1623), M.P. (1640), solicitor-general (1648–49), and attorney-general (1649–1659). He was consistently opposed to Charles I, and made noteworthy reforms in the postal service. See *D.N.B.*

158 E 112/328/55.

159 E 112/328/55.

160 E 112/328/63.

161 E 112/328/63.

162 See the next chapter.

163 Gilbert Jackson here mentioned as of Stanton St. John seems to have been born in 1640 and to have died in 1708. His wife Elizabeth (*née* Towersey) is said to have died in 1691 at the age of thirty-nine. His name is found in several other suits. He may have been a son of the William and Anne Jackson who were buried in St. Mary's Church, Oxford, and whose monuments Wood describes. The Anne Jackson who is mentioned below may

have been the latter. She may also have been the lady of that name who filed suits (as a widow) against various defendants in 1651 and 1652. She can hardly have been related to Gilbert except by marriage. Nor can this Gilbert very well have been the one who was sequestered for goods in Westminster in March, 1649. The marriage agreement of 1660 for Gilbert Jackson and Elizabeth Towersey (or Dowersey) is still preserved. The parties are Gilbert Jackson of Wheatley, Richard Eldridge of Shotover Wood, and Richard Dowersey of Holton. Either this date or Wood's statement that Elizabeth Jackson was thirty-nine years old in 1691 (and therefore born in 1652) is obviously wrong. Other documents to which Gilbert Jackson was a party, dated 16— and 1682, are in the same collection. See Wood, *Parochial Collections*, p. 284; Wood, *Antiquities of Oxford*, III, 123; C 5/142/1 (against Thomas Cox, 1697, about Long Crendon, Bucks); C 5/614/36 (against one Izard, about Cuddesdon and Milton, Oxford); C 5/378/104 (against John Jackson, 1651, about Cumberland); C 5/505/8 (against John Short, 1662, about Durham); *Calendar of the Committee for Compounding*, p. 92; Moulton, p. 70.

164 See Chapter IX.

165 C 5/44/90 (Whorwood's bill, 1662); C 5/76/27 (Powell's bill, 1691).

166 Montague Bertie, second Earl of Lindsay (1608?–1666) was, like the Powells, a thorough royalist. He served actively in the king's army during the Civil War, and as privy councillor and gentleman of the bedchamber accompanied Charles I in the Isle of Wight. On the Restoration he was again made a privy councillor and a judge in the trial of the regicides. See the *D.N.B.*, s.v. "Bertie, Montague."

167 C 5/44/90.

168 C 5/519/35.

169 *Calendar of Treasury Books, 1660–1667*, p. 7.

170 *Ibid.*, p. 64.

171 *Calendar of Treasury Books, 1681–1685*, part III, appendix I, pp. 1547, 1550–51.

172 *Ibid.*, p. 1582.

173 *Ibid.*, p. 1582.

174 *CSP Dom 1661–1662*, p. 149.

175 *Ibid.*, p. 246.

176 *Ibid.*, p. 264.

177 *Ibid.*, p. 272.

178 *Ibid.*, p. 303.

179 *Ibid.*, p. 506; G. A. Coppock and B. M. Hill, *Headington Quarry and Shotover* (Oxford, 1933), pp. 12–13.

180 *CSP Dom 1663–1664*, p. 92.

181 *Ibid.*, p. 94.

182 *Ibid.*, p. 465.

183 *CSP Dom 1665–1666*, pp. 113, 202.

184 *Ibid.*, p. 411.

185 C 5/44/90.

186 Little is known of James Parcall. His name occurs on a fine with Alexander Denton in property in Cuddesdon in 1637; C.P. 25 (2) Oxon, Trinity, 13 Charles I.

187 Richard Eldridge had been in 1618 a groom of the stable to James I, and he was associated with Richard Powell in several business affairs. See *Sixth Report of the Royal Commission on Historical Manuscripts*, appendix, p. 325; Masson, III, 478.

188 Thomas Tipping (born 1589) came of a family of some standing in Oxfordshire and Buckinghamshire. If I have identified him correctly, he was the great-grandson of William Tipping of Merton and Westcourt in Ewelme, Oxfordshire, the grandson of Thomas Tipping of Draycott (1544–1601), and the son of Sir George Tipping of Draycott and of

Worminghall or Worndall, Buckinghamshire. His brother William, vicar of Shabbington, Buckinghamshire, and author, nicknamed "Eternity" from one of his books, was buried in Waterstock, Oxford, in 1648/9; several cousins also held the living of Shabbington at various times. Another Thomas Tipping who might be an alternative identification, who lived in Wheatfield, the son of the former Thomas's brother John, married Elizabeth, daughter of Sir William Beconshaw of Hampshire, and died in 1693. This latter Thomas Tipping, a justice of the peace in 1680, was complained against in 1688 for not repairing "the Townesend gate that leadeth to Wheatley bridge." See *D.N.B.*, *s.v.* "Tipping, William"; *Oxford Justices*, pp. xxxviii, li, 67; Wood, *Parochial Collections*, pp. 289–291, 336–337; Wood, *Life and Times*, I, 143, 151–152; *ibid.*, III, 136; *48th Report of the Deputy Keeper of the Public Records*, appendix, p. 517.

[189] John Frinnor (variously spelled Finnor, Finmore, or Fynmore) was a malster of North Hinxsey, Abingdon, Berkshire. He was the grandson of William Finnor of Abingdon, Bachelor of the Civil Law and fellow of St. John's College, who died at North Hinxsey in 1646 at the age of eighty-seven. John's brother William, M.A. of Christ Church and archdeacon of Chester, died in 1686; his brother Richard was verger of Christ Church. John himself died in 1683 at North Hinxsey. See Wood, *Life and Times*, II, 377.

[190] Thomas Ball, B.A. of Oxford in 1621, became vicar of All Saints, Northamptonshire, in 1629, but died in 1659—too late to be the one named here. A Thomas Ball, however, was a witness to the will of John Cope dated April 5, 1659, and proved July 14, 1660 (113 Nabbes). A George Ball who may have been a relative witnessed a lease between John Rolle of London and Christopher Fyall of Stockenham, Devonshire, in 1648; it may have been the same George Ball who as executor signed Richard Powell's memorandum of August 21, 1634, asking respite from perfecting his grant of arms. He died in 1657, as his will (472 Ruthen) proves, and was buried at Forest Hill. He was tenant of Forest Hill under John Pye in 1650. See *Alumni Oxonienses, 1500–1714*, I (1891), 63; *Miscellanea Genealogica et Heraldica*, New Series, IV (1884), 39; Moulton, p. 197; Visitation of Oxford in 1634, Publications of the Harleian Society, V (1871), p. 334; Wood, *Parochial Collections*, p. 146; Hamilton, p. 86.

[191] A John Edwards, speaking as a "terræ filius" at Trinity College, Oxford, in 1663 was loudly hissed. Other John Edwardses are found: one an M.A. and fellow of Jesus College, who died 1678; another a fellow of Merton, who proceeded M.A. in 1678. The name occurs frequently in tax-lists of the 1660's in the city of Oxford. Our man is more likely to be the John Edwards of Forest Hill, who died in 1648, and whose will (1 Fairfax) was proved by his son John on January 1, 1648/9. A John Edwards of Littlemore died in 1635, and his will (82 Sadler) was proved in 1635. See Wood, *Life and Times*, II, 416, 420, 563; Salter, *Surveys and Tokens*, pp. 199, 224, 293.

[192] C 5/44/90.

[193] C 7/476/93.

[194] C 10/98/157.

[195] B.M. Add. MS. 24,501, f. 34.

[196] A John Spicer of Standon, Hertfordshire, was admitted to Gray's Inn in 1653. The family was settled at Little Offley, Hertfordshire. John Spicer brought a number of actions against various defendants. See *Gray's Inn Admission Register*, p. 264; C 5/559/19–24.

[197] C 7/483/43.

[198] Mary Morrison, *alias* Morris, of Blackfriars, was assessed £300 in February, 1647, by the Parliamentary committee; in April she was found to be the wife of Thomas Smith of Lime Street. See *Calendar of the Committee for Advance of Money*, p. 771.

[199] C 7/483/43.

[200] C 8/203/48 (the Powells' answer to Lowe, 1675.)

[201] Mary Roberts may be the woman of that name who sued Nicholas Curling in 1674, and the one who with her husband Richard sued Joseph Edlington in 1678. She may be the Mary, daughter of Sir William Glover, alderman of London, who married Barnes Roberts, who in turn died in 1610, though the dates make such identification almost impossible. Barnes and Mary Roberts had a daughter Mary, who died before 1634 without issue. Still another of this name was granted warrants for £20 on October 6, 1648, and on February 6, 1648/9, as co-payee with John Smith. See C 5/546/30; C 5/546/34; Middlesex Pedigrees, Publications of the Harleian Society, LXV (1914), p. 166; *Calendar of the Committee for Advance of Money*, pp. 1500–01.

[202] William Chilcott was the son of Robert Comyn *alias* Chilcott of Tiverton, Devonshire, and Ann, daughter of Waller Cade of London, merchant. He married Catherine, daughter of Thomas Billingsley of London, merchant, and had a daughter Ann and a son William. His brother Robert married Mary daughter of Robert Newman of London and had three children—William, Ann, and Sarah. It was probably the latter marriage which established the connection with Elizabeth and Osbaston Newman. See *Visitation of Middlesex in 1663*, ed. W. Ryley (1820), p. 12.

[203] The following pedigree, taken from the visitation of Middlesex in 1663 (ed. W. Ryley, 1820, p. 45), will show graphically the relationship of the various members of the Newman family concerned in this action.

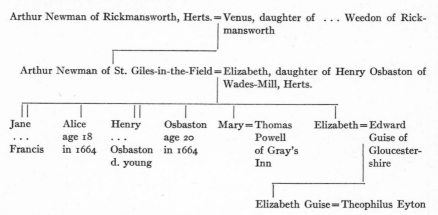

[204] C 7/572/42 (Powell's answer to Eyton, 1687).

[205] C 7/572/42 (Eyton's bill, 1687); C 5/176/2 (Newman's bill, 1688).

[206] George Lowe of Oxford was presumably identical with George Lowe of Calne, Wiltshire, M.P., who married Jane, daughter of Martin Wright, alderman of Oxford, as his second wife (she apparently having previously married Acton Drake). His wife died in 1655 or 1656. Their son Wright died in the Inner Temple in 1672. George Lowe himself, who in 1658 was a landholder in Oxford, and in 1673 was in Blome's list of gentry, died and was buried in Oxford in 1682 at the age of eighty-two. His heir and executor, Sir Edward Lowe of New College, Oxford, LL.D. and master in chancery, was the son of a Lowe of Fisherton, Wiltshire, by the sister of Edward Hyde, Earl of Clarendon. George Lowe was heavily assessed by the parliamentary commissioners in 1644 on his estate in Calne, but was discharged in 1647. See Wood, *Life and Times*, I, 198–199, 210; Wood, *Antiquities of Oxford*, I, 167; Salter, *Oxford*, pp. 12, 24; Blome, *Britannia* (1673), p. 416; *Calendar of the Committee for Advance of Money*, pp. 436, 726.

[207] See above, note 97.

[208] C 8/204/57.

[209] C 8/204/57.

[210] C 33/242, ff. 55, 111.

[211] *Britannia*, 1673, p. 417.

[212] C 33/242, f. 240v.

[213] C 5/519/35.

[214] Hope (or Hopton) Shuter was called to the bar in the Inner Temple in 1654, was called to the bench in 1672, was chosen reader in 1676, and after serving on various committees died and was buried in the Temple Church in 1677. He may have been Anne Powell's son-in-law, since one of her daughters married a Shuter. See *Inner Temple Records*, II, 313; *ibid.*, III, 84, 107, 451; above, Chapter VI, note 1.

[215] I have not found this document, but it is summarized in the following decree.

[216] Cooke was a Middle Temple man, called to the bar in 1654. He was master in chancery 1673–1699. See *Middle Temple Records*, II, 978; *ibid.*, III, 1070.

[217] C 33/242, ff. 322, 522.

[218] Keck may be either of two lawyers of the name. Samuel Keck was admitted to the Middle Temple in 1655, called to the bar in 1662, chosen bencher in 1681 and reader in 1689. He was master in chancery 1688–1711. Anthony Keck was called to the bar in the Inner Temple in 1659, and became bencher in 1677, knight in 1689, keeper of the seal in the same year, and M.P. for Tiverton in 1691. See *Middle Temple Records*, III, 1088, 1181, 1342, 1386; *Inner Temple Records*, II, 333; *D.N.B.*, *s.v.*, "Keck, Sir Anthony."

[219] C 33/242, f. 522.

[220] This honey-tongued Phillipps is impossible to identify without a Christian name, for many men of that surname were included on the rolls of the various Inns of Court.

[221] C 33/242, f. 765v.

[222] Sir Timothy Baldwin was master in chancery 1670–1682. Born in 1620, he was B.A. of Balliol College, Oxford, in 1638, and D.C.L. in 1652. He later became principal of Hart Hall, was knighted in 1670, became clerk of the House of Lords in 1680, and died in 1696. A conspicuous royalist, he is said to have encouraged Arthur Tillyard, the royalist apothecary, to sell coffee publicly, an act which almost caused a scandal. See *D.N.B.;* Wood, *Life and Times*, I, 201, 324, 328.

[223] Hewler has evaded my search.

[224] C 33/244, f. 358.

[225] C 7/598/77.

[226] A William Freeman, who married Susan, daughter of John Brent, counsellor-at-law, was rector of Stretton-on-the-Fosse, Oxford. Another William Freeman, described by Wood as "late of Preston Cromarch," married the daughter of John Biggs; in the church at Benson there was a brass to their son. A Ralph, son of William Freeman of London, entered the Middle Temple in 1640, the same year in which William, son of William Freeman of Blockley, Worcester, entered Gray's Inn. A William Freeman of Alpenden, Hertfordshire, is mentioned in the Visitation of London in 1634. Lowe's antagonist may be any one of these. See Wood, *Life and Times*, II, 370; Wood, *Parochial Collections*, p. 36; *Middle Temple Records*, II, 897; *Gray's Inn Admission Register*, p. 225; Publications of the Harleian Society, XVII (1883), 251.

[227] Ralph Manwaring may be the citizen and girdler of London whose will (124 Ruthen) was proved in 1657, or the Randulph Manwaring who was successively a sergeant-major, captain, and colonel under General Skippon, and whose son George became mayor of Chester in 1681/2. The Mainwarings were a populous and important family in Cheshire. See George Ormerod, *History of Cheshire*, II (1882), 429; *ibid.*, III, 80, 440.

[228] The name of John Clement appears frequently in records. One of Bridge Ward, London, was assessed £100 in 1644, and cleared his record in 1654. There were various John Clements in Plymouth in 1620. Another was rector of South Perrot, Somersetshire, in 1660, and a servant to the Marquis of Ormonde in 1685. The name appears often in Chancery suits of 1668, 1676, and 1677. See *Calendar of the Committee for Advance of Money*, p. 368; Visitation of Devon, Publications of the Harleian Society, VI (1872), 338; *Seventh Report of the Royal Commission on Historical Manuscripts*, appendix, pp. 101, 817; C 5/461/120–122.

[229] Possibly a mistake for Mary Roberts, or a relative.

[230] George Clarkson may have been related to the "seeker" Laurence Clarkson. In 1653 (?) he bought part of the estate of Sir William Fenwick in Northumberland. In 1660 he sued James and Dorothy Gibbons over money and property in Middlesex. See Masson, III, 153; *Calendar of the Committee for Compounding*, p. 2748; C 5/461/90.

[231] C 7/598/77.

[232] C 33/244, f. 358.

[233] C 33/244, f. 530.

[234] C 8/203/48.

[235] See Chapter IX.

[236] Simon Cleaver, probably the third son of Robert Cleaver of Over or Upper Bodington near Banbury, was born at Bodington in 1580. Another of the same name, possibly the one who matriculated as pensioner of St. John's College, Cambridge, in 1647, is mentioned by Wood as a witty blind preacher. See *Miscellanea Genealogica et Heraldica*, II (1876), 304; Wood, *Life and Times*, II, 244; Venn and Venn, *The Book of Matriculations*, p. 155.

[237] Thomas Bennett is probably Sir Thomas Bennet, judge, member of Gray's Inn, master in chancery 1635–1670. The family appears to have come from Berkshire. It was probably a different Thomas Bennett, who may nevertheless be Powell's creditor, who was assessed 7s. poll-tax in 1667 in St. Ebbe's parish, Oxford. See *D.N.B.*; Middlesex Pedigrees, 1634, Publications of the Harleian Society, LXV (1914), pp. 178–179; Salter, *Surveys and Tokens*, p. 306.

[238] Margery Lupworth (or Lapworth) was one of the large group of royalists in Oxford and other counties who lent money in December, 1648, for the king's service on the Oxford engagement. She may have been the wife of Edward Lupworth, Doctor of Physic of Oxford (born 1622), whose daughter Anne married William Lyde *alias* Joyner, who will appear later in this book. Another Margery Lapworth was buried in Oxford in 1643. See *Calendar of the Committee for Advance of Money*, p. 999; Wood, *Athenæ Oxonienses*, IV (ed. Bliss), col. 587; Wood, *Antiquities of Oxford*, III, 244.

[239] I have discovered no trace of Jane Cholder.

[240] A Thomas Overman matriculated at Cambridge in 1629, and proceeded B.A. in 1632–33, and M.A. in 1636. Either he or another Thomas Overman was a soap-boiler of Southwark, who was prosecuted in the Star Chamber in 1633, fined, imprisoned twenty-five months, and forbidden to work again at his trade. He reverted to it, however, and was often involved in suits and petitions later. The commissioners for sequestrations in the county of Surrey certified in January, 1650/1, that he was never sequestered nor questioned for delinquency, but that he had lived quietly and peaceably during the "troubles," and had borne his proportion in the public charge. Yet he had been heavily fined in 1643 and placed in custody in 1644. After some bother and after his death, the assessment laid on him in 1643 was finally cleared in 1654, and the "public faith" granted to his son Thomas Overman. See Venn and Venn, *The Book of Matriculations*, p. 502; *Fifth Report of the Royal Commission on Historical Manuscripts*, appendix, p. 88; *Sixth Report*, appendix, pp. 4, 42; *Calendar of the Committee for Compounding*, p. 403; *Calendar of the Committee for Advance of Money*, pp. 309, 317, 1015.

241 Robert Styles sued Robert Johnson in 1670 over a marriage contract. There were two families of Styles in London in 1634, and others in Kent, but no Roberts. See C 5/632/126; Visitation of London, Publications of the Harleian Society, XVII (1883), 272; Hasted, *History of Kent*, I (1886), 224.

242 A James Heath was admitted to Gray's Inn in 1633. Another was the royalist historian (1629–1664), author of *A Brief Chronicle of the Late Intestine War* (1661), later continued by Milton's nephew John Phillips (1676). See *Gray's Inn Admission Registers*, p. 200; *D.N.B.*

243 C 33/246, f. 283.

244 C 33/246, f. 505v.

245 C 33/246, f. 621v.

246 C 5/540/83.

247 C 5/540/83.

248 C 7/572/42.

249 C 7/572/42.

250 C 5/176/2.

251 C 5/176/2.

252 C 5/76/27.

253 A perambulation is the ceremony of officially walking around a territory for the purpose of asserting and recording its boundaries (*N.E.D.*).

254 John Ellston of Forest Hill was a close friend of the elder Richard Powell, in whose will he was named as executor in case Mrs. Powell refused the office. He may have been a B.A. of Corpus Christi College, Cambridge, in 1619, or a pensioner of Emmanuel College in 1642. He seems to have died and been buried at Holton in 1669, and his wife Elizabeth in 1651. See Masson, III, 636; Venn and Venn, *The Book of Matriculations*, p. 233; Wood, *Parochial Collections*, p. 179.

255 Samuel Symonds (or Symons) was perhaps a pensioner of St. Catherine's College, Cambridge, in 1640, who proceeded B.A. at Christ's College in 1643–44, and M.A. at Pembroke in 1647. Two other Samuel Symondses graduated from Oxford in 1653 and 1674. A Samuel Symonds was assessed £300 in 1644 on an estate near Oxford. See Venn and Venn, *The Book of Matriculations*, p. 609; *Alumni Oxonienses*, IV, 1451; *Calendar of the Committee for Advance of Money*, p. 471.

256 Edward Hillyard was called to the bar in the Inner Temple in 1673 and became a bencher in 1696. See *Inner Temple Records*, III, 94, 329.

257 C 5/76/27.

258 C 5/73/36.

259 Richard Towersey of Holton, whose daughter Elizabeth married Gilbert Jackson, was a royalist of Wheatley in 1643, when with John Robinson and another he furnished a mare for the king's service. A William Towersey, who may possibly be related, sued a Jane Towersey in 1673 over property in Long Crendon, Buckinghamshire. See *Calendar of the Committee for Advance of Money*, p. 1117; C 5/567/66.

260 C 5/101/31.

261 C 33/Hil. 4 W. & M./f. 296.

262 C 33/Hil. 4–5 W. & M./f. 209.

263 Jane Brokesby was undoubtedly the sister of Ann Powell, wife of the younger Richard Powell. She brought suit against Katherine Symonds (perhaps a relative of Samuel Symonds, clerk, mentioned above), widow, in 1704. There were Brokesbys in Oxfordshire and Leicestershire. See above, note 1; C 5/228/10; Visitation of Oxfordshire, 1634, Publications of the Harleian Society, V (1871), p. 210; John Nichols, *The History and Antiquities of Leicestershire*, III, i (1800), 406.

264 Samuel Grascome (1641–1708) was a non-juror, rector of Stourmouth, Kent, till

deprived in 1690, and the author of many strongly partisan theological pamphlets. See *D.N.B.;* Thomas Hearne, *Collections*, I, 120.

²⁶⁵ Richard Holt was the son of Robert Holt of Castleton, Lancashire, LL.D. and fellow of All Souls' College, who died in 1673. Richard matriculated at Brasenose College in 1663, at the age of seventeen; but he must have transferred promptly to Gray's Inn, where he was admitted in 1664. He may have settled later at Stoke Lyne, where there were Holts living in 1634. See Wood, *Life and Times*, II, 274; *Gray's Inn Admission Register*, p. 296; Visitation of Oxfordshire, 1634, Publications of the Harleian Society, V (1871), p. 173.

²⁶⁶ *Forest Hill Book*, p. 16.

²⁶⁷ *Ibid.*, p. 16.

²⁶⁸ *Ibid.*, pp. 10, 12, 13, 15.

CHAPTER VII. NOVERINT UNIVERSI

¹ The material in this chapter was first presented (in slightly different form) by the present writer in *Harvard Studies and Notes in Philology and Literature*, XX (1938), 61–73. Selected documents are included in the Columbia edition of *The Works of John Milton*, Volume XVIII.

² See John Cowell, *The Interpreter* (edition of 1637), under "statute staple."

³ C 152/61.

⁴ On the history, form, and nature of statutes staple, see *Select Cases Concerning the Law Merchant*, Vol. III, ed. Hubert Hall, Publications of the Selden Society, XLIX (1932), *passim*.

⁵ On William Hearne, see Chapter VI, note 37.

⁶ Sir Nicholas Hyde, chief justice of England 1627–1631, was the distinguished uncle of Edward Hyde (1609–1674), Earl of Clarendon, and of Sir Robert Hyde (1595–1665), chief justice of king's bench 1663–1665. Sir Robert was the great-uncle of Anne Hyde, who became Duchess of York and mother of Queen Mary and of Queen Anne. See *D.N.B., s.v* "Hyde, Sir Nicholas."

⁷ Sir Thomas Hampson was a member of Gray's Inn, having been admitted from Oriel College in 1609 and called to the "grand company" of that Inn in 1632. He is occasionally referred to as "clerk of the statutes" in state papers of 1638 and thereabouts. See *Gray's Inn Admission Register*, p. 122; *Pension Book of Gray's Inn*, p. 310; *CSP Dom 1625–1649*, pp. 580, 611; *ibid.*, 1636–1637, p. 310 (evidently misdated); *ibid.*, 1637–1638, p. 173.

⁸ The name Thomas Gemm is odd, and may be an abbreviation. If it could be read as Gewin (for the writing is not entirely certain), then the man who gains notoriety by identifying the greatest literary person of the age might be Thomas Gewen, an Inner Temple man who was called to the bar in 1614 and chosen steward for the reader's dinner in 1632. A Thomas Gimmer (which is a possible reading) matriculated in 1624 at Milton's own college (Christ's). Wood also tells of one Thomas Gawen, later a Catholic priest, who while traveling in Rome "sometimes fell into the company of John Milton." I offer these assorted possibilities hesitantly, without feeling at all sure that any one may be the man in question. See *Inner Temple Records*, II, 81, 195; John Peile, *Biographical Register of Christ's College* (Cambridge, 1910), I, 362; *Athenæ Oxonienses*, ed. Bliss, IV (1820), 130.

⁹ *Michaelmas Term*, II, iii.

¹⁰ See above, Chapter II.

¹¹ *Michaelmas Term*, III, iv.

¹² The only other certain specimens of Milton's handwriting later than 1651 are (1) his signature to a salary warrant of January 1, 1654/5, and (2) his signature to the marriage allegation of February 11, 1662/3.

[13] L.C. 4/200, p. 265. A briefer entry occurs on the Recognizance Roll, L.C. 4/56.

[14] See below, Chapter IX.

[15] *The Attourney's Academy* (1630 edition), pp. 66–67; *Select Cases Concerning the Law Merchant*, III, lxxxvi *et seq.*

[16] *The Interpreter* (1637 edition), *s.v.* "exigent."

[17] C 228/6. For further examples of similar documents, see *Select Cases Concerning the Law Merchant*, Vol. III.

[18] William Lenthall (1591–1662), speaker of the House of Commons and a commissioner of the great seal. See *D.N.B.*

[19] William Cope, sheriff of Oxford, belonged to the important Cope family which we shall meet later. He had been appointed sheriff on December 1, 1646, and together with George Greenwood, Robert Harris, John Packer (Milton's pupil?), William Draper, John Cartwright, and numerous others, whom we shall also meet later, a visitor of the University of Oxford to inquire into royalistic tendencies on May 1, 1647. He was thanked for apprehending spoilers on May 4, 1647. See below, Chapter X; *Journals of the House of Commons*, IV, 733; *ibid.*, V, 161; *Journals of the House of Lords*, VIII, 589b; *CSP Dom 1645–1647*, pp. 550–551.

[20] John Hunt was a common name. A Cambridge graduate of that name became rector of Fritwell, Oxfordshire, in 1608, but probably moved away too early to be our man. Two John Hunts of Oxford matriculated at Oxford University in 1621 and 1626 respectively, the latter being the son of Richard Hunt of Oxfordshire. Our juror might be the tapster at the Bear Tavern who in 1667 paid a poll tax of one shilling. He would probably not be the John Hunt who lent £50-9-6 for the king's cause in 1648 on the Oxford engagement. See Venn, *Alumni Cantabrigienses*, II, 433; *Alumni Oxonienses*, II, 771; Salter, *Surveys and Tokens*, p. 227; *Calendar of the Committee for Advance of Money*, p. 999.

[21] A Richard Phillips from Shropshire who was postmaster of Merton College in 1651 was expelled in that year, but later taken back. Since he proceeded B.A. in 1651, however, he was probably too young for jury duty; and in fact, we know that he entered Balliol College in 1646/7 at the age of eighteen. More likely the juror was a cordwainer of that name, mentioned in a list of 1641/2. He later served as bailiff of the city of Oxford (1658), holding that office the year preceding Thomas Hore's tenure; and in the hearth tax of 1665 he was rated at three hearths, which was just half the number of William Michell. See Wood, *Life and Times*, I, 135, 166; Wood, *Antiquities of Oxford*, III, 38; *Alumni Oxonienses*, III, 1158; Salter, *Surveys and Tokens*, pp. 187, 430.

[22] William Sadler was a man of some property. In the hearth tax of 1665 he appeared under St. Mary Magdalene parish for four hearths, but for the hearth tax of 1667 he was appointed an assessor, and in the latter year he paid one of the highest poll taxes in the parish. He was taxed on £100 in money, and his tax on himself, his wife, and their three children amounted to £1-5-0, than which few inhabitants of the parish paid more. See Salter, *Surveys and Tokens*, pp. 208, 214, 274.

[23] Triumph de St. Paul was apparently not a university man, and probably not a man of much wealth. In the subsidy of 1648, when he was living at 140 High Street, Oxford, he was taxed only ninepence, which was comparatively low. At that time he was a neighbor of William Michell and William Cooper, two other jurors, and also of James Chesterman, the friend of Richard Powell. His daughter Elizabeth was buried in St. Martin's Church in 1642, and his wife Ursula in 1643. See Salter *Surveys and Tokens*, p. 164; Wood, *Antiquities of Oxford*, III, 232–233.

[24] John Slatford was rated at four hearths in the tax of 1665. *Job* Slatford, who was town clerk in 1694 and who died in 1706, was probably a different man. Anthony Slatford, his grandfather, who might just possibly be the Anthony *Slatter* mentioned as another of

the jurors, was a cutler by trade, served as bailiff in 1646, and was taxed 2/6 in the subsidy of 1648. See Salter, *Surveys and Tokens*, pp. 166, 195; Wood, *Antiquities of Oxford*, III, 37, 57; Wood, *Life and Times*, III, 450, 478–479, 489; *ibid.*, IV, 85.

[25] William Cooper may have been a graduate of Oxford, since several persons of his name matriculated within a range of dates which would make it possible for them to be alive in 1646, but we have too little information available to select any one. Similarly, several possibilities appear in the list of Cambridge students of this time, but with the identical limitations. But a William Cooper who was probably this juror was taxed in the subsidy of 1648 in Oxford, and the same man (?) was bishop's registrar at Oxford in 1688. See *Alumni Oxonienses*, I, 325; Venn, *Alumni Cantabrigienses*, I, 392–393; Salter, *Surveys and Tokens*, p. 164; Wood, *Life and Times*, III, 267.

[26] William Yanning has not been found.

[27] The best-known John Wild of this period was a bencher of the Inner Temple in 1628, a sergeant-at-law in 1636, a commissioner of the great seal in 1643, recorder of Worcester in 1646, judge of assize in various counties in the same year and subsequently in Oxfordshire, a member of the Council of State in 1649 and 1650, and a chief baron of exechequer 1646–1653 and 1660. But he was probably not the Milton juror of 1646, who was more likely the John Wild who in the subsidy of 1648 was taxed sixpence in St. Aldate's parish, and who (if he was the same man) was a carpenter in the occasional employment of the University of Oxford in the 1650's and 1660's. See *D.N.B.*, *s.v.* "Wilde, John"; Salter, *Surveys and Tokens*, p. 169; Wood, *Life and Times*, IV, 63, 66.

[28] James Colkyer has not been found.

[29] Half a dozen William Michells entered Oxford between 1576 and 1631, any one of whom might be our juror, though the college records reveal no connection with Oxfordshire. Several Cambridge men might similarly qualify. A William Michell who is probably our man was taxed tenpence in St. Martin's parish, Oxford, in the subsidy of 1648, and was assessed for six hearths in the same parish in the hearth tax of 1665. See *Alumni Oxonienses*, III, 1009; Venn, *Alumni Cantabrigienses*, III, 182; Salter, *Surveys and Tokens*, pp. 164, 186.

[30] Thomas Hore (or Hoare) may very well have been Anthony Wood's shoemaker and convivial friend, who was bailiff of Oxford in 1659 and who died in January, 1690/1. He lived in St. Martin's parish in Oxford, where he was taxed in 1665. In 1665 also he took a lease of a messuage in Oxford. He may have come of the family settled in Marston, who occasionally come into records; and several Oxfordshire Hores entered Oxford University. See Wood, *Life and Times*, III, 352; Wood, *Antiquities of Oxford*, III, 38; Salter, *Surveys and Tokens*, p. 186; Salter, *Oxford*, p. 225; Wood, *Parochial Collections*, p. 203; Visitation of Oxford, Publications of the Harleian Society, V (1871), p. 280; *Alumni Oxonienses*, II, 745.

[31] Anthony Slatter may possibly be the Anthony *Slatford* mentioned above in note 24; otherwise he has not been found.

[32] Walter Symons was a collar-maker, whose will (672 Wootton) was proved in 1658. He may have been the Symons whose estate near Oxford was assessed at £300 in 1644 and was discharged in the same year, though it is unlikely. He may have been related to the Symeons (the name could easily appear in this form) who have already been met in land-transactions in this vicinity, or to Samuel Symonds, clerk. See *Calendar of the Committee for Advance of Money*, p. 471; above, Chapter VI.

[33] Many Richard Clarkes (or Clerkes) appear in lists of this time. He may have been the Richard Clerke who was taxed two shillings in the poll tax of 1667 in the city of Oxford, and he is pretty likely to have been the Richard Clarke "of Bister, no gent.," recorded in the Oxford Visitation of 1634. The daughter of this last-named married Harrington Danvers of Cothrope. See *Alumni Oxonienses*, I, 282–283; Venn, *Alumni Cantabrigienses*,

I, 345; Wood, *Fasti Oxonienses*, ed. Bliss, I, 389; *ibid.*, II, 209, 210; Salter, *Surveys and Tokens*, p. 245; Publications of the Harleian Society, V (1871), 304, 334.

[34] It is possible that Thomas Church was the man of that name who, the son of Richard Church of Nantwich, Cheshire (the residence of Milton's third wife), matriculated at Brasenose College, Oxford, in 1634, and proceeded B.A. in 1637 and M.A. in 1642. Appointed a fellow in the same year, he was ejected in 1648, was restored in 1660/1, later became rector of Hethersett in Norfolk, and died at Oxford in 1677. Another Church, whose Christian name is not given, an officer of the Levellers, was among those routed and shot by Oliver Cromwell at Burford in 1649. A Thomas Church and his son Richard are found in a deed of 1602. See Wood, *Life and Times*, II, 366, 467; *Alumni Oxonienses*, I, 276; Wood, *Parochial Collections*, p. 65; Moulton, p. 90.

[35] Of William Platt nothing is known.

[36] See above, note 14.

[37] Hamilton, p. 103.

[38] See p. 123.

CHAPTER VIII. A GREAT BUYER OF LAND

[1] The following pedigree of Sir Robert Pye is based chiefly on the following sources: *D.N.B.;* Visitation of Berkshire, 1665–1666, Publications of the Harleian Society, LVI (1907), p. 270; *The Visitation of Middlesex, 1663*, ed. W. Riley, (1820), p. 43; John Burke, *Genealogical and Heraldic History of the Extinct and Dormant Baronetcies of England* (1841), pp. 433–434.

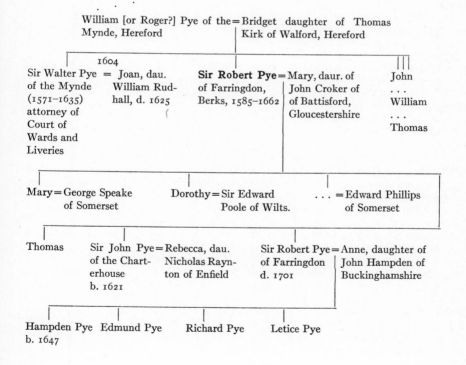

John Pye of the Mynde, Herefordshire

The Pyes, like Milton's other antagonists, were well acquainted with the courts. Without pretending to exhaustiveness I have collected notes on a good many suits in which they were involved. A list of some of them will suggest the background of the action against Milton. These references are taken from both manuscript and printed indexes in the Public Record Office.

PLAINTIFF	DEFENDANT	DATE	SUBJECT	REFERENCE
Attorney General	Robert Pye	Chas. I	Rickmansworth	E 112/232/75
Sir Robert Pye	Bevill	1634	Rickmansworth	C 2 Chas.I/P 6/32
Sir Robert Pye	Bevill	1634	Rickmansworth	C 2 Chas.I/P 55/17
Sir Robert Pye	Bevill	1638	Rickmansworth	C 8/41/9
Sir Robert Pye	Bevill	1638	Rickmansworth	C 8/73/62
Sir Robert Pye	Bevill	1638	Rickmansworth	C 8/83/85
Sir Robert Pye	Dr. Brideoke	1670	Farringdon	C 10/475/193
Sir Robert Pye	Simon Killigrew	1621	Laxton, Notts.	C 8/59/51
John Pye	John Lane	1663	Bradnemore	C 7/459/102
Sir Edmund Pye	Alice Moore	1650	Money	C 7/277/148
Michael Newman	Sir Robert Pye	1689	Westminster	C 5/90/8
Earl of Northampton	Sir Robert Pye	1687	Hardwick, Warw.	C 6/259/68
Earl of Pembroke	Sir Robert Pye	1652	Stepney, Msx.	C 6/149/50
Earl of Pembroke	Sir Robert Pye	1652	Stepney, Msx.	C 9/409/174
John Pye	Thomas Peck	1637	Debt	Req 2/389/331
Sir William Pelham	Sir Robert Pye	1639	Debt	Req 2/388/587
Sir Robert Pye	John Spragg	1654	Money	C 7/408/95
Robert Pye	T. Warr	1655	Marriage Contract	C 8/129/158
Robert Pye	J. Wodley	1656	Bosbury, Hants	C 8/121/140

In addition to these references, which I have not examined carefully, the name often occurs in the lists of the C2 Charles I proceedings, but I omit most of those here since without consulting the actual documents in addition to the indexes, as I had no time to do, it is impossible to discover more than the mere surnames of the parties. It might be added that Sir Robert Pye's name occurs occasionally among Oxfordshire fines. For example, he was concerned with Thomas Fettiplace in a transfer of property in Grafton in 1627/8, and with Thomas Prince in Grafton in 1630. He also held lands in Gloucestershire. See C.P. 25 (2) Oxon., Hilary, 3 Charles I, and Easter, 6 Charles I; *43rd Report of the Deputy Keeper of the Public Records*, appendix, p. 177.

² "To Master John Burges," *Underwoods*.

³ *Brief Lives*, ed. A. Clark, I, 422.

⁴ Wood, *Life and Times*, I, 63. Either Wood confused the Pyes, or the pun was a family affair, for on it Hoskyns based a farcical epitaph on Sir Robert's brother Sir Walter Pye, who died on December 26, 1635, and whom Hoskyns called "the Deuills Christmas Pye." See B.M. Add. MS. 23,229, f. 50, quoted in Louise B. Osborn, *The Life, Letters, and Writings of John Hoskyns* (New Haven, 1937), p. 87.

⁵ John Aubrey, *Remaines of Gentilisme and Judaisme*, Publications of the Folk-Lore Society, IV (London, 1881), 153–154.

⁶ Hamilton, pp. 85, 89; above, p. 81.

⁷ C 2 Charles I/P 10/15. The chief documents in this action were published by the present writer in the *LTLS*, 1935, p. 879, and 1936, p. 224; Milton's answer is included in Vol. XVIII of the Columbia edition of Milton's *Works*.

⁸ Bulstrode Whitelocke was a protégé of John Selden. Born in Buckinghamshire three years before Milton, he was admitted to the bar in the Middle Temple in 1626, chosen treasurer in 1628, elected M.P. for Stafford in 1626 and for Marlow in the Long Parliament, selected as chairman of the committee which managed the prosecution of Strafford, made parliamentary governor of Henley in 1644, and appointed one of the four commissioners of the great seal in 1648. He later held higher offices, and served widely in public affairs. He was also very busy as a private lawyer in 1647, being retained in thirty-nine cases in Abingdon, fifty at Oxford, thirty-eight at Shrewsbury, and thirty-six at Worcester.

Incidentally, he was to become a friend and colleague of Milton, one of whose letters to him has recently come to light. See *D.N.B.*; R. H. Whitelocke, *Memoirs, Biographical and Historical, of Bulstrode Whitelocke* (London, 1860), pp. 237–238; J. Milton French, "A New Letter by John Milton," *PMLA*, XLIX (1934), 1069–70.

⁹ "Kel. sen." is probably Robert Keylaway, master in chancery 1651–1660, though he might be any one of a number of people whose names begin with the letters "Kel" and appear in the registers of the various Inns of Court at about this time.

¹⁰ Lawrence Maydwell was six clerk 1629–1662.

¹¹ C 2 Charles I/P 10/15.

¹² Robert Aylett was master in chancery 1638–1655.

¹³ John Bradshaw was the famous regicide. After being called to the bar in Gray's Inn in 1627, and after several years as clerk to an attorney and as provincial barrister in Cheshire, he settled in London and rose to eminence. He served as counsel in several very important cases, such as the prosecution of the Irish rebels in 1641, the appeal of Lilburne in 1645, and the prosecution of Judge Jenkins in 1647. He was chosen commissioner of the great seal by the Commons in 1646, but the Lords refused to ratify his appointment. He became chief justice of Chester on the exact day of Milton's answer (February 22, 1646/7), and a judge in Wales a month later. He was subsequently to achieve notoriety by serving as lord president of the council appointed to try the king and by wearing the famous iron hat now on display in the Ashmolean Museum in Oxford. Milton's characterization of him is so fervent that it may pertinently be quoted here:

John Bradshaw (a name which will be repeated with applause wherever liberty is cherished or is known) . . . All his early life he sedulously employed in making himself acquainted with the laws of his country; he then practised with singular success and reputation at the bar; he shewed himself an intrepid and unwearied advocate for the liberties of the people . . . To a profound knowledge of the law, he added the most comprehensive views, the most generous sentiments, manners the most obliging and the most pure . . . . At home his hospitality is as splendid as his fortunes will permit; in his friendships there is the most inflexible fidelity . . . . If he undertake to plead the cause of the oppressed, to solicit the favour or deprecate the resentment of the powerful, to reprove the public ingratitude towards any particular individual, his address and his perseverance are beyond all praise. On such occasions no one could desire a patron or a friend more able, more zealous, or more eloquent.

This eulogy, though written years later, must have imbibed some of its warmth from the remembrance of Bradshaw's defense of him when Milton's own was a "cause of the oppressed," and when Milton must surely have had personal experience of the "splendid hospitability" here described. See *D.N.B.*; Milton, *Defensio Secunda, Prose Works*, ed. St. John (Bohn edition), I, 266–268.

¹⁴ C 2 Charles I/P 98/30.

¹⁵ C 33/192, f. 794.

¹⁶ E. A. Fry, *An Almanac for Students of English History*, pp. 136–137.

¹⁷ C 33/192, f. 794.

¹⁸ Wilcox may be Rowland Wilcox, who was admitted to the Middle Temple in 1598, or Sergeant John Wilcox of Wood Street, who died in 1652. See *Middle Temple Records*, I, 382; *The Obituary of Richard Smyth*, p. 32.

CHAPTER IX. MERCILESS TIGER

¹ The Ashworths were substantial people in Oxfordshire, of sufficient importance to have their pedigree entered in the visitation of 1634. Henry Ashworth, the son of Gervase Ashworth of Lancashire, married Ursula, daughter of John Edwards of Oxford, and had two sons. The elder, who married the daughter of Calibut Downing of Oxford, does not interest us; but Edward, the younger, does. He married twice: first, Elizabeth, daughter of Francis Duffield of Medmenham, Oxfordshire; second, also Elizabeth, daughter of Richard Wenman. By the first marriage Edward had two children, by the second, five.

Professionally, the family ran to medicine. Henry Ashworth received the degree of Bachelor of Medicine at Oxford in 1585, and of Doctor of Medicine in 1605. His son Edward got the first of these degrees, also at Oxford, in 1615. Henry died in 1633, long before the time of our story; his son Edward in 1648, six years before the first scene opens. About the former Anthony Wood tells one interesting fact. Together with John Cheynell of Christ Church, Ashworth was specially created a Doctor of Physic [or Medicine] on August 13, 1605, "because they were designed by the Delegates, appointed by Convocation, to be opponents in the disputations to be had before the King at his entertainment by the Muses in the latter end of the said month of August."

Henry Ashworth had also been party to a fine with one Richard Hodges over property in Shipton and Wychwood nearby in Oxfordshire in Michaelmas term, 1632. On February 21 of the same year Ashworth and his son Edward had also been sued by Sir William Cope of Hanwell over money. Cope protested that the Ashworths had put in suit against him at Common Law an ancient bond of 1613 for £200, though the bond had been paid long before. The Ashworths replied that it had never been paid,—as indeed it probably had not. The Cope family's business dealings, as we shall see, were so enormous and so intricate that with the best intentions Sir William could easily have been mistaken. See The Visitation of Oxfordshire in 1634, Publications of the Harleian Society, V (1871), pp. 251, 307; Wood, *Antiquities of Oxford*, III, 115, 235, 237, 242, 245; *Alumni Oxonienses*, I, 37; Wood, *Fasti Oxonienses* (1691), I, 171; indexes to wills in the Prerogative Court of Canterbury; C.P. 25 (2) Oxon., Michaelmas, 8 Charles I; C 3/399/85; below, chapter X. The following pedigree is taken from the same sources.

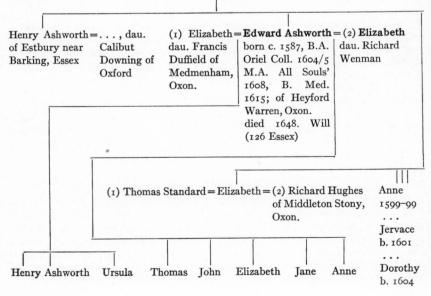

Gervase Ashworth of Lancashire = ...

Henry Ashworth, B.A. Oriel Coll. Oxon., = Ursula, daughter of John Edwards of Oxford, d. 1644; her will (71 Essex) pr. her 1572, M.A. 1577/8, B. Med. 1585, D. Med. 1605, died 1633, buried at Oxford. Will (109 Russell) | niece Anne Standard in 1648; buried at Oxford

Henry Ashworth = ..., dau. of Estbury near Calibut Barking, Essex Downing of Oxford

(1) Elizabeth = Edward Ashworth = (2) Elizabeth dau. Francis born c. 1587, B.A. dau. Richard Duffield of Oriel Coll. 1604/5 Wenman Medmenham, M.A. All Souls' Oxon. 1608, B. Med. 1615; of Heyford Warren, Oxon. died 1648. Will (126 Essex)

(1) Thomas Standard = Elizabeth = (2) Richard Hughes of Middleton Stony, Oxon.

Anne 1599–99 ...

Jervace b. 1601 ...

Dorothy b. 1604

Henry Ashworth　Ursula　Thomas　John　Elizabeth　Jane　Anne

² Symeon appears not infrequently in real-estate transactions in Oxfordshire. In one law-suit of the reign of James I he was named as mortgagor of Great Milton, Oxfordshire; and other fines and suits involving him and Oxford property have been noted in 1621–25, 1626, 1634, 1641, and later. See C 2 James I/A 8/1; C 3/330/24; C.P. 25 (2) Oxon, Mich., 2 Charles I; C.P. 25 (2) Oxon., Trinity, 10 Charles I; C.P. 25 (2), Oxon., Easter, 17 Charles I; and above, Chapter VI.

³ From a decree of June 5, 1657, C 33/207, ff. 1250–1251v.

⁴ See above, p. 77.

⁵ *N. & Q.*, XI, vii (1913), 21–22; *Inner Temple Records*, II, 239, 254.

⁶ Hamilton, pp. 128–130.

⁷ Thomas Estcourt was master in chancery 1653–1683.

⁸ C 10/44/2.

⁹ See above, p. 103.

¹⁰ See above, Chapter VII.

¹¹ See above, p. 73.

¹² C 22/759/17.

¹³ Sir Richard Crooke (or Croke) was later to achieve some reputation as a sergeant-at-law, a justice of the peace for Oxford in 1680, and a recorder of the city of Oxford. He married Elizabeth, daughter of Martin Wright, alderman and goldsmith of Oxford, and died in 1683. Wood says that he had a smooth, false, and flattering tongue, and that his religion was as venal as his tongue. He was the son of Unton Croke, also sergeant-at-law, a royalist; and his sons Wright and Charles Croke were both barristers of the Inner Temple. He was buried in Marston, Oxfordshire, with an inscription which describes him as "servientis ad legem per viginti annos Oxonii burgensis per triginta Recordatoris utrique Carolo dilectissimi Deo" (sergeant-at-law for twenty years, burgess of Oxford for thirty, recorder to both Charleses, and most dear to God). See *Oxford Justices*, p. li; Wood, *Life and Times*, I, 195–196; *Parochial Collections*, pp. 204–205.

¹⁴ George Bainger (or Banger), town clerk of Oxford, was the second son of Bernard Banger, esquire bedell in divinity in 1602, who died in Oxford in 1615. George's wife died in 1690, aged eighty or more. See Wood, *Life and Times*, I, 202; *Antiquities of Oxford*, III, 248.

¹⁵ Charles Holloway belonged to an interesting family of lawyers. Charles Holloway Sr., a sergeant-at-law of the Inner Temple, married Alice, daughter of Walter Darrell of Abingdon, counsellor-at-law, and died at Oxford in 1679, aged about eighty-four. He had a son Charles, a bencher in the Inner Temple, our present commissioner, born in 1627; a brother Richard, a barrister; an uncle, Richard, a notary; and a brother Francis, a mercer. They acquired a reputation partly complimentary and partly derisive, and Charles the younger was satirically nicknamed "Necessity" Holloway, because "necessity knows no law!" Wood gives amusing lines made on these five, matching the nickname or occupation of each with a punning description:

> Sergeant, Barrister, Necessity, Notary, Mercer—
> Gravely dull, ill-spoken, lawless, cum pergere, broken.

See Visitation of Oxford, 1634, Publications of the Harleian Society, V (1871), 290; Wood, *Life and Times*, II, 125–126, 469; *ibid.*, V, 48.

¹⁶ Edward Asteyn (or Aston, or Astyn) was an attorney of Oxford, a friend of Wood's. His wife was Grace Chesterman, daughter of John Chesterman and niece of James Chesterman, the friend of Richard Powell. His son James had matriculated at Queen's College, Oxford, in 1654, and was to become a barrister in Gray's Inn in 1664. See Wood, *Life and Times*, I, 40; *ibid.*, II, 269; *Alumni Oxonienses*, I, 39; above, Chapter VI, note 36.

¹⁷ C 22/759/17.

¹⁸ John Robinson was a man of fifty-five and a tenant to Milton in the premises under discussion. He was probably not too warm a friend of Milton's, for a few years before (1649–1650) he had been under investigation for lending money to raise a troop of horse for service under Prince Rupert. Though the prosecution had later been dropped for lack of definite evidence, the odium had probably clung to him. He was, however, to reappear in Milton's legal affairs nearly three years later, then to be described as of Horsepath, but still only fifty-five years old! He had been concerned in transfers of property in Wheatley in 1620, 1626, and 1639. He may possibly be the Oxford man who matriculated at Corpus Christi College in 1620 as the son of a clerk of Oxford; though since the editor of the registers of Oxford surmises that this John Robinson became vicar of Sonning, Berkshire, in 1628, such an identification may be erroneous. See *Calendar of the Committee for Advance of Money*, pp. 1117–18; C.P. 25 (2) Oxon., Easter, 18 James I; *ibid.*, Trinity, 2 Charles I; *ibid.*, Mich., 15 Charles I; *Alumni Oxonienses*, III, 1267; above, p. 139.

¹⁹ C 22/759/17.

²⁰ See above, Chapter VI, note 190.

²¹ It is tempting to identify this John Gadbury with the notorious almanac-maker (1627–1704), who was the son of a farmer, William Gadbury of Wheatley, and who in 1652 returned to Oxford from London, where he had studied under William Lilly, to work with Dr. Fiske. But the dates will not fit, for our deponent must have been born about 1611. He is more likely to be the person concerned in fines and Chancery proceedings of the 1620's and thereabouts. If so, he was party to a fine in Wheatley in 1623 and to one in Cuddesdon in 1629. He was the defendant in a suit about Garsington before 1624, and in another over money-affairs after 1625. He may, like the other John Gadbury, have been an almanac-maker, since Wood mentions one who died in 1668; and he may be the Gadbury who married a daughter of Richard Lyde *alias* Joyner of Cuddesdon. It seems a reasonably safe guess to venture that he may have been an uncle of the author of the *Ephemerides*. See Wood, *Athenæ Oxonienses*, ed. Bliss, IV, col. 9; *D.N.B.*, s.v. "Gadbury, John"; C.P. 25 (2) Oxon., Trinity, 21 James I; *ibid.*, Easter, 5 Charles I; C 2 James I/B 9/48; C 2 James I/B 16/58; C 3/412/153; Wood, *Life and Times*, II, 149; *ibid.*, III, 259.

²² I have found no information about John Trevis, unless he may be the John Travers who was a pensioner at Sidney Sussex College, Cambridge, in 1610, and B.A. in 1613/4; or the other man of the same name who matriculated as pensioner at Pembroke College in 1647. See Venn, *The Book of Admissions*, p. 676.

²³ Abraham Dickinson is known only through one trivial item, and that only by implication. In 1632 Leonard Diconson, son of Abraham Diconson of Sussex, S.T.D., *deceased*, was admitted to the Middle Temple. Our Abraham might possibly be a son of the deceased. See *Middle Temple Records*, II, 796.

²⁴ Nathaniel Hobart was master in chancery 1652–1673. The third son of Sir Henry Hobart, chief justice of the king's bench, he was admitted to Lincoln's Inn in 1615 and to the bar in 1622. His signature here looks like "Hoban," but must be "Hobart." See *Lincoln's Inn Admission Registers*, I, 170; *Black Books*, II, 236, 237.

²⁵ C 33/205, f. 1119v.

²⁶ Thomas Blount, *Glossographia*, 1670, p. 527, s.v. "publication."

²⁷ C 33/205, f. 989.

²⁸ *N.E.D.*, s.v. "de."

²⁹ C 33/207, f. 221 v.

³⁰ C 33/207, f. 809.

³¹ William Harrington was master in chancery 1655–1660.

³² C 5/405/2.

[33] Edward Peck was an Inner Temple man who had been called to the bar in 1642. See *Inner Temple Records*, II, 268.

[34] C 33/207, ff. 1250–1251v.

[35] Antony Collins was a Middle Temple man who had been admitted in 1639 and who was to become treasurer in 1676. See *Middle Temple Records*, II, 887; *ibid.*, III, 1299.

CHAPTER X. DICE OF THEIR BONES

[1] Since no account of Milton's transaction with the Cope family has been published (except for a few excerpts in Volume XVIII of the Columbia *Milton*), and since they were so influential and so litigious, it seems desirable to have some account of their pedigree and their legal activities. To avoid detaining the reader unduly in the text, I have relegated this account to the notes. Unless otherwise mentioned, the authorities for statements in this sketch are the following: (1) *Miscellanea Genealogica et Heraldica*, III, iv (1902), 208 ff.; (2) *ibid.*, New Series, I (1874), 240–241 (from Lady Elizabeth Cope's manuscript genealogy); (3) Wood, *Parochial Collections*, p. 30; (4) indexes to wills in the Prerogative Court of Canterbury; (5) indexes to inquisitions post mortem in the Public Record Office; (6) *Calendar of Patent Rolls*, 1494–1509, pp. 259–261 and *passim;* (7) private information. From the same sources, and principally from the first mentioned, comes the pedigree facing this page.

William Cope (1450–1513) of Banbury gained some little fame as cofferer (an officer next below the controller) to Henry VII, and in 1502 bought an estate at Hanwell near Banbury, the future Oxfordshire seat of the family. He was buried, however, in Banbury.

His son Sir Anthony (1491–1551; it will be observed that the favored masculine names among the Copes were William, John, and Anthony) was a noted traveler, spending a good deal of time abroad, visiting universities and learned men. He wrote a number of books, was the subject of an epigram by Mantuan, served as lord chamberlain to Queen Catherine Parr, died in 1551, and was buried at Hanwell (Wood, *Athenæ Oxonienses*, ed. Bliss, I, 192).

His grandson (for we may pass over his son Edward), also Sir Anthony (1549–1617?), illustrates some of the complexities of relationships which tangle genealogists. He married (1) Frances Lytton and (2) Anne Paston. His second wife later had at least two other husbands, and a daughter of one of them married his son by his first wife Frances Lytton. Lady Elizabeth Fane, wife of his grandson Sir John Cope, was married after the latter's death to his cousin William Cope of Icombe. Lady Elizabeth, Sir John, and their son Sir Anthony are the principal figures in the ensuing narrative.

Sir Anthony Cope was one of the foremost men of Oxfordshire, representing it in many Parliaments between 1571 and 1606. He was an ardent Puritan, as were the majority of his family, who in the seventeenth century led the persecution of an important rival family, the Catholic Stoners (*The Victoria County History of Oxfordshire*, II [1907], 46). Sir Anthony was sent to the Tower in 1587 for proposing in the House that all laws then in force touching ecclesiastical government be made void. He was knighted, however, in 1591, entertained King James at Hanwell in 1606 and 1612, held the office of justice of the peace for Banbury in 1608, and was created baronet in 1611. On his death in 1617, he was buried in Hanwell church. He made many enemies by his severity against recreations and country pastimes. John Danvers, then sheriff of Oxford, wrote to the lord chancellor in 1589 that Cope and others of Banbury, under the plea of religion, "were practising to abolish most pastimes used in the country, as May-poles, Morris-dances, Whitsunales, and others, to the great discontentment of Her Majesty's loving subjects" (W. R. Williams, *The Parliamentary History of the County of Oxford*, 1899, pp. 49–50).

His son Sir William (1577–1637), whose will (131 Goare) was proved by his son John, succeeded Sir Anthony in 1617 as second baronet. He was M.P. from 1604, with intervals, till about 1625, and held several minor governmental positions. He was admitted to Lincoln's Inn in 1614 (*Lincoln's Inn Admission Register*, I, 167). Joseph Chamberlain, whose letters to Sir Dudley Carleton furnish many intimate glimpses of people of the time, wrote in 1616 that Sir William Cope had missed being created baron by dallying too long about it (Williams, p. 51). In 1625 he was confined in Oxford Castle and later in the Fleet for debt, but was released to receive the king's visit at Hanwell (John Nichols, *The Progresses . . . of King James the First*, IV [1828], 1001).

Sir John Cope (1608–1638), son of this Sir William (his will, 179 Lee, was proved in 1638 by his relict Lady Elizabeth), forms one of the principal figures in our present study. Though a less important man than those we have been discussing, he married ambitiously —at least on the second occasion. His first wife was Mary, daughter of Sir John Walter, of whom little is known. In 1631, however, after her death, he married Elizabeth, daughter of Francis Fane, first Earl of Westmoreland (d. 1628), and Mary Mildmay his Countess. The earl in turn was the son of Sir Thomas Fane (died 1589), the politician, who was attainted for a share in Wyatt's rebellion but pardoned in 1554 and knighted in 1573 (*D.N.B.*, s.v. "Fane, Sir Thomas"). Lady Elizabeth would thus be sister to Mildmay Fane (died 1665), second Earl, royalist and poet (*D.N.B.*, s.v. "Fane, Mildmay"), and aunt of Sir Francis Fane (died 1689?), the dramatist (*D.N.B.*, s.v. "Fane, Sir Francis").

A few later members of the family may be briefly mentioned. A niece of Sir John Cope, Elizabeth, married in 1691 John Gouldsmith of Nantwich, and may thus have formed a very vague and distant connection with the Minshull family, which provided Milton with his third wife. A sister of Sir John's, Frances, married Robert Lee of Warwick, who will be mentioned later. Sir John's son Sir Anthony (1632–1675), locally famous as a scientific dilettante, a "great virtuoso," and a "miracle of ingenuity" (R. Plot, *The Natural History of Oxfordshire*, pp. 73, 127), plays a prominent part in the following proceedings. Finally, Sir John's son Sir John (1634–1721) fitly ends our account, since by marrying Anne Booth, a lodging-house keeper at Dunkirk, where he commanded a troop in 1660, he caused Hanwell to be willed away from their children. He succeeded his brother Sir Anthony as fifth baronet, however, and served as M.P. off and on from 1679 to 1700. He was also justice of the peace until removed in 1685, and was appointed deputy lieutenant in 1689. For a considerable part of his life he lived in Chelsea, but purchasing an estate in Hampshire in 1699, he was buried, on his death in 1721, at Eversley in that county (Williams, p. 64). A great deal more about the Cope family could be learned from a study of the many inquisitions post mortem in the Public Record Office, which I have not fully examined.

It has already been mentioned that the Copes were involved in many law-suits. I have collected a great many references to these, only a few of which, however, I have been able to study in detail. A hasty account of them, nevertheless, will illuminate the situation into which Milton precipitated himself by suing one of the family in 1654.

The earliest action which I have noted is of 1605, when Sir Anthony Cope put in his bill against Samuel Cockes touching claims on Wychwood, Oxfordshire (C 8/24/104). In 1610 he sued Thomas Gardiner about Enderby, Leicestershire (C 8/17/21), and Thomasine Greville about Sezincote, Gloucestershire (C 8/21/29). Between 1596 and 1616 Sir William Cope was sued by the University of Oxford over Oddington, Oxfordshire (C 3/283/86). In 1617 John and Sir George Symeon were plaintiffs and Sir William Cope defendant in an action over Great Milton and other properties in Oxfordshire (C 8/5/206; see also C 2 JI/C 12/72; C 2 JI/D 7/76; C 2 JI/D 9/11; C 2 JI/D 9/44). Edmund Webb sued Sir William Cope over Bainton, Oxfordshire, in 1619 (C 8/36/363; see also C 2 JI/A 3/2; C 2 JI/A5/30; C 2 JI/C 9/1). Sir William Cope in turn brought proceedings against R. Payne in 1620

Sir John Cope, who borrowed £150 from Milton in 1638. From the portrait at
Canon-ffrome Court, Ledbury, Herefordshire. Used by the kind permission of Mrs.
Sybil Hopton.

over a manor in Hethe, Oxfordshire (C 8/31/114). In 1621 he sued Sir George Coppyn and others over Wakering, Essex, about which there may have been earlier proceedings (C 3/304/4; C 8/55/212; C 2 JI/C 20/44). He was sued by Edward (or Edmund) Webb again in connection with Bainton between 1621 and 1625 (C 3/390/82), and by Henry Timberlake about Wakering between 1621 and 1625 (C 3/385/28-29). In the same years he or John Cope was sued by Sir John Rous about Farnborough, Warwickshire (C 3/375/25), by Henry Lord Mandeville over Tangley (C 3/366/55), and by Stephen Hall over Tangley (C 3/358/20). About this time, as if not already sufficiently worried from without, the Copes themselves began a civil war. Sir William sued George Cope in 1623 (C 8/23/35), George returned the compliment (C 3/342/46), and John sued Sir William over Farnborough (C 3/338/13), over Wakering (C 2 JI/C 4/54), over Bruern and Tangley (C 2 JI/C 14/55), and over Cottisford (C 2 JI/C 26/75), and George and Sir William over Carnokehill (C 2 JI/C 23/15). Richard Cope, son of Sir Anthony, sued Sir William over Tangley, etc. (C 2 JI/C 23/34). Sir William sued Sir John Lenthall in 1623 over Hardwick, Oxfordshire (C 8/23/30).

During the reign of Charles I there were endless actions, but since they are not always dated in the index, I omit many of them (the C2 Charles I series) here. Robert Holt, however, brought action against Sir William Cope in 1628 over Bainton (C 8/87/91), as did Edward Ewer in the same year (C 5/1/40). Sir William Cope sued Sir Simon Harcourt (probably a distant relative) in 1631 about Stafford (C2 Charles I/C 38/46), and was sued by William Styant about Wakering in 1631 (C 8/89/195). Early in 1632 Sir William Cope brought action against Drs. Henry and Edward Ashworth over a bond of 1613 which Cope asserted, but the Ashworths denied, he had paid (C 3/399/85). In 1632 Sir William Cope sued Ralph Holt over Bainton (C2 Charles I/C 12/6). In the same year he resumed his feud with Edward Ewer over Bainton (C 2 Charles I/C 40/9). In 1633 he sued Sir William Halton (C2 Charles I/C 28/59). In 1634 he sued one Garway over Wickham, Lincolnshire, evidently a quarrel resurrected from the previous reign (C 2 JI/C 22/82; C2 Charles I/C 58/41). In 1634 he sued one Nicholson over Marnham, Nottinghamshire (C2 Charles I/C 38/49), and Philip Holman about Warkworth, Northamptonshire (C 8/43/13), and was sued by Thomas Hill about another place in Northamptonshire (Req 2/390/623). Richard Cope of Banbury, a son of Lady Elizabeth and her second husband William Cope, brought a bill in 1634 against one Sprigge over Wakering (C2 Charles I/C 39/41). In 1635 Elizabeth Cope sued William Christopher over Compton, Gloucestershire (C 8/39/13), and was the defendant in a process begun by Thomas Bradley over Calston, Gloucestershire (C 8/38/86).

Full as this record seems, it is child's play in contrast to 1637 and 1638, which were jubilee years for the lawyers. In 1637 Lady Elizabeth Cope sued and was sued by Edmund Fisher over Wakering (C2 Charles I/C 76/9; C2 Charles I/C 86/7; C2 Charles I/F 27/63). Sir John Cope, now only twenty-nine years old but nearing his death, sued one Hobson over the Wool Keys in London (about which the Milton suit will have much to say— C2 Charles I/C 74/19), again sued Ewer over Bainton (C2 Charles I/C 66/66), was sued by Richard Evans over Hethe Manor (C 7/112/118), and sued Edward Cropley and others over the Wool Key in London (C2 Charles I/C 93/40). This last action concerned arrangements made by Sir William Cope in disposing of the Wool Key, Hartshorn Key, and property in All Saints Barking to Jasper Dartnoll in 1625, and frequently brings into discussion the names of Henry Timberlake and Richard Morer, of whom more will be heard later. It may be said in passing that in the London Directory of 1638 (T. C. Dale, *The Inhabitants of London in 1638,*—from Lambeth Palace MS. 272 [London, 1931], p. 5) the group of properties in All Hallows Barking which included the Custom House Key, Hartshorn Key, and the Wool Key were valued at £400, and that Jasper Dartnoll and William

Coltman, who came next on that list, were put down for £8 and £15 respectively. Finally, to keep up the family spirit, Sir William Cope sued Richard Cope over Hardwick (C 7/83/74), and also Lady Elizabeth Cope (C2 Charles I/C 4/56; C2 Charles I/C 71/55). This must have been nearly Sir William's last appearance in court, since he died in 1637.

In 1638 Sir John Cope sued Richard Morer over the Wool Key (C2 Charles I/C 82/26), and William Coltman about the same property (C2 Charles I/C 108/35). In reference to this last process there are some interesting certificates among the State Papers (*CSP Dom 1638–1639*, p. 493). George Scott, a grocer, certified in February, 1638/9, that Sir John Cope last year affirmed in his house in London that if Hartshorn Key were taken from Coltman, he was to abate him £220 a year of the rent he then paid. Nicholas Gibbon certified that Coltman told him, as they walked on the Custom House Key, that he rented Hartshorn Key and the Custom House Key together, and gave Sir William Cope £820 a year for the whole, that he could say more if he were compelled to, and that he could never talk with Sir William of renewing it under two, three, or even four thousand pounds. Other testimonies here and elsewhere (*ibid.*, p. 119) show that some of the proceeds of this property went to provide charity for the poor of Sevenoaks, Kent, probably in accordance with a testamentary provision in a will of some deceased member of the family.

Lady Elizabeth Cope also brought several actions in 1638 and 1639. She sued J. Child about Middlesex property (C 8/55/198), Elizabeth Stanhope about a bond of Sir John Cope to Sir John Stanhope for £150 dated 1631 (C 8/49/111), Richard Vivers about Banbury (C 8/254/23), Richard Stevens about Cottisford (C 8/86/102), and Jasper Dartnoll about the Wool Key (C2 Charles I/C 104/8).

In 1640 the actions continued, though with a slight abatement. Lady Cope sued Edward Fisher about Wakering (C 8/55/246; C 8/67/129; for depositions, see C 22/617/8) and about Potten, Essex (C 8/55/248), and was sued by Francis Ewre (C 8/56/83). In 1641 she was the defendant in a suit brought by Robert Rivers concerning Banbury and Hardwick (C 8/88/248). In 1642 or later another Sir William Cope, perhaps the son of our active but now deceased acquaintance, appeared as defendant in a suit brought by Partridge Ashton over lands in Lincolnshire(C 3/432/36). Thomas Cope became bound in 1641 to John Cope in a recognizance for £500 for property in Suffolk, and paid the debt in 1643 (L.C. 4/202, p. 256). Lady Elizabeth Cope was sued by George Shieras over Bainton (C 8/125/176). In 1643 Thomas Cope again gave a recognizance to John Cope, this time for £100, which he did not repay until 1647 (L.C. 4/202, p. 286). In 1645 Sir John Cope sued William Edwards over Tangley (C2 Charles I/C 23/40; C2 Charles I/C 35/6). In 1647 Sir Anthony and Lady Elizabeth Cope were sued by Martin Browne (C2 Charles I/B 42/17). In 1648 Sir Anthony Cope sued Robert Sheires (or Sheiras) over Bainton (C2 Charles I/C 64/64). In 1649 William and Elizabeth Cope sued Mary Cope over the estate of Anne Cope (C 8/314/16). William and Elizabeth Cope were in turn sued by Edmund Fisher over Wakering in 1650 (C 5/481/42). Sir Anthony Cope sued Thomas Bennet over Middlesex property in 1651 (C 8/106/75), and again in 1652 (C 7/83/135). In 1652 Thomas Baker sued William Cope, together with one Draper, one Loggin, and others over Oxford property (C 8/116/16). In 1653 Sir Anthony Cope sued Thomas Grant again over Hanwell (C 5/407/129; C 8/112/38), and John Cope was sued by Robert Jaques (C 5/378/99).

In 1654, the year in which Milton brought his action against Lady Elizabeth and Sir Anthony Cope, the former was being sued once more by Jasper Dartnoll over All Saints Barking, London (C 8/120/24). In 1656 Sir Anthony Cope sued Edward Sheirs (or Shieras), Loggin, and others over Stoke Lyne, Oxfordshire (C 8/55/159).

In 1658, out of all the welter of these mere lists and indexes, Sir Anthony Cope suddenly comes to life in a dramatic little incident told in the State Papers (*CSP Dom 1658–*

1659, pp. 69, 93). On June 22, 1658, Sir William Walter of Sarsden, Oxfordshire, petitioned the protector for redress against Sir Anthony Cope. Poor Walter had been bound to keep the peace under a general order for compounders for royalist properties, had been summoned to Oxford by Major Crook, and had been made a prisoner. On June 6, a Sunday, he went to the Carfax church and was placed where the mayor and aldermen sit. After the service Sir Anthony Cope came up to him and said, "Sir Walter, if I were not a good Christian, I would cudgel you; you are an unworthy fellow." Walter said nothing, but appealed for relief from such outrages. The council, much impressed, ordered out a warrant for Cope's arrest. When he came on July 13 in answer to the summons, it was ordered that Fiennes, Fleetwood, and the lord chamberlain should try to compose the differences between the two, and also that they should consider information against Cope in reference to Major Salway and others, and reprove and admonish him to prevent like occurrences in the future. Incidentally, Cope and Walter were relatives, since Sir John Cope, father of Sir Anthony, had married the daughter of Sir John Walter (*Miscellanea Genealogica et Heraldica*, Third Series, IV [1902], 214). There are two fine engravings of the Walters' seat at Sarsden in White Kennett's *Parochial Antiquities . . . of Ambrosden, Burcester, etc.* (Oxford, 1695), between pages 682 and 683.

In 1659 the proceedings of Edward Shieras against Sir Anthony Cope over Stoke Lyne were resumed (C 8/135/118). On February 13, 1659/60, when the petition of five thousand Oxford gentlemen, ministers, and freeholders was submitted to General Monk, begging that vacant places in Parliament should be filled, the secluded members admitted, no tax levied without their consent, the laws of land and property assured, the true Protestant religion defended, etc., the small group selected to deliver it included James Fiennes, Sir Anthony Cope, and Captain William Cope (*CSP Dom 1659–1660*, p. 361).

Here this recital may fitly end. Not that the legal actions cease with the Restoration: far from it. Sir John, Lady Elizabeth, Sir Anthony, Thomas, Anna, and other Copes continued to sue and be sued; the places concerned continued to include Wapping, All Saints Barking, Wakering, Hardwick, Hanwell, and Banbury. But the Restoration makes a fair stopping-place. Enough has been said to show that whereas Milton was in 1654 an amateur at law, the Copes were veterans. Though he might well have refrained from attacking so redoubtable opponents, he seems merely to have been, as with Salmasius and the Episcopalian opponents earlier, simply the more stimulated to energetic action.

[2] Robert Lee (or Leigh or Ley) was the husband of Sir John Cope's sister Frances. He was probably the Robert Leigh of Newnham Regis (or King's Newnham, just outside Billesley), Warwick, who entered Lincoln's Inn in 1616, and whose mother was Mary Egerton, daughter of Lord Chancellor Ellesmere. The Visitation of Warwick in 1619 does not give Robert's name, but it gives those of his parents and of several generations preceding; so that we can think of him as the son of Sir Francis of Newnham, the grandson of Sir William of Newnham, and the great-grandson of Sir Thomas, lord mayor of London in the first year of the reign of Queen Elizabeth. Sir Francis seems to have died about 1626 (his will, 15 Hele, was proved in that year; and another Sir Francis was created Baron Dumore in 1628), and Sir William about 1628 (his will, 52 Scroope, being presented for probate in that year, but incurring some litigation). There were related Lees in Middlesex and Buckinghamshire. A John Ley, who was born in Warwick in 1583, who became a prebendary of Chester, a member of the Assembly of Divines, a trier, and in 1656 rector of Solyhull, Warwickshire, and who later retired to Sutton Coldfield, where he died in 1662, was probably a relative. Robert Lee of Newnham appears in the royalist composition papers in 1654 as having an income from a rectory in County Flint. Altogether he seems to have been a man of some importance in his county. See *Lincoln's Inn Admission Registers*, I, 172; Publications of Harleian Society, XII (1877), 80–81; *ibid.*, LVIII (1909), 81;

ibid., LXV (1914), 159; *43rd Report of the Deputy Keeper of the Public Records*, appendix, p. 114; Wood, *Athenæ Oxonienses*, ed. Bliss, III, 569; *Calendar of the Committee for Compounding*, p. 3214.

[3] Thomas Offley is mentioned in records as a freeholder of Great Dalby, Leicestershire, in 1630, but not much is known of him. He may possibly have been the Thomas Offley, son of Robert Offley of London, who entered the Middle Temple in 1624, after the decease of his father. But the fact that his father was of London rather than Leicestershire, combined with the later circumstance that in 1649 this Thomas was still living in the Middle Temple, and in that year moving into Edward Eltonhead's chamber in Kellaway's Buildings, makes the identification unlikely. Most of the Offleys mentioned in wills filed in the Prerogative Court of Canterbury came from the Staffordshire family of that name, which of course may be related or even the chief branch of the family. Various Staffordshire Offleys were concerned in Chancery suits of the period following the Restoration. It was probably our Thomas Offley, however, who as servant extraordinary to the king took the league and covenant in 1644, paid a sequestration fine of £160 on property in Hertfordshire, and so was freed from further molestation. He was a party in 1635 to a marriage settlement concerning among others William Walter of Sarsden, a relative. See John Nichols, *The History and Antiquities of the County of Leicester*, Vol. III, part i (1800), p. 242; *Middle Temple Records*, II, 697, 976–977; C 6/78/42 (1676); C 6/70/60 (1668); C 5/622/8 (1703); *Calendar of the Committee for Advance of Money*, p. 484; *Journals of the House of Commons*, IV, 12, 29; Moulton, p. 26.

[4] Mary Mildmay, wife of Francis Fane, first Earl of Westmoreland (1583–1628), and mother of Lady Elizabeth Cope. Their son Mildmay, Lady Elizabeth's brother, became second earl, and his sons Charles and Vere succeeded him as third and fourth earls. See *D.N.B.*

[5] Lord Say and Sele was William Fiennes, first Viscount Say and Sele (1582–1662), a lifelong and powerful opponent of regal tyranny. He was a kinsman of the Copes, but I have not discovered the precise relationship. Clarendon characterized him as "a man of close and reserved nature, of a mean and narrow fortune, of great parts and of the highest ambition; but whose ambition would not be satisfied with offices and preferments, without some condescensions (and alterations) in ecclesiastical matters." He was made a viscount by the Duke of Buckingham in return for powerful aid, but he continued to lead the peers in their fight against king and court. He was an active director of colonization in America, founding Saybrook in Connecticut and Dover in New Hampshire, and he even contemplated settling here himself. But he was too ardent an aristocrat and anti-democrat despite his fight against tyranny. He was prominent in puritan councils, "the oracle of those who were called puritans in the worst sense" (Clarendon). The king tried to conciliate him by various preferments, including those of privy councillor, master of the Court of Wards, and commissioner of the treasury. But he became a lord lieutenant of Oxford and a commissioner of safety in 1642 and raised a regiment for the parliamentary side. When the popular cause threatened the life of the king, however, he cooled in his ardor, since he had "not the least thought of dissolving the monarchy, and less of levelling the ranks and distinctions of men" (Clarendon). After the king's death he retired from public life, though on the Restoration of Charles II he was appointed M.P. and a member of the privy council and lord privy seal. He died in 1662, having achieved such fame as an astute politician that he became known by the nickname of "Old Subtlety." See the *D.N.B.*; Arthur Collins, *The Peerage of England*, ed. Sir E. Brydges, VII (1812), 16–39.

[6] Cope's cousin Richard Knightley is mentioned in Lady Cope's genealogical notes of the family as one of the sponsors present at the christening of her son John in 1634. Either he or another of the same name was a member of Parliament in 1646 and 1648, the chair-

man of the Commons' committee on complaints in 1647, and a member of the Council of State appointed on February 23, 1659/60. He was also one of three trustees to whom, as friends of Penelope, Countess of Peterborough, Henry Mordaunt, Earl of Peterborough, conveyed various estates in Bedfordshire and Northamptonshire to secure her jointure on their marriage in 1648. Several Richard Knightleys had been admitted to Gray's Inn: one of Fawsley in 1584, another of Preston Capes in 1601, and the nephew (?) of the first in 1612. A possible though remote link with the family of Westmoreland appears in the fact that one Richard Knightley was the second husband of Mary, daughter of John Upton and Joane Stow. John Upton's first wife had been Elizabeth Bence; the wife of Vere, fourth Earl of Westmoreland, was Rachel Bence, to whom John Upton's second wife Joane Stow left a legacy in her will. Wills of several Richard Knightleys are preserved: Richard of Preston Capes (186 Harvey), proved in 1639 by his son Richard; and Richard of Fawsley (6 Grey), proved in 1651 by his son Richard. The latter is probably the Copes' friend, who was dead by 1656. His wife Jane appears to have died in 1658, when her will (538 Wootton) was proved. See *Miscellanea Genealogica et Heraldica*, New Series, I (1874), 240–241; *ibid.*, Second Series, III (1890), 156; *Calendar of the Committee for Compounding*, pp. 38, 125; *Calendar of the Committee for Advance of Money*, pp. 634, 644; *Journals of the House of Commons*, VII, 849; *Gray's Inn Admission Register*, pp. 61, 64, 101, 131; Arthur Collins, *The Peerage of England*, III (1779), 218–235.

[7] Giles Harris, formerly steward to the Copes, seems to have been a man of some means, whose home was in Churchill, Oxfordshire. He was one of a number against whom Alice Lady Moore brought information on March 5, 1650, to the commissioners. Although he was then deceased, the informer asserted that his wife enjoyed his personal estate to the extent of £3,000. The son of John Harris, who came from Gloucestershire, he married Judith, daughter of Walter Wallwin of Hereford; she survived him to die in 1654. Giles Harris died in 1647 and was buried in Churchill parish church. His wife Judith's will (348 Alchin) was proved in 1654 by her cousin Thomas Lodge. As we shall later meet a minister (of Drayton, Oxfordshire) named Thomas Lodge, and a Mrs. Elizabeth Wallin, these names may well be borne in mind. Henry Harris, also of Churchill, was brought in by Lady Moore under the same indictment as Giles, compounded for £30 on March 25, paid, and was discharged. In the same list occurs also the name of Richard Harris of Shorthampton, who had a personal estate of £200. The relationship between these three Harrises, though perhaps mentioned in the original papers, is not made clear in the calendars. See *Calendar of the Committee for Compounding*, p. 2209; Visitation of Gloucestershire, Publications of the Harleian Society, XXI (1885), 254; Wood, *Parochial Collections*, p. 94; below, p. 201.

[8] Robert Harris was a divine of some note. Wood calls him "a famed puritanical preacher," who, as minister at Hanwell, was one of the "chief promoters of the rebellion." A Gloucestershire man, he proceeded B.A. at Oxford in 1600 and B.D. in 1614. In the latter year Sir Anthony Cope offered him the living of Hanwell, which he obtained, against the wishes of Archbishop Bancroft, but not before he had taken an extensive examination from the bishop of Rochester, during which "they Greeked it till they were both run aground for want of words, upon which they burst into a fit of laughter, and so gave it over." His church was a favorite resort for Oxford students, and he also won fame in London as a preacher. Ejected from Hanwell in 1642 by royalist troopers, he went to London, became one of the Assembly of Divines, and got the living of St. Botolph's, Bishopsgate. He was a Visitor to the University for several years, received the degree of D.D. in 1648, and was chosen president of Trinity and rector of Garsington. His pluralities provoked derisive comments from the royalists, and his exorbitant fees for renewals of leases caused bitter feelings. Wood tells a scandalous story of him as president of Trinity, accusing him of appropriating two bags of money containing £200, concealed by a former president behind

the woodwork of the wall and discovered during Harris's redecoration. Harris published many sermons, collecting some of them into a volume in 1655. The most interesting in this connection is one entitled "Samuels Funerall," a sermon preached at the funeral of Sir Anthony Cope. In the epistle to the general reader Harris writes in the independent, puritanical tone which one associates with such poets as Wither: "as I never flattered him living, so will I not deify him . . . being dead. He had his wants, his faults, nor did we concur in all opinions; but . . . he much respected, and greatly countenanced every learned and unscandalous preacher; so most of all those that least favored his corruptions." See *D.N.B.*, *s.v.* "Harris, Robert"; Wood, *Athenæ Oxonienses*, III, ed. Bliss, 458–460; Wood, *Fasti Oxonienses*, II (ed. Bliss), 116; *The Workes of Robert Harris* (1635), pp. 207–229.

⁹ Edward Raleigh may be related to the Edward Raleigh of Burton-on-Trent, Staffordshire, of whose estate administration was granted to Michael Honyborne in 1635 (31 Sadler). More likely, however, he belonged to the Warwickshire family, in the pedigree of which several Edwards are recorded. An Edward, son of Sir Edward, early in the sixteenth century had married Anne, daughter of Sir William Chamberlaine, his daughter Bridget had married a Sir John Cope, and one of his great-grandsons had been Edward, possibly our man. See the Visitation of Warwickshire in 1619, Publications of the Harleian Society, XII (1877), 76–77.

¹⁰ John Draper was a servant of the Copes, a steward of high trust. We shall meet him occasionally later in the story. A William Draper who is probably a relative is often mentioned among composition papers as an active member of the county committee of Oxford, reporting in letters and receiving warrants, being in this work closely associated with the Thomas Appletree who caused Anne Powell so much distraction after her husband's death. He was an active parliamentarian, a captain of horse militia, a governor of Oxford, and a high sheriff of Oxford. John Draper, who was of Brewengrange, Oxfordshire, married a wife named Anne (who died in 1687), died himself in 1679, and was buried in Ascot under Wychwood. See Hamilton, *passim*; *Calendar of the Committee for Compounding*, pp. 152, 168, 172, 206, 576; *Journal of the House of Commons*, IV, 512; W. R. Williams, *The Parliamentary History of the County of Oxford* (1899), p. 55; Wood, *Parochial Collections*, p. 8.

¹¹ A Thomas Chaundler of Hyde Barton near Winchester (whose father George's will [26 Seager] was proved in 1634) was admitted to Gray's Inn in 1618. He petitioned in 1645 to compound as a delinquent and by 1647 had paid a fine of some £270. But since he died in 1650, he could not be the present deponent. The latter might however, be a son, or he might be related to the Thomas Chaundler of Stratton St. Margarets, Wiltshire, whose will was proved in 1656. See *Gray's Inn Admission Register*, p. 149; *Calendar of the Committee for Compounding*, pp. 970, 3264.

¹² There were several Richard Deanes. Three are mentioned in the composition papers, one a colonel and later a general, another a secretary to the army committee, and another a treasurer at war. Another again was a skinner and sheriff of London in 1619. The will of Richard Deane of London (345 Alchin), who was in the parliamentary service, and who owned lands at Sidenham, Oxfordshire, and elsewhere, was proved by his relict Mary in 1654. He may have been related to the Sir Richard, alderman of London, whose will (82 Sadler) was proved in 1635, and this latter in turn may have been identical with the previously mentioned skinner and sheriff. Of these various Richard Deanes, we cannot be sure which was the friend of Cope and the witness of his will; perhaps the one who owned lands in Oxfordshire is the best guess. See *Calendar of the Committee for Compounding*, pp. 120, 365, 2166, and index; *Gray's Inn Admission Register*, p. 155.

¹³ Elias Jackman belonged, as the indexes to wills prove, to a family with branches in

Oxfordshire, Northamptonshire, and probably elsewhere. The will of a Michael Jackman of Adderbury, Oxfordshire (92 Russell), was proved in 1633 by his sister Avis. Several Jackmans come into Chancery proceedings. For example, Alice Jackman brought action against Peter Yate in 1664 about Shipton under Wychwood, Oxfordshire, and Susan and Elias Jackman sued John Harrawell in 1662 over the estate of Martin Jackman of Northamptonshire. Elias Jackman's son William entered Trinity College, Oxford, in 1664 at the age of seventeen, received the B.A. from Gloucester Hall in 1668, and became rector of Wigginton, Oxfordshire, in 1683. In 1664 his father Elias was living in Drayton, Oxfordshire. See C 5/421/114; C 5/421/117; C 5/434/81; *Alumni Oxonienses*, II, 793.

[14] See p. 126.

[15] So many lawyers named Staunton attended the various Inns of Court that without knowing the Christian name it is impossible to identify Milton's lawyer with any certainty.

[16] Philip Smythe was six clerk 1644–1654.

[17] Two copies of the bill are extant: C 7/452/60 and C 8/120/72. The bill alone, with no other proceedings, is entered in the Six Clerks' Book, Ind 4106 (#2, Lambe). In slightly modernized form, it is published in the Columbia edition of Milton's *Works*, Vol. XVIII.

[17a] C 8/120/72.

[18] John Warrens are mentioned several times in the composition papers: one of that name as having a chamber in Gray's Inn in 1650, another of Symond's Inn as compounding and being fined £13-13-4 in 1651, and a third as of Bledington, Gloucestershire, who petitions about sequestered premises in 1652. Several John Warrens were of Gray's Inn: one admitted in 1610, another of Worcester in 1623, and another of Bedfordshire in 1634. One of Coventry was admitted to Lincoln's Inn in 1621. Various others, representing several other counties, appear among indexes to wills, and one of Westminster, cofferer's clerk to King James, is mentioned in the Middlesex pedigrees as the son of Thomas Warren of Stanton, Gloucestershire. The latter may very likely have moved to the adjacent county of Oxfordshire, and become the John Warren, gentleman, of Burford, whose death in 1660 is recorded by Wood, and who is probably our man. See *Calendar of the Committee for Compounding*, pp. 1860–61, 2249, 2795; *Gray's Inn Admission Register*, pp. 123, 171, 205; *Lincoln's Inn Admission Register*, I, 187; Publications of the Harleian Society, XXI (1885), 176; *ibid.*, LXV (1914), 39; Wood, *Parochial Collections*, p. 71.

[19] A William Webb was surveyor-general in 1649, another was lord mayor of London in 1591, another was a musician, another was archdeacon of Hereford, and still another was a bookseller in the parish of St. Peter's in the East, Oxford, in 1657. A William Webb of Wiltshire was admitted to Lincoln's Inn in 1589, and one of London to Gray's Inn in 1632. In the indexes of wills the roll of William Webbs is almost endless. With the exception of the bookseller, however, none of these is from Oxford, and therefore probably none of them is the commissioner of 1654. He was probably, however, the attorney of the King's Bench mentioned by Wood as having died in 1661, aged eighty, the father of ten children, and been buried in Burford; his wife Margaret died in 1667, also aged eighty. Two William Webbs, father and son, are frequently mentioned among the Burford records. It was probably a relative of the commissioner, a John Webb, who as a sequestrator in Oxfordshire in 1646 was partially responsible for the selling of Richard Powell's goods at Forest Hill. See *Calendar of the Committee for Compounding*, p. 164; Wood, *Athenæ Oxonienses*, ed. Bliss, III, 119; *ibid.*, 1691, I, xxvii; *Fasti Oxonienses*, ed. Bliss, II, 72; *ibid.*, I, 42; *Lincoln's Inn Admission Register*, I, 109; *Gray's Inn Admission Register*, p. 197; Wood, *Parochial Collections*, p. 75; R. H. Gratton, *The Burford Records* (1920), pp. 103, 214, 315, and elsewhere; Hamilton, pp. 88, 94.

[20] Wood mentions various Jordans of Asthall, Fulbrook, and Burford, and a John

Jordan of Whitney who died in 1692. The Burford man was probably the commissioner, since he was a man of considerable property and was associated with William Webb in property transactions. He may have been the John Jordan who petitioned in 1652 for the allowance of an indenture in Dorset. Blome in 1673 mentioned a John Jordan of Tangley. See Wood, *Parochial Collections*, pp. 9, 147, 186, 348; Gratton, *The Burford Records*, pp. 213, 214, 315, 403, 404, and elsewhere; *Calendar of the Committee for Compounding*, p. 2977; *Britannia*, 1673, p. 416.

[21] William Hastings has not been found, unless he was possibly (as is unlikely) the man of that name who, living in Dorset, petitioned in 1651 as an adherent of Parliament, and was granted the discharge from sequestration of a piece of property in Hampshire. See *Calendar of the Committee for Compounding*, pp. 2349–2350.

[22] C 8/120/72.

[23] The list of Sir John Cope's creditors has not been repeated in the text, since it is given in full in the appendix below. But this seems the logical place in which to furnish such biographical notes on them as have been found.

Of Alderman John Hilard, to whom Cope owed £200, I can find nothing. Various Hillards of Somerset, some of them named John, occur among the indexes to wills, but none that can be definitely identified with this alderman. Similarly several are mentioned in the London directory for 1638 and among the lists in Salter's *Surveys and Tokens*, but Cope's creditor cannot be tracked down.

Sir John Elloway (or Elwes, or Elwayes), to whom Cope owed £400, married the daughter and heir of Carew Raleigh. He was the plaintiff in several suits between 1669 and 1678, and had previously been involved in proceedings on sequestered estates. See Wood, *Life and Times*, III, 295; C 5/476/84–86; *Calendar of the Committee for Advance of Money*, p. 199.

A Mrs. Elizabeth Gay, perhaps the one who lent Cope £100, was the wife of William Gay of Hedd, Devonshire, and proved his will (186 Gray) in 1651.

Elias Jackman has been encountered before.

Sir John Hewet, to whom Cope owed £200, may have been a distant relative, since a Sir Thomas Hewett married Margaret, grand-daughter of a Dame Katherine Cope, whose will (20 Fines) was proved by Margaret in 1647. So many John Hewetts are found among indexes to wills that we can obtain no assistance from them. Cope's friend may have been Sir John of Headly Hall, Yorkshire, of Rickmansworth, Hertfordshire, and of Warsley, Huntingdonshire, who was created baronet in 1621. He may have been the Sir John Hewett whose case was under consideration by the House of Lords in 1641 and who was in hot water in his composition for sequestrated lands in 1651 on account of his supposedly having omitted some of his holdings in Rickmansworth. See Robert Clutterbuck, *The History and Antiquities of the County of Hertford*, III (1827), 202; *Calendar of the Committee for Advance of Money*, p. 1145; *Fourth Report of the Royal Commission on Historical Manuscripts*, appendix, pp. 58, 90.

I know nothing of Mrs. Mary Ridiard. A Thomas Ridiard of London, citizen and haberdasher, died about 1647, when his will (90 Fines) was proved by his relict Sarah. A Mrs. Mary Rudiard, who may be the lady we seek under a different spelling, and who was the widow of James Rudiard of London, proved his will (128 Fairfax) in 1649.

Thomas Offley and Edward Raleigh have already been identified.

Edward Fleet, of whom Cope borrowed £400, might be either the father or the son of a London family, since Edward Fleet married Mary Blagrave and had a son Edward. See Middlesex Pedigrees, Publications of the Harleian Society, LXV (1914), p. 75.

Sir Philip Stapleton (1603–1647), to whom Cope owed the largest debt, the huge amount of £6,000, was a parliamentary commissioner in Yorkshire in 1642, a colonel of horse in Essex's bodyguard and a leader in the campaigns of the first Civil War, and an opponent of the self-denying ordinance. For this latter recalcitrancy he was impeached in 1647, whereupon he escaped to Calais and remained there till his death later in the same year. His will (205 Fines) was proved in 1647 by his relict Lady Barbara and his sister Lady Margaret Wildgoose. From the size of the loan I judge that he was probably related to the Copes. See the *D.N.B.*

Mrs. Elizabeth Wallin, of whom Cope took £200, was probably a relative of Giles Harris's wife Judith, who was the daughter of Walter Wallwin of Hereford. She was probably the Mrs. Elizabeth Walwyn of Fifield, Oxfordshire, whose will (472 Ruthen) was proved in 1657.

James Libert has not been found, and no Malbon is mentioned among the printed lists of admissions to either the Middle or the Inner Temple. There were, however, several Malbons in London in 1638. See T. C. Dale, *The Inhabitants of London in 1638*, pp. 78, 189.

Robert Edwards, who loaned Cope £200, may be a relative of the John Edwards mentioned previously. He may, again, be the Robert Edwards of Denbighshire and Shropshire who died in 1651 (his will is 20 Grey). He was of Lledrod, where Sir John Cope held property. Or again he may be one of the Robert Edwardses who occur among indexes to wills as of Wiltshire, Middlesex, Southamptonshire, and other counties.

With Henry Jones of Chastleton we are on firmer ground. He was the son of Walter Jones (died 1632) and Eleanor Pope. He married Anne, daughter of Edmund Fettiplace of Childrey, Berkshire, died in 1656, and was buried beside his father in Chastleton. His son Arthur, listed by Blome in 1673 as of Chastleton, died of apoplexy in 1687. In Wood's time the lord of the manor of Chastleton was John Jones, and the patron of the living Thomas Greenwood, perhaps a relative of the George Greenwood to be named below. See Wood, *Parochial Collections*, pp. 84–85; *Life and Times*, II, 147; Blome, *Britannia* (1673), p. 416.

Sir Thomas Roe (1581?–1644) was a widely traveled public servant, ambassador to the Great Mogul in 1615–1617, to Constantinople in 1621, and later to various European capitals. He represented Tamworth in Parliament in 1614, Cirencester 1620–1621, and Oxford University 1640–1644. As ambassador to the East he helped to lay the foundations of the British Empire. His will (52 Fines) was proved in 1647 by his relict Lady Eleanor. Next to the £6,000 lent by Sir Philip Stapleton, his loan of £2,000 is the highest among the Cope debts. See the *D.N.B.*

Though Henry Cornish of Norton was a man of humbler rank than several of the preceding, he was a near neighbor of Cope's, and information about him is abundant. He was a burgess of the town of Chipping Norton and one of the signers of the report about that town at the time of the Visitation of Oxford in 1634. He founded a hospital nearby in 1640. He died in 1650, and his will (171 Pembroke) was proved in that year by his kinsman William Diston of Chipping Norton. Henry was a frequent name in his family. Henry, son of Henry, died in 1618, another Henry of Stanton Harcourt was canon of Christ Church, Oxford, and his son Henry was fellow of Lincoln College in 1683. Still another was sheriff of London and implicated in the "fanatic" plot of 1683. A William Cornish, undoubtedly a relative, with William Diston procured in 1635 a license to sell wines in Chipping Norton. See Publications of the Harleian Society, V (1871), p. 261; Wood, *Life and Times*, III, 68–70, 109, 131, 166; *Parochial Collections*, pp. 90, 93; *48th Report of the Deputy Keeper of the Public Records*, appendix, 542.

The family of George Greenwood, who (with Dr. Clapton) lent Cope £400, was of sufficient importance to be included in the Oxfordshire Visitation of 1634, in which he appears as George of Chastleton, second son of Thomas of Oxford, counselor-at-law, with a family in 1634 of two sons and three daughters. It is interesting to note that his wife was Elizabeth Jones, daughter of Walter Jones of Chastleton, father of the Henry Jones of Chastleton just mentioned, and that a Thomas Greenwood was at one time patron of the living of Chastleton. His will (65 Grey) was proved in 1651 by his relict Elizabeth. His son George lived till 1681, when he too was buried in Chastleton. See Publications of the Harleian Society, V (1871), p. 256; Wood, *Parochial Collections*, pp. 11, 58, 84, 85–86.

Dr. Clapton, co-furnisher with Greenwood of £400, was Anthony Clapton, B.D., who with George Greenwood, Sir Edward Clark, and Edward Lapworth, M.D., proved in 1630 the will (28 Scroope) of Anne, widow and executrix of William Lyde *alias* Joyner, who will reappear in the story further on.

John Draper has been mentioned before.

John Cartwright of Aynho, Northamptonshire, near Banbury, was a friend of Anthony Wood and a benefactor to Brasenose College; he died at Aynho in 1676. His son John of Aynho gave a collection of books to the town of Bloxham in 1685. See Wood, *Parochial Collections*, pp. 50, 113; *Life and Times*, II, 299, 357; *ibid.*, III, 299–300, 520.

Sir William Chauncy of Edgcote, Northamptonshire, proved the will of his father Sir Toby (77 Dorset) in 1609; his own (40 Twisse) was proved at Oxford in 1644 and two years later at London by his relict Lady Eleanor.

Robert Sanders, who furnished Cope £100, may possibly be the Oxford physician of that name whose will (74 Alchin) was proved in 1654. Probably the Deborah whose will (257 Brent) was proved in 1653 and the John, Doctor of Physic and provost of Oriel College, whose will (268 Brent) was likewise proved in 1653 were relatives. It may be noted, however, that Stephen Cope (born 1473) had married Ann Saunders of Oxford. See *Miscellanea Genealogica et Heraldica*, Third Series, IV (1902), 209.

John Dutton, who got a judgment on Cope for £140, cannot be positively identified. One of that name of Isleworth is mentioned in the Middlesex pedigrees, and many others appear in the Visitation of Gloucestershire. One of these was the son of Lawrence of Chedworth; another, son of William of Sherborne, born in 1594, had a sister Mary who married Sir Gerard Fleetwood of Woodstock Park, Oxfordshire. It is likely that Cope's creditor was related to this last branch. Incidentally, Lady Elizabeth Cope's elder sister Mary married Dutton, Lord Gerard. It is of course possible that our John Dutton may have been the father of William Dutton, Marvell's pupil and Cromwell's intended son-in-law. See Publications of the Harleian Society, XXI (1885), 53–55; *ibid.*, LXV (1914), 103; Arthur Collins, *Peerage of England*, III (1779), 218–235.

Omitting Lord Say and Sir Francis Fane, who have already been discussed, we can say little of "Katern Cull Cope," creditor for £5, whose name is so curious that one distrusts his own eyes on reading it. The nearest identification that I can offer is the Dame Katherine Cope just mentioned in connection with Sir John Hewett.

Peter Langston probably lived in Oxford. A certain Timothy Carter, making his will in 1632, bequeathed several houses in the parish of All Saints', Oxford, to his friend Peter Langston, "whom for his courteous and kind respects toward me I have adopted as my son." These kind respects extended also apparently to Sir John Cope, to whom Langston lent £24. The property bequeathed by Carter, unfortunately, later had to be mortgaged more than once, by either this same Peter Langston or possibly a son of the same name, then of Middle Aston, Oxfordshire. The mortgagor in 1682 was Anthony Wood's brother Christopher. John Aubrey, however, mentions a Langston who was an attorney in Worcestershire about 1614. See Salter, *Oxford*, p. 377; John Aubrey, *The Natural History of Wiltshire*, 1847, p. [118].

What precise relationship, if any, existed between the Lewis Harris who was Cope's creditor for £15 and the Harrises mentioned above has not become evident. The chances are that Lewis belonged to the Churchill branch of the family. At any rate, he married Alice, daughter of John Holloway of Oxford and of Alice, daughter of Myles Leigh of Oxford. I judge he is in no wise connected with the Lewis Harris of St. Martin's-in-the-Fields whose will (1 Harvey) was proved in 1638/9 and later (82 Harvey) contested; or with the Lewis Harris of Westminster and Carnarvonshire whose will (75 Evelyn) was proved in 1641. See Publications of the Harleian Society, V (1871), 290.

Thomas Lodge, minister of Drayton, was an Oxford man who matriculated in 1610 (or 1607), proceeded B.A. in 1611 at Magdalen College and M.A. in 1614, and became rector of Drayton in 1619. Here he remained thirty-two years, dying in 1651/2 at the age of sixty-one. He was probably a cousin of Judith Harris, wife of Giles Harris mentioned earlier; for his son Thomas Lodge (who proceeded B.A. at Oxford in 1639 and M.A. in 1642) proved her will in 1654, acting as her "cousin." See *Alumni Oxonienses*, III, 934; Wood, *Parochial Collections*, p. 127.

²⁴ C 8/120/72.

²⁵ The John Moore mentioned here was probably the son of Alice Moore of Henley-on-Thames, Oxfordshire, widow, whose will (92 Gray) he proved in 1651. Another John Moore appears as the deceased husband of Mary of Taynton, Oxfordshire, whose will (138 Bowyer) was proved in 1652. Probably related is Sir Francis Moore of Fawley, Oxfordshire, sergeant-at-law, whose will (98 Dale) was proved in 1621. A More was sued by a Cope during the reign of Charles I. Many John Mores (or Moores) appear in the indexes of wills and among lists of matriculations to the universities, but none of them from Oxfordshire. There was, however, a family of Moores, probably at least related, in Bicester. See C2 Charles I/C 23/52; Wood, *Parochial Collections*, p. 37.

²⁶ Thomas Loggin, who accommodated Lady Cope with £1,500, was probably of the family of the Loggins (or Loggans) of Idbury, Oxfordshire, where several monuments to them are to be found in the parish church. A John Loggan was vice-chancellor of Oxford University in Wood's time, and for a time incumbent of the livings of Adderbury, Hanwell, and Barford St. Johns and patron of Swalcliffe. Only the haziest information about Thomas has come to hand. A Thomas of Little Tew died about 1660, when his will (12 Nabbs) was proved, after he had proved the will of his uncle William of Swalcliffe (62 Pile) in 1636, and his son John had helped to prove that of his brother Robert of Idbury (411 Alchin) in 1654. The family was apparently on terms of close but not always harmonious intimacy with the Copes, since several suits between them have been found. John Loggin also sued John Barker in 1663 and was sued by Brome Whorwood in 1657. See Wood, *Parochial Collections*, pp. 1, 30, 162, 183, 291; R. Plot, *The Natural History of Oxfordshire*, 1677, p. 45; Blome, *Britannia*, 1673, p. 416; above, p. 192; C 5/411/58; C 5/411/57.

²⁷ Henry Timberlake was probably connected with the family of that name in Titchfield, Hampshire. The will of a Henry of Titchfield (63 Hele) was proved in 1626 by his relict Margaret and by William Styant, but various administrations on it were granted in 1639 and 1668 to his daughter Hester Jenour and to her granddaughter Hester Sawyer. A Henry Timberlake sued Sir William Cope between 1621 and 1625. Other Timberlakes who may be mentioned are John of Walton-on-Thames, Surrey (11 Pembroke, proved 1650), Thomas of Iver, Buckinghamshire (164 Bowyer, administration granted 1652), and Thomas of Hereford (1 Russell, proved 1633). Lady Elizabeth Cope's benefactor may have been the first-named Henry, or perhaps a son. See C 3/385/28–29.

²⁸ Sir Cope Doyley, it will be recalled from the Cope genealogy, was a distant cousin of Sir John Cope. His father, John Doyley, was the husband of Ursula, sister of Sir Anthony Cope, Sir John's grandfather. For generations the Doyleys had been settled at Chiselhampton, Oxfordshire. The will of a Cope Doyley (110 Russell) was proved in 1633. John, son of Sir Cope Doyley, who married Martha, daughter of James Quarles, procured license of entry on lands in Oxfordshire in 1635. See *48th Report of the Deputy Keeper of the Public Records*, appendix, p. 532, Visitation of Oxfordshire, 1634, Publications of the Harleian Society, V (1871), p. 325.

²⁹ *Lincoln's Inn Admission Register*, I, 167.

³⁰ *Gray's Inn Admission Register*, p. 112.

³¹ *Ibid.*, p. 133.

³² *Ibid.*, p. 187.

³³ Several Sanfords are eligible for identification as the Cope counsel. Thomas Sanford was admitted to Gray's Inn in 1586, Francis in 1606, and William in 1618; Henry entered the Middle Temple in 1618. See *Gray's Inn Admission Register*, pp. 70, 111, 149; *Middle Temple Records*, II, 628.

³⁴ C 33/204, ff. 475–475v.

³⁵ C 38/124.

³⁶ C 7/452/60.

³⁷ Thomas Blagrave was probably the same man who was one of the commissioners assigned to consider Anne Powell's petition in 1649. He was undoubtedly related to, perhaps a son of, the T. Blagrave of St. Ebb's parish in Oxford, groom of the privy chamber, who was buried in 1643, and who was probably the godfather of one of Anthony Wood's family. Another Blagrave, a bookseller of Oxford, is frequently mentioned by Wood in his journals. See Hamilton, p. 81; F. J. Varley, *The Siege of Oxford* (1932), p. 100; Wood, *Survey of Oxford*, III, 216; Wood, *Life and Times*, V, 8, and *passim*.

³⁸ C 7/452/60.

³⁹ There may be errors in the names of these places, for the spellings in Lady Elizabeth's answer make the towns difficult to locate. Most of them, however, are correct.

⁴⁰ C 38/127.

⁴¹ C 7/452/60.

⁴² By a stroke of irony two of these commissioners were sons of the man on whom they served the writ. James Fiennes, eldest son of "Old Subtlety," was admitted to Lincoln's Inn in 1628, became a member of Parliament and a holder of various offices, and succeeded his father in 1662 as second Viscount Say and Sele. Wood characterized him as "an honest cavalier and a quiet man." See *Lincoln's Inn Admission Register*, I, 205; W. R. Williams, *The Parliamentary History of the County of Oxford*, p. 53; *D.N.B.*, *s.v.* "Fiennes, Nathaniel," and "Fiennes, William"; *Collins's Peerage of England*, ed. Sir E. Brydges, VII (1812), 16–39.

⁴³ Richard Fiennes was a younger brother of James.

⁴⁴ William Dalby of Melcombe, Oxfordshire, was admitted to the Middle Temple in 1599 and left in 1604. See *Middle Temple Records*, I, 392, 402, 411, 428; *ibid.*, II, 450.

⁴⁵ When Barnabas Horseman's son Ralph (or Raphael) entered Lincoln College, Oxford, in 1681 at the age of sixteen, Barnabas was described as a "gentleman" of Banbury. Samuel, son of John Horseman of Banbury, gentleman, who followed Ralph to Lincoln College in 1699, was probably a relative. They were also probably related to the Horsemans of Haseley entered in the 1634 Visitation of Oxfordshire. John Horseman brought suit against Samuel Calcott about Banbury in 1678. Another relative may have been Nicholas Horseman, registrar to the Bishop and Archdeacon of Oxford, who supplied Anthony Wood in 1667 with some manuscripts which Wood desired to copy. The Horsemans may have been related to the Powells, Milton's in-laws, since in 1653 the will of Constance Horseman (235 Brent) was proved by her kinsman Richard Powell. See *Alumni Oxonienses*, II, 748; Publications of the Harleian Society, V (1871), 172; C 5/501/99; Wood, *Life and Times*, I, 325; *ibid.*, II, 121.

⁴⁶ C 7/452/60.

⁴⁷ Ind 1926, an index to Reports and Certificates (C 38).

⁴⁸ This John Williams is of course not the famous archbishop of York and lord keeper of the great seal, who, however, was an honorary member of Gray's Inn and of Lincoln's

Inn. But he may have been the John who was admitted to Gray's Inn in 1612, one of Monmouth admitted in 1634, or one of Anglesey admitted in 1635. Another was on a committee of Lincoln's Inn in 1658. John Williams of Dorset entered the Middle Temple in 1605, and one or two are mentioned in passing in the records of the Inner Temple between 1637 and 1654. The likeliest candidate here is John of Lincoln's Inn. See *Gray's Inn Admission Register*, pp. 130, 203, 208; *Black Books of Lincoln's Inn*, II, 422; *Middle Temple Records*, II, 459; *Inner Temple Records*, II, 234, 278, 310.

48a C 33/210, f. 310.

49 Williams, *The Parliamentary History of the County of Oxford*, p. 55.

50 C 33/210, f. 723v.

51 C 21/M 44/23.

52 William Dobinson has left little trace in contemporary records. In 1711, however, he (or a namesake) was living in Thame, Oxfordshire, as a "plebeian"; in that year his son Richard, later to be vicar of Fotheringay, Northamptonshire, entered Oxford. See *Alumni Oxonienses*, I, 408.

53 George Roberts was perhaps the man of that name who was bursar of Merton College, Oxford, in 1674, and who entertained Anthony Wood with scandalous tales about Sir Thomas Clayton, master of Merton. He was a boon tavern-crony of Wood's. See Wood, *Athenæ Oxonienses*, ed. Bliss, I, xlix; *Life and Times*, I, 390, 398, 433, 461, 507, *et seq.*

54 A Thomas Chamberlaine of Oddington, Gloucestershire, died before 1641, the year in which his will (18 Evelyn) was proved by his son John; but his son (?) Thomas entered Gray's Inn in 1653. A Sir Thomas Chamberlaine of Wickham and Banbury, Oxfordshire, died before 1627, when his will (20 Skynner) was proved; his son (?) Sir Thomas of Wickham died in 1681. A [blank] Chamberlaine of "Bishops Land," Oxfordshire, was the choice of the House of Commons for sheriff of Oxford in 1647. Many Thomas Chamberlaines of other counties occur among indexes to wills. The present commissioner is most likely to be either the sheriff or the younger Thomas Chamberlaine of Wickham. See *Gray's Inn Admission Register*, p. 264; Wood, *Life and Times*, II, 536; *ibid.*, III, 328; *Journals of the House of Commons*, V, 361, 372.

55 Richard Coxeter was probably a member of the family in Bampton, who were relatives by marriage of Anthony Wood. Wood mentions four of the name: (1) Richard of Cote in Bampton, who died in 1570; (2) his second son Richard, who married Margery Fowler; (3) the latter's second son Richard, who married Jane Woodroff; and (4) this Richard's eldest son Richard, gentleman commoner of St. Edmund's Hall, Oxford, in 1684, aged eighteen. Our examiner is very likely the third in this list, and perhaps also the Richard Coxeter of Bampton named in Wood's *Parochial Collections*. See Wood, *Athenæ Oxonienses*, ed. Bliss, I, cxxxix; *Parochial Collections*, pp. 16, 17; *Life and Times*, I, 42; *Alumni Oxonienses*, I, 342.

56 C 21/M 44/23.

57 C 24/835.

58 William Harington was master in chancery 1655-1660.

59 See p. 141.

60 Edmund Gyles was master in chancery 1655-1660.

61 See p. 142.

62 See above, note 15.

63 See above, note 18.

64 Johnson might be Ambrose Johnson, who was admitted to the Middle Temple in 1611; his brother William, who was admitted in 1614; or George of Wiltshire, who was admitted in 1645, called to the bar in 1654 and to the Bench in 1670, and chosen treasurer in 1679. Or he might be any of a large number who went to Gray's Inn. See *Middle Temple*

Records, II, 537, 581, 934; *ibid.*, III, 1070, 1251, 1323, 1355; *Gray's Inn Admission Register*, *passim*.

[65] Nothing has been learned of Thomas Richards.

[66] C 21/M 44/23.

[67] Richard Vesey (or Veysey) belonged to a family of Bampton and Chimney near Witney. He was perhaps the Richard Veysey, son of Walter of Bampton, "plebeian," who entered St. John's College, Oxford, in 1626 at the age of seventeen. There is no record of his having taken a degree. There were several Robert Veyseys who were undoubtedly related. The wills of two Roberts of Chimney, gentlemen, were proved in 1635 and 1656, respectively; and Wood mentions another who died in 1666. It was perhaps the first of these two who entered Oxford in 1618, and possibly his grandson Robert, named as son of Robert of Chimney, who entered in 1681. One Robert Veysey of Chimney signed a petition to the justices of the peace in Oxfordshire in behalf of a man who desired to set up an ale-house in Brittington (apparently a calling congenial to his family), and Wood commends him (or a namesake) for his charity in founding a free school in Bampton with an endowment of £300. A recent photograph of the George Inn, where the depositions were taken, may be found in Gratton's *Burford Records*, facing p. 64. See *Alumni Oxonienses*, IV, 1544; Wood, *Life and Times*, II, 88; *Oxford Justices*, pp. xxxvii–iii.

[68] Edward Lyde *alias* Joyner was the son of William of Cuddesdon or Horsepath, whose will (103 Hele) had been proved in 1626; and of Anne, daughter of Dr. Edward Lapworth, whose will (28 Scroope) had been proved in 1630 by a whole committee of executors, including Sir Edward Clarke, Dr. Edward Lapworth, George Greenwood, and Anthony Clapton, B.D. He was a brother of the William Joyner, fellow of Magdalen College, Oxford, who was the friend of Wood and Hearne; and a descendant of Robert Lyde *alias* Joyner of Dorchester, who married Anne, daughter of Richard Beauforest, and died in 1559. The family occasionally figures in Exchequer papers concerning this section of Oxfordshire. See Wood, *Life and Times*, III, 259; Wood, *Parochial Collections*, p. 116; *D.N.B.*, *s.v.* "Joyner, William"; Blome, *Britannia* (1673), p. 416; *38th Report of the Deputy Keeper of the Public Records*, appendix, pp. 221, 232, 288.

[69] Since the name of John Robinson is one of the three proverbially most common names in English, there is little hope of discovering him by ordinary casual search. There are, for example, thirty-five men of that name listed in the registers of Cambridge University between 1544 and 1659. It seems likely, however, that we can equate him with the John Robinson whose name occurs in land-transfers in Wheatley occasionally: *e.g.*, with Richard Powell in 1620 and again in 1626, and with Nicholas Field in 1639. He was probably also the John Robinson of Wheatley who was informed against in 1649 as a delinquent who had lent money towards raising a troop for Prince Rupert's regiment, but who was dismissed in 1650 for lack of sufficient evidence against him. See C.P. 25 (2) Oxon., Trinity, 2 Charles I, and Michaelmas, 15 Charles I; *Calendar of the Committee for Advance of Money*, pp. 1117–18. See also chapter IX, note 18.

[70] See above, p. 131.

[71] C 33/212, ff. 155–155v.

[72] C 24/835.

[73] In 1638 a William Bannister was living in Rood Lane, parish of St. Dionis Backchurch, London. A William Bannister received the LL.B. at Cambridge in 1632, being incorporated from Oxford. Many Bannisters are named in inquisitions post mortem in Lancashire. See T. C. Dale, *The Inhabitants of London in 1638*, p. 47; Venn and Venn, *The Book of Matriculations*, p. 37; Publications of the Record Society of Lancashire, Vols. III (1879), XVI (1887), XVII (1888), *passim*.

[74] William Lynn may possibly be the man of that name who was admitted to Emman-

uel College, Cambridge, in 1590 as a pensioner, but the fact that he is known to have been steward in 1659 to the Countess of Bath and Middlesex (Rachel Fane, sister of Lady Elizabeth Cope, who after the death of her first husband, Henry Bourchier, sixth Earl of Bath, in 1654, married in 1655 Lionel Cranfield, third Earl of Middlesex, who died in 1674; she lived till 1680) makes him almost too old for such an identification. He may, however, have been the William Lynn who in 1638 was living in Mincing Lane, St. Dunstan's in the East. See Venn, *Alumni Cantabrigienses*, II, 122; above, p. 143; G. E. Cokayne, *The Complete Peerage*, ed. V. Gibbs, II (1912), 19; *ibid.*, VIII (1932), 691–692; Dale, p. 49.

[75] William Sprigge was an attorney and a steward of New College, Oxford, and had been before that time a servant to Lord Say and Sele. His will (350 Alchin) was proved in 1654. According to Wood and to contemporary scandal, his son Joshua Sprigge was not only a noted Independent preacher but a gallant of Lady Say and Sele during the life of her husband, after whose death he married her. Later writers discount the scandal. See Wood, *Life and Times*, I, 177; *ibid.*, V, 71; Alfred Beesley, *The History of Banbury*, pp. 466–469; above, p. 191.

[76] C 33/212, f. 792v.

[77] C 24/835.

SELECTED BIBLIOGRAPHY

SELECTED BIBLIOGRAPHY

The following bibliography contains the titles of those books which are most often referred to in the text or which are most likely to be of service to the reader.

I. THE LIVES OF THE MILTONS

Athenæum (1880), I, 375–376, 565–566; *ibid.* (1884), I, 20; *ibid.* (1902), II, 722.
Documents concerning the elder Milton.

Darbishire, Helen (ed.), *Early Lives of Milton* (London, 1932).
Makes available the earliest biographies by Edward Phillips, Wood, Toland, Aubrey, the Richardsons, and the earliest anonymous biographer (whom the editor identifies with John Phillips).

Englische Studien, LV (1921), 40–45.
A fresh Milton-Powell document.

Hamilton, William Douglas, *Original Papers Illustrative of the Life and Writings of John Milton*, Publications of the Camden Society, LXXV (1859).
First publication of many composition papers connected with Milton's holdings of real estate during the commonwealth.

Hanford, James Holly, *A Milton Handbook* (New York, 1926, and later revised editions).
Sections on the biography and the bibliography of Milton.

Hunter, Joseph, *Milton. A Sheaf of Gleanings* (London, 1850).
Selected facts from Hunter's researches in the Public Record Office. Many other details are still virtually buried in his tantalizing manuscript, B.M. Add. MS. 24,501.

Marsh, John Fitchett, "Papers Connected with the Affairs of Milton and His Family," *Chetham Society Miscellanies*, I (1851).
First publication of various papers connected with the settlement of Milton's estate.

Masson, David, *The Life of John Milton*, 6 vols. and index (London, 1859 ff.).
The most extensive biography.

Notes and Queries, XI, ii (1910), 427.
New facts about the elder Milton as scrivener.

Parsons, Edward S. (ed.), "The Earliest Life of Milton," *English Historical Review* (January, 1902).
First publication of the anonymous biography.

Patterson, Frank A. (editor-in-chief), *The Works of John Milton*, 18 vols. (New York, 1931–1938).
Includes new biographical material, especially in Volume XVIII.

Raymond, Dora Neill, *Oliver's Secretary* (New York, 1932).
More factual than many recent books.

Richardson, Jonathan, *Explanatory Remarks on Paradise Lost* (London, 1734).
Some first-hand facts and traditions from Milton's circle.

Stern, Alfred, *Milton und seine Zeit*, 2 vols. (Leipzig, 1877–1879).
A mine of information about Milton.

Stevens, David H., *Milton Papers* (Chicago, 1927).
Newly discovered papers concerning real-estate transactions of the Miltons and other matters.

II. Law and the Courts

Baildon, W. P. (ed.), *Select Cases in Chancery, A.D. 1364–1471*, Publications of the Selden Society, X (1896).

    Though the material covered is far older than Milton's time, the procedure is similar and offers useful parallels and explanations.

British Record Society, Publications of the, 1888 ff.

    Useful indexes to Chancery proceedings, wills, etc.

Cowel, John, *A Law Dictionary, or the Interpreter* (1637, and earlier and later editions).

    Definitions of law terms.

Dowling, Margaret, "Public Record Office Research: The Equity Side of Chancery, 1558–1714," *R.E.S.*, VIII (1932), 1–16.

    A brief but helpful introduction to Chancery records.

Gilbert, Sir Geoffrey, *The History and Practice of the High Court of Chancery* (Dublin, 1758).

    Much information about legal actions.

Giuseppi, M. S., *A Guide to the Manuscripts Preserved in the Public Record Office*, 2 vols. (London, 1923–24).

    The official and complete guide to the records.

Gross, Charles, and Hall, Hubert (eds.) *Select Cases Concerning the Law Merchant*, (Publications of the Selden Society, XXIII (1908), XLVI (1929), XLIX (1932).

    Many illustrative documents and good introductions.

Hardy, Sir Thomas Duffus, *A Catalogue of Lords Chancellors, Keepers of the Great Seal, Masters of the Rolls, and Principal Officers of the High Court of Chancery* (London, 1843).

    I have used this volume constantly, without indicating specifically in footnotes, to identify officials of Chancery.

Herbert, William, *Antiquities of the Inns of Court and Chancery* (London, 1804).

Inderwick, F. A., *The King's Peace* (London, 1895).

    Essays on various English courts of law.

Leadam, I. S. (ed.), *Select Cases in the Court of Requests, A.D. 1497–1569*, Publications of the Selden Society, XII (1898).

    A companion volume to Baildon's (above) on Chancery.

Martin, Charles T., *The Record Interpreter* (1892).

    A concise dictionary of legal Latin, together with much useful information on contractions and similar matters.

Powell, Thomas, *The Attovrney's Academy* (1630, and earlier and later editions).

    Detailed contemporary notes on procedure in legal matters.

Public Record Office Lists and Indexes (1892 ff.).

    Indexes to Chancery proceedings, etc.

Tomlins, Sir T. E., *A Law Dictionary* (1810, and later editions).

    Similar to Cowel (above) but later.

Wright, Andrew, *Court Hand Restored*, tenth edition, ed. C. T. Martin (1912).

    Extensive glossary of Latin terms and names, with twenty plates of facsimiles of various kinds of writing, chiefly from legal documents.

III. Tenure of Property

Brown, W., *Modus Transferendi Status* (1698).

    Forms of fines and other means of transferring property.

Blackstone, Sir William, *Commentaries on the Laws of England*, 4 vols. (1765–69, and many later editions).
  The standard history of English law.
Lyttleton, His Treatise of Tenures, ed. Sir Thomas E. Tomlins (London, 1841).

IV. LAWYERS

Dugdale, William, *Origines Juridiciales* (1666).
  Describes the Inns of Court as they were in Milton's time.
Gray's Inn, The Pension Book of, ed. R. J. Fletcher (London, Vol. I, 1901).
Gray's Inn, The Register of Admissions to, ed. Joseph Foster (London, 1889).
  These two books, with several which follow, give chronological lists of members of the different Inns of Court. They are indispensable in identifying the various lawyers whose names constantly occur in the proceedings which are here presented.
Inner Temple Records, A Calendar of the, ed. F. A. Inderwick (London, 1896 ff.).
Lincoln's Inn, The Records of the Honorable Society of, (London, 1897 ff.).
Middle Temple Records, ed. C. H. Hopwood (London, 1904–05).

V. BIOGRAPHICAL REFERENCE WORKS

Aubrey, John, *Brief Lives*, ed. A. Clark (Oxford, 1898).
  Gossip about many seventeenth century people.
Calendars of State Papers, Domestic Series, passim.
County histories, proceedings of county historical societies, etc.
Dictionary of National Biography (1885 ff.).
Foster, Joseph (ed.), *Alumni Oxonienses*, 8 vols. (1887 ff.).
  The early series (Vols. I, II, III, 1891; Vol. IV, 1892) covers the years 1500–1714. Gives dates of admission and degrees and considerable supplementary information.
Harleian Society, Publications of the (London, 1869 ff.).
  Visitations of various counties, pedigrees, transcripts of many parish registers.
Historical Manuscripts, Reports of the Royal Commission on (1870 ff.).
  Full of information but laborious to use. An amalgamated index has been begun, but is complete only to the letter L.
Matthews, G. F. (ed.), *Year Books of Probate from 1630*, 8 vols. (1902 ff.).
  Offers possibilities of discovering further information through wills, administrations, etc. Covers the period 1630–1654 for the Prerogative Court of Canterbury only.
Miscellanea Genealogica et Heraldica, (1866 ff.).
  Genealogical items on thousands of persons.
Moulton, H. R., *Palæography, Genealogy, and Topography* (Richmond, Surrey, 1936).
  Reissue of 1930 sale catalogue of a large collection of original deeds, charters, indentures, etc. Thoroughly indexed.
Parish Register Society, Publications of the (1896 ff.).
  Transcripts of many local registers, chiefly in London.
Venn, John and J. A., *Alumni Cantabrigienses* (Cambridge, 1922 ff.).
  Lists, with considerable biographical information, of graduates of Cambridge University.

Venn, John and J. A., *The Book of Matriculations and Degrees . . . in the University of Cambridge from 1544–1659* (Cambridge, 1913).
  A companion volume for Cambridge to Foster's on Oxford.
Wood, Anthony, *Athenæ Oxonienses* and *Fasti Oxonienses* (1691–1692). The best edition is that edited by Philip Bliss (1813 ff.).
  Extensive biographical material on many people concerned in the present proceedings.
Wood, Anthony à, M.A., and Richard Rawlinson, D.C.L., Parochial Collections made by, ed. F. N. Davis, Oxfordshire Record Society, II (1920), IV (1922), XI (1929).
Wood, Anthony, The Life and Times of, ed. Andrew Clark, 5 vols. Oxford Historical Society (1891–1900).
  The last two collections furnish glimpses of hundreds of obscure figures of Milton's time, especially in the neighborhood of Oxford.
Wood, Anthony, *Survey of the Antiquities of the City of Oxford*, ed. Andrew Clark, Oxford Historical Society, I (1889), II (1890), III (1899).

VI. MISCELLANEOUS

Bartholomew, John, *A Survey Gazetteer of the British Isles* (1932).
  Useful for locating places mentioned in these actions.
Ordnance Survey Atlas of England and Wales (London, 1922).
Davies, Godfrey (ed.), *Bibliography of British History, Stuart Period, 1603–1714* (Oxford, 1928).
  Extensive list of informative books, well arranged.
Fry, Edward A., *An Almanac for Students of English History* (London, 1915).
  Useful calendars of all kinds.

APPENDIX
TRANSCRIPTS OF ORIGINAL DOCUMENTS

PREFATORY NOTE ON THE DOCUMENTS

IN the remaining section of the book are transcribed the principal documents on which the preceding narrative has been based. As explained in the introduction, the purpose has been to reproduce, as accurately as is reasonably possible, the form of the original manuscripts. Many scholars prefer to expand abbreviations, to normalize typography and spelling, and to correct obvious mistakes. Though I have completely modernized quotations in the text of the book, in a body of material like the following the opposite method seems preferable. For one reason, the reader is entitled—and probably desires—to have a minimum of editorial change separating him from the original records. Again, though errors of transcription are inevitable in any such compilation, they are likely to be minimized by the present technique. And it may not be of least importance that in this form the records may be of service to younger scholars as a closer and more realistic introduction to the study of manuscripts than transcripts which have been virtually rewritten.

One caution, however, must be added. No printed text can hope to reproduce with absolute fidelity a manuscript of the seventeenth century. Only a photographic facsimile can achieve such a result. Very few printing establishments are equipped with even a reasonable percentage of the multifarious contractions used by scribes of that period. No printer could reproduce exactly all the variations even in the placing of the superscript dashes which appear in an ordinary page of a bill or a decree in Chancery.

Nor is such exactness desirable in a book like this. The text here provided steers a hopeful course between the Scylla of photography and the Charybdis of complete modernization. No words have been extended: when "Defendant" appears in the manuscript as "Def^t", it appears here also as "Def^t." When "examined" is written "ēxd," it is also so printed. No letters, in short, have been added or subtracted by the editor, even though a grammatical disinclination to furnish a plural subject with a singular verb offers occasional temptations.

On the other hand, though all contractions have thus been retained, they have been somewhat simplified. The curious querks and twists and decorations which make some manuscripts look more like road-maps than the English language appear here in one or the other of three forms: an apostrophe, a superscript dash, or a superscript letter. Sometimes the particular choice is almost a matter for blind guessing, since one form often runs imperceptibly into another; but the editor has striven to be

as accurate as possible. Contractions have also been retained, such as
p for *per* or *par*, p for *pro*, ꝑ for *es* or *as*, and ȝ for *us* or *ue* (as *usqȝ* for
usque and *omnibȝ* for *omnibus*).

Because of these abbreviations, it is sometimes easy to mistake one
word for another which, fully extended, is radically unlike it. Thus *east*
and *defendant, domino* and *duo* become almost indistinguishable. A more
amusing mistake almost crept into these pages. The name of Edward
Lyde *alias* Joyner was first copied as Edward Lydeate, joiner, since the
alias appeared as *als* with a crossed *l* and was run closely into the Lyde.
If the reader desires an omnibus word combining the most common abbreviations, he may amuse himself with these two synthetic specimens:
ppūqȝ (*i.e.*, properumque) and pīꝑpibȝ (*i.e.*, parnipropibus).

So far, then, a well-equipped American press will go, though reluc-
tantly; but no further. With the help of such a book as Martin's *Record
Interpreter* or Wright's *English Court Hand Illustrated*, or even by a little
patient study of these transcripts, a student may get the feeling of the
system and in a very short time may move easily through these crypto-
graphic mazes.

The usage as to contractions is after all less erratic than might at
first appear, and a little practice soon makes a reader familiar with the
normal forms of words, though one should notice that each classification of documents has its own degree and method of shorthand. Familiar
letters use few abbreviations; Chancery proceedings about the same or
slightly more; common law records are pared almost to the bone. The
handwriting, incidentally, is different in these different classes, so that
one who is familiar with the chirography of the Close Rolls, let us say,
may need to learn all over before being able to read fines. Certain practices, however, are fairly general. Nasals frequently disappear, leaving
only a superscript dash, so that "examined" may be written as "exāied"
or "omnes" as "omēs." The ending "-tion" usually appears as "-cōn,"
as in "psecucōn" for "persecution." Common words like "complainant"
and "defendant" dwindle to "comp^lt" or "p^lt" and "def^t," with or without dashes above. To take a more radical example, in a decree "an attachment to the sheriff of Oxfordshire returnable within three weeks of
the feast of the purification" shrinks to "attachm^t Sherr Oxon ret tcō
purif."

The letters i, j, u, and v have been retained exactly as they appear in
the manuscripts, but long ſ has been uniformly altered to the modern
short s. Capitals and lower case letters, when I could feel sure, I have
printed regardless of modern usage, since the writers of these documents
were in this respect creatures of whimsy. Thus many sentences begin
with small letters, whereas unimportant prepositions may be dignified

Specimen deposition in Chancery (Ashworth *vs.* Milton). From the original
in the Public Record Office, London.

with flowing capitals. In many instances, however, I have been forced to choose. My consolation must be that the original writer's equanimity, if he could know about it, would not be seriously ruffled.

In many of the bills and answers there are spots which are utterly illegible. Sometimes a corner or a side has been torn away, sometimes the parchment or paper has become blackened so as to be unreadable, sometimes the handwriting is so cramped or written over or even (though not often) is so desperately bad that it cannot be deciphered. In such difficulties I have always printed brackets. If the missing words or letters can with reasonable assurance be supplied from comparison with similar documents, from other records in the same affair, or even from a justifiable conjecture, they have been included within the brackets, but no word or letter appears unbracketed which I have not felt reasonably sure was actually visible. Even when I could be positive what a word must be and could definitely read part of it, I have bracketed the invisible portion. When two or more copies of a record have been available, I have usually telescoped them into one composite text, wherever possible supplying illegible sections in one from legible places in the other, since the location of the blind spots seldom coincides. In such circumstances it has not seemed necessary to indicate which document is the source of each individual word or phrase.

The documents are grouped in the same order as the corresponding chapters of the text, with the individual items chronologically arranged within the groups. Each one is furnished with a heading consisting of several parts: (1) date, (2) brief descriptive title, (3) source (all references being to materials in the Public Record Office in London unless otherwise specified), and (4) modern reprints and discussions, if any. In most instances the last item does not occur, since few of these documents have previously reached print. For elucidation of classifications in the Public Record Office, the reader is referred to the Introduction (above). Since a few documents have been printed in Volume XVIII of the Columbia edition of *The Works of John Milton*, references to that volume are provided here.

The reader may be interested to know how these documents are arranged in the Public Record Office. To begin with, the proceedings proper are divided into several categories according to the time they cover or the six clerk who arranged them. Omitting those sets which fall entirely before or after the period in which we are interested, there are about nine sets of proceedings extant. The following table gives concisely the identification number and letter, the number of bundles, the dates covered, and the type of index available. (For further details, see Giuseppi, *A Guide*, I, 50–52.)

C2 James I	}				
C2 Charles I	}	2,240 bundles	{ 1603–1624	Printed index	
C3		480 "	1625–1649	" "	
C4		173 "	1557–1660	" "	
C5 (Bridges series)			Unlisted	No index	
C6 (Collins ")			Before 1714	Printed index	
C7 (Hamilton ")			" "	Manuscript index	
C8 (Mitford ")	3,615 "		" "	" "	
C9 (Reynardson ")			" "	" "	
C10 (Whittington ")			" "	Printed index	
			" "	Manuscript index	

The indexes to these proceedings vary a good deal in helpfulness. Some, as those to the C2 Charles I series, give no information beyond the last names of plaintiff and defendant. Others, as the C10 series, give in addition the full names of both parties and frequently the names of several other parties if there are such, the date of the suit, the place or matter of contention of the suit, and the county.

To find a suit may require the searching of the entire indexes from beginning to end. If one knows positively the name of the plaintiff, his task is comparatively simple. The names of plaintiffs in the index to each series are arranged in one alphabetical list, though not always in complete alphabetical arrangement within each letter. Thus one has merely to look through the names under the letter S to be sure to find a known action brought by John Smith. To be sure, he may have to search all ten sets before he finds the action, because there is no way of telling in which series it may be filed. And there is always the danger that the plaintiff he seeks may be accompanied by another, and that the action may be filed under the other name. If on the other hand he seeks a defendant, he must search the whole body of indexes till he finds it. The names of defendants, obviously, can not be alphabetized without making a second complete list; and that labor has never been deemed worth while. And if, as in the case of the present search, the scholar undertakes his task simply with the Micawberlike hope that something may turn up, he must perforce search the greater part of indexes, for both plaintiffs and defendants. Milton, for example, might easily have been (and was) either a plaintiff or a defendant; there being no evidence on record, both lists must be scrutinized.

One further fact which complicates the situation is that the different papers in one suit may, and often do, become separated. Theoretically, if one found the bill in a suit between John Doe and Richard Roe, it would be accompanied by the answer, and by such replications, rejoinders, pleas, or demurrers as were submitted. Actually, however, one frequently finds a bill in one bundle, an answer in another, and further papers elsewhere. They may even appear in different series. Thus in the Ashworth case below some of the proceedings are filed in the C5 series, and others in the C10. In the Cope case, some are in C7, others in C8. Thus the search becomes difficult.

Depositions covering our period are divided into three groups: C21, C22, and C24. The C24 are "town depositions," covering the period from 1535 to 1853, and consist of 2,508 bundles, arranged alphabetically by law terms. The C21 and C22 are "country depositions." C21 covers the period from Elizabeth to Charles I, comprises 767 bundles, and is arranged alphabetically. C22 covers 1649–1714, consists of 1,051 bundles, and is arranged alphabetically under each of the six clerks. All these sets are accompanied by manuscript indexes, but these are often very incomplete. To be sure of covering a period thoroughly, one would have to search through every bundle falling within the period. (Giuseppi, I, 50–52.)

There are 3,330 volumes of Reports and Certificates (C38), beginning with 1544 and ending with 1875. These are bound in volumes, within which the documents are alphabetically arranged within terms, and chronologically by terms. There are 267 manuscript volumes of indexes. (Giuseppi, I, 55.)

Decrees and Orders (C33) are entered in huge books measuring perhaps fifteen by twenty-five inches, and each containing 2,000 or more pages. The volumes are chronological in order, but within each volume the order is haphazard. The 1,262 books begin with 1545 and end with 1875, and are accompanied by 640 manuscript volumes of indexes. There is also a long series of decree rolls (C78–79), with corresponding indexes, but these are much less useful than the Books. (Giuseppi, I, 52–53.)

The Court of Requests, from which some of the material of the present book comes, was somewhat similar in function to that of Chancery. It was originally a court for poor men's causes only, but in the course of time came to take cognizance of almost every type of suit which could be brought in equity. Its life, however, was much briefer than that of Chancery. Whereas that court dates back to the dim antiquity of the reign of King John, and the extant proceedings come from as early as Richard II, there are no proceedings in Requests before Henry VII. And whereas the files of Chancery continue till 1875, when it was merged in the Supreme Court of Judicature, the Court of Requests was abolished about 1641.

Records of the Court of Requests are in a much more chaotic condition than those of Chancery. The Proceedings (Req 2) are arranged more or less by reigns, and comprise in all, from Henry VII to Charles I, 829 parcels. Approximately 150 of these have been arranged and indexed; to find anything in the others would require a search through every bundle and every document in every bundle. Since each bundle includes several hundred parchment bills and answers, such a task is virtually impossible. A rich harvest, however, may very likely await any enterprising searcher who ventures on such an undertaking. Such a search has been made once for the purpose of discovering Shake-speareana, which are now grouped in a separate category (Req 4). A few proceedings from the reign of James I and Charles I (including one set affecting Milton's father) are calendared in the manuscript index; the others remain virtually unavailable. (Giuseppi, I, 270–271.)

Accompanying these proceedings are the usual decree books, affi-davit books, witness books, and like records (Req 1). But, unlike the corresponding records of Chancery, these are incomplete, poorly pre-served, and very inadequately indexed. For that reason it is difficult to gather the complete records of a case in the Court of Requests.

The Court of the Exchequer (more accurately entitled the Court of Pleas in the Exchequer) had jurisdiction in all causes which concerned the king's profit or revenue. Process therein was open to any person who could show that his action against another person affected his debt to the king, and persons employed in the king's service at the Exchequer had the privilege of impleading and being impleaded in this court only. By legal fiction and the extension of opportunity similar to that which came about in the Court of Requests, it eventually became possible for a plaintiff to enter almost any personal action in the Court of Exchequer.

Process in this court was roughly similar to that in the other two courts just described: that is, by bill, writ, answer, and order. The bills, writs, and answers (E5) comprise 209 bundles, covering the period from 3 Edward III to 1855. Order Books (E12) in 81 volumes extend from 3 Edward VI to 11 George IV. (Giuseppi I, 173–177.)

CHAPTER I

AYLOFFE *VS.* MILTON

May 1, 1624

JAMES AYLOFFE SUES MILTON'S FATHER

Chancery Proceedings, C2 James I/A6/35

Primo Maij 1624
Euelyn

To the right honorable John Lord Bishopp of Lincolne Lord Keeper of the great seale of England.

Humbly complayning sheweth vnto your good Lordshipp your dayly Orator James Ayloffe of Melditch in the Countie of Cambridge Esquier That whereas one Edward Raymonde in or about the Moneth of ffebruarie in the ninetenth yeare of the Raigne of our Soueraigne the kingꝑ māᵗⁱᵉ that now is did borrowe and take vp at interest of one Joh Milton a Scriuener in London the suñe of ffiftie powndꝑ for six moneths for securitie whereof your Orator at the instance and requeste of the said Edward Raymonde and for his only and ꝓper debte and vppon his Confident affirmacōns to saue and keepe your Orator harmeles was Content to become bounde wᵗʰ the said Edward Raymonde as his suerty for the said money for six moneths onely and noe longer And accordingly the said Edward Raymonde together wᵗʰ your Orator as his surety did by their Obligacōn beareing date vppon or about the ninthe day of ffebruarie in the said nynetenth yeare of his Maiesties raigne become bound to one John llane in whose name the said Milton now affirmes he tooke the said bonde wᵗʰ Condicōn for repayment of the said fiftie powndꝑ wᵗʰ interest at the ende of the six months then next following or there aboutꝑ vppon the sealeing of wᶜʰ bonde Your Orator did declare to the said Milton that hee would not stand bounde as surety for that debte longer then only for six moneths and willed him that the said money might not be Contynued at interest vppon that bonde any longer then onely for that tyme when yf the said Raymonde fayled to make paymente he desiered him to make him accquainted therewᵗʰ to the ende your Orator might haue pʳssed the said Raymonde to haue satisfied that money and haue discharged him. But the said Milton for some rewarde given to him by the said Raymonde and by some agreementꝑ betweene them Did at the ende of those six moneths notwᵗʰstanding your Orators said Declaration receaue the interest then due for the said money and contynued the said money at interest for six moneths longer vpon

the said securitye and bonde w^{th}out the privitye or knowledge and
exp^rsly against the good will and likeinge of your Orator whoe for that
the said Raymonde tould him that the said money was then payed
And for that the said Milton neuer acquainted him wth the Contrarye
hee thought the same had bin satisfied by the said Raymonde soe as by
reason thereof your Orator resting secure that he was discharged did
not as otherwise he would haue done presse the said Raymonde to
satisffie the same but the same as your is since given to vnderstande
being by like agreement betweene the said Raymond and Milton and
for the like rewarde by the said Raymond given to the said Milton as
aforesaid at the ende of those sixe months Continued at interest for sixe
months longer and your orator whoe in the meane tyme had notice
that the said Debte was vnpayed at the ende of those last sixe moneths
pressing the said Raymond to make satisfaction of the said debte the
said Edward Raymonde and John Milton fell to a newe agreement concerning the said debte w^{th}out the privitie knowledge or assent of your
Orator whereby the said Raymonde agreed to pay pte of the said money
in hand or w^{th}in a fewe dayes after and to accknowledge a iudgment
for the residue and the said Milton did agree to deliuer vpp the said
obligacōn vppon the acknowledging of the said Judgm^t and to give the
said Raymonde longer dayes for the payment of soe much of the said
debte as was then vnpayd and to discharge your Orator from the same
or to such or the like effecte and accordingly the said Edward Raymonde
vppon or about the sixe and twentieth day of March in the one and
twentieth yeare of his ma^{ties} said raigne haueing before that payed a
great pte of the said debte to the said Milton or to some other to his vse
did acknowledge a Judgment before the Lord Mayor and aldermen of
the Citie of London in the Chamber of Gin-hale London to the said
John llane for one hundred powndǫ debt and one penny costǫ wch the
said John llane remitted to ffourty powndǫ wch iudgment though it were
in the name of the said llane yet as the said Milton nowe affirmeth yt
was for the benifyte and behallf of the said Milton and yt was by him
taken and accepted as in full discharge of the said Obligacōn and debte
therevppon And the said John Milton according to the said former
agreement did agree vnder his hand by way of defeazancing of the said
Judgment to stay execution for the residue of the said debte then
vnpayd wch came not to ffowerty powndǫ to be payd at ffower seuerall
dayes then to Come according to the former agreement and nowe all
past in the life tyme of the sayd Raymond by equall porcōns vppon the
accknowledgeing of wch Judgment allsoe the said obligacōn wherein
your Orator stood bound as suerty wth the said Raymonde was according to the said agreement deliuered vp to the said Raymond whoe

shewed the same to your Orator and tould him the same was discharged
after the accknowleging of wch Judgment the said Raymond satisfied
and payd to the said Milton all or wthin a small deale of the residue
of the said debte for wch the said Judgment was defeazanced as aforesaid vppon or very neere to the dayes agreed vppon soe as your Orator
neither is nor ought in equity to be Charged wth the said debte for w^{ch}
he stood originally bound wth the said Raymond as aforesaid But nowe
soe yt is may it please your good Lordshipp That not wthstanding the
said Judgment was taken and accepted by the said Milton in full discharge of the said Obligacon wherein your Orator as a suerty for the
said Raymond stood ingaged as aforesaid And that vppon acknowleging
of the said Judgment the said Raymond and Milton came to the said
newe agreement for the said debte as aforesaid And notwthstanding that
all or the most pte of the said debte for wch the said Judgment was
defeazanced as aforesaid either was or if yt were not might haue bin
satisfied in the life tyme of the said Raymond yf the said Milton either
had or would haue ᵽsecuted execution against him vppon the said
Judgment yet the said John Milton and John llane p^{r}tending that all
or the greatest pte of the said debte for wch your Orator stood bound as
suerty for the said Raymond as is aforesaid is yet vnsatisfied knoweing
that the said Raymond is lately deade soe as your Orator cannot make
proofe of the said agreement or payment℘ and haueing gotten into their
or one of their hand℘ the said obligacōn wch was formerly deliuerd vp the
said Milton hath ᵽcuered an action to be therevppon brought in the
name of the said Lane against your Orator at the Comon lawe and
intend℘ to recouer the penalty thereof against him contrary to all right
equitie and good Conscience, the p^{r}misses Considered And fforasmuch
as your Orator Cannot plead anything in barre to the said accōn nor can
be relieued against the same at the Comon lawe nor otherwise but in
equitie before your good Lordshipp in this honorable Court, nor hath
any securitie from the said Raymond or otherwise to saue him harm-
lesse from his said ingagement May it therefore please your Lordshipp
to relieue your Orator in equitie and to graunt vnto him his Maties
most gracious writt of subp^{n} to be directed to the said John Milton and
John llane thereby Cōmanding them and either of them at a certayne
day and vnder a certayne paine therein to be limitted to be and psonally
to appeare before your Lordshipp in his Maties most high Court of
Chauncerie then and there to aunswere the p^{r}misses and to stand and
abide such further order and direccōn therein as to your L$\bar{o}$^{p} in equitie
shalbe thought fitt/ And your Orator shall pray for your L$\bar{o}$^{p} longe lieff
and happines/

                                        Wm Gilbert. J

May 10, 1624

MILTON'S FATHER ANSWERS AYLOFFE'S BILL

Chancery Proceedings, C2 James I/A 6/35

Jurat.' Maij. 10. 1624.	The answere of John Milton Def^t. to
Jacobus Hussey	the Bill of Complainte of James Ayloffe
Saunders F	Complaynñte./

The said Def^t. saveing vnto himselfe all advantages of excepcōn to the incertaynetie, and insufficiency of the said Bill for answere therevnto saith; That true it is, That in or aboute the time in the bill of Complainte mencōned One Edward Raymond in the said Bill of Complainte named, and now deceased together wth the said Cōmp^{lt}. Ayloffe became bound by obligacōn to one John Lane in the sōme of One hundred poundꝑ for paym^t. of ffiftie two poundꝑ. and Tenn shillingꝑ On or aboute the Eleaventh daie of August then following. And this Def^t. beleeveth it to be true. That the said debte was the proper debte of the said Edward Raymond. and that the said Def^t. Ayloffe was onely bound as suertie for the same, And likewise saith that the said debte is truly and iustly due to him this Def^t. and that he vsed the name of the said John Lane as obligee in the said obligacōn only in trust for this Def^{tꝑ}. vse, But he this Def^t. doth absolutely denie, That the said Ayloffe did declare to him this Def^t That he would not stand bound as suertie for y^t debte longer then onely for Six monethes, or y^t he willed him this Def^t. that the said money might not be continued at interest vpon that bond anie longer then onely for that time as in the said Bill of Complainte is most vntruely suggested. And this def^t doth also denie y^t for anie reward giuen to him by the said Raymond, or by anie agreem^{tꝑ}. betweene them (other then the consideracōn for the said Six monethes paste) he did continue the said money at interest, but the money being payable on or aboute the Eleaventh daie of August in ye Nineteenth yeare of his Maties. raigne that now is of England, The said Def^t. was informed he colde haue no accōn in his Maties. Co^{rt}. of Comon pleas at Westm' against the said Raymond, and Ayloffe vntill Mīchas terme then folloing, and then this Def^t. sente to the said Raymond, and pressed him that in freindly and Curtuous mañ he wold repaie the said ffiftie poundꝑ or otherwise he should be compelled to comence suite both against him the said Raymond, and against the said Cōmp^{lt}. Ayloffe. And the said Def^t. haueing often called and sent vnto the said Raymond for his said Money, and finding that he cold not haue it by faire meanes in Hillary terme then following deliuered the said obligacōn to an Attorney in his said Maties. Co^{rt}. of Comon pleas at Westm' to comence suite against the said Raymond, and the said Cōmp^{lt}. Ayloffe But the said Attorney

acquainting the said Raymond therewth, he the said Raymond being
an Attorney in the same Co^{rt}.) intreated the said Attorney to make stay
thereof for that he intended to giue this def^t. p^rsent satisfaccōn. And
shortly afterwardę sent to this def^t. and entreated him either to forbeare
his money, or otherwise y^t he would bring his accōn in some Co^{rt}. wthin
the Citie of London to avoyde extraordinarie expences in suite of lawe,
And this def^t. (willing to spare the said Ayloffe as longe as he could
conveniently and to put the said Raymond to as litle charge as might
be) did accordingly bring an accōn in the Lorde Maio^{rs}. Co^{rt}. in the
Citie of London vpon the said obligacōn aboute the time in the bill
mencōned and pressing ye said Raymond either to haue a plea, or a
Judgem^t. He the said Raymond intreated the def^t to accepte of his
Judgement, and that he would grante him some respite of time for the
paym^t. of the said debte in respect (as he alleged) That if execucōn were
sued out against him, he should be forced to lye in prison, wch would be
his vtter ouerthrowe, and vndoeing, where vpon this def^t. (pittieing
his complainte) was content to accepte of Tenn poundę in hand, and the
remainder being ffourtie poundę to take by Tenn poundę a quarter,
and to loose the the forbearance, or interest thereof, (that is to saie) at
Midsomer laste Tenn poundę at Michās then following Tenn poundę at
Xrīmas laste, Tenn poundę, and the rest at the feast of Thannunciacōn
of the blessed virgin Marie then next following. and as this def^t. thinketh
there is a note entred vpon the said Judgem^t. but not anie defeizance at
all that if defaulte were made in anie of these paym^{tę}. then execucōn to be
prosecuted, And this defd^t saith That the said Raymond made paym^t.
of the said first Tenn poundę of the said remainder of ffourtie poundę
and dyed verry shortely after and soe there hath not beene anie other
paym^t. made sithence, And this def^t. doth absolutely denie, that he did
euer agree to deliuer vpp the said obligacōn vpon the acknowledging of
the said Judgem^t. or to discharge the said Cōmp^{lt}. of or from the same,
as is in the said bill of complainte most vntruely alledged howbeit he
saith that there was such a request made, but vpon advisem^t. of the
weaknes of the said Raymondę estate, he absolutely denied it, and sent
for the said obligacōn from his Attorney, and hath kepte the same euer
since himselfe, And this def^t. is verily pswaded in his conscience y^t the
said Cōmp^{lt}. Ayloffe doth certenly know, that he is not discharged of the
said obligacōn; And this defendant veriely beleeveth that the same
obligacōn, neuer came to the handę of the said Ayloffe or that the said
Raymond euer shewed him the same, or tolde him, that it was discharged, for that the same obligacōn to this Def^{tę}. knowledge was neuer
delieuered to anie, saueing to his svantę to carry to his Attorney to
prosecute the suite, and he is the rather induced to beleeue it to be true

for that the Cōmp^lt. Ayloffe as this def^t. is informed by his svantꝑ, shortly after the death of the said Raymond of his owne accord came to this def^tꝑ shopp, and desired to know whether he were discharged of the said debte, or no, and he was then answered that he was not discharged thereof, And this Def^t. thinketh that the said Cōmp^lt. would neuer haue sought after him this Def^t. if his Conscience had not accused him, or at leaste pswaded him y^t he was not discharged, And this def^t taketh it, That the said Cōmp^lt. Ayloffe doth offer him great wronge to put him to these vnnecessary vexacōns, and chargꝑ of suite for y^t. allwayes in loving and curteous mann̄ he required but the iuste somē that was due, and the interest & reasonable chargꝑ expended in & aboute the recouery of the same, and this Def^t made the said Ayloffe this offer before anie charge was expended, and is still willing, and ready to pforme the same, and to discharge the said Ayloffe of the said bond vpon paym^t. of the remainder of the said debte being Thirtie poundꝑ wth interest, and of ye Charge wch this def^t. hath expended in and aboute the getting of his money, And this def^t. doth much marvell that the said Ayloffe doth still psiste in his obstinate refusall of this def^tꝑ offers, and to put both him-selfe, and this Def^t to such vnnecessarie Charge, for that as the said Ayloffe confessed, he hath in his handꝑ of the estate of the said Ray-mond to the value of Sixteene poundꝑ or thereaboutꝑ, and likewise for y^t this def^t. was allwaies willing that the said Ayloffe might releeve himselfe vpon the said Judgem^t. recouered in the Lord Maio^rs. Co^rt. against ye admīstratrix of the said Raymond: And this def^t. endeavour-ing to haue eased the said Cōmp^lt. Ayloffe of the paym^t. of this debte did sue the admīstratrix of the said Raymond vpon the said Judgem^t. and her Attorney (as he affirmeth) had instruccōns to plead that she had satisfied as farr as the goodꝑ came vnto vpon other Judgem^tꝑ. before the said Def^t. did sue out his scire facias vpon his Judgem^t. and for that it would haue beene Chargeable to haue brought the same to a tryall, He desired the said Ayloffe to pay the said debte, and take an assignem^t. of the said Judgem^t. wch he refused to doe, and therefore this def^t. comēnced his accōn against the said Ayloffe at ye Comōn lawe, as it was lawfull for him soe to doe (as he thinketh) w^thout that that anie other matter, or thing in the said Bill of Complainte conteyned matteriall or effectuall in the lawe for this def^t. to Answere vnto, and herein and hereby not before sufficiently answered vnto, confessed, or avoyded, trauersed, or denyed is true, All wch matters, and thingꝑ this deft is and wilbe readie to averr, and prove as this hono^ble. Co^rt. shall award, and humbly prayeth to be hence dismissed wth his reasonable costꝑ and Chargꝑ in this behalfe most wrongfully susteyned:./

Edm. Breres

CHAPTER II

BURTON *VS.* MILTON

Hilary term, 1623/4

THOMAS PARADINE OBTAINS A JUDGMENT AGAINST EDWARD AND THOMAS WILLOUGHBY

Plea Rolls, 21/22 James I, CP 40/2137/m. 3030

london'ss Edwardus Willughby nup de london' Ar alias dcus' Edwardus Willughby de Sutton' Coldfeild' in Com' Warr' Armig' smn' fuit ad respondend' Thome Paradine de plīto qd' reddat ei trescentas libras quas ei debet & iniuste detinet &c Et vnde idem Thomas p henricum hodgkinson' Attorn' suu' dic qd' cum p'dcus Edwardus sexto die Novembris Anno regnī dnī Regis nunc Angl' Etc vicesimo apud london' in parochia bē marie de Arcubȝ in Warda de Cheape p queddam scriptum suī obligatorū concessisset se teneri' eidem Thome in p'dcis trescentis libris soluend' eidem Thome cum inde requisit' fuisset p'dcus tamen Edwardus licet sepius requisit p'dcas trescentas libras eidem Thome nondum reddiddit set' ill' ei' hujusqȝ reddere cont'dixit & adhuc cont'dic vnde dic qd' det'iorat' est Et dampn' het' ad valenciam quadranginta librar Et inde p'dus sectam &c Et pfert hic in Cur' scriptum p'dcm' quod deb'm' p'dcm' in forma p'dca' testat^{ur} cuius dat' est die & Anno sup'dcis &c.

Et p'dcus' Edwardus p Thomam Shakespeare Attorn' suu' ven' Et defend' vim & iniur' quando &c Et idem Attorn' dic' qd' īpe non est inform' p eundem Edwardum magrm' suu' aliquo respons' p eodem Edwardo p'fat' Thoma in loquela p'dca' dand' Et nichil aliud inde dic' p quod idem Thomas remanet vsus p'fat' Edwardum inde indefens' Jo' cons' est qd' p'dcus' Thomas recupet vsus p'fat' Edwardum deb̄m suu' p'dcm' & dampna sua occōne detencōnis debi' illius ad Centum solidas' . . . . eidem Thome ex assensu suo p Cur' his adiudicat' Et p'dcus' Edwardus in mia' . . .

[*This is then repeated word for word for Thomas Willoughby*] . . . Et quia p'dcus' Thomas Paradine in Curȝ dni' Regis hic recupavit deb'm & dampna p'dca' vsus quendam Edwardum Willughby de Sutton Coldfeild in Com' War' Armig'um qui similcum p'fat' Thoma Willughby p scriptum p'dcm' eidem Thome Paradine in debō p'dcō' tenet^{ur} & obligat^{ur} pnt' patet isto eodem Rotlō Jo p'dcus' . . . . Thomas Paradine vnicam tantum hēat execucōnem vsus p'fat' Edwardum & Thomam Willughby seu eor alt'um de debō & dampnis p'dcis &c.

Hilary term, 1623/4

WILLIAM SMITH OBTAINS A JUDGMENT AGAINST EDWARD, THOMAS, AND ROBERT WILLOUGHBY

Plea Rolls, 21/22 James I, CP 40/2137/m. 3030

... Edwardus Willughby ... smn' fuit ad respondend' Willō Smith de plīto qd' reddat ei ducentas libras quas ei debet & iniuste detinet &c vnde idem Will's p henricum hodgkinson' Attorn' suu' dic' qd' cum p'dcus Edrus' decimo sexto die Octobris Anno regni dnī Regis nunc Angli &c vicesimo ...

Et pdcus Edrus p Thomam Shakespeare Attorn' suu' ven' Et defend' ... Jo' cons' est qd' p'dcus' Will's recupet deb'm suu' ... & dampm' ... ad octoginta solidar. ...

[*Similarly William Smith against Thomas Willoughby for 80 pounds, and William Smith against Robert Willoughby for 80 pounds.*]

Et quia p'dcus Willūs in Cur' dnī Regis hic recupavit deb'm & dampna p'dca' vsus quosdam Edwardum Willughby de Sutton Coefield' in Com War' Armig'um & Thomam Willughby C'vem london' qui similcum p'fat Robtō Willughby p scriptum p'dcm' eidem Willo in debō p'dco' tenentur & obligantur pnt' patet isto eodem Rotlo Jo' idem Will's vnicam tantum hēat execucōnem vsus p'fat' Edwardum Thomam & Robt'm seu eor' aliquem de debō & dampnis p'dcis' &c.

May 10, 1626

SAMUEL BURTON BRINGS BILL AGAINST MILTON'S FATHER

Requests Proceedings, Req 2/387

To the Kings most excellent Maiestie./.

Jn all humblenes sheweth vnto Your most excellent Maiestie Your most loyall and dutifull Subiect Samuell Burton Archdeacōn of the Diocesse of Gloucester That whereas [about] Three Yeares laste paste one Robert Willoughbie late Citizen and Grocer of London Together wth Thomas Willoughbie the elder of Sutton Colefield in the Countie of Warrwicke gentleman, and [Edward] Willoughbie the Yonger Citizen and Linnen Draper of London became bound vnto one William Smith by his addition styled to bee Citizen and Mercer of London in the penall somme of two hundred pounds [condicōned] for the paimt of one hundred Pounds wth the Jnterest therevppon due at a Day now past and vnknowne vnto Your sayd Subiect The sayd William Smith being a Common Vsurer and one that employes great Sommes of money in that vsurious Course and practise, Vppon which sayd Bonde of Two hundred pounds as Your Subiect hath bin informed, the sayd Robert Willoughbie and Thomas Willoughbie the elder or one of them about Two Yeares since were arrested at the suite of the sayd William Smith, who therevppon tolde them that if they Could procure any other securitye They should not onely bee inlarged but allso absolutely Released of the sayd debt And therevppon the sayd Robert Willoughbie became a sutor vnto Your sayd Subiect to ioyne wth one Sr George Peckham of Shipley in the Countie of Derbie Knight to secure vnto the sayd William Smyth the sayd Somme of One hundred pound℘ affirming vnto Your sayd Subiect that hee and the sayd Sr George Peckham woulde satisfie the sayd debt, And that Your sayd Subiect should onely enter Bond to satisfie the Curiositie of the sayd Smyth, which seemed the more probable And that the sayd Smith allsoe did Conceiue the sayd hundred pound sufficientlie secured by the sayd Robert Willoughbie and the sayd Sr George for that the sayd Smith accepted of their securitie onely by the space of Two moneths or thereabouts before Your sayd Subiect became bound for the same which induced Your sayd Subiect the more willinglie and securely to enter into the sayd Bonde And so At the length Your Subiect being thus wrought vppon about May in the two and twentieth Yeare of our late Soueraigne Lord King James entred into a Bonde of the penall Summe of Two hundred pounds vnto the sayd Smyth Condicōned for the payment of one hundred and Tenn pounds at the now dwelling house of John Milton Scriuenor scituate in Broadstreete London on the Twentieth day of Aprill which then should bee in the Yeare of our Lord God One Thousand sixe hundred twentie & fiue Jn which sayd Bonde the sayd Robert Willoughbie as first and principall and the sayd Sr George Peckham as suerty together wth your sayd Subiect as another suerty doe stand bound ioyntlie and severallie for the paym^t of the sayd debt aforesayd, and which sayd Bond as Your Subiect taketh it beareth date the eighteenth day of Aprill in the sayd Two and twentieth Yeare of the Raigne of our Late Soveraigne Lord King James But now so it is May it please Your most excellent Maiestie That the sayd William Smith and Sr George Peckham having vnder these p^{r}tences gotten your Subiect to stand bound as a surety for the sayd moneyes as aforesayd doe Combine and Confederate together wth one John Milton a Scrivenor in London and a Broker for the letting out of the moneyes of the sayd Smithe how they may lay the whole penaltie of the sayd Bond of Two hundred pounds vppon Your sayd Subiect, or at the least the s'd somme of one hundred pound℘ wth Jnterest, whereas Your sayd Subiect hopeth to proue that the sayd Smith never lent one pennie of the sayd sōme of one hundred pound℘ and so in all equitie ought to have noe benefit of the sayd Bond nor to prosecute sute at Law therevppon, And Your Subiect hopeth allso to proue that the sayd Smith well knowing that hee depteth wth noe money vppon the sayd Bond doth not

Beare the charges of the sayd sute at ye Common Law, nor disburse
money in the same, but the sayd suite is meerelye prosecuted by the
sayd Sr George and the sayd John Milton or one of them hoping thereby
to gaine and make some advantage vnto themselues of Your sayd Subiect
who conceiveth allso that the sayd Smith is dead and that the same is
knowne vnto the sayd Milton or otherwise that he the sayd Smith by
the advise of the sayd Milton concealeth the place of his lodging or
dwelling from Your Subiect, so that hee cannot possiblie enquire out
where the sayd Smith lodgeth or dwelleth to the intent hee might serue
him wth the proces of this Court Albeit the sayd Milton hath every day
allmost recourse to the sayd Smith, if hee bee living, and knoweth where
hee dwelleth or lodgeth, and by Messengers sent by your Subiect to
him for that purpose, hath bin earnestlie intreated to shew & declare
vnto Your subiect when and where Your Subiect might haue Conference
wth the sayd Smith Yet doth hee for the Reasons aforesayd vtterlie
Refuse to acquaint Your Subiect with his sayd dwelling endeavoring
by all meanes to stripp and depriue Your subiect of all meanes for his
Reliefe heerein, and indeede minding nothing else but with all speede
possible to obtaine a Judgement against Your Subiect at the Comōn
Law for the sayd penaltie of Two hundred poundꝑ And Your Subiect
further sheweth that the sayd Sr George Peckham by the Combinacōn
aforesayd hath practised wth the sayd Smith and John Millton to forbeare all prosecution of Law vppon the sayd Bonde against him the
sayd Sr George, Who thereuppon [*here follows a passage, later cancelled*:
the sayd Smith hath secretlie receaued some recompence and Con-
sideracon from the sayd Sr George, vppon which the sayd Smith hath
promised him not to take any extreame Course against him by law
but onelie to Colour their vniust designes doth make seeme thereof
suing the sayd Sr George Peckham to an vtlarie, but purposeth to
proceede further therein in such fauorable manner as hee intendeth shall
not bee p^rudiciall to him, nor any way Compell him to make paim^t of
the sayd debt, by reason whereof the sayd Sr George] resteth so secure
that hee vtterlie neglecteth the paiment of the sayd p^rtended debt. Jn
tender Consideracōn whereof and forasmuch as Your sayd Subiect
was drawne into the sayd ingagements by the perswasions and faire
pretences of of the sayd [*cancelled*: William Smyth, and] Robert Willoughbie and Sr George Peckham And forasmuch as the security of the
sayd Sr George Peckham was principallie & Chiefely aimed at & regarded
by the sayd William Smith at the sealing of the said Bonde and was at
the first accepted of in satisfaction of the first bonde wthout Your
Subiect's sealing of the sayd second Bonde And yet the sayd first bond
is not deliuered vpp by the sayd Smith according to his promise made
vnto the sayd Robert Willoughbie as Yo^r subiect is informed [*cancelled*:

as your Subiect,] but by him [*cancelled*: the sayd Smith keepeth both the sayd Bondϼ] kept on foote, & wth intent to take benefitt vppon both the sayd securities; And forasmuch as the sayd Sr George Peckham is a man of great ability and sufficiencie having Lands worth at the leaste One thowsand pounds p annū and noe Charge of Children, and therefore verie well able to satisfie the sayd debt, And in respect the sayd Sr George Peckham was of neere affinitie to the sayd Willoughbie having married his the sayd Willoughbies owne naturall Sister both by the ffathers and Mothers side, Jt is most iust and Conscionable that the sayd William Smith might bee ordered to take his remedie by the Lawe for the Recouerie of the sayd debt against the sayd Sr George Peckham, & not against Your Subiect And to the intent and purpose that the sayd Sr George Peckham may vppon his oathe set forth whether hee knoweth of the paymente or receit of any moneyes receaued by the him selfe or the s'd Robtē Willoughbye of the s'd Smith and whether the s'd former bonds of the s'd Willoughbie were [given] vpp or no and to shew cause if hee can why hee should not satisfie the sayd debt, and disengage Your s'd Subiect therefrom, And to the intent & purpose the sayd John Milton may vppon his Aunswere set forth whether vppon the sayd Bond so entred into by your subiect, the sayd Smith payd any moneyes vnto the sayd Willoughbie or noe, or whether the sayd Smith bee living or dead, and in Case hee bee living where hee dwelleth, And to the intent and purpose the sayd William Smith and Sr George Peckham and John Milton may make true Aunswere to the premisses, May it please Your most excellent Maiestie the p^rmisses Considered to graunt vnto Your Subiect Your Maiesties most gratious wrytt of priuie Seale to bee directed vnto the sayd William Smith Sr George Peckham and John Milton Cōmaunding them thereby at a Certaine day and vnder a certaine paine therein to bee limited personallie to bee and appeare before yor Matie and your Highnes Counsaile in Your Maiesties Court of Whitehall then and there to aunswere the p^rmisses and also to stand to and abide such further order and direccōn as to Your Maiestie and Your highnes Counsaile shall seeme fitt As allso your Ma^tϼ most gratious wrytt of Jniunction to bee awarded against the sayd William Smith his Counsellors Attorneyes sollicitors and ffactors in the Law to stay all further proceedingϼ in his sayd suite at Lawe And Your Subiect shall allwayes pray for Your Maiesties long and prosperous Raigne ouer vs

Richard Townesend

[*Endorsed*] x° die Maij Anno Rñd Rϼ Caroli Anglie Scotie fr et hibñie secundo Defend Nncī p Nñt Camer

[*Endorsed elsewhere*] Burton plea' q' v^rss Peckham mil Smith et Milton Defts

June 27, 1626

COURT OF REQUESTS ISSUES INJUNCTION AGAINST MILTON'S FATHER

Req 1/32, p. 966

[*Since the edge of the page is torn away, the words supplied in brackets are conjectural.*]

P: xxvij° die Junij A°: &c. secundo./

Burton   Jn the matter of variance brought before the Kingȝ Matie: &
[Peckham]   his highnes Counsaill in his ho^ble: Court of Whitehall at
Westm^r by Samuel Burton Archdeacon of Gloucester Comp^lt against
S^r. George Peckham Knight Willm' Smith & John Milton def^tȝ, Being
in effect for the stay of the def^tȝ proceedingȝ at the Comōn lawe vpon a
Bond or Bill obligatorie of the penaltie of CC^li entred into by the Comp^lt
togeather with S^r. George Peckham Knight and one Rob't Willoughby
gent vnto the said Willm' Smith wth Condicōn for the payment of CX^lī
at a day now past, Jnto wch Bond the Comp^lt was drawne by the
pswasions of the said Robt Willoughby wth out receauin[g any con-
sideration] in respect thereof, and the same [upon a bond] of the said
John Milton, being [made out also] in the name of the other Def[endants
who are] altogeather vnknowne vnto the C[omplainant] Sr George Peckham & Robt W[illoughby] & kindred ought to satisfie [the penalty of the]
said Bond if any were [Now the Complainant show]eth the said Def^t
Milt[on ha]th attempted suit at t[he Common Law against the said
Co]mp^lt intending to recouer the penaltie [of the said bond against]
him contrary to all equitie & conscience As in & by [the said Co]mp^ltȝ:
Bill is more at lardge sett forth & declared [Now therefore upon] the
opening of W^ch same matter by M^r. Townesend of Counsell wth the Comp^lt
& upon consideracōn had of two seūall Affīd made in the said cause
whereby it doth appear that th[e said De]f^t Milton being warned by the
Messenger of this Court to appeare & answere at a day now past hath
not appeared accordingly, And likewise that the Def^t Smith is not
found whereby he may be serued wth any proces of this court to answere
the said Comp^ltȝ: Bill It is therefore by his Ma^tȝ: said Counsaill of this
Court ordered that they the def^tȝ theire Councello^rȝ Atturneis & Sol-
licito^rȝ & eu^ry of them shall surcease & stay & noe further psecute or
pceede at [Com]mon Lawe against the Comp^lt vpon the said bond in
question vntill such tyme as they the said def^tȝ shall haue appeared &
answered the Comp^ltȝ: Bill in this court & other & further order bee had
& made by his Maiesties said Counsaill of this court to the contrary
And it is lastly ordered that an Jniunccōn vnder his Ma^tȝ: Privie Seale
vpon payne of CC^li. to be levied &c be furthw^th awarded & directed vnto
the said def^tȝ Willm' Smith & John Milton theire Counsello^rȝ Atturnies
& Sollicito^rȝ & eu^ry of them for the due pformance of this order./

June 28, 1626

MILTON'S FATHER APPEARS IN COURT TO ANSWER BURTON

Court of Requests Appearance Book, Req 1/111, pt. 2, fol. 6

xxviij° die Junij A p^rdict. . . .

Johēs Milton psoñ compet corā cōm Rϱ p mandat Nuñ Camer. Ad sect Samuelis Burton Theologie doct.

November 15, 1626

MILTON'S FATHER AND SMITH APPEAR IN COURT TO ANSWER BURTON

Court of Requests Appearance Book, Req 1/111, pt. 2, fol. 10ᵛ

xv° die Novembris A°: &c. secundo. . . .

Willūs Smith et Johēs Milton psoñ compent corā cōm Rϱ p mañdat Nuntij Camer Ad sect Samuel Burton. cler, Et sup Respoñ Admissi sunt compere p Petrū Langley Geñ Atturñ suū cū cōm Mrī Hakewill./

November 15, 1626

MILTON'S FATHER ANSWERS BURTON'S SUIT

Requests Proceedings, Req 2/387

Langley p dēftϱ/	xv^{to} die Novembris Anno RRϱ Caroli Angl &c. secundo 1626 Sydney Moun-tague	The Joynt & seuerāll Answeare of William Smyth & John Mylton def^{ts}: to the bill of Cōmp^{lt} of Samuell Burton Clerke Cōmp^{lt}:/

The said Def^{nts} nowe & att all tymes hereafter sauinge to themselues & either of them all advantages of excepcōn vnto the vncerteyntyes & Jnsufficiencies of the said Bill of Cōmp^{lt} for Answeare therevnto the said Deft^{ts} saye & eyther of them for himselfe seuerally sayth, that they conceaue the said Bill to bee exhibited against them Causlessly, & of purpose to putt theis Def^{tp}: to vnnecessary suits & Chardges for the said Def^{te}: William Smyth sayth that he Did not or Doth knowe the said Robert Willoughby & Thomas Willoughbye in the bill named or either of them neither what bond or bondϱ they or either of them entred into vnto this Def^{te}: William Smyth nor for what some or somes money the same were soe made, nor whether the said Robert Willoughby & Thomas Willoughby or either of them, were Arrested therevpon, neither Did this Def^{te}: Smyth euer tell the said Robert & Thomas therevpon, that if they Could pcure any other securitye, they should not only be enlarged butt absolutely Released of the said Debte, for this Def^{te}: Smyth sayth that to his knowledge he neuer had any Conference either wth the said Robert Willoughby, Thomas Willoughbye, Sr George Peckham in the bill

named, or the said Cōmp^{lt}, or any of them, And this Def^t: Smyth
vtterly Denyeth that he is a Comōn vserer as in the said Bill is scandalously alleadged, And both theis Def^{ts}: William Smyth & John Mylton
Doe Deny that they or either of them, or Sr George Peckham in the bill
named (to their knowledge) Did vnder the p^rtences in the bill named,
or any other, gett the said Cōmp^{lt}: to stand bound as suerty for the said
moneys, And they Doe likewise Denye that they haue Combined &
Confederated togeather to laye the whole penaltye of the said bond of
twoe hundred poundꝑ in the bill named vpon the said Cōmp^{lt}: or att
least the some of one hundred poundꝑ, wth interest, as in the bill is
vntruely alleadged, And Yett theis Def^{ts}: knowe noe Reason (vnder the
fauo^r of this Hō^{ble} Courte) if any such bond were made, why the same
should not be sued aswell against the said Cōmp^{lt}, as thother Def^{ts} in
the Bill named & the P'^{lt} therein to take his Remedy against wch of them
he may soonest recouer his Debte, And this Def^t John Mylton for his
parte sayth that he putteth out noe money or euer Did for the said
Smyth, neither euer knewe any such man till they nowe mett togeather
to putt in this their aunswere or of the said bond of twoe hundred
poundꝑ, for the paym^t. of one Hundred poundꝑ made as aforesaid, how-
beitt this Def^t: Mylton confesseth that he hath heard that one Thomas
Paradyne Cittizen & Haberdasher of London did vse the said William
Smyths name in trust in such A bonde, for such a some of one hundred
poundꝑ, And this Def^t verely beleeueth the said Cōmp^{lt} hath beene longe
ere this told soe much, & as this Def^{te} beleeueth he well knoweth the
same to be true, & although the said Cōmp^{lt} (as this Def^{te} beeleeueth)
well knoweth the same to be a Just & true Debte, Yett nowe will not
he seeme to take notice thereof, butt vniustly molesteth & troubleth
these Def^{ts} aboute the same, thinking thereby (as theis Def^{ts} conceaue)
to perplex & hinder some lawfull Course wch the said Thomas Paradyne
in the name of the said Smyth hath taken against the Cōmp^{lt}, & the
other Def^{te} Sr George Peckham, for Recouery of his Just Debte Due
by the said bond Wth Costs & Damadges by him susteyned therein,
wch this Def^t; John Mylton beleeueth the said Thomas Paradyne
hath Done, & that he hath beene soe farr from any Combynācon Wth
the said Sr George Peckham to laye the said Debte vpon the said
Cōmp^{lt}, as the said Cōmp^{lt} vntruely Chardge theis Def^{ts} John Mylton &
William Smyth therewth, whoe knoweth little or nothinge of the same,
nor Doth the same any whitt them concerne, that (as this Def^t John
Mylton hath heard) he the said Thomas Paradyne hath sued aswell the
said Sr George Peckham, as the said Cōmp^{lt}, & that the said Sr George
hath beene soe stirred thereby that he hath paid fiftye poundꝑ of the
said some of one hundred poundꝑ, And this Def^t: John Mylton vtterly

Denyeth that he ᵽsecuteth the said suite or any suite at all against the said Cōmpˡᵗ, or hath any hand in the ᵽsecutinge of any suite whatsoeuer against the said Cōmpˡᵗ, sauinge this same, wherein he is thus vniustly constrayned to make Defence. And this Defᵗ John Mylton further Denyeth that to his knowledge the said Smyth is Dead, butt verylye thinketh the contrary, or that the said Smyth by this Defᵗᵉˢ. aduice concealeth the place of his lodginge, or Dwellinge from the Cōmpˡᵗ so that hee cannot serue ᵽces vpon him. Butt this Defᵗᵉ: John Mylton sayth that the Cōmpˡᵗ as he hath heard hath beene often told where the said Thomas Paradyne Dwelt, & that the said bond concerneth him, & that the said Cōmpˡᵗ accordinglie sente his man or some other vnto the said Thomas Paradynes house, & as it should seeme conferred wᵗʰ him, or his man aboute the said bond, And this Defᵗ. John Mylton Denyeth that he hath Dayly Recourse or any Recourse at all to the said Smyth for he hath not known, neither him, or his dwellinge till nowe this Defᵗ hath mett wᵗʰ him to putt in this their Answer as aforesaid And theis Defᵗˢ: William Smyth & John Mylton doe vtterly Deny that they or eyther of them haue or hath Combined wᵗʰ the said Sʳ George Peckham to forbeare all ᵽsecucōn against him the said Sʳ George & only to ᵽsecute the said Cōmpˡᵗ vpon the said bond, or any wise to meddle wᵗʰ him att all, for theis Defᵗˢ say they haue nothinge to Doe either wᵗʰ the said Sʳ George, or him the said Cōmpˡᵗ And this Defᵗᵉ: Smyth further Denyeth that he ᵽmised to Deliuer vp the said first bond in the bill named vnto the said Roberte Willoughby, or that he keepeth the same on foote wᵗʰ an intent to take benefitt vpon both the said securityes, as in the said bill is vniustly alleadged, for this Defᵗᵉ: Smyth sayth as formerly he hath, said, that he neither knoweth, or euer Did knowe of any such bond, or man, wᵗʰout that that any other matter or thinge materiall or effectuall in the lawe for theis Defᵗˢ: or either of them to Answeare vnto, & herein either not sufficiently Answeared vnto, confessed & avoided trauersed or Denied is true, all wᶜʰ matters or things theis Defᵗˢ, & either of them are ready to auerr Justifye mayntayne & ᵽue as this Hōᵇˡᵉ Courte shall award, & therefore humblye pray to be hence Dismissed wᵗʰ their Reasonable Costs & Chardges in this behalfe wrongefully & wᵗʰout Cause susteyned./

W: Hakewill

CHAPTER III

DOWNER *VS.* MILTON

April 26, 1631

ROSE DOWNER SUES MILTON'S FATHER

Chancery Proceedings, C2 Charles I/D 39/47

xxvj° die Aprilis 1631/

To the right hō^{ble}. Thomas Lord Coventry Lord Keeper of the great
Seale of England/

B   Henley

Jn all humblenes complayning sheweth vnto yor. good Lo^p. yor. Daylie
Oratrixe Rose Downer of London widdowe, That whereas yor. said
Oratrixe about fiue Yeares since having in her handρ of her owne moneys
the greatest ρte of her estate being the sūme of ffiftie poundρ and the
same being come to the knowledge of John Milton of London Scrivener
he repaired to yor. said Oratrixe about the said time and advised her to
put out the said ffiftie poundρ at interest rather then to imploye it any
other wayes, and vsed diuers pswasions vnto yor. said Oratrixe that he
might haue the putting of it forth telling her that shee should haue good
securitie for the payement of the same to hir againe, by meanes whereof
yor. Oratrixe was drawne to consent that hir said money should be put
forth at interest and that the said John Milton should haue the benefitt
of the brocage thereof, and of the making of the bondρ for the same, but
yet soe as your said Oratrixe would first know her securitie and would
haue time to consider of the same and to approue or dissalowe thereof
And the said Milton agreed and consented therevnto, and afterwardρ
within a very short time after the said conference betweene the said
John Milton and yor. Oratrixe, he the s[aid John] Milton did nominate
vnto yor. said Oratrixe a Principall and twoe suerties for the having and
taking of the said ffiftie poundρ at interest, and your said Oratrixe
having taken advise and consideracōn of the same was willing that hir
said money should be sett forth vpon that securitie, and willed the said
John Milton to prepare the bondρ and take the securitie and the money
should be deliūed, All which was done accordingly and yor. said Oratrixe
was well pleased and did acc[ept] of the same and afterwardρ. vīzt. in
or about the moneth of June one thousand six hundred twenty eight,
(the time being then expired and the said ffiftie poundρ growne due and
payeable) your said Oratrixe repaired to [the] said John Milton and desired him to call in the said money declaring vnto him hir urgent oc-

casion to vse the same, and to imploye it otherwise, and the said John Milton according to the declaracōn and request of your said Oratrixe did call in the said money out of the said securities handρ, and did desire your said Oratrixe to leaue the obligacōn in his handρ and he would receiue the money for your said Oratrixe and deliuer vp the said obligacōn vpon receipt of the said money and agreed to bee answereable for it, And your said Oratrixe therevpon did deliuer vp the said obligacōn to the said John Milton and did entrust him to receiue her money for her vpon his faithfull promise to pay it over forthwith after vnto your said Oratrixe, and therevpon the said John Milton receaved the said ffiftie poundρ and interest and having gotten the same into his handρ did leaue the same as he nowe p'tendρ in the possession of his then servant Thomas Bower to the end the same should be paid over to your said Oratrixe for supplie of hir occasions which was the mayne end of calling in the said money. And yoʳ. said Oratrixe further sheweth vnto your good Lordshipp that ymediately vīzt the next day after the said ffiftie poundρ was paid as aforesaid vnto the handρ of the said John Milton or vnto the handρ of the said Thomas Bower or some other by his the said John Miltons appointment and direccōn, your said Oratrixe repaired to the dwelling house of the said John Milton in Breadstreete in London to the end to have had and received the said money to furnish her occasions and there demaunded the said money but finding not the said John Milton then at home the said Thomas Bower did signifie vnto yoʳ. said Oratrixe that he had the money in his the said Bowers owne possession and in his deske and your said Oratrixe requiring him to pay the same vnto her, he the said Bower refused soe to doe albeit he knewe her vse and necessitie of the same, telling her that he thought she would put it out againe, and soe deferred the payment thereof, whereat your said Oratrixe being very much moved grew very angrie with the said Bower and then the said Milton came in and bade his man pay the money to your said Oratrixe bidding her doe with it what she would and seemed in shewe to be much offended that the said Bower should offer to withhold the said money from your said Oratrixe, but yet with such gesture and subtile cariage as your said Oratrixe did plainely perceiue that it was a meere confederacie and a combinacōn betweene them to deteyne her money from her, And your said Oratrixe being much discontented about this matter aswell for that she had not present meanes to goe through with her busines, as also that she suspected she was in danger to loose hir money and to be defrauded betweene the Scrivener and his man was inforced to goe home without her money and the next morning after your said Oratrixe had bene with the said Milton and his man vīzt in or about the tenth day of June 1628

the said Milton or Bower by the handợ of one other of his the said
Miltons servantợ sent to your said Oratrixe to his house an obligacōn
beareing date that day of the Penall sumē of One hundred poundợ
wherein twoe persons were bound to your said Oratrixe by the names of
Mathew Ewen and William Keymer esquires condicōned for the payement to your said Oratrixe of the sumē of ffiftie and twoe poundợ the
twelueth day of December then next enseweing at the said Miltons
house in Breadstreete aforesaid, which bond was sealed by the said
supposed obligators as the said Milton and his servantợ pretend in the
presence of the said John Milton Thomas Bower and James ffisher
And the said ffisher or one other of the said Miltons servantợ presenting
the said obligacōn to yoᵣ. said Oratrixe at your said Oratrixes house she
required of him what it was and he answered her, a bond for her money
meaning the ffiftie poundợ, that was in the said Milton or his man Bowers
hand as aforesaid, and she saying that she had occasion for her money
and would not haue it any longer at interest and therefore she had
called it in, the said ffisher replied that she could haue but good securitie
for her money and there it was, and cast the bond to your said Oratrixe
and depted but she refused to take it being taken without her consent,
and your said Oratrixe repaired to the said Milton and told him that
she would not accept of the said bond for that she was then to vse her
money and the suerties were men vnknowne to your Oratrixe, but must
haue her money in for present vse whereto he said the securitie was
good and he would see her paid her money and soe relyeing therevpon
she was driven to trie her frendợ to borrowe moneys for her owne
buisines expecting payement of her money from the said Milton and
Bower and noe other and renouncing the other pretended securitie
noīated in the said Obligacōn for that they were men not knowne to
Your Oratrix and whom she yet neuer sawe and dwelt farre remote in
Somersetshire and were vtterly disliked by yoᵣ. said Oratrixe, and at
the first six moneths end the said Bower being then the said Miltons
man entreated yoᵣ Oratrixe to forbeare the said money one halfe Yeare
more and promised her that his Master and he would paye in the said
ffiftie poundợ & the interest to Your said Oratrixe at the end of the then
next six moneths followeing wherevpon she was patient till that sixe
monethes end and then the money not coming in she addressed herselfe
to the said Milton for it whoe entreated her to sue the bond, yet promised
neuertheless to be her paymaster himselfe But soe it is right hōᵇˡᵉ that
the said Milton and Bower knewe and perceiued that your poore
Oratrixe was an ignorant poore old woeman and taking advantage
thereof, or in hope of her death combined togeather vtterly to defraude
your said Oratrixe of her money and paid not the same nor any pte

thereof at the end of the said second sixe monethes nor at any time since
nor any interest for the same but fedd her with faire wordρ and promises
albeit she in the interim called for her money of the said Milton and
Bower diuers times, insoemuch as the said money is still whollie oweing
to your said Oratrixe by the said Milton and Bower and your said
Oratrixe finding herselfe deluded by them from time to time and pressing for satisfaccon they the said Milton and Bower in conclusion declared that she must stick to her bond and get payement as she could,
albeit she neuer assented to the said latter putting of it forth nor was
privie therevnto, nor accepted the said bond for hir securitie. But relied
whollie vpon the securitie promises and agreementρ of the said Milton
and his man, and therefore she hath long since offered and is still readie
to make over the said bond to them, But the said Milton and Bower
haue refused the same and doe nowe pretend that what promise soever
they made at the first to yor. Oratrixe yet since (she had the bond which
was cast to hir as aforesaid without her acceptance) they hold themselues to be freed from the same against which subtile and vniust practize
she humblie praieth releife according to conscience Sheweing further that
at that verie instant when the said Ewen and Keymer became bound
in the said obligacōn the said Ewen and Keymer or one of them were
or was much indebted to the said Milton or some others which he delt
for, and that the said Ewen was then fallen into decay and was vpon
sale of his landρ which were not competent to pay his debtρ as the said
Milton and Bower then knewe, and that at that time he the said Ewen
did obscure himselfe, And that none or very little of the said ffiftie
poundρ came to the handρ of him or the said Keymer, but was deteyned
and defalked by the said Milton to supplie and satisfie debtρ or interest
to the said Milton or others of his ffreindρ clientρ and acquaintance and
that the said ffiftie poundρ was enforced from your said Oratrixe without
M^r. Ewens privitie & consent or request but subtillie by the said Milton
to hedge in some despate debt or interest of the said Ewens Jn tender
consideracōn whereof and to the end the said Milton and Bower may
be compelled to satisfie the said ffiftie poundρ and damages to your said
Oratrixe, And forasmuch as yor. said Oratrixe is vtterlie remediles by
the strict rules of the comōn lawes of this Realme to recouer her said
money of the said Milton and Bower or any other, and cañot make such
precise proofe of theire promises and agreement aforesaid as the said
lawes require but hopeth that the said Milton and Bower vpon theyre
Oathes will not denye the truth of the premisses, and to the end, the
same may be examined and that the said Milton and Bower may sett
downe and declare vpon theire answere to this complaint whither Yo^r.
Oratrixe did not call for her money in from the form^r securities, and

whither they or either of them received the same, and after put it forth
againe to the said Ewen and Keymer whither Yo^r. Oratrixe was privie
or assenting thereto, whither she did not require her mony in, at what
tyme the said Milton or Bower had the same in their or one of their
handℯ, and what promises and agreementℯ they made to and with Yo^r.
said Oratrixe, and what disposicōn was made of the said ffiftie poundℯ
vpon putting the same forth to the said Ewen and Keymer, and what he
the said Ewen then owed to the said Milton or any of his ffrindℯ and to
the intent the said Milton and Bower may pay Yo^r. said Oratrixe her
said money with the interest & charges or shewe good cause to the con-
trary: May it please Yo^r. hō^{ble}. good Lo^{pp}. to grant vnto Yo^r said
Oratrixe his Ma^{tℯ}. most gracious writt of Subpena to be directed to the
said John Milton and Thomas Bower thereby comanding them and
either of them at a day certeyne and vnder a certeyne paine therein to
be limitted psonallie to be and appeare before yor. good Lo^p in his
Maiesties high and honorable Court of Chancerye then and there to
answere all and every the premisses vpon their Corporall oathes, and
to stand to and abide such further order and direction therein as to
your honorable good Lordshipp in equitie and conscience shall seeme
meete. And your said Oratrixe shall daylie pray for your Lordshipp long
to continue in honor health and happines.

Goldsmythe

May 3, 1631

MILTON'S FATHER ANSWERS ROSE DOWNER'S BILL
Chancery Proceedings, C2 Charles I/D 39/47

Juratur 3° Maij 1631   The Severall answere of John Milton one of
Tho. Eden   the Defendantℯ to the Bill of Rose Downer
Maydwell   Widdowe Complaynant:/

The said Defendant saving to himselfe now and at all times hereafter, all advantages of excepcōn, to the vncertainties, and insufficiencies of the said Bill, for answere vnto soe much thereof, as concerneth him this Defendant to make answere vnto, He saith, That
he knoweth it, to be true, That the said somē of ffiftie poundℯ was
lent forth in the name of the said Comp^{lt}. vpon the securitie of the
said Mathewe Ewenℯ and William Keymer in the bill named, and the
bond sealed at this Defendantℯ shopp. But this Defendant saith for any
thing this Def^t. knoweth to the Contrary the same was soe lent by the
Comp^{lt} willingly, for that she received both the bond at the first and
the Jnterest as the same grewe dewe at severall dayes, and times after-
wardℯ, and that this Def^t. never knewe that she was vnwilling therevnto,
vntill now of late, And this Defendant, for further satisfaccōn of this

hōᵇˡᵉ. Court in the premises saith That one John Downer the Complaynantꝑ late husband, having beene this Defendantꝑ long acquaintance Did dispose of at this Defᵗꝑ. shopp at Jnterest, vpon securitie, to the good liking of him the said John Downer some moneys, But this Defᵗ doth not well remember the particuler somē or somēs soe lent, And the said John Downer dying long since the said Complaynant hath sithence continued the said moneys or some pt thereof at Jnterest voluntarily, and willingly till of late, and vntill this Defendant was desirous to have noe further dealingꝑ with her moneys, and to that end this Defendant perswaded the Complaynant to take in her moneys That this Defendant might be altogether quitt of her, and her moneys, And this Defendant denyeth that he ever repaired to the Complaynant, or did advise her to putt it forth at Jnterest, rather then to imploy it any other wayes, Or that this Defendant ever vsed, any pswasions to the Complaynant to any such purpose, As in the said bill is vntruly surmised, for the reputting forth of any moneys at Jnterest, or that vpon any such perswasions the Complaynant was drawne to putt the same forth at Interest, But this Defendant saith that the said somē of ffiftie poundꝑ in the bill named, was putt forth at Jnterest to such men, and vpon such security as was to the good liking of the Complaynant and this Defendant saith that the said ffiftie poundꝑ was paid in about the moneth of June One thowsand six hundred Twenty and Eight at this Defendantꝑ shopp vnto the other Defendant Thomas Bower, for the Complaynantꝑ vse, and to be at her disposing, And this Defendant beleeveth that the Complaynant, Did afterwardꝑ require the said somē of ffiftie poundꝑ, of the said other Defendant Thomas Bower in the Bill named, But what satisfaccōn the said Thomas Bower, gave to the said Complaynant, Or why he did not p̄ntely deliver the same, vnto the Complaynant, he this Defendant doth not knowe but leaveth to the said Thomas Bower, to give answere therevnto, And this Defendant saith, That he the said Thomas Bower was then noe servant, of this Defendantꝑ, but a ffreeman of London and was then, and still is, Partner with him this Defendant, in the benefitt wᶜʰ. accreweth by this Defendantꝑ trade, and is sufficient, (as this Defendant verely beleeveth) to answere the Companyant if he hath done her any wrong (as he verely beleeveth, he hath not done her any) And this Defendant, absolutely denieth any confedracie, and Combinacōn between this Defendant, and the said other Defendant Bower to deteyne the Complaynantꝑ money from her, Or that this Defendant Did vse any subtill gesture or Carriage, whereby the Complaynantꝑ said money might be deteyned from her, As by the said bill is falsely and scandulously surmised, And this Defendant beleeveth that the said bond was sealed by the said Ewens and

Keymer, and the said moneys lent to them, by the privity and approbacōn of the said Complaynant, And this Defendant saith That he did
knowe, that the said bond was afterwardꝑ sent vnto her the said Complaynant, But knewe not, that the Comp^{lt}. did refuse to accept of the
said bond, Or that this Defendantꝑ servant James ffisher Did deliver
the bond in such sorte as the Complaynant in her said Bill hath sett
forth, ffor if this Defendant had been informed thereof, he this Defendant would have given him Due correccōn for the same, And this
Defendant confesseth, That he this Defendant beleeving the said
moneys to be putt forth by the Complaynantꝑ privitie, subscribed his
name as a Witnes therevnto, As he vsually doth in like cases, And this
Defendant saith that if the Complaynant, had then made knowne her
dislike of the lending of her moneys As in the said Bill is alledged, and
had pñtely brought back the bond to this Defendant, He this Defendant
would have seene that the said Complaynant, Should have had her
moneys forthwith paid her, But this Defendant did, and doth verely
beleeve and conceive, that the same was fairely carried betweene the
Complaynant and the said Bower, and that her consent was had to and
for the lending of the said ffiftie poundꝑ vpon the security aforesaid
(for that the Plaintiffe to this Defendantꝑ knowledge,) Did not shewe
any dislike of the lending thereof, till long time after the same was
lent, But this Defendant denyeth that he ever promised, or vndertooke
to pay the Complaynant her moneys or to become her Paymaster,
either vpon the lending of the moneys or at any time before or afterwardꝑ, And this Defendant denyeth that the said Ewens (to the knowledge of this Defendant,) was fallen into decay at the time of the said
lending of the Complaynantꝑ money to the said Ewens and Keymer,
or that the said Ewens at that time did obscure himselfe, But this
Defendant did beleeve the security to have beene good and sufficient,
and confesseth that the said Ewens Did then owe some other moneys
at this Defendantꝑ shopp, but to what value this Defendant doth not
well remember, And this Defendant further saith That he beleeveth that
part of the said somē of ffiftie poundꝑ was disposed, and paid over to
Ewens his vse, and by his appointment, and in such sorte as he did
direct, and that the remainder was paid into his own handꝑ, And this
Defendant conceiveth that the said Comp^{lt}. hath not p^rferred the said
bill against this Defendant of her owne disposicōn & minde but by the
instigacōn of some other ill disposed ꝑson for that this Defendant saith
that the said Comp^{lt}. hath oftentimes in the hearing of this Defend^{tꝑ}.
servant Cleared this Defendant touching the lending of the said ffiftie
poundꝑ:/Without that, that there is any other matter or thing, Clawse,
sentence, article, or allegacōn in the said bill contenyed materiall, or

effectuall, in the Lawe, to be answered vnto, and not herein well & insufficiently answered vnto, or denied, traversed, or avoyded is true, All wch. matters this Defendant is ready to Justefie, and avowe as this hō^ble. Co^rt. shall award, and humbly prayeth to be dismissed out of the same, with his reasonable cost℈, and damag℈ in that behalfe wrongfully susteined:./

W Greene.

May 3, 1631

MILTON'S FATHER'S PARTNER BOWER ANSWERS ROSE DOWNER'S BILL
Chancery Proceedings, C2 Charles I/D 39/47

Jur' 3° Die Maij	The severall answere of Thomas Bower one of the
1631 J Mychell	Def^tp. to the Bill of Complaint, of Rose Downer
Maydwell	Widdowe Complaynant:/

The said Defendant saving to himselfe now & at all times hereafter all advantag℈ of excepcōn, to the vncertainties, & insufficiencies of the said Bill, for answere therevnto soe much thereof as concerneth him this Defendant, to make answere vnto, saith, That he verely beleeveth that the said bill of Complaint, against him this Defendant, into this Hō^ble. Court exhibited by the said Comp^lt. is of purpose, to vexe, molest, and troble this Defendant, and to putt him to vnnecessary charge, having thereby to drawe some moneys from him without any Just cause at all, Yett nevertheless for the satisfaccōn, of this most hō^ble. Court he this Defendant saith, That he was for the space of Eight yeares or thereabout℈ now past servant to the said John Milton Scrivener, the other Defendant in the bill named, and hath beene for the space of Six yeares now past, or thereabout℈ Partner with the said John Milton in the Profession which he now vseth, and hath within the said time beene a meanes of putting out many somēs of money at Jnterest, And that the husband of the Comp^lt. in his life time, had some moneys lent at Jnterest, at the shopp of the said Defendant John Milton, And further saith that true it is that the ffiftie pound℈ in the bill mencōned, was by the said John Milton and this Defendant, by and with the consent, and good liking of the said Complaynant, putt to Jnterest for the vse of the said Complaynant, into the hand℈ of one Master Leigh vpon sufficient securitie by bond in November One thowsand six hundred Twenty & ffower And continued till about August One thowsand Six hundred Twenty & Six And then with all Jnterest paid in, And not long after by and with the privity and consent of the Plaintiffe, the said ffiftie pound℈ was lent at Jnterest vnto S^r. ffulke Grevill Knight vpon good securitie, where the same continued till about June One thowsand Six hundred Twenty and Eight, And then was voluntarily paid in with

all Jnterest, therevpon due, And the said ffiftie poundę remayning in
the howse of the said John Milton whereof the Complaynant had notice,
At which time, Master Ewens, and Mr Keymer in the bill named had
occasion for a hundred poundę, whereof ffiftie poundę was then lent vpon
their security by one Master Bulteell vpon Jnterest for Six moneths
whoe liked them well, And the other ffiftie poundę was then lent by the
Complaynant vpon Jnterest for the like time, the said Ewens and Keymer being then reputed Gentleman of good worth, and sufficiency and
the meaner of them to have about ffive hundred poundę p Annū, And
both of them formerly having taken vp moneys at Jnterest, and delt
fairely and squarely therein from time to time, And vpon their request,
at that time there being such a some in the howse, This Defendant
moved the Complaynant to lett them have the said ffiftie poundę informing her that their security was good, And this Defendant was the
rather induced soe to thinke, for that their dealingę had been formerly
alwayes good and Currant, Vpon which report and informacōn she the
said Complaynant gave consent to and for the lending of the said ffiftie
poundę, vnto the said Ewens and Keymer, and a bond was then taken for
the same, and afterwardę by and with the consent, and good liking of the
said Complaynant, was continued for Twoe, or three Six monethę, and
the Jnterest duly paid her for the same time, and by her accepted of,
without any dislike at all, And this Defendant saith that the said Ewens
vpon thenseling of the said bond to the Complaynant for the said ffiftie
poundę Did appointe this Defendant to pay pcell thereof vnto certaine
psonę to whome he the said Ewens was then indebted, which was done,
accordingly and the remainder recd paid to the said Ewens himselfe,
But how much of the said ffiftie poundę was paid by the said Ewens his
appointm^t. and how much came to his owne handę this Defendant well
remembreth not, And this Defendant further saith, that this Complaynant was then soe farre from making such Complaynt for want of
money That about the same time, at this Defendantę request she the
said Complaynant Did lend vnto one Master Waring Thirtie poundę
at Jnterest for Six monethę, and soe continued the same till about the
moneth of June One thowsand Six hundred and Thirtie, But the said
Ewens, and Keymer, afterwardę failing in paying of the Jnterest of the
said ffiftie poundę, the Plaintiffe tooke excepcōns & called in for her
money And this Defendant hath divers times since very earnestly sol-
licitied and importuned the said Ewens, and Keymer for the payment
of the same accordingly, whoe have divers times faithfully pmised the
paym^t. thereof, And this Defendant verely beleeveth That the said
ffiftie poundę, with all the Jnterest due for the same, wthin a while may
be obteyned and he for his pt will doe his best endeavour to procure the

payment thereof, And this Defendant doth vtterly denye the deteyning of the said ffiftie poundρ, As in the said bill is falsely alledged, Neither that the bond was soe delivered as in the said bill is surmised Neither did this Defendant ever goe about to hinder or crosse her of the said ffiftie poundρ. And doth vtterly deny that ever he vndertooke to secure the said ffiftie poundρ or any part thereof Neither doth he or the other Defendant John Milton vse for to doe to any, having little reason for it, (in these evill times) But only doe their best endeavours to take good security for moneys lent, and afterwardρ with much travell paines and care Doe seeke to gett such moneys in againe to give the lenders what content they may And denieth that he knewe or ever heard, (at the time of the lending of the said ffiftie poundρ or of long time after) That the said Ewens and Keymer or either of them, were in any decay, in their estate, or did obscure themselves as in the said bill of Complaynt is alledged, And denieth any combinacōn with the other Defendant John Milton as is most scandalously sett downe;./ Without that That any other matter or thing in the said bill conteyned materiall to be answered vnto, and not herein sufficiently answered vnto, confessed, avoyded, traversed, or denied is true, All which this Defendant, is ready to averre, and prove as this hō^{ble}. Co^{rt}. shall award, and humbly prayeth to be dismissed out of the same, with his reasonable costρ and damagρ in that behalfe wrongfully susteined.:/

Steph: Atterbury/

September 19, 1631

DEPOSITION OF OLIVE STREET IN DOWNER-MILTON SUIT
Chancery Depositions, C24/574/40

19. die Septembris. 1631.   Ex parte Rose Downer vīd quēr versus
Anº: R: Rρ: Caroli. 7º./   Johēm Milton et āl dēftρ Testes examī^t: per
                              Martinū Basill in Cancellaria Examina-
                              torem./

Oliue Street of the parish of S^t: Andrewes in the Wardorb London Em-browderer, aged Twenty Six yeares or thereaboutρ sworne &c. and by direccōn examined vppon the 1.2.3.4.5.6.7. &.8th.

1. That he knoweth all the parties to this suite Cōmp^{lt}: and dēftρ, and hath knowne Rose Downer widdow named for Cōmp^{lt}:, for these Twenty yeares at the least., and John Milton and Thomas Bower named for dēftρ, for these Six yeares and vpwardes, And saieth that the Cōmp^{lt}: lives as A widdow on the smale meanes she hath and keepes onely one Maide Seruant, and the Two dēftρ are by their

ᵽfessions both Scriueno^{rs}, the dēft Bower, being heretofore the other
dēft Miltons Seruant or Apprentice, and at this time writes vnder
him in his Shopp, or did within these Three Monethes, And more-
ver saieth, that the Cōmp^{lt}; liveth on Audlin Hill, in the s'd parish
of S^t: Andrewes in the Wardorb, and the dēft Milton liues in Bredstreet London, But where the dēft Bower now lodgeth, this dept
saieth hee knoweth not, but saieth that within these Six Monethes
hee lodged in Long Lane, and did then write vnder the s'd Milton,
in his Shopp in Bredstreet./

2. That as hee hath credibly heard and beleiueth, the dēft Milton,
(haueing the report of an honest man in his ᵽfession) was hereto-
fore trusted by the Cōmp^{lt}: wth puting forth at interest for her, the
sūm of ffifty poundes, being (as was conceiued) the maine matter she
had to liue on, for this dept saieth, that the s'd dēft Milton hath
heretofore confessed to him this dept, that hee was soe trusted by
the Cōmp^{lt} with puting forth of ffifty poundes for her, And more over
saieth that as hee hath alsoe credibly heard, the Cōmp^{lt}, from time
to time, was made acquainted with the security, and the names of the
parties, to whome the s'd monie was lent, and that shee did vsually
giue allowance or approue of such security, before her monie was soe
lent./

3. That in or about the Moneth of Jun in the yeare. 1628. hee this dept,
did goe along with the now Cōmp^{lt}, to the dēft Miltons house in
Bredstreet, where this dept heard the s'd Cōmp^{lt}:, earnestly call
in for, and desire of the s'd Milton, to haue her s'd monie, saying she
could noe longer forbeare the same, in regard of her great occasions,
and want, that shee had thereof, and that therefore shee must have
the same in, or to that effect./

4. That both before and after the Cōmp^{lt}: was wth the s'd dēft Milton
to call in for her s'd monie, as is before deposed, hee this dept. (at the
request and entreaty of her the s'd Cōmp^{lt}) was diuers and sundry
times wth him the s'd dēft, And did from her the s'd Cōmp^{lt}, and in
her name, earnestly desire, and sollicitte the s'd dēft, to call in for
the s'd monie when the same grew due, to thend the Cōmp^{lt}. might
haue the same, to supplie her occasions withall, And this dept.
further saieth, that at all the times, that this dept was with the s'd
Milton to demaund the s'd monie as afores'd, he still ᵽmised this
dept:, as hee did the Cōmp^{lt}: when shee was with him as afores'd,
that shee should have in her s'd monie when the same was due, but
the very time or times, or how often this dept was with the s'd deft
Milton for the s'd monies, hee saieth hee is not now able to depose./

[*Signed*] Oliue Streete

5. That as the Cōmp^lt her self told him this dept: (at such time as hee this dept was with her when she called in for her s'd monies of the dēft Milton, and when this dept called in for the same, as is before deposed) that her s'd monie was in such securities handes, as shee very well liked of, shee further saying, that if shee had not had great occasion to haue vsed it, that shee would not have called for it in, shee liked the security soe well, or to that effect./

6. Tbat as the dēft Milton himself told him this dept:, the s'd ffifty poundes and interest therefore (according to the desire and request of the Cōmp^lt), was (at or about the time the same was due) paid vnto him the s'd dēft in his Shopp in Bredstreet, by the principall or suerties whoe stood bound for the same, to the s'd Cōmp^lt.

7. That as hee hath credibly heard, (after such time as the Cōmp^lt. had notice that the s'd monie was paied in, to the dēft Milton, or the s'd Bower his seruant) shee the Cōmp^lt did ymediately repaire to the s'd Miltons house in Bredstreet afores'd, and there demaunded her monie of him, wherevnto (as this dept hath likewise credibly heard) the s'd dēft made answer, what A stirr is here about yor monie, and withall willed the other dēft. Bower, to pay her, her monie, and saied hee would be ridd of her, and her monie, and (in shew) seemed angrie with the s'd Bower that he delayed to pay her the Cōmp^lt, And moreover saieth, that as hee hath alsoe credibly heard, the s'd Bower then answered, that hee had pmised to furnish A ffriend of his, with soe much monie, and that hee must have that monie of the Cōmp^ltꝑ hee further saying, that hee did knowe, that when shee had it, shee would put it forth againe, and therefore shee were, as good let his friend have it, as another man, and soe would not let her have it, And further or otherwise to the Inter^r hee saieth hee is not able to depose./

8. That not long after the s'd Cōmp^lt: had bene with the s'd dēftꝑ for her s'd monie, as before is deposed to the next Inter^r precedent, the s'd Milton or Bower, or one of them (as the Cōmp^ltꝑ then Seruant ffraunces Stacy told him this dept.) sent A Seruant of theirs, to the Cōmp^ltꝑ, house, wth an Obligacōn in the names of Mathew Ewens, and Will'm Keymer, for payment of ffifty poundes with Jnterest, at Six Monethes, vnto her the s'd Cōmp^lt: whereat (as the Cōmp^lt: s'd Seruant likewise told this dept) shee the Cōmp^lt, was very angrie, saying shee would not accept of the s'd Bond, shee must have in her monie to serue her occasions, as shee had oftentimes told them be-fore, And that then the dēftꝑ s'd seruant replied, and saied that the security was good, and that his M^r (meaning the s'd Milton) would make it good, as reason was hee should, and therevppon the dēftꝑ

s'd seruantᵽ, (against the Cōmpˡᵗ: will) did leaue the s'd Obligacōn
behinde him, saying shee could haue but good security for her monie,
and there it was, or to that effect./ And lastly saieth, that as the
Cōmpˡᵗᵖ: s'd seruant likewise told him this dept, the Cōmpˡᵗ was at
that time sicke in her Bedd, and not fitt to carry the s'd Obligacōn
back againe./ And more &c./

[*Signed*] Oliue Streete

September 19, 1631

DEPOSITION OF GEORGE BROOME IN DOWNER-MILTON SUIT

Chancery Depositions, C24/574/40

19° Sept Ao 1631   ꝑ Down'
Ao' Car Rᵽ. 7°

1 *George Broome* of the pʳcinct of Blackfriers London scriuen' aged
   51 yeares or thereaboutᵽ sworne & exañed &c. To the ffirst Jnt
   saith That hee doth knowe the widow Down' named for the
   cōmpˡᵗ & John Milton named for one of the defᵗᵖ & hath knowne
   the cōmpˡᵗ the space of seauen yeares or thereaboutᵽ & the defᵗ
   Milton some 27 or 28 yeares or thereaboutᵽ And doth know
   yᵗ the sᵈ Milton is by ᵽfession a scriuenoʳ living in Breadstreet
   London But to his rēmbrance doth not knowe the Defᵗ Thomas
   Bower, but hath heard & beleeueth yᵗ to be true hee was svant
   sometymes to the sᵈ Milton & did write vnder him in his the
   sᵈ Miltons shopp in Breadstreet aforesᵈ.

2 Hee hath credibly heard yᵗ the sᵈ Defᵗ Milton had the reputacōn
   of a very honest man in the ᵽfession of a scriuenoʳ And the
   sᵈ Defᵗ Milton hath confessed vnto this Dept yᵗ the cōmpˡᵗ did
   trust him the sᵈ Milton with the putting forth of ffifty poundᵽ
   at Jnterest of her estate & hath also confessed yᵗ hee the sᵈ
   Milton did putt forth the s'ᵈ 50ˡⁱ vnto & vppon such security as
   shee the sᵈ cōmpˡᵗ did allow & apᵽue of And this is as much as
   hee can depose to this Jnt hee this depᵗ. not knowing whether
   the s'ᵈ cōmpˡᵗ from tyme to tyme were made acquainted wᵗʰ the
   security & names of the pties to whom the same money was lent
   as by the Jnt is demaunded./

6 That the sᵈ Defᵗ Milton hath confessed & acknowledged vnto this
   depᵗ that the sᵈ 50ˡⁱ wᵗʰ. the Jnterest was p'd into the s'ᵈ Miltons
   shopp in Breadstreet aforesd to the vse of the now cōmpˡᵗ into
   the handᵽ of the sᵈ Defᵗ Bower at or about the tyme in this Jnt
   meant & intended And further to the Jnt hee cannot depose

7 That all y^t hee can depose to this Jnt is this vizt y^t the s^d def^t
Milton did acknowledge & confesse vnto this dep^t. y^t the s^d
Cōmp^lt not long after the s^d money wth the Jnterest therefore
was p^d vnto the s^d Def^t Bower at the s^d Miltons shopp in Breadstreet as afores^d did come & repaire vnto the s^d Milton & demaund
of him the s^d 50^lt wth Jnterest so p^d as afores^d vppon wch demaund
as the s^d Milton confessed vnto this dep^t. hee did will the s^d
Bower to pay the s^d money wth the Jnterest vnto the s^d widow
Down' & did by his owne confession seeme to bee very angry
saying y^t hee would bee ridd of her the cōmp^lt & her money or
wordρ to y^t effect And saith hee hath heard the s^d cōmp^lt say and
affirme y^t the said def^t Bower did refuse at y^t tyme to pay the s^d
money wth the Jnterest therefore, & the s^d Cōmp^lt did then further
say y^t shee was very much greeued & discontented y^t shee could
not then haue the s^d money to furnish her pñte necessities.

11.12 It is true y^t since the Comencing of this suite hee this dep^t had
speech & conference wth Mr Ewens in this Jnt named about the
lending of the s^d ffifty poundρ At wch tyme this dep^t saith the s^d
Ewens in this dep^tρ. opinion seemed to bee very sorry y^t the s^d
money was a widdowes & did directly manifest & declare vnto
this dep^t y^t it was all one vnto him the s^d Ewens to whom hee was
bound for as hee then confessed it was to pay Debtρ owing by
him at the s^d Miltons shopp & did then confesse & acknowledge
y^t none or very little of the money (if any at all thereof) came to
his handρ & y^t at y^t tyme hee had neu' seene the s^d widow And
the s^d Ewens did further say vnto this dep^t. y^t if the s^d def^tρ had
not been p'd by his the s^d Ewens entring into the s^d bond hee did
not know wch way to haue p^d them, & did then further confesse
vnto this dep^t. y^t the s^d def^tρ or one of them did moue & pswade
him the s^d Ewens to enter into the s^d bond, saying vnto him y^t
they hoped y^t they nor either of them should bee any loosers by
him the s^d Ewens. And further saith y^t at the s^d conference the
s^d Ewens did confesse y^t hee neu' pd any Jnterest for the s^d
money & y^t if any interest were p'd to her the s^d widow Down'
the same was p'd by the s^d def^tρ or one of them out of their owne
moneys And the s^d Ewens further s^d vnto this dep^t y^t the s^d def^tρ
or one of them durst not but pay Jnterest for the s^d money at the
first to theñd as hee confessed to bring the cōmp^lt w^thin com-
passe of accepting the s^d bond. or wordρ to the like effect. And
further saith y^t since the conferences afores^d wth the s^d Mr Ewens
this dep^t. did at the request of the s^d cōmp^lt demaund the s^d
money of the s^d Def^t Milton & did charge him the s'^d Milton w^th

a pmise y^t hee would see her p^d the s^d money, wherevnto hee answered y^t what pmise soeu' hee the s^d Milton made her at the first yet in regard y^t shee had accepted of interest for the s^d money hee held himselfe to bee discharged & s'd y^t shee might gett her money where shee could or to y^t effect And more To the rest not exañed by direccōn

[*Signed*] Geo: Brome.

September 23, 1631
DEPOSITION OF FRANCES STACY IN DOWNER-MILTON SUIT
Chancery Depositions, C24/574/40

23. die Septembris. 1631.   p Downer vīd:./
Anº: R: Rꝑ: Caroli 7º./

ffraunces Stacy of the parish of S^t. Andrewes in the Wardorb London Spinster, aged Twenty Two yeares or thereaboutꝑ sworne &c./ and by direccōn examined vppon the 1.2.5.6. and 8. Inter^{rs}./

1. That shee knoweth all the parties to this suite Cōmp^{lt}: and dēft^ꝑ, And hath knowe Rose Downer widdow named for Comp^{lt}. euer since this deptꝑ rememberaunce, shee being this dep^{tꝑ}: Aunt, and hath bred, and educated this dep^t from her Childhoode, And John Milton and Thomas Bower named for dēftꝑ, this dep^t saieth shee hath knowne for these ffower yeares or thereaboutꝑ And moreover saieth that the Cōmp^{lt}. is not of any pfession but liues on Audlin Hill, in the s'd parishe of S^t: Andrewes in the Wardorbb, on that smale meanes it hath pleased god to lend vnto her, And the dēftꝑ are both of them by their pfessions Scriueno^{rs}, and liue (as this dep^t taketh it) both togeather in one house in Bredstreet London, the dēft Bower, being heretofore (to this dēp^{tꝑ}: knowledg) seruant to the other dēft Milton, and did write vnder him in his Shopp in Bredstreet afores'd./

2. That by her liueing wth the s'd Cōmp^{lt}: her Aunt, shee knoweth, that shee the s'd Cōmp^{lt}: (vppon the good report and oppinion that went, and was concieued, of the dēft Miltons honesty and vpright dealeing in his pfession) did trust him the s'd dēft, with the puting forth at Jnterest, of the sūm of ffifty poundes, for her the s'd Cōmp^{lt}:, being A great part of her the Cōmp^{ltꝑ}: estate, And this dep^t. further saieth, shee alsoe knoweth, that the s'd Cōmp^{lt}, was from time to time, made acquainted with the securitie, and names of the parties, and their suerties, to whome the s'd monie was lent, and that she did vse to giue allowance and approue of such security before her s'd monie was disposed of, for this dep^t saieth, shee hath knowne the deft Milton send

vnto the cōmp^lt to knowe if shee would let forth her monie, vppon such and such security wch shee did either allow, or disallow of as she pleased.

5. Shee alsoe knoweth that the Cōmp^lt: haveing earnest occasion to vse her s'd monie (soe put forth at interest as afores'd) did call in for the same to the s'd dēf^t Milton, when the same should grow due although it was then in such mens hands, or shee had such security for the same, as shee very well liked of, shee the Cōmp^lt: saying (that had not her owne earnest occasion for monies compelled her thereto), shee would not haue called for the same in, shee liked the security soe well, or to that effect./ And further or otherwise to the Jnter^r, shee saieth shee is not able to depose./

6. That as shee hath credibly heard, the s'd ffifty poundes, (according to the desire and request of the Cōmp^lt:) was, at or about the time the same grew due), paied in to the deftϱ, or one of them, at the dēft Miltons Shopp in Bredstreet afores'd, by the principall, or suerties whoe stood bound for the same to the Cōmp^lt And further therevnto shee saieth shee cannot depose./

8. That within A day or Two, or thereaboutϱ, after the Cōmp^lt: had bene at the dēft Miltons s'd Shopp for her monie, the same being then due, the s'd dēftϱ, or one of them, sent one of their Seruantϱ with an Obligacōn in the Names of one Mathew Ewens, and Will'm Keymer, for payment of the s'd ffifty poundes with Jnterest, at Six Monethes, vnto her the Cōmp^lt And this dep^t further saieth, that the Cōmp^lt: was very angrie, wth the s'd Seruant, that brought the s'd Obligacōn and very much greiued, that shee could not haue her monie to serue her occasions, and saied shee would not accept of the s'd Obligacōn, for that shee must have her monie, as shee had oftentimes told them the s'd dēftϱ wherevnto the s'd Seruant (in this deptϱ heareing) answered, that the security was good, and that his M^r (meaneing as this dept conceiued the dēft Milton) would make it good as reason was hee should

[Deponent's mark?]

And therevppon the s'd Seruant (against the Cōmp^ltϱ will) did leaue the s'd Obligacōn behinde him vpon A Table in the Roome saying vnto her that shee could haue but good security for her monie, and there it was, or to that effect./ And this dept lastly saieth that the Cōmp^lt: was then ill at ease and very aged and not able to stire forth of doores to carrie back the s'd Obligacōn to the dēftϱ./ And more &c./ To the rest of the Jnter not to be examined

[Deponent's mark?]

September 26, 1631

DEPOSITION OF RICHARD SHERATT IN DOWNER-MILTON SUIT

Chancery Depositions, C 24/574/40

26 Septemb': 1631 Ao   p Downer

Rᵽ Car' 7ᵐᵒ:

Richard Sheratt Cittizen and Haberdasher of London dwelling within
the p'cinct of bridwell aged 67 yeares or therabouts sworne & exam-
1: ined &c To the 1 Jnt' saith That he doeth know Rose Downer wid'.
named for Cōmplt & soe hath done for the space of 20 yeares or
theraboutᵽ and doeth likewise know John Milton and Thomas
Bowre named for dēftᵽ and hath knowne the sd Milton some twelue
yeares or theraboutᵽ and the said Bowre ten yeares or theraboutᵽ
And saith yᵗ the said dēft Milton is by ᵽfession a Notarie and doeth
now live in Breadstreet neere Cheape side London & yᵉ sd Bowre
some 2 yeares since was a servant to the said dēft Milton & did writ
vnder him in his shopp in Breadstreet beforesaid but of late (as this
depᵗ hath credibly heard) the said Bowre is become an Attorney in
his māᵗᵖ Court of Comon pleas and did in Hillary Terme last past
lodge at an vpholdsters house in the Strand London but whether he
hath changed his Lodging since that tyme or noe this depᵗ knoweth
not

2: He doeth knowe it to be true yᵗ the Cōmplt did trust and imploye
the sd dēfte Milton in the puting forth the sūme of ffifty poundᵽ at
Jnterest being a maine or great pte of her estate the said Milton
being reputed and accompted to be a very honest and iust man in
his ᵽfession & dealing And saith that at the first putting forth of the
said money the said Cōmplt was made acquainted with the names of
the ptie & his suerties to whome yᵉ same was lente and did yeld her
consent to the putting forth thereof And further he cannot depose
to the Jnt'/.

3 He well remembereth that some short tyme before the end of six
monthes or therābtᵽ next after the first putting forth of the said
money as aforesaid being in or aboute the yeare 1628 (but whether in
the month of June or noe this depᵗ certainly remembereth not) the
said Compˡᵗ did diuerse and sundry tymes goe vnto the said dēft
Milton to haue in her said money to supplye her vrgent occasions
and did earnestly importune & call vpon the said Milton for the
same telling him in this depᵗᵖ hearing that she would not haue the
same to remaine any longer out of her owne handᵽ she hauing as
she said great want & vse thereof or vsed wordᵽ to the same effecte/.

4 That about yᵉ tyme aforesd the sd Cōmplt did intreate this depᵗ to
repaire to the said Milton & earnestly to solicitte him to call in the

said money to yᵉ end that the same might be paid vnto her the Cōmplt as the same should growe due and this depᵗ according to her desire and sundry and often tymes goe vnto him both with her the Cōmplt and alone and did speake with the said Milton to the purpose aforesaid And saith that the said Milton did allwayes answere this depᵗ that he would calle in the said money Jnsoemuch that at last he did seeme to be very angry with the Cōmplt for coming and sending vnto him soe often for it saying that she should not need to feare her money for ye security was goode enough or wordǫ to the like effecte but the p'cize tymes when or how often this depᵗ went vnto the said dēft Milton about it as aforesd he doeth not now re-member/.

5 That as the Complt hath diverse tymes told this depᵗ she had great and vrgent occasions to vse her said money when she first did calle the same in otherwise it should not as shee said haue bene taken out of theire handǫ to whom it was first lent And this depᵗ doeth vn-doubtedly beleeue that if she had bene minded to haue kept the same at Jnterest that she would never haue called it in out of theire handǫ whoe did first borrow the same but this depᵗ saith that the said Cōmpltǫ occasions were such (as she did often tell this depᵗ) that she was inforced to call in the said money & not to dispose the same out againe at Jnterest

6 That as before he hath deposed the said dēftǫ Milton and Bowre haue confessed to this depᵗ that according to the request & desire of the Cōmplt the said money was called in out of theire handǫ to whome it was first lent and was paid vnto them by ye principall or suerties or theire assignees whoe stood first bounde for the same vnto the Cōmplt but in what place the same was soe paid vnto them as by the Jnt' is demanded this depᵗ knoweth not But verily beleeueth that the said money came to the handǫ of the said dēftǫ by the Cōmpltǫ calling the same in as aforesd & by noe other meanes/.

[*Signed*] Rychard Shurratt

7 That he doeth not know whether the Cōmplt had any notice or noe that the said money was paid in vnto the said dēftǫ Howbeit saith that the Cōmplt supposing that the same was paid in at the tyme when it fell due did goe vnto the said Milton imeadiatly after it was due vnto his house in Breadstreet aforesd and did demande the same of him in this depᵗǫ hearing And therevpon the said dēft Milton did will the other dēft Bowre he being then his servant to pay the same vnto her further saying what a stire is here J wilbe ridd of her & her money too seeming to be very angry with the said Bowre because he delayed to pay it vnto her whervnto the said Bowre then made

answere that a freind of his had need of soe much money and he
had put the same forth againe vnto him for her saying that he knewe
that she would put the same forth againe to Jnterest and therefore
he were as good haue the disposing thereof as another man or vsed
wordℓ to that effecte. And therevpon did in effecte vtterly deny to
lett her haue her said money and sent her away much greved and
discontented And moreover saith that he doeth verily beleeue that
the said dēftℓ when the Cōmplt demanded her money as aforesaid
had the some in theire handℓ & might haue payed it vnto her if they
had pleased soe to doe And further he cannot depose to the Jnt'/.

9 That as this dept hath heard after the said dēftℓ had received in the
Cōmptℓ money from them to whome it was first lent as aforesaid the
said Bowre did put forth & lend the same vnto Ewen and Keymer in
the Jnt' named whoe did therevpon enter into the bond in the Jnt'
menconed to the Cōmplt at the Jnstance of the said dēftℓ or one of
them without the liking prvity or knowledge of the Cōmplt as this
dept vndoubtedly beleeueth but whether the said bond was entred
into in leiwe of certaine desprate debtℓ by the said Ewen & Keymer
then oweing & paiable to the said Milton or Bowre or to some of
those for whome they did then put out money as by the Jnt' is questioned this dept cannot say Howbeit saith yt he hath heard yt noe
more then the sūme of ffowreteene poundℓ of the Cōmpltℓ money
soe lent by the said dēftℓ as aforesaid did ever Come to the handℓ
of them the said Ewen and Keymer and this dept hath likwise heard
since the said money was lent vnto them as aforesaid that they were
men insolvent and Carles in what & to whome they became bounde
& indebted being both of them farr more indebted then theire estates
did amounte vnto and were vnworthy of creditt for any such sōme of
money but what theire estates were at the tyme when the said
money was lent vnto them as aforesaid this dept doeth not knowe
Neither doe this dept know or can tell what to beleeue touching the
dēftℓ Jntencōns or either of them to defeate the Cōmplt of her
money as by the Jnt' is demanded Nor can he otherwise depose for
satisfacōn thereof/.

10 That he well remembereth that some shorte tyme before this suite
began in this hōble. Cort that he this dept had some conferrence wth
the sd dēft Bowre in the prsence of the Cōmplt concerning the
said money And saith that he this dept did charge the said Bowre
with bad dealing and told him he offered but hard measure to the
Cōmplt she being an Jgnorant & simple woman in putting forth her
money against her will and to men vnknown vnto her and withall
this dept told the said Bowre yt the dēft Milton laid all ye fault vpon

him or word℘ to that effecte Whervpon the said Bowre seemed to be very angry with the said Milton saying that if he (meaning the Def^t: Milton) did tell he would tell something also or to the same effecte And saith that he this dep^t did moreover charge the said Bowre & told him that all but a small pte of the said money was to stopp & pay debt℘ due vnto him & Milton by the said Ewans And that but a small pte of the said money came to the hand℘ of the said Ewens vnto wch the said Bowre made little answere but said that indeed he thought that the said Ewans had but little pte thereof or that effecte And

[Signed] Rychard Shurratt

further saith that after the Conference & speeches aforesd the said dēft℘ did advise the Cōmplt to put the said bonde in suit against the said Ewans and Keymer But whether the same were trickes between the said dēft℘ to pay themselues or others some weake debt℘ due to them by the said Ewens & Keymer & so put the bond vpon her the pl't as by the Jnt' is demanded this dep^t is not able to depose but this dep^t beleeueth it was very hard measure & dealing offered by them the s^d dēf^t℘ to the Cōmplt And more matterially he saith he cannot depose for satisfacōn of any the pticalar questions in this inter: ppounded Nor more To the rest not to be examined by direccon

[Signed] Rychard Shurratt

November 21, 1631
AN AFFIDAVIT IS TAKEN IN THE DOWNER-MILTON SUIT
Registers of Affidavits, C 41/7, Michaelmas, 1631, #469

Rosam Downer Henry ffisher maketh oath that James ffisher this
vid q' Thomam Def^t sonn is at this tyme resideinge in the kingdome
Bower et āl of Ireland and that the said Deft℘ doe informe this
Deft℘ 469 Dep^t that the said James ffisher is a very materiall
witnesse to be examīed in this Cause on the s'd Deft℘
behalfes Jur' xxj° Novem 1631 Ro Riche

November 28, 1631
PUBLICATION OF DEPOSITIONS IN DOWNER-MILTON SUIT IS STAYED
Chancery Decrees and Orders, C 33/161, f. 171

L xxviii No [1631] . . .

D Rosa Downer vid fforasmuch as it appeareth by an Afft of one
q' Tho. Bower et al Henry ffisher that one James ffisher Who is A
r deft materiall witnesse for the Deft is at this tyme
resideing in Jreland Jt is therefore ordered
vpon the mocōn of Mr Maundrell being of the Deft℘ Councell that A
Comī be awarded into Jreland to examine the said James ffisher Re-

tournable the Last Day of the next tearme, and in the meane tyme publicacō is staied but then to passe pemptorily./

ex'

[Thomas?] R[oberts?].

April 14, 1632

COPIES OF DEPOSITIONS ARE MADE FOR ROSE DOWNER

Chancery Depositions, C 24/574/40 (endorsement of bundle)

(40

Downer vid' con Milton et al'

Rsē+Olive Street.

Rsē+ffrancꝓ Stacy.

Rsē+Richard Sherrat

Rsē+George Broomee

Copied the. 14. April. 1632. ffor Down' by Waad'

Michīms: Anᵒ: 7ᵐᵒ. Caroli Rꝓ.

June 20, 1632

MILTON'S FATHER GETS A JUDGMENT AGAINST HIS PARTNER BOWER

Chancery Decrees and Orders, C 33/161, f. 704

Mer xx Junij [1632]/

D   Rosa Downer vid q'   Whereby an order of the second of June
    Johes Milton et Tho.   instant taken vpon hearing of the Cause. Jt
r   Bower Deft   was ordered and Decreed that the Defᵗꝓ
                           should before thend of this tearme paie vnto
the p't 50 ˡⁱ and therevpon the pl't should assigne over vnto the Dēftꝓ
the bond in question to help themselues agᵗ the obligors Vpon opening of
the matter this pn̄te Day vnto this Court by Mʳ Estcott being of the
Deft Miltons Counsell Jt was alleadged that although it plainely appeared
at the said hearing that the Deft Bower lent the said 50ˡ wᵗʰout the
Deft Miltons consent and that the Deft Milton comaunded the said
Bower to pay the same vnto the pt', and although the intent of this
Court (as was alleadged) then was that the said Deftꝓ should paie the
said 50ˡⁱ equally and proporcōnably betweene them yet the said order
being left geñall and not setting downe in pticuler how much each of
them shall paie the Deft Bower refuseth to pay the moiety of the said
money although the said money miscarried thorough the fault and will-
fullnes of the said Bower. Jt is therevpon thought meete & soe ordered
in case the said Milton shalbe charged wᵗʰ the whole 50ˡⁱ that if the
Deft Bowers shall not vpon the retourne of a spā shew good cause to the
contrary then he shall pay A moiety of the said 50ˡⁱ vnto the said
Milton./

ex̄

[Thomas?] R[oberts?].

CHAPTER IV

COTTON *VS.* MILTON

November 25, 1630

RECEIPT BY THOMAS BOWER FOR BONDS TURNED OVER TO HIM BY
JOHN COTTON

B.M. Cottonian Charters 1/5/4

The Schedule of the Principall debtǫ

Mr Mort & others by bond dated the vith of Septembr 1628.... 100li

Mr Welby & othrs by bond dated the viith of Novembr 1627.... 200li

The Lord Strange & othrs p obl' Dat' viio Novembr' 1626...... 300li

Mr Marbury & othrs p obl' Dat' xijo Maij 1630............... 100li

Mr Bold & othrs p oblᶜᵒⁿ Dat' xiiijto April' 1625.............. 100li

Mr Lea & othrs p obl' Dat' xiijo Maij 1621.................. 100li

Sr Ric' Molineux & othrs p obl' Dat' xvijo Maij 1623.......... 100li

Sr Wm Norres & othrs p obl' Dat' xviijo Novembr' 1626........ 100li

Mr Wm Welby & othrs p obl' Dat' [?] Novembr' 1629.......... 100li

Mr Bannester & othrs p obl' Dat' xxjo Maij 1623............. 100li

Mr Sherfeild & othrs p obl' Dat' xxvjo Junij 1629.............. 100li

Mr Ewens & othrs p obl' Dat' xxixo Maij 1628................ 100li

Mr Vaudray & othrs p obl' Dat' xxxo Novembr' 1627........... 100li

Sr ffrancis Leigh & othrs p obl' Dat' vltimo Novembr' 1624.... 100li

Sr Robt Heath & othrs p obl' Dat' j Decembr' 1620.......... 100li

Mr Leigh & othrs p obl' Dat' xij Decembr' 1626.............. 050li

Sr Kenelme Digby & othrs p obl' Dat' vijo Augustj 1626....... 200li

Mr Dabridgecourt & othrs p obl' Dat' xvijo Decembr' 1627..... 100li

Mr Reed & othrs p obl' Dat' xxo Maij 1630.................. 100li

Mr Prewet & othrs p obl' Dat' xxjo Decembr' 1627............. 100li

Bonds in suite

Mr Erdiswick & others p obl' xjo Maij 1624.................. 200li

Sr Wm Sandys & othrs p obl' Dat' xviijo Maij 1620............ 100li

Mr Charnock & othrs p obl' Dat' xixo Novembr' 1620.,........ 200li

Mr Chetwode & othrs p obl' Dat' xxvijo Novembr' 1623........ 100li

Mr Clopton & othrs p obl' Dat' xxjo Junij 1626................ 100li

Sr Geo: Horsey & othrs p obl' Dat' vto Julij 1627.............. 100li

Sr Geo: Horsey & othrs p obl' Dat' xixo Decembr' 1626........ 100li

Mr Veale & othrs p obl' Dat' xxiiijto Maij 1626................ 100li

Mr Carrent & othrs p obl' Dat' xxviijo Novembr' 1622......... 100li

Mr Blacker & othrs p obl' Dat' xjo Octobr' 1627............... 100li

Mr Rodney & othrs p obl' Dat' xijo Decembr' 1626............ 050li

xxv^{to} Die Novembr' 1630

Rec' the same day & yeare of John Cotton of Londoñ Esqre all the particular bondꝑ above in this schedule menconed wch are all that are due at Mr Miltons shop in Bread streete J say rec^d all the said seũall bondꝑ

p Tho: Bower

May 28, 1636
SIR THOMAS COTTON SUES MILTON'S FATHER

(1) *British Museum Cottonian Charters 1/5/5*	*Masson I (1881), 627 ff.*
(2) *Requests Proceedings Req 2/630*	*Academy 6 (1874), 560*
	Athenæum, 1880, II, 15

[The following is a composite text combining the two, and supplemented in the list of bonds by Bower's receipt of November 25, 1630]

To the kings most excellent Ma^{ty}.

Humbly sheweth vnto your gracious Ma^{ty} your loyall & dutifull subiect S^r. Tho: Cotton of Sawtry in Yo^r highnes county of Huntington Baronet, executor off ye last will & testam^t of John Cottō esqꝫ deceased. That whereas ye s^d John Cotton vncle of yor s^d subiect being an old decripitt weake man of the age of fourscore yeares and vpwards did heretofore about five yeares sithence put into the hands off one John Milton of Breadstreet in yor ma^{ties} city of Londō scrivener and Tho: Bower seruant to the sayd John Milton dīv great sumēs of money, in trust to be lett out at interest aft^r ye rate of eight in the hundred by the sayd John Milton and Tho: Bower which sayd somes were by seuerall specialtyes put out by the sayd John Milton and Tho: Bower viz Mr Mort and others by bond dated the 6th of Sept: 1628 100^{li}. principall debt, Mr Welby and others by bond dated 7 of Nouemb: 1627 200 principall debt The Lord Strang and others, by bond dated 7 of Novemb 1626 300 principall debt &^c. Mr Marbury and others by bond dated the Twelueth [of] May one thousand six [hundred and thirty one hund]red poundꝑ principall debt. M^r. Bold & others by bond dated the ffourteenth of Aprill One thousand six hundred Twentie & ffive One hundred poundꝑ [prin]cipall debt. M^r [Lea and others by bond dated the thirteenth] of May One thousand Six hundred Twentie & one One hundred poundꝑ principall debt, Sr Richard Molineux & others by bond dated the Seventeenth of May One thousand [Six] hundred Twentie & three [one hundred poundꝑ] principall debt. Sr Will'm Norris & others by bond dated ye the Eighteenth of November One thousand six hundred Twentie & Six One hundred poundꝑ principall debt. [M^r] Will'm Welby & others [by bond dated y^e [?]tieth of November One thowsand six hundred Twentie Nyne One hundred poundϼ principall debt. M[r] Bannister & others by bond dated y[e] One & Twentieth [of] May One thowsand Six [hundred twenty three] One hundred poundϼ principall debt, M[r] Cherfeild & others by bond dated y[e] Six & Twentieth of June One thowsand six hundred Twentie Nyne One [hund]red poundϼ principall [debt M[r] Ewens & others] by bond dated the Nyne & Twentieth of May One thousand six hundred Twentie Eight One hundred poundϼ principall debt. M[r] Vaudray & others by bond [dated] the Thirtieth of November [One thousand six] hundred Twentie seven One hundred poundϼ principall debt, S[r] Robert Heath & others by bond dated the Tenth of December One thowsand six hundred & Twentie One hundred poundϼ principall [debt. Sir Francis] Leigh & others by bond dated the Last of November One thowsand Six hundred Twentie ffoure One hundred poundϼ principall debt, M[r] Leigh & others [by] bond dated y[e] Twelueth of [November One thousand] six hundred Twentie six ffiftie poundϼ principall debt. S[r] Kenelm Digby & others by bond dated the Seventh of August One thowsand six hundred Twentie six two hundred poundϼ [principall debt.] M[r] Dabridgecourt & others by bond dated the seventeenth of December One thowsand six hundred Twentie seven One hundred poundϼ principall debt. M[r] [Reed] & others by bond dated y[e] [Twentieth of May] One thowsand six hundred & Thirtie One hundred poundϼ principall debt. M[r] [Prewet] & others by bond dated the One & Twentieth of December One thowsand six hundred Twentie seven, One hundred [poundϼ] principall debt. M[r] Erdiswick & others by bond dated the Eleventh of May One thowsand six hundred Twentie ffoure Two hundred poundϼ principall debt. S[r] Willm Sandys and others by bond dated h[e] Eighteenth of [May One thousand] six hundred Twentie, One hundred poundϼ principall debt, M[r] Charnock & others by bond dated the Nynteenth of November One thowsand six hundred & Twentie Two hundred poundϼ principall debt. [M[r] Chetwode] & others by bond dated the seven & Twentieth of November One thowand six hundred Twentie three One hundred poundϼ principall debt. M[r] Clopton & others by bond dated the One & Twentieth day of June One thousand [six hundred] Twentie six One hundred poundϼ principall debt. S[r] George Horsey & others by bond dated the ffift of July One thowsand six hundred Twentie seven, One hundred poundϼ principall debt. S[r] George Ho[rsey & others by] bond dated the Nyneteenth day of December One thowsand six hundred Twentie six One hundred poundϼ principall debt. M[r] Veale & others by bond dated the ffoure & Twentieth day of May One thowsand six hundred Twentie six One hundred poundϼ principall debt. M[r] Carrent & others by bond dated the Eight & twentieth of November One thowsand six hundred Twentie Two One hundred poundϼ principall debt. M[r] Blacker & others by bond dated the Eleventh day of October One thowsand six hundred Twentie seven, One hundred poundꝑ principall debt. Mᵣ Rodney & others by bond dated the Twelueth of December [One tho]wsand six hundred Twentie six, ffiftie poundꝑ principall debt. All which somes togeather of principall debt amount to the full some of 3600ˡⁱ, for which sayd somes the sayd John Miltō and Tho: Bowre did bring to the sayd John Cotton your subiects said vncle halfe yearly the interest after the rate of 8 p cent for some yeares and did often renew call in and put out the sayd sumes as they thought best themselues euer pretending to the sayd John Cotton that the sayd partyes to whom the mony was put out were very sufficient and able men, and as in truth most of them were (as your subiect hath since learnd) But shortly after the sayd John Milton and Tho: Bower (finding the sayd John Cotton to be decripitt and vnable by reason of his great yeares) any wayes to follow his occasions (being constrained altogeather to keepe his chamber the sayd Milton and Bower did by yᵉ practise & direcciō off one Thomas Holchar an attorney at law Who was vsed by yᵉ sᵈ John Cotton in suing bonds forbeare to bring him in either the principall or most part of the interest of the said somes pretending that the partyes to whom the sayd somes were lett out were not sufficient By wᶜʰ practice of deteyning yᵉ sᵈ intrest money they did cause yᵉ sᵈ John Cottō to beleeue that both principall & interest were desperate & that yᵉ debtors were psons non soluent. And hauing so farre wrought vppō his conceit then they together wᵗʰ yᵉ sᵈ Tho. Holchar vsed pswasionꝑ to the sayd John Cotton that it would be more for his proffitt and ease if he toke some competent some of mony and deliuer vp to them or one of them his sayd bond. wherevppō they would endeuoᵣ to get yᵉ principall money, and in consideration therof they or one of them would giue him 2000ˡⁱ in hand which the better to effect they or one of them by yᵉ priuity & direcciō off yᵉ sᵈ Holchar did combine & plot with one Tho: Collwell esq in whose house the said John Cotton then lay & by reward of yᵉ sumē of 200ˡⁱ giuē to yᵉ sd Tho. Colwell by yᵉ sd Holchar Miltō & Bowᵣ or some of them they did draw yᵉ sᵈ Tho. Colwell to informe & often to alledge to yᵉ sᵈ Jo: Cottō, that yᵉ sᵈ detꝑ were despate & yᵉ pties to be dead nonsoluant or beyond yᵉ seas. and resident in the county Palatine of Chester and Lancaster where writtꝑ could not easily be serued & undᵣ these pᵣtences so pswade yᵉ sᵈ John Cottō to accept 2000ˡⁱ fro yᵉ sᵈ Miltō & Bowᵣ or one off them for yᵉ sᵈ principal detꝑ wᶜʰ amounted to 3600ˡⁱ. wᶜʰ accordingly the sᵈ Tho: Colwel did By wʰ sᵈ practice & combinatiō they did draw yᵉ sᵈ John Cottō for the sayd some of 2000ˡⁱ to deliuer vp in the handꝑ of the sayd Tho: Blower all the sayd bondꝑ that they sayd Tho Blower might renew the said bonds in his owne name or in the name of any other and take the

principall debt either to his owne vse or to the vse of any other which
sayd principall debt so referred to them to gather vp is expressed in a
scedule vnder the hand of the sayd Tho: Bower, And the sayd Tho:
Bower or he whose name the sayd Thomas Bower did then vse w^h was
done by ye priuity & agreem^t of ye s^d Holchar who vnd^rhand was a
share^r wth ye s^d Bower in ye s^d agreem^t & disbursed a great part of ye s^d
2000^li. (having the custody of the sayd bonds by ye s^d Holchars meanes
& psecuciō at law did call in to his or their own vse or renew most of y^e
s^d bond℈ for the said principall debt in his or their owne name, And not
contented with the sayd principall debt (being a debt of their owne making, and being sixteene hundred pound℈ more then the consideration
they gaue for it) they the said Thomas Bower & Tho. Holchar or they
or hee whose name hee or they vsed haue receaued off seūal psons dettors
by ye s^d obligacions att least 500 for the interest due before the sayd debt
came to their vse; Shortly aft^r w^h time the s^d John Cotton dyed, leauing
yor subiect his sole executor as afores^d who did vnd^rtake ye same And
since that time yor s^d subiect hath in freindly mañ^r requested ye s^d.
John Milton & Tho Bow^r to accept their 2000^li, & to pay ou^r to yor s^d
subiect ye s^d monies by thē receiued or secured vpon the s^d obligaciōns
& to deliu^r ouer the new securities by them taken for any of ye s^d det℈
And hath also requested thē & ye s^d Holchar to expresse what sumēs of
money haue beene by them or any other to their vses received off any
ye psōs in ye s^d obligatiō, obliged for intrest or principall debt money or
altered by new securities & whof ye s^d old obligaciōs remaine in their
hands, & that they would account to yor s^d subiect for the s^d 3600^li w^th
y^e [interest] received or secured It being noe reason that ye s^d Holchar
Miltō & Bow^r should by such practices & vndue cariage make so great
pfit to thēselfes. But they haue hith^rto & stil doe refuse to entr into y^e
s^d accompt. Now forasmuch as yor s^d subiect ought in equity compel y^e
s^d Holchar Miltō & Bow^r to account wth yor s^d subiect for ye s^d principal
det℈ & [inte]rest monies off ye s^d dett℈, but is:, wthout remedy elswhere,
for that he knoweth not ye certaine sūms by them receiued altered or
secured nor in whose name ye s^d bond℈ are taken, nor who receiued y^e
s^d sumēs. Jn consid^raciō of all wch p^rmises & for yor subiects releife
herein, may it please yor Ma^ty to grt to yor s^d subiect yor Ma^tyes pces of
privy seale or oth^r comāund to be directed to ye s^d Jo: Miltō & Tho:
Bower & Thomas Holchar &c. or such others as your sayd subiect shall
hereafter learne to be interested in the said money & by the said [writt]
thereby comānde[ing them . . . to] be & appeare bef yor Matie & yor
Counsell of yor highest Court of Whitehall at Westminster then & there
to ans[wer the premises and also to] stand [to and abide such further
ordēr and direction as to your Majesty and your Highness' Counsel

shall seem agreeable to] equity & good conscience [And] yoʳ subject [as in] dutie bound shall ever praye for yoʳ Maᵗˢ long & happy [Reign over us]

[Signature illegible]

[*Endorsed:*] Dat xxviij Die Maij Anno RRρ Caroli Duodecimo./

p Nunc./

[*Cottonian Charters 1/5/5 also includes what appears to be a first draft of this bill, much shorter but following the same general plan.*]

January 23, 1636/7

A WRIT IS ISSUED AGAINST MILTON'S FATHER

Court of Requests Process Book, Hilary 12th and Easter 13th Charles I, Req 1/186, f. 1ᵛ

1636 Termino scī Hillarij Anno Regni Rρ Caroli xij°./
xxiijᵗⁱᵒ die Januarij

[1ˢ. 8ᵈ. *cancelled*] A P. S¹. reñ to John Milton at the suite⎫
of Sʳ Thomas Cotton Barronett . . . ⎭ 1° febr

February 13, 1636/7

WILLIAM WITHERINGTON MAKES AFFIDAVIT OF SERVING WRIT
ON MILTON'S FATHER

Court of Requests Affidavit Book, Req 1/141, f. 198ᵛ　　　　*Masson, I (1881), 629*

Decimo Tertio die ffebruarij Anno RRˢ duodecimo . . .
Cotton.　　William Witherington of the Cittye of Westmʳ. señ maketh
Milton./　　oath that on the 27ᵗʰ. daye of Januarye last hee served John
　　　　　　Milton the elder with his Maᵗρ. Proces of P: S¹: issueinge forth
of this honōᵇˡᵉ. Court at the suite of Sʳ. Thomas Cotton Barronett by
leavinge the same at his dwellinge house./

March 10, 1636/7

MILTON'S FATHER IS ORDERED TO ANSWER COTTON

Requests Proceedings, Req 2/630

By the Kinge:/

Trustie and w[ell beloved] wee greete you well: And send vnto you
here inclosed a Bill of Cōmpt. vnto vs exhibited by Sʳ Thomas Cotton
knight pl't against John Milton defendant Wherevppon wee trusting in
your approued wisdomes learningρ and indifferencies [do command] you
that by authority hereof calling afore you in our name the said De-

fendant yee then do receaue his answeres vnto the contentꝑ of the said
Bill by his [oa]the in due forme of lawe sworne, and of the same his
answeres soe by you receaued in forme aforesaid, Duely to certifie vs
and our Councell by your Writeings with the said Bill vnder your Seales
in our Court of Whitehall att Westm': in the tresmaines of Easter: next
To th'intent that wee by thadvise of our said Councell [may] further doe
therein as the case rightfully shall require, Nott fayling hereof as yee
tender our displeasure and th'advance^{mt}. of Justice. Given vnder our
Privy [S]eale att our Pallace of West[minster the] tenth Daye of
Marche in the xij^{th}. [ye]are of our Raigne./

Willm. Parker dep^{t}: Tho. Parker

[*Endorsed:*] Executio istius Comīssionis patet in quadam Responsione
huic annex'

Tho Agar
John Agar

March 22, 1636/7

COURT ORDERS WRIT OF DEDIMUS POTESTATEM FOR ANSWER OF MILTON'S FATHER TO COTTON BILL

Court of Requests Order Book, Req 1/71, p. 227   *Masson, I (1881), 630*

xxij^{do} die Martij

Cotton.   Whereas in the Cause at the suite of Sr Thomas Cotton barrt
Milton   p^{lt} ag^{t} John Milton th'elder deft Jt was ordered vpon the
          xxiij^{th} of May last vpon p^{r}tence that the deft stood in contempt
& living w^{th}in 17 myles of Lond' That an Attach^{t} should be awarded
agt him ret [*undated?*] And that the deft for his delayeꝑ should pay the
p^{lt} xx^{s} Costꝑ Now forasmuch as it is alledged by the p^{ltꝑ} humble Peticōn
exhīted to Sr Edward Powell Knt & barronett one of his Ma^{tꝑ} Councell
of this Co^{rt} That the s'd deft is an old man about fowerskore yereꝑ of age
and is infirme & vnfitt for Travell & that he sent vp to his Atturnies to
appeare in due time And for that it appeares by the Certifficatt of George
Miller gent one of the Clarkꝑ or Atturneys of this Co^{rt} That about the
beginning of the last Terme he was reteyned to appeare for the s'd deft
& soone after having p^{r}pared a Coppy of the Bill vpon Affīft made that
the deft was aged & vnable to Travell made forth a ded. Potestat for the
taking of his Answere in the Countrey Jt is therefore ordered That the
s'd Attacht shalbe hereby staid And that the xx^{s} Costꝑ awarded by the
s'd former order shalbe suspended And the Dedimus Potestatem so
made as aforesaid shall issue forth for taking the s'd Deftꝑ Answere to
the p^{ltꝑ} said Bill accordingly./

April 1, 1637

CHRISTOPHER MILTON MAKES AFFIDAVIT HIS FATHER IS TOO INFIRM TO ATTEND COURT IN LONDON

Court of Requests Affidavit Book, Req 1/141, f. 218   {*Athenæum, 1880, II, 15–16*
                                                                {*Masson, I (1881), 631*

Primo die Aprilis 1637 . . .

Milton./   Whereas John Milton geñ hath bin served with his Ma^tp.
Cotton./   Poces of P: S¹; issueinge forth of this honō^ble. Court to answere
        to a bill of Comp[laint ag]ainst him exhibited by Sr Thomas
Cotton Barronet plt, Christopher Milton sonne of the said defendant
maketh oath, that his said father beinge aged about 74 yeares is not by
reason of his said aige and infirmitye able to trauell to the Cittye of
westm^r. to make his perfect answere to the said bill without much p^riu-
dice to his health hee livinge at Horton in the Countye of Buck about
17 miles distant from the Cittye of westm^r./

April 3, 1637

MILTON-COTTON SUIT MENTIONED IN LETTER TO SIR THOMAS COTTON FROM HIS ATTORNEY

British Museum Cottonian Charters, 1/5/5   {*Athenæum, 1880, II, 15*
                                                       {*Masson, I (1881), 632–633*

(Noble S^r.) for yor businesses vss/ Bower & Milton they stande thus.,
in Easter tearme, we serued Bower by the messenger, & ffiled our bill
the same tearme & tooke a P.S. vss Milton, and after renewed it twice
but only the laste was served; Laste tearme we tooke an attachm^t
against Bower for want of Aunswere and gott an order for his Comittm^t
& encrease of Chardges for his delayes & Contempt℘, wth an other order
vss Milton allmost to the same effect, The warden of the ffleete hath that
vss Bower who desires to be remembred vnto you, and hath vndertaken
to bring in his body wth the Costes & Awnswere, and w^t else is requisite
&c./ Milton since the tearme hath obtayned an order that o^r Costes
shall for the p^rsent be suspended, and that in regard of his age he maye
haue a dedimus potestat to take his Awnswere in the Countrey, as soone
as ever J heard of it J sent the name, of a gent that liues thereabout℘ who
to be putt into the dēd for you: who J hope will be p^rsent when the
Ans^r is taken., att the beginninge of next tearme you need not feare but
to haue both there Awnsweres, and the Cause to stand in a right & ready
way for further ℘ceedings as shall then be advised./ J have here sent you
newse of the chardges and Copyes of all the orders, whereby you may be
further satisfyed [that], when yor other bill comes J shalbe as carefull in

yt as [I] maye be/ And thus with my humblest service & respects vnto
you first

[?]ves 3 April 1637   Yo[r] Wor[sh] ever to be Comāunded
                                            Hen: Perry:

[*Endorsed:*] The right Worp[full] S[r] Thomas Cotton Baronett o[r] sent
these: [*In another hand:*] Tho Bower expresse in his answer what interest
was r[ecei]ued.

April 8, 1637

THOMAS BOWER MAKES AFFIDAVIT IN COTTON-MILTON SUIT

Court of Requests Affidavit Book, Req. 1/141, f. 220   *Masson, I (1881), 633*

8°. Aprilis 1637.

Bower./   Thomas Bower sworne &c saith that hee this deponent about
Cotton./   the end of Easter Tearme last tooke out A Coppye of a bill
          exhibited against him and one Milton in this honō[ble] Court by
S[r] Thomas Cotton Barronet and forthwith carried the same to his
Councell to drawe vpp an answere therevnto who shortlye after went
out of towne and by reason of the sicknes and the adiourninge of Mid-
sumēr and Michaelmas tearme came not to towne againe as this Deponent could by any meanes learne vntill the beginninge of Hillarie
tearme last who at his Cominge had lost the Coppye of the said bill
wherevppon this deponent about Candlemas last was inforced to take
out a new Coppye of the said bill wherevnto this deponent by reason of
sicknes and his extraordinarye occasions in his other buisines could not
till of late make answere./

April 8, 1637

MILTON'S FATHER'S ASSOCIATE, THOMAS BOWER, FILES ANSWER
TO COTTON SUIT

British Museum Cottonian Charters, 1/5/2   *Masson, I (1881), 633-635*

viij° die Aprilis Anno   The seuerall Aunsweare of Thomas Bower one of
R Rρ Caroli xiij°./.   the defendantρ to the Bill of Complaynt of S[r]
                          Thomas Cotton Baronett Cōmp[lt]./
Perry ρ Quer/   All advauntages of excepcōns. to the vntruthes incer-
Exaīat[r]./.   tentyes and manifest imperfeccōns vnto the said Bill
                         of Complaint vnto him this defendant now and att all
tymes hereafter saved and reserved for a full perfect & direct Answeare
vnto the said Bill of Complaint and to soe much of the materiall Contentρ
as anie way Concerneth him this def[t] to aunsweare vnto hee saith as
followeth That he beleeveth that the Complayn[t] is executor of the

last will and testament of the said John Cotton in the Byll named and
that the said John Cotton was decrepite weake and about the age of
eightye yeares; And this def^t saith hee was servant to John Milton in the
Bill named And doth beleeve and hath beene enformed by the said M^r
Milton that the said John Cotton for thirty yeares or thereaboutǫ did
ymploye the said John Milton to lett out att interest diuerse great
somēs of money after the rate of Tenne and eight in the hundred &
accordingly the said John Milton by the direccōn and assent of the said
John Cotton did lett out the said somēs to sundry persons But this defendant denyes that the said John Milton and this def^t or this defendant onely hadd wthin five or six yeares last past putt into the handǫ
of them or this defendant by the said John Cotton or his assignes any
somē or somēs of money whatsoeū to be lett out att interest, Jt is true
during such tyme as this def^t did serve the said John Milton which was
vntill or about seaven yeares last past this def^t as servaunt to the said
John Milton and together wth him the said John Milton did by the
advice and Consent of the said John Cotton and John Milton and each
of them putt out all the said seuerall somēs in the Bill mencōned to
the seuerall persons in the bill named in and by the seuerall specialtyes
about the seuerall tymes and dates in the bill sett forth, All which somēs
togeather of principall money amounted to three thousand and six
hundred poundes or thereaboutǫ And the defendant saith that the
said John Milton and this defendant or one of them did bring the said
John Cotton halfe yearly the interest after the Rate of eight poundes
per Centum for some yeares of all or most parte of the moneyes they or
eyther of them were imployed to putt out for the said John Cotton, And
this defendant togeather wth the said John Milton or one of them with
the approbacōn & direccōn of the said John Cotton did call in and putt
out the said somēs as they and the said Cotton thought best and not as
this defendant and the said John Milton or eyther of them thought best,
But this defendant sayth that the three Thousand and Six hundredd
poundǫ being in the handǫ of the said persons aforenamed many of
them did much decline in their estates and liued priuately and ob-
scurely and did neglect to pay the principall or interest for two or three
yeares togeather to the said John Cotton or to this defendant for his vse,
the said debto^{rs} being the Remaynder and worst in estate of twice or
three tymes soe many debto^{rs} as the said John Cotton had caused the
said John Milton and this defendant or one of them to put forth his
money at interest vnto, by Reason whereof the said John Cotton finding that many of the said Debto^{rs} were likely to proue desperate, and
not to be brought in without great trauayle and large expence and almost halfe the said three thousand and six hundredd poundǫ being due

by seuerall persons whoe inhabitted in the Counties Palatyne of Lancaster and Chester and would occasion an increase of trouble and expence for the recouering thereof, wherevpon the said John Milton from
tyme to tyme calling the said debto^{rs} and sending after them to most
of their habitacōns and not obteyning ether principall or interest the
said Mr Milton did in Easter tearme one thousand six hundred and
thirty accquaint John Cotton therewith wherevpon the said John
Cotton as this defendant beleeueth did make enquiry after the said
Debto^{rs} and did then offer to sell and assigne all the said debtℓ vnto the
said John Milton for one thousand and ffyue hundred poundℓ But the
said John Milton as this defend^t beleeueth did soe much mistrust the
seuerall abilityes of the said Debto^{rs} that hee would by noe meanes
condiscend to compound agree or giue him the said John Cotton one
thousand ffyue hundred poundℓ ready money for the said debtℓ of three
thousand and six hundredd poundℓ, Butt did diswade him the said
John Cotton from makeing any such Bargayne and after such tyme as
the said John Milton had refused the said bargayne the said John
Cotton and especially the Cōmp^{lt} in Mayster Cottons behalfe in
Michaellmas tearme one thousand six hundred and thirty did make
further enquiry both by friendℓ & also strangers after the said debto^{rs}
and found the same desperate as this def^t conceiues, and therevpon the
Cōmp^{lt} togeather with the said John Cotton did entertayne treaty and
comunicacōn to and wth this defendt about assigneing the said Dēbtℓ
of three thousand and six hundred poundℓ for ready money, And att
last the said John Cotton and your subiect by and with the consent of
the now Compltē did mutually and reciprocally to and wth each other
condiscend and come to an agreement by word of mouth to the effect
followeing (that is to say) that this defend^t shou'ld Jmēdiately satisfy
and pay two thousand poundℓ to the said John Cotton and that this
defendant should haue the three thousand and six hundred powndes
wth interest then due for the same to his vse in Manner followeing
(that is to say) he should haue power to renew any of the said bondℓ
for the said three thousand and six hundred powndes wth interest in this
defend^{tℓ} name or in the name or names of any person or persons to his
vse but should not haue power to sue any bond in the name of the said
John Cotton, But if there were Judgmentℓ vpon any of the said bondℓ
he this defend^t might to his owne vse, cause execucōn therevpon to be
made and executed, accordingly this defendant in Michaellmas tearme
one thousand six hundred and thirty did pay and satisfy vnto the said
John Cotton or his assignes the full some of two Thousand poundℓ
(whereof one thousand poundℓ the said John Cotton forthwth gaue and
deliuered the p'^{lt} in Consideracōn thereof the said John Cotton did

deliuer vnto this defendant all and euery the said Bondę for the payment of three thousand and six hundred poundę with interest, And
further the said John Cotton did then and thereby giue graunt and
assigne power to this def'ᵗ to sue execucōn vpon Judgmentę vpon the
bondę and to renew all and euery the said bondę to his owne vse, but
nott to sue any bondę in the name of the said John Cotton, other then
such as Judgementę were then had therevpon All which two thousand
poundę this defendant borrowed and paid interest for the greatest
parte thereof after the rate of Eight poundę per Centū with other great
gratuytyes for pcureing of parte thereof, frōm seūall parties, And the
said John Milton was not present at the bargayne made or att the payment of all or any of the said two thousand powndę, or payd anye of
the said two thousand powndę or had any thinge to doe therewith or
any parte thereof neyther did euer receiue any benefitt by the said
bargayne makeing And this defendant att such tyme as he bargained
with the said John Cotton by the assent of the said Complaynant
would not haue payd soe great a Somē, but that hee was in hope to gett
something thereby but this defendant had noe sooner paid his two
thousand poundę and concluded the said bargaine, but his feare was
greater then his hopes for he was exposed to such travayle and trouble
into seūall counteyes and to soe great chardges and Expences in solicite-
ing seūall persons and for such long tyme putt in soe little hope of
recouery against many of the said Debtoᵣˢ for three thousand and six
hundred poundę that this defendt was doubtfull he should haue been a
great looser in makeing the said bargaine. But att last after infinite
expence and great trauayle and much losse of tyme in his other busines
this defendant did gett all the three thousand and six hundred poundę
(saueing one hundred Markes debt due by one Charnocke and others,
and an hundred poundę debt due by Sᵣ Wīlliam Sandys and one hundred
poundę due by the Lord Mollineux and some other debtę amounting
with interest and Charges as this defendant beleeueth to the value of
ffuye hundredd poundę the perticulers whereof this defendant now
remembreth nott, And this defendt denyes that the said John Milton
to this defendtę knowledge or this defendant did euer dispose of the
said somēs amounting to three thousand and six hundred poundę or
any of them but by and wᵗʰ the Consent of the said John Cotton Jt is
true the said John Cotton was alsoe decreped and kept his chamber, And
the defendant confesseth that he of himselfe & togeather wᵗʰ the said
Milton Neyther did nor could bring to the said John Cotton eyther the
principall or most part of the intrest in respect the partyes to whom
the said moneyes were lett were then insufficient as this defendant then
feared and belieued they haueing not paid the same, Butt this de-

fendant denyes it was vpon any pretence or practice to deteyne the
principall and the said Jnterest money or any parte thereof neyther
did this defendant of himselfe or togeather With the said Milton euer
cause or procure the said John Cotton to belieue that the principall &
Jnterest of the said somēs were desperate neyther did the defendant
of himselfe or togeather with the said John Milton euer worke vpon
him or vse perswatiōn to the said John Cotton that it would be more
for his proffitt and ease if hee tooke some Competent somē of money and
deliuer vpp to this defendant and the said John Milton or one of them
the said Bondꝑ But it is true at such tyme as this defᵗ agreed wᵗʰ the
said John Cotton hee did say hee would do his indeavour to gett in the
principall and interest but it was not his offer but the offer of the Cōmpˡᵗ
and the said John Cotton to this defᵗ: that hee this defᵗ should haue the
said bargayne of three thousand and six hundred powndes wᵗʰ interest
for two thousand powndes And this defᵗ denyeth that hee of himself or
together wᵗʰ the said John Milton did ever Combyne or plott wᵗʰ
Thomas Collwell esquier in the bill named in whose house the said
John Cotton then lay, or did this defᵗ of himselfe or together with the
said Milton ever giue reward or sumē of Two hundred powndꝑ or any
money or somē whatsoeuer to the said Collwell or anie other person
or persons whatsoeū, neither did this defᵗ of himself or together wᵗʰ
the said Milton ever drawe or perswade the said Collwell to informe the
said Cotton that the said Debtꝑ or any of them were desperate or that
the partyes obligors or any of them were dead and non soluant or beyond the seas, Jt is true this defᵗ hath often said to the said Cotton that
a great parte of the said debtꝑ were due in the Countyes palatyne of
Lancaster and Chester where wryttꝑ could not easily be served but this
defᵗ of himself or together with the said Milton never said soe vppon
any pretence to perswade the said John Cotton to accept of the said
two thowsand powndes from the said Milton and this defᵗ or eyther of
them for the said principall Debtꝑ wᶜʰ amovnte to three thowsand & six
hundred powndꝑ Nor did this defᵗ ever wish or require the said Mʳ
Collwell to effect anie such buisines or was the said agreemᵗ and bargaine
aforesaid between the said John Cotton and this defᵗ to this defendantꝑ
knowledge done by the advice or meanes of the said Collwell, And this
defᵗ deyes all practise & Combynacōn to drawe the said John Cotton
for the said somē of two thowsand powndes to deliuer vpp into the
handes of this defᵗ all or any of the said Bondes that this defᵗ might
renewe the same in his owne name or in the name of any other but
whether there be any schedule vnder the hand of this defendant hee
knoweth not neither Can this defendᵗ now remember whose names were
vsed for the renewing of the said Bondes it being above six yeares since

the agreem^t making And this def^t denyeth that the said debt was a debt of this def^{tp} making but this def^t saith he beleeveth he gave ffive hundred powndes ready money more then any would haue given for the same it being before that tyme offered to and refused by others neither did this def^t or any one whose name this def^t ever vsed receive of all or any the seuerall debtors by the said obligacōns five hundred powndes or any sumē of money whatsoeuer due before the said debt Came to this def^t or to their vse or vses, Jt is true this def^t beleeveth the said John Cotton about a yeare since dyed & did make the Cōmp^{lt} his sole executo^r and the Cōmp^{lt} did vndertake the same But this def^t denieth that the Cōmp^{lt} did ever request this def^t by himself or together wth the said Milton to accept of Two thowsand powndes and to pay the Cōmp^{lt} all the moneys by them received or secured vpon the said Obligacōns or to deliuer over the new securytyes by them taken for any of the said debt_p neyther did this Cōmp^{lt} euer request this defendant to expresse what somēs of money hath been by this defendt of himselfe or togeather wth any other to his vse receiued of any the persons in the said obligacōns obliged for interest money or principall debt or renewed or altered by new securyty, this defendant saith he hath onely in his hand_p one bond for payment of one hundredd pound_p principall money which is vnsatisfyed And this defendt denyes to accompt wth the Cōmp^{lt}, for the said three thousand and six hundred pownd_p, for that this defend^t did vndergoe such a hazard as he did to disburse two thousand pound_p without any any practise or vndue carriage, which somē of two thousand pound_p might haue been all or most parte of itt lost, therefore if this defendt after his trauell Charge and long expence and adventure hath altered & compounded for all the three thousand and six hundredd pound_p, but three or ffower hundred pownd_p or thereabout_p, he hopeth to make appeare, that it was iustly gayned and therefore this defendt hopeth he ought not vnder fauo^r of this honorable Courte to giue accompt to the Cōmp^{lt} for the same and the rather for that the Cōmp^{lt} in the life tyme of the said Cotton was the partye that allured and perswaded the said Cotton and this def^t to Come to the said agreem^t and was the Agent actor and procurer of this def^t to condiscend thereunto the said Cōmp^{lt} having offered the same to others who refused to deale therein and if there had beene any iust cause why this def^t should make any such accompt as in and by the said Bill is required the said bargayne being made by and with the advice consent & approbacōn of the Cōmp^{lt} this defendant Conceives hee ought to haue bin questioned for the same in the life tyme of the said John Cotton who lived as this def^t hath beene enformed aboue five yeares after the said bargaine making in the house of the now Cōmp^{lt} and there about_p a yeare sithence dyed so that the now Cōmp^{lt} had tyme sufficient in the life tyme of the said Cotton to haue perswaded the said Cotton to Call this def^t to an accompt if there had beene any iust Cause for the doeing thereof And this def^t denyes all Combynacōn and practise laid to his Chardge and Without that that any other matter thing Article or allegacōn in the said bill of Cōmp^{lte} Materiall or effectuall in Lawe for this defendant to answere vnto and not herein or hereby sufficiently answered confessed [and] avoyded trauersed or denyed is true All which matters and chargꝑ this defendt is ready to averr and proue as this honorable Court shall award and therefore humbly prayeth to bee hence dismissed [with his] costꝑ in this behalfe most wrongfully [susteyned]

> fran: Walsted:
> Pedaell: Harlowe

[*An abstract of this answer, in much the same language, though shorter, is in Cottonian Charters 1/5/5.*]

April 13, 1637

MILTON'S FATHER ANSWERS COTTON'S BILL

Requests Proceedings, Req 2/630
British Museum Cottonian Charters, 1/5/1
[*The text is from the Requests copy, supplemented by the Cottonian*]

Academy, VI (*1874*), 560
Notes and Queries, II, x (*1860*), 34
Masson, I (*1881*), 635

The Answere of John Milton one of the defend^{tꝑ}. to the Bill of Complaynt of S^r. Thomas Cotton Baronett Executor of the last Will and Testam^t of John Cotton Esquyer deceased Complaynant The said defend^t. saving to himselfe now and at all tymes hereafter all advantages of Excepcon to the incertainty and insufficiency of the said Byll of Complaynt ffor answere therevnto saith That it is true that the said John Cotton in the Bill named was a man of good yeares but certeynly what age hee was of the defend^t. knoweth not but this defend^t. saith that hee was of good vnderstanding and memory at the tyme of the defend^{tꝑ}. knowledge of him and able to walke abroad and did soe oftentymes to this defend^{tꝑ}. shopp in London And was then noe wayes decreipte in bodye or defective in mynde to his this defend^{tꝑ}. knowledge And this defend^t. denyeth that about ffive yeares sithence the said John Cotton did putt into his handꝑ or to this defend^{tꝑ}. knowledge into the handꝑ of the said Thomas Bower then this defend^{tꝑ}. partner and not his servant as in the Bill is alleadged any such sōme or sōmes as in the Bill is pretended in trust to be lett out at interest after the rate of Eight poundꝑ p centum, by this defend^t. or the said Thomas Bower but this defend^t. sayth that before this defend^t. became partner wth the other

defend^t. Thomas Bower and after their Copartnership vizt, in all, for
the space of neere fforty yeares the said John Cotton did dispose of and
lend at the shopp of this defend^t scituate in Bredstreete in London divers
somes of money vnto a good value about Three Thousand pound℘
sometyme more sometymes lesse, before the loane whereof this defend^t.
as hee was moved by such person and persons as desyred to borrowe the
same did alwayes acquaint the said John Cotton of the security offered
therefore, Whereof the said John Cotton did take notice And by inquiry
otherwayes then by this defend^t. (as he supposeth), and as hee told
this Defend^t, would be and was satisfied of the sufficiency thereof, before hee would or did at any time dispose of the same or any some or
somēs of money at his this Defendaunt℘ shopp before and after the Copartnershipp, Between this defend^t. and the said Thomas Bower, And
the bond℘ and other assurances therefore taken ffor the most part were
made at his this Defendaunts shopp either by him or his servants before the said Copartnershipp or by them or their ioynt servants w^{ch}
manner of Dealinge betwixt this defend^t and the said John Cotton did
Continue before the Copartnershipp Betwixt this Deffendaunt and the
said Thomas Bower about the space of thirty and ffive yeares, as this
Defendaunt taketh it, and after this Copartnershipp for the space of
Two yeares or thereabout℘ Jn all which tyme the said John Cotton
sustayned noe losse at all of any of the moneys, hee soe disposed of there
or at least very little if any at all And this Defendaunt saith that what
sōme and sōmes of money of his the said John Cotton were lent and
disposed of at any tyme at this Defendaunts said shopp were disposed
of by him this Defend^t before his Copartnershipp wth the other
deffendaunt and afterwards by them both for ought hee knoweth as
aforesaid and not otherwayes And this Deffendaunt denyeth that the
said John Cotton reposed any such trust in him this defend^t as in the
Bill is alleadged or that this Deffendaunt did take the same upon him,
butt the said John Cotton from tyme to tyme acquainted this defend^t
what moneys he had in his hands, and wch hee desired to dispose of during the tyme aforesaid, and of his desire to dispose of the same at interest
at the rate aforesaid, And desired this defend^t. to help him to good security therefore, wch hee as occasion was offered from tyme to tyme,
did informe him of And vppon the approbacōn of the said John Cotton,
the moneys desired vpon such security as this def^t. informed him of
were disposed of from tyme to tyme by the said John Cotton and not
otherwayes, Soe that this defend^t had not the trust of Disposinge thereof
comītted vnto him as in the bill is vntruely alleadged, And soe, and in
such sort as aforesaid the said John Cotton Did lend and putt out
divers somes of money at his this defend$^{t℘}$ shopp, but the perticuler

somes lent the tymes when, and the perticuler persons that borrowed the same and to whome they were bound this defend^t. doth not now remember (his imploym^t. beinge greate that way and longe since he gave over his trade but this defend^t. confesseth hee thincketh it may be true that the same somēs in the Bill mencōned or most of them were by the said John Cotton lent out uppon interest to the said psons therein alsoe named and thincketh that they or the most of them are able men in estate but sayeth, that the said moneys were not putt into the hands of this defend^t. or the other defend^t. Thomas Bower about ffive yeares sithence it manifestly appeares by the pl'tꝫ owne Bill for that by the same it appeares the bondꝫ therefore taken beare date before that tyme and divers of them about ffiftene yeares sithence And this defend^t. doth not remember that the said John Cotton did dispose of any more moneys at the tymes in the said Bill mencōned at his this Defend^{tꝑ}. said shopp then the somē of Three Thousand and Three Hundreth pounds or thereaboutꝫ And this defend^t. saith that as the interest for the said moneys was received by him soone after it was paid alwayes by him or his appointment to the said John Cotton sometymes at the said shopp of this defend^t. and sometymes it was sent home to the said John Cotton And this defend^t. denyeth that he did ever receive call in or putt out the said somes or any of them or tooke the securityes for them or any of them in the byll mencōned wthout the approbacōn consent and good liking of the said John Cotton first had But this defend^t. confesseth that it is true he did at several tymes informe the said John Cotton that the partyes he tendred him for security were very sufficient and able men in estate as they were as he then conceaved and as the Complaynant by his owne Bill setts forth they were Whereby it manifestly appeares this defend^t. had respect to the satisfaccōn of the said John Cotton and care that he should be duely repayd his money againe together with the Consideracōn for the forbearance thereof And this defend^t. doth deny that he found the said John Cotton to be decreipte or vnable by reason of his greate yeares to follow his occasions beinge constrayned altogether to keepe his Chamber or that it was soe wth the said John Cotton or that in that reguarde he did forbeare to bring him the said John Cotton the principall or part of the interest of the said somes as in the said Bill mencōned pretending the partyes to whome the said moneys were lent were not sufficient or that by deteyning the same or by practize wth the other defend^t. Thomas Bower hee did cause the said John Cotton to beleeve that both principall or interest were desperate or that the debtors were non solvant or that having soe wrought vppon the said John Cottons Conceipt hee wthout or with the said Thomas Bower the other defend^t. perswaded the said John Cotton

that it would be more for proffitt and ease if hee the said John Cotton
would take some competent some of money and deliver vpp the said
bonds to him or to him and the other defend[t]. Thomas Bower or that
they in Consideracōn thereof would give him the said John Cotton
Two Thousand pounds in hand or that the better to worke the same hee
and the said Thomas Bower the other defend[t]. did combyne and plott
wth the said Thomas Collwell in the Bill named or that by reward or for
a sōme of Two Hundred poundℓ or any other sōme given to the said
Collwell by this defend[t]. and the saide Thomas Bower or either of
them to this defend[tℓ]. knowledge this defend[t]. did by himselfe or w[th]
the said Thomas Bower drawe the said Collwell to informe or alleadge
to the said John Cotton that the said debts were desperate or the
partyes that borrowed the same or any of them dead or non solvant or
beyond the seas or resident in the Countyes Palatine of Chester and
Lancaster or that this defend[t]. vnder such or any other pretences
perswaded the said John Cotton to accept Two Thousand poundℓ from
this and the other defend[t]. or one of them for the debt in the Byll
mencōned or any other the debts of the said John Cotton or that the
said Thomas Colwell did to the knowledge of this defend[t]. moove or
perswade the said John Cotton as by the said Bill is pretended or that
by any practize or Combynacōn this defend[t]. by himselfe or any other
did drawe the said John Cotton for Two Thousand poundℓ to deliver
vpp into the handℓ of the said Thomas Bower the other defend[t]. all or
any the bondℓ in the Byll mencōned that the said Thomas Bower might
renew the said bondℓ in his owne name or in the name of any other or
take the principall debt to his owne vse or that the said principall debt
or any other was referred to this defend[t]. and the said Thomas Bower
to gather vpp and expressed in a Schedule vnder the hand of the said
Thomas Bower to this defend[tℓ]. knowledge But this defend[t]. confesseth
that the said John Cotton in his life tyme out of what reason this defend[t].
knoweth not but conceaveth it to be out of timorousnes and feare that
he might loose some of his said Debts did voluntarily make an offer to
this defend[t]. to accept of Two Thousand poundes in lieu of all such
monneys as were lent or mannaged for him at this defend[tℓ]. shopp
being as this defend[t]. conceaveth Three Thousand and Three Hundred
poundℓ or thereabouts And vrged this defend[t]. to agree wth him to that
purpose w[ch] this defend[t]. did vtterly refuse And was much greeved at
the same And tooke it very ill of the said John Cotton that he should
make such an offer as well in reguard that he would not that the said
John Cotton should susteyne any losse at all by non payment of the
moneys by him soe lent As alsoe that it was a greate disparagement to
this defend[t]. and his said Trade and shopp And this defend[t·] thought

himselfe much iniured thereby And told the said John Cotton that hee did very much wronge him this defend^t. and himselfe thereby ffor that the obligors and debtors were very sufficient men in estate and there was noe cause whie hee should doe soe or feare the losse of any part of his moneys then disposed of at his this defend^{tp}. shopp and soe hee departed from this defendt^t. And what hee did therein afterward$\wp$ this defend^t. knoweth not But it should seeme the said John Cotton persisted in his feare and doubt of losse of all or parte of the said moneys disposed of att this defend^{tp}. shopp as aforesaid ffor this defend^t. hath heard (but doth not knowe the same of his owne knowledge) that after the Defend^t. refused the said offer of the said John Cotton hee dealte wth the other defend^t. Thomas Bower wthout the privity or consent of this defend^t but the perticulers of what they did agree vppon this defend^t. certainely knoweth not nor ever had any benefitt or proffitt thereby neither doth hee knowe whether ever any such thing were don or not but by the reporte of others And this defend^t. saith hee hath heard that the said John Cotton made the like offer to the said Thomas Bower for the better performance whereof this defend^t. hath heard that the said Thomas Bower did ioyne with one Thomas Holker an Attorney in the Comon pleas whoe procured certaine moneys of S^r. Thomas Middleton late Alderman of London wch were paid to the said John Cotton vppon a bargaine for the said bond$\wp$ but what and how much this defend^t. knoweth not neither doth this defend^t. knowe that the said Thomas Bower the other defend^t. or any other whose name the said Thomas Bower vsed having the custody of the said bond$\wp$ did call in to his or their owne vse or renewe most part of the said bond$\wp$ for the principall debt in his or their owne name neither doth this defend^t. knowe that the said Bower or any other whose name hee vsed, or might use received ffive hundred poundes for the interest due before the said debts came to their hand$\wp$ or any other some therefore neither doth this defend^t. knowe that the said Complaynant is Executor to the said John Cotton but referrs himselfe to the Will and Probate of the Will of the said John Cotton in that behalfe if any such be And this defend^t. denyeth that the Complaynant ever requested this defend^t. to accept of the said Two Thousand poundes and to pay over to him the moneys received vppon the said bond$\wp$ or to deliver over any new security taken for the said debts or to expresse what som$\bar{e}$s of money had bin receaved of any of the persons bound in the said obligac$\bar{o}$ns in the byll menconed for interest or principall or renewed or altered by new security or wch of the said obligac$\bar{o}$ns remayne in this defend^{tp}. hand$\wp$ or that this defend^t. would accompte to the Complaynant for the said Three Thousand and sixe Hundred pound$\wp$ with the interest received or secured neither did this defend^t. ever refuse to enter into any such accompt And this defend^t. denyeth all practize and Combynacon whatsoever with the said Bower or any other in about or concerninge any the matters in the Byll mencōned And this defend^t. sayeth although hee and the said other defend^t. Bower were Copartners in the Trade of a Scrivener yett they were never partners in or concerninge the said bargayne or agreem^t. pretended by the said Byll to be made by theis defēnd^{tp}. with the said John Cotton if any such bargayne or agreement were made nor had this defendant ever any benefitt by any such bargaine or agreem^t. if any such were Without that that any other matter or thing in the said Byll of Complaynt materiall for this defendant to make answere vnto And herein not sufficiently answered confessed and avoyded traversed or denyed is true All wch this defend^t. is ready to averr and proove as this honorable Court shall award And humbly prayeth to be dismissed from forth the same wth his reasonable costs and charges in this behalfe wrongfully susteyned.

Whitfelde

Jūr xiij° die Aprilis 1637 coram nob

Tho Agar
John Agar

between April 8 and December 5, 1637
SIR THOMAS COTTON OFFERS EXCEPTIONS TO THOMAS BOWER'S ANSWER

British Museum Cottonian Charters 1/5/5 [torn and partially illegible. The words supplied in square brackets are conjectural]

Jntρ Thōm Cottō [versus] Thōm Bower
Exceptions to ye deftρ answeare.
The bill chargeth. That ye deft by practice did pswade John Cotton deceased to accept 2000^{li}, frō ye deft or one Miltō for ye s^d principal detρ, naming thē in pticulρ, wch amounted to 3600^{li}. By wch practice they drew him to deliu^r ye bondρ, wch were exp^{r}ssed in a schedule. & hau[e since that time] receiued ye money therevppō. And not only y^e [principal money, but] hath receiued of seu^{r}al psonρ dettorρ by ye s^d obligaciōρ, at least [500]^{li} for ye interest due before ye s^d det came to his vse.

They haue beene requested to exp^{r}ρ what monies they haue receiued for intrest mony or principal money.

Resp. That ye principal mony was 3600^{li} [fol]. 4. That miltō offred but 15[00^{li} for these] detρ off 3600^{li}. 8. He did get [bonds for] 3600 [pounds principal money,] amounting wth intrest & chargeρ to [over 4100.^{li}] He denieth to haue receiued off all or any ye dettorρ 500^{li}. or any sumē of money whatsoeu^r due before ye s^d det came to this deft. fol. 22.

Except. He hath not set forth what intrest he hath receiued frō euʳy of yᵉ sᵈ dettorₚ, due before the sayd principall dett came to his vse wᶜʰ he ought to doe, Jt being [a pl]aine questiō iff yᵉ bondₚ be wel granted and yet [he sh]al not haue such intrests as were due before the bondₚ were [granted], Jt being no pte of yᵉ [360]oˡⁱ put ouʳ.

2ˡʸ. Jn this point, yᵉ answeare is cautelous, That he did not receiue 500ˡⁱ or any sumē due, before yᵉ sᵈ det cāe to him. Whereas he should haue shewed what intrest he hath receiued since the sayd dettₚ came to his vse which were due before, Jt is not likely that he should receiue any before yᵉ det came to him. The Court must Judge wethʳ Jt belongₚ to him, or not.

[*The folio references are to the designated pages in Thomas Bower's answer, B.M. Cott. Ch. 1/5/2.*]

November 30, 1637

THOMAS BOWER IS TO APPEAR TO ANSWER COTTON BILL

Court of Requests Appearance Book, 13th-14th Charles I, Req 2/117, p. 124

xxx° Die Noūebris. . . .

Thomas Bower psonal' compet corā Coño Rₚ virtute ordinis adₚ Thomæ Cotton [*an illegible word*] quer' postea vizᵗ: quinto Die Decembris anno predto admiss est compere p Noel Boteler geñ atturñ suū cū coño Mrī Walsted.

December 5, 1637

THOMAS BOWER'S FURTHER ANSWER TO COTTON BILL

British Museum Cottonian Charters 1/5/3   *Academy, VI (1874), 560–561; Athenæum,*
Requests Proceedings, Req 2/630   *1880, II, 15*

[*The text, as before, is a composite*]

Quinto die decembris   The further Answere of Thomas Bower de-
Anno R Rₚ Caroli xiij°   fendᵗ to the bill of compˡᵗ of Sʳ Thomas
                     Cotton Baronet./

The sayd defendᵗ for a full Answer to the sayd Bill and to the exceptions taken to this defendᵗ ᵖ former Answere hee this defendᵗ sayth that in and by his this defendᵗ ᵖ agreement to and wᵗʰ John Cotton esquire in the Bill named the sayd John Cotton did Assigne & put ouer to this defendᵗ all & euerie the seuerall principall sūmes of money and also all and euÿe the seuerall vse & Interest money then due & owing to the sayd John Cotton by vertue of all and every the seūall Obligacōns in the Bill mencōned for the considerations in this defendᵗ ᵖ former Answere set forth And this defendᵗ was in and by the sayd agreement to haue all & euerie the Jnterest money then due & owing at the Tyme of the said

Assignem^t and putting over of the said Bondꝑ Obligacōns and specealties but how much vse or Jnterest money was then due vpon all and every or any of the sayd Bondꝑ and Obligations at the Time of the sayd Assignement & putting ouer to this Defend^t of all and every the sayd Bondꝑ in the Bill mencōned hee this defend^t knowes not but beleeues hee hath receiued since the sayd John Cottons Assignement & putting over of of the sayd Bondꝑ to this defend^t of all & euery the sayd seuerall debtors by vertue of the sayd Bondꝑ for Jnterest and of money due vpon the sayd Bondꝑ before the sayd Assignement and putting over the sayd Bondꝑ the sumē of an Hundred and Three score poundꝑ or thereaboutꝑ & noe more but of wch of the sayd Creditors or debtors in perticuler by vertue of all or any the sayd Obligations or how much vse or Jnterest money in pticuler was then due or oweing before or att the tyme of the sayd Assignement of the sayd bondꝑ for or by reason of all or any the sayd Bondꝑ or how much thereof this Defend^t or any person or persons to his vse receiued since the sayd Assignem^t: or putting over of the same this defendt knoweth not it being seauen Yeares since or thereaboutꝑ but this defend^t nor any person or persons to his vse did ever receiue before the sayd Assignement or putting ouer the sayd bondꝑ any Jnterest or Vse money due vpon all or any the sayd bondꝑ in the bill menconed & this defendant conceiueth the Jnterest money due vppon all and every the sayd bondꝑ vntill the sayd Assignement and putting ouer of the same to this defend^t. did not belong to the sayd John Cotton & the complaynant or either of them but to this defend^t by the agreem^t & Assignement of ye sayd bondꝑ by the sayd John Cotton as aforesayd therefore not materiall to the comp^{lt} to know how much thereof this defend^t receiued or of whome

ff. Weelsted

[Endorsed:]   Respons:
              Bower
              adv'^s
           Sr Tho: Cotton Bar:
              S

February 1, 1637/8
COURT DISMISSES COTTON-MILTON SUIT

British Museum Cottonian Charters 1/5/5   { *Athenæum, 1880, II, 15*
                                             { *Masson, I (1881), 660–661*

Primo die ffebruarii Anno RRꝑ Caroli decimo tertio./ Whereas Sr Thomas Cotton K^t. long since exhibited his bill of Comt vnto the Kings Matie before his highnes Councell in his ho^{ble} Court of Whitehall att Westm' ag^t John Milton Defend^t Vnto wch bill the s'd Def^t the same

Tearme answered wth wch as it seemeth the s'd Cōmplt resteth satisfyed for that hee hath by the space of two whole Tearmes last past and vpwardꝑ fayled to replye or otherwise to ꝓceede in the said cause whereby to bring the same to hearinge as by the ordinary Course of this Court hee ought to have done, Therefore it is by his Ma^tys said Councell of this Court ordered that the same matter shalbe from henceforth out of this Court Cleerely and absolutely dismissed for ever (for want of ꝓsecucōn) and the said Defend^t as concerninge the same is discharged of any further attendance in this behalfe and lycensed to depart att his lībtie (sine die) and that the said Cōmplit Sr Thomas Cotton shall p'sentlie vppon sight or knowledge hereof content and pay vnto the s'd Defend^t Milton or to his assignes demaundinge the same the full somē of Twentie shillingꝑ of Currant English money for his costꝑ herein wrongfully susteyned

Concordat' cñ Regnō et exām
J. W. lane dep Regr'

CHAPTER V

MILTON *VS.* DUCK

November 31, 1636

ARTHUR DUCK IS FINED £50 IN EWENS SUIT

Chancery Decrees and Orders, C 33/171, f. 4°

31 No. [1636] . . .

D Arthurū Duck Aʳ. quer' ⎫ The pˡᵗ is adiudged to pay to the
Allexanderū Ewens Andreā ⎬ deftꝑ 50¹ costꝑ for Want of a
Ewens et Johēm Ewens deft ⎭ Bill

Carne

February 16, 1636/7

MILTON'S FATHER AND THOMAS BOWER SUE ARTHUR DUCK

Chancery Proceedings, C2 Charles I/M 78/26

[Some words, torn away, have been conjecturally restored]

To the Right Honōᵇˡᵉ Thomas Lord Coventrey Lord
Keeper of the greate seale of England &c

xvj° Die ffebruarij 1636.

Maydwell

Humbly Complayneing sheweth vnto your Lordshipp your Orators
John Milton and Thomas Bower of London Scriveners that whereas
Rose Downer late of [London] now deceased in her life tyme (vizᵗ)
in or about June one thousand six hundred twenty eight at the earnest
Jmportunitie of Mathewe Ewins of Northcadburie in [the county of]
Summersett Esq₃ now also Deceased did lend vnto the said Mathewe
Ewins the some of ffiftie pounds of lawfull English mony to be repayd
againe at six Monthes followein[g And in] Consideration for forbearance
Thereof And for Assurance of Repayment of the same accordingly the
said Mathewe Ewins together with William Keymer of Pendower in
Pxiij° the same County of Summersett Esq₃ as his surtie became Joyntly
and severally bound to the said Rose Downer in one hundred poundꝑ
by obligation bearing date the tenth day of June in the fowrth yeare
of the Raigne of our now Soueraigne Lord King Charles Conditioned
for payment of the said some of ffiftie pounds to the said Rose downer
together with Consideracōn according to the rate of eight poundꝑ in
the hundred on the twelvth day of December then next ensueing the
date of the said obligacōn as named by the said obligacōn and Condicōn
doth and may more fully appeare and they the said Mathewe Ewins

and William Keymer not payeing the said ffiftie pound$\wp$ nor vse for the same at the tyme limited by the Condicōn of the said Obligacōn shortly after the said Mathew Ewins made his last will and testament in writeinge and thereby Constituted and ordayned Mathew Ewins his sonne and heire his Execut^r and shortly after died leaueing a great estate behinde him both in land$\wp$ and goods after whose decease the said Mathewe Ewins the sonne tooke vpon his the execucōn of his said fathers will and in due forme of lawe paid the same and by virtue whereof he possessed himselfe of all his said fathers good$\wp$ and personall estate and entered into all and singuler the Mannors land$\wp$ and tenem^{ts} his said father died seized of being of very great value as aforesaid and notwithstandinge did neglect to pay the said ffiftie pounds and vse for the same to the said Rose Downer wherevpon shee the said Rose in or about the tearme of the holy Trinitie in the Seaventh yeare of his Maties: Raigne that now is exhibited her Bill of Complaynte into this Honō^{ble} Courte against your Orators thereby alleadging That shee the said Rose Downer did deliuer vnto your Orato^r Milton ffiftie pound$\wp$ to be put out for her at Jnterest vpon $\wp$mise by him made that he should $\wp$cure good securitie to be given vnto the said Rose downer for the same which the said Milton did accordingly And that at the day of payment of the said money the said Rose downer left the bond which was giuen for repayment of the said ffiftie pound$\wp$ and vse with Your Orator Milton who receiued the money and deliuered the same to your other Orator Thomas Bower his then partner for the vse of her the said Rose Downer And your Orators put forth the same at vse for the said Rose Downer vnto the said Ewins and Keymer who paid Jnterrest for the same to your Orators for two six monthes who payd the same to the said Rose Downer But shee dislikeing her securitie required the money of your Orators who not withstandinge Continued the same at Jnterest to the Obligors vpon that securitie for repayment thereof to the said Rose and the said obligo^{rs} became Jnsolvent the said Rose alleadginge further by her said Bill that your Orators did refuse to pay the said ffiftie pound$\wp$ to the said Rose downer to which said Bill of Complainte your Orators answered which Cause $\wp$ceeded to hearing and in the month of June in the eight yeare of his Ma$^{tie}\wp$ Raigne and vpon hearing of the said Cause this Honō^{ble} Co^{r}te was satisfied that your Orators did put forth the said ffiftie pounds to the said Mathew Ewin$\wp$ and William Keimer themselues without the Consent of the said Rose Downer wherevpō it was thoughte meete ordered and decreed by this Honō^{ble} Courte that your Orators should pay vnto her the said Rose Downer the said ffiftie pounds and that therevpon the said Rose Downer should Assigne ouer vnto your Orators the said bond whereby they might be

inabled at there owne Charges to helpe themselues against the said
persons to whome your Orators had soe put forth the said ffiftie pounds
as in and by the said Bill and Answere, the said other pceedings in the
said Cause and the decree therevpon remayneing vpon record in this
Honõ^{ble} Courte more at large appeareth and in obedience to the said
decree your Orators vpon the twentith day of June in the said eight
yeare of his Maties. said Raigne did pay vnto the said Rose Downer
the said ffiftie pound℈ as by her receipt vnder her hand vpon the coppie
of the said decree appeareth And shee the said Rose downer the said
twentith day of June did Assigne ouer the said Bond to your Orators
as was inioyned her by the said decree And shortly after your Orators
haueing vnderstood that the said Mathewe Ewins the sonne takeing
vpon him the discharge and payment of his said fathers debts was also
willinge to satisfie the said Debt of ffiftie pounds soe to him lent in the
name of the said Rose Downer and therevpon he the said Mathew
Ewins the sonne the better to inable him soe to doe made sayle of some
parte of the said Mannors land℈ and p^rmisses his said ffather died soe
seized of as aforesaid vnto Arthur Ducke Docter of the Civill lawe and
William Child of London Scrivener or one of them and by sayle thereof
raysed a great some of Money sufficient to pay all his said fathers Debts
with a great surplusage a good parte whereof hee tooke into his owne
possession and two or three thousand pound℈ residew thereof he left
in the hand℈ of the said Arthur Ducke and William Child or one of
them for satisfaction of the said ffiftie pound℈ soe lent in the name of
the said Rose and of the forbearance thereof and of other debts oweing
by his said ffather and for disingageing of the said Manno^{rs} Land℈ and
tenements of Jncumbrances wherewth the same were lyable and shortly
after and before the said Debts satisfied he the said Mathewe made
his last will and testament and thereby made Constituted and appoynted
Alexander Ewins his brother and Cathrine Ewins and Barbara Ewins
his sisters his execto^{rs} and then died leaueing diverse good℈ of his
said ffather vnadministred and did also leaue all the said monyes soe
remayneing in the hand℈ of the said Arthur Ducke and William Child
or one of them vndisposed of by them and after the decease of the said
Mathewe the said Alexander soly tooke vpon him the execuc̃on of his
said brothers will and in due form of Lawe pued the same (power being
reserued to the said Cathrine and Barbara to ioyne with him in the
probate thereof if they pleased) And the said Alexander Ewins by
reason of the probate of the said will possessed himself of all the good℈
of the said Mathew the father and of the said money wch did still remayne
in the hand℈ of the said Arthur Ducke and William Child for satisfaction of the said debte soe due to your Orators and others by the said

Mathew the ffather as aforesaid all which your Orators Vnderstandinge
did soone after the payment of the said ffiftie poundℓ to the said Rose
Downer and assignem^t of the said Obligacōn to them by her (that is
to say in or about the tearme of St Michaell in the nineth yeare of his
now Ma^{tieℓ} Raigne exhibite there bill of Comp^{lt} in this Courte against
the said Docter Ducke and William Child Allexander Ewins Katherine
and Barbara Ewins to be releeued of in vpon and Concerninge the
p^{r}misses vnto which bill the said Docter Ducke and William Child
Answered and Confessed that there was moneyes left in theire handℓ
part of the monyes which should haue bene paid for the purchase of the
said Mannors and p^{r}misses or of some of them to the some of two
thousand poundℓ or thereabouts and after the said Bill exhibited and
before the said Cause came fitt for hearing she the said Rose Downer
died farr remote from the Cittie of London soe that your orators Cannot learne how or to whom she disposed of her estate or what will shee
made nor who hath taken Administration of her estate but humbly
desire they may be admitted to make the said executo^r or admīstrato^{rs}
pties to this bill when they shalbe discovered And for that by reason
of the death of her the said Rose the said bond soe entered into to her
the said Rose for payment of ye sayd fifty powndℓ & vse Cannot be
put in suite at lawe against the said Allexander Ewins but in the name
of the said Executor or admīstrator of the said Rose and for that that
the said Executor or admīstrator is vnknowne to your Orators so that
yor Orators cannot pcure any assignem^t of the said bond or warrant to
sue [at the Common Lawe] and for that it will as your Orators hope
stand with the equitie of this Honō^{ble} courte that sithence by the decree
thereof your Orators were inioyned to pay the said ffiftie poundℓ vnto
the said Rose downer and shee to Assigne the said bond to your Orators
both which were done accordingly as aforesaid and after the said
Assignem^t became defective by the strict Course of the Common lawe
therin that your Orator should take the full beniffitt of the intention
of the said decree by haueing the said money paid vnto them and a
full Assignem^t of the said debt whereby to recouer the same against
the said Allexander Ewins who hath so possessed himselfe of the personall estate of his said father and brother as aforesaid And the said
Arthur Ducke and William Child or one of them are possessed of the
said monyes left in there or one of theire handℓ as aforesaid for payment of the said Mathew Ewins the fathers debts and Clearing the said
mannors landℓ and p^{r}misses of Jncumbrances and yet doe not nor any
of them doth make payment to your Orators of the said some of ffiftie
poundℓ soe before lent in the name of the saide Rose by reason whereof
your Orators are likely to loose the said debt of ffiftie pounds and the

forbearance thereof haueing noe meaneꝑ for recouery thereof but by
the order of this Honōᵇˡᵉ Courte Jn tender Consideracōn whereof and
for that your Orators Cannot discouer the perticuler personall estate
of the said Ewins the father left behind him nor where the same is neither
the perticuler landꝑ the said Ewins the father died seized of nor what
estate he had therein at the time of his death nor what estate did
Discend vnto the said Mathew the sonne nor Doe your Orators knowe
what parte of the monyes soe left vpon the purchase of the sayd landꝑ
doe remaine as aforesaid in the handꝑ of the said Arthur Ducke and
William Child or one of them for payment of the said debt due vpon
the obligacōn entered into to the said Rose Downer and for that your
Orators were inforced to pay her the said Rose in readie money and your
Orators have bene from the said twentith day of June in the said eight
yeare of his Maties Raigne out of purse the said ffiftie poundꝑ and noe
parte of principall or Jnterest payd to your Orators [and] for [that] the
said Mathew Ewins the sonne knowinge the Justnes of the said debt
due by the said Bond entered into to the said Rose Downer and other
debts of his said ffather [in] order for payment and satisfaction of the
same as aforesaid and Disingageing the said Landꝑ of Jncumbranceꝑ
the same discendinge to the said Mathew Ewins the sonne [al]soe he [as]
heire to his said ffather being lyable and Chargable to satisfie the said
Debt to the said Rose downer And to the end that the said Arthur Ducke
and William Child may accordinge to the trust reposed in them and
accordinge to theire Agreemᵗ with the said Mathew Ewins vpon the
purchase of the said land pay the said Debt due by the said obligacōn
entered into to the said Rose Downer as aforesaid with damages for
the same And that the said Allexander Ewins Barbara and Kathrine
Ewins may discouer and sett forth the perticulers of the personall estate
and the true value thereof whereby it may be made lyable to the payment of the said debt due by the said obligacon as aforesaid, and for
that your Orators bee remediles herein at the Comon Lawe Jt may
therefore please yoʳ Loᵖᵖ to graunt vnto your Orators his Maties most
gratious writt or writts of Subpena to be directed to the said Arthur
Ducke William Child Allexander Ewins Barbara Ewins and Katherine
Ewins & to yᵉ Executor or admīstrator of yᵉ sᵈ Rose when they shalbe
discouered and euery of them Comanding them and every of them at a
certaine day and vnder a Certaine payne in the said writt to be lymitted
personally to appeare before your Loᵖᵖ in his Matⁱᵉꝑ: High Court of
Chauncry then and there to Answere the pʳemisses and to shew Cause
why they or some of them should not forth with make payment of the
sᵈ Just and due debt by the said obligacōn with theire reasonable
forbearance and Costs which they have bene putt vnto for recouery

thereof and to stand to and abide such order in the p^rmisses as to your Lo^ppp graue wisdome shall seeme meete & agreeable to your Conscience and your Orators as in al dutie bound shall ever pray &c./

R[oberts?]

March 16, 1636/7
ARTHUR DUCK AND WILLIAM CHILD ANSWER MILTON'S FATHER'S BILL

Chancery Proceedings, C2 Charles I/M 78/26

[*One section is badly rubbed and illegible in spots; bracketed restorations are conjectural.*]

Arthurus Duck iur.	The Joint and severall answeres and de-
16°. Martij. 1636.	murrer of Arthur Ducke Docto^r. of lawes
John Page.	and William Childe Two of the Defendants to
Robinsonn	the bill of Complaint of John Milton and Thomas
	Bower Complaynant℘./.

The said Defend^tℓ saveing to themselues now and at all tymes here-after all manner of advantage and benefitt of excepcōn to the incer-teyntyes insufficiency and manyfold imperfeccons of the said Com-playnants Bill of Complaynt [for answer] vnto soe much thereof as concerneth them these Defend^tℓ: to make answere vnto They these Defend^tℓ. say and each of them saith That they doe not know that Rose Downer in the bill named did lend vnto Mathew Ewins [the] ffather [in the bill] named the somē of ffifty Pound℘ in the bill mencōned or any somē of money at all nor for what tyme the same was lent if any such were nor what obligacōn or security shee tooke for repaym^t: thereof wth Jnterest for the vse [of the same] when the same was payable neither doe these Defend^tℓ: know of any of the passages orders proceeding℘ or decrees in the said Bill of Complaint mencōned to be had or made betweene the said Rose Downer and the Complaynants either in this Court or elsewhere about the said debt if any such were, Neither doe these Defend^tℓ: know of any assignem^t: of the said debt p^r.tended by the Complaynant℘ to be to them made by the said Rose Downer [and these] Defend^tℓ. say if any such were they were mere strangers to them And therefore these Defend^tℓ: therein leave the said Complaynant℘ to such proofe thereof as they shalbe able to make And these Defend^tℓ say that th[ey believe it] to be true that the said Mathew Ewens the ffather in his life tyme made his last will and Testam^t: and thereof con-stituted Mathew Ewens his sonne and heire in the Bill named Executo^r: and about the tyme [in the bill] named dyed But what estate the said Mathew the father left behind him or what he was indebted at his death they these Defend^tℓ. know not, And they beleiue it also to be

true that the said Mathew the sonne p[roved the] said will And that
after the decease of his said ffather he the said Mathew the sonne as
heire to his said ffather entred into the Manno^{rs}: landρ and tenem^{tρ}:
Whereof his said ffather dyed seised as was [lawful for] him to doe, But
of what parsonall estate belonging to his said ffather he possessed
himselfe these Defend^{tρ}. know not nor whether he neglected to pay
the said ffifty poundρ wth: Jnterest to the said Rose Downer [as the
same] were due as by the said Bill of Complaint is supposed And these
Defend^{tρ}. further say true it is That this Defend^t: Docto^r. Duck for
valuable consideracōns did about the moneth of December in the ffift
yeare of his Ma^{ts} [reign] that now is purchase and buy of the said
Mathew Ewens the sonne the Manno^{rs}. of North Cadbury and South
Cadbury in the bill mencōned And this Defendant Docto^r. Duck did
truely satisfie and pay vnto the said Mathew [Ewens the son] or to
others by his appointm^t: All the money agreed vpon for the purchase
thereof saveing the somē of Two Thousand Poundρ which by agreem^t:
betweene the said Mathewe and this Defend^t. Docto^r. Duck was deliūed
to the [other defendant] William Childe to lye deposited in his handρ
for the space of Seaven yeares as a security against such incombrances
as might rise vp or happen to be discovered against the said purchased landρ and to defray and beare such [expenses and] charges as
these Defend^{tρ}. might susteyne or be put vnto about cleering and
discharging such incombrances as within the tyme aforesaid might rise
vpp against the said purchased landρ Which Two Thousand Pounds or
[as much] thereof as should remayne in the handρ of the said Defend^t:
William Childe at the end of the said Seaven yeares the incombrances
Jn the meane tyme appearing and the aforesaid Costρ and charges to
be expended there[from being] thereout deducted and allowed true it is
was by the said agreement to be paid vnto the said Mathew the sonne
his executo^{rs}. admīstrators or assignes, Out of which said somē of Two
Thousand Poundρ this Defend[ant William] Childe saith That the said
Mathew Ewens the sonne in his life tyme did receave for supplie of his
occasions the somē of five hundred Poundρ or thereaboutρ And these
Defendantρ doe absolutely denie That the said somē of Two Thousand
Poundρ or any parte thereof was left in the handρ of either of these
Defendantρ vpon any trust reposed in th[em or either] of the[m] for
satisfaction of the debt p^r:tended to be owing to the said Rose Downer
and the forbearance thereof or for satisfaction of any other debtρ owing
by the said Mathew Ewens the ffather and Mathew E[wens the] sonne
or any other wayes then is expressed or that the said Mathew the sonne
tooke any order with these Defendantρ or either of them for satisfyeing
the same out of the said money as by the [bill] is vniustly surmised

And these Defendantρ further say that they beleive it to be true that
the said Mathew the sonne alsoe made his last will and Testament in
writing and thereof did [appoint the] Defendantρ Alexander Ewens
Katherine Ewens and Barbara Ewens Executors and dyed After whose
decease these Defendnantρ beleive the said Alexander and Barbara
did prove the said [will and took] vppon them the execution thereof
but what goodρ either of the said Mathew the father vnadministred by
the said Mathew the sonne or of the said Mathew the sonne came to
his handρ thereby or [of what value] the same were these Defendantρ
know not nor either of them knoweth And these Defendantρ further
say that divers persons pᵣtending themselves to be Creditors to the said
Mathew the ffa[ther and] Mathew the sonne for divers somēs of money
farr surmounting in all the aforesaid sumē of Two Thousand Poundρ
divers of them alsoe as they alleadge haveing obteyned seuāll [judgments
against the] said Mathew the ffather and Mathew the sonne and against
the said other Defendant Alexander as executoʳ. to the said Mathew the
sonne have exhibited their Bills of Complaint into this Honᵇˡᵉ Co[urt
against these] Defendantρ and against the said Alexander Ewens and
Barbara to be releiued for their said pʳ.tended debtρ and demaundρ
out of the Remainder of the said money soe deposited as aforesaid which
suitρ [?] And these Defendantρ say that true it is that amongst others
the said Rose Downer about the tyme in the Bill mencōned Did exhibite
a bill of Complaint into this Honᵇˡᵉ: Court against the sd Defendants
[and the] others in the said Bill named to such or the like purposes as
in the said Bill of Complaint now exhibited are sett forth for certeinety
wherein these Defendantρ referr themselves to the said Bill made [of]
Record in this Honᵇˡᵉ: Court to which these Defendantρ did make
answere Which suite as these Defendantρ are informed by their Councell
is abated by the death of the said Rose Downer And the said assignemᵗ
[of the] said debt pʳ:tended by the Complainantρ to be to them made
by the said Rose Downer if any such were as these Defendantρ are
informed is become also Defective and void And as to the Remainder
of the said sume of [Two] Thousand Poundρ and the satisfaction which
the said Complainantρ by their bill of Complaint pʳ.tend in equity
ought to be made vnto them by these Defendantρ for the aforesaid debt
by them pretended to be [owing unto the] said Rose Downer out of the
aforesaid somē of Two Thousand Poundρ deposited in the handρ of
this Defendant William Childe or out of the Remainder thereof if any
should be, for that it appeareth by the Com[plainants] owne shewing
in and by their said Bill of Complaint That the said Alexander Ewens
one other of the Defendantρ in the said bill of Complaint named was
by the said Mathew Ewens the sonne nōmted and [appointed to be]

one of the executo^rs. of his last will and Testament and that he the said Alexander proved the said will and tooke vppon him the execuçõn thereof And by reason thereof as by the said Compla[inant by his own] shewing appeareth he the said Alexander possessed himselfe of the aforesaid money which remained in the handꝑ of these Defendantꝑ whereby these Defendantꝑ by the Complainantꝑ owne shewing are acquited of an[y money] remaining in their handꝑ wherewith to make the Complainantꝑ satisfaction if their should be any reason or cause therefore And the Complainantꝑ are wholly to resort to the said Defendant Alexander Ewens for [satisfaction And] These Defendantꝑ doe demurr in Law and humbly craue the Judgement of this hon^ble. Court whether they shalbe compelled to make any further or other answere therevnto. Without that that any other matter or [thing] whatsoever in these Complaynantꝑ bill sett forth and herein not sufficiently answered vnto confessed or avoided traversed or denyed is true in such manner and forme as in and by the said bill of Complaint [is set] forth or in any other manner whatsoeuer All which matters these Defendantꝑ are and wilbe ready to averr mainteyne and prove as this Honorable Court shall award and humbly prayeth to be dismissed out [of this Court with] their reasonable Costꝑ and Charges in this behalfe wrongfully and without iust cause susteyned././

Maie Hil ter

Tho[mas Roberts?]

June 9, 1637

WILLIAM CHILD IS ORDERED BY COURT TO PAY ALEXANDER
EWENS £20 IN DUCK-EWENS SUIT

Chancery Decrees and Orders, C 33/171, ff. 414–414^v

V. 9 Junij [1637]

D   Arthur Ducke Legū   Vpon opening of the Matter this p̃nte daie
L   Doctor et Ws Child   vnto this Court by Mr Edward Hide of
   q' Alex' Ewens Deft   Councell wth the Deft Alexander Ewens Jt was
    informed that Mathew Ewens the deft Alexanders Late brother in his life time conveyed divers Manno^rs & Landꝑ in the bill mençõned to the Deft Doctor Ducke in consideraçon of 11300^li and by agreem^t 2000^li of the purchase money was Deposited in the handꝑ of the said Mr Child for 7. yeares after the sd purchase for discharging such Jncumbrancꝑ as might be in that time Discovered and for bearing such chargꝑ as should arise thereaboutꝑ and if in that time none should appeare then the said 2000^li wth Damagꝑ should be repaid vnto the said Mathew Ewens and it was further informed that there being A suite here in this Court betweene one Thomas ffarewell

p't and Doctor Ducke and others Deftᵱ concerning severall somēs of
money for wᶜʰ the said Mathewe Ewens stood bound in severall bondes
vnto the pl't ffarewell vpon wᶜʰ the pl't had Judgmtȝ and Demaunded
satisfaccōn out of the 2000ˡⁱ Deposited as aforesaid, and the Cause
coming to hearing Jt was ordered that Mʳ Dr Ducke and Mʳ Child
should paie vnto the said pl't his said principall monies and Damages
to be cast vpp and ascertained by Mʳ Page &c Now forasmuch as the
said tearme of 7 yeares is expired and the said Deft Alexandʳ Ewens
being willing to satisfie all Jncombrances incident to the said Lands and
all his brothers the said Mathew Ewens his iust debtᵱ soe as he may
haue the Remaindʳ of the 2000ˡⁱ soe deposited wᶜʰ he Claimes as Executor
to his said brother Jt was humblie moved that the said Alexandʳ may
haue the Jnterrest of the sd Remʳ of the 2000ˡⁱ vntill this Cause come to
hearing, but vpon hearing Mʳ ffountayne being of Councell wᵗʰ the
Creditors of the said Mathewe Ewens who alleadged that the greatest
part of the said Deposited money will be taken away by the said Doctor
Ducke for discharge of Jncombrances, and that there are diuers other
Judgmᵗᵖ and debtᵱ to be satisfied out of the said money Jt is never-
theles ordered that the said Mʳ doe forthwᵗʰ expedite his Certifft according to the said recited order and the Mʳ. is to expedite his report
by thend of this tearme, and in the meane tyme the said Mʳ Child in
respect of the Deftᵱ present necessities is to paie and deliver vnto the
said Alexander Ewens the some of xxˡⁱ. and the said Mʳ. Child is hereby
discharged for the same/
    ex'   [John] Ch[urchill?]

July 6,1637
MILTON'S SUIT AGAINST DUCK MENTIONED
Chancery Reports and Certificates, C 38/86

Jnter Arthurū Ducke legū Doctor et Willm' Child q'ᵗᵉˢ Alexandr'
Ewens executor' Mathew Ewens et al' Creditor' dict Mathei
defendᵗᵉˢ.
6° Julii 1637 . . .

[*Three folio pages stating suits against Duck and the creditors of Ewens,
showing that Child has too little money to meet all the claims. Part way
through is the following:*]

Jn May. 1635. Rose Downer exhīted a bill for a debt of 50ˡⁱ· wᵗʰ
Jnterest lent to Mathew the ffather in June. 4°. Cār & is since dead, since
whose death in ffebr'. 1636. Milton & Bowers Scriveners that putt forth
that money & by Decree of this Cʳᵗ had paid Downer have exhīted a
bill for the same debt . . .

John Page.

June 12, 1640

MILTON'S FATHER'S SUIT AGAINST DUCK IS DEFEATED

Chancery Decrees and Orders, C 33/173, f. 349

M   Johem Milton et Thomam   Lune xij° Junij
L   Bower q' Arthurum Ducke   Vpon openinge of the matter this
     in Legib; Dctor et Wm'   p'sent Day by M' ffountaine of Co:
     Childe Deft   with the Deft vpon theire Demurrer
                    put into the pt' Bill

Jt was alleadged that the pt' by theire Bill sett forth that one Mathew
Evans being indebted vnto Rose Downer vpon a bond for 50ˡⁱ the pt
paid the same to Mʳ. Downer and Had the Bond assigned to them but
before any satisfaccōn hereof made Mathew Ewens Died and left
Mathew Ewens his sonne his heire & extōr whoe to satisfie his ffathers
Debtᵱ made sale of his ffathers Lands to the Deft Dʳ Ducke for a greate
some of monie which hee received all to twoe or three thousand pound
which was left in the Deft hands to satisfie amongst others the said
50ˡⁱ out of which monie to haue satisfaccōn of the said 50ˡⁱ from the
Deft is the scope of the p't Bill to which the Deft have Demurred and
say that the said p't have in their Bill set forth that Allexander Ewens
one of the Deft was by the said Mathew Ewens Deceased appointed
extor of his will whoe proved the will and tooke vpon him thexecucon
thereof and possed himselfe of the monie remaininge in theire hands
whereby the Deft alleadge they are acquited of the same and the p't
are to Demaund satisfaccōn from the said Allexander Ewens Jt is here-
vpon ordered that vnles the said p't shall by thend of this Terme shew
good cause to the contrary then the said Bill shall stand clearelie Defaulted out of this Courte & the p't payinge the Deft the ordinary
Costᵱ./

CHAPTER VI

MILTON, POWELL, AND FOREST HILL

[*Since this chapter is based on so large a number of documents, and since many of them are so distantly related to Milton personally, it seems better not to attempt to print them. For the few which are of close concern to Milton, see the following chapter.*]

CHAPTER VII

MILTON AND POWELL

June 11, 1627

RICHARD POWELL GIVES A STATUTE STAPLE TO MILTON

Certificates and Recognizances, C 152/61

Harvard Studies and Notes in Philology and Literature, XX (1938),
61ff., *as also the later documents in this transaction which follow. The
statute is also reprinted in the Columbia edition of Milton's Works*, XVIII,
419.

Noūint vniuʳ si p pñtes nos Ricūm Powell de fforest Hill in Cōm Oxōn
gen'osum et Will[mum] H[earne] Aurifabr' Londoñ, teneri et firmiter
obligari Johī Milton de vniūsitat Cantabr' geños' [in] Qu[ingentas
libras de] legalis monete Anglie solveñd eīd Johī, aut suo certo Attorñ
hoc script ostedeñ heredibus vel executor' suis in festo Natiuiᵗᵖ: scī
Johīs bāpte px' futur' post dat' pñciū, Et si defecerimus in solūcoe debit
p'd volumus et [concedimus quod tunc] Currat sup nos et utrumqȝ
ñrum heredes et executor' ñros pena in Statuto Staplē de debit puicandiss
in eād [empt] recupañd ordinat' et pviss Dat' vndecimo die Junij, Anno
regni dnī nrī Caroli [dei grā re]gis Anglie S[cotie] ffranc' et Hibñie fidei
defensor' &c Tercio.

Ric Powell'   [*seal*]

William Hearne [*seal*]

[*blank*]   [*seal*]

Ni: Hyde   [*seal*]

June 11, 1627

STATUTE STAPLE FROM RICHARD POWELL TO MILTON RECORDED

Lord Chamberlain's Recognizance Book, L.C. 4/200, f. 265

[Powell   vndecimo die Junii Anno regni dnī nrī Caroli dei grā regis
Hearne   Anglie Scotie ffranc et hibnīe fidei defensor &c Tercio Ricūs
H: Powell de fforrest Hill in Cōm Oxoñ geñ et Willmūs Hearne
cancelled]   Ciuis et Aurifabr' London, Coram Nichō Hide mīl &c
           Recogñ st debere Johī Milton de vniūsitat Cantabr' geñ
Quingentas Libras sō¹ in festo Natiuiᵗᵖ. sci Johīs bapte px' Et si &c./

June 11, 1627
POWELL-MILTON STATUTE STAPLE RECORDED
Recognizance Roll, L.C. 4/56

M'd q'd xj° die Junij Anno p'd Ricūs Powell de fforest Hill in Cōm Oxōn geñ et Willmūs Hearne Civis et Aurifabr' London. Coram Nīchs Hide mīl &c Recogñ se debere Johī Milton de vniūsitat Cantabr' gen Quingentas libras sōl in festo Natiui^ts: scī Johīs Baptē px':/ [*marginal note*:] 91

December 16, 1646
MILTON OBTAINS A CERTIFICATE ON POWELL'S STATUTE STAPLE
C 152/61 (dorso)

Cert' in Canc' Dnī regis per me Thomā Hampson Barronettū Clīcu &c Decimo Sexto Die Decembris Año xxij^do Caroli Regni.

Lord Chamberlain's Recognizance Book, L.C. 4/200, f. 265

Cer in Canc. Dnī Rρ per me Thomā Hampson Barronettū Clīcu &c xv^to die Decemb^r A°: xxij^do. Car Rρ &c

July 16, 1647
MILTON OBTAINS ORDER TO EXTEND PROPERTIES OF RICHARD POWELL AND WILLIAM HEARNE IN OXFORD
Certificates on Statutes Staple, C 228/6

Carolus dei grā Angl' Scotie ffranc' & hibñ' Rex fidei defensor &c vic' Oxōn sal'tm Cum Ricus Powell' de fforest hill' in Cōm tuo gen' & Will's hearne Civis & Aurifabr' london vndecimo die Junij Anno regni nrī tcīo coram Nichō hide Milite tunc Capitali Justic' nrō ad plīta coram nōb tenend' assign' recogn' se debere Johī Milton de vniūsitat' Cantebr' gen' quingent' librī' quas eidem Johī soluisse debuissent in ffesto Natiuitatis scī Johīs Baptē tunc p'x futur' Et eas ei non soluer' vt dicebat^r Per brē ñrm tibi nup p'cepim^s qd' corpora p'dcōr' Ricī Powell' & Willī hearne (si laici essent) capi & in prisona ñra donec eidem Johī de debito p'dcō satisfecissent saluo custodiri & omīa t'ras & catalla ipōr' Ricī & Willī in balliua tua p sacr'm pbor' & legāl homī de eadem balliua tua p quos rei vītas melius sciri potuisset iuxta verum valorem eor'dem diligent' extendi appciari & in manū ñram seīri fac' vt ea p'fat' Jōhi quousq3 sibi de debito p'dcō plene satisfc'm foret libāri fac' iuxta formam statuti apud West'm p hmoī debit' recupand' inde edit' & puis Et qualit' dcm' p'ceptum ñrm fores execut' scir' [fac'] nōb in Cancellar' nrām ad c'tum diem iam pt'it' vbicunq3 tunc foret p lrās tuas sigillat'. Et qd' hēres ibi dcm' brē ñrm, Ad quem diem in dcō brī ñro content' tu nōb in

Cancellar' nrām p'dcām retorn' qd' pñoīat' Ricūs Powell' mortuus est
Tibi igit[r] p'cipim[s] qd' corpus pd'ci Willī hearne (si laicus sit) capi & in
prisona nrā donec eidem Johi de debito p'dcō plene satisfecit saluo Custodiri & omīa t'rās & catalla ipīus Willī in balliua tua necnon tam omīa
t'rās & ten' que fuerunt p'dcī Ricī Powell' dcō tempore recognicōis
debiti p'dcī aut inqūi postea nisi alicui hered' infra etatem existen' iure
hereditario discenderunt quī omīa boni & catalla que ferunt p'dcī Ricī
tempore mortis sue in dcā balliua tua p Sacr'm pbor' & legal' hoīm de
eadem balliua tua p quos rei vītas melius sciri potit iuxta verum valorem
eor'dem diligent' extendi & ap'pciari & in manū ñram seīri fac' vt ea
p'fat' Johī milton quousqȝ sibi de debito p'dcō plene satisfac'm fuīt
libāri fac' iuxta formam Statuti p'dcī Et qualit hoc p'ceptum ñrm fuis
execut' scir' fac' nōb in Cancellār' nrām p'dcām a die scī michīs, pᵈx
futur' in tres septimanas vbicunqȝ tunc fuīt p lrās tuas sigillat' Et hēas
ibi hoc brē T'me ipō apud West'm xvj° die Julij Anno r'ñ vicesimo
t'cio./

lenthall' P.

[*Endorsed*] Execūco ipsius brīs' patet in quadam Inquisicōne huic brī'
annēx.

Will's Cope Ar'
vic'

August 5, 1647

THE SHERIFF OF OXFORD ORDERS AN INQUISITION ON POWELL'S PROPERTY IN WHEATLEY

Proceedings on Statutes Staple, C 228/6

Oxōn ss Inquisicō indentat' capt' apud Civitat' Oxōn in Cōm pd'
quinto die Augusti Anno regni dnī nrī Caroli dei grā Anglī Sccie ffranc'
& hibñie Regis fidei defensoris &c' vicesimo t'cio coram me Willō Cope
Ar' vic' Cōm pd' virtute brīs dcī dnī Regis mihi directi & huic In-
quisicōni annēx' & Sacr'm Johīs hunt Ricī Phillips Willī Sadler Triumph
de St Pauli Johīs Slatford Willī Cooper Willī Yannynge Johīs Wild'
Jacobi Colkyer Willī Michell' Thome hore & Anthīj Slatter pbōr' &
legl'm hominū de ballīa mea Qui dicunt sup Sacr'm suū qd' Ricus Powell
geñ in brī p'dcō noīat' die Recognicōnis debī in brī p'dcō mencōnat'
scilt' vndecimo die Junij Anno regni dcī dnī Regis nunc Anglī &c' t'cio
in brī p'dcō mencōnat' seīt' fuit in dmcō suo vt de feodo de & in tota
illa porcōn decimar' grani cum ptiñ in Whateley in pochia de Cuddesdeñ
in Cōm pd' clari Annui valoris in omibȝ exit' vltᵃ reprīs viginti sex
librar' triū solidōr' & quatuor denar' Ac de & in vno mesuagio duōbȝ
horreis vno Cottagio & vñ virgat t're & dimid' vnius virgat' terr' contineñ triginta & septem acras & vnam Rodam t're tres acras prati

& octo acras & dimid' vnius acre pastur' cum ptiñ iaceñ & existeñ in
villa & Campis de Whateley pd' in pōch de Cuddesden' pd' clari Annui
valoris in omībȝ exit' vltie repris' quindecim librar' Ac vlt'ius Jur'
p'dcī sup Sacrm' suū p'dcm' dicunt qd' p'dcūs Ricūs Powell' post pd'⋅
diem Recognicōnis debī p'dcī in eōdm brī mencōnat' scīlt p'dcō vndecimo
die Junij Anno t'cio sūpdcō & ante diem Capcōnis huius Jnquisicōnis
seīt' fuit in d'mcō suo vt de feodo de & in duōbȝ virgat' t're cum ptiñ'
iaceñ & existeñ in Whateley pd' contineñ quadragint' octo acr' & vñ
rod' terr' arabili & quatuor acr' prati cum ptin' clari Annui valoris in
omībȝ exit' vltie repris' tres decem librar' sex solidor' & octo denarior'
Ac de & in vno Cottagio cum ptin' in Whateley p'd' modo in tenur' siue
occupacōne cuiusdam Walt'i Symons clari Annui valoris in omībȝ exit'
vltie repris' viginti solidor' Ac de & in vno alio Cottagio cum ptin' in
Whateley pd' modo in tenur' siue occupacōne cuiusdam' Rīci Clarke
clar' Annui valoris in omībȝ exit' vltie repris' viginti solidor' Ac de & in
vno mesuagio cum ptin' in Whateley pd' in tenur' siue occupacōne
cuiusdam Thome Church clari Annui valoris in omībȝ exit' vltie repris'
viginti solidor' Ac etiam de & in vno alio Cottagio cum ptin' in Whateley
pd' in tenur' siue occupacōne Cuiusdam Willī Platt clari Annui valoris
omībȝ exit' vltie repris' tresdecim solidor' & quatuor denarior' Ac
vltius Jur' p'dcī sup Sacr'm suū p'dcm' dicunt qd' Anna Powell vid'
que fuit vxor p'dcī Ricī seit' existet de & in t'cia parte omñ & siñglor'
p'missor' p'dcōr' cum ptin' vt de lībo teñto ꝑ t'nno vite sue vt dote
sua ex dotacōne p'dcī Rīci quondam viri sui qdqȝ p'dcā Anna adhuc
supstes & in plena vita existit vidēlt apud Whateley p'dcām Omnia
que quidem p'missa p'dcā cum p'tin' ego p'fat' vic dcō die Capcōnis
huius Jnquisicōnis in manus dcī dnī Regis cepi & seīri feci Deniqȝ Jur'
p'dci' sup Sacr'm suū p'dcm' dicunt qd' p'dcus' Ricūs Powell tempore
mortis sue nulla hūit bona seu catalla nec hūit aliqua alia siue plura
terr' senteñta in dcā ballīa mea ad noticiam Jur' p'dcor' que extendi
aut seiri possunt Jn cuius rei testimonie tam ego p'fat' vic' q'm Jur'
p'dcī huic Jnquisicōni Sigilla nrā die & Anno primo sup'dcis apposuimˢ./

Will's Cope Ar'
vic'

November 29, 1659
POWELL-MILTON STATUTE STAPLE IS CANCELLED
C 152/61 (dorso of recognizance of 1627)

Memorañd that vpon the nyne and Twentieth day of November in
the yeare of our Lord one thousand six hundred ffiftie and nyne Before
the keepers of the liberty of England by authority of Parliament did
come the within named John Milton and did acknowledge himselfe to

be fully satisfied the within mencōned ffiue hundred pounds and all the damages costs and expences any waies susteined in and aboute the recovery thereof And therevpon he the said John Milton instantly requireth that this wryteing obligatory may be Cancelled and made voide Att whose instance this said wryteing obligatory is altogether Cancelled vacated and made voide.

J know the aboue named John Milton

Tho: Gemm'/

[The following note is written crosswise on the right-hand edge; much of it is illegible but has been restored by comparison with the similar note in the Lord Chamberlain's books]

Discharged the [29th day of November] 1659: because J saw [the said recognizance] in the hands of Richard Powell [esquire].

[Just below the last note, perpendicular to it, and almost running into it, is Milton's own signature:]

John Milt[on]

Lord Chamberlain's Book, L.C. 4/200, f. 265

Discharged in this booke the 29th Day of Nouember 1659 at the request of Richard Powell Esq₃ because J saw the said Recognizance cancelled in his hands:

CHAPTER VIII

PYE *VS*. MILTON

February 11, 1646/7
SIR ROBERT PYE SUES MILTON
Chancery Proceedings, C2 Charles I/P 10/15

LTLS, Dec. 21, 1935, p. 879

To the right Honble the Comm^{rs} of the Great Seale of England.
Vndecimo die ffebruarij. 1646./
   Maydwell
Humbly complayning sheweth vnto yor Hono^{rs}, your daily Orato^r
Sr Robert Pye of Westm^r in the County of Midd'ǫ knight That whereas
Richard Powell of fforsthill in the County of Oxōn Esqr did, by his
deed Jndented bearing date the thirtieth day of June in the sixteenth
yeare of the Raigne of o^r Soūaigne Lord King Charles, for and in consideracōn of the sume of One thowsand ffour hundred poundǫ payed
vnto him by yor Orato^r graunt vnto yor Orato^r All that Manno^r or Lo^{pp}
of fforresthill āls fforstill āls ffosthill, with diuers other Landǫ in fforsthill
aforesayd. To haue and to hould all the sayd Landǫ and p^rmisses to
yor Orato^r his exec^{rs} Adm^{rs} and Ass's for and dureing the terme of one
and thirty yeares, with a Prouiso therein conteyned that if the sayd
Richard Powell his ex^{rs} or adm^{rs} or any of them should well and truly
satisfie, and pay or cause to be satisfyed and payd vnto yor Orato^r his
Executo^{rs} or adm^{rs} the full sumē of ffifteene hundred pōwndǫ & ten on
the first day of July Anno 1641. That then the estate, and terme of one
and thirty yeares to cease and bee voyd as in and by the sayd recited
Jndenture, ready to bee shewed to this Honble Court more att large may
appeare. Which sayd sumē of ffifteene hundred & ten poundǫ or any
parte thereof was not satisfyed att the sayd day limitted in the sayd
recited Jndenture nor att any tyme since vnto yor Orato^r, whereby the
sayd estate, and terme of One and Thirty yeares of and in the p^rmisses
is become absolute. But now soe it is May it please yor Hono^{rs} that
yor Orato^r hauing lately had and taken possession of the p^rmisses soe
conueyed to him as aforesayd, is now, and lately hath binn hindered,
and interrupted in the peaceable injoym^t thereof by one John Melton
of London geñ who p'^rtendǫ that hee hath some former Jnterest, and
Estate of and in the same p^rmisses by and from the sayd Richard
Powell by Mortgage Statute Recognizance Judgment, or some other
Tytle Estate or Jnterest deriued from the sayd Richard Powell p^rcedent
to yor. Orato^{rs} said Estate. And the sayd John Melton being often in

a friendly manner desired by your Orato^r to discouer, and make knowne
vnto him what estate Title Jnterest or Engagement hee hath or may
clayme of or in the premisses or any parte thereof from the sayd Richard
Powell, hath from tyme to tyme and still doth vtterly refuse to discou^r
and make knowne the same vnto yor Orato^r whereby yor Orato^r cannot
injoy the p^{r}misses according to his Estate before menc̄oed, and sett
forth contrary to Lawe, and Equity. Jn Consideracōn whereof, and for-
as-much as yor Orato^r hath noe remedy by the Common Lawe of this
Realme to know the truthe of such engagem^{tp} if any such bee whereby
hee may bee releeued for his sayd debt vnlesse the sayd John Melton
shall or will upon his Corporall Oath discouer and sett forth what
Statute Judgem^t Recognizance Mortgage or other Estate or Jnterest
hee hath or may clayme in, out of, or vnto the p^{r}misses or any parte
thereof by from or vnder the sayd Richard Powell. And vpon what
Consideracōn the same was obtained And whether the same bee not,
or ought not to bee vacated released and determyned. To the End
therefore that the sayd John Melton may vpon his oath sett forth the
truth thereof, and may also make a full and pfect answer to all and
singuler other the p^{r}misses. May it please your hono^{rs}. to graunt vnto
your sayd Orato^r his Ma^{tp} most gratious writt of Subpena to bee directed vnto him the sayd John Melton commaunding him att a certeyne
day, and vnder a certeine payne therein to bee limitted psonally to bee
and appeare in his M^{tp} high Court of Chauncery then and there to
answere the p^{r}misses And to stand to, and abide such further Order and
direction therein as to yor Hono^{rs} shall seeme most agreable to equity
and good Conscience. And your Orato^r shall: &c./
Kel: sen./

Jntr.
Bulstrode Whitelocke.

February 22, 1646/7
MILTON ANSWERS PYE'S BILL

Chancery Proceedings, C2 Charles I/P 10/15   *LTLS, March 14, 1936,
p. 224; Columbia edi-
tion of Milton's Works,
XVIII, 398.*

The answere of John Milton gent to the Bill of Complaynt of S^r
Robert Pye Knight Complaynaunte./
Jurat 22°. ffeb.
1646. Rob't. Aylett
   Smythe./
The said Defeñdt saueinge to himself nowe and all tymes hereafter all
advantage of exception to the vncertaintie and insufficiencie of the

said Bill of Cōmplt for answere therevnto hee this Defeñdt sayth That
hee this Defeñdt. Doth not knowe That Richard Powell in the said
Cōmplts said Bill named did at anie tyme for anie Considerracōn at all,
or otherwise by his Dede in the Bill pretended or otherwise graunt, or
otherwise Convey vnto the said Complainaunte. All or anie parte of
the mannor or Lordshippe of fforesthill al's. fforsthill al's. ffosthill in
the said Bill mencōed or anie other lands in ffosthill aforesaid for anie
terme whatsoeu^r or vppon anie pvisoe whatsoeu^r to bee voide or Determined, for non payment of anie sumē of money whatsoeu^r, Nor Doth
this Defendant Knowe that the same or anye such terme or estate as
in the said Bill is mencōed, became absolute for the same, or anie such
Cause as in the said Bill is pretended. Howbeit this Defendant saith
That hee this Defendant Conceiveth it to bee true That the sayd
Richard Powell in his life tyme was lawfullye seised in his Demesne as
of ffee or of some other good and lawfull estate of inheritance or otherwise was possest of some longe terme of yeares yett to come of and in
the said mannor lands and premisses in the said Bill mencōed enablinge
him to make the graunt hereafter mencōed./ And that the said Richard
Powell, beinge thereof soe seised or possessed as aforesaid and beinge
iustly and truely indebted vnto this Defeñdt in the sumē of three hundred pounds of lawfull English money for repayment whereof with
Damages, for the forbeareance thereof, Hee the said Richard Powell
togeather with one William Hearne of London gouldsmith did by one
statute staple bearinge date on or about the elleventh Day of Julye in
the third yeare of his ma^{ties}. Raigne that nowe is become bound to this
Defeñdt in the sumē of five hundred pounds to bee paid at middsomēr
then next, which said statute was Defeazansed to bee void vppon payment of three hundred and twelue pounds to this Defendant his heires
executors or administrators on or about twelueth Day of December
next after the Date of the said statute as by the said statute
and Defeazance readdye to bee shewed to this hōble Court, whereto
for more Certaintye therein this Defeñt referreth himselfe is Doth and
may more fully, and at large appeare./ And, this Defeñdt further saith,
That the said three hundred and twelue pounds or anie part thereof
was not paid accordinge to the said Defeazance the twelueth Day of
December or at any tyme since to or to the vse of this Defeñdt But all
the said three hundred and twelve pounds togeather with Damages
for the forbearance thereof for Divers yeares last past is iustly and
truely oweinge vnto this Defeñdt, which the said Richard Powell from
tyme to tyme hath refused or neglected to pay though hee hath often
bene in all freindlye manner thereto required by this Defeñdt where-
fore and for that this Defeñdt hath now present occasions for his said

moneys true it is, That hee this Defendt intendeth and indeauoureth
by Due Course of lawe to putt the said Statute in execution, for the
recouerye of his said iust true Debt and Damages aforesaid, as hee
hopeth vnder the favour of this hōble Court is lawfull for him this
Defendt to Doe without anie wronge at all as hee Conceiveth to the
Cōmplt whose tytle to the premisses sett forth by the said Bill is of
his owne shewinge subsequent to the said statute, Nor Doth this
Defendt knowe of anie possession the Cōmpt hath or ought to haue in
the premisses or anie part thereof or howe or when hee entred, or that
this Defendt hath any wayes Disturbed interrupted or Disquieted him
therein, or intends soe to Doe otherwise then in a legall waye for recouerye of his Debt and Damages aforesaid./ And saith that hee Claymeth noe other tytle estate or interrest whatsoeuer in or to the premisses,
but by vertue of the said statute which hee neuer refused to Discouer or
sett forth to the said Cōmplt, And this Defendt saith That the said
statute ought not to be vacated released or Determyned for the reasons
aforesaid But vppon receipt of his said Debt of three hundred pounds
with Damages for the forbearance thereof yett vnsatisfyed togeather
with this Defendts Costs at Lawe and Charges in this hōble Court
occationed by the non payment of the said Debt in tyme hee this Defendt
is and wilbe readdye and willinge to Deliuer vpp the same to be Cancelled./ Without that, That anie other matter or thing Clause sentence
Article or allegacōn in the said Bill of Complt conteyned and not before
herein sufficiently answred vnto confessed and avoided denyed or
Traversed is true soe & in such sort manner and forme as in & by the
said Bill of Complt the same are sett forth & alledged All which matters
& things this Defendt is & wilbee readie to averre iustify maintaine &
prove as this hōble Cort shall award And prayeth to bee thence dismissed wth his reasonable Costs & charges in this behalfe most wrongfully
sustained./

Jo: Bradshawe.

November 27?, 1647
SIR ROBERT PYE REPLIES TO MILTON'S ANSWER

Chancery Proceedings, C2 Charles I/P 98/30   *LTLS, March 14,*
1936, p. 224

Maydwell   The Replicacōn of Sr Robtē Pye Kt Complaynant to the
                 Answere of John Melton geñtl Defendt./
The said Complaynñt for Replicacon saith, that hee doth & will averr,
maintaine & iustifie his said Bill of Complaint & all & everie the matters
thingp & allegacōns therein Contayned to bee just true, Certaine &
sufficient in the lawe to bee Answered vnto, And that the Answere of

the said Defend^t is verie vntrue incertaine & insufficient in the lawe to
bee Replied vnto for the manifest faultꝑ & impfeccōns therin contayned,
And for further Replicacōn this Repliant saith in all & everie thinge
& thingꝑ as in his said Bill of Complaint hee hath sayed, wthout that y^t.
anie other matter thing or thingꝑ materiall in the said Def^{tꝑ} Answere to
bee Replied vnto, and not heerin sufficientlie Replied vnto is true, All
wch matters & thingꝑ this Repliant is readie to averr & prove as this
honōᵇˡᵉ Court shall Award, and prayeth as in his said Bill of Complaint
hee hath alreadie praied.

Smith. Hīll: 22° Car Rꝑ./

[*Dated from the decree of June 16, 1649, q.v.*]

June 16, 1649

COURT DISMISSES PYE-MILTON SUIT

Chancery Decrees and Orders, C 33/192, f. 794   *LT LS, March 14,*
1936, p. 224

Sābb 16° Junij

P.   Ro. Pye mil. q' ⎞   fforasmuch as this co^{r}t was this pñte Day
       Johēs Milton geñ ⎬ informed by M^r. Wilcox being of the p^{tꝑ}
L C   Def   ⎠ c: that the p^t excted his bill into this c^{r}t ag^t.
                            the Def in Hill tearme 1646. to wch the Def
apped & in March following putt in his answ^r. Wherevnto the said p^t.
replied the 27th of No: 1647 but hath not since pceeded in the said cause
as appeth by Cert from the Deft^{tꝑ} Att yt was therfore prayed that the
said bill might be dismissed wth ordinary costꝑ wch is ordered accord-
ingly/

CHAPTER IX

ASHWORTH *VS.* MILTON

February?, 1653/4
ELIZABETH ASHWORTH SUES MILTON

*[The bill has not been found; the following is a transcript of the summary
of it given in a court degree of June 5, 1657, q.v.]*

. . . the Pl't by her bill settρ forth that Richard Powell Decēd did about
January 7°. Car Borrowe of Henry Ashworth Decēd 400ˡⁱ at Jnterest
at 8ˡⁱ. p Cent the said Powell being then seised in his Demease as of
ffee by purchase from Sʳ George Symeon Knᵗ: Discharged of all Jncumbrances of one Messuage one Cottage, the Moyety of Three yard Landρ
and of all the Tythes of Corne and other thingρ in Wheatley & Grove
Leaze scituate in Cuddesden or Holton worth 100ˡⁱ. p anñ, and of the
Reūcon of yᵉ pʳmisses and for security of the Repayment of the said
400ˡⁱ. and of yᵉ Jnterest for one yeare the said Powell made the said
Henry Ashworth and the Pˡᵗρ late husband a Lease of the pʳmisses for
99. yeareρ to comence from the 13ᵗʰ of January 1632. wᶜʰ Jndenture
was Dated 10ᵐᵒ. Jañ. 7°. Car betweene the said Powell & Ashworth
whereby the said Powell did Demise vnto the said Henry Ashworth
Deceased & the p'ˡᵗρ said husband, and the Survivoʳ of them, and the
Execūtōʳρ of the Survivoʳ of them the said pʳmisses Dureing the said
Terme, wᵗʰ a Provisoe that if the said Powell or his heires should pay
vnto the said Henry Ashworth or the p'ˡᵗρ said husband or the survivoʳ
of them or the Execūtōʳˢ of the Survivōʳ of them the said 400ˡⁱ. vpon ye
13ᵗʰ; of January 1632. that then the said Demise was to be voyd. But
the said Powell fayleing in paymᵗ of the said 400ˡⁱ according to the said
Provisoe the said Demise became absolute, Notwᵗʰstanding which the
said Henry Ashworth and the p'ˡᵗρ said husband suffered the said
Powell and his vnder Tenantρ to enjoy the pʳmisses, and Henry Ashworth dying made Edward Ashworth the p'ˡᵗρ said husband his Execūtōʳ.
who proved the will, and thereby became intituled to the said money,
and lyable to the paymᵗ of his Debtρ, And that 6 yeareρ since the p'ˡᵗρ
said husband receiued 100ˡⁱ in pte of the said 400ˡⁱ. and the Jnterest
untill January 1644. for the 300ˡⁱ. remd'ʳ of the sd 400ˡⁱ. Since wᶜʰ tyme
neither principall nor Jnterest hath byn payd, and that the sayd Powell
ffather of the dēfte Richard Dyeing seised of the pʳmisses they came to

the Dẽfte Richard Powell as his Sonne and heire, and that afterwardꝑ about 1648. The P'ˡᵗꝑ said husband made his last will & Dyed, haueing made the P'ˡᵗ his Executˣ & Disposed of the said 300ˡⁱ. & the Damages due for the same for the benefit of his younger Children, and that the Dẽft Milton Did about August in the 23ᵗʰ. yeare of the late King Charles extend all the pʳmisses soe Demised to Henry and Edward Ashworth as aforesaid vpon a Statute of 500ˡⁱ. acknowledged to him by the said Richard Powell Decẽd about June 3ᵗᵒ. Cãr and found the Landꝑ at a very low rate chardgable wᵗʰ the Thirdꝑ for the Dẽft Anne being the late wife of the said Powell Deceased, and the Deft Milton haueing for those 6 yeares last past recẽd 100ˡⁱ. p Anñ for th'extended Landꝑ Soe that the said Statute was satisfied out of the pffittꝑ of the said Landꝑ whereby the Creditõˢ of the said Powell were like to be Defeated of their Debtꝑ, Soe as the scope of the P'ˡᵗꝑ Bill is that the Deftꝑ Milton, and Rĩch. and Anne Powell may sett forth what Jncumbrãces were vpon the pʳmisses, and whether the monyes Due therevpon were not paid, and what Estate Milton had in the pʳmisses, and whether hee were satisfied his pʳtended Debt chardged vpon the pʳmisseꝑ and that hee may accompt for what hee hath recẽd. . . .

[*Scattered bits may be extracted from references in the other papers in this action.* (*1*) *From Milton's answer of February 22, 1653/4*:]

. . . hee [Milton] hath possessed himselfe . . . of Cattell household stuffe money plate Jewells or any other the goods and chattells of the said Richard Powell . . . any Statute or Recognizance or Mortgage . . . made or Acknowledged by the said Richard Powell to the said Sʳ John Powell . . . the said Mortgage statute or Recognizance . . . was att any time Ante dated . . . hee [Milton] hath forborne or doth forbeare the Raiseing and levyeing of the said debt . . . combinacõn and confederacy . . .

[(*2*) *From Anne and Richard Powell's answer, May 26, 1657*:]

. . . Combinacon with Sʳ John Powell . . . or with John Milton Esqʳ . . . Richard Powell dẽcd and one William Herne by a Wryting or Recognizeance in the nature of a Statute Staple beareing date on or about the Eleaventh day of June in the third Yeare of the raigne of the late King Charles became bound vnto the other dẽft. John Milton in the Sũme of five hundred pounds of Lawfull money of England defeazeanced for the payment of three hundred pounds principall Debt . . . and twelve pounds for Jnterest thereof vpon the Twelfth day of December then next following . . .

February 22, 1653/4
MILTON ANSWERS ELIZABETH ASHWORTH'S BILL

Chancery Proceedings, C 10/44/2   *Columbia edition of Milton's
                                                     Works, XVIII, 401*

Sworn the 22th. of ffeb. 1653.   The severall Answeare of John Milton
     Tho: Estcourt   Esqr one ye Deftᵖ to the bill of Complaint
                                 of Elizabeth Ashworth Widdow Compˡᵗ.

The said Deft now and att all times hereafter saving to himselfe &c
All Advantages of Excepcōn to the incerteintie and insufficiencie of the
said bill of Complaint ffor Answeare to soe much thereof as concerneth
him this Deft to make answere vnto saith that hee knoweth not that
Richard Powell the elder deceased in the bill named did Att any time
make or Agree to make any lease of the messuage and lands in the bill
mencōned Or of any other lands or Tenements whatsoever vnto Henry
Ashworth in the bill named and the Compˡᵗˢ husband Edward Ashworth
in the bill alsoe named or either of them by way of Mortgage as in the
bill is pretended or otherwise howsoever Neither doth this Deft know
that the said Richard Powell did at the time in the bill menconed or at
any other time borrow of the said Henry Ashworth the some of fower
hundred pownds in the bill mencōned Or any sumē whatsoever And this
Deft doth deny that hee hath possessed himselfe or in any wise Jnter-
medled with or disposed of any stocke of Cattell household stuffe money
plate Jewells or any other the goods and chattells of the said Richard
Powell for the Ends and purposes in the bill pretended Or for any other
end or purpose whatsoever or that this Deft either by himselfe or with
any other person or persons whatsoever hath att any time sett on foote
Any ancient or other Mortgage whatsoever as in and by the said bill is
most vntruly suggested But this Deft saith that true itt is That the said
Richard Powell and one William Hearne by A wryting or Recognizance
in the nature of A statute Staple bearing date the Eleventh day of June
in the Third yeare of the late King Charles Acknowledged before Sr
Nicholas Hide deceased, then Lord Cheife Justice of the kings bench
att Westm' became bound vnto this Deft in the Some of fiue hundred
pounds of lawfull English money defeazanced for the payment of Three
hundred pownds principall debt and Twelue pownds Jnterest for the
same vpon the Twelueth day of December then next following Which
said Three hundred pownds principall was for the like some then iustly
and truely lent vnto the said Richard Powell by John Milton deceased
ffather of this Deft in his life time And this Deft sayth that the said
Three hundred pownds principall debt was not payd vnto this Deft
nor Any parte thereof vpon the said Twelueth day of December Ac-

cordinge to the purport and Jntent of the said Defeazance nor hath
the same or any parte thereof been payd att any time since the said
Twelueth of December but hath bin forborne continually from time to
time Att the Earnest request of the said Richard Powell But this Def^t
Alsoe sayth and verely beleeueth that the said Twelue pownds Jnterest
was payd vpon the said Twelueth day of December Or soone after
And that the growing Jnterest for the forbearance of the said Principall
debt was for some yeares then following likewise payd And soe continued
to bee payd vntill June Jn the yeare of our Lord One Thousand six
hundred ffortie and ffower Att What time the said Richard Powell failed
not onely in the payment of the Jnterest then due and payable and from
thence growing due and payable butt of the said principall debt of three
hundred pownds also Wherevpon this Def^t Did take out severall Extents
vpon the said Statute before hee could gett any of the Lands and Tenements of the said Richard Powell duely extended Butt this Def^t saith
that after the death of the said Richard Powell by vertue of an Extent
and An Inquisicōn therevpon taken before the Sherriffe of the County
of Oxōn in the Citty of Oxōn by the oath of lawfull men of the said
County vpon the fifth day of August Jn the yeare of our Lord One
Thousand six hundred ffortie and seaven itt was then and there found
that the said Richard Powell att the time of the Acknowledgement of
the said Statute That is to say vpon the Eleventh day of June in the
said Third yeare of the late king was seized in his Demesne as of ffee of
and in All that porcōn of tithes of Corn with the Appurtennances in
Whately in the parish of Cuddesden in the County aforesaid of the
cleare yearely value in all yssues Over and aboue All Reprizes Twenty
six pownds three shillings and foure pence And also of and in One
messuage Two barnes One Co[ttage] and One Yard land and A halfe
conteyning Thirty and seven Acres and One Rood of land three Acres
of meadow and Eight Acres and A half of pasture with the Appurtennances lying and being in the Towne and ffeilds of Whateley aforesaid
in the parish of Cuddensden aforesaid of the cleare yearely value in all
yssues over & aboue Reprizes fflfteene pownds And that the aforesaid
Richard Powell after the day of the Acknowledgement of the said
Statute and debt aforesaid to bee payd as aforesaid And before the day
of the takeing of the said Jnquisicōn was seized in his Demesne as ffee of
and in Twoe yard land with the Appurtennances lyeing and being in
Whateley aforesaid conteyning forty and Eight Acres and One Rood of
Arrable land And fower Acres of meadow with the Appurtaññces of the
cleare yearely value in all yssues Over And Aboue Reprises thirteene
pownds six shillings and Eight pence and of and in one Cottage with the
Appurtennances in Whateley aforesaid then in the Tenure or Occupacōn

of One Walter [S]imonds of the cleare yearely value in all the yssues ouer
and Aboue reprizes Twenty shillings and of and in other Cottage with
the Appurtennances in Whateley aforesaid then in the Tenure Or Occupacōn of One Richard Clorke of the cleare Yearely value in all yssues
over and Aboue Reprizes Twenty shillings And of and in One messuage
with the App^rtennances in Whateley aforesaid in the Tenure or Occupacōn of One Thomas Church of the Cleare yearely value in all
yssues over and Aboue Reprizes of Twenty shillings And also of and in
one other Cottage with the Appurtennances in Whately aforesaid in
the tenure Or Occupacōn of William Platt of the cleare yearely value
in all yssues Over and Aboue Reprises of Thirteene shillings and ffoure
pence And that Anne Powell widdow which was the wife of the said
Richard was then seized of and in the Third parte of all and singuler
the premises aforesaid with the Appurtennances as of her ffreehold ffor
Terme of her life as her dower by the Jndowement of the said Richard
her former husband And that the said Anne was then surviving that is
to say in Whateley aforesaid All which premises aforesaid the Sherriffe
aforesaid the said day of the takeing the said Jnquisicōn did take and
seize into the hands of the said King And itt was further found by the
said Jnquisicōn that Richard Powell aforesaid the said Time of his
death had noe goods or chattells nor any other or more lands or Tenements in the said County to the knowledge of the said Jurors of the
said Jnquisicon which might bee seised or Extended As by the returne
of the said Jnquisicōn vpon the files of Record in this honōble Courte
more fully may appeare By vertue of which extent Jnquisicōn and a
liberate therevpon had Retornable ffifteene Dayes after St Martin in
the Said Twenty Third yeare of the raigne of the said late king the said
porcōn of tithes with the Appurtennances and alsoe All and singuler
the lands Tenements Cottages and premises with their Appurtennances
vpon the Twentieth day of November in the Twenty Third yeare aforesaid were delivered to this Def^t by the said Sherriffe to hold to him and
his assignes as his ffreehold vntill hee should bee fully satisfied of his
said Debt with all damāges costs and chardges in that behalfe And this
Def^t saith that the totall of all his costs and chardges and expenses in
Rideing Journeying ffees to the Sherriffe and others and also in other
chardges costs and expences necessarily layd out in and about the
execucōn and perfecting the said Extent Amounts in the whole to the
some of fforty and nine pounds Twelue shillings att the least As by
severall billes ready to bee produced to this honorable Court may
Appeare And this Def^t also further sayth that att the time of the
Delivery of the said Tithes lands and premises vnto him by vertue of
the Extent and Jnquisition aforesaid there was due unto him besides

the said Three hundred powndes principall debt for three yeares and a quarters Jnterest vpon seaventy Eight pownds which said principall debt of Three hundred pownds and seventy eight pownds interest with the said fforty nine pownds and Twelue shillings costs before mencōned Amount in the whole to ffowre hundred Twenty seaven pownds and Twelue shillings And this Def^t further saith that by An Act of Parliament of the fift of August Jn the yeare one Thousand six hundred and ffiftie enioyning all persons who were seized or possessed of the Estates of Delinquents by Extent or otherwise to compound for the said Estates or to fforfeit and loose the same this Def^t was Enforced to compound about our Lady day then following for the said Tithes landes Tenements and premisses for that the said Richard Powell in his life tyme was reputed A delinquent And had not compounded for the same for which Composicōn as aforesaid this Def^t was Ordered to pay by the then Cōmittee for Compositions the sume of One hundred and Thirty pownds which this Def^t paid Accordingly and did Also lay out and disburse in necessary Chardges for the perfecting the said Composition the some of Two pownds One shilling and six pence As by An Order of the said Cōmittee and this Def^{ts} bills of chardges ready to bee produced to this honorable Court may Appeare which some of one hundred and Thirty Two pownds One shilling and sixpence out of the Rents yssues and proffitts of the said premisses soe compounded for as aforesaid is to bee Allowed vnto this Def^t not onely by the Order of the said Cōmitee butt by the expresse provision of the saide Act which said some of One hundred Thirty Two pownds One shilling and six pence being Added to the former some of foure hundred Twenty seven pownds and Twelue shillings Amounts in All to fiue hundred ffifty nine pownds Thirteene shillings and six pence And this Defendant further saith that the said Tithes landes Cottages and premises being delivered vnto him by vertue of the said Extent as aforesaid in the said Month of November being in the yeare One Thousand six hundred fforty and seven this Def^t that winter season could not make any thing thereof saue onely Two powndes and Thirteene shillings rent out of the Cottages not being Able to lett the rest of the premises vntill the Lady day following Att what time this Def^t did lease the said Tithes and Cottages to John Robinson E[sq of] Whateley aforesaid for six yeares from thence fully to be compleat & ended reserveing the yearely rent of threescore pounds and the said lands Tenements and rest of the said premisses to John Gadbury and Graland Page for ye same terme of yeares att the severall yearely rents of Twentie pounds a peice And this Def^t saith that Accordingly hee hath received of the said Tennants from halfe yeare to halfe yeare Taxes and the Dower of the said Anne being deducted as followeth

That is to say Att Michalmas One Thousand six hundred ffortie and eight (the said leases con[tinuing] from the ffiue and Twentieth of March before) Thirty and One pownds Thirteen shillings and Eight pence vpon the ffiue and Twentieth of March One Thousand six hundred fforty and nine Thirty One Pownds ffoureteene shillings and nine pence Att Michalmas One Thousand six hundred ffortie and nine Thirty One pownds Three shillings and Tenn pence vpon the fiue and Twentieth of March One Thousand six hundred and ffifty Thirty One pownds and Tenn shillings Att Michalmas One Thousand six hundred and ffifty Thirty Two pownds Two shillings vpon the ffiue and Twentieth of March One Thousand six hundred ffifty and One about which time this Def^t made the Composicōn aforesaid vpon which Composition this Def^t was ordered to Receiue the whole proffitts of the said Tithes lands and premises without deducting any parte thereof for the Dower of the said Anne as formerly the said Anne not being Admitted to any Composition This Def^t received fforty and seven pownds Twelue shillings and foure pence Att Michalmas One Thousand six hundred ffifty and One This Def^t Receivd of the said Tenen^{ts} fforty ffiue pownds Eighteen shillings and Eleven pence vpon the ffiue and Twentieth of March One Thousand six hundred ffifty and Two fforty seauen pownds Two shillings and seven pence Att Michalmas One Thousand six hundred ffifty and Two fforty Eight pownds and six shillings vpon the ffiue and Twentieth of March One Thousand six hundred ffifty and Three fforty seven pownds ffifteene shillings and foure pence Att Michalmas One Thousand six hundred ffifty and Three fforty seven pownds ffourteene shillings and six pence which is all this Def^t hath received to the best of his knowledge and which Amounts in the whole to ffour hundred fforty ffiue pownds seauen shillings and fiue pence And which being deducted from fiue hundred ffifty [nine] pownds Thirteene shillings and six pence there Remaynes yet due and payable out of the Rents yssues and proffitts of the said Tithes lands premises besides all the growing Jnterest from the time of the said Extent the some of One hundred and fourteene pownds six shillings and One peny whereof vntill hee this Def^t shalbee fully satisfied hee doubteth not butt hee may iustly hold and Enioy All the said premises According to Law Equitie and good conscience Butt this Def^t knoweth not of any Statute or Recognizance or Mortgage att the Time in the bill mencōned or att any time before or since made or Acknowledged by the said Richard Powell to the said Sr John Powell in the bill named Or to Any other person or persons whatsoever condicōned or defeazanced as in the bill is sett forth or otherwise howsoever And this Def^t doth vtterly deny that hee did ever giue out in speeches that the said Mortgage Statute or Recognizance or any of them or any

such like were att any time assigned to him this Def^t or to any others
to this Def^ts knowledge as in and by the said bill is most vntruely suggested And this Def^t Alsoe vtterly denyeth that the said Mortgage
statute or Recognizance in the bill mencōned or any other Mortgage
statute or Recognizance to this Def^ts knowledge was att any time Ante
dated as this Cōmp^lt most vntruely suggesteth And this Def^t hopeth
this honō^ble Court will giue him very good costs for the said false and
scandalous suggestion surmised causelesly without any grownd to de-
fame and discredit this Def^t And this Def^t saith that the statute aforesaid was Dated and extended and the moneys therefrom haue been
levied and received in such manner as hath been already declared and
not otherwise And this Def^t claymeth not any estate or Jnterest in the
said Tithes lands and premises or in any other the lands or Tenements
of the said Richard Powell otherwise than [by the said] statute and
extent in such manner as hath been Already sett forth And this Def^t
saith that the said Tithes lands and premises were for ought this Def^t
knoweth to the contrary duely extended and found att an equall and
true value by the oath of lawfull men [however] this Def^t hath as aforesaid given A true and iust Accompt what monneys haue been raised and
received by him out of the Rents issues and proffitts of the said lands
and what remaynes behind and vnpayd by which itt plainely Appeares
that the said debt and interest with costs and chardges in that behalfe
by this Def^t susteyned Are not yett satisfied as they ought to bee and
therefore the Extent not yett Dischardged as by the said bill is supposed And this Def^t denyeth that hee caused the said Tithes lands and
premises to bee chardged with the Dower of the said wife of the said
Richard Powell named in the said bill by the name of Elizabeth but
intended as this Def^t conceiveth by Anne aforesaid the Relict of the said
Richard this Def^t not knoweing of any other wife that the said Richard
had And this Def^t conceiveth that the said Tithes lands and premises
were chardged by the said Jury with the Dower of the said Anne vpon
the said Annes makeing knowne her clayme and Right therevnto by
reason whereof her said Dower was Allowed vnto her by this Def^t as
hee conceiveth Rightfully vntill vpon his composicōn aforesaid and
the Refusall of the Comīttee to Admitt the said Anne to Any composicōn
And their expresse Order to this Def^t to take and Receiue the whole
Rents yssues and proffitts of all the sayd Tithes lands and premises As
by the said Order Appeareth this Def^t then Refused Any longer to Allow
the said Dower to the said Anne and hath since Received the whole
proffitts And hath Accounted for the same as aforesaid But this Def^t
saith hee knoweth nothing of Any Joynture either before or since
Marriage made by the said Richard to the said Anne As in the said

bill is pretended true itt is this Def^t hath heard of some bond entred into by the said Richard Powell to that purpose but what Or how this Def^t knoweth not Or what benefitt the said Anne hath Reaped by the said bond if Any such bee And this Def^t knoweth not of any other lands Tenements or hereditaments of the said Richard besides the premises before mencōned lyable to the payment of the debt aforesaid or otherwise And this Def^t Denyeth that hee hath forborne or doth forbeare the Raiseing and levyeing of the said debt as in and by the said bill is most vntruely suggested This Def^t vseing All the meanes hee cann for his most speedy satisfaccōn and the levying of his said Debt damāges and chardges And this Def^t doth vtterly deny all combinacōn and confederacy wherewith hee is chardged in the said bill And All Combinacōn and confederacy whatsoever without that that any other matter or thing in the said bill mencōned materiall for this Def^t to make answeare vnto and herewith well and sufficiently answeared vnto confessed Avoyded traversed or denyed is true to the knowledge of this Def^t All which matters and things this Def^t is ready to Averr and proue as this honō^{ble} Court shall Award And humbly prayes to bee dismissed from forth the same with their reasonable costs and chardges in this behalfe wrongfully susteined.

Chr'. Milton

December 3, 1655

A WRIT IS ISSUED TO EXAMINE WITNESSES IN ASHWORTH-MILTON SUIT

Chancery Depositions, C 22/759/17

Oliver Lord Protecto^r of ye Comōnwealth of England Scotland and Ireland and ye Dominions thereto belonging To Richard Crooke esq^r. George Bainger gent Charles Holloway the younger esq^r and Edward Astyn gent greeting Know ye that we reposeing speciall trust and Confidence in your fidelity and care haue assigned you & doe hereby give vnto you or any three or two of you full power and authority haveing first administred an oath each to other according to ye forme and effect of the Ordinance in that behalf appoynted to examine all witnesses whatsoever aswell on ye parte & behalfe of Elizabeth Ashworth widdowe plainetiffe as on the behalfe of John Milton Defendant or on ye behalfe of either of them on certain Jnterrīes to be exhibited to you or any three or two of you And we give vnto you or any three or two of you power & authority to administer an oath to ye Clarke or Clerkes attending you or any three or two of you at the Execucōn of this o^r Comission to write downe the Deposicōns of ye said witnesses truely and Jndifferently wthout partiality And therefore we comānd you or any three or two of you that you call or sumōn the said witnesses to come and appeare

before you or any three or two of yo^u at such days & places as you shall
appoint for this purpose And that you or any three or two of you examine the said witnesses & every of them by themselves severally vpon
ye said Jnterrīes, they haueing first taken their corpall oathes vpon h^e
holy Gospells of God before you or any three or two of you And that
you receive their examinacōns and reduce them into wryting in pchm^t
And when you haue soe done that you send them distinctly and plainely
closed vp vnder the Seales of you three or two of you to vs in our Court of
Chancery from the day of St Hillary next comeing in eight Dayes wheresoever itt shall then be together wth the Jnterrīes aforesaid and this writt
Witnes ourselfe at Westm^r the third day of December in the yeare of
our Lord 1655. Hen Martyn W.

> This Comīssion is to be executed eight dayes before the return
> thereof vpon 14 dayes notice to be given to the Def^t.

[*Endorsed on the back:*]

The execucōn of this Comīssion appeares in C^{r}taine schedules herevnto
annexed.

December or January, 1655–56
INTERROGATORIES ARE PREPARED TO BE ADMINISTERED TO
WITNESSES IN ASHWORTH-MILTON SUIT

Chancery Depositions, C 22/759/17

2 & last be [?] Lond.

On the pl^{tp} p^{tp}./   Interrogatoryes to bee administered to y^e Wit-
                          nesses pduced on the pte & behalfe of Elizabeth
Ashworth Widdowe Cōmpl^t: ag^t: John Milton Esq$_3$ Dēf^t:/

1 Imprimis. doe you knowe the ptyes Pl'^{t}: & Dēf^t: or either of them, &
   did you knowe Richard Powell late of fforresthill in the county of
   Oxōn Esq$_3$. deceased, & did you knowe Henry Ashworth late of y^e
   vnīv^{r}sity of Oxoñ Doctō^r: in Physicke, Deceased; & Edwards Ashworth eldest sonne of the said Doctō^r: alsoe deceased sett forth how
   longe you did knowe them, or either of them, & whether y^e said Edwards Ashworth overlived his said ffather; & how longe hee lived after
   ye decease of his said ffather?

2 Item doe you knowe ye messuage lyeing in Whateley in the said
   county of Oxoñ wch ye said Richard Powell purchased to him & his
   heires from S^r: George Symeon of Baldwin Britewell in the said
   county of Oxoñ Kn^t: togeather wth a Cottage there, & all that y^e
   moetye of three yard Lands wth thapp^{r}tñces scituate in Whatelye

aforesaid comōnly occupyed wth ye said Messuage, & ye tythes of corne graine and other thinges of & in Whately aforesaid & groveleyes in ye said county of Oxoñ: & other ye p^rmisses held & enioyed Wth ye said Messuage Lands & tythes, if you doe knowe them sett forth ye true yearely value of ye said messuage Lands & tythes, & What yearely rente ye same have been sett for for the space of seaven yeares last past or Longer sett forth yor whole knoweledge to this Jntērgatory?

3. It'm sett forth what you doe knowe ye said Messuage lands & Tythes to bee yearely worth more then ye said Def^t: doth lett ye same for, sett forth what you would give, for ye said p^rmisses in case you might quietly enioy them for ye space of seaven yeares or more?

4 It'm whether are you tenant at this p^rsent to ye said Def^t: of ye said messuage Lands & tythes, if yea? sett forth how longe you have rented ye same p^rmisses & what yearely rente you doe pay or give for ye same, & how much you have payd ye Def^t: in rentes for ye said p^rmisses since you first tooke it, to Lady day next one thousand six hundred fiftye six, & what will then bee due, sett forth ye whole trueth to each pte of this Jntērr?

5 It'm sett forth, Whether you are to beare & pay all ye taxes, or how much for ye said Lands & Tythes & Whether you have any abatem^t: out of the yearely rente for ye said Taxes, or whether you beare all taxes over & above ye yearely rente you pay for the p^rmisses sett forth ye trueth to each pte of this Jntērr?

6 It'm whether did you see this Jndenture now shewed vnto you at ye time of this exaiācon, & bearing date ye tenth day of January in ye seaventh yeare of ye raigne of ye late Kinge Charles sealed & deliv^red by the said Richard Powell as his acte & deed, whether doe you knowe ye names of ye Witnesses, or any of them y^t were p^rsent at ye sealing & deliū^ry of ye said Jndēnt^r: if yea sett forth whether they or any of them, & wch of them are living, & whether they are psons of good creditt & report & whether theire names bee not ye pper hand writinge of ye said witnesses sett forth what you knowe to this Jntērr: & what you beleive therein?

7 It'm sett forth whether ye said Edwards Ashworth did survive & ov^rlive ye said Henry Ashworth his father, if yea? sett forth how Long ye said Edwards Ashworth outlived his said ffather, & in what manner hee disposed of his int^rest in ye said messuage Lands & p^rmisses sett forth what you knowe therein?

8. Item, whether doe you knowe y^t ye Dēf^t: payd any moneys for a fyne

for yᵉ Composicōn of Rich: Powell esq; Deceased, & what moneys did hee pay vpon yᵉ said Composicōn for the said pʳmisses or any pte thereof, Declare what you knowe beleive or have credibly heard therein?

9 Item if there bee any other māttʳ or thinge materiall for you to depose for & on the behalfe of yᵉ Pʹltᵗ, in this mattʳ of variance, declare what you knowe beleive or have heard therein?

Charles Holloway Ju
George Banger

[*Endorsed on the back*:]

Ashworth coñ Milton, Aᵒ: 7ᵒ. Cār 2ᵈⁱ.
Ashworth agᵗ Milton Deposicōns . . . Quarta ps A . . . 4ᵃ ps. A

January 11, 1655/6

DEPOSITIONS OF WITNESSES IN ASHWORTH-MILTON SUIT

Chancery Depositions, C22/759/17

On yᵉ pte of   Deposicōns of Witnesses taken att Oxford yᵉ Eleaventh
yᵉ pˡᵗ.   Day of January in yᵉ yeare of oʳ Lord One Thousand
                six hundred fiftye five by vertue of a Comission out of
Highnes Courte of Chañcy to Richard Croke Esqʳ and George Banger gent Charles Holloway yᵉ younger Esqʳ & Edward Astin gent directed for yᵉ exaiācon of Witnesses in a cause there depending between Elizabeth Ashworth Widow pˡᵗ & John Milton defᵗ. wᶜʰ said Comīssionʳˢ according to the late acte were sworne:/

John Robinson of Whately in the countye of Oxon'. gent aged fifty five yeares or thereabouts deposeth as followeth:

4 & 5 To yᵉ fourth & fifth Jntērries this deponent saieth that hee is att this pʳñt tenant to yᵉ dēfᵈᵗ. of yᵉ Messuage Lands & tithes in yᵉ Jnterrogatory menconed & that hee hath rented yᵉ Messuage & Landes for a yeare & vpwards & yᵉ Tithes for seaven yeares & vpwards & that this deponᵗ. doth pay to yᵉ dēfᵈᵗ yearely threescore & tenne pounds for yᵉ said Messuage Lands & tythes Contribucōns & taxes being deducted, & that this deponᵗ. hath paid yᵉ dēfᵈᵗ. Two hundred & fowrescore pounds or thereabouts in rents for yᵉ said Tythes since hee first tooke it as hee remembreth & that this deponᵗ. hath & is to pay at our Lady Day next one Thousand six hundred fifty six threescore & five pounds & vpwards for yᵉ said Messuage Lands & tythes & further to this Jnterrogatory this deponent Cannot depose.

8   To yᵉ Eight Jntērr: this deponᵗ. further saieth that hee hath heard yᵉ defᵈᵗ. say that hee payd one hundred thirty three pounds to take of yᵉ sequestracon of Richard Powell Esqʳˢ estate deceased for his Land & tythes in Whately & further Cannot depose

John Robinson:

1   George Ball of forresthill in yᵉ County of Oxon gent aged ffifty fowre yeares or thereabouts deposeth as followeth To the first Jntērrie this deponent deposeth that hee knoweth yᵉ pties pˡᵗ. & dēfᵈᵗ. & did knowe all yᵉ other pties in yᵉ Jntērrie mencined & did knowe them for divers yeares last past, but l [*sic*] wheither or noe yᵉ said Edward Ashworth outlived his said ffather this deponᵗ cannot sett forth

2   To yᵉ second Jntērrie this deponent saieth yᵗ hee doth knowe yᵗ yᵉ said Richard Powell did purchase yᵉ Messuage in this Jntērrie mencōned to him & his heires from Sʳ George Symeon in this Jntērrie mencōned & also one Cottage & yᵉ moetye of one yard Land & a halfe wᵗʰ. Thappteñces in Whately aforesaid comōnly occupied wᵗʰ yᵉ said Messuage & Tythes & this deponᵗ further saieth yᵗ hee hath heard yᵉ said Mʳ Powell say yᵗ yᵉ tythes now in question were worth fifty pounds by yᵉ yeare & vpwards, but as to his owne pticuler knowledg this deponᵗ saieth yᵗ hee knoweth nothing of yᵉ value of yᵉ said tithes, & this deponᵗ further saieth yᵗ hee hath heard yᵗ yᵉ dēfᵈᵗ hath beene bid thirty & fower pounds a yeare for yᵉ said Messuage & Lands & farther to this Jntērrie cañott depose.

3   To yᵉ third Intērrie this deponᵗ cannot depose

6   To yᵉ sixth Jntērrie this deponᵗ saieth that hee doth not knowe yᵗ yᵉ Jndentʳ now shewed unto him bearing date yᵉ tenth day of January in yᵉ seauenth yeare of yᵉ late Kinge was sealed & delivered by yᵉ said Richard Powell deceased but doth know yᵉ names of yᵉ Witnesses yᵗ are subscribed on yᵉ said Jndenture & doth beleive yᵗ they are all dead & doth conceive that they were psons of good Creditt & Report & further to this Jntērrie cannot depose

7 & 9   To yᵉ seauenth & Nineth Jntērryes this deponᵗ cannot depose.

George Ball

John Gadbury of Whately in yᵉ County of Oxon' gent' aged five & forty yeares or thereabouts deposeth as followeth

2   To yᵉ second Jntērrye this deponent saieth that hee knoweth yᵉ Messuage Cottage moetye of Three yard Lands with thapptēncs & tithes in this Jntērrie mencōned were heretofore in yᵉ possession of Richard Powell Jnterrogated but of whome this dēfᵈᵗ purchased yᵉ same this deponᵗ. knoweth not & that yᵉ said Messuage Cottage moetye of three yard Lands & tithes were lett for six yeares last past or thereabouts for fourescore pounds a yeare & further to this Jntērrie cannot depose

3   To yᵉ Third Jntērrie this deponent saieth yᵗ hee knoweth not what yᵉ Messuage Lands & Tythes in this Jnterrie mencōned are lett att but yᵗ hee would give fowrescore & tenne poundes by yᵉ yeare for yᵉ same if hee might quietly enioy yᵉ same for yᵉ tʳme of seauen yeares & further to this Jntērrie cannot depose

9   To yᵉ Ninthe Jntērrie this deponent cannot depose further then hee hath pʳdeposed

John Gadbury

John Trevis of Whately in yᵉ said County of Oxon gent aged fifty [blank] yeares or thereabouts deposeth as followeth

2 & 9   To yᵉ second Jntērrie this deponent saieth that hee doth not knowe yᵗ Richard Powell in this Jntērrie named Purchased any Messuage or Cottage in Whately of Sʳ George Symeon neither doth hee knowe yᵉ value of yᵉ moety of yᵉ three yard Lands there wᵗʰ th'appʳtnces are yearely worth neither doth hee knowe what yearely rent yᵉ same haue beene sett for, for yᵉ space of seauen yeares last past or longer & farther to these Jntērryes cannot depose

The marke of
John Trevis ⸦

Charles Holloway Ju:
George Banger

[*Endorsed on the back:*]

Ashworth agᵗ Milton . . . Ashworth a Milton . . . 22ᵗʰ of January 1655 by the oath of Abraham Dickenson gen'

Na[thaniel] Hobart

May 10,1656
MILTON IS WARNED IN ASHWORTH SUIT
Chancery Decrees and Orders, C 33/205, f. 1119ᵛ

10 May

A   Eliza. Ashworth widd'   Jf the Deft shew no cause for stay of
pl' John Milton Deft   publ' by this day seavenight then publ' is graunted.

May 13, 1656
MILTON OBTAINS STAY IN ASHWORTH SUIT

Chancery Decrees and Orders, C 33/205/ f. 989   *Columbia edition of Milton's*
                                                              Works, XVIII, 417

Tu. 13 May

A   Eliza Ashworth widd'   Vpon opening of the matter this pn̄te day
    pl't John Milton esqʳ   by Mʳ Milton being of Co. wᵗʰ the deft
    Anne Powell widd' and   John Milton Jt was alleadged on the
    Rich. Powell esqʳ deft   behaulf of the said deft that the other
                                 deft Anne and Richard were onely named
by the pl't in her bill to take away their testimoney they being materiall
witness for the deft Milton in this cause. and that the said deft were
neū served wᵗʰ any pcesp to aunswʳ the said bill Jt was therefore praied
that the said deft Anne Powell and Rich. Powell may be exed de bene
esse on the behaulf of the said deft Milton in this cause and that the
Deft may have time to examine them vntil the first Day of the next
Tearme wᶜʰ is ordered accordingly and in the meane time publ' is to
stay./

    ex
                                                    H[enry Scobell?]

December 2, 1656
MILTON PROTESTS THE ASHWORTH SUIT IS SCANDALOUS

Chancery Decrees and Orders, C 33/207, f. 221ᵛ   *Columbia edition of Milton's*
                                                              Works, XVIII, 418

Tuesd: 2d Decēm

A   Elizabeth Ashworth   fforasmuch as this Court was this pʳsent
L Co.   p't John Milton and   day vnto this Court by Mʳ Milton being
        other Defts   of the defts Councell that the pl'te bill
                                Conteines in it matter of imptinency and
scandall against the Deft Milton Jt is ordered that the Mʳˢ of this Coʳt
doe looke into the plts bill and examine and certifie whether the same
bee scandelous or not Wherevpon such further order shall be taken as
shall bee meete/

    ē
                                                    J[ames?] E[dwards?]

May 4, 1657
ANNE AND RICHARD POWELL ARE ORDERED TO ANSWER
ASHWORTH BILL

Chancery Decrees and Orders, C 33/207, f. 809

Mond 4 May

A   Elizabeth Ashworth   This Cause standing in the paper
L Co: widd. Extrix of Ed-   to bee heard this day and Councell

ward Ashworth her husband whoe was Extoᵣ of Henry his ffather Deced pl' John Milton Richard Powell Esqʳ and Anne Powell wid: Dēfts

on both sides attending for that purpose vpon entring into the heareing thereof fforasmuch as it appeared that the scope of the pl'ts bill is to redeeme a morgage and that the Heire of the morgagee and his mother who are parties to this suite and whome the matter pply concernes have not as yett Answered

Jt is ordered that the said Dēfts Richard and Anne Powell shall in a fortnight next Answer the said bill and examine their witnesses soe as publicacōn may passe the first day of the next terme and the Cause bee heard the last weeke of the same terme/

ē

W[illiam?] G[oldesbrough?]

May 26, 1657

RICHARD AND ANNE POWELL ANSWER ELIZABETH ASHWORTH'S BILL

Chancery Proceedings, C5/405/2

Both sworne the 26ᵗʰ. of May 1657. Wᵐ. Harrington Dᵈ Aᵒ 59 13ᵃ ss A²

The Joynt & seūall Answeres of Anne Powell widd': & Richard Powell Esqʳ. defendants to yᵉ Bill of Cōmplt. of Elizabeth Ashworth, complainant./

The said Defendants now and att all times hereafter saveing to themselves all advantages of Excepcōn to the Jncertainty and Jnsufficiency of the said Bill of Cōmplᵗ. for Answeare to soe much thereof as concerneth them these dēfts or either of them to make Answeare vnto They these dēfts say That Richard Powell late of fforresthill in the County of Oxoñ Esqʳ. deceased in the Bill named, (husband to the dēft Anne and father to the dēft Richard) was in his life time Lawfully seized in his Demeasne as of ffee by Purchase from Sʳ. George Symeon Knᵗ. in the bill named and by other good right and title of and in the Messuages or Tenements in Wheatly in the County of Oxōn in the bill of Cōmplᵗ. on that behalfe mencōed And also of and in the Moyety of Three yards of Lands with thappurtenances and of and in all the Tythes of Corne Grayne and other things att of or in Wheatly aforesaid and Groveleyes in the said County of Oxoñ in the Bill of Cōmplᵗ. on that behalfe more perticulerly mencōed of the Yearely value of about Seventy pounds and also of other Lands & Tenemᵗˢ. in Wheatly aforēsd & in Cuddesden in yᵉ s'd County of Oxford And these dēfts further say, That They belieue it to bee true That the said Richard Powell dēcd did att the time in the bill mencōed borrow of Henry Ashworth or Edward Ashworth in the Bill named the Sumē of ffowre hundred pounds and that

for Security of repayment of the said fowre hundred pounds hee the said
Richard Powell dēcd did by his Jndenture beareing date att or about
the time in the Bill mencōed Demise Grant bargaine and sell to the s^d
Henry and Edward Ashworth and to the Survivo^r of them and to the
Ex'^rs. and Administrato^rs. of the Survivo^r. of them the s^d Messuage
Cottage moyety of the said three yard Lands & Tythes with tha'ppurtenances in the bill on that behalfe mencōed for the terme of ffourescore
and Nyneteene yeares from and after y^e. thirteenth day of January in
the Yeare 1632. with provisoe therein contayned in Effect, That vpon
payment of the Sumē of foure hundred pounds vpon the aforesaid
thirteenth day of January 1632. then the said Demise and grant to bee
absolutely void; But these def'^ts. doe deny that the said Richard Powell
dēcd did make any Agreem^t. with the s^d. Henry & Edward Ashworth or
either of them to borrow the said foure hundred pounds att Jnterest
after the rate of 8^li. p Cent or any other rate whatsoeū or did by the
aforesaid Jndenture secure the repayment of any Jnterest whatsoever
for the said foure hundred pounds att the End of one yeare then ensueing
or att any other time whatsoeū And these dēfts dēfts doe likewise beleive
that the said Richard Powell did fayle in payment of the said 400^li:
according to the said Provisoe Yet hee did afterwards (as these dēfts
belieue) pay vnto the Cōmp^lts husband the said Edward Ashworth the
Sūme of One hundred pounds in part of payment of the said debt of
400^li: as in the said bill is set forth And all interest of the remaineing
three hundred pounds wch from time to time grew due vntill the death
of him the s^d Richard Powell dēcd. And these dēfts deny all & all manner
of Combinacon with Sr John Powell in the bill named if any such person
there bee or with John Milton Esqr. in the bill likewise named or with
any other person or persons whatsoeū to defeate or defraud the Cōmp^lt
of any Sūme or sūmes of money which are & shall appeare to bee justly
due vnto her or of the s^d security soe as aforesaid made and given for
the said originall debt of foure hundred pounds by any wayes or meanes
in the Bill most vntruely Suggested or by any other wayes or meanes
whatsoeū And whereas the said Cōmp^lt by her said Bill doth Craftily
and most Jnjuriously endeavo^r. to Asperce them these dēfts & the other
def^t. John Milton and to Charge them with the Antidating of some
Mortgages Statutes or Recognizeances these dēfts and either of them doe
vtterly deny that they or either of them haue Antidated or Caused to be
antidated any Mortgage or Mortgages Statute or Statutes Recognizeance
or Recognizeances or other Deeds or Evidences whatsoever And hope
that this Court will allow them good Costs for that most false and
Scandalous Jmputacōn And these defts further say That they beleive
it to bee true that the said Richard Powell dēcd and one William Herne

by a Wryting or Recognizeance in the nature of a Statute Staple beareing date on or about the Eleaventh day of June in the third Yeare of the raigne of the late King Charles became bound vnto the other dēft. John Milton in the Sūme of five hundred pounds of Lawfull money of England defeazeanced for the payment of three hundred pounds principall Debt (which said Sūme of three hundred pounds was as these dēfts belieue really and truly Lent vnto the said Richard Powell dēcd by John Milton dēcd father of the other deft John Milton) and twelve pounds for Jnterest thereof vpon the Twelfth day of December then next following for non payment of which said Reall and just principall debt of three hundred pounds and the Jnterest for the forbearance thereof for seūall yeares (but how many neither of these dēfts. Canne certainly set forth) the said other dēft. John Milton did about the time in the bill on that behalfe mencōed cause the said Lands Tythes and pᵣmisses in the bill mencōed and likewise the said other Lands of the said Richard Powell dēcd. in the parish of Wheatly or Cuddesden aforesaid to bee Extended att the values (as theise dēfts. beleive) in the sᵈ. dēft. Miltons Answeare, (wherevnto for the more certainty of all pticulers touching the sᵗᵈ. Extent these dēfts refere) set forth And that since the sᵗᵈ. Extent the dēft Anne late wife of the sᵗᵈ Richard Powell dēcd did receive the profitts of the third part as shee belieueth of all & singuler the said Extended pᵣmisses with tha'ppurtenances for about the space of two yeares as shee conceiveth was Lawfull for her to doe And these dēfts say That on or about the thirteenth day of December in the Yeare of our Lord one Thousand Six hundred fforty Six the aforesaid Richard Powell dēcd made his last will & Testament in wryting and therein and thereby amongst other things bequeathed All the said Messuages Lands Tythes and pᵣmisses vnto the dēft Richard Powell for the payment of his the said Testatoᵣˢ. debts and to other the vses intents and purposes in the sᵗᵈ. last will specified and set forth and thereof made the said dēft sole Executoᵣ. And in Case the said dēft Richard should not take vpon him the Executoᵣshipp Then his will was that the other dēft: Anne should bee sole Executrix vnto whom hee gaue (amoungst other things) the said Lands and pᵣmisses to the vses and purposes aforesaid and shortly after dyed, After whose death the said dēft Anne (in regarde the other dēft. Richard did not Accept of the said Executorshipp) proved the said will in due forme of Law and took vpon her the burthen and Execucōn thereof and thereby became intituled amoungst other things to All the said Lands and pᵣmisses subject neūtheless and lyable to the payment of the said Testatōᵣˢ. just dēbts which Trust these dēfts alwayes haue bin and still are ready to performe and in pursuance thereof these dēfts doe say, That what shall appeare to bee justly due vnto the said Cōmp^{lt}: to bee Computed according to the seūall Statutes with the vsuall abatement and moderation of Jnterest during the Warres and deducting likewise what hath bin rēcd by her the said Cōmp^{lt}. or by the said Henry Ashworth or Edward Ashworth dēcd or any to her or their or either of their vse or vses of the said Richard Powell dēcd or any to his vse or by his direccōn and what they or either of them haue or might haue rēcd without their respectiue wilfull defaults out of the Rents Jssues & proffitts of the p^r'misses (They ye said Edward Ashworth & y^e. sd' Complñt or one of Them hauing had y^e. possession of y^e. sd' demised p^r.misses for some time since or lately before y^e. death of y^e. s'd Richard Powell decēd) They these Dēfts are and shall bee ready to pay the same vnto the s^d. Cōmp^{lt}. within such reasonable time as this honō^{ble} Court shall thinke fitt to appoint And these dēfts doe further say that if the other dēft M^r. Milton bee satisfyed his just debt which (if hee bee, the same) will appeare by this Accompt as hee ought to make and giue vnto these dēfts touching the Rents jssues & proffitts of the said Extended p^r'misses rēcd by him or any to his vse) Then the possession of all and eūy the sd p^r'misses togeather with the Rents jssues and proffitts thereof ought to bee and remayne vnto and with these dēfts or one of them and if any Lease or Leases of all or any the p^r'misses haue bin made by the s^d other dēft M^r. Milton for any terme or number of yeares yet to come and vnexpired such Lease and Leases, as these dēfts conceive ought to stand and bee from henceforth voyd, Cancelled and of none Effect, his the said M^r. Miltons vndertenañt or Vnder-tenants of all or any the p^r'misses haveing Convenient time allowed him or Them for removeing takeing off and Carrying away his or their Stocke or Cropp from of the p^r'misses All which these dēfts hope shalbee De-creed accordingly Without that, that any other matter or thing in the Cōmp^{lts}. said bill of Cōmplt. conteyned, materiall or Effectuall in the Law for these dēfts to make Answeare vnto and herein not sufficiently Answeared vnto confessed and Avoyded Traūsed or denyed is true All which matters and things these dēfts are and wilbee ready to Averre justifie maintaine and proue as this honō^{ble}: Court shall Award and humbly pray to bee hence dismissed with their reasonable Costs & Charges in this behalfe wroungfully and needlessely susteyned./

Chr': Milton.

Ed Peck

June 5, 1657
FINAL DECREE IN ASHWORTH-MILTON SUIT
Chancery Decrees and Orders, C 33/207, ff. 1250–1251^v

ffrid: 5th. June.

A   Elizabeth Ashworth wīdd

L. Co: Exec^x. of the last Will
and Testam^t. of Edward
Ashworth Decēd pl't: John
Milton Esqr Richard Powell
Esqr, & Anne Powell widd' Exec^x.
of the last Will & Testam^t
of Richard Powell Esqr
Decēd Dēfd^{tp}.

Whereas this Cause came to be heard before the Lordɵ Com^{rs} vpon the 4th. Day of May last past, and forasmuch as it then appeared that Two of the Dēftɵ most proply concerned had not answered the pl'tɵ Bill, it was therevpon ordered that the said Defd^{tp} Richard & Anne Powell should in a ffortnight then next following answere the said bill & examine their Witnesses soe as publicacōn might passe the first day of the then next terme, and the Cause to bee sett downe to be heard the last weeke of the said terme, And forasmuch as the Pl't by her bill settɵ forth that Richard Powell Decēd did about January 7⁰. Car Borrowe of Henry Ashworth Decēd 400^{li} at Jnterest at 8^{li}. p Cent the said Powell being then seised in his Demease as of ffee by purchase from Sr George Symeon Kn^t: Discharged of all Jncumbrances of one Messuage one Cottage, the Moyety of Three yard Landɵ and of all the Tythes of Corne and other thingɵ in Wheatley & Grove Leaze scituate in Cuddesden or Holton worth 100^{li}. p anñ, and of the Reūcon of ye p^{r}misses and for security of the Repayment of the said 400^{li}. and of ye Jnterest for one yeare the said Powell made the said Henry Ashworth and the P^{ltp} late husband a Lease of the p^{r}misses for 99. yeareɵ to comence from the 13th of January 1632. wch Jndenture was Dated 10mo. Jañ. 7⁰. Car betweene the said Powell & Ashworth whereby the said Powell did Demise vnto the said Henry Ashworth Deceased & the p^{ltp} said husband, and the Survivō^r of them, and the Executō^{rp} of the Survivo^r of them the said p^{r}misses Dureing the said Terme, wth a Provisoe that if the said Powell or his heires should pay vnto the said Henry Ashworth or the p^{ltp} said husband or the survivo^r of them or the Executō^{rs} of the Survivō^r of them the said 400^{li}. vpon ye 13th: of January 1632. that then the said Demise was to be voyd. But the said Powell fayleing in paym^t of the said 400^{li} according to the said Provisoe the said Demise became absolute, Notwthstanding which the said Henry Ashworth and the p^{ltp} said husband suffered the said Powell and his vnder Tenantɵ to enioy the p^{r}misses, and Henry Ashworth dying made Edward Ashworth the p^{ltp} said husband his Executō^r. who proved the will, and thereby became intituled to the said money, and lyable to the paym^t of his Debt℘, And that 6 yeare℘ since the p^{ltℓ} said husband receiued 100^{li}. in pte of the said 400^{li}. and the Jnterest untill January 1644. for the 300^{li}. rēmd^r of the sd 400^{li}. Since wch tyme neither principall nor Jnterest hath byn payd, and that the sayd Powell ffather of the dēfte Richard Dyeing seised of the p^{r}misses they came to the Dēfte Richard Powell as his Sonne and heire, and that afterward℘ about 1648. the P^{ltℓ} said husband made his last will & Dyed, haueing made the P^{lt} his Execut^x & Disposed of the said 300^{li}. & the Damages due for the same for the benefit of his younger Children, and that the Dēft Milton Did about August in the 23th. yeare of the late King Charles extend all the p^{r}misses soe Demised to Henry and Edward Ashworth as aforesaid vpon a Statute of 500^{li}. acknowledged to him by the said Richard Powell Decēd about June 3to. Cār and found the Land℘ at a very low rate chardgable wth the Third℘ for the Dēft Anne being the late wife of the said Powell Deceased, and the Deft Milton haueing for those 6 yeares last past recēd 100^{li}. p Anñ for th'extended Land℘ Soe that the said Statute was satisfied out of the pffitt℘ of the said Land℘ whereby the Creditō^{rs} of the said Powell were like to be Defeated of their Debt℘, Soe as the scope of the P^{ltℓ} Bill is that the Deft℘ Milton, and Rīch. and Anne Powell may sett forth what Jncumbrāces were vpon the p^{r}misses, and whether the monyes Due therevpon were not paid, and what Estate Milton had in the p^{r}misses, and whether hee were satisfied his p^{r}tended Debt chardged vpon the p^{r}misse℘ and that hee may accompt for what hee hath recēd,—Wherevnto the said Milton by his Answere sett℘ forth that by vertue of an Extent taken vpon the 5th. day of August 1647, Jt was found that the said Powell Deceased acknowledged a statute dated 11°. Junij. 3°. Caroli (at wch tyme the said Powell was seised of all the said p^{r}misses), by vertue of wch Extent he the said Milton became pōssed of the p^{r}misse℘ and enioyed the said p^{r}misse℘ soe extended, and tooke the benefitt thereof, and that he recēd for the seūall yeare℘ hee wa℘ soe in pōssion 445^{li}. 7^s. 5^d. as appeare℘ by his Accompt in the said Answere sett forth, wch Accompte of the Dēft^e Miltons ended Michās 1653. And the said Deft℘ Richard and Anne Powell by their Answere offering that they are ready to pay vnto the pl't all such monyes as shall appeare to be due vnto the P^{lt} as this Court should appoynte—Therevpon, and vpon heareinge what was alleadged by the said pties on either side, Jt is this Day ordered and decreed by and wth the consent of the P$^{l't}$ and the said Deft℘ That the said Defd^{tℓ} Richard and Anne Powell, their Exēc^{rs}, Adm'^{rs} or Assignes shall pay vnto the said Cōmp^{lt} her Executō^{rs} Adm'^{rs} or Assignes the sūme of 560^{li} being the same agreed vpon to be due not only for the principall money in question but alsoe for all Damages and Cost℘ due vpon the said Mortgage, wch said sume of 560^li is by and wth the like consent of the said Cōmp^lt and the Dēft℘ Richard and Anne Powell agreed to bee paid as hereafter is lymĩtted & appoynted, that is to say the sũme of 300^li. of Lawfull money of England at or vpon the 23th. day of octōb^r next ensueing the Date hereof at or in an Jnne in Oxford comonly called the signe of the Beare there, and that the rest and residue of the said 560^li soe agreed to be due & paid, being 260^li. of like money at or vpon the 23th Day of January next following, And it is further ordered and Decreed that in case the Deftd^t℘ Richard & Anne Powell their Executō^rs Adm'^rs or Assignes, shall fayle in paym^t of the said Sũmes or either of them, it shall & may bee lawfull to & for the said Cōmp^lt her Exēc^rs, Adm'^rs, & Assignes into & vpon the said mortgaged p^rmisse℘ to enter, and the same to hold and enioy Dureing. the residue of the Terme of 99. yeare℘ aforesaid freed & dischardged from all Equity of Redempcōn ag^t the said Dēf^t℘ Richard & Anne Powell, and all claymeing by from or vnder them or either of them, or vnder the said Rīch. Powell Decēd late ffather of the said Dēft Richard, and all claymeing by from or vnder him, And the said Dēft℘ Ann & Richard Powell are hereby ordered and Decreed to saue and keepe harmeles the sd' Cōmp^lt from all Costs ag^t the Deft Milton by reason of this suite And alsoe vpon payment of the said sũme of 560^li. the s'd Cōmp^lt shall convey & assigne to the s'd Dēft℘ Richard & Ann Powell the said Mortgaged p^rmisse℘ freed & Dischardged of & from all Jncumbrñs made done or suffered by the said Cōmp^lt or the said Henry or Edward Ashworth or any claymeing by from or vnder them or either of them, But if it shall happen that the said Def℘ Richard or Anne shall pay or cause to be paid the said 560^li. at the tyme p^rfixed for the first paym^t. of the said money, then the said Cōmp^lt. is to abate soe much of the said 560^li. as the Jnterest of 260^li. doth amount vnto from ye said 23th. of octob^r vntill the said 23th of January then following, And forasmuch as it appeares vnto this Court that the Defte Milton hath already justly accompted wth the said other Dēf^t℘ Richard & Anne for all proffits recēd by him vpon his said Extent, and for that it is agreed by & betweene the said Dēf^t℘ that vpon the said Dēf^t Miltons Receipte of the Rents & proffit℘ Due at Michās last ye said Milton was fully satisfied his Debt Jnterest and chardges, and that being alsoe allowed out of the said last Michās Rent all the Cost℘ and expenses in this Suit, wch hee can reasonably Demand there will yet remayne in his hand℘ vpon the Receipt of the said Rent an ouer plus of 4^li-17^s-4^d the said Milton being fully satisfied as aforesaid, Therevpon it is further ordered and Decreed by consent of all the said pties p^l't & Dēft℘ That the said Milton shall forthw^th Deliver vpp the pōssion of the s'd ex-

tended p^rmisses to the said other Def^{tᵨ} or one of them, and alsoe forth^wth
pay vnto the said Dēf^{tᵨ} or one of them the said overplus money, And
that the said Dēf^{tᵨ} Richard and Anne are likewise to haue & receiue all
the Rents & profitt_ᵨ Due for the said extended p^rmisses at O^r Lady day
last past, deducting the vsuall iust & lawfull allowances to the Tenant_ᵨ,
And this Court Doth by & wth the consent aforesaid also confirme &
approue of the Acc^t. before mencōned to be made by y^e Dēf^t Milton to
the said other dēf^{tᵨ}, and the Cost_ᵨ to him allowed vpon the same as
aforesaid, and doe thinke fitt & soe order, That the said Dēf^t Milton bee
hereby Dischardged & saued harmeles by the said other Def^{tᵨ} of & from
all other & further Accompt_ᵨ either to the s'd Cōmp^{lt} Ashworth or any
other pson whatsoever, and from all suits or troubles for or by reason
of the p^rmisses, and his takeing or receiueing the profitts thereof soe
accompted for as aforesaid vpon the Extent aforesaid.

An: Collin_ᵨ p q'

John Milton
Ann Powell   W[illiam?] G[oldesbrough?]
Richard Powell/

ēx
W G.

CHAPTER X

MILTON *VS.* COPE

February 1, 1637/8 (?)

SIR JOHN COPE GIVES MILTON BOND FOR £300

*[The original has not been found. This note comes from Milton's bill, June 16, 1654,
C 8/120/72]*

... Sʳ John Cope late of Hanwell in the County of Oxōn deceased togeather with Robert Lee of Bilseley in yᵉ County of [Warwick?] Esqȝ
and Thomas Ofley of greate Doulby in yᵉ County of Leicester alsoe
Esqȝ by their Obligacōn or writinge Obligatory bearinge date yᵉ first
day of ffebruary in yᵉ thirteenth yeare of yᵉ late Kinge Charles and in
yᵉ yeare of our Lord god *1637* became ioyntly & severally bound to yoʳ
Oratoʳ in yᵉ penall sumē of 300ˡⁱ. of lawfull English money Condicōned
for yᵉ paymᵗ. of 150ˡⁱ principall money lent & 3ˡⁱ Jnterest for yᵉ same
vpon yᵉ third day of May then next ensueinge ...

1654 (?)
MILTON'S ACTION AT COMMON LAW AGAINST SIR ANTHONY COPE FOR DEBT IS BLOCKED

*[The original documents have not been found; but see Milton's bill of June 16,
1654, C 8/120/72]*

And yᵉ s'd Sʳ Anthony Cope alsoe ... hath lately pleaded to yoʳ Oratoʳ
in barr of an accōn of debt longe since brought by yoʳ Oratoʳ vpon yᵉ
s'd bond or writinge obligatory yᵗ yᵉ s'd Sʳ Anthony ... yᵗ noe Land℘
Tenemᵗ℘ or other hereditamᵗ℘ are descended vpon him in ffee simple as
heire vnto yᵉ s'd Sʳ John Cope ...

[See also Cope's answer to Milton's bill, October 21, 1654.]

... Wᶜʰ land℘ at Marshland this Defte Sʳ Anthony Cope hath confessed
in his plea to the Accōn broughte at Lawe by the said Complaynante
against this Defendᵗ as heire to his father Sʳ John Cope.

June 16, 1654
MILTON BRINGS SUIT AGAINST LADY ELIZABETH AND SIR ANTHONY COPE

Chancery Proceeding, C 8/120/72 and C 7/452/60
*[Neither is completely legible; but one being a copy of the other, the text here given
is a composite.]*

Columbia edition of Milton's
Works, XVIII, 409

To the Right honōᵇˡᵉ the Lordρ Comissioners for the Custody of the
    greate Seale of England
                The xviᵗʰ of June 1654
72   Smythe/
humbly Complayninge sheweth vnto your Lordshippes yoʳ Oratoʳ John
Milton of Westminster in yᵉ County of Middlesex Esqʳ, That whereas
Sʳ John Cope late of Hanwell in the County of Oxōn deceased togeather
with Robert Lee of Bilseley in yᵉ County of [Warwick] Esq₃ and Thomas
Ofley of greate Doulby in yᵉ County of Leicester alsoe Esq₃ by their
Obligacōn or writinge Obligatory bearinge date yᵉ first day of ffebruary
in yᵉ thirteenth yeare of yᵉ late Kinge Charles and in yᵉ yeare of our Lord
god *1637* became ioyntly & severally bound to yoʳ Oratoʳ in yᵉ penall
sūme of 300ˡⁱ. of lawfull English money Condicōned for yᵉ paymᵗ of
150ˡⁱ principall money lent & 3ˡⁱ Jnterest for yᵉ same vpon yᵉ third day
of May then next ensueinge yᵉ date of yᵉ said Obligacōn or writinge
Obligatory & aboute A yeare after [the date] thereof yᵉ s'd Sʳ John Cope
beinge seized in his demeasne as of ffee of and in divers Messuages Landρ
Tenemᵗρ & other hereditamᵗρ of A very greate yearely value and being
alsoe pōssed of A very greate psonall estate in Leases ready money
plate household stuffρ Corne Cattle & other goodρ & chattells to A very
greate value made his last will & Testamᵗ in wrytinge & did therein expresse & declare his will to be yᵗ as for his Landρ wᶜʰ were nott entayled & wherein hee had power to dispose they should be disposed of
for yᵉ payinge of his debtρ & for the raisinge of porcōns for his yonger
children & for his sisters whom hee there particulerly named and by his
said will gave full power & authority to yᵉ Lady Elizabeth his wife to
yᵉ Right honōᵇˡᵉ the Countess Dowager of Westmerland to Wᵐ. Lord
Say and Seale being his kinsmen & Rich Knightley Esq₃ & Gyles Harris
of Churchill in yᵉ County of Oxōn gent to sell sett or otherwise dispose
of all yᵉ Landρ nott entayled for yᵉ payinge of his debtρ & raisinge of
porcōns as aforesaid in and by his s'd will declareing & expressinge yᵗ
by a Deed vnder his hande & seale hee had conveyed yᵉ said Landρ
to yᵉ vses intentρ & purposes aforesaid as in & by yᵉ same will & Testamᵗ
relacōn beinge therevnto had it may & doth more att lardge appeare
& of this his last will & Testamᵗ hee yᵉ s'd Sʳ John Cope made & or-
deined yᵉ s'd Lady Elizabeth his wife sole executrix & soone after dyed
after whose death yē said Lady Elizabeth ρued yᵉ s'd will in due forme
of Lawe & by vertue thereof pōssed herself of all yᵉ Leases bondρ bills
wrytinges monie & plate iewells houses & household stuff Corne Cattle
& of all other yᵉ goodρ Chattles & psonall estate whatsoever of the
s'd Sʳ John Cope her said husband and as your Orator is informed is
since marryed to [*blank*] Cope Esqʳ Nowe so it is may it please yoʳ
Lōppes that yᵉ said Lady Elizabeth intendinge to defraud yoʳ Oratoʳ

& ye rest of the Credito^{rs} of their iust & due debtℓ & to convert the said personall estate to her owne vse hath by divers secrett meanes conveyed the same to psons vnknowne to yor Orato^r & secretly disposed thereof to ye Jntent y^t the s'd psonall estate may remayne vndiscoũed & concealed from yor Orato^r & ye s'd Credito^{rs} soe y^t neyther yor Orato^r nor any of the said Credito^{rs} might bee able to chardge her ye s'd Elizabeth wth Assetℓ in any accõn wch they should Comẽnce att Lawe for ye recovery of theire s'd iust & due debts & thereupon hath nott onely given out in speeches but likewise pleaded to severall psons whoe for ye recovery of their iust debtℓ have Comẽnced accõns at Lawe ag^t her as executrix of the said Sr John Cope her late husband y^t shee hath fully Administered & hath nothing in her handℓ to satisfy ye s'd debtℓ whereas in trueth she ye s'd Dame Elizabeth hath Assettℓ in her handℓ of the said psonall estate to satisfy & pay all ye debtℓ whatsoever due by ye s'd Sr John Cope her late husband with A very greate overplus And yor Orato^r also sheweth vnto yor Lõppes y^t ye s'd Lady Elizabeth ye s'd Countesse Dowager of Westmerland ye said William Lord Say & Seale ye s'd Richard Knightley & Gyles Harris by combinacõn & Confederacy amongst themselves & wth Sr Anthony Cope sonne & heire of the s'd Sr John Cope contrary to ye good intent & meaninge of ye s'd Sr John & contrary to ye trust by him reposed in them, ever since ye death of the said Sr John Cope have or some or one of them hath taken and received eyther to their owne or some of theire owne private vse & benefitt or to ye vse & behoofe of the said Sr Anthony all ye rentℓ yssues profitts of all ye s'd Messuages Landℓ Tenem^{tℓ} & other hereditam^{tℓ} whereof the said Sr John was seized in his demeasne as of ffee & whereof hee had power to dispose & wch hee did dispose as afores'd & in particuler they ye s'd Trustees have or some or one of them hath ever since ye death of the said Sr John Cope taken and received to their or some of theire private vse and benefitt as aforesaid severall rentℓ to ye yearely value of 500^{li} or thereaboutℓ due payable & yssuinge out of ye Messuadge or house called ye Custome house in London and ye Wharfe or Key there & out of divers Tenem^{tℓ} & houses therevnto neare adioyning or scituate in ye streetes Lanes or places neere thereaboutℓ beinge pte of those Landℓ & hereditam^{tℓ} whereof hee was seized in his demeasne as of ffee att ye tyme when hee made ye pvision aforesaid for ye paym^t of his debtℓ afores'd & being according to his true intent and meaninge included within ye s'd pvision of ye sd Sr John Cope & within ye purport & intent of ye s'd will & deed before menconed to be made for y^t purpose And yor Orato^r further sheweth y^t notwithstandinge ye s'd Sr John Cope left such A great psonall estate sufficient to satisfy all his debtℓ & legacies with A greate overplus wch ye s'd Lady Elizabeth hath gott into her põssion & secretly conveyed & imbeizilled as aforesd &

alsoe notwithstandinge yᵗ yᵉ s'd Ladye Elizabeth & yᵉ rest of yᵉ Trustees
aforesaid have [either] taken & received yᵉ rentȹ yssues & ꝑfittȹ of all
the s'd Landȹ Tenemᵗȹ & other hereditamᵗȹ intended & Allotted by yᵉ
s'd Sʳ John Cope for yᵉ Paymᵗ of his debtȹ as afores'd & converted yᵉ
same to theire or some of theire private vse & benefitt or suffered yᵉ
sd Sʳ Anthony to take & receive yᵉ rentȹ yssues & profittȹ thereof or of
A greate pte thereof or have secretly sould & conveyed yᵉ same to
psons vnknowne to yoʳ Oratoʳ & yᵉ moneyes raysed vpon such sale &
conveyance deteyne & keepe in theire or some of theire owne handȹ &
convert to theire or some of theire owne vse & benefitt yett nott onely
yᵉ s'd Elizabeth but yᵉ other trustees before named alsoe & yᵉ s'd Sʳ
Anthony Cope sonne & heire att Lawe of yᵉ sd Sʳ John Cope hath and
every of them hath hitherto vtterly denyed & refused & still doe &
every of them doth vtterly refuse & deny to pay or satisfy or cause
to be payd or satisfied vnto yoʳ Oratoʳ his said iust and due debt of 150ˡⁱ
or any parte thereof or any Jnterest for yᵉ forbearance of yᵉ same notwithstanding yᵗ all yᵉ s'd pties well knowe & soe yᵉ trueth is yᵗ neyther
yᵉ s'd principall debt of 150ˡⁱ nor any pte thereof nor any Jnterest due
for yᵉ forbearance of the same since November 1641 hath beene paid
or satisfied vnto yoʳ Oratoʳ or any other for his behalfe either by yᵉ sd
Sʳ John Cope in his life tyme or by yᵉ s'd Robert Lee and Thomas
Offley or eyther of them or by any other pson or psons whatsoever before or since his death & yᵗ yᵉ s'd principall debt with Jnterest as aforesaid remaynes to this day wholly vnpaid & vnsatisfied to yᵉ greate
losse & Damage of yoʳ Oratoʳ & yᵉ better to culloʳ yᵉ vniust [deteyning?]
of yᵉ s'd debt & Jnterest from yoʳ Oratoʳ & to discourage yoʳ Oratoʳ in
ꝑsecucōn of his lawfull Accōn for yᵉ recoūy of his sd iust & due debt shee
the s'd Lady Elizabeth doth give out in speeches & affirme yᵗ shee hath
nott Assetts in her handȹ of yᵉ psonall estate of yᵉ s'd Sʳ John Cope
her late husband whose executrix shee is as afores'd to pay or satisfy
yᵉ s'd debt whereas in truth yᵉ s'd psonall estate of yᵉ s'd Sʳ Jo: Cope is
amply sufficient fully to pay & satisfy nott onely yoʳ Oratoʳ but all
other yᵉ Creditoʳˢ of yᵉ s'd Sʳ John if yᵉ s'd Lady Elizabeth would discover yᵉ true value thereof & have nott wasted imbeizilled or by some
secrett waies & meanes fraudulently conveyed away to some person or
psons in trust for her & to her private vse & benefitt or to & for yᵉ vse
& benefitt of yᵉ said Sʳ Anthony her son or of some other of her children
And yᵉ s'd Sʳ Anthony Cope alsoe whoe came very lately to his age of
21 yeares doth give out in speeches & hath lately pleaded to yoʳ Oratoʳ
in barr of an accōn of debt longe since brought by yoʳ Oratoʳ vpon yᵉ
s'd bond or writinge obligatory yᵗ yᵉ s'd Sʳ Anthony as heire att Lawe
vnto yᵉ sd Sʳ John Cope yᵗ noe Landȹ Tenemᵗȹ or other hereditamᵗȹ
are descended vpon him in ffee simple as heire vnto yᵉ s'd Sʳ John Cope

his ffather, except Landℰ to yᵉ yearely value of 40ˡⁱ or thereaboutℰ whereas in truth although noe Landℰ Tenemᵗℰ or other hereditamᵗℰ bee actually descended vpon him in ffee simple from his said ffather in regard yᵉ s'd Sʳ Jo: Cope his s'd ffather did convey & dispose of all his s'd ffee simple Landℰ as afores'd yett seeing yᵉ s'd Lady Elizabeth & yᵉ s'd other Trustees before named have nott imployed yᵉ same according to yᵉ trust reposed in them by yᵉ s'd Sʳ John Cope for yᵉ paymᵗ of his debtℰ but have pmitted & suffered yᵉ s'd Sʳ Anthony to receive & enioye yᵉ rentℰ issues & profittℰ of yᵉ s'd Landℰ Tenemᵗℰ & hereditamᵗℰ or of yᵉ greatest ptᵉ thereof to his owne vse & benefitt yoʳ Oratoʳ therefore humbly conceives yᵉ s'd Sir Antho: ought in all Conscience & equity to bee as iustly chardgable & lyable to yᵉ paymᵗ of his sd ffathers debtℰ as of yᵉ sd Landℰ Tenemᵗℰ or other hereditamᵗℰ the profittℰ whereof hee doth soe receive & enioye as aforesaid were actually descended vpon him in ffee simple from his said ffather otherwise the good & honest intencōn & pvision of yᵉ s'd Sʳ John Cope his ffather for yᵉ true paymᵗ & satisfaccōn of his debtℰ wyll nott onely bee frustrated & diūted but may bee wrongfullie made vse of by yᵉ s'd Sʳ Anthony for his advantage to defraud and delude yoʳ Oratoʳ & yᵉ rest of yᵉ Creditoʳˢ of his said ffather by descent from whom besides yᵉ s'd ffee simple Landℰ hee yᵉ s'd Sʳ Anthony doth likewise enioy diūse Messuages landℰ tenemᵗℰ & other hereditamᵗℰ of A very greate yearely value wᶜʰ beinge intayled are nott lyable by yᵉ strict course of Lawe to any of yᵉ debtℰ of his s'd father And yᵉ s'd Lady Elizabeth & yᵉ rest of yᵉ s'd Trustees before named doe alsoe pʳtend & giue out in speeches yᵗ they have sould & disposed of yᵉ sd Landℰ accordinge to yᵉ intent of yᵉ said Sʳ John Copes last will & have accordingly paid & satisfied his debtℰ whereas in trueth if they have paid any of yᵉ said debtℰ it is onely some fewe speciall psons whome they had A desire to pleasure, & if they have sould or disposed of any pte of yᵉ s'd Landℰ for yᵉ purpose aforesaid it is onely some small parte & yᵗ att very great vndervalues & nott accordinge to yᵉ true worth thereof & vpon some secret Condicōn reservacōn or trust and yᵉ residue of yᵉ said Landℰ they have secretly conveyed to divers psons vnknowne to yoʳ Oratoʳ vpon Confidence & in trust yᵗ they or some of them or yᵉ sd Sʳ Anthony Cope or some other pson or psons by his theire or some of their appointmᵗ or on his theire or some of theire behalfe should take & receive yᵉ rentℰ Yssues and profittℰ thereof To yᵉ end yᵗ they or some of them may convert yᵉ same to theire owne private benefittℰ to yᵉ greate wronge & damage & iniury of yoʳ Oratoʳ & yᵉ sd Creditoʳˢ & contrary nott onely to yᵉ good intencōn & meaninge of yᵉ s'd Sʳ John Cope but to all Justice & equity & good Conscience Jn tender Consideracōn whereof & for yᵗ yoʳ Oratoʳ by reason of yᵉ sd secret & fraudulent practizes and Contriveances aforesaid is vnable directly to chardge

eyther yᵉ s'd Lady Elizabeth or yᵉ sd Sʳ Anthony with Assettꝑ in their
severall capacityes accordinge to yᵉ strict rules of yᵉ Comōn Lawe of
this Nation & for yᵗ alsoe yoʳ Oratoʳ cannot ꝑply be releived elsewhere
then in this honōᵇˡᵉ Courte agᵗ. yᵉ s'd Lady Elizabeth & yᵉ other Trustees
before named to compell them or any of them to pay & satisfy vnto yoʳ
Oratoʳ his iust & due debt afores'd accordinge to yᵉ trust reposed in
them by yᵉ sd Sʳ John Cope as afores'd & yᵉ true intent & meaninge
of his s'd will And to yᵉ end yᵗ yᵉ s'd Lady Elizabeth beinge executrix
of the last will & testamᵗ of yᵉ s'd Sʳ John Cope as afores'd may sett
forth & discover what goodꝑ Chattles money plate houshold stuffe corne
cattle bondꝑ billꝑ writeingꝑ or either personall estate whatsoever of
yᵉ s'd Sʳ John Cope her late husband or in any wise belonginge to him
or to his estate hath att any tyme come to yᵉ handꝑ or pōssion of yᵉ
s'd Lady Elizabeth or to any other ꝑson or ꝑsons in trust for her or to
her vse or in right of her s'd executorshipp & of what value yᵉ said goodꝑ
Chattles & ꝑsonall estate soe come to her or theire handꝑ as afores'd
nor are or where, & how shee hath disposed of yᵉ same & what debt or
debtꝑ of yᵉ s'd Sʳ John Cope shee hath really satisfyed or p'd wᵗʰ or out
of yᵉ same & to what ꝑson or ꝑsons & how & vpon what Consideracōn
yᵉ s'd debt or debtꝑ or any of them became due & payable yᵗ it may
appeare whether there bee Assettꝑ remayninge in her handꝑ to pay &
satisfy yoʳ Oratoʳ his s'd debt of 150ˡⁱ wᵗʰ interest for yᵉ forbearance
thereof or nott And to yᵉ end alsoe yᵗ yᵉ s'd Sʳ Anthony Cope may
cleerely & truely sett forth & discover what messuages Landꝑ Tenemᵗᵖ
or other hereditamᵗᵖ are descended vpon him as heire to yᵉ s'd Sʳ John
Cope his ffather & of what yearely value & whether there bee any ꝑson
or ꝑsons whatsoever seized of any Messuages Landꝑ Tenemᵗᵖ or other
hereditamᵗᵖ wᶜʰ at any time were yᵉ Landꝑ Tenemᵗᵖ or hereditamᵗᵖ
of yᵉ s'd Sʳ John Cope his ffather by any Conveyance from his s'd ffather
or otherwise in trust for him yᵉ sd Sʳ Anthony or vpon Confidence yᵗ
hee yᵉ sd Sʳ Anthony should take & receive yᵉ rentꝑ yssues & ꝑfittꝑ
thereof or vpon any other trust & confidence whatsoever & of what
yearely value yᵉ s'd Messuages Landꝑ & Tenemᵗᵖ are And whether he
doth nott vpon some trust or otherwise take & receive yᵉ rentꝑ yssues
& ꝑfittꝑ of any Messuages Landꝑ Tenemᵗᵖ or other hereditamᵗᵖ whereof
his said ffather Sʳ John Cope was seized in his demeasne as of ffee &
what Messuages Landꝑ Tenemᵗᵖ or other hereditamᵗᵖ they are yᵉ rentꝑ
yssues & ꝑfittꝑ whereof he doth soe take & receive as afores'd & of what
yearely value they are And whether there bee not Assettꝑ eyther actually
descended vpon him in fee simple from his father to pay & satisfie yoʳ
Oratoʳ or by culloʳ of some trust as afores'd taken & enioyed by him in
yᵉ rentꝑ yssues & ꝑfittꝑ thereof And to yᵉ end alsoe yᵗ yᵉ s'd Lady
Elizabeth Sʳ Anthony son or either of them may sett forth & discover

whether yᵉ s'd Sʳ Jo: Cope at yᵉ tyme of his death or some short tyme
before was seized in his demeasne as of ffee of or in certeyne Messuages
Tenemᵗᵖ or houses & of Wharfes, Keyes, or some other hereditamᵗᵖ
at in or neere yᵉ Custome House afores'd & wᵗ yᵉ s'd Messuages tenemᵗᵖ
Wharfes Keyes or hereditamᵗᵖ are & of what quality & yearely value
And whether yᵉ said Messuages Tenemᵗᵖ Wharfes Keyes or other
hereditamᵗᵖ did not descend vpon yᵉ s'd Sʳ Anthony as heire vnto his
said ffather, or how yᵉ s'd Sʳ John Cope did dispose of yᵉ same, & what
estate or Jnterest hee had therein & who take & receive or att any
tyme since yᵉ death of yᵉ s'd Sʳ Jo: Cope hath taken & received yᵉ
rentρ issues pfitρ thereof or of any pte thereof And whether the afores'd
Lady Eliz Cope and Sʳ Anthony Cope or eyther of them or any other
by theire or eyther of theire direcōn or appointing or to theire vse or
in trust for them or eyther of them doe take or receave or att any time
haue taken or rēcd yᵉ rentρ issues pfitρ of yᵉ s'd Messuages tenemᵗᵖ
Wharfes, Keyes or other hereditamᵗᵖ: or of any other Messuages Tenemᵗᵖ
Wharfes Keyes or other hereditamᵗᵖ at in or neere yᵉ Custome house
afores'd & wᵗ right & authority they or any of them doe or haue taken
& rēcd yᵉ same & who they be yᵗ soe take & receive or have taken &
received yᵉ same by theire direccōn & appointmᵗ or in trust for them
of any of them as afores'd And lastly yᵗ yᵉ said Lady Elizabeth yᵉ s'd
Countesse Dowager of Westmerland yᵉ sd William Lord Say & Seale
Richard Knightley & Gyles Harris & every of them may truely & cleerely
sett forth & discoū wᵗ Messuages Landρ Tenemᵗᵖ or other hereditamᵗᵖ
soere conveyed settled or assured to or vpon them or any of them either
by yᵉ s'd last Will & Testamᵗ of yᵉ s'd Sʳ John Cope & yᵉ deed under yᵉ
handρ & seale of yᵉ said Sʳ John therein mencōned or eyther of them or
by any other Deed or deeds in trust for yᵉ paymᵗ of yᵉ debtρ of yᵉ said
Sʳ John Cope & [what?] yᵉ true & cleere yearely value of yᵉ said Messuages Landρ tenemᵗᵖ or other hereditamᵗᵖ so settled conveyed & assured as afores'd & whoe take & receive or att any tyme since yᵉ death
of yᵉ s'd Sʳ John Cope have taken & received yᵉ rentρ yssues hereof or
of anie parte thereof And whether they yᵉ said Trustees or any of them
have sold conveyed sett lett or otherwise disposed of yᵉ s'd Messuages
Landρ Tenemᵗᵖ & other hereditamᵗᵖ or any of them or any parte thereof
& to whome they have sould conveyed sett lett or disposed of yᵉ same &
how & in what manner yᵉ s'd Sale conveyance Lease or disposall hath
bin made & vpon what Consideracōn, & what money or moneyes they
or any of them have raised or received by or vpon yᵉ s'd sale Conveyance
Lease or Disposall as afores'd and what rentρ yssues & pfitρ & to wᵗ
vallue they or any of them or any other by theire or any of theire license
direccōn or appointmᵗ or interest for them or any of them since yᵉ death
of yᵉ s'd Sʳ John Cope have taken levyed or received vpon or out of yᵉ s'd

Messuages Landꝑ Tenem^{tꝑ} other hereditam^{tꝑ} or any of them & what
debtꝑ they ye s'd Trustees or any of them have satisfied or paid accordinge to ye trust in them reposed as aforesd & whome, & when y^e
s'd debts were paid & how and vpon [what] consideracōn they or any
of them became due & payable And y^t all ye sd parties may alsoe discover what sumē or sumēs of money are remayninge in theire or any of
theire handꝑ arrisinge out of ye sale or other disposall of ye sd pᵣmisses
or any parte thereof And may shew cause if they can why yor Orato^r
should nott bee satisfied & paid his said iust debt & Jnterest eyther out
of the personall estate of ye s'd Sr John Cope or out of ye Landꝑ descended vpon ye s'd Sr Anthony Cope or out of ye said Messuages lands
tenem^{tꝑ} or other hereditam^{tꝑ} conveyed appointed & allotted by ye s'd
Sr John Cope for ye paym^t of his debtꝑ as afores'd or by some other
lawfull wayes or meanes accordinge to equity & good Conscience. May
it therefore please yor Lordshippes to graunt vnto yor Orato^r A Writt
or Writtꝑ of Subpena to bee directed to ye said [blank] Cope Esq₃ y^e
Lady Elizabeth Cope William Lord Say & Seale [blank] Countesse
Dowager of Westmerland Richard Knightlie Sr Anthony Cope & such
other Confederates as shall be hereafter discovered thereby Comāndinge
them & every of them vpon A certeyne day & vnder A certeyne pain
therein to bee Lymītted psonally to appeare before yor Lōppes in y^e
high Courte of Chancery [then &] there to Answeare ye said pᵣmisses
truely & particulerly vpon theire & every of theire corporall oathes And
to stand to & abide such further order & direccōn therein as to yor
Lordshippes seeme agreeable to equity & good Conscience. And yor said
Orato^r shall ever pray Etc.
                                                          Chr Milton
Staunton

June 22, 1654

A WRIT TO EXAMINE COPES AT MILTON'S SUIT IS ISSUED

Chancery Proceedings, C 8/120/72

Oliver lord protector of ye commonwealth of England. Scotland, &
Ireland & ye dominions thereto belonging To John Draper John Warren
William Webb John Jordan and William Hastings gentlemen greeting
Whereas John Milton complaynante hath exhibited his bill of complaint before vs in our court of chauncerie against the Lady Elizabeth
Cope and Sir Anthony Cope defendants And whereas wee have by our
writt lately commaunded ye said defendants that they should appeare
before vs in our said chauncerie at a certaine day now past to answere
ye said bill Knowe ye, that wee much trusting to your fidelities haue
appointed you, and by these presents doe giue you, or any three, or two
of you power & authoritie to examine diligently ye said defendants vpon

yᵉ matter of yᵉ said bill (yᵉ tenor whereof we send to you inclosed in theise presents) And therefore wee commaund you, three, or two of you, that at such certaine tymes & places as you shall think fitt you goe to yᵉ said defendants (if they cannot conveniently come to you) & diligently examine them vpon theire corporall oathes to be taken before you, three, or two of you, vpon yᵉ holie Evangells of God touching yᵉ matter of yᵉ said bill: and that you receiue theire answeres to be made therevnto & reduce them into writing in parchment: and when you haue so taken them that you send them distinctly & plainly vnder yᵉ seales of you, three, or two of you to vs in our said chauncerie three weekes after the feast of Saint Michaell next comeinge wheresoever it shall then be, together with yᵉ tenor aforesaid & this writt. Witnes our selues at Westm' the 22ᵗʰ Day of June 1654/

Leñ Leñ[thall?]

[*On an attached end:*]
John Draper John Warren Wᵐ Webb John Jordan and William Hastings gent three or twoe of you to take the answeres of the Lady Eliz: Cope & Sʳ An: Cope Defᵗᵖ at the suite of John Milton ret 3 weekᵖ aft Michal

[*Endorsed:*]
The execucōn of this Comīssion appeares in a certeyne answere herevnto annexed./

John Draper
Will'm Webbe./

October 21, 1654
LADY ELIZABETH AND SIR ANTHONY COPE ANSWER MILTON'S BILL
Chancery Proceedings, C 8/120/72

The ioynt and severall Answeres of the Lady Elizabeth Cope and Sʳ Anthony Cope Barronett twoe of the Defendᵗᵖ to the bill of Complaynt of John Milton Complaynant./
The said Defendᵗᵖ savinge to themselves and either of them nowe and at all tymes hereafter all advantage of excepcōn to the incertenties and insufficiencyes of the said bill of Complaynt for Answere therevnto theis Defendᵗᵖ severally say That they or either of them doe not knowe nor beleive that the said Sʳ John Cope Baronett in the bill named Did at any tyme become bound vnto the said Complaynant in any bond of the penall sōme of three hundred poundes or any some at all for the paymᵗ of one hundred and fiftie poundes or any sōme of money at all for his owne proper debte; But as theis Defendᵗᵖ have heard the said Sʳ John Cope was bound only as suerty wᵗʰ the said Sʳ Robert Lee and Thomas Oflye in the bill named or as suertie for one of them Wᶜʰ said Sʳ Robert Lee and Thomas Oflye are both livinge and of abilitie to pay

the said p^rtended debte as these Defend^tp have heard and beleeve if any
such debte be truly owinge vnto the said Complaynant as by the said
bill of Complaynt is p^rtended or they or one of them was or were for
many yeares after the entringe into such p^rtended bond and since the
death of the said Sr John Cope (whoe Dyed in October in the yeare of
our lord One thousand sixe hundred thirtie and eighte) able to pay the
said debte if reall, the said bond beinge of the Compl^tp owne shewinge
entred into the first day of ffebruary in the yeare of our lord One thousand sixe hundred thirtie and seaven (nowe about seventeene yeares
since) and the mony by the Condicōn of the said bond (by the Cōmpl^tp
owne shewinge in and by the said bill of Complaynt) made payable vpon
the third Day of May then nexte; And the said Lady Elizabeth Cope
and Sr Anthony Cope severally say and Deny that to their or either of
their respective knowledges the said Sr John Cope Dyed seized in fee
simple of any Manno^rs Messuages landes tenementp or hereditamentp
other then what they have herein after sett forth; And the said Lady
Elizabeth Cope for her selfe saith and Denyeth that the said Sr John
Cope to her knowledge Dyed possessed of a greate personall estate either
in Messuages landes leases moneys Debtes goods houshold stuffe corne
cattle or chattles as by the said bill of Complaynt is p^rtended or of any
other or greater personall estate then is sett forth in and by this her Answere and in and by the Jventorye of such his personall estate vnto this
her Answere aññexed, W^ch Jnventory this Defend^t doth averre and say is
a true Jnventorie of what came to her handes or to the handes of any
other to her vse to her knowledge other then a lease of a Messuage in
Covent garden secured by Sr John in his life tyme to the late Countesse
of Westmerland for the payment of fifteene hundred poundes w^th
Collaterall security for the paym^t thereof Which the said Countesse
made over to S^r ffrancys ffane and this Defend^t after the death of S^r
John Cope sould the said lease for Eighte hundred and twenty poundes
to one Mr Tomson W^ch was the most shee could sell the same for and
this Defend^t over and besides the said eighte hundred and twenty
poundes paid six hundred and thirtie poundes more in all ffowerteene
hundred and fiftie poundes to S^r ffrancys ffane in discharge of the said
Debte, wch lease was not put into the said Jnventory beinge made over
by Sr John for securitie of money as aforesaid and was not of value to
satisfie the said debte by much as aforesaid by wch said Jnventorie the
said personall estate appeareth to amounte vnto Twoe thousand Nyne
hundred thirtie twoe poundes fourteene shillinges and five pence if
rightly Cast or thereaboutp W^ch was not sufficient by many thousand
poundes to satisfie and pay the proper Debtp of him the said Sr John
Cope besides his legacyes Devised by his will W^ch Did amounte vnto the
sōme of 3145^li—6^s o^d or thereaboutp And this Defend^t the Lady Eliza-

beth sayth that shee doth not beleeve that the personall estate was vndervalued but was valued at higher rates then the same could be solde for and a higher rate was sett vpon the same then in truthe the same were worth for the Honour of the said Sr John Cope as the appraysers Did after affirme and confesse; And this Defend^t the Lady Elizabeth sayth That the said Sr John Cope on or about the eleventh Day of October One thousand six hundred thirtie and eighte made his last will and testament in writing and Did thereby expresse himselfe in theis wordes vidēlt: And for the rest of my landes that are not intayled and wherein J have power to dispose of my will is that they be wholy Disposed of for the payment of my debtρ and for the raysinge of porcōns for my younger children: And for the payinge of my sister Mary Cope seven hundred poundes and for the payinge of my sister Vrsule Cope five hundred poundes W^{ch} by this my will J freely give vnto them; And my will is that my sister Mary shalbe paid her seven hundred poundes Wthin twoe yeares nexte after my Decease and my sister Vrsule shalbe paid her five hundred poundes when shee shall accomplishe the age of eighteene yeares and by this my will J give full power and authoritie vnto my lovinge and carefull wife and my noble frendρ the righte Hono^{ble}. the Countesse Dowager of Westmerland the lord Say and Seale Richard Knightly Esquier and Giles Harris gent to sell sett or otherwise Dispose of all the said landes not intayled for the payment of my said Debtρ and for the raysinge of porcōns for my said younger Children and for the payinge of my said twoe sisters And by a deede vnder my hand and seale J have conveyed the said landes to those vses and purposes and thereby gave and Devised Diverse other legacyes and thereby made this Def^{te} his sole executrix. And by a Codicell annexed to such his will Did amongest other thinges recite that whereas his Daughter Anne Cope had Twoe Thousand poundes assured to her out of the Custome house or otherwise and likewise Twoe hundred poundes given her by her two Grandmothers in case the Twoe thousand poundes be not paid accordinge to the security that then it shall be paid by his executrix to the trustees nomynated in his will to the vse of his said Daughter & they to pay it to her at the Day of her marriage or one & twenty yeares of her age, As in & by the said last will & Codicell remayninge in the Prerogative Court to wch this Defend^t referreth her selfe for more certenty in every pticular appeareth; And this Defend^t sayth that the said Sr John Cope wthin some shorte tyme after Dyed and this Defend^t proved the said will and tooke vpon her the said executrixship and possessed her selfe of his psonall estate sett forth in the inventory herevnto annexed and in this her Answere acknowledged & noe more to her knowledge: And this Defend^t beleeveth that the said Sr John Cope Did sōme short time before his death make sōme Deede or writing to

such purpose as he Declared by his last will but had not power to make
over or assure any other the landes and hereditam^tᵖ therein conteyned
then Tangley the same beinge formerly conveyed and Devised away
by Sʳ Will'm Cope Grandfather to this Defend^t Sʳ Anthony Cope; And
this Defend^t Denyeth that shee Doth or Dyd ever intend or goe about
to defraud any the credito^rs of the said Sʳ John Cope of their iust and
Due debtᵱ or hath wasted imbecilled or any way converted or conveyed away to any pson or psons whatsoever in trust for her or to her
owne vse or benefitt or to or for the vse of Sʳ Anthony Cope or any other
of her Children any parte of the psonall estate as is pʳtended or disposed
or any parte thereof contrary to the Dutie of an executor but this
Defend^t hath paid for the Debtes of Sʳ John Cope her late husband
more then his psonall estate and the inheritance of the landes chargeable
for paym^t of debtᵱ doth amounte vnto by many thousand poundes if
sold to the vttermost value thereof as by her Accompte to this her
Answer annexed appeareth And this Defend^t doth say and iustly that
shee hath not Assettᵱ and hath pleaded to seūall psons who have sued
this Defend^t as executrix to her said late husband that shee hath fully
administred and doth averre & say that shee hath not any thinge of the
estate of the said Sʳ John Cope to pay his Debtᵱ but hath paid more by
sōme thousandᵱ of poundes then shee could any way be lyable to pay
for his debtᵱ and yett his Children not provided for wth porcōns But his
estate reall and psonall imployed to paym^t of debtᵱ was not of value
to rayse moneys to satisfie the same And the said Defend^tᵖ the Lady
Elizabeth Cope & Sʳ Anthony Cope seūally say & deny that they or
either of them Doe knowe that the said Sʳ John Cope was at the tyme
of his death seized of any other Manno^rs Messuages landes tenem^tᵖ or
hereditam^tᵖ in fee simple and not intayled other then the landes herein
after mencōned (that is to say) That the said Sʳ John Cope in his life
tyme was seized in fee of the Manno^r ffarme or Grange of Tangley in
the County of Oxford of the yearely value of One hundred poundes or
thereaboutᵱ W^ch said ffarme or Grange the said Sʳ John Cope in his life
tyme about the Nyne & twentyeth day of Marche in the year of our
lord 1637 Did Mortgage vnto John Moore Esquier for about Nynety
yeares to begynne ymediately from and after the seūall and respective
ends & determynacōns of such severall and respective estates as the
Lady Elizabeth Cope his wife (this Defend^t) and Sʳ William Hatton
knight or any other pson or psons to their vses have or are to have out
of or in the premyses or any parte thereof for or by reason of any Demyse
or graunte then before made vnto them or any of them or vnto any other
pson or psons for their or any of their vses wch said Mortgage was made
for the security of five hundred poundes borrowed by the said Sʳ John
Cope longe before his Decease and the interest thereof wch said Mort-

gage became forfeited in the lifetyme of the said Sr John Cope soe that Duringe such estates and the said terme soe made to the said John Moore the said trustees could not as shee is informed by her Councell make any assurance thereof for the raysinge of any considerable sōme of money And the said Defend^t the Lady Elizabeth Cope sayth that shee this Defend^t Did wth her owne prop moneys & estate redeeme the said lease out of the handρ of the said John Moore and paid in all for principle & interest five hundred Nynety eight poundes and this Defend^t was inforced to borrowe vpon the said landρ & such other security as this Defend^t gave the sōme of ffifteene hundred poundes of one Mr Loggin wch this Defend^t paid or to the value thereof for the satisfyinge of the debtρ of her said late husband, and this Defend^t hath out of her owne estate paid & satisfied of the reall debtρ of her said late husband more by sōme thousandρ of poundρ then the value of the said landes & personall estate Doth or canne amounte vnto the landρ beinge solde to the vtmost value thereof as doth appeare by this Defend^{tρ} accompte annexed to this her Answere wch accompte this Defend^t doth averre to be true. And the said Sr Anthony Cope for himselfe sayth that he was an infant & very younge at the death of his said father & did atteyne his full age not full a yeare since & Duringe the tyme of his infancy or since Did not medle or make wth the said landes or the rentρ thereof nor wth the psonall estate otherwise then nowe of late he hath hired the said house at Tangley to live in wth his family and some pte of the said groundes therevnto belonginge at the yerely rent of Thirty poundes by the yeare And the said Lady Elizabeth sayth & Doth confesse that in pursuance of the power to her given shee hath Disposed of the said landρ at Tangly & hath disposed of the moneys and a farre greater sōme then the value & inheritance of those landes are bona fide worth to be sould as aforesaid as by her accompte of her paym^{tρ} herevnto annexed will appeare, But this Defend^t Denyeth that shee hath Disposed of the said landes for the vse & benefitt of ye said Sr Anthony Cope; And as for the Messuages called Custome house & any houses Wharfes or keyes there or thereaboutρ this Defend^t the Lady Elizabeth sayth saith that Sr Will'm Cope father to the said Sr John Cope Did in his life tyme and longe before the Death of the said Sr John Cope mortgage the said Messuages wharfes and keyes there & thereaboutρ to one Mr Tymberlacke for a greate sōme of money & by a decree made in this Ho^{ble}. Court against the said Sr William Cope the said Tymberlacke was to hould and enioy the said Messuages wharfes & keyes & the Cranes therevnto belonginge wth the App^{r}tenñces vntill the said debte should be thereby & out of the rentρ & profittρ thereof satisfied wth the interest thereof at the rate of Nyne poundes for every hundred poundes by the yeare W^{ch} said debte beinge cast vp & made certeyne by a master of this

Hono^{ble}: Court accordinge to an order of this Court directinge the said
Master soe to doe the same Did amount vnto fower thousand & odd
poundes or thereaboutp, And after the death of the said Sr Will'm & S^r
John Cope this Defend^t was advised by her Councell to pcure sōme frend
to buy in the said Decree & mortgage out of the handp of the executo^{rs}
of the said Tymberlacke to save the said Messuages landes & p^rmyses
otherwise the same had bene vtterly lost by reason the yearely rent of
the said Messuages & p^rmyses would not pay the interest of the said
Debte, And this Defend^t did by the advise of her Councell pcure some
frend to buy in the said mortgage & decree & this Defend^t bona fide paid
for the same fowre thousand & twoe hundred poundes & doth confesse
that shee hath received the rentp & profittp thereof ever since toward
the satisfaccōn of the said fowre thousand & twoe hundred poundes
& the interest thereof as shee hopeth is lawfull for her to doe vntill
shee shall receive the said fowre thousand & twoe hundred poundes
wth Damages accordinge to the Decree of this Hono^{ble} Court And the
said Sr Will'm Cope notwthstandinge such mortgage by him made &
decree against him Did in the yeare one thousand six hundred thirty &
one in consideracōn of the marriage of the said Sr John Cope wth this
Defend^t the Lady Elizabeth and a greate marriage porcōn of five thousand & five hundred poundes settle & intayle the said Messuages wharfes
& keyes wth the app^rtennces as in & by the said Jndenture of settlement to wch this Defend^t referreth her selfe appeareth, And this Defend^t
saith that the wharfe tenem^t & buildinges therevnto adioyninge called
Hartshorne key was but a lease for certeyne yeares at & vnder a yerely
rent & expired soone after the said Sr Will'm Cope Dyed, and this
Defend^t since such tyme hath for a greate fyne by her paid to the
ffeoffees or trustees of the schole of Senocke in Kent renewed the said
lease for her owne benefitt as is lawfull for her to doe, and by reason
thereof claymeth the rentp & profittp of the said wharfe called Hartshorne key to her owne vse, And the said Sr Anthony Cope sayth that
after the money Due on the Decree wth Damages bee satisfied this
Defend^t Doth Clayme the inheritance of the said Messuages wharfes
& keyes wth the appurtannces other then Hartshorne key by vertue of
the said setlement made by this Defend^{tp} said Grandfather vpon the
marriage of this Defend^{tp} said father & Mother: And theis Defend^{tp}
the lady Elizabeth & Sr Anthony Cope severally say that they Doe not
knowe that the said Sr John Cope had any other Messuages lands
tenementp or hereditamentp in ffee simple at the tyme of his Decease
then the said landp at Tangley as aforesaid and one parcell of land
in Marshland in the County of Northfolke wch landp at Marshland this
Defte Sr Anthony Cope hath confessed in his plea to the Accōn broughte

at Lawe by the said Complaynant against this Defend^t as heire to his father Sr John Cope: And this Defend^t saith that in the fowrth yeare of the raigne of the late Kinge Charles the said Sr Will'm Cope Did assure all his Manno^{rs} Messuages landϼ & hereditamentϼ other then Tangly to Sr Cope Doyly and others & their heires, and after vpon the marriage of this Defend^{tϼ} father & mother the said Sr Will'm Cope & the said Sr Cope Doyly and others Did assure the said Messuages wharfes & keyes wth the App^{r}tennces and all other the Manno^{rs} Messuages and landes this Defend^t Doth Clayme to have intayled vpon him, and the said Sr Will'm Cope by his will and otherwise Did Dispose of all other his Manno^{rs} landϼ & hereditamentϼ to others of his Children as by his will and other his settlem^{tϼ} if this Defend^t had the same to ϸduce would more at large appeare. And this Defend^{tϼ} severally say and Deny to pay the said Compl^{tϼ} p^{r}tended debte for the reasons aforesaid. And the Defend^{tϼ} severally Deny that the said Defend^t Sr Anthony Cope hath receaved & enioyed the rentϼ issues and ϸfittϼ of any the said landes to his owne vse or benefitt as in and by the said bill of Complaynt is falsly p^{r}tended or hath receaved the rentϼ issues and profittϼ of any Manno^{rs} Messuages landes tenementϼ or hereditam^{tϼ} other then such as were intayled vpon him vpon the marriage aforesaid, And the Defend^t the Lady Elizabeth sayth that shee hath Disposed of the value of the said landϼ as aforesaid accordinge to the true intent of the said Sr John Cope for shee hath Disposed of the said landϼ and the value of the said landϼ wth a greate overplus for the paym^t of the debtϼ and in performance of the last will of the said Sr John Cope as by her accompte herevnto annexed appeareth. And the said Defend^{tϼ} the Lady Elizabeth and Sr Anthony Cope severally say and Deny that they or either of them knowe that the said Sr John Cope made any conveyance in trust as by the said bill is pretended or any trust or confidence whatsoever other then as aforesaid and the said Defend^t Sr Anthony Cope Denyeth that he doth by colour of any trust take or enioy any rentϼ or profittϼ of any landϼ or hereditam^{tϼ} whatsoever And theis Defend^{tϼ} severally say & Deny that they Doe knowe or beleive that the said Sr John Cope was ever seized of any the Messuages wharfes or keyes in or nere the Custome house in the bill mencōned and Deny all combynacōn and confederacy whatsoever wth any person or persons laid to their or either of their Charge: Wthout that that any other matter or thinge clause sentence article or allegacōn in the said bill of Complaynt conteyned materiall or effectuall for these Defend^{tϼ} or either of them to Answere vnto and not herein and hereby sufficiently answered vnto confessed and avoyded traversed or Denyed is true to the knowledge of theis Defend^{tϼ} or either of them. All wch matters and thinges theis Defend^{tϼ} and either of them are ready to averre maynteyne and prove as this Hono^ble: Court shall award and humbly pray hence to be Dismissed wth their Cost℘ and charges in this behalfe most wrongfully susteyned./

Eliza: Cope
Ant: Cope

This Answere was taken and the Defend^tℓ the lady Elizabeth Cope and Sr Anthony Cope were sworne at Brewerne in the County of Oxōn vpon saturday the one & twentyeth Day of October in the yeare of our lord 1654 before vs John Draper & Will'm Webb by vertue of a Comission to vs & others Directed

John Draper
Will'm Webbe./

[*Endorsed:*] 26th of october 1654 by the oathe of Thomas Collier Cler the 26th day of october 1654 by the oathe of Thomas Collier/[?] ffor John Warren at the sixe Clarkes office in Chancery lane./

1654?

LADY ELIZABETH COPE'S INVENTORY OF SIR JOHN COPE'S ESTATE

Chancery Proceedings, C 8/120/72

A true note and Jnventory of all the goods. and Chattles of Sr John Cope Barronett that Came to the handes of the Lady Elizabeth Cope his Executrix and one of the Defend^ntℓ to the Bill of Complaynt:

	lı	s	d
ffirst his weareing Apparrell.............................	100–	0–	0
Alsoe in ready Money...................................	337–00	–00	
Allsoe Rent℘ due at his Death...........................	786–	3–00	

	lı	s	
Allsoe in plate after the rate of ffive shilling℘ the Ounce.....	509–19–	1	

	lı	s	d
Allsoe pewter Dishes fflaggons Candlesticke℘ and all other sort℘ weighing ffive hundred seauenty pound℘ and a halfe.	24–	0–	6
Allsoe fflander℘ Brasse.................................	4–00	–00	
Alsoe pott brasse.......................................	11–00	–00	
Allsoe dripping panne℘..................................	2–10	–00	
Allsoe yron ymplem^tℓ.................................	4–00	–00	

Jn the Hall: at Brewerne

Allsoe three Table℘ six fourme℘ and Eleauen picture℘......	4–00	–00	

Jn the Dineing Chamber

	lı		
Allsoe ffoure peece℘ of hanging℘ ffive Turkey worke Carpett℘ on Couch of Red Cloath twelue Chayre℘ and six lowe-stoole℘ suteable....................................	14–00	–00	

Allsoe ffourteene other Chayreꝑ fowre old windowe Cusheans
and foure Tableꝑ..................................... **li s d**
4–16– 8

Allsoe one paire of brasse Andirons, fire shovell tongeꝑ and
belloweꝑ.. **li**
2–00–00

Allsoe three sconceꝑ of gild leather three Windowe Curtayneꝑ
and three Curtaine roddꝑ............................ **li s d**
01–16– 8

Jn the Withdraweing roome to the dineing Chamber

Allsoe the Hangingꝑ four Turkey Worke Carpettꝑ foure windowe Curtayneꝑ and two Curtaine roddꝑ.............. **li s d**
033– 3– 4

Allsoe one Coutch eight Chaireꝑ and one square carpett all of
greene Cloth imbroidered with gilt leather suteable..... **li**
3–00–00

Allsoe one Sconce and one frame for a Chimney & peece of
gilt leather....................................... **d**
00–16–00

Allsoe one greate lookeing glasse, two little Tableꝑ and one
paire of brasse Andirons............................ **li**
2–00–00

In the best Chamber

li s d

Allsoe ffive peeceꝑ of hangeinꝑ....................... 20– 0– 0

Allsoe one ffeild bedsteed with tester headpeece vallons and
Counterpoint two Chaireꝑ six stooleꝑ and two carpetꝑ all of
plush suteable.................................... **li**
50– 0– 0

Allsoe two twiltꝑ one boulster two blankettꝑ two pilloweꝑ
three windowe Curtayneꝑ two Curtaine roddꝑ and a lookeing glasse.. **li s d**
3–13– 4

Allsoe two footꝑ carpettꝑ two lowe Tableꝑ and one livorie
Cupboard... **li s**
1– 6– 8

Allsoe one paire of Andyrons fire shovell & tongeꝑ wᵗʰ brasse
knobꝑ and one paire of belloweꝑ..................... **s d**
00– 6– 8

In the inner Chamber to the best Chamber

Allsoe one livory bedsteed with a Canopy one ffeather bed,
one boulster, one Rugge, two blankettꝑ, the Chamber
hanged with Daruix & other odd thingeꝑ.............. **li s**
3–10– 0

In the Chappell Chamber

Allsoe one bedsteed tester headpiece vallons Curtaine Counterpoint and six stooleꝑ of Damaske, two Chaireꝑ and one
little Carpett of other stuff.......................... **li s d**
45–00–00

Allsoe one ffeather bed one boulster, one twilt, two pilloweꝑ
two blankettꝑ, and one Coverlett..................... **li s d**
4–00–00

Alsoe three peeceρ of hangingρ foure Windowe curtayneρ two
Curtaine roddρ, one paire of Andyrons fire shovell tongeρ
and belloweρ:.....................................   li   s   d

                  6–13– 4

In the jnner Chamber to the Chappell Chamber

Allsoe one livory bedsteed one Canopy one ffeather bed boulster and other furniture.............................   li   s   d

                  3–10–00

In the vpper Chappell

Allsoe chaireρ, stooleρ Cushians Andyrons fire shovell tongeρ
and belloweρ.....................................   li

                  2–00–00

Jn the Bryde Chamber

Allsoe one bedsteed with tester vallons and a headpeece of
Cloth of Bodkin ffive Tuffata Curtayneρ two ffeather bedρ,
two ffeather boulsterρ one Twilt foure blankettρ & two   li   s   d
Ruggρ...   13– 0– 0

Allsoe the Chamber hanged with stript stuffe, five chaireρ
seaven stooleρ, one Table one livory Cupboard, one lowe
bedsteed one paire of Andyrons fire shovell tongeρ and   li
belloweρ:.......................................   4–00–00

Jn the vpper Chapple Chamber

Allsoe one bedstead with tester, headpeece vallons and Curtayneρ of greene stuff one ffeather bed one boulster one   li   s   d
rugge two blankettρ and two pilloweρ..................   7–00–00

Allsoe the Chamber hanged with striped stuffe six Chaireρ
one Table one livory Cupboard, one paire of Andyrons fire   li   s   d
shovell tongeρ & belloweρ...........................   2–00–00

Jn the greene Chamber

Allsoe one bedsteed tester headpeece vallons Curtayneρ and
Counterpointe of Kersie one ffeather bed one boulster one   li
twilt two blankettρ two pilloweρ and one Coūlett........   10–00–00

Allsoe six peeceρ of hangingρ, three Chaireρ, fowre stooleρ
two Carpettρ, one Mappe one paire of Andryons, and fire   li   s   d
shovell tongeρ and two tableρ.......................   10– 0– 0

Jn the Jnner Chamber

Allsoe one livorie bedsteed, one feather bed one boulster one
rugge, two blankettρ one Canopy, the Chamber hanged   li
with Darnix and one Chayre.........................   4–00–00

Jn the Armory Chamber

Allsoe one bedsteed one ffeather bed one boulster one blan-
kett and one Coūlett...............................

li s d
1—10— 0

Jn the Armory

Allsoe one Horsmans Armour, one greate Saddle wᵗʰ the
furniture one buffe Coate Eight head peeceꝑ eight Muskettꝑ
and other peeceꝑ.....................................

li
8—00—00

Allsoe two old ffeather bedꝑ one old twilt one bedsteed and
other lumber......................................

li s d
2—00—00

Jn the new Chamber

Allsoe one bedsteed with tester vallons head peeceꝑ &
Curtayneꝑ of stripped stuffe one ffeather bed one boulster
one rugge two blankettꝑ two pilloweꝑ, one Chayre three
stoleꝑ one little Table Andirons fire shovell and tongeꝑ...

li s d
4—00—00

Jn the darke Chamber

Allsoe three bedsteedꝑ three ffeather bedꝑ three ffeather
boulsterꝑ two wooll boulsterꝑ five blankettꝑ one rugge
three old Coūlettꝑ................................

li s d
5—00—00

Jn the lowe parlour

Allsoe one bedsteed wᵗʰ tester vallons Curtayneꝑ and Counterpointe of Kersie, one ffeather bed one boulster one pil-
lowe two blankettꝑ one Table two stoleꝑ and some old
hangingꝑ:...

li s d
6—13— 4

Jn the two bed chambers

Allsoe two bedsteedꝑ two ffeather bedꝑ, one woolbed two
boulsterꝑ foure blankettꝑ and two old Coūlettꝑ and one
Chaire...

li s d
2—00—00

Jn the Falknerꝑ chamber

Allsoe one bedsteed one ffeather bed one boulster one Wool-
boulster two blankettꝑ and one coverlett...............

li s d
02—00—00

Jn the Porterꝑ chamber

Allsoe two bedsteedꝑ one ffeather bed one Woolbed one
ffeather boulster two Woolboulsterꝑ fowre blankettꝑ & two
Coūlettꝑ..

li s d
01—00—00

In the stewardꝑ Chamber

		ĺi	s	d
Allsoe one bedsteed one ffeather bed one boulster two blankettꝑ, one Coverlett, one table and one stoole		3—00—00		

Jn the Bayliffeꝑ chamber

	ĺi
Allsoe one bedsteed one ffeather bed one boulster two blankettꝑ and one Coverlett	02—00—00

Jn the old Parlour

Allsoe one bedsteed with tester, headpiece vallons Curtayneꝑ & Counterpointe of Needle Worke a Carpett fiue Chaireꝑ & foure stooleꝑ all of needle Worke suteable to the bed: . . . . . .   ĺi 10— s 0— d 0

Allsoe two ffeather bedꝑ two boulsterꝑ three pilloweꝑ fowre blankettꝑ one rugge one Coūlett one Canopy the Chamber hanged wth old hangingꝑ one Turkey Carpett two Tableꝑ Andirons fire shovell and tongeꝑ . . . .   00— 0— 0   0— 0— 0   ĺi 0— 0— 0   10—00—00

Jn the Scoole chamber

	ĺi
Allsoe one bed with the furniture one livory Cupboard one Table one Chayre three stooleꝑ and the Chamber hanged . .	5—00— 0

Jn the Maydꝑ chamber

	ĺi
Allsoe two bedstedꝑ one downe bed one ffeather bed two two boulsterꝑ fowre blankettꝑ, two ruggeꝑ fowre trunkꝑ & other lumber	8—00—00

Jn the passage at the staireꝑhead

	ĺi	s	d
Allsoe seaven old trunkeꝑ and one prsse	1—15— 0		

Jn the Nursery

	ĺi	s	d
Allsoe three bedsteedꝑ three ffeather bedꝑ five boulsterꝑ & theire furniture three peiceꝑ of hangingꝑ one livorie Cupboard two sumpture trunkeꝑ and other lumber	8—00—00		

Jn the Dineing Parlour

	ĺi	s	d
Allsoe thirteene Chayreꝑ one Coutch three stooleꝑ one rownd table, two livory Cupboardꝑ, one fourme foure carpettꝑ twelue Cushians fowre Windowe Curtayneꝑ curtaine roddꝑ Andirons fire shovell tongeꝑ and belloweꝑ	8—00—00		

Jn the Draweing Chamber to it

Allsoe one coutch eight Chaireρ one table one payre of doggeρ
fire shovell and tongeρ.............................

lï   s   d
3–00–00

Jn Mʳ Will: Copeρ Chamber

Allsoe one bedsteed two feather bedρ two boulsterρ two pilloweρ fowre blankettρ two Coūlettρ one table one Chaire
and fowre stooleρ.................................

lï   s   d
4–00–00

Jn his studie

Allsoe one Table one Chaire, one deske one standish and Certayne bookeρ.....................................

lï   s   d
6–13– 4

Jn the chamber over the parlour

Allsoe six peeceρ of hangingρ fowre Windowe curtayneρ two
Chayreρ two stooleρ one stove and Clocke & one truncke

lï   s   d
7–00–00

Jn Mʳᵖ Maryes chamber

Allsoe two bedstedρ two feather bedρ two boulsterρ foure
blankettρ two Coūlettρ two stooleρ, one table Andyrons,
fire shovell tongeρ and belloweρ...................

lï   s   d
4–00–00

Jn the little chamber

lï   s   d

Allsoe one bed with the furniture...................
2–00–00

Jn Mʳ Harry chamber [*first written* Henryeρ *but erased*]

Allsoe one bedsteed with tester, headpeece vallons & Cur-
taineρ of Kersie, one livory Cupboard one table one
Chayre and three stooleρ..........................

lï
2–00–00

Jn the Jackemanρ chamber

Allsoe one bedsteed one ffeather bed one boulster two blankettρ one Coūlett three Curtayneρ...................

lï   s   d
2–00–00

Jn the Butlerρ chamber

Allsoe one bedsteed one ffeather bed one boulster two blankettρ and one Coūlett..............................

lï   s   d
2–00– 0

Jn the Wardrobe

Allsoe two pressρ wᵗʰ one Counterpointe one rugge Certayne
vallons testerρ curtayneρ & other peeceρ of seūall stuffeρ

one Chayre fowre stooleꝑ ten foot Carpettꝑ certaine peeceꝑ
of hangingꝑ one downe bedd and boulster, two feather
bedꝑ & two boulsterꝑ fiue pilloweꝑ, two twiltꝑ & Certaine
other thingeꝑ and lumber:............................. 40—00—00

li s   d

Jn the Gallery

Allsoe one Table one bedsteed, sixteene Chaireꝑ and stooleꝑ
and other lumber:................................. 2—00—00

li s   d

Jn the Boyeꝑ Chamber

li   s   d

Allsoe one bed with the furniture:..................... 00—10—00

Jn the Kitchinge

li

Allsoe three Dresserboardꝑ, one Cupboard, one Mustard Mill
and other lumber................................. 2—00—00

Jn the larder

li   s   d

Allsoe powdereing tubbꝑ and Ceaverꝑ.................. 2— 0— 0

Jn the stove house

Alsoe one table one luncke, two bings & one safe.......... 00—13— 4

Jn the Bakehouse

Allsoe one Kneadinge trough two moulding boardeꝑ and
other implemᵗꝑ................................... 1—00—00

Jn the Brewhouse

Allsoe one furnace with the brewinge vessell.............. 10—00—00

Jn the boulting house

Allsoe one boulting trough, one hutch one mouldinge table
and other lumber:................................. 1—00—00

In the Fish loft

Allsoe one payre of scaleꝑ with an yron beame, wᵗʰ leaden
weightꝑ and other lumber:........................... 1—00—00

Jn the Henne house

Allsoe one vergis pʳsse hen pennes and lumber........... 00—13— 4

Jn the Cheese chamber

Allsoe two Cheese rackeꝑ and Cheeseꝑ.................. 2—10—00

Jn the Dairy

Allsoe one Cheese presse, two Churmρ couleρ cheesfastρ
payleρ and other lumber:............................ 1–10–00

Jn the Washouse

Allsoe one furnace couleρ Ceaverρ and lumber............. 2–00–00

Jn the Paintrey

Allsoe one binge one Table one glasse case one Cupboard,
blacke Jackeρ Juggρ and glasseρ:..................... 2–00–00

Jn the Sellers

Allsoe ffive and fortie hogsheadρ and buttρ, six Rundletρ ten
dozen of bottleρ and st[e]llρ:....................... 6–10–00

Jn the stable

Allsoe two Barbery Horsseρ............................ 50–00–00
Allsoe two saddle Mareρ.............................. 24–00–00
Alsoe one gray Geldinge.............................. 12–00–00
Allsoe one Pyde Geldinge............................. 4–00–00
Allsoē five Coach Horseρ............................. 40–00–00
Allsoe one Coach and six harneiρ..................... 15–00–00
Allsoe tenn saddle geldingρ and Mareρ................. 24–00–00
Allsoe one gray Nagg and one blacke.................. 2–13– 4
Allsoe saddleρ bridleρ and horseclotheρ............... 2–10–00
Allsoe tenne milch kine.............................. 40–00–00
Allsoe all the Hay.................................. 30–00–00
Allsoe all the wood and Coaleρ....................... 30–00–00
Allsoe tenn sheepe.................................. 5–00–00

Linnen of all sortes

Allsoe one suite of Damaske........................... 6– 8–00
Allsoe another suite of Damask........................ 5– 2– 4
Allsoe anothe suite of Damaske........................ 4–19–00
Allsoe one suite of Diaper............................ 3– 5–00
Allsoe another suite of Dyaper........................ 12– 8–00
Allsoe fowre wrought pillowbeareρ, two Cushian clotheρ and
six sweete baggeρ................................... 1–10–00
Allsoe five payre of Holland sheeteρ three table clotheρ
fowre cupboard clotheρ and fiue Hall clotheρ............ 3–10–00
Allsow fowre & twentie payre of flaxen sheeteρ nine payre of
pillowbeareρ eight payre of Holland Pillowbeareρ Eleaven
towellρ three and twentie paire of ordinarie sheeteρ and
Nine Cupboard clotheρ............................... 41–00–00

Allsoe ffifteene table Clotheρ & Cupboard clotheρ five towellρ
    eighteene Dozen of fine Napkinρ foure Dozen of Course
    Napkinρ and one plate Cloth............................ 17‒00‒00

Allsoe one table Cloth two Cupboard clotheρ three towellρ
    and one Dozen of Napkinρ all of Damaske............ 5‒00‒00

Allsoe one table cloth two Cupboard Clotheρ two towellρ and
    twelue Napkins all of Damaske and three Holland pillow-
    beareρ... 4‒00‒00

Allsoe one table Cloth two Cupboard clotheρ two towellρ &
    Nine and twentie Napkins:.......................... 02‒10‒00

Allsoe two Clotheρ one towell and twelue Napkins all of
    Diaper...

Alsoe fiue other suiteρ of Diaper a long Cloth two short
    Clothρ and a towell to eūy suite...................... 5‒00‒00

Allsoe five other clotheρ and tenn dozen of Napkinρ all
    Diaper.. 5‒00‒00

Allsoe three Holland table Clothρ seaven Holland towellρ six
    flaxen table Clothρ and tenne flaxen Cupboard clotheρ.... 3‒10‒00

Alsoe six towellρ six Dozen of ordinary Napkins fourteene old
    table clotheρ six hall Clotheρ eight Course towellρ fowre
    and twentie Dozen of Napkins of all sorteρ six old Dresser
    clotheρ and fowre plate clotheρ...................... 4‒00‒00

Allsoe twelue paire of fine sheeteρ ffifteene paire of Course
    sheeteρ and seaven paire of pillowbeareρ with some other
    course linnen.. 11‒00‒00

Allsoe all other thingeρ not pticularly sett downe:.......... 10‒ 0‒ 0

	li	s	d
Allsoe two Clotheρ ... Diaper	2‒00‒	0	

Some is M M D C lv^{li} x^s v^d
Jn his house at London

	li	s	d
ffirst three old bedsteedρ.....................	00‒	7‒	6
Allsoe three ffeather bedρ & three boulsterρ..............	2‒00‒00		
Allsoe three payre of blankettρ.....................	0‒10‒00		
Allsoe two Coverlettρ home made...................	0‒ 8‒00		
Allsoe three little Tableρ.......................	00‒ 5‒00		
Allsoe three Jron Andyrons...................	0‒ 2‒ 6		
Allsoe eight pewter Disheρ.................	0‒12‒00		
Allsoe six sawcerρ...................	0‒ 1‒00		
Allsoe three slye plateρ...................	0‒ 2‒00		
Allsoe two tinne sconceρ and six tinne Candlestickeρ......	0‒ 2‒ 6		
Allsoe one pewter Chamber pott...................	00‒ 1‒00		
Allsoe fowre new pewter disheρ.................	00‒ 8‒00		
Allsoe two paire of pewter Candlestickeρ................	00‒ 3‒00		

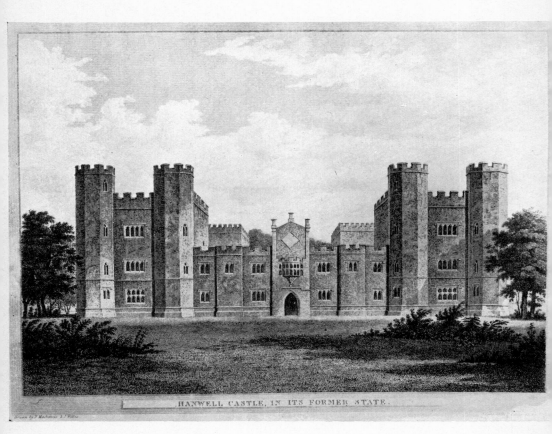

HANWELL CASTLE, IN ITS FORMER STATE.

Hanwell Castle, seat of the Cope family. From *Skelton's Engraved Illustrations of the Principal Antiquities of Oxfordshire* (1823 ff.), "Bloxham Hundred," Plate VIII.

Allsoe five curtayneȝ a payre of vallons tester & headpeece foure knobȝ, furniture for a bed of Watchett perpetuana layd with Yellow lace six bedsteedȝ & three curtayne roddȝ.. 2—00—00

Allsoe one high chayre two lowe stooleȝ suitable to the Bed with watchett cotten coverȝ........................... 00— 8—00

Allsoe twelue high backe Chayreȝ and six lowe chaireȝ of greene Kersie wth ffringe and Yellow Nayles, & greene cotten Coūrȝ:...................................... 4—00—00

Allsoe twelue other backchayreȝ wth brancht velvit........ 1—10— 0

Allsoe ffive leather back chayreȝ....................... 00— 8— 4

Allsoe three Windowe Curtayneȝ of Watchett stript with yellowe... 00— 6—00

Allsoe one gilt Arme two paire of belloweȝ.............. 00— 2— 6

Allsoe two fire shovellȝ two paire of tongeȝ with brasse knobbȝ... 00— 4—00

Allsoe one plate baskett & matt for a chamber........... 00— 6— 8

Allsoe fowre greene Cushians........................... 00— 4—00

Allsoe five pieceȝ of Arras hangingȝ.................... 7—10— 0

Allsoe one round baskett two skuttleȝ................... 0— 1—00

Alsoe two kettles two skillettȝ a brasse pott.............. 1—00—00

Allsoe a Chaffingdish a brasse ladle...................... 00— 1—00

Allsoe a brasse skimmer................................ 00—00— 8

Allsoe two fire forkeȝ a tinne Dripping panne............. 00— 2—00

Allsoe an Jron before the fire........................... 00— 1—00

Allsoe one Jron grate one buckett two boulȝ............. 00— 4—00

Allsoe one Cleaver one Closse stoole and panne and one hamper....................................... 00— 6—00

Allsoe one trunke wth linnen in it a suite of Damaske........ 3—00—00

Allsoe a suite of Diaper................................. 2—00— 0

Allsoe other old linnen in that truncke.................. 3—14— 6
som is xxxij^{li} xij^s

ｌｉ　ｓ　ｄ

Att Hanwell.

Jn the Hall

ffirst three Tableȝ, one Cupboard and fourme one paire of Andyrons, two brasse sconceȝ and one and thirty holberts. 4—00—00

Jn the parlor

Allsoe one table one Cupboard, one Couch two Chayreȝ six-teene stooleȝ, one skreene one payre of brase Andyrons, fire shovell & tongeȝ................................. 3—00—00

Jn the greate chamber

Allsoe two tableꝭ one Cupboard one Couch two fourmeꝭ two Chayreꝭ, twenty stooleꝭ, one Yron grate one paire of brasse andyrons & one footstoole....................   8–10–00

Jn the Draweing roome

Allsoe one livorie Cupboard, one Coutch two Chayreꝭ foure stooleꝭ, and foure pictureꝭ.........................   5–00–00

Jn the two Gallirieꝭ

Allsoe two Chestꝭ one paire of virginallꝭ one Chaire eleaven stooleꝭ, and six & twentie pictureꝭ....................   6–00–00

In the Gallery chamber

Allsoe one bedsteed one ffeather bed one boulster five blankettꝭ, one Coverlett, one Cupboard one Chayre and one stoole...   2–10–00

Jn the White chamber

Allsoe one table and Cupboard, two curtayneꝭ two curtaine roddꝭ andirons, fire shovell & tongeꝭ.................   00–10–00

Jn the next chamber to it

Allsoe one bedsteed with tester head peece and vallons of sattin foure sarcenett curtayneꝭ one feather bed one boulster two blankettꝭ one coūlett two Chaireꝭ three stooleꝭ, one Cupboard one mappe and three peeceꝭ of stripped stuffe...   4–10–00

Jn the chamber at the stairehead

Allsoe one Cupboard one bedsteed, one feather bedd one boulster, two blankettꝭ one rugge one Closse stoole Andyrons and tongeꝭ.................................   2–10–00

Jn Mr Dodꝭ chamber

Allsoe two bedsteedꝭ with testerꝭ vallons and seaven Curtayneꝭ...   1–10–00

Jn the Cooks chamber

Allsoe two bedsteedꝭ and one Coutch....................   00– 6– 8

Jn the parlor chamber

Allsoe one Cupboard one table one Mappe............... 00—10—00

Jn the Gallery stower chamber

Allsoe one bedsteed one feather bed one boulster two blankettρ one rugge one settle bed two Cupboardρ one stoole
fowre Curtayneρ five pictureρ and one payre of tongeρ.... 3—00—00

Jn the Queeneρ chamber

Allsoe one bedsteed one ffeather bed one boulster two blankettρ one rugge one chaire five stooleρ one Mappe and a
payre of Andyrons................................. 3—10—00

Jn the Garden chamber

Allsoe one bedsteed one ffeather bed one boulster two blankettρ, one rugge one Cupboard, one Mappe and ffive curtaine roddρ....................................... 3—00—00

Jn the upper Tower chamber

Allsoe one bedsteed and p^{r}sse one truncke one stoole and
one Table.. 00— 6— 8

Jn the blacke chamber

Allsoe one bedsteed one featherbed one boulster two blankettρ one rugge one tester vallons & Curtayneρ two
chaireρ, two stooleρ one mappe andirons fire shouell and
tongeρ... 4—00—00

Jn the Nursery

Allsoe one bed steed one Chayre two stooleρ Andyronρ fire   ℔   s   d
shovell and tongeρ................................ 00—15—00

Jn the next chamber

Allsoe one bedsteed with tester head peece and vallons of
stuffe one trundle bedsteed one Chayre and two stooleρ.... 00—10—00

Jn the two chamberρ in the Entry

Allsoe two bedsteedρ and one table..................... 00— 6— 8

Jn the entry

Allsoe fowre trunckρ................................. 00—10—00

Jn the Kitchin

Allsoe one Jron grate foure pothangerρ one payre of pot-
hookeρ two rackeρ Nine spittρ two Dripping panneρ one
Morter & one pestle,...............................   2—00—00

Jn the back kitchen & pastery

Allsoe one furnace two tableρ and lumbʳρ...............   0—19—00

Jn the Larder

Allsoe one beame and scaleρ and fiue leadden weighteρ with
other lumber......................................   00—10—00

Jn the Wash house & long house

Allsoe two old tableρ wood and lumber.................   1— 2— 7

Jn the Paintrey

Allsoe two tableρ one Cupboard one bing, one glasse Case
one safe one forme blacke Jackeρ juggeρ and glasseρ.......   1—00—00

Jn the Sellerρ

Allsoe twentie hogsheadρ and stellρ....................   2—00—00

Pewter of all sortes

Allsoe one and twentie pie plateρ two basons and ewerρ and
two voydʳρ.......................................   1—10—00

Allsoe tenn Dozen of Disheρ and three and twenty sallett
Disheρ..   7— 3—00

Allsoe twelue sawcerρ, twelue small plateρ two Cullenderρ,
two basons one salt and two tunneρ...................   00—12—00

Allsoe eighteene Candlestickeρ ten Chamber pottρ three
stoolepanns and two still headρ......................   2— 2—00

Brasse of all sortes

Allsoe seaven pottρ and two posnettρ....................   6—13— 4
Allsoe two brasse panneρ and five kettleρ................   2—16— 8
Allsoe other implemᵗρ belonging to the kitchin...........   1—00—00

Jn the Armory

Allsoe Armeρ Caleevereρ Pistollρ and other Implemᵗρ and
lumber..   100—00— 0

Jn the Warderobe

Allsoe two Downe bedₚ and boulsterₚ seauen ffeather bedₚ
and boulsterₚ, thirteene pilloweₚ one twilt three mat-
teresse, one Wooll bed and five Wool boulsterₚ...........   31–00–00

Allsoe one Counterpointe seaven blankettₚ seaven Coūlettₚ,
one skreene cloth eighteene Cushians eight Windowe
cushians......................................   7–00–00

Allsoe one bedsteed two chesteₚ and six trunkₚ with vallons
testerₚ, curtayneₚ certayne peeceₚ of linnen not pticularly
sett downe....................................   10–00–00

Jn the Brewhouse

Allsoe the furnace and breweing vessellₚ.................   6–13– 4

Allsoe two small pcellₚ of Hay.........................   00–15–00

Allsoe boardₚ and other lumber about the house herein not   00–00–00
pticularly sett Downe...........................   5–00–00

some is C C xliiij^{li}–xi^{s}–x^{d}

The some totall Cometh to M M ix^{c} xxxij^{li} xiiij^{s} v^{d} yf Rightly Cast vp

Eliza: Cope

[*The totals and the final note seem to be in the hand of Lady Elizabeth
Cope; the rest is by a professional scribe*]

1654?

LADY ELIZABETH COPE'S INVENTORY OF SIR JOHN COPE'S DEBTS

Chancery Proceedings, C 8/120/72

A true note and accompt to the knowledg of the Lady Elizabeth Cope
what Debtₚ Sr John Cope in the bill named did owe at the time of his
death and to whom and vppon what securitie And what Debtₚ the sayd
La Elizabeth Cope his Executrix and one of the defendantₚ to the bill
of Complaint hath payd and to whom and vppon what securitieₚ and
of other moneys she hath payd as Executrix to her late husband

A pticuler of soe maney of the Debtₚ oweing by Sr John Cope at the
time of hiₚ Death as are Com to the knowledg of the sayd Lady Elizabeth Cope his sayd executrix

	li	s	d
ffirst to Alderman John Hilard by bond................	200–	0–	0
To Sr John [?Elloway] by bond.......................	0400–	0–	0
To M^{rₚ} Elizabeth Gay by bond.......................	0100–	0–	0
To Mr Elias Jackman by bond.......................	0080–	0–	0
To Sr John Hewet by bond..........................	0200–	0–	0

To Mʳᵖ Mary Ridiard by bond...................... 0200– 0–0
To Mʳ Thomas Offly by bond........................ 1000– 0–0
To Mʳ Edward Rawly by bond....................... 0060– 0–0
To Mʳ Edward ffleet by bond....................... 0400– 0–0
To Sʳ Philip Stapleton by bond........................ 6000– 0–0
To Mʳᵖ Elizabeth Wallin by bond..................... 0200– 0–0
To Mʳ James Libert by bond........................ 0200– 0–0
To Mʳ Malbon of the temple by bond................. 0200– 0–0
To Mʳ Robert Edwardᵖ by bond...................... 0200– 0–0
To Mʳ Henry Jones of Chastleton by bond............. 0200– 0–0
To Sʳ Thomas Roe by bond........................ 2000– 0–0
To Mʳ Henry Cornish of Chipping norton by bond....... 0200– 0–0
To Mʳ Georg Greenwood and to Dʳ Clapton by bond..... 0400– 0–0
To Mʳ John Draper by bond......................... 0200– 0–0
To Mʳ John Cartwright by bond..................... 0600– 0–0
To Sʳ willm Chancy by bond....................... 0200– 0–0
To Robert Sanderᵖ by bond........................ 0100– 0–0
To John Dutton esq₃ by Judgmᵗ..................... 0140– 0–0
To the Lord Say by bond............................ 0700– 0–0
To Sʳ ffranciᵖ ffane by Covenant vnder hand and seale to be
     payd by 200ˡⁱ a yeare for 7 yearᵖ and a halfe and bond for
     performance thereof................................ 1500– 0–0
To katern Cull cope by bill vnder hand and seale.......... 0005– 0–0
To Mʳ Peeter Langston by bill vnder hand ad........... 0024– 0–0
To Mʳ Lewis Harris a bill........................... 0015– 0–0
To seuerall personᵖ vppon book Debtᵖ and billᵖ......... 0700– 0–0
To hiᵖ servantᵖ for wagiᵖ at the time of hiᵖ Death....... 0082– 3–4
Legacieᵖ giuen to seuerall personᵖ and to the pooer........ 3145– 0–0
the funerall exspenciᵖ and Chargiᵖ incident theirevnto 0360– 0–0
the charge of proueing the will........................ 0006–13–4
passinge the accompt in the prerogatiue Court........... 0005– 0–0

The some totall if Rightly Cast vp Cometh Twentie thowsand twentie
     two powndᵖ **sixteen shillings eight pence**

A perticuler of the Debtᵖ of the sayd Sʳ John Cope payd by the sayd
lady Elizabeth Cope the sayd Defendant and hiᵖ sayd Executrix

                                                         lî   s   d
ffirst to Alderman Hilord by bond..................... 0105–13–0
To Mʳ John Ellowayes by bond........................ 0228– 0–0
To Mʳᵖ Elizabeth Gay by bond....................... 0051–13–4
To Mʳ Elias Jackman by bond....................... 0080– 0–0
To Sʳ John Hewet by bond........................... 0128– 0–0

To M^rᵖ Mary Riddiard by bond...................... 0132– 0–0
To Mr Thomas Offly by bond........................ 0500– 0–0
To Mr Edward Rawly by bond....................... 0050– 0–0
To Mr Edward ffleet by bond........................ 0224– 0–0
To Sr Phillip Stapleton by bond..................... 3303– 0–0
And for the Intrest of a leuen hundred pounds J borrowed
   in ffebruary 1638 for wch J hau payd Jntrest vntill this
   time the some of................................. 1256
To M^rᵖ Elizabeth wallin by bond for principall and Jntr.... 0226– 0–0
To Mr James Libbert by bond....................... 0109–14–6
To Mr Malbon of the Temple by bond................ 0150– 0–0
To Mr Robert Edwardᵖ by bond..................... 0113–10–0
To Mr Henry Jones of Chastleton by bonde........... 0152– 0–0
To Sr Thomas Ro by bond........................... 1900– 0–0
To Mr Henry Cornish of Chiping norton by bond........ 0104– 0–0
To Mr Geo greenwood and to Dr Clapton by bond....... 0402– 0–0
To Mr John Draper by bond......................... 0200– 0–0
To Mr Cartwright by bond.......................... 0385– 7–6
To Sr William Chancy by bond...................... 0112– 0–0
To Robert Sanderᵖ by bond.......................... 0100– 0–0
To John Dutton Esqȝ by Judgm^t..................... 0140– 0–0
To m^rᵖ Mary Cope 225^li and to m^rᵖ vrsula Cope 225^li to m^rᵖ Ann Cope
100^li and for Jntr 205^li and vpwards And this waᵖ due vppon bond from
the sayd Sr John Cope to the lord Say in trust for the Sayd Mary Vrsula
and Anne Cope and is in all pd 755^li–0^s–0^d
To S^r ffrancis ffane by Covenant vnder hand and seale to pay
   200^li a yeare for 51 yearᵖ and a halfe And farther secured
   by by bond and two Tenamentᵖ in Covent garden w^ch   li   s   d
   Tenamentᵖ J sold for 820^li and hau pd in all.......... 1450– 0–0
To Katern Cull cope by bill vnder hand and seale....... 0005– 0–0
To Mr Peeter Langston by bill vnder hand.............. 0024– 0–0
To Mr Lewiᵖ Harriᵖ by bond........................ 0015– 0–0
To seuerall personᵖ vppon billᵖ and booke debtᵖ......... 0700– 0–0
And allsoe pd to hiᵖ servantᵖ for wagiᵖ oweing by him at
   the time of hiᵖ death.............................. 0082– 3–4
pd the ffunerall exspenciᵖ and chargiᵖ Jncedent theirvnto... 0360– 0–0
The Charge of proueinge of the will................... 0006–13–4
The charge of passing the first accompt in the p^rrogatiue
   Court... 0005– 0–0
To M^rᵖ Mary Cope her legasie giuen by will............ 0700– 0–0
And allsoe for educacōn Diat clothing and other accomo-
   dacōnᵖ for M^rᵖ Ann Cope the eldest Daughterᵖ of S^r

John Cope since hiꝑ death for 16 yearꝑ at 50^{li} by the yeare   0800– 0–0
And allsoe that J payd for the Diat clothing educacon and
   other accomodacon for m^r John Cope second sonn to S^r
   John Cope sixteen yearꝑ at fforty pownds by the yeare . . .   0640– 0–0
And allsoe that wch J payd for the Diat clothing educacōn
   and other accomodaconꝑ for Elizabeth Cope second   ̇li
   Daughter to Sr John for 16 yearꝑ at 30^{li} by the yeare 0480– 0–0

                                                                    ̇li
More to the pooer a legacy giuen them 20– 0–0
To Mr Harriꝑ the Minester of Hanwell his Legacie 05– 0–0
To Mr Lodg the minester of Draiton his legacie 05– 0–0
To Mr Harriꝑ the minester of Brewen his Legacie 10– 0–0
To Mr Gyles Harriꝑ of Churchill his Legacie   05

The some totall if Rightly Cast vp Cometh to sixteene thowsand two
   hundred and twentie powndꝑ and ffyften shillingꝑ

                                                                Eliza: Cope

*[This list may be in the handwriting of Lady Elizabeth Cope herself: the
writing resembles that of her signatures here and elsewhere]*

                              February 6, 1654/5

          MILTON THROUGH HIS BROTHER CHRISTOPHER AS LAWYER
            EXCEPTS TO THE COPES' ANSWER TO HIS BILL

          Chancery Decrees and Orders, C 33/204, ff. 475–475^v

                         Tuesday vj^{th} ffebr

M   John Milton Esq pl't   fforasmuch as this Court was this daie
L Co   Dame Elizabeth Cope   informed by Mr Milton being of the
         & o^{thrꝑ} Dēfts   pltꝑ Co. that the pl't haveing put in
                                     Excepconꝑ to the insufficiency of the
deftꝑ answeare the s'd dēftꝑ have not amended the same by the tyme
limitted Jt is therefore ord^red that Mr Estcourt on exc doe consider of
the pl'tꝑ bill the dēftꝑ answeare & the pl'tꝑ Excepconꝑ taken therevnto
& certifie whither the same bee suff't in the poyntꝑ Excepted vnto or not
if not then a spñ is awarded agt the s'd dēftꝑ to make a pfect & direct
answer to the pl'tꝑ bill according to the s'd Mrs Report therein to bee
made/

                         W[illiam?] G[oldesbrough?]

February 28, 1654/5

MILTON'S EXCEPTIONS IN COPE SUIT SUSTAINED

Chancery Reports and Certificates, C 38/124

The 28th of ffebruary 1654 Between John Milton Esqr. pl't Dame Elizabeth Cope and oth[ers] Dēfts According to an Ord^r of the 6th day of ffebruary instant J have after heareing Councell on both sides Considered of the p^{ltp} Bill the said Dēfts Joint and seuerall Answers and the pl'ts excepcōns taken therevnto, And ffind the said Answers insufficient as to the Dēft the Lady Cope, ffor that she doth not set forth to whome the Deed of Settlem^t in the Bill mencōned ffor paym^t of Debts was made nor what Lands, were thereby Conveyed nor the value thereof nor the Estate thereby Settled, but onely saith he had not power to Convay any the Lands therein mencōned saveing Tangly which is worth One hundred poundρ p Anñ, Nor doth she set forth the Perticuler Messū[ages] Wharfes or Keyes or yearly Value thereof in or near the Custome Howse which she saith were Mortgaged by Sr William Cope. Nor of Hartshorn key. All which J humbly certifie and submitt to the graue Judgem^t of this Ho^{ble} Court./

Tho: Estcourt.

[*Endorsed:*]
Milton ag^t Cope
Hillary Terme 1654
Estcourt.

May 28, 1655

WRIT ORDERING FURTHER EXAMINATION OF THE COPES IS ISSUED

Chancery Proceedings, C 7/452/60

Oliver Lord Protector of y^e. comōnwealth of England Scotland & Ireland & ye dominions thereto belonging To John Draper John Warren William Webb Elias Jakeman John Jordan and Thomas Blagrave Gentlemen Greeting Whereas John Milton esq^r Cōmplte hath exhibited his bill of Comp^t before vs in o^r. Co^{rt}. of Chancery ag^t. the Lady Elizabeth Cope and Sir Anthony Cope Barr^t defend^{tp} & whereas wee have by o^r. writt lately cōmanded the said defend^t. that they should appeare before vs in o^r. said Co^{rt}. of Chancery att a certaine day now past to answere ye said bill knowe yee that wee much trusting to yor. fidelities have appointed you & by vertue of these p^{r}sents doe give you or any three or two of you power & authority to examine diligently ye said defend^t vpon y^e. matter of ye said bill y^e. tenor whereof wee send you enclosed in these p^{r}sents And therefore we comānd you three or two of you that att such certaine times & places as you shall thinke fitt you goe to y^e

said defend^t if they cannot conveniently come to you & diligently examine them vpon theire Corporall oathe to be taken before you three
or two of you vpon ye holy Evangelists touching y^e matter of y^e said bill
& that you receive theire said answeres to be made therevnto & reduce
them into writeing in parchment & when you have soe taken them that
you send them distinctly & plainely vnder y^e seales of you three or two
of you vnto vs in our Chancery aforesaid eight daye$_p$ after the holy
Trinyty next comeinge wheresoever itt shall then be together wth. y^e.
tenor aforesaid & this writt witnes our selfe att Westm^r. the 28th Day
of May 1655./

Len' Len'[thall?]

June 18, 1655

ELIZABETH COPE MAKES FURTHER ANSWER TO MILTON'S SUIT

Chancery Proceedings, C 7/452/60

The further severall Answeare of the Lady Elizabeth Cope one
of the Defend^{nts} to the Bill of Complaynt of John Milton Esq$_3$
Complayn^t

The said Defend^{nt} as formerly soe now and att all times hereafter
saveing to her selfe the benefitt and aduantage of Excepcōn to the
Manifold Jncertaintyes & insufficiencies of the said bill for further
Answere therevnto and to the Exepcōns taken to this Defend^{ntp} former
Answere and in obedience to the reporte made by Mr Egcourte late one
of the Masters of this Honnour^{ble} Courte saith that the said Deede of
settlement made by the said Sr John Cope is a deede poll and beares
date the Tenth Day of October in the ffourteenth Yeare of the Raigne
of the late King Charles and in and by the said Deede itt is thereby
Mencōned that hee the said Sr John Cope aswell for the better payment
of his Debt$_p$ and rayseing and payeing of porcons for his Sisters and for
his Yonger Children as alsoe for and in Consideracōn of ffiue shilling$_p$ to
him in hand, paid by the [*blank*] Right Honnourable Mary Countesse
of Dowager of Westmerland William Lord Say and seale Richard
Knightley and Gyles Harris did graunt Aliene bargaine and sell enfeoffe
& Confirme vnto the said Countesse Lord Say Richard Knightley and
Gyles Harris and theire heires all that the Manno^r Grange or farme of
Tangley in the Countie of Oxōn with thappurtenaunces and all that
the Rectory of South & North marnham in the County of Nottingham
with all the gleabland$_p$ tent$_p$ and other the appurtenaunces whatsoeuer
all that the toft close and parcell of land Meadow or pasture in March
land called Crosse Keyes in the County of Norfolke all that Capitall
Messuage in Hounslowe in the County of Middlesex all that the Rectory

or parsonage of Mellther Kennocke in the County of Brecknocke with
the Appurtenaunces all that the Rectory of Winterngham with Certayne
tythes of Wooll and lambe in Winterngham Newton Linton and Knapton with the Appurtenaunces in the County of Yorke all that tith Corne
and all those tithes of Corne in Knattingley in the said County of
Yorke all those tithes of the sea fish in Winthornesey in the said County
of Yorke the Rectory of Middle Reaseing in the said County of Lin-
corlne the Rectory of Kidwelly in the County of Caermarthen with
all the tithes, and Glebes therevnto belonging, and the tythes of Millρ
in Kidwelly aforesaid the Rectory of Miller and Mabee in the County
of Cornewall the parsonage of Mount and Llethered in yᵉ County of
Cardigan with all the Appurtenaunces: To haue and to hold the said
Mannoʳρ Rectorees psonages hereditaᵐᵗρ Whatsoeū and all other the
pʳmisses with theire and eūy of theire Appurtenaunces vnto the said
Mary Countesse Dowager of Westm'land William Lord Say Richard
Knightley and Gyles Harris theire heires and assignes for euer to the
onely Vse and behoofe of the said Lady Mary Lord Say Richard
Knightely and Gyles Harris theire heires & assignes for ever as in and
by the said recited Deede if the same may be produced to this Honnourable Court may more at large appeare And Concerneing the vallue
of the said Landes this Defendⁿᵗ saith that shee conceues the said
Mannoʳ farme and Grange of Tangley is of the Yearely Vallue of One
hundred poundρ or thereaboutρ as in her former answere shee hath sett
forth, And shee hath heard that the said Marshland in Norffolk is of the
Yearely Vallue of ffortie shillings, And hath heard that the Messages
in Hounsloe was of the Yearely Vallue of ffower poundρ or thereaboutρ,
And that the rectory of Marnhamρ is of the Yearely Vallue Thirty
pownds or thereaboutρ, And that the rectory of Miller and Mabee is
of the Yearely Vallue of Twentie pounds or thereaboutρ, And for the
vallue of Mether Kennocke, she Cannot sett forth the said rectory being
solde by Sʳ William Cope in his life time and before the Death of the
said Sʳ John Cope: And Further saith shee doth not knowe or hath euer
heard what the tythes of sea ffish taken in Withornsie in the County
of Yorke aforesaid are worth: And ffurther saith shee hath heard that
the said Rectory of Winteringham was of the Yearely value of six
poundρ or thereaboutρ. And that the Rectory of Kidwelly is of the
Yearely value of Thirty ffive poundρ sixteene shillingρ and ffive pence.
And that the said Rectory of Mount Llethered is of the Yearely Vallue
of ffive pounds or thereaboutρ as this Defendⁿᵗ hath heard, And that
the said Rectorie of Middle Resing is of the Yearly Vallue of ffourteene
poundρ, And that the Rectory of Knottingly is of the Yearely Vallue
of Nyne poundρ or thereaboutρ as shee this Defendⁿᵗ hath heard And

this Defend^nt cannott assertayne the vallues of the said Landes and p^rmisses otherwayes then as aforesaid and as to that part of the reporte whereby it is required that this Defend^nt should sett forth the estat hereby settled she saith she Cannot sett forth the estate thereby settled otherwise then she hath in and by her fformer Answare and by this her answar and this defendant sayth that longe before the time that he the said Sr John Cope made such Writeing that shee hath heard that Sr William Cope his ffather was amongst other manno^rs and Landes seised of the said Mannor of Tangley and other the Messuages landes heredita^mts and p^rmisses Mencōned And being soe seised did Convey and assure the same to and vppon the said Lord Say Sr Cope Doyly & Richard Knightly and theire heires; And this Defend^nt saith that vppon the Mariage of the said Sr John Cope with this Defend^nt the said Sr William Cope the said Lord Say and the then surviveing trustees did in the seaventh Yeare of the Late king Charles settle divers of his Mannors messages landes and Hereditam^tρ Vppon the said Sr John Cope: And this Defend^nt part to this Defend^nt for her Life for her Joynture and all vppon the heires Males of the body of him the said Sr John Cope by this Defendant onely the said ffarme of Tangley hee settled vppon the said Sr John Cope and his heires, And this Defend^nt hath heard and is informed that the said Sr William Cope and the said trustees, or the survivor of them by his the said Sr William Copes appoint^mt and Direccōn in his life time or since his Death by his appoint^mt did sell dispose and Convey away other the Manno^rρ Messuages landes & heredita^mtρ not setled in the seaventh Yeare of the Late King as aforesd to severall other psons: And this Defendant saith that shee verely beleeveth that the said Sr John Cope about a day or two before his decease and at the time of makeing the said Deede being Very Weake and sicke, had a desire to make some provision for pay^mt of Debtρ and rayseing porcons for his sisterρ and Children And this Defend^nt beleeveth that the pty that Drew the said deede for the said Sr John might phapps not knowe that the said Rectoryes and p^rmisses were before setled sould or Conveyed away as aforesaid hee then being as this Defend^nt beleeueth a stranger to the estate of the said Sr John Cope, And as Concerneing the particular Messuages Wharfes and Keyes and the Yearly vallue thereof, this Defend^nt saith that shee Cannott otherwise pticularily sett the same forth saveing then by the name of the new Wooll Key and the old wooll Key and the Cranes cellars & Warehouses thereto belonginge but the pticular Wharfes Keyes shopps Cellars roomes Chambers & Warehouses thereto belongeing shee saith shee Cannott otherwise sett forth for shee this Defend^nt did never take such p^rcise notice thereof more particularly to expresse the same then as aforesaid: And as for the pticulars of the said Hartshorne Key shee saith shee Can noe moore pticularly sett forth the same then shee hath by her former answeere, onely this Defend^{nt} saith that the lease wch the said Sr William Cope had thereof expired by effluxīon of time in Septemer One Thousand six hundred thirtie and Eight, And this Defend^{nt} saith that after a suite and decree in this Honnour^{ble} Court this Defend^{nt} for a Considerable fine paid by this Defend^{nt} obtayned a new lease thereof for this Defend^{nt}ρ owne Vse for diuers Yeeres Yet to Come, And shee this Defend^{nt} Clayms the lease thereof, to her owne Vse, as a purchaser as in her former Answere is expressed. And as Concerneing the Yearely vallue of the said Keyes and Wharfes, this Defend^{nt} saith that there is payable out of the said Key called Hartshorne Key wch this Defend^{nt} hath by Lease as aforesaid to the scoole of Sevenocke the Yearely Rent of on hundred and Twentie pownds and out of the said Keyes Called the New Wooll Key & old wooll Key the ffee farme rent of ffiftie three powndρ thirteene shillingρ fower pence yearly, And this Defend^{nt} saith that the said Key Called the old wooll Key and the new wooll Key and the Hartshorne Key aforesaid weare formerly and vntill the Lady Day last demised for the Yearely Rent of ffower hundred poundρ over and above the said Yearely Rentρ thereout reserved but Cannott Distinguish the Yearely vallue of the said Custome house Cranes & Keyes, and Hartshorne Keyes for that they haue beene alwayes dureing the tyme of this Defend^{nt}ρ re-membraunce demised together without that, that any other matter or thinge Clause sentence Article or Allegation in the said Bill of Complaynt Conteyned Materiall or effectuall in law for this Defend^{nt} to make Answeare vnto and not herein and hereby and by her former answeare sufficientlye answeared vnto Confessed & avoyded travissed or denyed is to the knowledge of this Defend^{nt} trew all which Matters and thingeρ this Defend^{nt} is & wilbe ready to aver Mayntayne and prooue as this Honnour^{ble} Courte shall award, And humbly prayeth hence to bee Dismissed with her Costρ in this behalfe susteyned:

Eliza: Cope

[*This signature seems to mean that she wrote the answer herself. Such documents are usually signed by counsel*]

This Answeare was taken and the Defend^t above named was sworne at Brewerne in the County of Oxoñ vpon the eighteenth of June 1655 before vs./

Will'm Webbe./
Tho. Blagrave./

[*Endorsed:*] The 20th day of June 1655 [by] the handρ of Wm Webb gent' one of the Com^{rs}.

July 14, 1655
MILTON'S EXCEPTIONS IN COPE SUIT OVERRULED AND MILTON IS CHARGED COSTS
Chancery Reports and Certificates, C 38/127

Saturday the 14th day of Julij 1655 Betweene John Milton Esqr p[lte] And the Lady Elizabeth Cope defend[t]

The Excepcōneȝ taken by the P[lte] to the Defend[t] Answeare Comeing this day to be hearde in the presence of M[r] Milton of Councell with the P[lte] & of M[r] Sandforde for the Defd[t] vppon openinge the Bill Answeare & Excepcons the same were ouerruled and the P[lte] is in respecte thereof to pay to the Defd[t] ffortie Sixe shillingȝ & eight pence for Costȝ:.//

W[m] Lenthall./

[*Endorsed:*]
Milton ag[t] Cope
Trinity: Terme 1655
Cert M[r] Rolles

November 27, 1655
WRIT TO EXAMINE LORD SAY AND SELE IN MILTON-COPE SUIT IS ISSUED
Chancery Proceedings, C 7/452/60

Oliver Lord Protecto[r]. of y[e]. comōn wealth of England Scotland & Ireland & y[e]. dominions thereto belonging To James ffienes [and] Richard ffienes Esq[rs] William Dalby [and] Barnabas Horseman genr' Greeting whereas John Milton Comp[lt] hath exhibited his bill of Comp[lt]. before vs in o[r]. Co[rt]. of Chancery ag[t]—William Lord Viscount Say and Seal, Def[t]. & whereas wee have by O[r]. writte lately comānded y[e] said Def[t]. that he should appeare before vs in o[r]. said Co[rt]. of Chancery att a c[r]: taine day now past to answere y[e]. said bill know yee that wee much trusting to yo[r]. fidelities have appointed you & by vertue of these p[r]sents doe give you or any three or two of you power & authority to examine diligently yee said Def[t] vpon y[e]. matter of y[e]. said bill y[e]. tenor whereof wee send you enclosed in these p[r]sents And therefore wee comānd you three or two of you that att such c[r]:taine times & places as you shall thinke fit you goe to y[e] said Def[t]. if he cannot conveniently come to you & dliigently examine him vpon his corporall oathe to be taken before you three or two of you vpon y[e]. holy Evangelists touching y[e]. matter of y[e] said bill & that you receive his said answere to be made therevnto & reduce it into writeing in parchm[t]. & when you have soe taken it that yo[u] send y[e] same distinctly & plainely closed vp vnder y[e] seales of you three or two of you vnto vs in o[r] Chancery aforesaid in Eight dayes after hillary next cominge wheresoever itt shall then be together wth. y^e. tenor aforesaid & this writt witnes o^r. selfe att Westm^r. the seaven and twentith day of November 1655

Lenth: Prid.' Bett.'

[*Attached end:*]

To James ffiennes [and?] Richard ffiennes Esq^{rs}, William Dalby and Barnabas Horseman gent 3 or 2 of y^u a Com' to see the r^t ho^{ble}. William Lo: viscount Say and Seale to an[sweare the complai]nt⸗ of John Milton, r^o viij dayes after Hill'

Lenth: Prīd: Bett'

[*Endorsed:*]

The execucōn of this Comission is extant in a certaine Schedule here-vnto annexed

James Fiennes
Richard: Fiennes

January 16, 1655/6

LORD SAY AND SELE ANSWERS MILTON'S BILL

Chancery Proceedings, C 7/452/60

The severall answere of the right honourable William Lord Say and Seale one of the Dēfd^{ts} to the bill of Cōmpl^t of John Milton Esquire Complaynant

The said Dēfd^t saveing & reserving vnto himselfe both now and att all times hereafter all advantages and benefitt by waye of Excepcōn or otherwise to the manifest incertenties vnthruths and insufficiencies in the said bill of Cōmpl^t conteyned for answere therevnto or to soe much thereof as any way materially or effectually toucheth or concerneth the said Dēft to make answere vnto, hee saith that hee doeth not knowe that Sr John Cope late of Hanwell in the County of Oxōn deceased together with Robert Lee of Bilsley in the County of warwick Esquire and Thomas Offley of greate Dauby in the county of Leicester also esquire by their obligacōn or writing obligatory beareinge date the first day of ffebruary in the thirteenth yeare of the late King Charles and in the yeare of our Lord one thousand six hundred thirty and seaven became Joyntly and severally bound vnto the said Compl^t in the penall some of three hundred pounds of lawfull English money condicōned for the paym^t of one hundred ffifty pounds principall money lent and three pounds interest for the same vpon the third day of May then next ensueing the date of the said obligacōn or writeing obligatory as in the said bill is sett forth nor in any other debt att all Neither doth this Dēfd^t knowe whether the said Sr John Cope was seised in his demeasne as of ffee of and in divers Messuag⸗ lands Tenements and hereditaments of a great yearly value or of any value or of a greate personall estate in leases ready money plate household stuffe Corne Cattle and other goods to a very greate value yet this Dēfd^t beleeveth that the said Sr John Cope made his last will and Testament in writeing and did therein expresse and declare his will to bee that as for his lands that were not intayled and wherein hee had power to dispose they should bee disposed of for the paying of his debts and raysing of porcōns for his yonger children and for his sisters and gave power to his wife the Countesse Dowager of Westmerland this Dēfd^t Richard Knightly and Giles Harris in the will named to sell sett or otherwise dispose of all the said lands not intayled for the paying of his debts and raysing of porcōns as aforesaid thereby declareing & expressing that by a deed vnder his hand and seale hee had conveyed the said lands to the vses intents and purposes aforesaid and made the Lady Elizabeth his sole executrix as by the said bill is sett forth as hee verily beleeveth And this Dēfd^t furtheι saith that by an Jndenture beareing date the first day of September in the sixteenth yeare of the raygne of the late King Charles made betweene him this Dēfd^t of the one parte and the said Giles Harris of the other pte (reciteing that whereas the said Sr John Cope By his deed pole beareing date the tenth day of October in the fowerteenth yeare of the raygne of the said late King Charles for the consideracōns therein mencōned graunted infeoffed and confirmed vnto the said countesse sithence deceased this Dēfd^t Richard Knightly sithence deceased and Giles Harris their heires and assignes All that the mannor grange or ffarme of Tangly in the county of Oxōn All that the rectory or Parsonage of south and north Marnhams in the County of Nottingham All that Toft Close & parcell of land meadowe and pasture called the Crosse keyes scituate and being in Marshland in the County of Norffolke All that Capitall Messuage or Tenem^t with the appurtenñc$\wp$ scituate and being in Hounslow in the County of Midd' All that Rectory or Parsonage of of Meather Cannock in the county of Breācon All that the Rectory of Winteringham in the County of Yorke All that the Rectory or Parsonage of Middle raysing in the County of Lincolne And all the Rectory or Parsonage of Kidwelly in the county of Carmarthen All those the tithes of the mills in Kidwelly aforesaid All that yearely pencōn goeing out of the Rectory of Penbray to the said late Priory of Kidwelly belonging All that Rectory and Parsonage of Milde and Mabee in the County of Cornewell And all that the Parsonage or Rectory of mount and Llethred in the County of Cardican To hold all the said recited premisses vnto the said Countesse this Dēfd^t Richard Knightly and Giles Harris their heires and assignes forever to their onely proper vse and behooffe) hee this Dēfd^t did by his said Jndenture declare that the said Deed pole was made without the

knowledge or privity of this Dēfd^t and that att the time of the makeing
of the aforesaid deed pole hee did not nor att any time sithence hath not
consented agreed vnto accepted of or taken the said estate but this
dēfd^t did thereby refuse and disclayme and doth hereby further disclayme any trust or estate soe conveyed or intended to bee conveyed and
settled vpon him and others of in and vnto the said Mannor Rectories
Parsonages Tythes and all other the p^{r}misses by force and vertue of the
said Deed pole & this Dēfd^t did thereby remise release and forever quite-
clayme vnto the said Giles Harris his heires and assigns All the estate
right title and interest vse benefitt clayme and demaund whatsoeū which
hee this Dēfd^t then had or claymed or might or should thereafter have or
claime or p^{r}tend to have or clayme of in and to the said mannors Rectories Parsonages Tythes hereditam^{ts} & p^{r}misses or any of them or any
pte or pcell of them by force and vertue of the said recited Deed pole or
the last will and Testam^t of the said Sr John Cope and not otherwise
whatsoever As by the said Jndenture of Disclaymer if the same were
produced to this honoble Co^{r}t would more att large appeare And this
Dēfd^t saith that the reason why hee did not accept of the said trust from
Sr John Cope but did disclayme the same by his said Jndenture of
Disclaymer as aforesaid was for that Sr William Cope Knight and
Baronett father of the said Sir John by his Jndenture dated the fower
and twentith day of September 1628 and in the fowerth yeare of the
Raigne of the said late King Charles made betweene him of the one parte
& this Dēfd^t Sr Cope Doyly Knight and Richard Knightly Esq₃ of the
other parte for the consideracōn therein mencōned Did graunt vnto this
Dēfd^t Sr Cope Doyly and Richard Knightly Seūall manno^{r}s Lord'pps
lands Tenem^{ts} and hereditam^{ts} in the Counties of Oxōn Notingham
Essex and other Counties To hold to them and their heires foreū Never-
theles vpon this trust that as well out of the yearely profitts of the said
Mannors Lord'pps lands Tenem^{ts} hereditam^{ts} and P^{r}misses As by the
sale of any of the said Mannors Lord'pps lands Tenem^{ts} & hereditam^{ts}
amongest other payments therein mencōned should pay and discharge
all such sume and sumes of money and debts as the said Sr William
Cope then or thereafter should stand indebted and for severall other
trusts therein declared and after performance of the said severall trusts
then to Convey such lands as were in their hands vnsold as the said S^r
William Cope should appoynt in his life time or by his last will and testament as in the said last recited Jndenture are mencōned expressed and
declared vnto the which recited Jndenture relacōn being therevnto had
for more certenty thereof this Dēfd^t referreth himselfe may appeare And
the said Sr William Cope by his last will & testam^t in writeing dated the
third day of May. 1637. Did give to his sonne Jonathan Cope his manno^{r}s

lands Tenem^ts and hereditaments in great Wakering and little Wakering
in the County of Essex & severall other Mannors & lands And all such
Messuages lands Tenem^tp and hereditam^ts in the Custome house the
old Wooll Key and newe Wooll Key as were not settled vpon his sonne
John And all other his parsonages in the Kingdome of England and
dominion of Wales And did therein give severall other gifts and legacies
As by the said last will if it were produced to this hono^rable Co^rt would
more playnely and att large appeare And this Dēfd^t absolutely denieth
that hee hath Combined and confederated with the said Lady Elizabeth
Cope the said Countesse Dowager of Westmerland & Richard Knightly
or any of them or with Sr Anthony Cope in the bill named or that hee by
any such Combinacōn & Confederacy or otherwise contrary to the good
intent and meaning of the said Sr John Cope or to the trust by him
reposed in this Dēfd^t Did ever since the death of the said Sr John Cope
receive either to his owne private vse and benefitt or to the vse and
benefitt of the said Sr Anthony Cope or the Lady Elizabeth Cope or
for any other person whatsoeū all or any the rents issues and profitts of
the said Messuagp lands and Tenem^ts or of any pte or pcell thereof or of
any of the lands appoynted by the said Sr John Cope to bee sold either
by the said Deed Pole or by the said Will of the said Sr John Cope ffor
this Dēfd^t did wholly disclayme to medle therewith or to accept of the
trust reposed in him by the said Sr John Cope as this Defd^t hath herein
before sett forth And this Dēfd^t also denieth that hee hath ever since the
death of the said Sr John Cope taken and received to his private vse
and benefitt severall rents to the yearely value of five hundred pounds or
thereabouts due payable and issueing out of the Messuage or house called
the Custome house in London & the Wharfe or Key there and out of
divers Tenem^ts & houses therevnto neare adioyning or scituate & being
in Temes streete or in any streete neare thereaboutes or in any other
place whatsoever or that hee this Dēfd^t had any int^rest in the said houses
and lands by vertue of the deed pole or will made by the said Sr John
Cope And this Dēfd^t denieth that hee hath secretly or otherwise sold or
conveyed all or any of the said lands Tenem^tp or hereditaments by vertue
of the said deed pole or will of the said Sr John to aney person or persons
whatsoeū or that hee doth deteyne any moneys raysed by any such sale
in his hands or convert the same to his owne vse and behooffe but this
Dēfd^t saith that by vertue of the said Jndenture soe made by the said
Sr William Cope to him and other trustees as aforesaid and of the will
of the said Sr William Cope he hath sold and Conveyed to and for the
vses mencōned in the said deed and will of the said Sr William Cope
severall lands and tenem^tp in the said Deed pole mencōned but by
vertue of the said settlem^t formerly made by the said Sr William Cope

as hee hopeth it is lawfull for him to doe & conceiveth and is advised by his Counsell hee is not bound to give an accompt of his doeings therein to the said Cōmpl^t having disclaymed the trust in him reposed by the said Sr John Cope as aforesaid and hereby further disclayme the same. And this Dēfd^t denieth that hee p^rtendeth and giveth out in speeches that hee hath sold and disposed of the said lands according to the intent of the said Sr John Copes last will and hath accordingly paid and satisfied his said debts as by the said bill is surmised or that he by vertue of the said deed pole or last will of the said Sr John hath sold or Disposed of any parte of the said lands for the purpose in the bill mencōned or otherwise or vpon any secret or other Condicōn reservacōn or trust or Conveyed to divers or any persons vpon confidence & in trust that hee or the said Sr Anthony Cope or any other person by his or their appointm^t or behalfe should take & receive the rents issues and profitts thereof to thend to convert the same to his or their owne private Benefit As by the said bill is alsoe surmised by vertue of the said Deed Pole and last will of the said Sr John Cope or of any settlem^t deed or writeing made to him by the said Sr John Cope And this Dēfd^t alsoe denieth all and all manner of secret & fraudulent practices & contrivancꝑ & Combinacōn & Confederacy wherewith hee in and by the said bill of Cōmpl^t stands any way charged or chargable And this Dēfd^t saith that to his knowledge there were noe other Messuages lands Tenements or hereditaments conveyed settled or assured to or vpon him either by the said last will and Testam^t of the said Sr John Cope or the deed vnder the hand and seale of the said Sr John Cope or by any other deed or deeds in trust for the paym^t of the debts of the said Sr John Cope then what hee hath herein before sett forth and disclaymed to meddle therewith And this Dēfd^t saith as before hee hath said & sett forth that hee disclaymed and hereby doth further disclayme to medle with the deed poll or will of the said Sr John Cope or to sell or dispose of any of the manno^rs Messuagꝑ landꝑ & Tenem^{ts} therein mencōned by vertue of the said Deed and will or of either of them and therefore hee hath not nor did sell dispose or medle with any of the Messuagꝑ Lands Tenem^{ts} and hereditamentꝑ therein mencōned by vertue thereof & conceiveth vnder the favo^r of this hono^rable Co^rt that what Manno^{rs} lands Tenem^{ts} & other hereditam^{tꝑ} hee hath sold or otherwise settled or disposed of by vertue of any power to him given by the said Jndenture made by the said Sr William Cope as aforesaid or the said will of the said Sr William Cope in pursuance of his said trust hee is not to give an accompt thereof to the said Cōmpl^{lt} as hee hath before sett forth And this Dēfd^t denieth that he hath received any rents and profitts or that any other pson or psons by his this Dēfd^{ts} license direccōon or appoyntm^t or in trust for him since the death of the said Sr John Cope hath or have received any rents or profitts out of the said Messuages Lands Tenem^ts or other hereditam^ts by vertue of the said Deed pole and will of the said Sr John Cope & this Defd^t saith that hee hath not satisfied any of the debts of the said Sr John Cope without that that there is any other matter or thing in the said bill of Compl^t conteyned materiall or effectuall in the law for this Defd^t to answere vnto & not in this his Answere sufficiently answered vnto confessed or avoyded traversed or denied is true to the knowledge of this Defd^t All which matters and things this Defd^t is and wilbee willing and ready to averr Justify mayntayne and prove as this honōble Court shall award and humbly prayeth to bee dismissed hence with his reasonable costs and charges in this behalfe most wrongfully and causelessely susteyned:

The Right hoñ^ble William Lord Viscount Say & Seale the defd^t abovenamed deliūed in this his answere vpon his Honor the sixteenth day of January in the yeare of o^r Lord 1655 before us

James Fiennes.
Richard: Fiennes

[*Endorsed:*]
ffebr: the 6th. 1655 by the handǫ of Barnabas Horsman gent one of the Com^rs.

January 12, 1657/8
MILTON'S WITNESS IN COPE SUIT IS ATTACHED
Chancery Orders and Decrees, C 33/210, f. 310

Tuesd: 12° Jan [1657/8]. . . .

M John Milton pl'te   John Williams made oath that John Draper
   Cope Dēft   hath not attended to be exaīed as a witnes in
                       the Cause on the pl'ts. behalfe therefore At-
                       tachm^t Sherr Oxon ret tcō purif/.

May 17, 1658
SHERIFF OF OXFORD IS REPRIMANDED IN MILTON-COPE SUIT
Chancery Decrees and Orders, C 33/210, f. 723^v

Mond. 17° May [1658]

M John Milton pl'te   fforasmuch as the Sheriffe of Ox-
   Lady Cope and others Dēftǫ   fordshire hath had a writt of At-
                                  tachm^t deliūd to him ag^t John Drap
and hath made any returne thereof therefore Satturday next is a further day given the said Sheriffe to returne the said writt otherwise he is awarded to pay 5^li for a fine/

September 21, 1658

A WRIT TO EXAMINE WITNESSES IN MILTON-COPE SUIT IS ISSUED

Chancery Depositions, C 21/M 44/23

Richard Lord Protector of the Comonwealth of England Scotland &
Ireland & the Dominions & Territories therevnto belonging, To Will'm
Dobinson George Roberts Thomas Chamberlaine & Richard Coxeter
gent' greeting Knowe ye that we much trusting to your fidelityes &
prudent care have assigned you & doe hereby give vnto you three or
twoe of you full power & authoritie diligently to examyn all witnesses
whatsoever aswell on the behalfe of John Milton Esqr plte as on the
behalfe of Dame Elizabeth Cope widd' & execx Def^{tp} or on either of
their parts on certeine Jntērrs to be ministred or delivered to you three
or two of you And therefore we comānd you three or twoe of you that
at such certeine dayes places as you shall thinke fitt you cause to come
& call before you the said witnesses & that you diligently examyn them
& every of them severally by themselves vppon the Jnterr^{rs} aforesaid
vppon their severall corporall Oathes first taken before you three or
two of you vppon the holy Gospells of God And that you receive their
said Examinacōns & reduce them into writing distinctly & plainly in
pchment And when you have soe done that you send the same closed
vpp vnder the seales of you three or twoe of you to vs into our Court of
Chancery in three weekes after Michās next comeing Wheresoever it
shall then be togeather with the Jnterr^s aforesaid & this writt Witnesse
our selfe at Westm^r the xxith day of September in the yeare of our Lord
1658

Lenth. S^{r}my

[*Attached end:*]

To Wm Dobinson George Roberts Thomas Chamberlaine & Richard
Coxeter gent or 2 of them to ēx witnesses on Jnterr^{es} to be ministred
aswell for Milton Esqr pl't as for the Lady Cope & other deft^s on xiiij
dayes notice to the deft ret 3 weekes [after Michas?]

Lenth S^{r}m

[*Endorsed:*]

The execucōn of this Comission apperρ in certaine Schedules herevnto annexed

W^m. Dobinson
Geo: Roberts
Richard Coxeter.

September (?), 1658

INTERROGATORIES ARE PREPARED FOR LADY ELIZABETH COPE'S WITNESSES

Chancery Depositions, C 21/M 44/23   *Photostats in Harvard College Library*

Interrogatories to bee Administred to wittnesses to bee produced on the part and behalfe of the Lady Elizabeth Cope and Sir Anthony Cope Barr^t defendants at ye suit of John Milton Complaynant

1) ffirst doe you knowe the partyes Comp^lts & defend^ts & wch of them and did you know Sr Wm Cope & Sr John Cope deceased the grandfather and father of the said Sir Anthony declare the truth:/

2 Doe you know a certaine place scituate in London called by the name of the New Woll key & the Old Woll key wth theire appurtenances comonly called the custome house was nott the said p^rmisses setled by a decree made in the high Courte of Chancery by the consent of the said Sr Wm Cope deceased for the paym^t of a debt of Three thousand pounds wth interest att nine poundes p cent: due from the said S^r W^m to be paid to one Timberlake; or how much was the sūme that was to bee paid, by the said Decree to the said Timberlake declare ye truth./

3 Was: the said sūme of Three thousand poundes & the interest thereof paid by the said Sr Wm Cope in his life time; how much was oweing to the said Timberlake att the time of the Death of the said S^r W^m, either principall money or interest that was due by vertue of the said Decree, and how doe you knowe what money was soe due did not the said Timberlake or some other pson to whome the interest in the said Decree was assigned sell the same & to whome was the interest thereof sold, & how much hath been paid for the benefitt of the said Decree, and by whome? what was the reason the said Decree was soe bought in & the money paid that was due thereupon, what interest or estate had Sr John Cope in that parte of the Custome house in London called by the name of Hartshorne key wth the appurtenances att the time of his death, did not the Lease of Hartshorne key determine by effluccion of tyme soone after the death of Sr William Cope who hath the present interest thereof and who purchased the same & how much rent is yearly payd for the said key called Hartshorne key & to whome declare the truth hereof:/

4 What part of the old Woll key & the new Woll key being part of the Custome house in London hath the defend^t Sr Anthony Cope purchased in his owne name or in the name of some other pson for his benefitt and of whome was the same soe purchased, declare the truth:/

5 Was this Jndenture now shewed vnto you att the time of your examinacōn made between the ptyes in the said Jndenture mencōned upon the marriage of Sr John Cope to the def^t the Lady Elizabeth Cope & were you a witnes therevnto, doe or did you knowe whose names are thereunto sett & doe you know or beeleeve theyre names to bee of theyre owne hand writeing whoe else by name were witnesses thereunto declare the reasons of such your knowledge and conceale nothing:/

6 Doe you know that Sr John Cope did in his life time mortgage the ffarme or Graunge called by the name of Tangly to one m^r John More for ninety nine yeareȝ were you a witnes to any such deed of mortgage and is this writeing now shewed vnto you att the time of your examinacōn the same writeing that was soe sealed & delivered by the said Sr John Cope to the said m^r More declare the truth:/

7 Doe you know that the said Mannor graunge or farme of Tangley became forfeited by the said Sr John Cope in his life time to the said Mr Moore for nonpaym^t of the money therein mencōned & was not such Mortgage of the said Mannor farme or graunge of Tangly since purchased by the Lady Elizabeth Cope after the decease of the said Sr John Cope of the said Mr Moore & what sūme of money did the said Lady Elizabeth Cope pay to the said Mr Moore for the same were you and who else by name wittnesses to any such writeing declare the truth herein at large

8 Were you a wittnes and who else by name besides your selfe to the writeing now shewed unto you to what purpose was the said writeing made & was not the Mannor farme or graunge of Tangly aforesaid made over or setled upon one Mr Thomas Loggyn for the securing of a debt of fifteen hundred pounds wch was borrowed of the said Mr Loggyn by the said Lady Elizabeth Cope who was executrix to Sr John Cope dē^{cd}, did the said Lady Elizabeth Cope really borrow fifteen hundred pounds of the said Mr Thomas Loggyn for what purpose did shee borrow the said money & how did shee dispose or imploy such money that shee soe borrowed as you know beleeve or haue heard:/

9   Doe you know what moneys was really paide to Mr Thomas Loggyn
     when he assigned the lease of ninty nine yeares made by Sr John
     Cope to Mr Moore of the mannor farme or graunge of Tangly de-
     clare the truth and by whome was the said money payd/

10   What sūme or sōmes of money hath the defend^ts Sir Anthony Cope
     paid or secured to bee paid to the said Lady Elizabeth Cope his
     mother an other of the defend^tp for the revertion of the inheritance
     of Tangly aforesaid after the expiracōn of the said lease of ninety
     nine yeares declare the truth:/

11   Did you examine the paper writeing now shewed unto you att the
     time of your examinācon conteyning [blank] sheetϸ of paper with
     the originall writeing wch was sealed by the said Sir John Cope
     is the same a true coppy thereof doth the orrignall deed beare the
     same date as this paper coppy doth by whome was the said or-
     riginall deed sealed & delivered & was there livery & seisen executed
     thereupon by whome declare the truth

12   Was the Lease of the houses in Covent garden Mortgaged by S^r
     John Cope in his life time & to whome was the said Lease Mortgaged
     & for how much money and for what debt & how else was the said
     debt secured was the said Lease of the said houses in Covent garden
     sold att a full value and forasmuch as the said Lease was worth
     and for what sūme was the said Lease soe sold and by whome declare
     the truth hereof a Large,/

13   What Rectoryes or Parsonages either in England or Wales which
     were Sr Wm Copeϸ hath been sold either by the Lord Say or any
     other pson or psons that had power to sell the same either before
     the death of Sir John Cope or since and from whome had they power
     to sell these Rectoryes declare the truth:/

14   Doe you know in whome the right or interest of the houses in
     Hownsloe was att the time of the death of Sr John Cope mencōned
     to bee conveyed by Sir John Cope in one Deed Poll dated the tenth
     of Occtober in the fourteenth yeare of the late King Charles did
     Sir John Cope ever receive any rent for the said houseϸ in Hownslowe
     as you know beleeve or haue heard:/

15   How long is it since the said Sr John Cope departed this life declare
     the truth:/ at large

16 Doe you know of any agreement which was att any time made between the said defend^t the Lady Elizabeth Cope & one m^r Robert Lee concerning the paym^t of certaine debts which Sr John Cope & Mr Robert Lee stood bound or ingaged to any pson one for the other was not the said defend^t the Lady Elizabeth Cope to disingage the said m^r Robert Lee from all ingagements whatsoever which hee any way stood bound as surety for him the said Sr John Cope and was not the said m^r Lee to free and disingage the said Lady Elizabeth Cope from all manner of ingagementȝ which hee the said Sr John Cope stood bound as surety for the said m^r Lee and howe long it is since such agreement [was] made and did not the said Lady Elizabeth Cope performe what on her part was to be performed in relacōn to such agrements as aforesaid and was not the said Mr Lee at the tyme of the makeinge of such agreem^t of abillyty to haue payd the debt now claymed by the said Complt? declare yor knowledge herein/·

17 Haue you seen the defend^t the Lady Elizabeth Copes accompt annexed to her Answeare put into the Compl^ts Bill in this Courte and haue you perused the same accompt & is the same accompt that is soe putt in and annexed to her Answeare a true accompt as you know or beleeve declare your knowledge & the reason thereof

18 Hath not the Lady Elizabeth Cope paid a great deal of money more for the debts of Sr John Cope then the personall estate of Sr John did amount unto & by how much more hath shee soe payd was nott such money as the said Lady Elizabeth Cope paid over & above what the psonall estate did amount vnto paid out of such estate as of right did belong vnto her declare the truth:/

19 Haue you ever seen any the deeds writeings or evidences which concerne the estate either of the defend^tȝ the Lady Elizabeth Cope or of Sr Anthony Cope upon what occasyon were such writeings shewed vnto you and how long since declare the truth/

Wm Dobinson
Richard Coxeter
Geo: Robertȝ

[*These interrogatories have been very much written over, crossed, and corrected. The erasures have been so carefully done that it would be virtually impossible, if worth while, to decipher the clauses so deleted.*]

September (?), 1658

INTERROGATORIES ARE PREPARED FOR MILTON'S WITNESSES

Chancery Depositions, C 21/M 44/23   *Photostats in Harvard College Library*

Jnterrogatories to be administred vnto Witnesses to be produced on the part and behalfe of John Milton Esqr Cōmplt ag^t Dame Elizabeth Cope widd' and Sr Anthony Cope Barr^tt. Dēfts./

1st Doe yo^u know the pties Cōmpl^t & Dēfts or either & which of them and how long haue yo^u soe done and did yo^u know Sr John Cope late husband to the Dēft Elizabeth and father to the other Def^t Sr Anthony: How long did you knowe the said Sr John before his death?

2^d Alsoe Did yo^u see the Obligacōn and now shewne vnto yo^u purporting that the said Sr John Cope wth the other psons therein named standρ bound to the Cōmplt in Three hundred poundρ for the payment of One hundred & ffifty poundρ wth interest Sealed and delivered by the said Sr John Cope as his Act & Deed to the Cōmplt to his vse and is yor Name subscribed as a Witneρ to the same of yor hand writeing.

3^d Was the said Sr John Cope at the time of his death or any other pson or psons in trust for him and who by name possest of any messuages Landρ Tenem^tρ or other hereditamentρ in Lease for any Terme of yeareρ, of what Messuageρ Landρ Tenemtρ or other hereditam^tρ in pticular was the said Sr John Cope and such other pson or psons soe possessed and what were then or at any time since the seūall yearely valueρ of the said Messuages Landρ Tenem^tρ or other hereditamentρ declare yor knowledge herein & in what parisheρ & County such Messuageρ Landρ Tenem^tρ and hereditam^tρ lye, and in whose possession they were at his death & since and every other circumstance tending to make such a discovery thereof as that the Cōmplt may haue his iust benefitt thereof more especially who hath received the profittρ thereof and to whom haue ye same bin answered.

4 Alsoe haue you pvsed the Jnventory of the psonall estate of the said Sr John Cope now shewne vnto yo^u being a Coppie of that wch is annexed to the Dēftρ answeres, Js any and what pte of the psonall estate wch Sr John Cope had at the time of his death either ready money securityeρ for money debtρ due to him or other goodρ and Chattellρ omitted out thereof, Jf soe expresse such sōmes of ready money, securityes for money debtρ and other thingρ pticu-

larly and all circumstances about every one of them whereby soe pfect a discovery may be made thereof as that the Cōmplt may haue a iust benefitt thereof.

5 Alsoe of the pticulars in the Jnventory expressed wᶜʰ of them were vndervallued, And what would yoᵘ haue given for any & wᶜʰ of the pticulers herein contayned more then the prices they are therein rayted att expresse them all. And alsoe which of the pticulers therein expressed haue been sold for greater and how much greater prices then they are therein rayted att, expresse the pticulerꝑ herein and the severall prices they were sold att.

6 Alsoe haue yoᵘ pvsed the Schedule or Schedules now shewne vnto yoᵘ conteyning (amongst other thingꝑ the debtꝑ of the said Sʳ John Cope and the Deft Dame Elizabeth for payment thereof; Did you pay or receive any and wᶜʰ pte or ptes thereof expresse the pticulerꝑ and tymeꝑ when and the Names of the pticulers to & of whom and the severall summeꝑ that you payd or received And whether the Deft Dame Elizabeth really and bonâ fide payd to the seūall psons the full severall summeꝑ to whom it is expressed in the said Schedule shee did soe pay the same, or deduct any lesser summeꝑ to any and which of them express the Names of the psons who received lesse and the summes how much less they received therein mencōned in the said Schedule, declare yoʳ knowledge therein and the reasons thereof.

7 Alsoe Did the said Sʳ John Cope make any and what Deed of settlemᵗ. and vpon whom and of what Landꝑ Tenemᵗᵖ or hereditamᵗᵖ. for the payment of his debtꝑ or did he make any and what pvision for the paymentꝑ thereof by his last Will & Testamᵗ And what is be- come of such Deed or Will, and when & where did yoᵘ last see either and wᶜʰ of them and in whose handꝑ expresse the truth.

8 Alsoe haue yoᵘ pvsed the further severall answere of the said Dēft Dame Elizabeth were the Messuages Landꝑ Tenemᵗᵖ and heredit- amentꝑ therein for that purpose expressed those wᶜʰ Sʳ John Cope conveyed for the paymᵗ of his debtꝑ? was Sʳ John Cope then seized thereof or of any and which of them in fee simple and who was the pson that made or directed to bee made or engrossed such Deed, expresse yᵉ Names of every one of them.

9] Alsoe haue yoᵘ knowledge of the Manner graung or farme of Tangley wᵗʰ the appurtenances in the County of Oxford what is the vtmost or true yearely value thereof and what are the Demesne Landꝑ rentꝑ issueꝑ services and pfittꝑ of the sayd Mannoʳ worth by the yeare one yeare wth another and who enioyeρ or receiveρ the same and hath soe done since the death of Sr John Cope who are and have since that tyme been the Teñtρ thereof, and what yearely rentρ haue they payd, and to whom, or by whose vse expresse the severall nameρ of the psons who paid the same and to whom and for whose vse and what annuall rent or summe of money every or any of the Tenantρ of any pte or ptes of the sayd Manno^r haue payd and what other pfitt hath bin made thereof since the death of the said Sr John Cope by the said Dēftρ or either of them by fines or otherwise, expresse yor knowledge herein and the reasons thereof.

10 Alsoe have yo^u any knowledge of the Rectory or Rectories of South & North Marnhead in the County of Norff; what is the yearely vallue thereof & of the Gleabe landρ Tenem^{tρ} and appurtenñcρ therevnto belonging who hath held the said rectory or rectoriρ and Landρ ever since the death of the said Sr John and haue been Lessors and Lessees thereof and who now receives the rentρ issueρ and profitρ thereof, and what proffit or advantage thereof hath been made by fineρ vpon Leaseρ or otherwise since the said Sr John Copeρ death rēcd or had such ffines and other advantages expresse the Nameρ of the psons the fines pfittρ or advantageρ had or received and the time when.

11 Doe yo^u know the toft Close or pcell of Land in Marchland [named] Krosse keyes or by what other name soever it is called in the County of Norffolk wch was Sr John Copeρ at the tyme of his death, What is the true or vtmost yearely vallue of the s'd pcell of land who haue beene Lessors or Lesseeρ thereof or hold the same ever since the death of Sr John Cope, and to whom haue the rentes issues and pfittρ thereof beene answered or to whose vse payd.

12 Alsoe have yo^u any knowledge of the Capitall Messuage or house in Hunsloe in the County of Middle what is the yearely vallue thereof who hath held the said Messuage or house ever since the death of the said Sr John and haue bin Lessorρ and Lesseeρ thereof and who now receives the rentρ issueρ and proffitρ thereof or what profitt or advantage thereof hath bin made by fineρ vpon Leases or otherwise since the said Sr John Copes death who haue paid and who have received or had such fines and other advantages expresse the Names of the psons the fines pfittρ or advantageρ had or received and the tyme when

13 Alsoe have yo^u any knowledge of the Rectoryρ psonages and Tythes or any of them hereafter in this Jnterrogatory mencōned that is

to say of the Rectory or psonage of Mether Kennocke in the County of Brecknock of the Rectory of Wintheringham and of the Tytheρ of Wintherngham Newton Linton and Knapton in the County of Yorke and of the Tith corne in Knattingley in the said County and of the Tithes of Seafish in Winthernsey in the same County what is the yearely vallue thereof and of the Rectoryρ psonages and tytheρ therevnto belonging and who hath held the said Rectoryρ psonages or Tytheρ ever since the death of the said Sr John and haue bin Lessors and Lessees thereof and who now receives the rentρ issueρ and profittρ thereof and what profitt or advantage thereof hath beene made by fines vpon Leases or otherwise since the said Sr John Copeρ death who hath payd and who haue received or had such fines and other advantageρ expresse the Names of the psons the fines pfittρ or advantageρ had or receiued and the tyme when.

14 Alsoe haue yo^u any knowledge of the yearely vallue of the Rectoryeρ psonages & tythes heereafter in this Jnterrogatory mencōned or of any of them that is to say of the Rectory of Middle Reaseing in the County of Lincolne of the Rectory of Kidwelly in the County of Carmerthen what is the yearely vallue thereof and of the tythes of the Mills in Kidwelly aforesaid therevnto belonging who hath held the said Rectorieρ psonageρ Tytheρ and Gleabes ever since the death of the said Sir John and haue been Lessors and Lessees thereof & who now receives the rentρ issues and profitρ thereof and what profitt or advantage thereof hath bin made by fines vpon Leaseρ or otherwise since the said Sr John Copes death who hath paid and who hath received or had such fineρ and other advantages, expresse the Names of the psons, the fines profittρ or advantageρ had or received and the tyme when

15 Alsoe haue yo^u any knowledge of Miller & Mabee in the County of Cornwall what is the yearely vallue thereof who haue held the sayd Miller & Mabee ever since the death of the said Sr John and haue bin Lessors & Lessees thereof and who now receiveρ the rentρ issues and profittρ thereof and what pfitt or advantage thereof hath bin made by fineρ vpon Leaseρ or otherwise since the said Sr John Copeρ death who hath payd and who hath received or had such fines & other advantageρ expresse the Nameρ of the psons the fineρ profittρ or advantageρ had or received and the tyme when./

16 Alsoe haue yo^u any knowledge of the Parsonage of Mount and Lethered in the County of Cardigan what is the yearely vallue thereof who haue held the sayd Parsonage of Mount & Lethered ever since the death of the said Sr John and haue bin Lesso^rρ and

Lesseeρ thereof and who now receiveρ the rentρ issueρ and pfittρ
thereof and what pfitt or advantage thereof haue bin made by
fineρ [upon] Leaseρ or otherwise since the said Sʳ John Copes death
who hath paid and who hath received or had such fineρ and other
advantageρ expresse the Nameρ of the psons the fines pfittρ or
advantageρ had or receiued & the time when./

17 Alsoe haue yoᵘ any knowledge if the said Sʳ John Cope att the tyme
of his death was seized in fee of any Messuageρ or houseρ or of any
Wharfes cranes or Keyes in or neere the Custome house in London
by what name or signe are or were the said Messuages houseρ
wharfeρ craneρ or keyeρ knowne or distinguished, what is the yearely
vallue thereof who haue held the sayd Messuageρ houseρ wharfeρ
craneρ or keyeρ ever since the death of the said Sʳ John and haue
bin Lessorρ and Lesseeρ thereof and who now receives the rentρ
issues and profittρ thereof and what profitt or advantage thereof
haue bin made by ffines vpon Leaseρ or otherwise since the sayd Sʳ
John Copes death who hath received or had such fines and other
advantages expresse the Names of the psons the fines profittρ or
advantages had or received & the time when./

Wᵐ: Dobinson   Richard Coxeter
Geo: Robertρ

18 Alsoe haue yoᵘ any knowledge of the seūall Keyeρ in this Jnterrogatory hereafter named that is to say the old wool key the new
wool key & harthorne key what is the yearely vallue thereof who
haue held the said keyes ever since the death of the said Sʳ John
and haue been Lessorρ and Lesseeρ thereof and who now receiveρ
yᵉ rentρ issueρ and pfittρ thereof and what pfitt or advantage thereof
haue bin made by fineρ vpon Leaseρ or otherwise since the said
Sʳ John Copeρ death who hath payd and who hath received or had
such fineρ & other advantages expresse the Nameρ of the psons the
fineρ pfittρ or advantages had or receiued and the time when.

19 Alsoē Doe yoᵘ know of any fine levyed or recovery suffered of any
and wᶜʰ of the said Messuages Landρ Tenementρ hereditamᵗρ &
pʳmisseρ in the said Dēft Dame Elizabeth farther answere or in
the precedent Jnterrogatory expressed within Eight yeareρ before
the death of Sʳ John Cope by whom were such fine or fineρ recovery
or recoveryeρ leived or suffered and to whom & of wᶜʰ of the pʳmisses
and for what causeρ or consideracōns and in what yeare or yeareρ
expresse yoʳ full knowledge therein.

20 Doe yoᵘ know of any house in Covent garden whereof the said
Sʳ John Cope was att the time of his death possest for any terme or

or number of yeareꝑ and for what terme of yeareꝑ and by what Lease and when dated and by whom granted and what is the yearely vallue of the said Messuages or houseꝑ att the tyme of Sr John Copeꝑ death and who hath received the rentꝑ issueꝑ and proffittꝑ thereof or any of them since the death of the said Sr John to whose vse by what right & by whose appointment are or haue been the said rentꝑ and ꝓfittꝑ soe received.

21 Was the said Sr John Cope att the time of his death indebted to the late Countesse of Westmoreland in any summe or summeꝑ of money and in what summe how or vpon what consideracōn did the same grow due, what security did the sayd Sr John Cope giue for the same who hath paid the said debt and how hath the same bin paid Declare what yo^u know beleive or haue heard hereof wth the groundꝑ and reasons thereof.

22 Was the said Sr John Cope att the tyme of his death indebted to John Moore Esqr in any and in what summe or summes of money how and vpon what consideracōn did the said debt grow due how was it secured by the said Sr John Cope to the said Mr Moore and by whome was it paid and to whom and when and how much money was paid in satisfaccōn thereof declare yor knowledge herein & reason thereof.

23 Alsoe Doe yo^u know any estate either reall or psonall or vallueable thinge whatsoever that was Sr John Copes att the time of his death and was liable after his death to pay his debtꝑ more then yo^u haue already beene examined vnto or haue discovered, Jf soe expresse such Estate or thinge vallueable & the true vallue thereof and where it is and how it hath bin disposed of and by whom and to whom.

24 Doe yo^u knowe the Manno^r of Tangley in the County of Oxōn with itts rights members and apptenñcs what the yeareley value thereof Hath ye same bein lett & sett att an vndervalue if soe vnto whome & for what reason or cause was the same soe lett & sett att an vndervalue sett forth the truth of yor knowledge herein att large.

25 Doe you knowe or have heard what sūme or sōmes of money was lent vnto Sr John Cope deceased by D^r. Clapton & M^r: Greenewood for ye vse of M^r: William Joyner how longe was the same soe lent & what interest was paid for the same & to whom when was the said monies Repaid & by whome what was the sōme soe Repaid & vnto whome was the same Repaid declare what yo^u knowe or have heard touchinge the same.

W^m: Dobinson
Richard Coxeter
Geo: Robertꝑ

October (?), 1658
DEPOSITION OF THOMAS RICHARDS FOR LADY ELIZABETH COPE

Chancery Depositions, C 21/M 44/23   *Photostat in Harvard College Library*

On the Defeñd^{te} parte

Thomas Richardꝑ of Lynt in the County of Wiltꝑ gent aged sixty yeares or thereaboutꝑ sworne and exaīed deposeth as followeth;/

1 To the first Jñt^r this Depon^t saith that he doth knowe the defeñd^t Sir Anthony Cope Barr^t in the Jñt^r named and did knowe Sir John Cope late father of the said Sir Anthony./

6 To the sixth Jñt^r this Depon^t saith that hee doth knowe that Sir John Cope in the Jñt^r named did in his life time by the name of John Cope Esqr mortgage the farme or Grange called by the name of Tangley for nynety nyne yeares. And that hee this Depon^t was a witnesse to A deed of Mortgage to that purpose And that this Deed or writeing now shewed vnto him this Dep^t at the time of his Ex-aminacōn is the same writeing that was soe sealed and delivered by the said Sir John Cope to the said More, and the name of this Depon^t subscribed as a witnesse therevnto is of his this Depon^{te} owne prop handwriteing./

W^m: Dobinson
Richard Coxeter
Geo: Robertꝑ

[*The numbering of the answer reveals that this deposition was taken on the earlier rather than the revised interrogatories. In the former, question 6 concerns the mortgage of Tangley and the deed to be showed to the witness; in the latter, this has been renumbered 7*]

October (?), 1658
REVISED INTERROGATORIES ARE PREPARED FOR LADY ELIZABETH COPE'S WITNESSES

Chancery Depositions, C 24/835   *Photostats in Harvard College Library*

[*The new interrogatories follow those given previously (C 21/M 44/23), with slight variations of spelling, punctuation, phraseology, and the like, except for the variants noted below. The numbering has been slightly re-vised. Number 5 is broken in the middle and numbered 5 and 6. Numbers 6, 7, 8, and 9 have been altered to 7, 8, 9, and 10. Number 10 has been in-cluded with number 9, so that numbers 11, 12, 13, 14, and 15 remain un-changed. Number 16 is included with 15, causing numbers 17, 18, and 19 to be altered to 16, 17, and 18. Number 5 omits* and conceale nothing. *Number 9, after* Tangly, *adds* and what is the true yearely vallue thereof;*]

and after said money payd, *adds* and for whose vse was ye s^d lease assignd. *Number 10 adds at the end* of your knowledge herein at large. *Number 11, in the blank space, supplies* two. *Number 12, after the sixth word,* houses, *adds* late the said Sr John Copeρ scituate. *Number 14, after* Hounsloe, *adds* late the houseρ of the s'd Sr John Cope. *Number 17, after the first* accompt, *adds* and her Jnventory of Sr John Copes estate and the. *Before later occurrences of the word* accompt *the words* Jnventory and *in some form are added. After* beleeve, *it adds* and is this paper book nowe shewed vnto you a true coppy of the said Jnventory or accompt so put in and annexed to the Lady Copeρ answere. *After the last word of the interrogatory follows* or how much doe knowe of the said Accompt to be just and true? *Number 18 omits by erasure everything after the first* did amount unto, *and adds* or that was any way raysed by the benifitt of the mortgage of Tangley or by the sale of the Jnheritance thereof Declare what you knowe and the reasonρ of such yor knowledge and what of your beleife herein/. *The signatures of the three commissioners are omitted.*

Various notes of the examination of witnesses have also been jotted down in blank spaces. At the head, before number 1, is John Drap sworne 10th ffēb 1658 Wm Harrington. *After the first interrogatory follows* Thomas Chaundler sworne 24th ffēb 1658 Edm Gyles. *After number 2 comes* Hugh Candish sworne 10th June 1659 Wm Harington. *On the back is noted,* The pap booke or Jnventory mencōned was r'd back by me this 11th of ffēb: 1658/ John Draper/ r'd C Drap 26 iiij^d Cope ad^s Milton. rd 10th ffēb 1658 shew Staunton Mr Warren Johnson noe ffees Mr Warren noe ffee Chandler noe ffee Candish./ All the seūall deedes & writings in this cause mencōned J rēcd back againe this 21th of June 1659

John Draper.]

October (?), 1658

JOHN DRAPER IS EXAMINED AS WITNESS FOR MILTON IN COPE SUIT

[*Though the original record has not been found, it is mentioned in his deposition for Lady Elizabeth Cope, February 10, 1658/9*]

"John Draper of Brewengrange in the Countey of Oxford gent aged 58 yeares or theraboutρ being formerly sworne and examined on ye part and behalfe of the nowe Comp^lt in the suite . . .

[*See also the Chancery Decree and Order of January 12, 1657/8, and that of May 17, 1658. By the first, Draper is to be attached for not appearing as a witness for Milton; by the second the sheriff is to be penalized for not serving the attachment.*]

October 12, 1658
DEPOSITIONS OF MILTON'S WITNESSES, EDWARD LYDE *ALIAS* JOYNER AND JOHN ROBINSON

Chancery Depositions, C 21/M 44/23   *Photostats in Harvard College Library*

On the Cōmplts behalfe/

Deposicōns of wittnesses taken att the howse of Richard veysey Jnholder Comonly knowne by the name of the signe of the George scituate in Burford in the County of Oxōn on the twelveth day of October in the yeare of oʳ Lord one thowsand six hundred fifty & Eight Before vs William Dobinson George Roberts & Richard Coxeter Gent By virtue of a Comission out of the high Court of Chauncery vnto vs and vnto Thomas Chamberlayne Gent' directed for yᵉ exaiacōn of wittnesses in a Cause there dependinge betweene John Milton Esqʳ. pl't. and yᵉ Lady Cope & others defts as followeth.

Edward Lyde āls Joyner of Horsepath in yᵉ County of Oxōn Gent'. aged 39 yeares or thereabouts sworne & exēd Deposeth as followeth.

1   To the first Jnterrogatorie he saith that he doth not neither eū did certeinly knowe yᵉ pties in this Jntērr named or either of them but hath often heard of them.

2   To the Sixt Jntērr this Depᵗ: saith that hee hath lately pvsed the Schedule now shewed forth vnto him at the time of this his exaiācon and hath now alsoe seene yᵉ same and saieth that whereas in & by the same Schedule there is mencōn of an Accompt made of 402ˡⁱ: to bee paid by the Dēfte Dame Elizabeth Cope to Mʳ. George Greenewood and Dʳ. Clapton (both since deceased) by bond hee this Deponant saith that he verily beleeveth in his Conscience that the said Defᵗˢ. Dame Elizabeth Cope Did not pay to yᵉ sayd Mʳ: Greenewood & Dʳ Clapton yᵉ full sōme of 402ˡⁱ: as in & by the sayd Schedule is mencōned and the reason of such this Depᵗˢ. beleife is for that the sayd Mʳ: Greenwood & Dʳ. Clapton beinge Execʳˢ in trust of the last Will & Testament of Anne Lyde āls Joyner Widd' deceased this dēpᵗˢ late Mother and this deponant being pʳsent at & haveinge now pvsed seūall accompts of yᵉ sayd Mʳ: Greenewood & Dʳ. Clapton doth by yᵉ same accompt vnder the hand of yᵉ said Dʳ. Clapton & Mʳ Greenewood finde that they did lend to yᵉ sayd Sʳ: John Cope in the yeare of oʳ Lord one thowsand six hundred Thirty Eight the sume of 200ˡⁱ: & noe more and that the said Dēfᵗˢ. the Lady Cope did pay to yᵉ

s^d. M^r: Greenewood & D^r: Clapton or one of them the sōme of 16^{li}: for one yeares Jnterest due the eight day of october 1639 for the sayd some of 200^{li} lent as aforesayd and that shee the sayd Dēf^t. Did alsoe pay to them the sayd M^r: Greenewood & D^r: Clapton the further sōme of sixteene pownds for one other yeares Jnterest due for the sayd 200^{li}: at the eighth of octōb: 1640 and the further sōme of eight pownds for the Jnterest thereof in the yeare of o^r Lord 1641 And further saith that ye sayd M^r: Greenewood in or about the yeare of our Lord 1643: tould this Dep^t. that hee had receaved of the sayd Dēf^t. Dame Elizabeth Cope the sōme of 200^{li}: which hee paid (as hee the sayd M^r: Greenewood then affirmed) to Willīm Lyde āls Joyner this Dēp^{ts}: brother in pte of his Legacie to him given in & by the sayd last will & Testament of his this Dep^{ts}. sayd late Mother deceased and that his this Dep^{ts}: sayd brother accordingly acknowledged to this dep^t. the receipt thereof in or about the sayd yeare of o^r Lord 1643. And this Dep^t further saith that the sayd M^r: Greenewood was a man of greate Jntegrity & neū as this Dep^t. beleeveth reecē^d. ye forfiture of any bond and the sayd M^r: Greenewood often affirmed to this Dept that hee recēd of ye sayd Lady Cope noe more but the aforesayd Sōme of two hundred pownds & the Jnterest thereof vntill the same were paid./

John Robinson of Horsepath in the Countie of Oxōn Geñt Aged 55. yeares or thereabouts sworne & exēd Deposeth as followeth./

1 To the first Jntērr he saith that he knoweth ye Cōmplt & hath knowne him for ye space of 10 yeares last past or vpwards but doth not knowe thother psens in this Jntērr named./

9 To the 9th: Jntērr this Dep^t: saith that he this dep^t: doth not knowe ye Manno^r Grainge or farme of Tangley in this Jntērr mencōned but saith that hee this Dep^t: hath Diligently Enquired Concerninge the Worth or yearely value thereof & saith that hee hath bine Credibly informed by the neighbours therevnto adiacent that the same Manno^r Grainge or farme is accompted worth 160^{li}: p anñ & is & hath bin Charged & Taxed for Contribucōn & other payments after that rate or value./

W^m: Dobinson
Richard Coxeter
Geo: Robertρ

[*Endorsed:*] Milton con Cope &c.

November 11, 1658

SIR ANTHONY COPE'S PETITION FOR NEW COPIES OF INTERROGA-
TORIES FOR WITNESSES IN MILTON'S SUIT IS GRANTED

Chancery Decrees and Orders, C 33/212, ff. 155-155ᵛ

Satt 11ᵗʰ: No:

M: Milton p'ᵗ   Vpon the humble petecon of the s'd
    Sʳ Anthony Cope Barrᵗ   defendᵗ this day Ex'ted vnto the Rigᵗ
    and others defts   hono^{ble} the Mʳ of the Rolles thereby
                                             shewing that a Com' yssued in this Cause
the last vacacōn for Examicōn of witnesses wherein the deftꝑ Joined
and diuʳse witnesses were Exēd on both sideꝑ but since that by some
accident the dēftꝑ have lost theire paper draught of the Interrʳˢ Execūed
on their pte at the Execōn of the s'd Comm' and soe now the dēfte
havinge occasion to renewe the s'd Com' to Exaīne other witnesses cannot pceed therein vnlesse the Clerke for the pˡᵗ will produce the s'd
Com' before some Mʳ of this Courte whereby the same may bee opened
and the int'rrs soe Exēd bee deliuʳed to the dēfts Clerke to take a coppy
thereof wherevpon it is ordered by this lōpp that Mʳ Eltonhead one of
the Mʳˢ &c be attended to the end the said Com' bee opened that the
dēftꝑ might haue the Jnterrʳˢ to coppy whereby to Exaīne theire other
witnesses:/

R[obert?] D[ods?]

February 10, 1658/9

DEPOSITION OF JOHN DRAPER ON LADY ELIZABETH COPE'S BEHALF

Chancery Depositions, C 24/835   *Photostats in Harvard College Library*

ffebr yᵉ 10ᵗʰ. 1658   Wittnesseꝑ examined on yᵉ part and
[showed by Mʳ Johnson,   behalfe of the Lady Elizabeth Cope
cancelled] formerly examined and Sʳ Anthony Cope Barronett De-
by the pˡᵗ.   fendant against John Milton Complt by
                                         Robert Shiers Esqʳ Examiner in Chan-
cery/ John Draper of Brewengrange in the Countey of Oxford gent aged
58 yeares or theraboutꝑ being formerly sworne and examined on yᵉ part
and behalfe of the nowe Compˡᵗ in the suite and nowe sworne and examined on yᵉ part and behalfe of the Deftꝑ in the suite deposeth and
saith./

(1 That he doth very well knowe the ptyeꝑ Defendᵗꝑ in the suite in
the title of the Jntērrꝑ named and hath seene the Compˡᵗ John
Milton but hath little or acquaintance with him And saith that he
did knowe Sʳ William Cope and Sʳ John Cope deceased the Grandfather and father of the Defᵗ Sʳ Anthony Cope when they were
liveing./

(2 That he doth knowe A certaine place in London called by the name of the newe wooll key and the olde wooll key with their appurtenance¢ comonly called the Customehouse the wch said p^{r}misse¢ were settled by A Decree of thi¢ honorable Court made by the Consent of the said Sr William Cope deceased for ye Payment of A debt of three thousand pound¢ with interest at nine pound¢ p cent to be paid by the said Sr William by one Timberlake as appeare by the said decree to wch for his full certainety therein he referreth himselfe./

(3 That he doth beleeve that the said debt of 3000^{li}. due by vertue of the said Decree and Agrem^{t} part of the interest therof was vnpaid and remayning due to the said Timberlake at the tyme of the death of the said Sr William Cope for that by A Report made about that time by Sr Robert Rich knight deceased late one of the m^{r¢} of this honorable Court to wch sd report this Deponent referreth himselfe the same debt with interest for the same amounted to 4000: or thereabout¢. And this Deponent saith that the Executors of the said Timberlake after hi¢ decease or some other persons who had an interest in the said Decree by vertue of such Executorshipp assignem^{t} or otherwise did sell and Assigne over vnto the Def^{t} the Lady Elizabeth Cope or to some other for her vse or by her appointem^{t} the said Decree and all his or their interest therein or benefitt therof for and in Consideracōn of fower thousand pound¢ and vpward¢ paid by the said Dame Elizabeth Cope for the same And he saith that the reason why the said Decree was soe bought in as aforesaid and the money therevpon paid was for that the said debt and interest wa¢ growne soe great being settled by the said Decree at 9^{li}. p Cent. that the Jnheritance of the said keye¢ would not have beene sufficient to have paid the same together with the Cheefe Rent and taxe¢ therout payable as thi¢ Depon^{t} beleeveth And thi¢ Deponent saith that he beleeves that the said Sr John Cope had noe interest or estate in that part of the Custome house called Hartshorne keye with the appurtenance¢ at the tyme of his death for that the said Hartshorne Keye wa¢ held by A lease from the ffree schoole at Seavenoake in the Countey of Kent made to the said Sr William Cope or to Sr Walter Cope his vnckle the wch expired by efffluxion of tyme much about the death of the said Sr William and for that the said Sr John Cope liveing but A short tyme after his said ffather could not procure A newe Lease of the said premisse¢ from the said Schoole And for y^{t} the said Deft Dame Elizabeth Cope soone after the death of

John Draperr

the said Sr William did procure A new Lease for ye terme of 40 yeareσ of the said premisseσ from the said schoole at the yearely rent of 120^{li}. payeing fiftey poundσ for A ffine All wch thiσ Deponent is the better enabled to depose as aforesaid for that this Deponent ever since the death of the said Sr William Cope as Agent for ye now Def^{tσ} hath beene privey vnto (or otherwise imployed in or concerning) the seūall matters and thingσ before declared./

4 That the Def^t Sr Anthoney Cope hath boughte of his vncle Jonathan Cope yonger sonn of the said Sr Will'm Cope in the name of some other person or persons for his vse and benefitt all such part of the said Custome house as came vnto the said Jonathan Cope by vertue of the last will of the said Sr William Cope and wch was not settled vpon the said John Cope late ffather of the said Sr Anthony vpon the great deede of settlemen^t made vpon the marriage of the said Sr John Cope vnto the nowe Deft Dame Elizabeth Cope dated the 20th of January in the seaventh yeare of the raigne of the late King Charles and more saith not to this Jntērr/

(5 That he doth beleeve that the Jndenture now produced and shewed
6 vnto him thiσ Depon^t at the tyme of his examinacōn beareing date the 20th day of January 1631 and in the 7th yeare of the raigne of the late King Charleσ is the very same deede that was made (betweene the ptyes therein named to be partieσ therevnto) vpon the marriage of the said Sr John Cope to the nowe Deft Dame Elizabeth Cope for that this Deponent was very well accquainted with Sr William Cope in his life tyme and with the Lady Westm'land in her life tyme and Sr Cope Doyley and Richard Knightley in their respective life tymeσ and doth knowe William Lord Viscount Say and Seale; Mildemay Earle of Westm'land, and the Deft the Lady Elizabeth Cope all ptyes to the said deede and is very well acquainted wth the hand writing of the said Sr William Cope, William Lord Viscount Saye and Seale and the Lady Elizabeth Cope, whose nameσ (together with the nameσ of other the ptyeσ to the said deede) are respectively subscribed to the said deede the wch he beleeveσ for his reason before declared to be of the respective prop hand writing of the said Sr William Cope William Lord Viscount Say and Seale and the Lady Elizabeth Cope and saith y^t he beleeves that Giles Harris Will'm Banister William Lynn and William Sprigg were present and wittnesseσ to the sealeing and deliūy thereof for y^t he findeσ their seūall and respective names therevpon endorsed as wittneσ to the same with whose hand

writing this Deponent is very well acquainted and for that the
said Mr William Lynn one of the said wittnesseρ (and the only
wittneρ that this Deponent knoweth of or can finde to be liveing
of all the ptyeρ whose nameρ are endorssed as wittnesseρ therto)
haveing beene sent for to come vp to London from Tavestock
neere Barstable (where he lyeth sick) to prove the said produced,
Deede, (haveing proved the same vpon A former examinacōn in
thiρ honorable Court) did write vp word that he was not able to
come soe great A Journey without danger of his life and therein did
likewise affirme that he was A wittneρ to the sealeing and deliūy
of the said deede and more saith not to these Jntērrs/

John Draperr

(7:8 That the said Sr John Cope did in his life tyme Mortgage the
ffarme or Grange called by the name of Tangly to m^r John Moore
in the Jnterr named for 99 yeareρ wch said mortgage became forfeited to the said John Moore in the life tyme of the said Sr John
Cope for non payment^t of the money therein mencōned wch said
Mortgage was purchased by the Def^t the Lady Elizabeth Cope
after the decease of the said Sr John Cope of the said m^r moore and
paid him for the same the sūme of ffive hundred and fowerscore
poundρ or thereaboutρ thiρ Deponent being privey to the makeing
of the agreem^t touching the said purchase and payem^t of the money
for the same the same being to the best of hiρ remembrance and
as he beleeveρ paid by the handρ of thiρ Deponent for and in the
behalfe of the said Def^t Dame Elizabeth Cope and further he deposeth not to these two Jntērrρ/

10 That he doth knowe that the Def^t Sr Anthony Cope did pay vnto
m^r Thomas Loggins (who had purchased the sd mortgage of Tangley heretofore made by the sd Sr John Cope vnto the said Moore)
the sūme of 1500^li for the said mortgage made by his late ffather
to the said John Moore as aforesaid the said 1500^li being paid
to the said Loggin by the handρ of this Deponent wch said mortgaged p^rmisses have beene lett for 120^li: A yeare out of wch the
Landlord hath paid or allowed taxes and other payem^ts chargable
vpon the same./ And saith that the said Lease or Mortgage vpon
the payem^t of the said 1500^li. as aforesaid was Assigned over to
or for the vse of the said Def^t Sr Anthony Cope And this Deponent
saith that the said Def^t Sr Anthony Cope after he came of Age
did Agree with the other Def^t Dame Elizabeth Cope for the purchase of the Jnheritance of the said mannor Grange or ffarme
of Tangley aforesaid the wch the Def^t Dame Elizabeth had in

reūsion after the expiracōn of the said Lease of ninety yeareꝑ And
the said Def^t Sr Anthony did therevpon agree and vndertake, for
and in consideracōn of the same purchase to paye and secure to
paie the sūme of 1550^{li}. or theraboutꝑ wch waꝑ formerly the proper
debtꝑ oweing by the said Sr John Cope to seūall persons by bond
and hath since the said Agreem^t and in pursuance therof paid
by the handꝑ of this Deponent the sūme of fowerteene hundred
poundꝑ or theraboutꝑ of the said 1550^{li}. and the rest he hath secured by bond as namely the 150^{li}. residue of the said 1550^{li}. and
more saith not to this Jntērr/

(12 That the leaseꝑ of the houseꝑ late the houseꝑ of the said Sr John
Cope scituat in Covent garden were mortgaged by the said Sr John
in his life tyme to the Lady mary Countess Dowager of westmerland for and in Consideracōn of the sūme of fowerteene hundred
and fiftey poundꝑ secured by bond to be paid vnto the said Countess Dowager or her Assigneꝑ by 200^{li}. A yeare at halfe yearely
payem^{tꝑ}. and saith that the nowe Def^t Dame Elizabeth after the
decease of the said Sr John Cope as the Relict and Executrix of
the said Sr John did sell the said leaseꝑ for the sūme of eighte
hundred and twenty poundꝑ or theraboutꝑ wch he beleeves was
asmuch money as could be gott for the same and more saith not to
this Jnterr/

                                              John Draperr

(13 That this deponent doth beleeve that all the Rectoryeꝑ or Parson-
ageꝑ either in England or Waleꝑ wch were heretofore Sr William
Copeꝑ and mencōned to be Conveyed to seūall psons in trust by
A deed dated in or about 10° Oct. 1638 by Sr John Cope and w^{ch}
were not Conveyed and settled by the said Sr William Cope (vpon
the marriage of the said Sr John with the said Def^t Dame Elizabeth) by the great deede mencōned in this Deponentꝑ answere to
the 5th and 6th Jntērrꝑ preceedent have since beene sold and Conveyed away by the Lord Say by the Direccōn of the said Sr William Cope in his last will and Testament and in pursuance of A
former trust in him and otherꝑ reposed by the said Sr William
Cope and not by any trust or power receaved by him from the
said Sr John Cope he the said Lord Say haveing disclaymed the
trust later made vnto him by the said Sr John and more saith not
to this Jntērr/

(14 That the right and interest of the houseꝑ in hounslowe in the
Jntērr mencōned at the tyme of the decease of the said Sr John
Cope mencōned to be Conveyed as in the Jntērr is expressed was

in Robert Lee Esqr and ffrance⟨p⟩ his wife Daughter of the said
Sr William Cope and sister of the said Sr John And this Deponent
doth beleeve that the said Sr John did not receave any rent at
all for the said house⟨p⟩ in hounslowe aforesaid for that all the
Accompt⟨p⟩ of the said Sr John hath from tyme to tyme since the
decease of the said Sr William Cope come to the hand⟨p⟩ of thi⟨p⟩ Deponent wch concerned the rent⟨p⟩ by him the said Sr John or by
other⟨p⟩ for his vse receaved and doth not therby finde nor doth it
appeare that the said Sr John or any for him did at any tyme
receave any the rent⟨p⟩ of the said house⟨p⟩/

(15 That the said Sr John Cope departed this life in or about October
1638 And saith that the said Sr John Cope and Mr Robert Lee
Esqr in the Jntērr named were in their life tyme⟨p⟩ engaged one
for the other in seūall obligacōns and imediately after ye death
of the said Sr John Cope the said Mr Robert Lee did make an
agreement with the said Dame Elizabeth Cope that the said Dame
Elizabeth should discharge or disingage the said Lee of all these
bond⟨p⟩ wherein the said Lee stood bound for the said Sr John Cope
for hi⟨p⟩ the said Sr John debt⟨p⟩ and that the said Robert Lee should
then discharge the said Def^t Dame Elizabeth Cope of and from
all bond⟨p⟩ or engagem^{t⟨p⟩} whereby the said Sr John Cope was any
bound or engaged a⟨p⟩ for the debt⟨p⟩ of him the said Lee And thi⟨p⟩
Deponent saith the said Def^t the Lady Elizabeth did on her part
pforme the said Agreement by discharging or Dissingageing the
said m^r Lee And the said m^r Lee did likewise on his part dissingage
the said Def^t Dame Elizabeth as from soe many bond⟨p⟩ or en-
gagem^{t⟨p⟩} as she knewe of or could finde out by enquirey made at
such Scriuener⟨p⟩ shopp⟨p⟩ here in London where they vsed to take vp
money together and he doth verily beleeve that the said m^r Lee
was at that tyme of abillity to have payed the debt now in question and did say to thi⟨p⟩ Deponent that he did scorne to be soe much
beholding to the Def^t (meaning the Def^t Dame Elizabeth) that
she should stand engaged for any money for him and more saith
not to this Jntērr/

John Draperr

(16 That this Deponent hath seene the Accompt and Jnventory of the
estate of the said Sr John Cope annexed to her answere put in to
the Comp^{lt⟨p⟩} bill in thi⟨p⟩ honorable Court and thi⟨p⟩ Deponent hath
very lately pvsed the same and doth beleeve the said Jnventory
and Accompt to be true but saith that as touching the pticuler
debt⟨p⟩ mencōned in the said Accompt to be paid for ye debt⟨p⟩ of

the said Sr John Cope he well knoweꝑ were the prop Debtꝑ of the
said Sr John Cope and that the same were paid accordingly/the
wch he iꝑ induced to depose for that he thiꝑ Deponent did receave
all rentꝑ and moneyeꝑ due to the said Def^t Dame Elizabeth and
made payem^tꝑ for her accordingly of all wch thiꝑ Deponent did
keepe A booke of Accompt; the wch said pticuler debtꝑ mencōned
in the said Accompt to be paid for the debtꝑ of the said Sr John
Cope as aforesaid thiꝑ Deponent hath lately Compared and
examinacōn with thiꝑ Deponentꝑ said booke of Accompt and doth
finde the same to agree therwith And thiꝑ Deponent further saith
that the paper booke now produced and shewed vnto thiꝑ Deponent at the tyme of hiꝑ examinacōn is A true Copie of the Jnventory
and Accompt annexed to the answere of the Def^t Dame Elizabeth
put in the to the said Comp^ltꝑ said bill of Comp^lt for he saith that
he did examine the said produced paper booke with the said
Jnventory and Accompt soe annexed and therby knoweth that the
same doe agree/and more saith not to thiꝑ Jntērr

                                        John Draperr

[*Endorsed on the back, which serves as the cover of the whole bundle of
depositions:*] 28 Cope & others at ye suite of Milton 26 John Draper—
paid Hugh Candish Thomas Chandeler Hillary terme 1658

[*See the endorsements on the interrogatories*:] John Drap sworne 10th
ffēb 1658/Wm Harington. The paꝑ booke or Jnventory mencōned was
r'd back by me this 11th of ffēb: 1658/John Draper/r'd C Drap 26 iiij^d

February 24, 1658/9
DEPOSITION OF THOMAS CHANDLER FOR LADY ELIZABETH COPE

Chancery Depositions, C 24/835   *Photostat in Harvard College Library*

ffebr ye 24th. 1658   ffor ye Lady Elizabeth Cope and otherꝑ
shewed by m^r Johnson   Dēf^tꝑ ādv^ꝑ John Milton p^lt
Thomas Chandeler of the pish of St Andreweꝑ holborne London gent
aged 70 yeareꝑ or theraboutꝑ being produced A wittneꝑ &c Deposeth
and saith/

(1 That he doth knowe the ptyeꝑ to thiꝑ suite in the title of the Jntērrs
   named. And did well knowe Sr William Cope and Sr John Cope deceased the Grandfather and ffather of the said Def^t Sr Anthony
   Cope./

(2 That he doth knowe the place scituat in London called by the name

of the new wooll keye and the olde wooll key comonly called the
Custome house wᶜʰ said pʳmisseρ as he beleeveρ were by A Decree
made in this honorable Court settled by the Consent of the said
Sʳ William Cope deceased for paiemᵗ of such debt of 3000ˡⁱ as is
menconed in the Jnterr with interest at 9ˡⁱ p cent to be paid by the
said Sʳ William Cope to one Timberlake for that thiρ Deponent
did heare asmuch but did never see the said Decree and therefore
cannot further or otherwise more directly depose to this Jntērr/

(5 That the Jndenture now produced and shewed vnto him at the tyme
of his examinacōn dated yᵉ 20ᵗʰ of January 1631 was made betweene
the ptieρ therein mencōned vpon yᵉ marriage of Sʳ John Cope to
the nowe Defᵗ the Lady Elizabeth Cope but this Deponent was not
A wittneρ to the same,/ but saith that the reason that induceth
thiρ Deponent soe to depose iρ aforesaid for that the endorsemᵗ
beginning in these wordρ on yᵉ backside of one of the skinnes of
Parchmᵗ part of the said deede to witt Tangley was Aunciently
the Jnheritance of henry Bridgeρ &c) is of the hand writing of
thiρ Deponent and for yᵗ thiρ Deponent hath often tymeρ had the
said produced Jndenture from the handρ of the said Sʳ John Cope
late ffather to the now Defᵗ Sʳ Anthony Cope to shew vnto Councell
vpon some speciall occasion this Deponent being servant to the
said Sʳ John Cope for diverρ yeareρ together when he waρ liveing/

7 That Sʳ John Cope in the Jnterr named did in his life tyme mortgage
the ffarme or Grange called by the name of Tanley to one mʳ moore
for the terme of ninety nine yeareρ but thiρ Deponent waρ not A
wittneρ to the said deede of mortgage, but saith that he is doth
verily beleeve that the the Jndenture or parchmᵗ writing now produced and shewed vnto him at the tyme of his examinacōn beareing
date the 29ᵗʰ daye of march 1637 and purporting to be such deede of
mortgage as is mencōned in the Jntērr was sealed and deliūd by
the said Sʳ John Cope to the said mʳ Moore for that he thiρ Deponent
being well accquainted with the Character of the hand writing of the
said Sʳ John Cope (as being servant to him by the space of twentey
yeareρ together in his life tyme) is very confident that the name
John Cope subscribed to the said deede of mortgage or writing now
produced) is of the prop hand writing of the said Sʳ John and for
that thiρ Deponent did well knowe some of the witnesseρ whose
nameρ are endorsed on the backside of the said deed as wittnesseρ
therunto as namely Thomaρ Moore and Gileρ Harriρ whoe he beleeveρ were present and wittnesseρ to the said deede./ and more
saith not to thiρ Jntērr/

(9 That he is very confident that the Manno^r ffarme or Grange of
Tangley waꝑ made over or settled vpon Mr Thomaꝑ Loggin in the
Jnterr named for securing of A debt of 1500 borrowed of him the
said Loggin by the Def^t the Lady Elizabeth Cope the said 1500^{li}.
being as he beleeveꝑ really borrowed of the said Loggin by her the
said Dame Elizabeth to paye vnto the said m^r moore for the redempcōn of the mortgage of the p^rmisseꝑ to him made as is before
mencōned and more saith not to this Jntērr/

Tho: Chandelēr

(11 That he this Deponent did examine the paper writing now produced
and shewed vnto him at the tyme of his examinacōn Conteyning two
sheeteꝑ of paper and beareing date the 10th day of October in ye 14th
yeare of the reigne of the late king Charleꝑ) with the originall therof
(wch was sealed and deliūd by Sr John Cope therein named in the
presence of thiꝑ Deponent (and wherein thiꝑ Deponent did endorss
or subscribe hiꝑ name as A wittneꝑ) and saith that the said paper
writing is A true Copie of the said Originall deede and that the said
Originall deede doth beare the very same date as is mencōned or
expressed in the said Copie to witt the tenth day of October in y^e
14th yeare of the late King Charleꝑ And he saith that Liūy and seizin
waꝑ afterwardꝑ executed thervpon on ye 11th daye of October 1638 as
thiꝑ Deponent beleeveꝑ according as is mencōned or expressed in the
said produced paper writing or Copie before mencōned and more
saith not to this Jntērr/

(14 That he cannot depose thervnto/.

(15 That the said Sr John Cope dyed as he remembreth the tyme in
yeare of our Lord 1638 and further hee cannot materially depose
of hiꝑ owne knoweledg for satisfaccōn of any the questions of thiꝑ
Jntērr/

(16 That he cannot depose therevnto as not knoweing what Jnventory or
Accompt is annexed by the Def^t the Lady Elizabeth to her answere
put in to the Comp^{ltꝑ} bill in thiꝑ honorable Court nor haveing any
such paper booke produced vnto him as is mencōned in the Jntērr/./
nor more saith in thiꝑ behalfe/

To the rest/
Tho: Chandelēr

[*See the note also on the sheet of interrogatories:* "Thomas Chaundler
sworne 24th ffeb 1658 Edm Gyles."]

June 10, 1659

DEPOSITION OF HUGH CANDISH FOR LADY ELIZABETH COPE

Chancery Depositions, C 24/835   *Photostat in Harvard College Library*

June yᵉ 10ᵗʰ 1659   ffor Dame Elizabeth Cope and Sʳ Anthony
shewed by mʳ Johnson   Cope Deftρ at yᵉ suite of Milton pˡᵗ
                                       Hugh Candish of Shipton vnder Whichwood in
the Countey of Oxōn gent aged 40 yeareρ or theraboutρ being produced
A wittneρ &c Deposeth and saith./

(1 That he doth knowe the ptyeρ Deftρ in thiρ suite in the title of the
Jntērrρ named and did knowe Sʳ William Cope and Sʳ John Cope
deceased in the Jntērr named and enquired of late Grandfather
and father of the said Sʳ Anthony but the Cōmptˡᵗ John Milton
thiρ Deponent knoweth not/

5:6 That he doth verily beleeve that the nameρ of Gileρ Harriρ and
William Sprigg (with whome this Deponᵗ was very well accquainted) endorsed on the backside of the Jndenture now produced
and shewed vnto him is of the respective prop hand writing of the
said Gileρ Harriρ and William Sprigg the said Sprigg being an
Attorney at Lawe and the said Harris haveing heretofore some
Relacōn to the ffamily of the Copeρ as their Steward who afterwardρ lived vpon his meaneρ in the Country as A private gent and
dyed; and thiρ Deponent vpon further pvsall of yᵉ said Jndenture
findeing the name William Lynn endorsed also aρ A wittneρ to
the said Jndenture saith that he beleeveρ the same is of the prop
hand writing of one Mʳ William Lynn who is of thiρ Deponent
Accquaintance and now Steward to the Countess of Bathe and
middlēsex. and beleeveρ that the said seūall persons before named
were wittnesseρ with otherρ to the sealeing and deliūy of the said
produced Jndenture beareing date the 20ᵗʰ Daye of January 1631
and more saith not to these Jntērrρ/

(7 That he doth now knowe but doth beleeve that the said Sʳ John
Cope did in his life tyme mortgage the ffarme or Grange called
Tangley to one mʳ Moore in the Jntērr named for ninety nine
yeareρ./ and more saith not to thiρ Jntērr/

9 That the Defᵗ the Lady Elizabeth Cope did to the knowledg of this
Deponent borrowe of mʳ Thomas Loggin in the Jntērr named the
sūme of ffifteene hundred poundρ for the redeeming of the said
ffarme or Grange called Tangley out of the handρ of the said mʳ
moore to whome the same were as thiρ Deponent beleeveρ mort-

gaged as aforesaid but thiϱ Deponent doth not knowe or remember that he was A wittneϱ to any writing made by the said Lady Eliz: Cope for the securing of the said 1500ˡⁱ. to the said Loggin but is very Confident that the said 1500ˡⁱ waϱ by the said Lady Cope secured to the said Loggin by some deede or mortgage or other Conveyance Assurance or Assignemᵗ of the said ffarme or Grange called Tangeley and doth knowe that the said 1500ˡⁱ was paid by the said Lady Cope or her order vnto the said mʳ moore accordingly and more saith not to this Jntērr there being noe such writing left to be shewed vnto him at the tyme of his examinacōn as he is informed by the Examiner/ as is menconed in the Jntērr/

(10 That by the accknoweledgmᵗ of the said mʳ Loggins himselfe and one Mʳ John Draper Steward to the now Dēftϱ there waϱ paid by the said Draper by the appointemᵗ of the defᵗ Sʳ Anthony to the said Mʳ Loggin at such tyme aϱ hee the said Loggins Assigned the lease of ninety nine yeareϱ mencōned in the Jntērr to be made by the said Sʳ John Cope to the said mʳ moore of the said mannor ffarme or Grange of Tangely (wᶜʰ said pʳmisse he conceaveϱ to be of the value of 140ˡⁱ. A yeare or thereaboutϱ) the said sūme of ffifteene hundred poundϱ with interest for the same and that the said lease waϱ soe Assigned by the said Loggins for yᵉ only prop vse of the said defᵗ Sʳ Anthony Cope And thiϱ Deponent saith that he both knowe it to be true that the sᵈ Defᵗ Sʳ Anthony hath further paid and secured to be paid to the said Defᵗ the Lady Elizabeth Cope his mother for the Revercōn of the Jnheritance of the said ffarme or Grange of Tangely aforesaid after the expiracōn of the said Lease of ninety nine yeareϱ the sūme of ffifteene hundred poundϱ or vpwardϱ and more saith not to thiϱ Jnterr/

Hugh Candish

13 That he hath heard that the Lord Saye since the death of Sʳ John Cope aϱ he remembreth (as A ffeeoffee in trust for the paiemᵗ of the debtϱ of the said Sʳ William and Sʳ John Cope) did sell seūall Rectoryeϱ or Parsonageϱ wᶜʰ were heretofore Sʳ William Copeϱ both in Waleϱ and England as namely the Parsonage of midwim in the Countey of Carmarrthen the Parsonage of Llanghangell in the said Countey of Carmarthen and the Parsonage of Llangahangell in the Countey of Brecknock the Parsonage of merthood in the said Countey of Brecknock with two other Parsonageϱ in the said Countey besideϱ other Parsonageϱ neere Bristoll and in yorkesheire the nameϱ wherof doth not at present remember and more saith not to thiϱ Jntērr/

(15 That it is twentey yeareȝ ageoe since the said Sʳ John Cope departed thiȝ life and more saith not to thiȝ Jntērr/

(18 That this Deponent hath heretofore and of late time seene the deedeȝ writingȝ or evidenceȝ wᶜʰ concerne the estate both of the Deftȝ the Lady Elizabeth Cope and of the said Sʳ Anthony Cope but vpon what occasion the said writingȝ were shewed vnto him thiȝ Deponent doth not remember nor saith to thiȝ Jntērr or in thiȝ behalfe/

To the rest
Hugh Candish

[*See the note after no. 2 of the revised interrogatories mentioned above:* Hugh Candish sworne 10ᵗʰ June 1659 Wᵐ Harington. *Also the endorsement on the same document:* r'd 10ᵗʰ ffēb 1658 . . . noe ffee Candish.]

June 11, 1659

DECREE IN MILTON-COPE SUIT

Chancery Decrees and Orders, C 33/212, f. 792ᵛ

11 June [1659]

M   Millton pᵗᵉ   If the defᵗ shewȝ noe cause for stay of publicacōn
Cope Bar defᵗ   by this day sevenight then publicōn is graunted./

June 21, 1659

JOHN DRAPER RECEIVES BACK ALL THE PAPERS IN THE MILTON-COPE SUIT

Chancery Depositions, C 24/835 (a note on the sheet of interrogatories)

All the seūall deedes & writings in this cause mencōned J rec'd back this 21ᵗʰ of June 1659

John Draper

SUPPLEMENT

TWO ADDITIONAL RECORDS OF MILTON'S FATHER

October 8, 1623

DEPOSITION OF MILTON'S FATHER IN WALTHEW-SHARES SUIT

Chancery Depositions, C 24/501

viijᵒ octobr' Aᵒ. xxjᵒ Jacobi Rᵱ. 1623.
John Mylton of the pishe of Allhallowes in Breadstreete London scryvener
aged 6o. yeres or thereaboutᵱ sworne & exd

1. 1. That he doeth well knowe Mʳ Sheres & Mʳ Walthewe named for
   the ptyes complt & defft to this suyte and hath knowen them these
   xx yeres past or thereaboutᵱ

12. That true it is that he doeth fynd a note in a booke wᶜʰ he keepeth
    for such purposes that the Defft Robert Walthewe by an obligacōn
    dated the xxvijᵗʰ day of ffebruary Aō Dnī 1607. did become bound
    to the plt in the penall somme of fower hundred poundᵱ condicōned
    for the paymt of CCxxˡⁱ to the complt at the shoppe of the depont
    in Breadstreete london vpon the first day of March Ao Dnī 1608. as
    by the said booke may appeare wherevnto for more certenty he
    doeth referre himself And sayth that he verely beleeueth that the
    defft or some for him did afterwardᵱ satisfy and pay to or to the vse
    of the complt the said CCxxˡⁱ in discharge of the said bond or
    obligacōn at or about the tyme lymitted for the payment thereof
    in & by the condicōn of the said obligacōn And more or otherwise
    he sayth he can depose nothing certen or materiall to any the other
    questions of the Jnterr' vpon his nowe pʳsent rēmbrance To the rest
    not exd by direccōn

                                              [*Signed*] Jo: milton

April 9, 1630

DEPOSITION OF MILTON'S FATHER IN PECK-RANDOLPH SUIT

Chancery Depositions, C 24/566

9: Aprilis 1630. Ex pte Christopheri Pecke et Susannæ vxoris ejus
6. Caroli Reg' q'tes, Cont' Edmudū Randolph Armī Defte testes
                exāte p RI. CHILD in Comettī exoñ.
John Milton. of the prish of All hallowes in Bredstreete London. scriuener
of the age of 67. years or thereabouts sworne & exēd deposeth & sᵗʰ.

1. That hee doth know. Edmound Randolph. esqʳ named for defendᵗ
   in the suite & hath: seene the Complt Christopher Pecke but hath
   little knowledge of him, but Susan his wife the other complt thiᵴ
   dponᵗ sᵗʰ hee Doth not know:

2. That hee doth know. that John Collins of Lincolnes Jnn in the Countye of midlesex. esq^r. did hertofore p^{r}tend to bee seised of certeine howses in Scroopes Courte in the prish of s^t Andrewes Holburne London; but what money hee pd for the same or what they were worth when the Defend^{ts} bought the same this dpon^t sth hee knoweth not; nor doth he know what money or rent the s^d defend^t was to pay vnto the s^d John Collins for the same; howbeit hee sth that hee doth remember that about 8 or 9 years. sithence hee this depōn^t did offer the s^d John Collins. money for the s^d houses, wch as hee taketh itt was about 12 years pchase. & soe much hee would then haue given for the same; & what the particular rents of the s^d howses. then were this dpon^t. sth he now remembreth not, but as he taketh itt all the s^d houses. were letten for about 120^1 p ann̄; & this is as much as hee cann depose to the questions of this Jnt for he sth hee doth not well remember how much rent S^r. Henrye Colt Knt pd for one of the s^d houses. but as he thinketh hee pd 45^1 by yeare; nor doth hee remember what money Docto^r Poe. & the rest of the creditors of the s^d Collins receiued;

[*Signed*] Jo: milton:

INDEX

The following index comprises all the proper names which occur in the text, footnotes, bibliography, and appendix, as well as a few common terms chiefly concerning the law and taken from Chapter I. In view of the wide variations in spelling of names in the seventeenth century, generous cross-references have seemed necessary; but the main entry has been placed under the spelling which is most common. Titles of books and articles are entered under the most important, not necessarily the first, words. References to two or more people of the same name are consolidated into one entry, so that "Coxeter, Richard," for example, covers several men of that name.

THE MONOGRAPH SERIES

A discount of one-third from the list-price is allowed to Members of the Association. Orders from the U.S. and Canada should be addressed to the Executive Office. Orders from abroad should be addressed to Humphrey Milford, Oxford University Press, Amen Corner, London, E.C.4.

I. LES PROPHECIES DE MERLIN
Edited from MS.593 in the Bibliothèque Municipale of Rennes
By Lucy Allen Paton

Published 1926 and 1927.
Part One: Introduction and Text (xl+496 pp.).
Part Two: Studies in the Contents (iv+406 pp.).
} Price $9.00.

Wm. A. Nitze (*Mod. Phil.*, Aug., 1929): This is an important book not merely for Arthurians but especially for students of medieval history and of Franco-Italian literature. Essentially a piece of Venetian propaganda, the *Prophecies de Merlin* consists of historical and romantic prognostication, attributed to the Arthurian seer, and mingled with narratives of knightly adventure taken, in large part, from the Vulgate cycle, the *Prose Tristan*, and the *Palamedes* . . . One closes those two volumes with a sense of admiration and gratitude for their learned author, who promises further studies on the legend of Merlin, an event to which all Arthurian scholars will look forward with much interest.

II. DRAMATIC PUBLICATION IN ENGLAND, 1580–1640
A Study of Conditions Affecting Content and Form of Drama
By Evelyn May Albright

Published 1927 (vi+442 pp.). Price $4.50.
Sir Edmund Chambers (*Mod. Lang. Review*, Jan., 1928): Miss Albright has succeeded in collecting a great deal of interesting material on many topics relating to play publication; on the regulation of the stage; on the censorship both in its general and in its dramatic operation; on copyright and stage right; on the sources of dramatic copy; on the methods of the printing houses; on contemporary notions of typographic accuracy . . . .

III. WRITINGS ASCRIBED TO RICHARD ROLLE HERMIT OF HAMPOLE AND MATERIALS FOR HIS BIOGRAPHY
By Hope Emily Allen

Published 1927 (xvi+568 pp.). Price $7.50.
The British Academy awarded the Rose Mary Crawshay prize in English Literature to Miss Allen for this work.
Howard R. Patch (*Speculum*, October, 1929): For a number of years scholars have have eagerly awaited the publication of this work . . . . And it is really an honor, not only to Miss Allen, but also to the scholars who initially guided her research, and to the foundation which is responsible for its publication. Every document ascribed to Rolle has been minutely examined and its claim to authenticity duly tested from every point of view. The editions and manuscripts are fully listed, and the evidence for the materials regarding the mystic's life properly scrutinized.

IV. THE CONSECUTIVE SUBJUNCTIVE IN OLD ENGLISH
By Morgan Callaway, Jr.

Published 1933 (110 pp.). Price $1.50.
George O. Curme (*JEGP*, July, 1934): This treatise on the use of the subjunctive in Old English in clauses of result . . . shows conclusively that the subjunctive here is due to the meaning of the subordinate clause itself.
J. R. Hulbert (*Mod. Phil.*, August, 1934): This most recent publication of Professor Callaway shows the same painstaking care and thoroughness, the same impeccable technique as all its predecessors, and, like them, is a valuable contribution to our knowledge of Anglo-Saxon.

V. THE REAL WAR OF THE THEATRES
Shakespeare's Fellows in Rivalry with the Admiral's Men, 1594–1603
By Robert Boies Sharpe

Published 1935 (viii+260 pp.). Price $2.50.
Mario Praz (*Rev. Eng. Stud.*, October, 1937, p. 228): . . . the value of Professor Sharpe's

contribution . . . [lies] in the light he throws incidentally on the taste of the period, in his tentative characterization of the kind of audience for which each company catered, in his brief but excellent surveys of such *motifs* as the Jew on the stage, the girl-page device, the domestic crime plays, the Greek plays, etc.

T. W. Baldwin (*JEGP*, April, 1937, p. 275): It is clear from the facts assembled by Professor Sharpe that there were certain distinctive tendencies both literary and political within the two companies.

A. Brandl (*Archiv*, Dec., 1935, p. 252): . . . Sicher ist Sharpe ein sehr vielseitiger Kenner und ein sehr scharfsinniger Vergleicher auf diesem engen, aber reichen Literaturgebiete . . .

VI. PETER IDLEY'S *INSTRUCTIONS TO HIS SON*
By Charlotte D'Evelyn

Published 1935 (vii+240 pp.). $2.50.

J. R. Hulbert (*Mod. Phil.*, August, 1936, p. 98): The volume contains all the essential apparatus of a good modern edition—an introduction of seventy-eight pages on the author, his book, its date, language, and manuscripts, the text (printed from one manuscript with significant variant readings from the other six), a brief body of notes, and an index.

Howard R. Patch (*Speculum*, April, 1936, p. 295): Miss D'Evelyn has supplied a masterly introduction, setting forth the facts about Peter's life, the sources of his work, and the date, dialect and manuscripts of the poem, together with sensible and useful notes which follow the text.

G. D. Willcock (*Mod. Lang. Review*, Jan., 1937, p. 86): This is a strenuous, textually accurate and on the whole well-proportioned edition of a mid-fifteenth-century text, of which only brief extracts have so far appeared in print, and of the author of which nothing was known except the name and one or two details deducible from the poem itself.

VII. CHARLES TIMOTHY BROOKS, TRANSLATOR FROM GERMAN, AND THE GENTEEL TRADITION
By Camillo von Klenze

Published 1937 (viii+114 pp.). Price $1.50.

Harold Lenz (*German Quarterly*, Nov., 1938, p. 217): The book is written with vigor and circumspection. Numerous marginal and general questions are treated *passim* with keen insight. There are chapters on Mme de Stael, Carl Follen, Carlyle, foreign reactions to German literature. The documentation is profuse, almost anxiously so. Two appendices contain, respectively, a list of Brooks' unpublished works and ten previously unpublished letters.

H. G. Atkins (*Mod. Lang. Review*, Oct., 1938, p. 617): It is a very scholarly and stimulating little book, written with complete command of the field with which it deals.

VIII. THE VOYAGERS AND THE ELIZABETHAN DRAMA
By Robert Ralston Cawley

Published 1938 (xiv+429 pp.). Price $4.00.

J. H. Walter (*Mod. Lang. Review*, Jan., 1939, p. 87): The final estimate of Mr. Cawley's extensive labour must wait until he has published his deductions from the evidence he has so painstakingly sought out and arranged in this volume.

IX. ARTHURIAN LEGENDS IN MEDIEVAL ART
By Roger Sherman Loomis and Laura Hibbard Loomis

Published 1938 (vii+155 pp.+420 illustrations). Price $12.00.

G. H. Gerould (*Speculum*, April, 1939, p. 254): In conclusion, let me emphasize the great interest and value of the work in which Mr. and Mrs. Loomis have so happily collaborated. They have produced a book of permanent value. After their patient toil it cannot fail to be a satisfaction to them to have the monuments they have studied reproduced so admirably in the magnificent album of illustrations, that others may see what they have seen.

Howard R. Patch (*Romanic Review*, April, 1939, p. 193): It is something especially to be grateful for that so systematic and thorough an investigation should be presented in a style never dull and often touched with humor and a sense of proportion.

J. J. Parry (*JEGP*, Jan., 1939, p. 156): In every case Professor Loomis seems to have examined the object at first hand besides making use of the literature of the subject.